NORTH, SOUTH, EAST AND WEST— RESOUNDING PRAISE FROM EVERYWHERE!

"Fresh and distinctive . . . reading it is sheer joy."
—*The New York Times*

"Bruce Catton is doing the same job on the Civil War that Carl Sandburg did for Lincoln . . . a magnificent account which reads like a modern *Iliad*."
—*Miami Herald*

"Catton writes as though he owned the War. It could not be in better hands."
—*Little Rock Arkansas Gazette*

"Racing, exciting narrative . . . a great book that reflects in full measure Catton's rare combination of talent as writer and historian"
—*The Kansas City Star*

Published by POCKET BOOKS

Bruce Catton

THIS HALLOWED GROUND

PUBLISHED BY POCKET BOOKS NEW YORK

POCKET BOOKS, a Simon & Schuster division of GULF & WESTERN CORPORATION
1230 Avenue of the Americas, New York, N.Y. 10020

Copyright © 1955, 1956 by Bruce Catton

Published by arrangement with Doubleday & Company, Inc.

ISBN: 0-671-83315-4

First Pocket Books printing February, 1961

20   19   18   17   16

Trademarks registered in the United States and other countries.

Printed in the U.S.A.

To Nellie Catton

Contents

viii / *Contents*

List of Maps

THIS HALLOWED GROUND

THE WESTERN THEATER

THE EASTERN THEATER

York
SUSQUEHANNA R.
DELAWARE R.

NEW JERSEY

MARYLAND

Baltimore

Annapolis
Ft. Stevens

DELAWARE

POTOMAC R.

Chesapeake Bay

Atlantic Ocean

RAPPAHANNOCK R.

YORK R.
CHICKAHOMINY R.
Williamsburg
Yorktown
JAMES R. Ft. Monroe
Monitor vs. Merrimac
Norfolk   HAMPTON ROADS

1.

The Hurricane Comes Later

1. Sowing the Wind

THE SENATOR was tall and handsome, with wavy hair to frame a proud ravaged face, and if hearty feeding had given him the beginning of a notable paunch he was erect enough to carry it well. He had the easy grace of a practiced orator —his speeches, according to spiteful enemies, were carefully rehearsed night after night before a mirror in his chambers, while an awed colored boy stood by with a lighted candle —and there was a great humorless arrogance about him, for he had never been blessed with a moment of self-doubt. He liked to say that he was in morals, not in politics. From this the logical deduction was that people who opposed him, numerous though they undoubtedly were, must be willfully wrong.

Such a deduction Senator Charles Sumner was quite capable of drawing for himself. He would draw it today in the Senate chamber. In his speech, he had told a friend, he would "pronounce the most thorough philippic ever uttered in a legislative chamber."

It was an ominous promise. The date was May 19, 1856, and although there was still a little time left it was running out fast, and angry words might make it run faster. Yet angry words were about the only kind anyone cared to use these days. Men seemed tired of the reasoning process. Instead of trying to convert one's opponents it was simpler just to denounce them, no matter what unmeasured denunciation might lead to.

The point at issue was, at bottom, simple enough: how to

1

legislate so that Kansas might someday become a state. But Kansas was a symbol rather than a territory. Men saw what they feared and hated, concentrated on its wide empty plains, and as they stared they were losing the ability to see virtue in compromise and conciliation. The man on the other side, whatever one's vantage point, was beginning to look ominously alien. He could not easily be dealt with, and perhaps it was best simply to lash out at him. In the charged atmosphere thus created the lightest act could be fateful. All of the things that were slipping beyond hope of easy solution—sectional enmities, economic antagonisms, varying interpretations of the American dream, the tragic unendurable race problem itself—all of these, somehow, might hinge on what was done about Kansas, so that the wrong phrase in an enacting clause could mean earth's best hope lost forever.

In Senator Sumner's view the wrong phrase was on the verge of adoption. The bill which the Senate was about to pass would, as he saw it, mean that Kansas must eventually become a slave state. In addition, it would give a great deal of aid and comfort to slavery's advocates, wherever they were. It was not to be thought of calmly; it was not merely wrong, it was an actual crime. Furthermore, it was no common crime; it was (he solemnly assured the Senate) a fearful thing, "the crime against nature, from which the soul recoils, and which language refuses to describe." Yet if language could not describe it the senator could, and he would do so.

He was a man of breeding and education, given to much study of the classics; and he stood now in the Senate chamber, looking imperiously about him as one who has glimpsed the tables of the law on the mountaintop, and he dwelt extensively on "the rape of a virgin territory, compelling it to the hateful embrace of slavery." The South, he said, was guilty of a "depraved longing for a new slave state, the hideous offspring of such a crime." Force had been used, he declared, "in compelling Kansas to this pollution."[1]

The desk in front of Senator Sumner was empty. It belonged to Senator Andrew Butler of South Carolina, and when Sumner first became a senator, white-haired Butler had been pleasant and cordial—so much so that Sumner wrote to a friend that he had learned, from the old gentleman's kindness, "to shun harsh and personal criticism of those from whom I differ." But that had been years ago, when men from Massachusetts and South Carolina could still exchange courtesies in the Senate chamber; and in any case Sumner was always ready to denounce even a close friend, and in the most unmeasured terms, if he suspected that the friend had fallen into error. Butler was a spokesman for slavery, he had had his part in the crime against nature, and the fascinating exercise of discussing political opposition in terms of sexual depravity could be carried on—by this bookish man, still unmarried at forty-five—with Butler as the target. Sumner addressed himself to the absent Butler.

The South Carolina senator considered himself a chivalrous knight, but Sumner had seen the truth: "He has chosen a mistress to whom he has made his vows, and who, though ugly to others, is always lovely to him; though polluted in the sight of the world, is chaste in his sight—I mean the harlot slavery. For her his tongue is always profuse with words. Let her be impeached in character, or any proposition made to shut her out from the extension of her wantonness, and no extravagance of manner or hardihood of assertion is then too great for this senator."

There was quite a bit more of this, ranging all the way from Senator Butler to the ancient Egyptians, "who worshipped divinities in brutish forms," with due mention of the "obscene idols" to which the Aztecs had made human sacrifices; the connection of these latter with the harlot slavery not being of the clearest. At one stage Sumner interrupted himself to cry: "Mr. President, I mean to keep absolutely within the limits of parliamentary propriety"; and then he went on, his speech still unfinished at the session's end.

The senator managed to reach his conclusion the following day, reminding the presiding officer (perhaps unnecessarily) that "an immense space has been traversed," and in closing he came back from brutish idols and obscene Aztecs to Senator Butler, from whom he had learned not to let political arguments get personal. There was not, he said, "any possible deviation from the truth" of which Butler was innocent, although fortunately these deviations were made in the heat of such passion "as to save him from the suspicion of intentional aberration." Still, there it was: "The senator touches nothing which he does not disfigure—with error, sometimes of principle, sometimes of fact."[2]

A philippic, as he had promised. No single vote had been changed by it; the Senate would decide, at last, precisely as it would have done if he had kept quiet. But he had not been trying to persuade. No one was, these days; a political leader addressed his own following, not the opposition. Sumner had been trying to inflame, to arouse, to confirm the hatreds and angers that already existed. In the North there were men who from his words would draw a new enmity toward the South; in the South there were men who would see in this speaker and what he had said a final embodiment of the compelling reasons why it was good to think seriously about secession.

At the very end Sumner had a gloomy moment of insight.

The fight over Kansas, he said, spreading from the western plain to the Senate chamber, would spread still farther; would go to a nationwide stage "where every citizen will be not only spectator but actor."[3]

There is a rowdy strain in American life, living close to the surface but running very deep. Like an ape behind a mask, it can display itself suddenly with terrifying effect. It is slack-jawed, with leering eyes and loose wet lips, with heavy feet and ponderous cunning hands; now and then, when something tickles it, it guffaws, and when it is made angry it snarls; and it can be aroused much more easily than it can be quieted. Mike Fink and Yankee Doodle helped to father it, and Judge Lynch is one of its creations; and when it comes lumbering forth it can make the whole country step in time to its own frantic irregular pulse-beat.

Senator Sumner had invited it out with his fine talk. So had the eminent clergyman, the Reverend Henry Ward Beecher, who had told the world that a Sharps rifle was a greater moral agency than a Bible, as far as Kansas was concerned. Yet these men need not have bothered. Rowdyism was coming out anyway, having been invited by men of the

South as well as by men of the North, and the spirit of rowdyism was talking in the spirit of Sumner's and Beecher's exhortations without the fancy trimmings. It was saying now, south of the slavery line, that "we will continue to tar and feather, drown, lynch and hang every white-livered abolitionist who dares to pollute our soil," and in Kansas it had legislated that anyone who denied the legality of slave ownership in the territory should get five years in prison.[4]

In Kansas there was a town called Lawrence. It had existed for two years, and although it was so new, it was solid and substantial, with buildings of brick and stone, including a hotel that was massive enough to serve as a fort. (In point of fact, the hotel had been built with that end in mind.) The town was a piece of New England set down in the prairie, but it was a New England all distorted, as if someone were seeing bizarre dream-shapes that were slipping into nightmare. In place of white steeples and colonial doorways it had grim buildings and men who carried "Beecher's Bibles"— Sharps rifles, named with a cynicism matching that of the reverend clergyman himself—and it was expressive of the stern New England purpose that had planted it there. It was named for a Massachusetts millowner who had given money to fight slavery, and it was the stronghold and rallying point of all Kansas settlers who believed that the extension of slavery must be stopped at the Missouri line.

As such, it became a focal point for hatred. The tension had been building up for months. There had been arrests and shootings and all manner of bloodthirsty threats and shouts of defiance, for nothing could be more hateful just then, to a certain attitude of mind, than the simple belief that one man ought not to own another. A territorial grand jury with pro-slavery leanings had asked that the town's leading citizens be jailed for treason, and it had added a rider to the effect that both of the town's newspapers ought to be suppressed as public nuisances and that its fortress hotel should be torn down.

Now, on May 21—one day after Senator Sumner had finished his excellent speech—there was a posse on hand to see that the grand jury's thoughts were properly embodied in action. This posse numbered perhaps a thousand men. A great many of them came from Missouri, for Lawrence was not far from the state line, and they rejoiced in the collective title of Border Ruffians. They owed dim allegiance to a United States marshal who had certain arrests to make in Lawrence and they were heavily armed. Unlike most posses, they dragged along with them five cannon.

For once the people of Lawrence were on their good behavior. They offered no resistance when the marshal came in, and the arrests he wanted to make were made. The marshal thereupon dismissed his posse, which was immediately called back into service by a Kansas sheriff, a cover-to-cover believer in slavery, who announced himself as a law-and-order man and who said that he had a job of his own to do in Lawrence. The transformed posse was addressed briefly by former Senator David R. Atchison of Missouri, the great spokesman for slavery in the West, who cried: "Be brave, be orderly, and if any man or woman stand in your way, blow them to hell with a chunk of cold lead." The sheriff then led the posse into town and the fun began.[5]

Various rounds from the cannon were fired at the hotel. It had been well built—and the cannon, perhaps, were aimed and served inexpertly—and nothing in particular seemed to happen. The sheriff's helpers then swarmed all over the town, setting fire to the hotel, raiding the two offending newspaper offices and dumping press and type into the river, ransacking homes and getting drunk and in general having a high old time. The home of a man who presumed to call himself the free-state governor of Kansas was burned, two men who apparently stood in the way were killed by flying pellets of lead, a certain amount of lesser damage was inflicted, various female free-staters were scared half out of their wits (though not, it would appear, actually harmed), and there was a great round of shouting and speechifying and wobbly-legged parading and rejoicing. If rowdyism could settle the matter, it had been demonstrated beyond recall that Kansas was slave territory and would someday be a slave state and that the writ that made it treason to doubt the legality of the proslavery government of the territory would run henceforth without interference.[6]

Lawrence was sacked by men with a genius for putting the

worst foot forward. There were in Lawrence—and would arrive in droves in the next few days—certain newspaper correspondents who wrote from deep abolitionist conviction and who had access to the front pages of some of the country's most influential newspapers. These men had something to write about now, and they would make the most of it. And there stood on the record now one more indication that the disagreement between sections might not finally be settled by the ordinary processes of reason, debate, and compromise.

Next day was May 22, and Senator Sumner sat at his desk in the Senate chamber, the Senate having adjourned for the day. The senator was large, the fixed chair under his desk was high, and the base of the desk itself was screwed to the floor. The senator sat all hunched over, ankles hooked behind chair legs, intent on his correspondence. As always, he was serious, concentrating on the job at hand. He once told a friend that he never left his apartment to go to the Senate without taking a last look around, to make certain that everything he owned was just as he would wish it to be if the slave power should suddenly strike him down and he should never return to the place. Presumably he had taken such a look today.

The chamber where the Senate met was nearly empty. A few senators lounged about near the doorways, chatting, or worked at their desks. Sumner scribbled away, and then he realized that someone was standing beside him, trying to get his attention.

"I have read your speech twice over, carefully," this man was saying. "It is a libel on South Carolina and on Senator Butler, who is a relative of mine."

Then the man raised a walking stick high in the air and brought it down as hard as he could on Senator Sumner's head.

The man with the cane was a South Carolina congressman, Preston Brooks, nephew to Senator Butler; a youthful six-footer of robust frame, sometime cavalryman in the Mexican War. He struck again and again with a full-arm swing, and a man who saw it said that he came down with the cane like a dragoon using his saber and striking to kill. Caught between the chair and the immovable desk, Sumner tried desperately to get up. He was heard to gasp: "O Lord!"—and then, with a great convulsive heave, he wrenched the desk loose from its fastenings and reeled to his feet. Brooks struck again; the cane broke, and Brooks went on clubbing him with the splintered butt.

Now Sumner was on the floor, blood on his head and clothing, and men were running down the aisle to him. Brooks stopped beating him and strolled away, remarking: "I did not intend to kill him, but I did intend to whip him." Sumner was helped to his feet and made his way to the lobby, where he fell on a sofa, half unconscious. A doctor came and dressed his wounds—the scalp was badly cut, the doctor said afterward, but beyond that the wound did not seem very severe—and someone helped Sumner to a carriage and got him back to those rooms that were always maintained in perfect order in anticipation of some violent incident.[7]

Sumner disrobed, found his clothing saturated with blood, and sent for his own doctor—who, after examination, took a much graver view of his injuries than the doctor in the Senate lobby had done. He pronounced Sumner's condition most serious and ordered him to get into bed and stay there.

Concerning which there was much argument, then and later—the idea perhaps being that to pound a senator into speechlessness was no especial threat to the processes of democratic government unless the man's life was actually endangered. The doctor who had treated him in the lobby declared contemptuously that as far as he could see Sumner might have ridden by carriage all the way to Baltimore without ill effect if he had wanted to—his wounds were not critical. But Sumner's own doctor disagreed violently, and so did all of Sumner's friends, and so for the matter of that did Sumner himself. For three years he did not return to the Senate chamber. He traveled to England and France for medical treatments, some of which were agonizing; his spine had been affected, the foreign specialists told him, and for a long time he walked and talked like a man who had had a partial stroke.

Thus there would be many who would consider Sumner a tragic martyr, just as others would call him a faker who had been properly beaten for loose talk; and young Brooks would be a hero in the South, the recipient of innumerable gifts of canes, one of which bore a plate with the inscription: "Hit him again." He did not have long to live, this impulsive young congressman; within a year he would die of a bronchial infection, clawing at his throat for the air his lungs could not get; and in the days that were left to him he grew heartily sick of the kind of fame he had won, for he did not like to be considered a bully. He was a friendly, warmhearted man of good family, and he had grown up in a society in which a man might be held to render a physical account for any words he had used. He would have challenged Sumner to a duel, he said, if he had any notion that the man would accept, but since he knew that he would not he had felt obliged to use either a cane or a horsewhip. He had chosen the cane, and undeniably he had done what he set out to do—that is, he had worked off his own anger and he had compelled Sumner to shut up—but the final effect was wholly disastrous.⁸

For this particular method of replying to Sumner's speech was the one method above all others most certain to make many folk in the North overlook the provocation that the speech had contained. The slave power (it would be said) could not be reasoned with; the man who tried it would be bludgeoned almost to the point of death.

Violence in Kansas, violence in the Senate chamber; the infection was spreading.

The week was not over. One day there had been an elegantly phrased appeal to hatred, the next day a Kansas town had been sacked, the day after that a senator had been beaten to insensibility. Now it was May 24, forty-eight hours after the grim scene in the Senate chamber, and men with drawn swords were climbing through the shadows of early night in the ravines bordering Pottawatomie Creek in Kansas.

As weapons go, these swords had an odd history. They were shorter than cavalry sabers, straight in the blade, and some forgotten armorer had made them originally to government order as artillery broadswords. (In the old days all gunners wore swords for defense against attack by charging dragoons.) Then, in a sale of surplus property, the swords had been bought by a harebrained secret society in Ohio which called itself the Grand Eagles and which fuzzily imagined that one day it would attack and conquer Canada. The society's plans came to nothing, and when a cranky, hard-mouthed farmer-turned-sheep-trader came through the state muttering that the way to keep slavery out of Kansas was to go out there and "meddle directly with the peculiar institution," the swords had been turned over to him. They were made of good steel, and the society which had had such grand plans for them had had ornamental eagles etched on the blades.

Tonight the swords would be used, for the lanky Ohio farmer who proposed to meddle with the peculiar institution lived with strange fever-haunted dreams and felt an overwhelming compulsion to act on them. He was a rover, a ne'er-do-well, wholly ineffectual in everything he did save that he had the knack of drawing an entire nation after him on the road to unreasoning violence. He climbed the wooded ravines in the darkness this night, seven men at his heels—four of them were his own sons—and the naked metal of the swords glimmered faintly in the starlight. The man and his followers were free-state settlers from the town of Osawatomie. The grim farmer in the lead was named John Brown.

They had taken up arms two or three days earlier, along with other men, in a dimly legal free-state militia company, to go to the defense of Lawrence. By good or evil chance they got there too late, and all of the company but Brown and his chosen seven disbanded and went home. But Brown was obsessed. He declared that "something must be done to show these barbarians that we too have rights," and he and the seven turned a grindstone and ground their broadswords to a fine cutting edge. Some other militia leader saw and came over to warn Brown that he had better behave with caution.

"Caution, sir!" growled the old man. "I am eternally tired of hearing that word caution. It is nothing but the word of cowardice."

The eight men headed for Pottawatomie Creek, where proslavery settlers lived; and as they went they met a man who had seen late dispatches from Washington, and this man told them how Bully Brooks had beaten Senator Sumner. One of the party wrote of this news long afterward: "The men went crazy—*crazy*. It seemed to be the finishing, decisive touch."

For John Brown no more than a touch was needed. In some shadowy way the old man had got the idea that five free-state men had been killed at Lawrence, and he felt bound to balance the account. An eye for an eye, a life for a life; if five had been killed, five more must die; the logic that would kill an abstraction by striking at the living men is direct, unthinking, and grisly.[10]

John Brown and his band went stumping along through the night. They were in pro-slavery land now, and any man they saw would be an enemy. They came to one lonely cabin, saw lamplight gleaming under the door, and pounded for admittance. There was a noise as if someone were cocking a gun and sliding the muzzle through a chink in the logs, and the men slipped away from there—it was not precisely open combat that they were looking for. They went on, and after a time they came to a cabin occupied by a family named Doyle.

The Doyles were poor whites from Tennessee. They had come to Kansas recently, and although they believed in slavery—as men counted their beliefs in those days—they did not like to live too close to it; it appears that they had migrated in order to get away from it. Brown hammered on the door. It was opened, and he ordered Doyle and Doyle's two grown sons to come outside. The three men obeyed, the door was closed behind them, and Brown's band led the three away from the cabin. Then there were quick muffled sounds, brief cries, silence and stillness and darkness, and Brown and his followers went off down the road. In the morning the bodies of the three Doyles were found lying on the ground, fearfully mangled. They had been hacked to death with the Grand Eagle swords, which were to have been employed in the conquest of Canada but which had found strange other use. The father had been shot in the head.

Next the men went to the home of one Wilkinson, a noted pro-slavery leader. Knock on the door again: Wilkinson, ready for bed, came and opened up without bothering to put on his boots. The threat of death was in the very look of the terrible old man who peered in from the night, and Mrs.

Wilkinson—sick in bed with measles—cried and begged that her husband be spared. No pity: Wilkinson was taken out into the yard, the door was shut, and again the swords came down with full-arm swings—like the cane of Bully Brooks, only heavier and sharper. The men left Wilkinson dead in his dooryard and went on to another cabin.

Here they found William Sherman, Dutch Bill, known as one of the Border Ruffians. Dutch Bill, like the others, was dragged out into the darkness for the fearful work of darkness. In the morning he was found lying in a stream, his head split open, a great wound in his chest, one hand cut off—apparently he had put up a fight for his life.

It was past midnight now. Old Brown had planned to get five, and five he got. He and his men washed their swords in Pottawatomie Creek and went off to their homes.[11]

2. *Where They Were Bound to Go*

There were these things that happened in one week in the month of May 1856. The wind was being sown, and the hurricane would come later; and yet, all in all, these things were not so much causes as warnings—the lightning flashes that set evil scarlet flares against the black clouds that were banked up along the horizon. Somewhere beyond the lightning there was thunder, and the making of a great wind that would change the face of a nation, destroying much that men did not want destroyed. A doom was taking shape, and it seemed to be coming on relentlessly, as if there was nothing that anyone could do to prevent it. The republic that had been born in an air so full of promise that it might have been the morning of the seventh day was getting ready to tear itself apart.

Yet fate can move in two directions at once. At the same moment that it was driving men on to destroy the unity of their society it was also making certain that they would not be able to do it. Men who were whipping themselves up to the point where they would refuse to try to get along with one another were, at the same point of time, doing precisely the things that would bind them together forever whether they liked it or not. The impulse to disunion was coming to a land that, more or less in spite of itself, was in the very act of making union permanent.

The year 1856 saw many happenings that are much easier to interpret now than they were then. It saw wild appeals to anger and hate, convulsive moments of violence, heralds of a storm that would take five hundred thousand lives; it also saw the workings of a force greater than any storm, an incalculable thing that the wind and the lightnings could hardly touch. For even as they quarreled and learned to hate each other, Americans were in the act of entering upon a continental destiny. They were pouring out unfathomable energy upon a mighty land that was stronger than themselves. They were committing themselves to that land, and in the end it would have its way with them.

The steamers came down from Lake Superior that spring, carrying iron ore to furnaces on the lower lakes, and this was the first spring it had happened. Always before, Lake Superior had been landlocked—forever blue, forever cold, the scent of pine in the clean winds that blew over the water. In the mountains by the lake there was a great wealth of metals, but this wealth was locked up, out of reach, and the St. Mary's River came tumbling down in white foam through a green untouched wilderness. A few schooners had been hauled overland, creaking on rollers, dozens of oxen leaning into heavy wooden yokes. Some of these vessels, once afloat on the upper lake, brought small deckloads of red iron ore down to the Soo, where it was shoveled into little cars that ran on wooden rails, with teams of horses to haul the cars down below the rapids, where the ore was loaded into schooners that had come up from Lake Erie.

In midsummer Indians would camp by the rapids, to cast their nets for whitefish, having week-long feasts in the little clearings by the riverbank. Some venturesome merchant from lower Michigan came up every year with huge iron kettles and hired the Indians to pick tubfuls of wild blackberries, from which he made jam to sell in the cities on the lower lakes; and the clear air would be fragrant with the odor of broiling fish and bubbling blackberry jam—as pleasant a scent, probably, as the north country ever knew. Jesuits in their

black robes had been here in the old days, and trappers
bound for the beaver country, and a handful of soldiers—
soldiers of the French King once upon a time, and then
British redcoats, and at last United States regulars. Below the
rapids there was a meadow where sailors from the lower
lakes schooners camped on the grass and sang fresh-water
chanteys as they relaxed, backwoods-style, around the fire in
the evening:

> *And now we are bound down the lakes, let 'em roar—*
> *Hurrah, boys, heave her down!*

And the river and the land about it were empty, the north
wind murmuring across a thousand miles of untouched pine
trees, the whole of it as remote (as Henry Clay once contemptuously pointed out in the Senate) as the far side of the
moon, and as little likely to affect anything that happened
in the rest of the country.[1]

All of that was changing. A canal had been dug around the
rapids in the St. Mary's, with two locks in it—men hauled the
lock gates around by hand, and the water came burbling in
to rock the little wooden vessels that were being locked
through—and now the steamers could go all the way from
Cleveland and Detroit to the new ports of the Marquette
range, to bring ore down to the new furnaces. Eleven thousand tons of it would go down this year, ten times as much
as had ever gone down before, and nothing would be the
same again. Nothing would be the same because the canal
and the shipping were the visible symbols of a profound and
unsuspected transformation.

The puffing wooden steamers, stopping at the old sailors'
encampment to take on wood for fuel (three hundred cords
of it at a time, for a fair bunkerful), were part of a vast
process that nobody had planned and that nobody could stop;
a process that was turning America into an entirely new sort
of country which could do practically any imaginable thing
under the sun except divide into separate pieces. In Ohio and
Pennsylvania the blast furnaces and foundries and rolling
mills were going up, railroads were reaching from the forks
of the Ohio to the Lake Erie shore to take coal one way and

iron ore the other, and there would be more trains and steamers and mills and mines, year after year, decade after decade. America would cease to have room for things like an empty wilderness at the Soo, with sailors lounging by campfires in lazy waiting, with Indians netting fish from a flashing river while ripe berries simmered in the iron kettles at the edge of a silent forest, the timeless emptiness of unclaimed land and unfretted leisure running beyond vision in every direction. It would have no room, either, for a feudal plantation economy below the Ohio, veneered with chivalry and thin romance and living in an outworn dream, or for the peculiar institution by which that economy lived, or for the hot pride and the wild impossible visions that grew out of it. The old ways were going, an overpowering compulsive force was being generated, and the long trails of smoke that lay on the curving blue horizon of Luke Huron were the signs of it.[2]

It was not just iron ore. The Illinois Central Railroad was finishing the seven hundred miles of its "charter lines," running from Chicago down to the land of Egypt, where the Ohio met the Mississippi, with a crossline belting the black prairie from east to west with a terminus at Dunleith on the upper Mississippi. It was running fabulous "gothic cars" for sleepers, with staterooms and berths, and washrooms fitted in marble and plate glass, and in Chicago it had just built the largest railroad station in the world. (Too large by far, said eastern railroaders, and here on the edge of nowhere not half of the station would ever be used. Within a decade it would be outgrown, needing enlargement.) In two years the railroad had sold more than eight hundred thousand acres of land to settlers, and its elevators on the river were already stacked with wheat brought down by steamer from Minnesota, where newcomers in this one year would take up a million acres of new farm land.

Wheat was the word, along with iron. America was beginning to feed Europe, and the price of grain had gone up and up. Farmers were driving a hundred miles or more, in Illinois and Wisconsin, to reach railroad stations and lake ports with wagonloads of grain, and there were long lines at the elevators; often enough a man had to wait twenty-four hours before he could discharge his load. On the lakes a grain schooner could earn her cost in a single season. With new mechanical reapers and with steel moldboard plows, men could till more land and reap bigger harvests than ever before, and the lake and river states were drawing people in by the thousand, from the East and from the South and from faraway Europe.[3]

For here was something new in the world, a great land promising everything men had hoped for, the very air and sunlight seeming keener and brighter than the air and the light in other places. On the docks at New York were crowds of immigrants, many of them knowing no single word of English except for some place name like Milwaukee or Chicago; somehow they found their way to the comfortless trains that would take them West, and at Buffalo they boarded the creaking side-wheelers, barrels of bedding and crockery and crates of furniture on the decks, wagon wheels lashed in the rigging, to finish the journey to something that they could find nowhere else on earth.

In addition to wheat and iron, there were people. Not all of them came from overseas. In America there was a continual surging and shifting, with New Englanders going to Ohio, Kentuckians to Illinois, Hoosiers to the black-soil country west of the Mississippi. They were looking for the same thing the immigrants were looking for—a chance to make life a little better for themselves—and they saw their destiny in this great western land tied by natural law to the destiny of the whole country.

In this year 1856 there was a typical family opening a new farm in Iowa, and this family's story expresses the whole of it.

For a quarter of a century this family had lived in Indiana, settling there when a good farm could be bought from the government for two dollars an acre, building in the wilderness a home that was almost entirely self-sufficient; one man recalled that "we could have built a Chinese wall around our home and lived comfortably, asking favors of no man." This was sturdy frontier independence, romantic enough when seen from a distance, but nobody wanted to put up with it any longer than he really had to. For there were no markets —"no demand and no price." A drove of hogs might be chivvied 150 miles through the woods to Cincinnati, to be sold there for $1.50 per hundred pounds; what could be bought with the money thus obtained was costly, with calico selling for 40 cents a yard and muslin for 75 cents, and with tea costing $1.50 a pound.[4]

As the western country opened, this isolation ended. As roads were built and people moved in and cities and towns sprang up, with steamboat and railroad lines handy, new markets were opened; crops could be sold for a decent sum, necessities and luxuries could be bought; and the mere fact that there were people all around brought prosperity, so that this particular family at last sold its Indiana farm for $100 an acre and moved on to Iowa, to do the whole thing over again.

As they went west they saw thousands of others doing the same, and a young man remarked that "Old America seemed to be breaking up and moving west."[5] The die had already been cast. In the East men who looked to the Pacific coast looked overland now, and not around the Horn. The great day of the clippers was over. The noble winged *Sea Witch* was a forgotten wreck on a reef off the Cuban coast, the *Flying Cloud* lay idle at her wharf for want of a charter, and it no longer paid to build ships that could advertise ninety days to California. California was peopled and fully won, the great leap to the Pacific had been made, and what was important now was to fill in the empty space.

A few years earlier Stephen A. Douglas had tried to say it in the Senate: "There is a power in this nation greater than the North or the South—a growing, increasing, swelling power that will be able to speak the law to this nation and to execute the law as spoken. That power is the country known as the Great West—"[6]

Yet men see things late, and it may be that at times an evil fate drives them on. In 1856 what seemed to be important was the great and sublimely irrelevant argument, the great fear and the great surge of emotion; unforgivable words self-righteously spoken, blows brought down from behind on a defenseless head, a drunken mob rioting across a frontier town, long knives slashing and hacking in the moonlight. Out of this, heralded by this and much more like it, men would pay half a million lives to go, finally, where they were bound to go anyway.

3. *Light over the Marshes*

The substance and the shadow went in opposite directions, and it was hard to say which was real and which was no more than a shred of mist blowing from the land of haunted impossible dreams; and there was, meanwhile, a great pentagon of masonry built on a reef at the entrance to the harbor of Charleston, South Carolina, where the orderly sequence of events was about to be crossruffled by exploding violence.

This was Fort Sumter, which had been built in a routine way to adorn the coast of a country that expected never to go to war, and the fort stood at the precise spot where the hurricane was going to break. In the fort there was a company of artillerists of the regular army, seventy-odd of them in all, commanded by a grave Kentucky major named Robert Anderson. They had hired out to do a job, and in the ordinary course of things the job was simple enough: to stand guard over government property, looking vigilantly to seaward for an enemy who would never come by water, and to walk post in a military manner permitting no nuisances. When the early months of 1861 came along this routine job developed an extraordinary tension.

For the bitterly divided men who, unable to phrase a nobler appeal, had asked fear and anger to judge between them were being compelled to cope with an issue greater than any of them. They had not chosen to cope with it; they had been willing to go to almost any length to avoid coping with it; but it was there, and now it had to be faced. At the very bottom of American life, under its highest ideals and its most dazzling hopes, lay the deep intolerable wrong of slavery, the common possession not of a class or a section but of the nation as a whole. It was the one fatally limiting factor in a nation of wholly unlimited possibilities; whatever America would finally stand for, in a world painfully learning that its most sacred possession was the infinite individual human spirit, would depend on what was done about this evil relic of the past. Abraham Lincoln had once called it "the great Behemoth of danger,"[1] and now it was forcing men into war.

Yet for a long time men would refuse to admit that this was the dreadful inevitable beneath all of their differences. They would look instead at symbols; at swaggering Border Ruffians, at gaunt John Brown, or at something else. And in April 1861, Fort Sumter itself had suddenly become the most compelling of these symbols.

When southern men looked at the fort they saw a squat, ugly obstacle standing in the path of romantic destiny, the visible sign that there were cold and designing folk who would not let the lovely, white-pillared, half-imaginary past perpetuate itself; they lined the mud flats and the sand dunes around Charleston Harbor with batteries, and eager young men in gray uniforms tossed palmetto flags into the wind, until Major Anderson at last calculated that if his government ever tried to force its way in to rescue him it would need all of its navy and an army of twenty thousand men besides.

Most Northerners, so far, were hardly looking at the fort at all. Secession had been threatened for years and now it was here, but there was something unreal about the situation. Sumter was no more than an unpleasant reminder of a distasteful possibility. Yet there it was, a solid block of a thing, holding the national flag in the light between Charleston and the sunrise, and the indifference of the North was only apparent. For beneath everything else, North and West, there ran a profound, unvoiced, almost subconscious conviction that the nation was going to go on growing—in size, in power, in everything a man could think of—and in that belief there was a might and a fury that would take form instantly at the moment of shock. If just one of these encircling guns should be fired an immeasurable emotional flood would be released.

But for the time there was an uneasy equilibrium. The regulars did their best to go on as usual. Some months earlier they had noticed that the people of Charleston were courting them—were courting even the enlisted men, who in ordinary times had a dog's berth and expected nothing better and so were not courted by anybody. There is a record of a banquet in Charleston (held in the autumn of 1860, before things had quite come to a head) with high privates seated with their betters at a great table, and one mercenary in uniform, full of good food and southern whiskey, got up on the table and stalked at full stride from one end to the other, scattering meat and drink and broken china, scandalizing the elect; yet pride was swallowed and nothing was done to him, because hired soldiers might change flags if they were treated softly. In the end the hired soldiers changed no flags; instead they moved their own flag from obsolete Fort Moultrie, which could never be defended, into Fort Sumter, which perhaps could be; and now they waited in their stronghold, in a situation odd enough for anyone.'

There was no war. As far as the government in Washington was concerned, the men in Sumter had not an enemy in the world. Yet they were in fact besieged, and as they worked to perfect their defenses they knew perfectly well that the besiegers could take the place any time they cared to make the effort. The food the garrison ate, the mail it received, the very orders it got from the War Department, all came to it entirely by sufferance of the southern Confederacy—which clearly was refraining from bombarding the fort into submission only because it seemed possible that Washington could be pressured into giving it away without a fight.

This seemed possible to Winfield Scott, among others—Winfield Scott, commanding general of the United States Army, old and pompous and dropsical but pretty much all soldier just the same. Early in the winter Scott sat at his desk in Washington, proudly wrote "headquarters of the Army" at the top of a sheet of paper, and expressed himself in a memorandum to the Secretary of War. As always, Scott wrote of himself respectfully in the third person:

"Lieutenant General Scott, who has had a bad night, and can scarcely hold up his head this morning, begs to express the hope to the Secretary of War"—that Fort Sumter be held, provisioned, reinforced and given the help of a couple of first-class warships. Two days later the old general wrote a letter to President James Buchanan, who was all but totally immobilized by the twin beliefs that the southern states could not legally secede and that the Federal government could not legally stop them if they tried it. To Buchanan, General Scott wrote:

"It is Sunday; the weather is bad, and General Scott is not

well enough to go to church. But matters of the highest national importance seem to forbid a moment's delay, and if
misled by zeal he hopes for the President's forgiveness"—and,
in fine, it was vital to reinforce the Sumter garrison at once,
sending in more weapons and stores and calling on the navy
for help.[3]

All of this got nobody anywhere. To be sure, Sumter was
not abandoned and a steamer was sent down with stores and
men; but it was not convoyed by naval forces, the coastal
batteries drove it away, and as spring came Major Anderson
and his men were still locked up in their fort. They did what
they could to make the place strong, bricking up embrasures
that they could not defend and hoisting the heavy barbette
guns to their emplacements on top of the fort, and they ate
their way through their dwindling supply of provisions. In
mid-March there was an odd incident, which went all but
unnoticed: a young Negro slave, sensing no doubt that what
with one thing and another there might be a new meaning
for men like himself in ground held by the United States
Army, broke away from his lawful owner in Charleston, stole
a canoe, and in the darkness paddled out to Fort Sumter to
find refuge. The officers there promptly sent him back to his
owner, not realizing that they had in their hands, months before the expression would have any meaning, the first of
thousands upon thousands of *contrabands*.[4]

On the same day President Abraham Lincoln, newly
inaugurated, wrote to his Secretary of War:

"Assuming it to be possible to now provision Fort Sumter,
under all the circumstances is it wise to attempt it?"

Under all of the circumstances, the Secretary replied, it
would not be wise; would not, in fact, even be possible. The
best brains in the army held that it would take an expedition of
such size and scope that four months would pass before it
could even be assembled.[5] Major Anderson called for a report on the quantity of food remaining in the fort and
learned that there were six barrels of flour, six more of hardtack, three of sugar, two of vinegar, two dozen of salt pork,
and various odds and ends, including three boxes of candles.
Out in the marshes the sandbag parapets kept on growing,
with black metal visible in the apertures, and the ring grew

tighter and tighter. Then the garrison was notified that no more supplies could be bought in Charleston. Mr. Lincoln sent a messenger to tell the governor of South Carolina that Washington meant no particular harm but that a cargo of food for Sumter's garrison would be coming down directly, and then the government of the Confederate States of America formally demanded of Major Anderson that he haul down his flag and surrender.[6]

Major Anderson replied that he would obey no such demand. He added, however, that if the Confederates cared to be a little patient his men would be out of food in a very few days and would have to give up anyway. Trim officers in swords and sashes went back and forth between the fort and the encircling batteries that evening. There was grave, courtly politeness between besieged and besiegers, with solemn handshakes and farewells on the fort's wharf by torchlight, and word came back at last that what the major had said was not good enough: he must surrender now, and do it under the gun. This, said the major, he could not do; and so, after midnight, the final word came out from the mainland: Our batteries will open on the fort in one hour precisely.[7]

War: the word had been said, and the business could go just one way. In the black hours of early morning the United States officers stood at the parapet atop Fort Sumter and looked off in the darkness toward the place where, they knew, the nearest guns had been planted. The candle flame was guttering out fast and it was very close to the socket, but as long as it continued to flicker the America of the old days still lived, the America that was cemented to a heritage from the past with a dream born of pride and careless waste, of lazy beauty and cruelty, its face turned away from the future—a dream that would begin to die the moment its impassioned defenders pulled on the lanyard of one of the surrounding cannon.

And at last there was a quick flash, like heat lightning, off beyond the unseen marshland, and a sullen red spark climbed up the black sky, seemed to hang motionless for a final instant-directly overhead, and then came plunging down, to explode in great light and rocking sound that would reverberate across the land and mark an end and a beginning.

2.

Not to Be Ended Quickly

1. *Men Who Could Be Led*

IN THE state capitol at Columbus, Ohio, senators were talking their way through a desultory session when one of their number came hurrying in from the lobby. There was some note of urgency in his manner, and the debate died down. Catching the eye of the presiding officer, he called out: "Mr. President, the telegraph announces that the secessionists are bombarding Fort Sumter!" There was a stunned silence in the chamber for a moment. Then, far up in the gallery, a woman sprang to her feet and screamed ecstatically: "Glory to God!"

The woman was a devout abolitionist, convinced that nothing mattered but to set the Negro free and that only war could do it, and most people in the North did not see it that way. Yet her terrible cry, ringing out without premeditation, somehow spoke for men and women all across the land, and they surged out into bannered streets to cheer and laugh and exult. There had been all of these years of doubt, of argument, of bewilderment and half-stifled anger; the moment of disaster brought wild rejoicing, as if an unendurable emotional tension had at last been broken.

For Abraham Lincoln, to be sure, the news from Fort Sumter brought no release.

He had said that his policy was to have no policy; that he did not control events but was controlled by them; that his task was heavier than the one Washington had carried; and now he had to act firmly and swiftly in a contingency not provided for by the founding fathers. What he could do, he did without delay. On April 15 he announced that "combina-

23

tions too powerful to be suppressed" by any U.S. marshal or *posse comitatus* had taken possession of various southern states, and he called on the states to send seventy-five thousand militia into Federal service for three months to restore order. He summoned Congress to meet in special session on July 4. He announced a blockade of southern ports, from South Carolina to Texas. (Something of a mistake, this announcement, for the navy could not for months begin to make the blockade fully effective, and the announcement automatically gave the Confederacy a belligerent's status and almost seemed to admit that it was in fact a separate nation.) Not least important was Lincoln's act in promptly going into consultation with Stephen A. Douglas, idol of the northern democracy. From Douglas there came a firm pledge of support for any warlike acts needed to restore the Union. Douglas was worn out, less than two months away from death, but he went across the Midwest rallying men to the cause; and as he spoke, in a voice whose dimming vitality still carried magic, he laid at rest the danger that the war might seem to be purely a party matter, to be opposed by northern Democrats as a matter of straight politics.[2]

Having done the things immediately required of him, President Lincoln could only wait for the country to respond.

It responded with a wild enthusiasm that was almost beyond belief. The quick outpouring of emotion surprised even the people who were at the center of it.

In Washington, sober Senator John Sherman wrote that the actual arrival of war "brings a feeling of relief: the suspense is over." A Bostonian considered the crowds, the ringing church bells, and the awakened drums and trumpets and noted that "the heather is on fire," while a newspaper correspondent telegraphed that the war spirit in the West exceeded anything the most hopeful Republicans had expected. A New York woman looked at the cheering crowds and felt the wild excitement, and wrote that "it seems as if we never were alive till now." An Ohio politician, looking back long afterward, remembered the outburst of jubilant feeling that swept across the North as "a thrilling and almost supernatural thing."[3]

Supernatural it may perhaps have been; for when men

looked about them, in the strangely revealing light of the exploding shell, they saw something that was to carry them
through four years of war. It is hard to say just what it was,
for nobody bothered to be very explicit about it and time has
dimmed it anyway, but apparently what they saw—briefly but
clearly, after so many years in which nothing was clear—was
the fact that they did have a country and that their common
possession of it was the most precious thing in the world. For
a time this lifted them up, so that they went off to war joy-
ously, as if the moment of crisis had lifted a burden instead of
imposing one; and what was seen was long remembered, the
memory of it a rod and a staff to lean upon when the path
led down through the valley of shadows.

There was in all of this a bright innocence, and a losing of
innocence, and nothing quite like it ever happened again, or
ever can happen. Except for a few veterans of the war with
Mexico, no one knew what organized war could be like, and
even the middle-aged men who had fought in Mexico had
nothing in their experience by which to foretell the sweep
and terror of the war that was beginning now. The land was
used to peace, and in the ordinary way its experience with
military matters was confined to the militia muster—awkward
men parading with heavy-footed informality in the public
square, jugs circulating up and down the rear rank, fires lit
for the barbecue feast, small boys clustering around, half
derisive and half admiring—and if war came the soldier was
a minuteman who went to a bloodless field where it was always the other fellow who would get hit.

Just before Fort Sumter the Michigan legislature had been
debating an act permitting the governor to raise two new
regiments of militia. Secession had come and war was near,
and it seemed wise to prepare for it; yet the legislators
somehow could not quite take the project seriously, and
their humor rose because the bill contained a provision for
"field officers"—technically, regimental officers above the rank
of captain. Amendments were solemnly introduced to change
the title to "corn-field officers," the sense of urgency evaporated in a chain of rude jokes, and in the end the legislature adjourned without voting any money to make the act
effective. A week after Fort Sumter the state was enlisting

volunteers as fast as the men could be sworn in, and the money needed for equipment, which the legislature had gaily refused to appropriate, was raised by popular subscription—eighty-one thousand dollars of it in a few days in the little city of Detroit alone.⁴

As in Michigan, so in all other states. The thing had suddenly become serious, and yet everyone was gay about it. The call for troops looked like a summons to high adventure, a prodigious lark to be held under government auspices and at government expense. To thousands and thousands of young men it seemed the chance of a lifetime. War was all music and flags and cheering crowds, the bands were playing "Yankee Doodle" and "The Girl I Left Behind Me," and "Dixie"—not yet a southern war song, "Dixie"; it piped many a Yankee regiment off to war—and the man who enlisted felt that he was lucky beyond all natural expectation. So the recruiting stations were crowded, and all that mattered was to be young and to share in the vibration of a common enthusiasm.

In New York City the tattered flag that had been flown over Fort Sumter was displayed to a vast crowd, and Senator Edward Baker of Oregon, old-time friend of Abraham Lincoln, was on a rostrum to demand that the national flag be hoisted again "over every rebellious fort of every Confederate state." The Union, he cried, must conquer a peace and dictate its own terms, and whether it cost seven thousand lives or seven hundred thousand was no matter—"We have them!" He looked out over the crowd, tossed his head in the practiced orator's gesture, and shouted: "My mission here today is to kindle the heart of New York for war—short, sudden, bold, determined, forward war!"⁵

(Senator Baker would presently become a soldier himself. The bullet that would kill him had already been molded; on the brow of a wooded bluff above the Potomac the place where he would fall had been appointed; he had, as he made this speech, about four more months to live.)

In Iowa twenty times as many men as could be taken came forward to volunteer. Because this frontier state had few railroads, men came in by farm wagon or on foot, some of them taking ten days for the trip, and those who were turned away raised a great clamor, so that the state authorities had to beg the War Department to increase the quota—the rejected volunteers would not go home, but stayed around the enlistment centers and demanded admittance. Men who were accepted went to camps where contractors fed them on fresh beef and soft bread. So primitive was their frontier background that many of these lads from the back lots promptly became sick from eating food too rich for them; at home their diet was mostly salt pork and corn bread.*

Everywhere there were more men than the army was prepared to take. Many companies were raised locally, to be assembled into regiments later, and often enough the companies were far above the legal size when they went to camp. In such cases the roster would be pruned and some men would be sent home; and an Illinois veteran recalled that this led to "a great deal of very wicked swearing," with some of the men who had been dropped threatening to shoot the colonel. In Indiana many companies that had been ordered to stay at home went off to camp regardless, making such an uproar that the state authorities had to admit them in sheer self-defense; and in Boston men climbed in through the windows of Faneuil Hall to join companies that were using the building as a drillroom. The country's overcharged patriotism led to odd aberrations here and there. A newspaper correspondent reported that Illinois businessmen were raising money to support the families of volunteers, insisting that "none shall fight the battles of their country at their expense"; a number of railroads in Indiana announced that they would carry all soldiers free, and Company H of the 11th Massachusetts marched up in a body to take a pledge of total abstinence for the duration of the war, officers and men, explaining that "their business is to fight, not drink."*

The training these volunteers got, once they reached camp, was often very sketchy. Company and regimental officers at that stage of the war were elected, and in most cases they knew no more about military matters than the recruits they were supposed to instruct. It was not uncommon to see a captain on the parade ground consulting a book as he drilled his company, and after the war a survivor from those early days wrote that he and his fellows "had some fun that the boys missed who went out after things were in good shape and the officers had learned the tactics." Boys who had been on a first-name basis with their officers all of their lives could see no point whatever in military formalities. In a New York regiment one recruit who thought the drill had gone on long enough on a warm spring day called out to his captain: "Say, Tom, let's quit this darn foolin' and go over to the sutler's." A Massachusetts veteran remembered that his company bore the name of "The Savages" and wore dark green uniforms, and said that "our drill, as I remember it, was running around the old Town Hall in West Newbury, yelling like devils and firing at an imaginary foe." Men in a Wisconsin company were quartered for weeks in a small-town hotel, from which they were in the habit of emerging at midnight, whooping and laughing, to hold a "night-shirt drill" in the town's main street.[8]

At times the whole business seemed like an extended picnic. An Ohio soldier looked back, long after the war, at "those happy, golden days of camp life" and said the only worry was the fear that the war would end before the regiment had a chance to prove itself under fire. (It was a needless worry, he recalled dryly; by war's end more than a third of the regiment's total enrollment had become casualties, and 150 more had died of disease.) An Irish boy remembered "the shrill notes of the fifes and the martial beat and roll of the drums, as they played in unison at early daylight," as the sweetest music he ever heard, and an Illinois soldier wrote to the folks back home: "I never enjoyed anything in the world as I do this life." The drill, he said, was very light, and the regiment was leading "an awful lazy life"; and he concluded rhapsodically that it was wonderful to be where "a fellow can lay around loose with sleeves up, collar open (or shirt off, if it suits him better), hair unkempt, face unwashed, and everything un-everything. It beats clerking ever so much!"[9]

It did beat clerking. Boys in a Wisconsin regiment, whose roster was not yet full, used to ride about the country in wagons, seeking recruits, with drummer and fifer to play them along, the cavalcade riding into towns with all hands yelling: "Fourth of July every day in the year!" There would be a war meeting in town hall or village grove, with speeches and music, and afterward a barbecue. Girls would urge their swains to enlist. These Wisconsin soldiers remembered one meeting at which a girl cried out to her escort in a voice all could hear: "John, if you don't enlist I'll never let you kiss me again as long as I live! Now you mind, sir, I mean what I say!"[10]

Every regiment was formally given a flag sooner or later, usually by a committee of ladies, with the mayor and leading citizens looking on and with some orator present to make suitable remarks. The flag was generally handed to the colonel by some pretty girl, and it was fairly standard procedure for the entire regiment to take a solemn oath that they would not return "until our flag could wave in triumph over all our land." It was a sentimental age, much given to dramatic tableaux. Men in a New York regiment recalled that when they finally boarded the cars to start off for Washington their train passed a species of rocky knoll not long after leaving the depot; and on the knoll, togged out in Revolutionary War regimentals, there posed a white-haired man waving a flag, while two small girls dressed in white knelt on each side of him, their arms stretched out and their eyes raised as if in prayer.

Some regiments took on especial characteristics. The New York 7th was a dandy outfit, private soldiers wearing tailor-made gray uniforms as trim as so many West Pointers, with hired cooks to prepare the meals. The 33rd Illinois, organized largely through the efforts of Charles E. Hovey, principal of the State Normal University, who became its colonel, had many college students and teachers in its ranks and was known, inevitably, as the "Brains regiment." All sorts of tales were circulated about it; privates discharged from its rolls for mental incapacity, it was said, promptly won officers' commissions in less brilliant regiments. The 8th Wisconsin was famous as the "Eagle regiment," because its Company C came to camp with a live eagle as mascot. A T-shaped perch was devised, and the bird—known as "Old Abe"—was carried between regimental and national flags wherever the regiment went. Old Abe was even taken into battle later on; liked artillery fire and would flap his wings and scream loudly, but grew depressed and nervous under musketry fire. The eagle survived the war and was taken back to Wisconsin and became an essential feature of innumerable post-war veterans' reunions.[11]

Military drill, where it was taken seriously, was a nuisance to be endured. An Illinois soldier spoke of "that most exasperating and yet most useful institution of the early army, the German drill sergeant," and in a labored attempt to transcribe high-Dutch brogue he quoted the sergeant as forever crying: "Eyes vront! Toes oudt! Leetle finger mit de seam de bantaloons! Vy shtand like a —— —— haystack? You neffer make a soldier." In a Wisconsin regiment a recruit wrote to his parents that his drillmaster "is a proud bugger in his brand new suit of blue," and confessed that army life "is harder work than farming." Yet the ardor that took the men to camp sometimes made even the drill seem pleasant, and when a spanking new Ohio regiment was given muskets and introduced to the manual of arms one soldier noted that "the boys take to it as natural as a three-months calf to a pail of warm milk." Nor was military routine always repellent. Most recruits were fascinated by the lights-out ritual. At nine o'clock in the evening the regimental band would play "tattoo," after which the roll would be called. Half an hour later came "taps," which meant that everyone must be in bed with lights out; and "taps," according to old-army procedure, was given by a drummer, not by a bugler. In the silent, darkening camp a lone drummer would stand at the head of the regimental street and tap out the single drumbeats that gave the business its name. A certain rhythm was always followed, and the men fitted words to it: "*Go* to bed *Tom! Go* to bed *Tom! Go* to bed, go to bed, go to bed *Tom!*"[12]

Needed equipment often was lacking. An Illinois regiment could get no more muskets than were needed to arm the camp sentries, and for quite a time—until the first enthusiasm wore off, anyway—the men eagerly competed for the right to take a musket and stand guard; a state of mind which they recalled with amused wonder a year later. In Iowa, recruits were told to bring no change of clothing to camp as Uncle Sam would provide everything. One regiment had to wait for more than a month before Uncle Sam provided as much as a spare undershirt, and a generation later the regimental historian was remembering that month with wry distaste. In Ohio the first recruits to reach Camp Dennison found that the camp consisted entirely of a huge pile of raw lumber and a very muddy cornfield; before anyone could get shelter the men had to build their own barracks.[12]

The first volunteers were enlisted for ninety days only and were technically state militia called temporarily into Federal service. Long before most of them were ready to leave training camp—on May 3, actually, little more than a fortnight after Fort Sumter—President Lincoln issued a call for three-year volunteers. These regiments were raised and organized by the states and, when complete, were mustered into Federal service, after which they were entirely out of state control; and as the men enlisted under this call reached camp, things began to look a little more businesslike, with less of the flavor of an old-time holiday militia muster.

Yet matters never did reach what a modern soldier would consider proper military tautness. Some of the new volunteer regiments had colonels and lesser officers from the regular service, and in these a fair degree of impersonal discipline and formality was sometimes attained, but for the most part—especially among the western regiments—discipline was and remained fantastically loose. Boys from the small town and the cornfield simply could not make themselves look on their officers with awe, and a lieutenant or a colonel—or, for that matter, even a general—could exercise very little control just by virtue of his shoulder straps; he had to have solid qualities of leadership within himself or he did precious little leading.

For it never entered the heads of most of these volunteers that a free American citizen surrendered any appreciable part of his freedom just by joining the army. An Indiana soldier put it quite bluntly: "We had enlisted to put down the rebellion and had no patience with the red-tape tom-foolery of the regular service. Furthermore, our boys recognized no superiors except in the line of legitimate duty. Shoulder straps waived, a private was ready at the drop of a hat to thrash his commander; a feat that occurred more than once." In Missouri, men of a volunteer regiment which was camped next to a regular army regiment looked on in horror when one of the regulars was "bucked and gagged" for some infraction of discipline. When one of the regular officers ("a dudish young fellow") came out and ordered the volunteers to go away and stop making a scene over it, they threatened to untie his prisoner and set him free. One of the volunteers remembered: "We told the officer that they might do that to regulars, but that they could not do that sort of thing to free American citizens." An Illinois soldier, recalling the slack discipline that always prevailed in his regiment, frankly justified it:

"While all the men who enlisted pledged themselves to obey all the commands of their superior officers, and of course ought to have kept their word, yet it was hardly wise on the part of the officers in volunteer service to absolutely demand attendance upon such service, and later on it was abandoned."[4]

This free-and-easy quality the Civil War soldier never lost. It remained with him to the end, and although it was less marked in the eastern regiments, generally, than in those from the West, and varied a good deal from regiment to regiment in each section, it was always, and predominantly, the great distinguishing characteristic of the volunteer armies. For better or for worse, the armies of the Civil War had that devil-may-care, loose-jointed tone to them. They could be led—by the right man, anyway—but they could not often be driven. Their members straggled freely, foraged and looted as the mood seized them, sometimes deserted in droves—and, in the end, carried the load that had been given them, which was not a light one.

. . . They had, at the very top, a commander-in-chief who understood their point of view perfectly because he had had firsthand experience of it: Abraham Lincoln. (Jefferson Davis was West Point, and a self-made patrician to boot, and he never quite understood the enlisted Confederate, who was very much like his northern counterpart, if not a good deal more so.) Lincoln had been captain of a volunteer company in the Black Hawk War: a hard set of men, who cried out "Go to hell!" in response to the first order Lincoln ever gave them. They got badly out of hand—or, to be more accurate, they never got into hand—and Lincoln was ordered by a court-martial to carry a wooden sword for two days because he had been unable to keep his company from robbing the regimental whiskey cache and getting drunk. To keep his men from murdering an Indian peddler who wandered into camp, Captain Lincoln once had to take off his coat and offer to thrash each soldier personally. Later, when he was in Congress, Lincoln made a speech ridiculing his own military experience and his pretensions to command.[15]

Yet the experience may have been one of the most valuable of his life. In the Civil War, Lincoln called into service rather more than a million and a half young men, the bulk of whom were his Black Hawk War company all over again. From first to last, he knew them—knew what they could do, how much they could stand, knew how they could be persuaded to surpass themselves on occasion.

2. *In Time of Revolution*

Abraham Lincoln was not all brooding melancholy and patient understanding. There was a hard core in him, and plenty of toughness. He could recognize a revolutionary situation when he saw one, and he could act fast and ruthlessly to meet it.

Long-range, his problem was to take the formless, instinctive uprising of the northern people and develop from it a firm resolve that would outlast the tempest and make the Union secure. First of all, however, he had to keep the war from being lost before it had well begun. For there was a considerable danger that the Confederacy might make its independence good before the first militia regiments had got fairly settled in their makeshift training camps.

To begin with, the call for troops to suppress those "combinations too powerful to resist" had driven Virginia, Arkansas, North Carolina, and Tennessee into secession. Shortly after Fort Sumter those states joined the Confederacy, and from his White House window the President could look across the Potomac and see a landscape which—rolling to the south in hazy blue waves under the warm spring sunlight—was now, by the will of the people who lived in it, part of a foreign country.

What Virginia had done the border states might possibly

do, and if they did the game was probably lost beyond recall.

Maryland, Kentucky, and Missouri were slave states of divided sentiment, many people strong for secession, many more equally strong for the Union. With the western part of Virginia—where, it was beginning to appear, most people were unhappy over the state's act of secession—these states lay in a long wide ribbon, reaching from tidewater to the Nebraska country. This ribbon might swing either way. If it swung south, then the Confederacy's frontier lay along the Ohio River and the Mason and Dixon line, southern Indiana and Illinois could probably be pinched off, Washington itself would be wholly surrounded by hostile territory, and the Unionists' task would be hopeless. On the other hand, if this area stayed with the Union, the way was open for a thrust straight into the heart of the Confederacy. The whole war might well be determined by what happened in the border states, and there the only certainty was that whatever happened was going to happen rather quickly.

Things came to a head first in Maryland. On April 19, less than a week after the surrender of Fort Sumter, the first of the new militia regiments to go to Washington, 6th Massachusetts, gay in its new uniforms, marched cross-town through Baltimore to change trains and got into a street fight with a mob of furiously secessionist civilians. Brickbats and paving stones were thrown, pistols were fired, soldiers fired their muskets; militiamen and civilians were killed, and southern sympathizers in and near the city came storming out in wild anger, destroying bridges so that no more of the despised Yankee regiments could profane their city. Temporarily the capital's connections with the North were broken.

The Lincoln government wasted no time. The appeal of the Unionist-minded governor of Maryland, Thomas H. Hicks, that no more troops be sent through Baltimore, was complied with—it had to be, for a while, since the bridges were gone—but a heavy hand came down hard on the Maryland secessionists. A shifty, cross-eyed Massachusetts lawyer-politician named Benjamin Butler appeared in major general's uniform with troops at his command, and after he had restored northern communications with Washington by way of Annapolis, he moved up and occupied Federal Hill, overlooking downtown Baltimore. The city's mayor and nineteen members of the state legislature (which had just denounced the unholy war upon the South) were thrown into jail, along with a good many indignant citizens. When Chief Justice Roger Brooke Taney issued a writ of habeas corpus to set one of these free, President Lincoln blandly ignored it. Eastern Maryland, where secessionist sentiment ran the strongest, was firmly held by Federal troops—and, all in all, by mid-May or a bit later the government had things pretty well in hand. The Supreme Court had indeed been flouted, the Constitution had been stretched, perhaps even broken (depending on one's point of view), scores of people were being held in prison without due process of law, and an ardent son of Maryland was writing a flaming war poem, apostrophizing his state with the cry: "The despot's heel is on thy shore!" No matter. Maryland was not going to go out of the Union, and what Maryland might have done if all of the legal niceties had been observed made no difference at all.[1]

The new administration, in other words, was not afraid to act. Yet it knew how to walk softly and speak in a soothing voice, as well, and while it was inflicting Ben Butler and unfeeling Yankee militia on eastern Maryland it was being most scrupulously considerate and correct just a little farther west.

As far as western Virginia was concerned, to be sure, the administration had very little to worry about. The people beyond the mountains owned few slaves and had no great admiration for the tidewater aristocracy, and Virginia had hardly seceded from the Union when they began casting about for means to secede from Virginia. For the moment, Washington needed to do nothing about them except indicate approval and stand by to lend a helping hand when necessary. But in Kentucky things were very different.

Kentucky needed very delicate handling. Its governor, Beriah Magoffin, had flatly refused to send troops to Washington for "the wicked purpose" of subduing the South and was known as a secessionist. The legislature, however, was Unionist, or largely so, and when the Confederates invited Governor Magoffin to send them some troops he had to decline, on the ground that it was beyond his power to do so. Then he issued a proclamation announcing that Kentucky would be wholly neutral in this war, and both factions within the state sat back to wait each other out, to jockey for position, and in general to see what would happen next.

It seemed fairly clear that most Kentuckians favored the Union. But it was equally clear that this was no time to jiggle Kentucky's elbow, since any abrupt coercive move might turn everything upside down. For the time being both Abraham Lincoln and Jefferson Davis were happy enough to let Kentucky be neutral if that was what Kentucky wanted.

What Kentucky would finally do, in fact, would probably depend a great deal on what Missouri did; and although the situation in Missouri was almost fantastically complicated, with a great many factors at issue, Missouri's decision—as this fateful month of April drew toward its close—was going to be affected very powerfully by a sandy-whiskered, wiry, blue-eyed little captain of regular infantry named Nathaniel Lyon.

Born in Connecticut, Lyon was forty-two; an intense, pugnacious character who from childhood had wanted only to be a soldier. Graduating from West Point in 1841, he had taken into the army a strong detestation for higher mathematics—the calculus, he insisted, "lies outside the bounds of reason" and had doubtless been invented by someone of disordered imagination—and an orthodox faith in the Democratic party. This latter stayed with him through the Mexican War, in which he was wounded and got a brevet· captaincy for bravery in action, and led him to vote for Franklin Pierce in the presidential election of 1852. The faith withered and died, however, in the mid-fifties, when he was assigned to duty at Fort Riley, Kansas, and saw the Border Ruffians in action. He became an ardent Free-Soiler, wrote pro-Lincoln pieces for a Kansas paper in 1860, and by the beginning of 1861 he was declaring that he would rather have war than see "the great rights and hopes of the human race expire before the arrogance of the secessionists." He was also hoping that he might be transferred from the frontier to some spot where he could enjoy "the legitimate and appropriate service of contributing to stay the idiotic, fratricidal hands now at work to destroy our government."

He was transferred to St. Louis, which, as it developed,

was just the place where his dream could come true. In St. Louis he met Francis P. Blair, Jr., the one man in the state who could give him the leverage with which he could act to the best effect.

Blair was one of *the* Blairs of Maryland, son and name-sake of Andrew Jackson's trusted adviser of the long ago, brother of Montgomery Blair, who sat in Lincoln's cabinet; a powerful man of strong opinions, almost unlimited political influence in Washington, and a passion equal to Lyon's own. He had been a principal organizer of the Republican party in Missouri; working closely with the anti-slavery, pro-Unionist German population in St. Louis, he had set up a little committee of public safety which, although entirely unofficial, was nevertheless relied on by Lincoln as a potential action arm in case matters came to a showdown. He and Lyon—who, technically, was on the scene merely to command a company of regulars in the U.S. Arsenal—quickly discovered that they could work together. They shared many traits, among them a conviction that what was going on in the country was in fact a revolution, and an instinctive feeling that a time of revolution was no time for crippling legalisms.

The legalisms would not bother them very much. Governor of Missouri was Claiborne Jackson, strongly secessionist, who tried to get a state convention to take the state out of the Union, saw the convention controlled by a Unionist majority, and was quietly waiting for a more favorable turn of events. Like Blair, he kept his eyes on the arsenal. It contained sixty thousand muskets, a million and a half ball cartridges, a number of cannon, and some machinery for the manufacture of arms. If the secessionists could seize it they could equip a whole army and control the entire state. To prevent such a seizure there was nothing much but Blair's iron determination and the presence of energetic little Captain Lyon.

Pulling wires that led to Washington, Blair moved to make the arsenal safe. Lyon's superior officer there seemed to feel that if the state government should call on him to surrender the arsenal he could do nothing except comply, so Blair had him transferred to other parts, and defense of the arsenal was entrusted to Lyon. Top Federal commander at St. Louis was Brigadier General W. S. Harney, a hard-boiled old Indian-fighting regular who was thoroughly loyal to the Union but who could not make himself believe that Governor Jackson actually meant any harm. Blair sent more messages to Washington, and late in April—after Fort Sumter had been surrendered, after Governor Jackson flatly refused to raise troops for war against the Confederacy—Harney was suddenly called to Washington. (En route the old soldier managed to get himself captured by Confederates when his train stopped at Harpers Ferry, Virginia, where a thriving government arsenal had just been taken over by Virginia troops. The experience prolonged Harney's absence from St. Louis and may have given him a new insight into the things that could happen to government property in a time of crisis.)[3]

In his absence command of everything in and around St. Louis devolved on Lyon, who then got as extraordinary a set of instructions from the War Department as any mere infantry captain ever received. To maintain order and defend national property he was empowered at his discretion to enroll up to ten thousand citizens of St. Louis and vicinity in the military service. (These could be none other than Blair's Germans, who had been zealously drilling, often with Captain Lyon's aid, in *Turnverein* halls all winter.) In addition, Lyon was told that if he, Blair, and Blair's committee of public safety thought it necessary he could proclaim martial law.

Decidedly, this was stretching military regulations past what would ordinarily be considered the breaking point. Old Lorenzo Thomas, lanky and crotchety adjutant general of the army, was seen coming out of a White House conference on the matter looking very grave and shaking his head dolefully. "It's bad, very bad," he said. "We're giving that young man Lyon a great deal too much power in Missouri." General Winfield Scott, older and more decayed than Thomas but much more able to see to the heart of things, took it in stride. Across the bottom of Lyon's instructions he scribbled: "It is revolutionary times, and therefore I do not object to the irregularity of this."[4]

Not long thereafter things began to happen.

Governor Jackson called out some seven hundred troops

of the state militia and put them into camp on the edge of St. Louis—for routine instruction, said the militia commander; to seize the government arsenal and take Missouri out of the Union, said Blair and Lyon. Lyon began swearing the Germans into U.S. service. It was hard to do this regularly, since in the ordinary course of things a state government formally offered troops to the Federal government; offered them, and looked after their clothing, pay, and equipment. None of this could happen in the case of the Germans, but they were sworn in anyway, larger irregularities having already been swallowed. Then Lyon reflected that Harney would sooner or later be getting back from Washington and decided that it was time to take steps.

His first step was to have a look at the state militia camp. He was an unlikely character for the part of female impersonator, but it seems that he tried it: dressed up in black bombazine dress, sunbonnet, and heavy veils (the better to hide his bristling whiskers), he rode through the camp in a rustic buggy, a basket of eggs in his lap, like any farm woman who had come in to bring some extra rations to a soldier son. Hidden beneath the eggs in the basket were half a dozen loaded revolvers, just in case. Lyon saw what there was to see, including company streets named after Jefferson Davis, Beauregard, and other Confederate heroes, and then he hurried back to the arsenal, where he called Blair and the committee of public safety into meeting. Shedding sunbonnet and bombazine and regaining the dignity of a proper army officer, Lyon announced that on his tour of the camp he had seen, through the veils and over the eggs, Missouri militiamen with weapons in their hands—weapons which, as he detected, had recently been taken by Louisiana insurgents from a government arsenal at Baton Rouge and which therefore rightly belonged to the Federal government. It was necessary, said Lyon, to occupy the camp, hold the militiamen as prisoners of war, and recover all of this government property forthwith.

This touched off an argument. Two members of the committee insisted that things ought to be done legally; if Captain Lyon wanted the munitions which were held by the militia and could show that these did in fact belong to the Federal government, let him go to court and get a writ of replevin.

. . . But Blair and the others rode them down. The government had lost a number of arsenals in the last few weeks by clinging to legalities while men with guns in their hands went out and took what they wanted. The same thing could happen in St. Louis; if it did, the Union cause was as good as done for—and, as Lyon remarked, whatever was done had better be done quickly because Harney would be back any day now and he was unlikely to do anything at all, since he believed that a state governor had every right to camp his militia in his own state when and where he chose.[5]

Winfield Scott had said it; the times were revolutionary, and there was no sense in quibbling over irregularities. So on the morning of May 10, Captain Lyon marched out with several thousand troops—a few companies of regulars, plus various regiments of the recently enrolled German guards—surrounded the militia camp, and demanded its surrender.

Things went smoothly enough at first. General D. M. Frost was the militia commander. He made formal protest and statement of innocence, then gave in to superior force. Lyon marched two companies of regulars into camp, disarmed the seven hundred militiamen, seized a number of cannon, twelve hundred muskets, twenty-five kegs of powder, and odds and ends of military equipment—some of it, he noted darkly, bearing the stamp of the Baton Rouge arsenal—and then he prepared to take the prisoners down to the arsenal where they could be paroled. What might have been done with bailiffs and a writ had been done by the soldiery and, it appeared, had been done peacefully and in good order.

The trouble began when Lyon himself was knocked down by the kicking and plunging of an unruly horse. He was not badly hurt but he was stunned and out of action for a few minutes. He had nobody in particular for staff officers, and until he was himself again the proceedings came to a halt. This was unfortunate, because a crowd began to gather: a passionately secessionist crowd, which waved sticks, threw stones, and called down curses on the heads of the German home guards. (One of these regiments called itself "Die Schwarze Garde," which the sidewalk demonstrators translated freely as "Damned Dutch blackguards.") By the time Lyon finally had things moving—prisoners marching in column, with files of troops on both sides and armed detachments moving ahead and in the rear—he was at the storm center of a revolving mob which was likely to break out in open violence at any moment.

Some chance spark touched it off, as usually happens in such cases. A drunk tried to force his way through the military cordon, damning the Dutch, and was bounced back with unnecessary verve. Various people had been waving pistols for some time, and one of these pistols was fired, a soldier fired in reply, and presently there was a regular riot, with shots and screams and curses and the scuffling of heavy feet on the cobblestones, smoke billowing up past the house tops— and, in the end, with twenty-eight people lying dead and many more badly hurt.[6]

The militia had been disarmed, the lost government property had been reclaimed, the threat to the security of the arsenal had been lifted—and authentic civil war had gone raging through the streets of St. Louis, just as it had raged through the streets of Baltimore a few weeks earlier. There was a portent in it, a significance easy to overlook: in this war between the sections the first serious battles, producing bloodshed and corpses, were battles between soldiers and civilians, on city streets, at opposite ends of the long belt of border states. Regular troop action could come later; it all began with men in uniform fighting men not in uniform.

Harney got back to St. Louis in a couple of days and tried to pick up the pieces. He ordered the German troops out of the city, proposed to Frank Blair that they be disbanded— apparently not realizing that in this highly irregular war they had already been sworn into Federal service—and then he tried to work out a truce with the state authorities.

Commander of Missouri troops now was General Sterling Price, former governor of the state, a Virginia-born Mexican War veteran, a stout, serious-minded man of vast personal popularity. He was raising state troops, apparently for eventual use against United States troops; he was also conferring with the general commanding the United States troops, and out of this curious conference there came presently something along the lines of a cease-fire agreement. Both state and national forces would try to keep order and prevent bloodshed, the defense of the rights and property of all Missourians would be the concern of both sides, and any evilly disposed persons who tried to make trouble would be squelched; on this uneasy agreement perhaps the peace could be kept in Missouri.

But to men like fiery Nathaniel Lyon the keeping of the peace was the last thing that mattered. This truce (as Lyon saw it) had been arranged with men who favored secession—favored it, and would strike for it the moment they saw a good chance; the only possible thing to do with such people was to smite them hard and at once, and to treat with them at all was to come mortally close to recognizing the right of secession. Lyon fumed and wrote that "the Government seems unwilling to resist those who would cut its throat, for fear of exasperating them." Blair wrote some more letters to Washington, and two documents soon after this came west—one, a brigadier general's commission for Captain Lyon, the other a White House writ to Frank Blair giving him the power to remove General Harney if he saw fit.[1]

Blair saw fit, and by the end of May, Harney had been transferred away from Missouri forever, with Lyon formally taking his place. Lyon and Blair at once called a meeting with Governor Jackson and General Price to review this business of a truce. The two Missouri officials offered to disband their troops and keep all Confederate armies out of the state if, in return, the Federals would disband their home guards—the Dutch blackguards, so offensive to southern sympathies—and if the Federals would promise not to occupy any part of Missouri that Federal troops did not already hold. In effect, they were offering at least a temporary neutrality as far as Missouri was concerned.

Lyon turned this down contemptuously. The Federal government, he announced, would move its troops where it pleased, asking permission of nobody, and it would retain in its service any and all home-guard levies it wished to keep, blackguard Dutch or otherwise; and he personally would see every man, woman, and child in Missouri six feet under the ground before he would admit that this or any other state could impose any conditions at all upon the Federal government. He had, further, one final word for Governor Jack-

son and General Price: they had a war on their hands and it
was beginning in earnest as of that moment.[8]

Within two days Lyon was marching on Jefferson City, the
state capital, with several thousand troops. Governor Jackson,
who had gone back to the capital immediately after the St.
Louis conference ended, fled as Lyon approached and tried to
set up shop in Boonville, fifty miles to the northwest. Lyon
drove on after him, attacked and scattered Jackson's hastily
assembled militia, and sent Jackson off to the west and south,
a governor with nothing that he could govern. General Price,
who had gone west to Lexington to recruit an army, fled south
when Jackson went—and by mid-June the Federals were
ahead of the game in Missouri. They had played it irregularly,
as General Scott admitted, but they had not been bound by
legalisms. In Frank Blair and Nathaniel Lyon the Lincoln
government had two men who were not afraid to act like
revolutionists once a revolution had begun.

3. *The Important First Trick*

The war had hardly started, yet the most momentous single
decision had already been made. As far as the Federal government was concerned, it was going to be a war to the
finish.

There had been street fighting in the cities, governors and
legislators had been driven in flight or put under arrest,
earnest home guards were tramping clumsily into state capitals, and what it all meant was that secession had been accepted as revolution. There could be no compromise with it;
it would be fought whenever necessary with revolutionary
weapons, which in effect meant with any instrument that
came to hand. The South could win its independence only by
destroying the government of the United States.

The stakes, in other words, had become immeasurable,
and most of the ordinary rules had been suspended. If the
war could be ended within a few months, none of this would
matter very much; but if it should go on—and on—if there
should be no quick and easy ending to it—anything at all
could happen. The country had gone to war gaily, it was

all abubble North and South with flags and oratory and bands and training camps where life beat clerking all hollow; but ahead there was unutterable grimness, not simply because a great many people were going to die but because, before the war had properly begun, it had been determined that no price for victory would be too high.

It was the Lincoln administration that had made this decision, but the country at large accepted it, instinctively and without stopping to reason about it. Of all the misunderstandings that had produced the war, no single one had more tragic consequences than this—that the men of the South had completely failed to realize how deeply the concept of nationality had taken root in the North. The great wagon trains had gone rolling west, a wilderness had been opened, new towns and farms had sprung up, limitless hopes and great sacrifices had been invested in the development of a rich new land, and out of it all had come a conviction that the national destiny involved unity. Whatever the North might do to win the war—and it would do just about anything it could lay its hands to—would be done with the conviction that this attempt at secession was morally wrong, a blind attempt to destroy something precious, a wanton laying of hands on the Ark of the Covenant. The Southerners were not merely enemies; they were traitors, to be treated as such.

And the new levies continued to come in, gay and full of high spirits, brandishing their weapons as if they were playthings for holiday use. A Connecticut regiment came cruising up the Potomac by side-wheeler steamboat, the men lining the rails to cheer every schooner, sloop, or barge that displayed the United States flag. If they met one flying no flag, the men would level their muskets and order: "Show your colors! Show your colors!" When the flag was hoisted—as it always was, with all those fidgety fingers under the trigger guards—the men would give three cheers, and laugh, and peer ahead for the next chance to enforce a display of patriotism. Girls met troop trains in upstate New York, offering kisses in exchange for brass buttons, and some regiments went off to war all unbuttoned and buttonless. Young infantry captains knelt on Boston Common and wept with emotion as little girls presented company flags; a Pennsylvania father presented his officer son with a new sword and enjoined him not to return until the weapon was "stained to the hilt," and one of Lyon's volunteers in Missouri looked about him and declared that campaigning was "war in poetry and song and set to music."[1]

It was not quite unanimous. A young esthete graduating from Yale delivered a "commencement poem" whose sole allusion to the war was the scornful line: "What is the grandeur of serving a state, whose tail is stinging its head to death like a scorpion?" After graduation, the question presumably being unanswered, he took ship for California, not to return until the unpleasantness had died down. A Wisconsin boy found with dismay that his regiment was sent to western Minnesota to fight the Indians and not to the Deep South to fight Rebels, recalled that in his home state he had always been good friends with Indians, and wrote to his parents: "I can't help thinking of the wrong-doing of the government toward the Indians . . . It must be I ain't a good soldier."[2]

For the most part, though, things went with a whoop and a holler, and if there was much lost motion in the way the new regiments were recruited, equipped, and drilled—western boys used to firearms came almost to mutiny when harassed supply sergeants outfitted them with clumsy Belgian muskets in place of the rifles they demanded[3]—the government was moving with remarkable effectiveness to make the long fringe of the border states secure.

In Maryland there was Ben Butler, his troops camped on Federal Hill overlooking Baltimore Harbor, himself camped at Annapolis, opening a new road to Washington; Ben Butler, who had worked energetically for southern rights in the Democratic convention of 1860, all out for the Union now, grinning sardonically with eyes that did not mesh, revolving monstrous ambitions in his mind as he followed a new political tack; Ben Butler, with his lawyer's mind and his flair for administrative detail and his whole-souled lack of scruple, contriving to make capital for himself out of this war that cut him loose from his old moorings, a one-time friend of the South who was presently to become the most hated man in the entire Confederate legend.

In Washington itself there had been uneasy moments in the

days just after Fort Sumter's surrender, when the cutting of railroad and telegraph lines through Baltimore left the capital temporarily isolated. There were hardly any soldiers in the city, and it was easy to imagine armed Virginians coming across the Potomac and bringing the war to a quick end by seizing capital, President, and government entire. That period quickly passed, and now Washington was full of troops—state militia, for the most part, called in for ninety-day service, poorly trained and almost totally unorganized, but impressive nevertheless with their bright uniforms, their cocky airs, and the numbers of them. Detachments of these before long were sent across the Potomac to occupy the high ground on the southern shore, and Federal soldiers pitched their tents on an estate known as Arlington, lately the home of Robert E. Lee.

While Arlington was occupied, other troops were sent a few miles downstream to seize Alexandria. The outfit chosen for this job was the 11th New York, a flamboyant and slightly riotous organization wearing the baggy pants, short jackets, and turbans of the Zouaves: the Fire Zouaves, as they were called, since most of the members had been recruited from various New York fire companies.

Colonel of the Fire Zouaves was young Elmer Ellsworth, who had made something of a profession of being an amateur soldier; his Chicago Zouave drill team had given exhibitions all over the North in the year or so just before the war. Ellsworth was dashing, eager to win fame and glory, was perhaps a little headline-happy, and apparently he was destined to have a spectacular role in this war. As he led his men into Alexandria, Ellsworth spied a southern flag on a stump of a flagpole on the roof of a hotel. Full of dramatic ardor—a correspondent for the New York *Tribune* was along—Ellsworth drew his sword and dashed into the building to cut the flag down . . . and died ingloriously when the hotel proprietor, a mere civilian but a staunch secessionist, met him on the stairway, thrust the muzzle of a shotgun against his belly, and pulled the trigger. The hotel man was promptly bayoneted, Ellsworth's body was brought back to Washington to lie in state in the White House, and the North mourned a lost hero.[4]

Meanwhile the army authorities were trying desperately to make an army out of the assortment of militia units in Washington. The job fell to Brigadier General Irvin McDowell, a tall, plump, serious-minded regular who had studied in France, owned a good Mexican War record, and had served on Scott's staff. He had a very hard assignment. He had to organize his regiments into brigades and divisions, had to find some way to instruct them in brigade and division tactics—very intricate, calling for innumerable hours on the drill field; he lacked anything resembling an adequate staff, and the War Department's inefficiency was raising serious problems of supply and equipment. Worse yet, people were beginning to demand that he move out at once and capture Richmond, first defeating a Confederate army that was in camp near Manassas, some two dozen miles from Washington. The fact that this army was in no better shape than his own was cold comfort: before he had his carefree militia regiments organized and drilled enough to make any sort of cross-country march possible (let alone a formal battle) the terms of service of a great many of them would begin to expire. The United States Army has not had very many generals as unlucky, all things considered, as Irvin McDowell.

In Ohio there was a very different man—short, stocky, handsome young George B. McClellan, West Pointer, Mexican War veteran, official observer for the War Department in the Crimea when the British and French fought the Russians; an ambitious, brilliant man who had left the army to become a railroad president and who now held a major general's commission. He commanded everything along the Ohio line, he was revolving elaborate plans for a down-the-Mississippi invasion of the South, and he was moving now to slice western Virginia off from the Old Dominion and create a new state between the Alleghenies and the Ohio River.

McClellan was worth a second look. If his fellow West Pointers had balloted on a "most likely to succeed" classmate, they would almost certainly have elected him. He had brains, connections, a winning personality, the quality known as brilliance. Putting together the new Ohio regiments, he was showing a definite knack for organization and administration; leading them across the river and into western Virginia—as he was doing this June—he was also showing powerful qualities of leadership, with a marked ability to make his troops believe in themselves and in him. His campaign was going well, and it was one of the Union's most important moves this summer.

Leading twenty-seven regiments, mostly from Ohio and Indiana, McClellan struck at a Confederate force that had come west with the dual intent of holding this part of Virginia for the Confederacy and of cutting the Baltimore and Ohio Railroad line, which connected Washington with the West. He had chosen his troops wisely—ninety-day regiments they were, for the most part, selected so that they might do a little service before their time expired while the three-year volunteers got a little more seasoning—and if these men were imperfectly drilled, the Southerners they were going up against were in no better case and in addition were substantially fewer in numbers.

Campaigning in the picturesque mountain country struck the ninety-day soldiers as exciting, even though the men did make disparaging remarks about the region as "a land of secession, rattlesnakes, rough mountains and bad whiskey," and when they were finally led up to the Rebel outposts around Rich Mountain they still had their enthusiasm. Actual fighting, to be sure, turned out to be a little different from what they had imagined it would be. One Ohioan whose regiment had to attack a log blockhouse wrote indignantly that the Southerners were "cowardly dogs" who fired through loopholes in the log walls instead of coming out in the open and fighting like men. To their surprise, the men looked at the prisoners they took and discovered that Virginia boys looked exactly like Ohio boys; and they concluded that if all Southerners were like these "we have no mean enemy to contend with."[5]

In the end McClellan's troops swept the Confederates off the mountain range and out of the valley that lay beyond it, driving them all the way back to the main ridge of the Alleghenies; and if their victory was not especially spectacular—except in McClellan's prose: his message of congratulations to his soldiers sounded like something Napoleon might have said after an especially good campaign—its effects were permanent. There would be a spatter of skirmishes, advances, retreats, and sullen little mountain battles in this area for months to come, but the Confederates had lost western Virginia for good. Creation of the new state of West Virginia would follow in due course.

Kentucky was a strange no man's land as spring drew on into summer. Governor Magoffin was as ardently pro-Confederate as ever and his legislature, along with a good majority of the voters, was equally hot for the Union. Officially, the state was neutral. Everybody was watching everybody else, and neither the Washington nor the Richmond government was willing to make the first move.

Kentucky had a state guard commanded by General Simon Bolivar Buckner, a former regular army officer who, back in the mid-fifties, had in New York run into an old classmate just back from the West Coast, broke and in disgrace, and had lent him money to get back to his home in Ohio—an obscure ex-captain of infantry named Ulysses S. Grant. In Washington it was hoped that Buckner would eventually go with the Union, but Union men in Kentucky were sure he would turn up on the side of the Confederates; to hamper him, the legislature refused to vote any money for the arming and equipping of his state guard. As a counterweight, in Louisville and elsewhere, semi-official home guards of a strong pro-Union cast were organized.

These home-guard companies presently found themselves assembling at a central rendezvous, Camp Dick Robinson, between Lexington and Danville, where they came under the command of a breezy three-hundred-pound giant named William Nelson. Nelson had been a lieutenant in the navy. Resigning when the war broke out, he stopped off in Washington long enough to wangle a brigadier general's commission and the authority to draw on the Federal government for ten thousand stand of arms; then he hurried to his home state of Kentucky to see what could be done about organizing Union troops. He was bluff, blustering, profane, a driver and a martinet, and the home guards were not enthusiastic about him. They were wild young men, these home guards, with even less taste for discipline and drill than most recruits of that innocent day; their ideas of military life, a veteran recalled afterward, had been drawn exclusively from "the glowing accounts of the fertile pens of historians and the more exciting works of fiction," and Nelson was bearing down hard on them.[6]

Recruiting for both armies was going on openly. Confederate recruits were assembled in camp just over the Tennessee line, and Unionists—aside from Nelson's amorphous home-guard outfits—were put in camp just north of the Ohio River, in Indiana; it was not uncommon for rival groups of recruits, heading for their respective training camps, to pass one another on the streets of Louisville. Once a passenger train pulled out of a town in the central part of the state with a carful of Union recruits and at the next station picked up a carload of Rebels; company officers met on the platform and arranged a truce for the duration of the ride. Symptomatic was the case of Senator John J. Crittenden, who had struggled hard, and in vain, during the winter to work out a compromise that would avert war. Of his two sons, one was to become a general in the Confederate Army, the other a Union general.[7]

From President Lincoln the situation got very careful handling. If he did not formally recognize the state's neutrality, as Confederate President Jefferson Davis did, he was careful not to disturb it. When southern-minded Kentuckians protested that Nelson's presence at Camp Robinson was a violation of neutrality, Lincoln blandly replied that no coercion was implied or intended; the home guards there were Kentuckians, not Federal troops, and they were entirely under the control of the state legislature. Meanwhile he made a brigadier general out of Robert Anderson, the sorely-tried regular who had commanded in Fort Sumter, and stationed him in Indiana with a command which—on paper, and rather on an if-and-when basis—embraced the state of Kentucky.

It was a queer summer in Kentucky. And yet, although nothing much seemed to be happening, the Confederates were playing a losing game. Whether they realized it or not, they had to have Kentucky. While it stayed neutral the rest of the border was being nailed down for the Union, and if western Virginia and Missouri were firmly held by the national government, Kentucky would eventually be held also, even though southern leaders would ultimately go through the motions of voting the state into the Confederacy. From Kentucky the road to the Deep South would be wide open.[8]

By the middle of July, in fact, the Lincoln administration had taken the all-important first trick. It had the border states—not firmly, as yet, by any means, and either military reverses or political clumsiness (both of which would be encountered) might easily lose them—but the first big danger had been passed. The time for serious fighting was approaching, and when it came the North would be operating with a solid advantage.

4. *The Rising Shadows*

Nearly four years later, when he was just five weeks away from the casket with the bronze handles, the echoing capitol dome above, the blue-coated soldiers standing with sober and disciplined unease in the flickering purple twilight, Abraham Lincoln tried to sum it up.

"Neither party," he said, "expected for the war the magnitude, or the duration, which it has already attained. . . . Each looked for an easier triumph, and a result less fundamental and astounding."[1]

The easy triumph did not look very far away in the early summer of 1861. There was going to be a short war, and it would be romantic and glorious—crowned, of course, with victory. In the Confederacy people held to the belief that one Southerner could whip five Yankees; in the North it was supposed that secession would collapse once a blue battle line came over the hills with the sunlight glinting on polished musket barrels; and no one, as Lincoln remarked, could see that what was going to happen would be fundamental and astounding, a tearing up and a breaking down, a consuming tragedy so costly that generations would pass before people could begin to say whether what it had bought was worth the price.

The price . . . Well, what do you pay for an American Civil War? What is the cost of development from national adolescence to manhood; for the idea that the oneness of all people must run unbroken all through the national fabric, for a notion of citizenship that draws no line of color, birth, or where your grandfather's people came from? The coins are various: a boy dying of typhoid in a cold tent, trampled grass growing up around the legs of his cot, a careless steward offering salt pork and hardtack for a final meal; another boy falling in a swamp with a slug of hot lead in his lungs; a home disrupted, with the goods that were to keep a family through the winter trampled on by grinning hoodlums; a woman on a farm in Indiana, or Mississippi, learning that the child who used to run barefooted across the meadows in spring has gone under the turf in some place whose name she never heard before . . . These are some of the coins, bloodshed and suffering and a deep sorrow in the breast, spent prodigally by folk who had not wanted to buy anything at all but who had just hoped to get along the best they could, winning a little happiness out of life if their luck was in: the total of these coins high beyond counting, the payment exacted from people who had made no bargain, the thing bought a mystic intangible dim in the great shadows.

But the payment had hardly begun in July of 1861, and what lay ahead looked easy, looked like something that would soon be over.

It was time, northern patriots believed, to whip the South and end matters. Specifically, it was time for General McDowell to take his army down to Manassas Plain, crush the rebellion, and march triumphantly on to Richmond. A clamor of press and oratory informed him that he would have to get moving. One battle, and then it would all be over.

General McDowell knew better. The processes of nineteenth-century warfare were as intricate as the weapons themselves were simple. A regiment of infantry consisted of ten companies. With much training, these ten could be taught the ballet-dance movements by which the regiment could maneuver as a unit rather than as a loose aggregation of semi-independent commands. The men could be taught the cumbersome business of loading and firing their muskets (it went by the numbers, with "tear cartridge!" as the first order, the whole line grounding musket butts and swinging the limber metal ramrods together), and there were involved proceedings by which the regiment could change its shape and its direction, maneuvers called for by orders such as "Change front forward on the first company!" "Advance firing!" and "Forward, by the right of companies!" All of this business could be learned, and many of the bright new soldiers had gone quite a way with their schooling.

But that was only the beginning. McDowell had some thirty-five thousand men in his army, and when they went down to Manassas to crush rebellion they would not be going as companies or as regiments. They would march and fight by brigade and division, all of the involvements of battalion drill multiplied by ten, and they had learned almost none of the business by which this would be done. They could perhaps just manage the chore of marching across a smooth drill ground and shaking their marching column out into a line of battle; they could not begin to comprehend that the actual doing of it, finally, would involve a shambling column a mile long, proceeding down a winding dirt road bordered by brambles, swampy patches, and dense second growth, this column suddenly required to fan out into a double rank stretching all across the meadow-and-woodlot complex of the nearest farm . . . with smoke in the air, everybody excited, menacing racket beating on the eardrums and drowning out the words of command, invisible enemies firing missiles that would whine horribly just overhead, some elements in every regiment missing the signals entirely, every man absorbed in his own attempt to master panic. They could not picture this yet and they could not do it, but it was what they would have to do the moment they were committed to battle.

Worse yet would be the matter of changing position on the battlefield. The means by which a fighting line could transform itself into a marching column without losing its cohesiveness, so that it could move from one field to another, follow an invisible diagonal to support a hard-pressed line of guns, or simply get itself in an orderly manner out of a spot that had become too hot to stay in—of all of this the men understood almost nothing because there had been no time to teach them and hardly any men who knew how to do the teaching. These soldiers might be shoved into battle if the authorities insisted, but what would happen after that would be totally unpredictable.

All of this McDowell knew, but the impassioned patriots who from a safe distance were providing the pressure for the great march on Richmond neither knew nor cared about any of it. They wanted action; action was ordered, and on the afternoon of July 16 McDowell hauled his regiments out of camp, got them strung out on the road, and headed for Manassas. Two days later he had his men more or less concentrated at Centreville, twenty miles from Washington, half a dozen miles from the place where the Confederates were waiting.[2]

There were not as many Confederates as there were Federals, but they occupied good ground behind a wandering little river named Bull Run, and—despite the strange notion of their commanding officer, the ambitious General Beauregard who had pounded Fort Sumter into surrender and who fancied now that he would cross the river and smite the Yankees in the flank—their function was to stay put and await attack: a much easier job for pea-green soldiers than to try to take the offensive. McDowell sent forward skirmishing and scouting details, who did their work clumsily enough but who at least gave him a fair idea where the enemy was, and he concluded correctly that a head-on assault on the Confederate lines would be a very bad gamble; better to feign a frontal attack and send half of the army around to come in on the Confederate left.

So ordered; and on July 21 two divisions of McDowell's army—twenty infantry regiments, plus a handful of cavalry and some artillery—were sent marching upstream, to cross Bull Run a couple of miles beyond the end of the Rebel line and move down in battle array. The move was made—hours late, for the thing was managed poorly, and the soldiers simply had not had enough training to make an ordinary cross-country march without lopping all over the county—and by the middle of the morning the flanking division came in on a Confederate battle line on the hills behind Bull Run and the big fight was on.

There is an unreal quality to most accounts of this battle because they tend to describe it in terms of later battles which

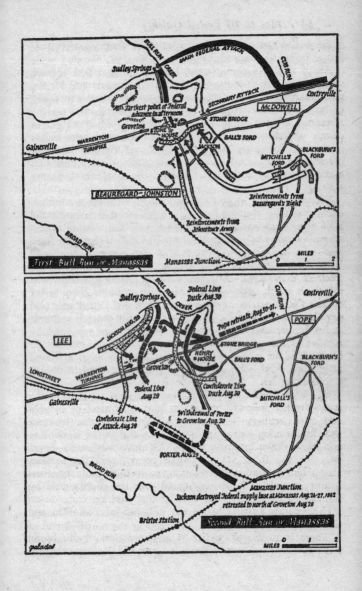

First Bull Run or Manassas

MAIN FEDERAL ATTACK
Sudley Springs
BULL RUN CREEK
CUB RUN
Centreville
SECONDARY ATTACK
McDOWELL
Farthest point of Federal advance in afternoon
Groveton
STONE BRIDGE
STONE HOUSE
BALL'S FORD
JACKSON
WARRENTON TURNPIKE
Gainesville
BLACKBURN'S FORD
MITCHELL'S FORD
BEAUREGARD-JOHNSTON
Reinforcements from Beauregard's Right
Reinforcements from Johnston's Army
BROAD RUN
Manassas Junction
MILES 0 1 2

Second Bull Run or Manassas

Federal Line Dusk Aug.30
Sudley Springs
BULL RUN CREEK
CUB RUN
Centreville
Pope retreats, Aug.30-31.
POPE
LEE
JACKSON Aug.28
STONE BRIDGE
HENRY HOUSE
BALL'S FORD
BLACKBURN'S FORD
Groveton
LONGSTREET
WARRENTON TURNPIKE
Federal Line Aug.29
Confederate Line Dusk Aug.30
MITCHELL'S FORD
Gainesville
Confederate Line of Attack Aug.29
Withdrawal of Porter to Groveton Aug.30
PORTER Aug.29
BROAD RUN
Manassas Junction
Jackson destroyed Federal supply base at Manassas Aug.26-27, 1862 retreated to north of Groveton Aug.28
Bristoe Station
galantos
MILES 0 1 2

were fought after generals and soldiers had learned their trade, and it was not like those battles at all. Nothing went the way it had been planned, except for that first clumsy lunge around the Confederate left. After that, for Northerners and Southerners alike, it was simply a matter of pushing raw troops up to the firing line and hoping for the best.

The men stood up to it better than anyone had a right to expect. A good many of them lost heart and hid in the woods on the way up to the firing line, and a good many more ran away at the first shock, but that happened in every battle all through the war, even with veteran regiments; the amazing thing about Bull Run is that so many of these untested holiday soldiers dug in their heels and fought with great courage. They knew so little about their business that men in the front rank were on occasion shot by their own comrades farther in the rear. An officer who tried to shift a regiment from one place to another ran the risk of seeing it fall completely apart, and since most of the generals were as inexpert as the privates the matter of moving up supporting troops was bungled. In the end, about half of McDowell's army failed to get into action at all. But although a great deal was said afterward about the disgraceful rout at Bull Run, the simple fact is that for most of the day the soldiers stood up manfully under a great deal of pounding.

What really turned McDowell's battle into a defeat was something that had happened in the Shenandoah Valley a few days earlier.

The Confederates had some ten thousand soldiers in the valley. With them was General Joseph E. Johnston, an able tactician, who held over-all command for the Confederates along the Virginia frontier. Johnston and his men were sixty miles from Manassas, but they had a direct railroad connection with the place and it had been clear from the start that, when McDowell moved down toward Bull Run, Johnston would quickly bring his men down to Beauregard's aid unless somebody stopped him.

The man who was supposed to stop him was General Robert Patterson, Federal commander at the northern end of the valley, who had fifteen thousand men in and around Charles Town, not far from Harpers Ferry. The general idea was that he would keep pressing Johnston so that no Confederates could be sent from the valley to Bull Run.

Unfortunately, however, Patterson was semi-moribund, in a military sense. Old and fragile and bewildered—he had fought in the War of 1812, long before most of the Bull Run soldiers had been born—he proved quite unable to keep in touch with Johnston, and that officer had very little trouble in slipping away from him and bringing most of his men down to the battlefield. As the final elements of the valley army detrained at Manassas, their most direct route to the battlefield brought them into action right where they were needed most—on the right flank of McDowell's attacking force—and as the afternoon wore along, McDowell's assault was first stopped and then driven back.

Realizing that his big effort had failed, McDowell ordered a retreat. Then the trouble began. His raw troops had fought well enough, but to make an orderly withdrawal under fire from a losing field was too much for them—not so much because they were demoralized as because they just had not had enough practice in the involved maneuvers that were necessary. Brigades and regiments dissolved, and what had been a stout line of battle turned into a disorganized crowd of individuals, lost and discouraged, walking back toward the rear—not exactly running away, but irretrievably out from under anybody's control.[3]

There was little actual panic at first. But as the men got out of the battle zone the confusion multiplied. Not far to the rear—well back on the "safe" side of Bull Run—a fantastic sort of picnic had been going on, with a big crowd of Washington civilians enjoying basket lunches in the fields and getting the thrill of battle from a convenient distance. As the retreat began, these piled into their carriages and started for Washington at their best speed. A few miles down the road there was a bridge over a little stream named Cub Run, and this bridge collapsed. The carriage drivers grew frantic; and all of a sudden there was a frenzied traffic jam, with army wagons, caissons, guns, and ambulances jouncing up into the melee, straggling soldiers all round, everybody swearing, mass desperation rising higher every minute. A few casual Confederate shells exploded not far away, and chaos became complete. Now there was just a mob scene, miles long and a hundred yards wide, and there was no way to restore order until everybody had got back to Washington—which everybody undertook to do just as rapidly as possible.

So there developed a national belief that the troops at Bull Run had disgracefully fled in terror from a field they might have won. It was underlined by a singular development. On July 20, the day before the big fight, while all of the skirmishing was going on, two militia regiments pointed out that their ninety-day periods of service had expired, asserted their rights, and marched off to Washington—going to the rear, as McDowell indignantly commented, to the sound of the enemy's cannon. The story of what they did got mixed up with the story of the rout itself, and the legend became fixed: untrained troops had either refused to fight at all or had fled in panic once the fighting started, and the whole battle had been a blistering national disgrace.'

A disgrace, in sober truth, and a painful licking to boot; out of which the people of the North drew shame, indignation, and the beginning of wisdom. It was not going to be a short war after all, and there would be no quick and easy triumph won by jaunty militia boys looking for something that would beat clerking. Beyond the battle smoke and the red casualty list with its twenty-five hundred names there was rising the indecipherable shadow of something fundamental and astounding, and now the shadow began to touch people. Bull Run was both a lesson and a portent.

If that was not enough, there was another battle in Missouri that carried its own shadows.

Nathaniel Lyon had driven Missouri's fugitive Governor Claiborne Jackson off into the southwestern part of the state; a governor fatally handicapped in his attempt to take Missouri out of the Union and into the Confederacy by the fact that he had been chased away from all of the machinery of state government (except for the great seal of the state, which an underling thoughtfully brought along). He had called for fifty thousand Missourians to rise and expel the Yankee disturbers, and although he was not getting fifty thousand, he was getting quite a few; enough so that by the first of August

Lyon found that the armed Rebels in his immediate vicinity greatly outnumbered his own forces.

Lyon had got all the way to Springfield by this time. His base of supplies was at the town of Rolla, at the end of the railroad that came over from St. Louis, and Rolla was 120 miles away from Springfield, over some very bad roads. It was clear that Lyon would have to retreat, but he hoped that he could strike a quick blow first, before his enemies had concentrated all of their troops.

Like all armies at this date, Lyon's was a mixed one. It contained two small battalions of regular infantry and a few companies of regular cavalry, three batteries of regular artillery, three of the semi-irregular Missouri regiments recruited from among the Germans in and around St. Louis, and two volunteer regiments from Kansas and one from Iowa. Altogether it amounted to fifty-eight hundred men. Except for the regulars, with their hard discipline and precision drill, these men were no better trained than the men who had fought at Bull Run.[5]

They were at least learning how to manage a cross-country march, for they had done a power of walking since Lyon started chasing Governor Jackson, and if they were not getting much time on the drill field they were learning soldiering on the hoof. Lyon had them breaking camp and hitting the road well before sunrise, and the volunteers were not sure that they liked this. Army life had several aspects they had not counted on. The army mule, for instance, had a way of beginning to bray at midnight, and he was likely to keep it up for hours—a habit that (as a diarist asserted) was finally broken by a Mexican War veteran, who said that mules would not bray in the night season if weights were tied to their tails: a trick that was tried and actually seemed to work. The volunteers were awed by the regulars; they detested what they saw of regular army discipline (whose punishments they considered too revolting and brutal for free-born Americans), but they greatly admired the way the regulars looked and marched, and they strove to be like them. In Lyon's army there was a ninety-day outfit, the 1st Iowa, whose time was due to expire early in August. The Iowans said that they did not want to go home without getting into one good fight, and they offered to stick around for an extra week or so in the hope that maybe there would be one.[6]

There would be. On August 10, Lyon took his army down to Wilson's Creek, an unpretentious little stream that meandered cross-country ten miles from Springfield, where twelve thousand Confederates under General Sterling Price and a former Texas Ranger captain named Ben McCulloch were waiting. Lyon had a distinguished subordinate, a former German brigadier named Franz Sigel, who had defied the Prussians in the revolution of 1848, had led troops against them, and had fled for his life to America when the revolution was suppressed. Sigel was told to take his men in a big sweep around the Federal left and get in rear of the Confederate line of battle. When Sigel's guns were heard the rest of Lyon's men would make a frontal attack.

It could have worked, but it did not, quite. Sigel got his men where he was supposed to get them, but unhappily it turned out that although he was a devoted and a high-minded man he was almost totally incapable of handling troops in the field. His men opened fire, got Confederate fire in return, and then somehow went all to pieces, tumbling back across dreary woods and stumpy meadows in complete rout, leaving the rest of the army to fight its way out of the battle which their firing had commenced. The rest of the army did its best, but its best was not quite good enough, and the day ended in disaster.

Before the battle began Lyon went through the camps, talking to the men like an undersized red-whiskered father: "Men, we are going to have a fight. We will march out in a short time. Don't shoot until you get orders. Fire low—don't aim higher than their knees. Wait until they get close. Don't get scared—it's no part of a soldier's duty to get scared." Then he swung them out into line of battle and sent them into action.[7]

The Confederates were banked up four ranks deep, and the firing started with the rival lines no more than fifty yards apart—murderously close range, for the clumsy muzzle-loaders that constituted the infantry weapon in those days were deadly at anything under two hundred and fifty yards. The Iowa boys, who had hoped they could have one good fight before they were paid off, got their wish. They stood next to a battery of regular artillery, six guns commanded by an uncommonly hard-boiled West Pointer, Captain James Totten, who went into action with a canteen of brandy at his hip. Even in the excitement of their first battle the Iowans marveled at the profane fury with which Captain Totten stormed at his lieutenants and his gunners—"Forward that caisson, God damn you, sir! . . . Swing that piece into line, God damn you, sir!"—as his guns slammed canister and case shot into an advancing Rebel line and blew it apart.

The Rebels withdrew briefly, the smoke lifted from the field, and the volunteers found themselves facing an empty pasture with a snake-rail fence on the far side. A lone Confederate was perched on this fence, defiantly swinging a Confederate flag, and when the Iowans prepared to shoot him their officers went along the line ordering them not to: he was too brave, something about his valiant posture made it indecent to take pot shots at him. Captain Totten's regulars felt otherwise; an Irish gunnery sergeant swung a piece around, got the Rebel in his sights, pulled the lanyard, and blew the man all to fragments—and with an angry yell the Confederate line surged forward in a new assault. The Kansans came in to help repel this attack, smoke settled close to the ground, everything was a wild clangor of beaten metal and shouting men, and a remarkable number of the northern volunteers got shot. For untaught soldiers it was rough, and men fought blindly, not knowing what they were doing; an officer came on one man who was loading his musket feverishly, firing straight up into the air, reloading and firing again, an automaton acting entirely by blind instinct.[8]

Lyon came along the line, bleeding from two wounds, his shaggy whiskers clotted with blood. He was profoundly depressed: a third of his men were down, Sigel's attack had gone completely astray, no help was in sight, all the Rebels in Missouri seemed to be coming in on him. When Totten offered him a pull at the brandy he waved him aside, and to an aide he muttered: "Major, I fear the day is lost." The aide said something hopeful, and Lyon galloped off to bring up a few companies he had been holding in reserve. He got them up to the front, and some of the untried young hotheads shouted that if he would lead them they would charge with their bayonets and chase the Rebels all the way to Arkansas. Lyon was the man for that. He swung his hat, wreaths of smoke floating about him, blood on his hair and blood on his uniform, and he wheeled to lead them—and then a stray bullet whacked into his heart and killed him. The charge died before it got started, and it developed that there was no surviving Union officer above the rank of major.'

The principal major turned out to be one Samuel D. Sturgis. He looked things over, concluded that the little army had about fought itself out, and took it away in retreat with the regulars to bring up the rear. Eventually the army arrived at the railhead at Rolla. There the 1st Iowa found a consignment of new uniforms, together with orders to head back home and get paid off. The boys took a bath in the nearest pond, threw away their filthy old uniforms, put on the new, and set off for Iowa, glad they had been in that one battle. At Burlington twenty thousand people were waiting to welcome them home, and they paraded down the streets singing a tune called "The Happy Land of Canaan."[10]

3.

Men Who Shaped the War

1. *The Romantics to the Rescue*

WINFIELD SCOTT was an old man, vain and ponderous, drop-sical and infirm, a swollen and grotesque caricature of the brilliant soldier who had won the Mexican War and who, because he once so perfectly acted the part of the proud soldier, had been known half affectionately as "Old Fuss and Feathers." He was mixed up now in a war that had come too late for him, a bewildering sort of war that saw his pet enemy, Jefferson Davis, and his pet soldier, Robert E. Lee, making common cause against the country that had all of his loyalty. He was greatly partial to the regular army, believed that volunteer troops needed many months in training camp be-fore they could take the field, and doubted that cavalry would be of much account in this war; everybody knew that it took a full two years of drill to turn an ordinary recruit into a competent trooper. He blamed himself for having let political pressure make him send McDowell's unready army out on the disastrous expedition to Bull Run, and his own physical disabilities—getting in and out of the chair behind his desk, with much puffing and wheezing, was about all he could manage—must have been a painful reminder that this war was in process of slipping out from under the commanding gen-eral of the army.

Yet the old man had a clear eye. Others might talk about the one swift blow that would end the rebellion. Bright young General McClellan, for instance, had proposed a quick stab up the Kanawha Valley, across western Virginia, and over the mountains to Richmond, and since he proposed that this be done with the ninety-day men, he had obviously been thinking of a short war. But Scott saw it differently. The Confederacy, he believed, would never be subdued by piecemeal; it would have to be enveloped and throttled. The job could hardly be begun before the enlistments of the ninety-day men had expired, and it was time to think in terms of the long pull.

Let the navy (said Scott) blockade the southern coasts. The army, then, must drive down the Mississippi, opening the river all the way to the Gulf, splitting the western states from the Confederacy and holding the valley in such strength that the blockade of the Southland would be complete. With rebellion isolated, it could then be crushed at leisure.

The proposal got to the White House and was talked about, and before long it was being discussed in the press. It called up the picture of a gigantic constrictor tightening a deadly inexorable grip about the seceding states, and it became generally known as the "Anaconda Plan," under which title it was widely derided by impatient patriots who looked for a quick and easy war. Scott, they complained, believed that the war could be won without fighting—visible proof that he was a senile old fumbler who had lived beyond his usefulness. "On to Richmond" had more of a swing to it.

But Scott had something. He had submitted a general idea, not an actual strategic plan, and he was not suggesting that the war could be won without fighting. Instead, he was trying to show the things that would have to be done before a really effective fight could be made. And although his idea was scoffed at, it did take root in the mind of Abraham Lincoln. In the end, the Anaconda idea became the basis for the Federal war effort.[1]

By midsummer it appeared that the lieutenants through whom most of the spadework for this plan must be done would be chiefly two—George Brinton McClellan and John Charles Frémont.

The army in 1861 hardly possessed two more completely different soldiers—and yet, in an odd way, they had certain traits in common. They came into their new posts as ready-made heroes, welcomed by a land that wanted heroes to worship. They had the gift for making fine phrases, and so for a time they could express perfectly the spirit with which men of the North were going to war. A great many men believed in them passionately and went on believing in them long after failure had come. They had color and dash, romance seemed to cling to them, and at bottom each man was essentially a romantic. That was their great handicap, for this was not going to be a romantic war and it would never be won by romantics.

The romantic in McClellan was buried under a layer of crisp, energetic efficiency. Called to Washington immediately after Bull Run and given command of all the troops in and around the capital, he seemed the very model of the business-like, self-reliant administrator. He found the town overrun with men in uniform who drifted about the streets (and jammed the saloons) in aimless confusion, not knowing what they were up to or what was expected of them, conscious of the shame of panic and defeat. He detailed regular army soldiers to police the place, got the wanderers back into camp, saw that the camps were properly laid out and intelligently managed, ironed out the kinks in the commissary system so that everyone got plenty to eat; and set up a regime that involved endless hours of drill. In short, he restored order, made the men feel like soldiers, and before long he instituted a series of grand reviews in which the new soldiers could look at themselves in the mass and could begin to realize that they were part of a powerful, disciplined, smoothly functioning army.

The transformation was taking place. The Bull Run fight had taken off a little of the pressure, and McClellan was doing what McDowell had never had a chance to do; he was creating an army, and it had a name, a name that would cast long shadows and stir great memories before the end came—the Army of the Potomac. More often, though, the newspapers spoke of it simply as "McClellan's army," and that was the way the men themselves thought of it. They were McClellan's men, and in spirit most of them would continue to be that as long as they lived.

For McClellan had touched their spirits. To the men who had lived through Bull Run he brought back pride and self-respect. To the newcomers, who did not carry Bull Run in their memories, he gave the feeling that it was grand to be a soldier. To all he gave a sense of belonging to something big and powerful that was going according to plan.

The men did not set eyes on him very often, to be sure. Instead of living in camp he rented a large house in downtown Washington not far from the White House, and he lived in considerable splendor, giving elegant dinner parties for important people, his doors guarded by swanky regulars, with glittering staff officers and aides following him wherever he went. The average soldier saw him only at the big reviews, and at such times McClellan always made a dramatic entrance. There would be the great level field, long ranks of men in blue standing at attention (the men secretly proud of their ability to stand and march and look like real soldiers), carriages full of senators and diplomats and starchy womenfolk waiting on the far side of the field, officers with drawn swords poised immobile in front of their commands, everybody tense with expectancy. Then the jaunty little man on his big black horse would come galloping down the line, his escort trailing out after him, and the whole field would break out in a wild shout of enthusiasm . . . and all at once army life would be just as exciting and romantic and wonderful as it had seemed to be when one stood with raised hand before the mustering officer, and all the drudgery and annoyance of training camp would be forgotten.²

A Massachusetts recruit summed it up.

"The boys are happy as clams at high water," he wrote to his family. They were being drilled hard, but somehow it seemed good: "I never done anything yet that I like so well as I do soldiering." There was a bond between private soldier and commanding general, a bond that became almost tangible as the general rode down the lines: "He has got an eye like a hawk. I looked him right in the eye and he done the same by me. I was bound to see what he looked like and I think I would know him if I should see him again." The general was "Our George" or "Little Mac," and he would not put his boys into action until he was sure that everything would be all right with them: "He looked like a man that was not afraid of the cry On to Richmond. . . . The rank and file think he is just the man to lead us on to victory *when he gets ready* and not when Horace Greeley says to go. For my part I think he is just the man, and"—using a colloquialism that apparently expressed the ultimate—"the kind of a man that can keep a hotel."[3]

Everybody was getting ready. Infantrymen were discovering the ins and outs of brigade and division drill, were learning that doing guard duty was not quite as much fun as they had expected it to be, and were beginning to realize that a great many volunteer officers were not up to their jobs; a regiment that had any regular officers would consider itself lucky, since the regulars knew how to make camp routine go more smoothly. Budding artillerists fired their guns in target practice and blinked in awe at the discovery that a gunner, if he looked closely, could see his missile from the moment it left the muzzle until it ended its flight. (A few were slightly sobered by the reflection that if you could do this you probably could see the enemy's shells approaching as well, which would be pretty nerve-racking.) Green recruits trying to become cavalrymen complained that government-issue saddles, high before and high behind, gave a soldier a perch like a two-pronged fork astride a round stick; he couldn't easily fall off, but he couldn't exactly be said to be sitting on anything, either. The new troopers found that their horses caught onto the drill as fast as the men did. When the bugles sounded "March!" or "Halt!" or "Wheel!" most of the horses would respond without waiting for their riders to guide them.[4]

Even the drummer boys were practicing, working at mysteries known as the double and single drag, learning all of the irregular syncopated beats that carried orders to marching men; a crack regiment, it seemed, was one that could maneuver all over a parade ground without spoken orders, the commands being transmitted entirely by the drums. Precocious infants not yet old enough to shave, the drummers took great pride in their work. Long afterward one of them remembered it: "When a dozen or more of the lads, with their caps set saucily on the sides of their heads, led a regiment in a review with their get-out-of-the-way-Old-Dan-Tuckerish style of music, it made the men in the ranks step off as though they were bound for a Donnybrook Fair."[5]

And if all of this made for the men a living, shifting panorama of bright color and taut anticipation, it is clear that it did the same for McClellan himself. The man had basic traits of the true romantic: the ability to see, each moment, the fine figure he must be cutting in other men's eyes, and the imperative need to play his part in such a way that he himself can look on it with admiration. In his letters to his young wife (he had been married only a little more than a year) McClellan was forever reciting with a kind of bemused wonder the details of his own sudden rise to fame; inviting her to look, he could stand by her shoulder and look also.

"I find myself in a new and strange position here; President, cabinet, Gen. Scott and all deferring to me," he would tell her. "I seem to have become the power of the land. . . . It seems to strike everybody that I am very young. . . . Who would have thought, when we were married, that I should so soon be called on to save my country?"[6]

To save it singlehanded? Possibly. Washington was full of strange talk in that summer of 1861, and McClellan had been there less than a fortnight when he was hearing some unusual suggestions. He told his wife about them:

"I receive letter after letter, have conversation after conversation, calling on me to save the nation, alluding to the presidency, dictatorship, etc. As I hope one day to be united with you forever in heaven, I have no such aspiration. I would cheerfully take the dictatorship and agree to lay down my life when the country is saved. I am not spoiled by my unexpected new position. I feel sure that God will give me the strength and wisdom to preserve this great nation; but I tell you, who share all my thoughts, that I have no selfish feeling in this matter."[7]

Clearly enough, it was a magnificent and enchanting vision that was dancing before the young general's eyes, and he was luxuriating in it as a tired man luxuriates in a warm scented bath. Yet if this romantic indulgence might in time narrow his field of vision and place limits on the things he might do, it was not at the moment keeping him from buckling down to a solid job of work. He was surrounding Washington with forts, he was training an army of high morale, and if he was at bottom a romantic he was at least a romantic of high administrative capacity.

This, unhappily, was a good deal more than could be said for the other principal in Scott's team of lieutenants, Major General John Charles Frémont.

Frémont was a skyrocket; a man who rose fast, seeming to light all the sky, and then went plunging down into darkness. Right now he was on the way up, and giving off sparks, with the great darkness still ahead of him; but he had had his ups and downs before. As a dashing young lieutenant of topographical engineers in the 1840s, the son-in-law of powerful Senator Thomas Hart Benton of Missouri, he had led spectacular exploring sorties across the Far West and had become known all over America as "the Pathfinder." The precise value of his explorations may have been open to some question, but his talents as a publicist were not; and if he did not actually find very many new paths through the West, he at least centered national attention on paths other people had found, and he and the Far West became famous together.

It appears that fame went to his head. In the Mexican War he got into California in time to have a hand in detaching that territory from Mexico, and he enjoyed brief glory as an empire-builder; then, when the army sent a full-fledged general out to California to take charge, Frémont refused to obey his orders, and the army cracked down hard. Frémont was recalled to Washington, court-martialed, and dismissed from the service. To rebuild his reputation he led an expedition that was to find a route for a railroad from St. Louis to San Francisco. He elected to march into the worst of the Colorado Rockies in the bitterest winter the West had known in years, lost more than a fourth of his men through cold and starvation, saw the expedition evaporate completely, and went on to California by himself over the well-traveled southern route —and on his arrival found that the new gold rush had made him a multimillionaire, pay dirt having been struck in quantity on a ranch he had bought a year or two earlier.

Then he became a senator, and in 1856 the new Republican party made him its first candidate for President, and the North throbbed to the drumbeat chant: *Free soil, free men, Frémont!* Clearly, he was a man the Republican administration had to reckon with, and he was one of the very first men to be commissioned as major general after Fort Sumter fell. (The date of the commission was extremely important, as far as rank was concerned, since a major general automatically outranked all other major generals whose commissions bore later dates than his.) When old General Harney was finally pulled out of St. Louis, Frémont seemed the obvious person to put in his place.

His job was fully as big as McClellan's. He had command of what was called the Western Department—everything between the Mississippi and the Rockies, plus the state of Illinois, with the promise that Kentucky would be added as soon as Kentucky's gossamer-thin neutrality was torn apart. He had the support of the powerful Blair family, and in a personal conference Lincoln had given him a broad charter of authority—"Use your own judgment and do the best you can"—and in general terms Frémont was responsible for saving the West and winning the Mississippi Valley for the Union.[3]

He received his assignment on July 3. It took him three weeks to get from Washington to St. Louis, since he went by way of New York and tarried there to attend to various business matters, and when he reached St. Louis late in July he found himself stepping into an uncommonly tough spot. The Confederates were putting on a big push to retake the state. In the south and southwest they had perhaps as many as fifty thousand men under arms, with five thousand more ominously waiting at New Madrid, on the river, and an undetermined number concentrated somewhere in western Tennessee. It was believed that a Confederate army of ten thousand was about to attack Cairo, Illinois, where the Ohio joins the Mississippi. (At that moment there was probably no spot in the United States, outside of Washington itself, whose retention was more vital to the Union than Cairo.) The northeastern counties of Missouri were boiling with guerrilla bands whose night ridings and bridge burnings seemed likely to spill all the way over into Iowa if they were not checked, and St. Louis itself was full of Rebel sympathizers who would seize the city if they had half a chance.

To deal with all of this Frémont had in his command just

twenty-three thousand men, more than a third of whom were ninety-day soldiers who were about to go home. He had no arms or equipment for any new troops, the military war chest was about empty, and it developed that the government's credit in St. Louis was exhausted.[9]

Altogether, it was a situation in which the Federal commander needed a rich variety of talents, including the ability to make bricks without straw. These talents Frémont did not have. He could strike an attitude and he could send fine words glinting down the wind, and while these qualities had taken him far they might not be adequate to carry him through a civil war in Missouri.

2. *Trail of the Pathfinder*

Frémont tried to meet the immediate threats first, and here he did perhaps as well as anyone could have done under the difficult circumstances.

The big thing, of course, was to hold the river. Frémont began by going up to take a look at all-important Cairo. He learned to his horror that although the Federal garrison there consisted of eight regiments, six of them were ninety-day detachments that were due to go home. Of the balance, nearly everyone was sick, nobody had ever drawn any pay, morale had almost entirely vanished, and all in all there were but six hundred men on duty under arms.

In one way or another he scraped together thirty-eight hundred troops and got them up to Cairo. He saw to it that enough men were sent to the northeastern counties of Missouri to suppress secessionist outbreaks there, and with the help of the German irregulars (with whom his name had powerful magic) he held onto St. Louis. All of this was good, but it did mean that no reinforcements could be sent to Nathaniel Lyon in Springfield, so the blazing little man with the red whiskers took the path that led him down to the smoky bottom lands along Wilson's Creek. Flushed with their triumph, the Rebels who had killed him went surging up the western part of the state, pinching off and capturing a Union force of thirty-five hundred men at Lexington. But at least St. Louis and the river were secure.[1]

Now it was up to Frémont to collect his forces and squelch all of this secessionist activity; but first he had to get organized, and the assignment might easily have dismayed a much abler man. Frémont had been calling frantically for reinforcements, and midwestern governors were sending regiments to St. Louis as fast as they could be mustered in—men without tents or blankets, many of them without uniforms or weapons, nearly all of them completely untrained. With these necessitous thousands arriving week after week the army's purchase and supply arrangements in St. Louis were swamped. The War Department was too busy outfitting McClellan's army to be very helpful, and anyway, Washington was a long way off. Frémont needed everything from tugboats and mules to hardtack and artillery, and he had been told to look out for himself.

If it was a prosaic job, he at least gave it the romantic touch. The commanding general's headquarters were soon famous as a place of unrestrained pomp and spectacle. It seemed to Frémont that he needed officers, and he began to hand out commissions generously, overlooking the rule that officers' commissions could legally come only from the President. Foreign adventurers of high and low degree began to blossom out in blue uniforms with gold braid and sashes, and the problems of Missouri were analyzed and argued in all the tongues of middle Europe. An émigré Hungarian officer named Zagonyi showed up as organizer of a crack cavalry guard, explaining in high pidgin English: "Was the intention now to form a body of picked men, each to be an officer. As was raised regiments, could be taken from this corps welltrained officers." Another émigré Hungarian, General Asboth, scoffed at the call for tents: "Is no need of tents. In Hungary we make a winter campaign and we sleep without tents, our feet to the fire—and sometimes our ears did freeze." Needing a bandmaster, Frémont took a musician from a local theater, commissioned him as captain of engineers, and put him in charge of headquarters music. There were guards and sentries everywhere, and a surgeon sent from the East to join Frémont's staff learned that he could not get near the commanding general. He found Frémont making a speech to admiring Germans from the balcony of the building, and when the speech ended saw Frémont "surrounded by a queer crowd of foreigners, Germans, Hungarians and mixed nationalities. . . . There was much jabbering and gesticulation, and the scene was most un-American."

To a general who was trying to improvise command arrangements in a hurry—a general known in Europe as a fighter for freedom, his name a magnet to displaced revolutionaries, titled idealists, and plain adventure-seekers—much could be forgiven. Yet the broken-English bustle and gold-laced glitter, the sheer ostentatious foreignness around headquarters, made a queer contrast with unvarnished Missouri reality, and what Frémont had surrounded himself with was sharply out of key with the men he commanded. Frémont's army was not an army at all, as a European would understand the word. It was just the Middle West, unexpectedly in uniform and under arms, getting ready in its own way to take charge of a little history.

It was, for instance, the 43rd Ohio, whose members in their camp by the Mississippi found life dull and felt homesick for something that would remind them of familiar things back in Ohio and so built birdhouses out of cracker boxes and nailed them to trees and posts all around, attracting a huge population of martins; and the regiment for the rest of the war was known as the Martin Box Regiment, all through the western armies.

It was the 8th Wisconsin Infantry, parading before a general under an officer not long off the farm. Passing the general, the column was supposed to swing to the right, but its commander found himself suddenly unable to think of the proper command and so in desperation at last bawled out: "Gee! God damn it, *gee!*" Farmers to a man, the regiment understood and made the right turn snappily enough; but the general did ask the officer afterward if he customarily steered his command about as if it were a team of oxen.

It was the 15th Illinois, restless in a Missouri outpost, complaining angrily about the colonel who commanded the post because, outranking the 15th's own colonel, he ordered a detail from the regiment to clean his own regiment's camp.

They had not, said the 15th, enlisted to do menial labor like so many slaves, and they would not on any account do it. They protested so stoutly that the colonel at last shrugged and canceled his order, but for some months thereafter the 15th had no use for him. His name, as it happened, was Ulysses S. Grant.[5]

It was the 51st Indiana, which liked to yell just because it was young and yelling was fun, and set the pattern for the whole army. A veteran recalled that the 51st yelled at everything it saw or heard, and added: "When another regiment passed, they yelled at them; they scared the darkies almost to death, with their yelling; as they tumbled out to roll-call in the morning, they yelled; as they marched out of camp their voices went up in a muscular whoop; when they returned, after a hard day's scouting, they were never too tired to yell. If a mule broke loose and ran away his speed was accelerated by a volley of yells all along the line; and if a dog happened to come their way they made it livelier for him than could the most resonant tin can that ever adorned his tail. Indeed, our whole army was blessed with this remarkable faculty. Sometimes a yell would start in at one end of the division, and regiment after regiment and brigade after brigade would take it up and carry it along; then send it back to the other end; few knowing what it was about, or caring."[8]

. . . Into St. Louis toward the end of August came a plump balding young regular army officer, Major John M. Schofield, who had been Lyon's chief of staff; a serious-minded officer deeply interested in physics, whose spare-time pursuit it was to try to "work out the mathematical interpretation of all the phenomena of physical science, including electricity and magnetism," and who was approaching now to tell the commanding general about what had happened at Wilson's Creek. Schofield came to headquarters with Frank Blair (who owned a colonel's commission by now), and after some delay the two were admitted to Frémont's presence. To their surprise, Frémont asked not a question about the recent battle or about Lyon. Instead he led them to a big map spread out on a table and for a solid hour he talked enthusiastically about the great campaign he was going to have just as soon as he got everything ready—a march down through southwestern Missouri and Arkansas to the valley of the Arkansas River, a swing thence to the Mississippi, and eventually the capture of Memphis. This would turn all of the Rebel defenses on the lower river, the Confederate armies would be scattered, and the watchword for Frémont's command this fall and winter would be: "New Orleans, and home again by summer!"

Somewhat dazed, Schofield and Blair got out at last and went off down the street. Blair finally asked the inevitable question: "Well, what do you think of him?" Schofield took a deep breath and replied in words which, he confessed later, were too strong to print. Blair nodded and said that he felt the same way himself.'

It was an evil omen for Frémont. Missouri was a Blair fief, as far as the administration in Washington was concerned. Blair had struck the first blow there; he had raised Lyon from infantry captain to brigadier general and he had had distinguished General Harney deposed. The commander in St. Louis, whatever else he might do, had better show that he could get along with the Blair family. Frémont had come to St. Louis with Blair support, but he had already lost some of it. During the next few weeks he was to show a positive genius for losing all the rest of it.

For one thing, there were contracts to be signed. Of necessity, Frémont was buying enormous quantities of goods —doing it in a most irregular manner, the old-line quartermasters complained, with improperly commissioned officers signing orders that no right-minded quartermaster or disbursing officer could honor, and with rumors of graft and waste and favoritism spreading all across the Middle West. This was bad, although in view of the general disorganization and the imperative need for haste, it is probable that no officer in Frémont's position could have avoided trouble. What was worse, as far as Frémont's personal fortunes were concerned, was the fact that the innumerable contractors who bore Frank Blair's endorsement could not seem to get aboard the gravy train at any price. Blair's rising distaste for Frémont began to harden into active opposition.'

Then, too, there was Jessie.

Jessie was Mrs. Frémont—Jessie Benton Frémont, daughter of the famous Senator Thomas Hart Benton, a strong-minded and imperious woman who was completely devoted to her husband's advancement and who was used to having her own way. She was often in view at headquarters; she liked to be there, she found it "a stirring, eager, hopeful time," and she liked to see the halls and offices "humming with life and the clank and ring of sabre and spur." She worked with her husband, a cross between confidential secretary and executive assistant. When he was away Jessie actually seemed to be in charge of the army, and she wrote fondly of her husband's habit of "referring all manner of work and duties to me as acting principal in his absence." She would issue orders in his name, and he would send messages to her: "Thank you for the sabres and guns; send any such things forward as best you can." She shared his belief that a great victory was in the making. To her he confided: "My plan is New Orleans straight . . . I think it can be done gloriously."[9]

It could be done gloriously. The adverb was to be emphasized; war was still a matter of romance and great words, it went to "the clank and ring of sabre and spur," officers with golden sashes and foreign titles swung naturally in the orbit of the daring Pathfinder, and if the Pathfinder and his wife felt impelled to take the general direction of things out of the hands of the President in Washington, the times were, as General Scott had admitted, revolutionary. Also, the general had once been a candidate for Lincoln's own office, he was still the great hero of the anti-slavery men, and anyway, it was time to give tone and definition to the nation's war aims. General Frémont must issue a proclamation.

General Frémont did so, on August 30; a turgid document, issued on a to-whom-it-may-concern basis, composed the night before by an inspired general by the midnight oil, cups of strong tea at hand. It announced that rebellion in Missouri would be put down with a heavy hand. Martial law was proclaimed, enemies of the Union found with arms in their hands inside the Union lines would be shot, and the slaves of all Missourians who favored secession were declared to be free men. Immediate emancipation, in short, was to be the price of rebellion.[10]

Admittedly the situation was confused. Mrs. Frémont had written that "St. Louis was the rebel city of a rebel state," and it was easy for a Federal commander there—reflecting that the devoutly anti-slavery Germans were the hard core of loyalist support—to feel that the war needed to be put on an anti-slavery basis. Yet Missouri was not in fact a Rebel state. It had flatly refused to become one. Lyon could never have got away with his high-handed program if it had not, somewhere and somehow, touched majority opinion. Nor was St. Louis necessarily a Rebel city. The 8th Wisconsin infantry, equipped by its native state with uniforms of gray instead of blue, was showered with bricks, eggs, dead cats, and other things when it disembarked there that fall and marched through the streets to its barracks; the citizens mistook it for a Confederate regiment and would have none of it, and the mob scene ended only when the soldiers remembered that they were carrying overcoats of proper Union blue and put them on in spite of the heat.[11]

Indeed, the whole point of everything that had happened in the border states thus far was the demonstration that a deep, mystic feeling for an undivided country did exist and that even in slave territory it could rise above all other feelings. Men who would have no part of an attempt to fight against slavery would take up arms to fight for the Union. By his proclamation Frémont was in effect telling them that they were wrong, was saying that the whole of Lincoln's winning gamble along the border was a mistake that had to be canceled.

From Washington to St. Louis came a hurry-up message for Frémont over Abraham Lincoln's signature. The business of shooting civilians would lead to reprisals of indefinite extent and was altogether too risky: therefore, the general would execute no one without referring the case to Washington and getting specific authority. Also, the emancipation proclamation would probably cancel out the substantial patches of Union sentiment in the South and along the border and "perhaps ruin our rather fair prospect for Kentucky." Would not the general, therefore, voluntarily withdraw it?[12]

Frémont would not. He had thought this up by himself, he had done it because he believed it to be right, he still felt that way about it, and if he took it back now it would look as though he were admitting an error. He would withdraw the offending proclamation only if the President publicly ordered him to do so. Having put all of this down on paper, Frémont sealed the letter, gave it to Jessie, and told her to set out for Washington at once and deliver it personally to President Lincoln.

Thus far into unreality could posturing and a sense of drama carry a man. Jessie made the trip and had what appears to have been an extremely unpleasant interview; for the man she met in the White House was not the kindly sentimentalist of legend but a coldly furious executive who was not going to let any general, not even one whose fame exceeded his own, tell him how to shape the top policy of the war. He greeted her with a cold "Well?" and did not invite her to sit down. She gave him the letter, argued her husband's case, and hinted broadly that if the people had to choose between Lincoln and Frémont they would choose Frémont. Then she left, and off to St. Louis went the orders Frémont had specified: orders from the President, revoking the premature proclamation of emancipation.[13]

It was beginning to be pretty clear by now that in a military sense nothing much was apt to be accomplished in Missouri under Frémont. The Confederates themselves were the first to catch on; a bit later their Secretary of War was to write contemptuously of Frémont, "whose incompetency, well known to us, was a guarantee against immediate peril."[14] From the War Department in Washington came a top-level mission to look into the charges of graft and corruption that were piling up around the St. Louis headquarters. (The mission found much real waste and mismanagement, much probable graft, but no dishonesty involving Frémont personally; the man was a romantic made dizzy by his own altitude and dazzled by his own reputation, but he was never a grafter.) Meanwhile the break between Frémont and the Blair family became complete. Ever since Frank Blair and Schofield had paid their visit Blair had considered Frémont a dithering incompetent. In return, Frémont looked on Blair as an unscrupulous alcoholic, and he presently put him under arrest for insubordination. Rookie soldiers of the 16th Ohio Artillery, marking time disconsolately because Frémont was unable to provide them with any cannon, were assigned to stand guard over Blair's tent. They found him a pleasant sort of prisoner; one rainy night he even invited the soldier who was guarding him to come into the tent and have a drink, and he appears to have been mildly shocked when the soldier virtuously refused.[15]

Only one thing could keep Frémont in command: a speedy and decisive victory over a Confederate army in the field. This Frémont set out to achieve. He had plenty of troops by mid-September, and if all sorts of equipment were still lacking there was enough to get moving. (After all, in Hungary the revolutionists had campaigned without tents; and, as Jessie recorded, it was considered that the army could seize cattle and corn along the way and so could move without an extensive supply train.) So by the early part of October an army of forty thousand men set off for southwest Missouri, where the Rebel forces were somewhat loosely concentrated under Sterling Price. Frémont was still thinking in terms of the capture of New Orleans, and he wrote to Jessie (who was in effective charge of army headquarters at St. Louis) that this "would precipitate the war forward and end it soon and victoriously."[16]

This it might possibly do. But the simple lack of know-how at the top was a fearful drag on the army's movements and a depressant for army morale as well. The green soldiers could not help seeing that Frémont and his staff seemed much more concerned with military pomp and display than with the more prosaic business of keeping the army fed and moving. Full of enthusiasm though it was, the army began to feel that it was almost helpless—poor weapons, inadequate training, and bad leadership—and an Iowa soldier remarked that they were being led straight into the heart of the enemy's country with "an inferior quality of unserviceable foreign-made guns, a lamentable lack of military method in the plans for the campaign, a want of confidence and harmony among the commanders who were to lead the army, and in many regiments discipline little better than that of an armed mob." Illinois soldiers grumpily declared that the best they could say about this campaign in Missouri was that it was better than being in hell, and one volunteer wrote angrily about the failure of supplies and concluded: "If there ever was an empty, spread-eagle, show-off, horn-tooting general, it was Frémont."[17]

With infinite effort the loose-jointed army plowed on down toward the southwest. Substantially outnumbered, the Confederates drew back from before them, and by the end of October Frémont had his troops in and around Springfield. A couple of incidental skirmishes, dignified in Frémont's later reminiscences as "admirably conducted engagements" and "a glorious victory," had been fought, but although Frémont believed he was on the verge of bringing the main Confederate force to battle the chance actually was remote. Instead of being concentrated at Wilson's Creek, nine miles away, where Lyon had been killed—which is where Frémont innocently supposed they were—the Confederates were a good sixty miles away, easily able to retreat further if they chose in case Frémont tried to come to grips with them.

Frémont's objectives were two: to catch and destroy the Confederate army, and then to capture Memphis as a step toward New Orleans. Remote as Washington was, it was obvious even in the White House that he was never going to do either of these things, the way he was going. So to one of his subordinate officers in St. Louis, late in October, there came from Washington a sealed packet with instructions to get it into Frémont's hands as quickly as possible.

But Lincoln had made this delivery subject to one condition —an extremely interesting one for the light it sheds on Lincoln's attitude, even at that stage of the war, toward an erring strategist. If, when the messenger reached Frémont, "he shall then have, in personal command, fought and won a battle, or shall then be actually in a battle, or shall then be in the immediate presence of the enemy in expectation of a battle," the envelope was not to be delivered; instead, the messenger was to keep it and check back for further instructions.[18] Lincoln had had enough, in other words, but if Frémont would actually get into a full-dress fight all would be forgiven. . . . Then and throughout the war, inability to get in close and fight was the trait in a general that Lincoln could not forgive. One good battle could always cover a multitude of military sins.

The messenger took off. Because it was commonly understood in St. Louis that Frémont had made arrangements to keep any order of recall from reaching him, the messenger was disguised as a Missouri farmer and was under orders to follow a little stratagem. He presented himself at Frémont's camp and told the sentries that he was a messenger with information for the general from within the Rebel lines. He got at last to some of Frémont's staff officers, who told him he could not see the general but could give them any information he had. He refused to do this—what he had to tell the general was for the general's own ears—and after a whole day of this the staff finally decided that he was harmless and took him to Frémont's tent. There the man produced the envelope and handed it over. Frémont opened it, asked wrathfully how this person had ever got through his lines, and read the bad news: over the signature of Winfield Scott, he was ordered to turn over his command to his ranking officer—a surly regular named David Hunter, who had long been convinced of Frémont's total ineffectiveness—after which he was to report to Washington, by letter, to see if anybody had any further orders for him.[19]

For the time being, at least, the Pathfinder had come to the end of the trail.

3. *He Must Be Willing to Fight*

There had been the romantic General Frémont, and there still was the romantic General McClellan. In addition there was General U. S. Grant, who was not romantic at all—a stooped, rather scrubby little man whom nobody in particular had ever heard of—and the war was giving him a chance to make a modest new start in life.

In a way, Frémont was responsible for him. Grant had gone off to war that spring as colonel of the 21st Illinois Infantry, which put in a month or two in the summer guarding railroads in eastern Missouri, and he had been promoted chiefly because the inscrutable ways of Republican party politics entitled an Illinois congressman named Elihu B. Washburne to name one brigadier general. Washburne knew Grant and liked him and sent in his name; and somewhat to his surprise—for he had had a hard time getting into the war at all, that spring—Grant became a general. And what Frémont had done for him was to lift him out of a railroad-guarding billet in Missouri and give him command of the military district of southeastern Missouri, whose headquarters were in Cairo.

Like Grant himself, Cairo was more important than it looked. It was a muddy, untidy little place snugged down behind the levees at the angle between the Ohio and the Mississippi, and it had been a troop center right from the start. The first volunteer regiment raised in Illinois was sent down there, and others came soon afterward, so that before the war had fairly got started the Federals had a modest troop concentration at this key point, facing south.

Grant's arrival at Cairo was not impressive. When his promotion came through he gave away his colonel's uniform and sent for a brigadier's outfit, and the new togs had not yet arrived; he showed up in civilian clothing, looking like anything but a soldier, and he wandered into the office of Colonel Richard Oglesby, the commanding officer, and wrote out an order relieving Oglesby and assuming the command himself. Oglesby looked at the order and then looked at Grant, and for a time he was undecided whether to obey the order or put this strange civilian under arrest as an impostor.[1] He finally obeyed the order, whereupon a key piece in the machinery of the Civil War dropped quietly into place and began to function.

Frémont said afterward that he appointed Grant because he saw in him "the soldierly qualities of self-poise, modesty, decision, attention to details"; qualities which he was not seeing much of in the flamboyant crowd around headquarters in St. Louis. Other officers had warned Frémont not to do it, "for reasons," said the Pathfinder primly, "that were well known." Grant was a West Pointer and he had served in the war with Mexico, and the officer corps of the little regular army was a clubby group in which everybody knew and gossiped about everybody else. In all of this gossip Grant had been typed—a drunkard and a failure, a man who had been forced to resign as infantry captain on the west coast in 1854 because he could not keep his hands off the bottle, and who had come back to an excessively undistinguished civilian career as Missouri farmer, St. Louis real estate agent, and most recently as manager of his father's harness shop in Galena, Illinois. But Frémont was not impressed by this gossip. He was no West Pointer himself, and the regulars had never admitted him to the club, and, said Frémont, something about Grant's manner was "sufficient to counteract the influence of what they said." Anyway, he made the appointment, and as September began Grant was installed at Cairo.²

He was not yet the Grant of the familiar photographs. An army surgeon who came on from the east coast about this time found him short, spare, and somewhat unkempt, with a long flowing beard and puffing constantly on a big meerschaum with curved ten-inch stem; a man who did not seem to have much to say and who would sit quietly at his desk, methodically going through his paper work as if he were turning all sorts of things over in his mind. He was unprepossessing at first glance but there was something about him that made a man take a second look, and the surgeon wrote: "As I sat and watched him then, and many an hour afterward, I found that his face grew upon me. His eyes were gentle, with a kind expression, and thoughtful."³

Grant was at Cairo, which was becoming one of the great gateways to the war. Immense quantities of army stores were beginning to cram its warehouses, and the place was alive with blue-coated soldiers; one of these said it was like the mouth of a vast beehive, with a never-ending coming and going of recruits. . . . "They came on incoming trains and up-river steamboats. They went away on outgoing trains and down-river steamboats, and meantime they crossed and crisscrossed the town in every direction. They crowded its stations, hotels, boarding houses and waiting rooms, and, if it must be said, its saloons as well."⁴

Eight miles up the Ohio was the town of Mound City; a tiny place which had come into being as part of a real estate boom that it had never been able to live up to and which had been equipped by hopeful speculators with a range of brick warehouses to accommodate a river trade that had not developed. Grant's medical director seized on these and converted them into a huge army hospital—one was badly needed because the hot river valley was unhealthy and there was much sickness. In the course of outfitting the place the doctor learned that it was all but impossible to get any work out of the soldiers who were detailed to help. To these Westerners, sweeping and scrubbing and setting up beds was women's work, and they simply would not do it. He learned, too, that these boys from the farm and the small town, self-reliant to a fault at ordinary times, became totally helpless when they fell ill, requiring much more nursing than the civilian patients of his past experience.[5]

Mound City had a shipyard, in which four ironclad gunboats were being built; big snub-nosed craft with two and one half inches of armor on their slanting sides, pierced for thirteen guns, three of which were heavy-duty eight-inch Dahlgrens. It had been clear from the start that war could not be fought along the great rivers without warships, but Washington (to the navy's intense disgust) had decreed that all of these inland operations should be under army control. So the War Department was having the gunboats built, the navy would man and operate them, and skippers and squadron commanders were required to take orders from the army. Thus, when he took over at Cairo, Grant found that he had a budding fleet under his control.

Part of it was already afloat and in operation: three river steamers hastily converted into gunboats, powerfully armed but very vulnerable to enemy fire because their boilers were above the waterline and they had nothing but five-inch oak bulwarks for armor. Since the Confederates had no gunboats at all in this part of the world, these fragile steamers were having no trouble, but they could not for five minutes stand up against shore fortifications, and therefore they could control the river only if the army occupied the banks.

To command its Mississippi squadron the navy had sent out Flag Officer Andrew Foote, a salty person with an engaging fringe of whiskers jutting out around a heart-of-oak face; a devout churchman who not infrequently delivered sermons to his crews and who was so well liked by the rank and file that he was even able to stop the grog ration without creating trouble. Luckily for the cause of the Union, he and Grant took to each other at once, and—in a command situation almost guaranteed to generate friction—they got along in perfect harmony.[6]

Grant had been at Cairo almost no time at all before he began to get action.

Across the river was Kentucky, and Kentucky was still neutral, but nobody imagined that the neutrality was going to last very much longer. Somebody was bound to violate it; if the Union and the Confederacy were going to make war on each other along the underside of the Middle West, Kentucky was bound to become involved, and the only real question was when and how it would happen. At Cairo, Grant was looking down the river, turning over plans for a thrust toward Tennessee; and in northwestern Tennessee there was a Confederate army under Major General Leonidas Polk, former bishop in the Episcopal Church, who had gone to West Point with Jefferson Davis and who now was responsible for keeping Yankees from coming down the Mississippi.

On the Mississippi there was a little Kentucky town named Columbus, important for two reasons: it was the northern terminus of a southern railroad line, and it was perched on high bluffs which, if properly fortified, no northern gunboats could pass. Bishop Polk suspected that the Federals were about to put up works on the opposite Missouri shore, and he decided to beat them to the punch. On September 4 he acted, disregarding Kentucky neutrality and sending troops over the state line to occupy and fortify Columbus.

Grant learned of this at once, and the surgeon who had been watching him with growing interest discovered that one of his early judgments was correct—the man could act swiftly in an emergency.

Grant began by sending a telegram to the Speaker of the Kentucky House of Representatives at Frankfort, telling him that the lawless Confederates had wantonly violated the state's neutrality. Then he got off another wire to Frémont in St. Louis, announcing that unless he was quickly ordered not to he would that night move up the Ohio and occupy the Kentucky city of Paducah. When he got no reply—he did not wait very long for it—he loaded two regiments on river steamers, got Foote to bring up two of the converted wooden gunboats, and at midnight his flotilla set off.[7]

Paducah was another key spot. It is situated where the Tennessee River flows into the Ohio, not far upstream from Cairo, and the Tennessee was an obvious highway to the heart of the South. Broad and deep, it was easily navigable all the way to northern Alabama; and if Kentucky was no longer to be a no man's land, the Tennessee River was of first importance. A Federal base at the mouth of the river would make possible a formal invasion of the Deep South a bit later on.

Grant reached Paducah, disembarked his troops, saw that the town was made secure, and hurried back to Cairo. There he found a message from Frémont, authorizing him to do what he had just done. Then he got another wire, rebuking him for communicating directly with the Kentucky House of Representatives—that was a job for the department commander, and in doing it himself he had been insubordinate and out of line. Then he was notified that Paducah would be put under the command of General Charles F. Smith, and although Paducah was in Grant's district Smith was being ordered to by-pass Grant and report directly to St. Louis.

Smith was an old-timer, with a record of thirty-five years' service. He was tall, slim, and straight, with great piratical white mustachios that came down below the line of his chin, a man with ruddy pink cheeks and clear blue eyes, a strict disciplinarian and a terror to volunteers; the very incarnation of the pre-Civil War regular army officer. Among the regulars, indeed, there were many who considered him the best all-around man in the army. He had been commandant of cadets when Grant was at West Point, and although Grant outranked him—and would soon have him in his command, for Frémont's order was before long rescinded—Grant always felt a little humble and school-boyish in his presence. He remarked once that "it does not seem quite right for me to give General Smith orders," and some of the regulars felt the same way about it; Grant, they said, owed his rise to political pull, and Smith had spent a lifetime in uniform and ought to be top dog. It never bothered Smith, however. He was frankly proud of his former pupil and had confidence in him.[8]

Something of Smith's quality comes out in a story told by Lew Wallace.

Wallace as a boy had longed to go to West Point, and when that dream failed he tried earnestly to become a novelist. That failed too—the train of thought that would eventually become *Ben-Hur* had not yet taken shape in his mind—and so he turned to the law and politics, and when the war began he was made colonel of the 11th Indiana. He was sent to Paducah soon after the place was occupied by Union troops, and—his political connections being first-rate—it was not long before he learned that he was being made a brigadier general. This unsettled him a bit, and he went to General Smith to ask advice.

Smith had taken over a big residence for headquarters, and Wallace found him sitting by the fire after dinner, taking his ease, his long legs stretched out, a decanter on the table. Smith was, said Wallace, "by all odds the handsomest, stateliest, most commanding figure I had ever seen." Somewhat hesitantly Wallace showed him his notice of promotion and asked if he should accept.

Smith had worked thirty-five years to get his own commission as a brigadier, and the idea that any officer might hesitate to accept such a thing stumped him. Why on earth, he asked, should Wallace not take it?

"Because," confessed Wallace, "I don't know anything about the duties of a brigadier."

Smith blinked at him.

"This," he said at last, "is extraordinary. Here I have been spending a long life to get an appointment like this one about which you are hesitating. And yet—that isn't it. That you should confess your ignorance—good God!"

Then Smith reached for the decanter, poured Wallace a drink, and told him to accept the promotion and stop worrying. He dug into a table drawer, got out a copy of the United States Army Regulations, and declared that a general should know these rules "as the preacher knows his Bible." Then he went on to sum up his own soldierly philosophy in words which Wallace remembered:

"Battle is the ultimate to which the whole life's labor of an officer should be directed. He may live to the age of retirement without seeing a battle; still, he must always be getting ready for it exactly as if he knew the hour of the day it is to break upon him. And then, whether it come late or early, he must be willing to fight—he *must* fight!"

Rebel troops were in Columbus, another column was coming up into Kentucky through the Cumberland Gap, and a growing Union force was established in Paducah. Kentucky's neutrality by now had completely evaporated. The pro-Union legislature made it official, adopting a resolution directing Governor Magoffin to issue a proclamation ordering the secessionists out of the state. Magoffin, strong for the Confederacy, indignantly vetoed the measure, whereupon the legislature passed it over his veto, formally invited the Federal government to help expel the southern invaders, and ordered volunteers recruited to meet the state's quota. The Richmond government countered by sending General Albert Sidney Johnston out to take top command in the West, and a Confederate force occupied Bowling Green and sent out patrols which burned a bridge within thirty-three miles of Louisville. Fort Sumter hero Robert Anderson established Union headquarters in Louisville; then his health collapsed and he had to retire from active duty, and Federal command passed to another of General Smith's old protégés, a red-haired bristling general named William Tecumseh Sherman.

Sherman had inherited a perplexing job. Except for Smith's forces at Paducah, which was out of his bailiwick, there were very few responsible troops in Kentucky, most of the mid-western levies having been sent either to Missouri or Virginia during the period of Kentucky's neutrality. Sherman had a couple of thousand of the Kentuckians who had been training on the Indiana side of the Ohio River, he had scattering groups of home guards, and there were a few regiments which the prodigious William Nelson had been assembling at Camp Dick Robinson. None of these was ready for active service, and the green regiments which Indiana's Governor Morton was hurrying down were in no better case. The 38th Indiana, as a sample, was sent to Kentucky just three days after it had been mustered into service, and one of its members wrote acidly that "all the regiment lacked of being a good fighting machine was guns, ammunition, cartridge boxes, canteens, haversacks, knapsacks, blankets, etc., with a proper knowledge of how all these equipments could be used with effect."[10]

All the information Sherman could get indicated that large, well-equipped, adequately trained Confederate armies were about to come sweeping up from Tennessee to overrun the entire state. (The rumors were wild exaggerations, but Sherman did not know that until later.) For a short time Louisville itself seemed to be in danger; Confederate Simon Buckner was advancing on the city along the line of the Louisville and Nashville Railroad. (His force was so small that two troop trains served to carry it, but the Federals did not realize this.) Providentially, Buckner was delayed—by a patriotic citizen who removed a rail from the track, thus derailing the leading train—until Sherman could get a makeshift force out to meet him; upon which Buckner withdrew, and the panic was over. But it did seem clear that the Rebel commanders in the West had most aggressive intentions.

Sherman was in a bad mood. He was tense, nervous, given to worry; the grim singleness of purpose that marked him later in the war had not yet appeared. Like Grant, he had something to live down. He had resigned from the army in the 1850s and had tried various business ventures, all of which had failed. In St. Louis, a couple of years before the war, Sherman had referred to himself bitterly as "a dead cock in a pit"; now he may have been uneasily conscious that his general's commission had come to him largely because his more successful brother, John Sherman, was an important Republican senator.

Sherman worried most about the enlisted men in his command. They were woefully untrained, and it seemed to him that to send them into battle—which he might have to do any day—would be plain murder. The sketchy Kentucky cavalry regiments were so busy scouting and patrolling that they had no time for drill. The 1st Kentucky, hastily recruited by a lawyer-politician named Frank Wolford, rode about the countryside without uniforms, armed with infantry muskets, so innocent of proper military usage that when Wolford wanted them to start marching he shouted: "Git up and git!"

while he got them from marching column into line of battle by ordering: "Form a line of fight!"[11]

The farm boys who were grouped together in the volunteer regiments were suffering from the usual camp diseases such as measles. Sanitation and proper medical care seemed to be nonexistent in most camps, and regimental officers who owed their commissions to politics (as practically all of them did) knew not the first thing about taking care of them. An officer in the 53rd Ohio, reporting to Sherman about this time, was surprised to hear the general bark: "How long do you expect to remain in the service?" The officer replied that his regiment had enlisted for three years and expected to serve out its time. "Well, you've got sense," said Sherman. "Most of you fellows come down here intending to go home and go to Congress in about three weeks." When the officer asked where the regiment should camp, Sherman gestured at the surrounding landscape and said: "Go anywhere—it's all flat as a pancake and wet as a sponge." (This, said the regimental historian, was entirely true.)[12]

Problems of discipline were peculiar. The 3rd Ohio went into camp minus its colonel, who preferred to linger in Louisville. In his absence the lieutenant colonel, who had ideas about discipline, reduced a number of incompetent noncoms to the ranks and stirred up so much antagonism that the enlisted men circulated a petition calling on him to resign and roused all the folks back home—lifelong friends and neighbors of the luckless officer—to write indignant letters to him. The missing colonel then let the men know that if the harsh lieutenant colonel were just dismissed he himself would take the regiment back to Ohio to rest and recruit and would see to it that it was outfitted with gaudy Zouave uniforms. In the end, Sherman got the colonel sent home and the unpopular lieutenant colonel was retained and supported, but the whole flare-up was symptomatic. The raw material of the Federal army in Kentucky had no idea whatever of what soldiering was going to be like.[13]

It seemed to Sherman that these untaught boys were going to be sacrificed, and his feeling came out now and then in unexpected ways. An Indiana sergeant was detailed for a job at headquarters. When he finished it, Sherman said:

"Sergeant, I hear you are short of rations over in your camp." The sergeant said that this was so, and Sherman told him to wait and went bustling out to the kitchen. He came back in a minute with two slabs of buttered bread, a thick cut of ham between them, and two red apples. Giving these to the sergeant, he said: "There, that will put some fat on your ribs."[14]

If the regimental officers were incapable of training their soldiers, professionals who could do the job were beginning to appear; most notably a West Point classmate of Sherman (and thus still another of General Smith's former charges) named George Thomas, who was put in charge of operations at Camp Dick Robinson.

Thomas was a Virginian, forty-five years old, tall and stout and reserved in manner; he rarely laughed or raised his voice, he had a majestic full beard and a general air of kindly sternness, he moved with ponderous deliberation, and altogether he was extremely impressive in appearance. His army friends called him "Old Tom," and his troops referred to him as "Old Slow Trot"—he had hurt his spine in a railroad accident a few months earlier, and it gave him excruciating pain when his horse moved faster than a walk. He was inclined to distrust volunteers and he was very stiff about matters of training; not for months would his men give him the affectionate title, "Pap," by which he was to become famous.[15]

He had been much admired by Jefferson Davis when Davis was Secretary of War, and in 1855 when the crack 2nd Cavalry was organized with Albert Sidney Johnston as colonel and Robert E. Lee as lieutenant colonel, Thomas became one of its majors. In January 1861 he suspected that his spinal ailment might make active duty impossible, and in casting about for possible employment he wrote to the superintendent of the Virginia Military Institute, applying for the post of commandant of cadets there. This was remembered against him in Washington after Virginia seceded, and the War Department was inclined to doubt his loyalty. Sherman himself had vouched for him; now Thomas was under him, helping get troops ready for the serious fighting which everybody knew must begin in the spring.

It would begin, actually, long before the spring, and when

it began it would be very rough. And there were, here in this Kentucky sector, these generals who had imbibed old General Smith's doctrine: ". . . he must always be getting ready for it . . . And then, whether it come late or early, he must be willing to fight—he *must* fight!"

4.

To March to Terrible Music

1. *Sambo Was Not Sambo*

THERE WAS a significance in the crossing of the Ohio River. North of the river was the familiar Middle West; beyond it there was nothing less than the South itself, mysterious, romantic, threatening, strange. The nearest Confederate armies might be scores of miles away, with no faintest intention of coming any closer. No matter: when a soldier crossed the river he felt that he was in the war.

Thousands of sunburned boys in ill-fitting blue uniforms were crossing the Ohio this fall, for Kentucky was the destined point of departure and the government was hastening to build up Union strength in the state. Nervous General Sherman had warned the Secretary of War that before they got through they would have to have two hundred thousand soldiers on this front. His panicky overestimate unsettled the authorities so much that they concluded Sherman was too flighty for his job, and he was replaced by the less emotional General Don Carlos Buell; and for a time Sherman hovered unhappily on the fringes of the war, a general without portfolio, alleged by unfriendly newspaper correspondents to be insane. But although his estimate of required strength had been rejected, the government nevertheless was getting troops into the state as fast as the training camps could send them. (By the war's end it would turn out that Sherman's wild appraisal was tolerably accurate, after all.)

The new arrivals were the greenest of recruits, and they came into Kentucky peering nervously about for enemies, tasting the wild excitement of the road to war, seeing a miraculous tonic quality in the sunrise and the crisp autumn wind. Even their officers felt it, even the West Pointers. Ormsby Mitchel, who had been graduated from the military academy in the same class with Robert E. Lee, had left the army to become an astronomer of note and now came to Kentucky as a grizzled brigadier bearing the nickname of "Old Stars"—even Mitchel felt it as he looked about his brigade camp at dawn and saw a haunting mist on the landscape: "Reveille is just sounding from forty drums and fifes and from twenty bugles, all over an area two miles square. It is just coming daylight, but the moon makes it bright as day even at this early hour. The smoke of the campfires spreads a gauzy veil over the white tents sleeping in the moonlight, illumined here and there by an early fire. . . ."[1]

They were a heavy-handed and irrepressible lot, these Unionists. There was the 18th Illinois, which was under orders to march away from Cairo when one soldier murdered a comrade. The soldiers immediately took things into their own hands; hustled the colonel off to town on some trumped-up errand, then formed an impromptu court, appointed members of the regiment as attorneys for prosecution and defense, tried the culprit, and forthwith sentenced him to death. The lieutenant colonel led them into a wood, where the murderer was immediately hanged from a convenient tree. When someone suggested that after hanging a proper length of time the man ought to be given a grave, the officer agreed: "Damned good idea. Dig one under him as he hangs and drop him into it." It was done, the lifeless body was buried, the colonel presently came back from town, and the regiment went off to the wars.[2]

The impatience was characteristic, although the results were not often so grim. Another Illinois regiment, training at Cairo, was sent across the Mississippi each day to practice the manual of arms, loading and firing with blank cartridges, and after a few days of it the colonel went to General Grant with a complaint:

"General, I can't take my boys over there to practice any more unless you will furnish us with some real cartridges. For two days past they have attacked those —— —— weeds and there they stand, as saucy and defiant as ever." Grant chuckled and issued ball cartridges. Next evening the colonel reappeared, all jubilant, to report: "General, there isn't a —— weed left standing in front of my command. Now you can turn us loose on the southern Confederacy as quick as you please!"[3]

As far as the soldiers were concerned the Confederacy began on the southern border of the Ohio River. That Kentucky had maintained a painful neutrality for months meant nothing; that a majority of her citizens now favored the Union rather than the Confederacy meant nothing, either; it was a slave state, and although they had not enlisted to put down slavery, these Middle Westerners felt instinctively that slave territory was enemy territory. As they disembarked at Louisville and marched off through the town the files looked about them in nervous excitement for signs of hostility. The 51st Indiana chuckled when one private, thus marching up a city street, remarked aloud that he wished he could see one real, live Rebel. Instantly a two-hundred-pound Amazon of a woman stepped out from the pavement, came up to him with brandished fists, and cried: "Well, sir, here's one! What do you want?"

Camp life was taking on its own routine. The big conical Sibley tents, each one large enough to house an entire squad, dotted the meadows, set off by crude charcoal signs: "Bull Pups," "Bengal Tigers," "Wild Cats." At dawn the camps rang with a rhythmical, tinny clangor as the men took the unground coffee beans that made up such an important part of their rations, put them in tin pails, and ground the beans by pounding them with musket butts. Sutlers set up their tents near the company streets, selling indigestible pies, gingerbread, and candy, and it was noticed that hungry boys who patronized them lost appetite for army hardtack and bacon, came down with digestive upsets, and trailed off on sick call. Stray colored men, somehow escaped from bondage, began to filter into the camps, and many of these were pressed into service as company cooks. It was learned that surplus coffee from the army ration was as good as money, and soldiers used it to buy Dutch ovens, potatoes, vegetables, and chickens for these cooks to use.[4]

The colored people were beginning to influence men's

attitude toward war. Most of these western regiments had very little anti-slavery sentiment as such. They had enlisted to save the Union or because, being young, they had had a special receptivity to the drums and trumpets and cheering crowds, or perhaps just plain for fun, and the peculiar institution had meant nothing much to them one way or the other. Yet here they were, in what they considered to be the South, and there were colored folk all about them; and it began to seem that in the great fight to put down disunion these colored folk were allies, pathetically eager to help, very useful on occasion. Company E of the 33rd Illinois remembered a tour of duty in Missouri when a collection of rifles and a handful of Confederate recruits had been rounded up on somebody's plantation. Unable to think of anything better, the company commander had equipped the plantation's slaves with the rifles and had them march the captives back to camp, only to draw a stiff reprimand from army authorities, who castigated him for doing "what the President of the United States had not seen fit to do—liberate and arm the slaves." The prisoners had been released and the slaves had been sent back to servitude, and Company E still felt that there was something about the deal that was not quite right.[5]

Runaway slaves would come into camp, and the men would try to hide them—moved, apparently, by nothing much more than sympathy for men who had found every man's hand against them. It was official policy at that time to return all fugitives to their lawful owners, and in most detachments the policy was enforced. Little by little the soldiers began to feel that returning fugitive slaves was helping the rebellion; they objected to it, and some outfits were brought almost to mutiny by the orders, although under ordinary circumstances the men were as ready as any to draw the color line. Slowly but surely the idea began to dawn: these slaves are on our side, and in a state where people keep both Union and Confederate flags and display the one which on any given day seems most likely to be advantageous, these men with dark skins are the ones we can count on as friendly.

Not that the colored people got much out of it. The soldiers felt themselves to be immeasurably superior to all people whose skins were not white, and they had much pride of race. The 77th Illinois laughed at a group of officers who, touched by feelings of romance on a moonlight evening, went to the handsomest mansion in town, stood beneath its windows, and sang sentimental serenades very prettily (encouraged by handkerchiefs and scarves waving from opened windows) until their wind gave out; after which a colored maid came to the front door, thanked them for their effort, and said she was "sorry de white folks weren't at home to hear it." A Wisconsin soldier moodily confessed in a letter home: "The black folks are awful good, poor miserable things that they are. The boys talk to them fearful and treat them most any way and yet they can't talk two minutes but tears come to their eyes and they throw their arms up and praise de Lord for de coming of de Lincoln soldiers." This same Wisconsin boy admitted that he was greatly surprised to find that none of these slaves had ever heard any of Stephen Foster's "colored" songs.[6]

It was the beginning of wisdom, perhaps. For this was not the land of Old Black Joe and My Old Kentucky Home, with gay darkies picturesquely melancholy over long shadows dropping on the plantation lawn, Uncle Ned hanging up the shovels and the hoe after a life of faithful service, Nelly Gray gone down the river to the tune of quavering male quartet vocalizing, Swanee River curling lazily south with the romantic sadness of a faint tug at the heartstrings. This was not minstrel-show land, after all. These midwestern soldiers had grown up knowing only the stage Negro—the big-mouthed, grinning, perpetually carefree Sambo who loved watermelons and possum, had peculiar gifts for wielding the razor (always on other Sambos, who did not much mind being slashed, having been born for it), and who liked to eat fried chicken and drink more gin than he could properly manage. Mr. Bones was out of his depth here, and there were emotional values under the surface that Stephen Foster had not quite touched; when Negro music was heard it had a wild quality and a jungle drumbeat, fit to be punctuated by the thudding of heavy guns and the cries of men desperately in earnest. This was real, there was a life force welling up here, and these illiterate men and women whose English was a queer gumbo of mispronounced words and faulty grammar nevertheless were actually trying to say something. This was not picturesque Sambo, faithful Old Black Joe, the grinning darky who was gay in the autumn sunlight; this was *a man* struggling to stand upright as a man should and to be master, as far as a weak mortal may, of his own destiny, as precious to him as to any white boy from Wisconsin farm or Ohio city. It was something nobody had been prepared for, and it was inordinately disturbing.

What the Westerners were beginning to run up against, indeed, was the inexorable fact that the Negro was going to have a controlling effect on this war for union . . . simply because he was there. His presence, ultimately, had been the cause of the war; the war could not be fought and won without taking him into account; when the settlement finally took place, he would have to be in it.

On the day after Bull Run, Congress had solemnly decreed that the war was not being fought to disturb "the established institutions of the states," and the radical Republicans had not ventured to object; yet the solemn resolve was becoming a dead letter, for the established institution which the resolution had been designed to protect was being disturbed more and more every day and there was no way to avoid disturbing it. Freedom and union were bound up together, whether man wished it so or not; and freedom was not a word that could ever be used in a limited sense. It was an idea, not a word, and there was no way to keep the people who wanted freedom the most from absorbing the idea.

If it did nothing else, slavery gave Union soldiers the notion that when they were in slave territory they were in land that somehow was foreign. This was as true in the Army of the Potomac as in Kentucky and Missouri. Private Chase of the 1st Massachusetts Artillery—a man who worshiped McClellan and who did not believe that abolition had any rightful part in this war—was writing home at this time that Virginia was a fine country in which, if there was no war, he would like to live. Yet he felt compelled to add: "I think if they could have a lot of New England farmers settle here they could show them how to raise a heap of stuff." The war, he admitted, was ravaging the Virginia countryside fearfully, but perhaps that was all for the best: "I hope when it is done it will be a permanent thing and the Question settled that there is such a thing as Union."'

McClellan himself—McClellan, who went by the book of Napoleon and saw all the rebellion as something formalized, to be settled by professionals who went by the old chivalric tradition—was beginning to learn this fall that this war could not be fought without some reference to the slavery issue. He was learning it just now in a very hard way, by means of a lost battle in which men were killed, by which bright reputations could be tarnished.

McClellan had troops occupying the Maryland country along the upper Potomac, northwest of Washington, with Confederates in unknown strength across the river. Late in October he got word that Confederate troops in Leesburg, Virginia, were making ominous moves, and he ordered a Union force to scout across the river, feel them out, and see what was developing. His orders went down to a division commander, Brigadier General Charles P. Stone, and Stone had a few regiments go over the river at Harrison's Island, scale the muddy heights at Ball's Bluff, and on October 21, 1861, perform the maneuver known to military men as a reconnaissance in force.

General Stone's detachment went over under command of Colonel Edward D. Baker, the same who had orated gloriously in springtime New York, calling for bold and determined war and scoffing at battle deaths as matters of small account. On the fringe of a wood atop the bluff Baker inexpertly led his men into a more powerful Confederate force, which promptly cut the command to pieces, shooting down scores, capturing hundreds, and driving a disorganized remnant back across the river in headlong flight. Altogether the action cost the Union army nine hundred casualties, among them Baker himself, shot through the heart at the height of the battle.

In an official Washington which still had painful memories of Bull Run, this was exactly the sort of disaster for which somebody was going to be made to sweat; especially so since Baker himself had been a man of considerable political consequence—a close friend of Abraham Lincoln (who had named his second son for him), a leading west-coast Republican, and a member of the United States Senate. House and

Senate joined to name a committee to look into the business, and this committee—which before long would become a fearsome Jacobin creation, the Joint Committee on the Conduct of the War—selected as the chief culprit General Stone, who had not been present at the battle but who seemed to be mostly responsible for the move.

General Stone himself had a certain standing. During the previous winter James Buchanan had commissioned him colonel and had given him responsibility for maintaining order at the inauguration of President Lincoln; an important assignment, as men saw it then, for the capital had been full of rumors about a secessionist attempt to keep the ceremony from taking place. Lincoln knew Stone and trusted him, and Stone enjoyed McClellan's full confidence, but none of this helped him now. The Joint Committee scented something very fishy about the whole Ball's Bluff operation; suspected, in fact, that Baker and his command might have been purposely sacrificed by a Federal officer secretly in sympathy with the Confederacy—an officer who, under the circumstances, could not be anyone but General Stone, who had ordered the crossing in the first place. The committee collected a quantity of ominously vague testimony about mysterious flags of truce and the passage of messages back and forth between Union and Confederate commanders along the upper Potomac. It reflected also that during the last couple of months Stone had won a certain unhappy prominence by ordering his men to return to their owners all fugitive slaves who came within his lines; a course of action that had involved him in violent argument with Governor John Andrew of Massachusetts and with that afflicted lion of the antislavery cause, Senator Charles Sumner himself. As more and more testimony came in, it seemed clear to the members of the committee that Stone was probably disloyal.

Stone was never actually accused of anything. He was simply wrapped in suspicion; the War Department took note of it, and in time Stone was quietly removed from command and locked up in prison, where he had to stay for quite a number of months. He was released eventually—not exactly cleared, because there had never been any charges that could be either replied to or canceled, but at least released—but his career was ruined.

General Stone had run into very bad luck and had suffered atrocious injustice. Yet what had really wrecked him was not so much the vengeful suspicion of ruthless politicians as the sunken reef of the slavery issue. He had been taught, suddenly and with great brutality, what other soldiers were being permitted to surmise for themselves—that that issue was not going to stay submerged, that it was going to become central, that sooner or later the war was going to adjust itself to it.[8]

Like the lamented Colonel Baker, the principal men in the Republican party believed in bold and determined war, and it did not seem to them that they had been getting it lately. It had been hard enough for them to keep quiet while McClellan leisurely perfected his army's organization and training; they found it altogether unendurable when the first aggressive move made by any piece of that army proved to be the halfhearted thrust at Ball's Bluff, productive of shameful disaster. When the man responsible for that fiasco turned out to be one who had steadfastly refused to let his part of the army take an anti-slavery stand, the inference seemed irresistible.

For the Republican leaders in Congress—men like Ohio's Senator Ben Wade, Michigan's Senator Zachariah Chandler, Pennsylvania's Congressman Thaddeus Stevens—believed not only in hard war but also in the abolition of slavery. Hard war meant smiting the Confederacy quickly and with vigor; also, as they saw it, it meant destroying what the Confederacy stood on, the institution of slavery. The two *must* go together, and a general who had no interest in striking down slavery probably had no real interest in striking down the Confederacy either. That the President of the United States had flatly refused to let abolition be made official policy made no difference. Notice had been served that softness on the slavery issue would ultimately be equated with softness in regard to victory itself.

. . . In which, perhaps, there was less political scheming and plain human cussedness than may appear. The innocent enlisted man who went to Kentucky fancying that colored folk were burnt-cork clowns who expressed their deepest feelings with the music of Stephen Foster or Dan Emmett was beginning to learn that the reality was a little grimmer than that. He was discovering, in fact, that the contraband who tried to hide in a Union camp was a fugitive from slavery and not just from a minstrel show; and he was also beginning to sense that it was going to be very difficult to wage war against the society from which those men were trying to escape, without in one way or another taking a stand on the problem of the men themselves. Ben Wade and Thad Stevens and men like them had lost their innocence far back in the unrecorded past, but the same force that was pressing on the midwestern recruit was also pressing on them. Sambo was not Sambo any longer, and the land was going to march to more terrible music than any minstrel had yet sung. Slavery had been a factor in the events that had brought on the war, and now there was no way on earth to keep it from being a factor in the war itself. Both senators and private soldiers were beginning to respond to that fact.

2. War along the Border

Among those who would feel the pressure was General George B. McClellan.

It would come a bit later, of course. The prestige he had brought to Washington—a prestige which was at least partly due to the fact that everybody hopefully expected so much of him—was not yet dimmed. There were a few private mutterings, to be sure. McClellan had had a good deal of time to get his Army of the Potomac into shape—a good deal by pre-Bull Run standards, anyway—and he was steadfastly refusing to do anything with it. Rebel armies were still camped in the Bull Run region, defiant Rebel batteries closed the Potomac River to commercial traffic, and "On to Richmond" (which hardly anyone was saying out loud these days) had a rather hollow sound.

But actually the war was making progress, even though the country's principal army was not moving.

Shortly after Fort Sumter, Lincoln had proclaimed a blockade of the southern seacoast. There had been at the time no way to make even a respectable pretense of enforcing the blockade, and the whole business had looked a little ridiculous —the more so when, before half the spring was gone, the Confederates seized the naval base at Norfolk, Virginia, capturing enough big naval guns to equip forts all over the South and possessing themselves of the disabled hulk of one of the nation's first-line warships, U.S.S. *Merrimac;* a hulk that could be raised, remodeled, and put back into service under the Confederate flag. There had been times during the last few months when the only blockade worth talking about seemed to be the one which the Southerners themselves were maintaining on the water route to the Federal capital.

The administration, however, had no intention of letting things remain in this unhappy condition, and early in August it began to take steps. These steps were not very well co-ordinated at first, and there was a certain amount of pulling and hauling in opposite directions, but eventually the army and navy found themselves carrying out a logical, co-ordinated plan for sealing off the Confederacy. Old General Scott's "anaconda" idea had taken root.

As was the case with a number of things in this war, the operation seemed to begin with Ben Butler.

After his crackdown on Baltimore and eastern Maryland, Butler had been sent to take command at Fortress Monroe, at the entrance to Chesapeake Bay. In a purely military way he had very little to do there, but his fertile lawyer's mind had made one great contribution to the handling of the fugitive-slave problem. Runaway slaves who came within his lines, he held, were, as far as he was concerned, simply a species of property owned by men in rebellion; property which could have a direct military usefulness and whose owners, by the act of rebellion, had forfeited title; contra-band of war, in other words. As contraband, fugitive slaves could be collected and used by a Union army just as any other property could be collected and used, and nobody was in any way committed on any side of the slavery issue itself. This interpretation proved enormously handy to harassed Federal commanders everywhere, and the word itself caught on at once. For the rest of the war runaway slaves and dis-placed colored folk in general were contrabands.

Late in August an amphibious expedition with troops under Butler and warships under a lean, irritable flag officer named Silas Stringham sailed from Hampton Roads, dropped down the Carolina coast, and without great difficulty captured two forts which the Confederates had built at Hatteras Inlet, where there was a good entrance to the vast enclosed area of the North Carolina sounds. Leaving a garrison for the forts and a tiny fleet of light-draft vessels, general and flag officer returned to Hampton Roads. The foothold they had gained could be exploited whenever the government chose.[1]

Government would choose just as soon as it could get everything ready, for the advantages of amphibious warfare were beginning to become evident. While Butler and Stringham were cracking Hatteras Inlet, the navy was thinking about seizing a good harbor farther down the coast to serve as a fuel and supply base for blockading squadrons. It set aside its best warships and gave them to Flag Officer Samuel du Pont, a sailor whose social and financial standing was quite impeccable. Du Pont decided to make a descent on Port Royal, South Carolina, and asked the War Department to stand by to provide troops. McClellan objected bitterly; this was a side show, the troops ought to be sent to his own Army of the Potomac, for the issue would finally be settled in Virginia and there should be no diversions. He was overruled, however. Lincoln wrote to the Secretary of War that the expedition must get moving in October, and twelve thousand soldiers were earmarked for the job, under General Thomas W. Sherman. (Not William Tecumseh; it was Thomas W.'s misfortune, by the end of the war, to be known simply as the other General Sherman.)

Inspired by this or by cogitations of his own, General Ambrose E. Burnside next went to McClellan with a proposition.

Burnside was an easy-going West Pointer from Rhode Island; a big, handsome, likable chap whose visible assets included an intimate friendship with McClellan, a set of the best intentions in all the world, and a fantastic growth of well-sited whiskers; and he asked permission to recruit along the New England seaboard a division of troops familiar with the coasting trade and the handling of small boats. With such men, he said, and with proper help from the navy, he could go in through Hatteras Inlet, dismantle every Confederate installation on the sounds, and forever end the danger of any blockade-running in that area. Furthermore, the army would be established on the mainland not too many miles south of Richmond if the expedition was a success.[2]

McClellan had just got through objecting to the Port Royal expedition, but he went for this one with enthusiasm and Burnside was told to go ahead. Hardly had this been done when the navy picked up a couple of Ben Butler's regiments and a battery of artillery and whisked them down into the Gulf of Mexico, to occupy desolate Ship Island, a sprawling sand dune dotted with marsh grass and scrub oaks and pines, which lay a few miles offshore some little distance west of the entrance to Mobile Bay. The original idea seems to have been to hold the place as a coaling depot for light-draft gunboats, with which the navy hoped to break the Confederate traffic between New Orleans and Mobile. But the men and guns deposited on Ship Island were hardly seventy-five miles in an air line from New Orleans itself, largest city in the Confederacy, and they were an equal distance from the entrance to the all-important Mississippi River; a fact that was bound to call itself to strategic attention before long.

Thus by the middle of the fall the government was beginning to get on with the war even though most of the progress was as yet invisible. If McClellan's army was doing nothing in particular in Virginia, the Confederate army in that state was keeping equally quiet; and although the idea would never have dawned on McClellan, it is just possible that by keeping quiet in Virginia his army was fulfilling its most important function. The strategy by which the Confederacy would eventually be destroyed was taking shape that fall—seal off the coast, strike down the Mississippi, destroy secession state by state, working east from the West—and the unhappy Army of the Potomac, which was to do the worst of the fighting and suffer the heaviest casualties, was not, in the end, actually required to do anything more than hold the line in front of Washington.

What was to happen would bear a striking resemblance to Scott's original Anaconda Plan, but Scott himself would not be around to see it—except dimly, as an outsider, from afar. The old man had obviously grown too old and infirm to command the country's armies. Also, McClellan, who was still on his way up, looked on him as an encumbrance and by-passed him whenever possible. Finally, early in November, Scott grew tired of being continually snubbed by his subordinate and went off into retirement, and McClellan was put in his place. Now McClellan had it all; immediate command of the Army of the Potomac, top command of all the country's armies. He said stoutly, "I can do it all," when Lincoln suggested that the burden might be too heavy; yet he did know a moment of humility when, with his staff, he went to the railway station to see Scott off, was touched by the sight of a once-great soldier shuffling sadly away into the discard, and reflected that unless things broke right he himself might someday be in Scott's position, riding dejectedly away to make place for another man.[3]

But that would be a long way off. For the time being all the war was in McClellan's hands, and the moments of self-doubt that plagued the brilliant young general were kept hidden from the multitude. Aside from the coastal operations, he had three principal theaters for action—Virginia, Kentucky, and the Missouri-Mississippi valley area—and he was resolved not to let political pressure force him, as it had forced McDowell, to move before everything was ready.

In Virginia he had unwittingly shouldered a great handicap; he had given himself Allan Pinkerton, the famous detective, as chief of military intelligence. Pinkerton was expert at catching bank robbers, railway bandits, and absconding fiduciaries, but he was almost completely incompetent at giving the general-in-chief the data he needed about the opposing army. He was telling McClellan now that Joe Johnston, Confederate commander in northern Virginia, had a large and aggressive army, and since what he told McClellan fitted perfectly with McClellan's own native caution, McClellan soon came to believe that he was actually outnumbered. In actual fact, McClellan had just about twice as many men as Johnston had, they were fully as well trained as Johnston's men, and in matters of supply and equipment they were ever so much better off; but it seemed to McClellan that he must be very careful what he did, and although President and Cabinet kept pressing him to make some sort of aggressive move before winter came, McClellan would not be hurried. He would always need two or three more weeks before he could start his campaign; would need them, partly because the ability to take quick, decisive action had been left out of his make-up, and partly because military intelligence kept telling him that the enemy was stronger than he was and would crush him if he made the slightest mistake.'

In the West, unfortunately, McClellan's two chief subordinates turned out to be men as cautious as himself.

Romantic Frémont was gone, of course, and the petulant David Hunter who had taken his place was himself superseded shortly afterward by a flabby, moon-faced general who was to become one of the minor enigmas of the Civil War—Henry Wager Halleck, known to the regulars as "Old Brains," a solemn, rumbling-portentous pedant in uniform who had the habit of folding his arms and rubbing his elbows whenever he was the least bit perplexed, and who took into high command a much better reputation than he was finally able to take out of it.

Halleck had written military textbooks and had translated other texts from the French, he had retired from the army in gold-rush California to make money as a lawyer, and he was a born gossip and scold; nature had designed him to fill the part of a paper-pushing bureaucrat, and his mind was as orderly and tidy as its range was limited. What McClellan might be able to do about sending an offensive column down the Mississippi would in the end be largely up to Halleck. For the moment, however, Halleck's primary function was to pick up the litter left by Frémont and to make certain that military housekeeping was restored to an orderly basis. This much he could do, and he could also put Federal troops on the march across those parts of Missouri where rebel sympathies seemed to be strong. He was stopping waste and graft and he seemed to be restoring order; his capacity for waging aggressive war and directing troops in the field remained to be seen.

Halleck was supposed to work in harness with the other principal commander in the West, Don Carlos Buell, who had replaced Sherman in Kentucky. It was unlikely that real co-operation between these two men would come spontaneously, for each man was convinced that the other ought to be subordinate to him, but for the moment they were co-equals, with distant McClellan bearing responsibility for co-ordination of their efforts.

Buell was much like McClellan, except that the spark of personal magnetism was missing. He was one more of those diligent officers whom the old army labeled "brilliant," and he should have been a first-rate general. He was methodical, careful of details, an able disciplinarian and organizer, the very model of a sound professional soldier. But he tended to be somewhat prissy. He had spent thirteen years in the adjutant general's office, was fascinated by military routine, considered military problems wholly divorced from politics and other civilian realities, and—hating untidiness and military slackness above all else—he had little use for volunteer soldiers and their officers; which was unfortunate, since these made up all but a tiny fraction of his army. He knew moments of sheer horror occasionally when confronted with the civilian in arms in all his native rudeness. Once in Kentucky he saw by the road a mounted man in slouch hat, hickory shirt, and homespun breeches, spurs on naked heels, two revolvers in his belt, a rifle in his hands; and when a staff officer remarked that the man was doubtless a Federal cavalryman on duty, Buell indignantly bet fifty dollars that he was nothing but an unenrolled mountaineer. Buell lost; the man was a regular member of the 1st Kentucky Cavalry, on duty; and the loss of the money apparently hurt Buell much less than the realization that this unmilitary character was actually a trooper under his own command.[5]

The enlisted men sensed Buell's disapproval of volunteers, and they considered him very reserved and aloof and refused to warm up to him. They might have admired one odd trick which Buell used to indulge in to display his physical strength. In his home, with guests present, he liked to take his wife by the elbows, lift her off the floor, and place her on the mantelpiece—something of a feat, one guest observed, since the lady weighed at least 140 pounds and the mantel was nearly as high as Buell's head.[6]

The war, to Buell, was a business of maps, of military maxims carefully studied and observed, of conscious application of basic principles. It would be possible, he argued, to win an important campaign without fighting a single general engagement; battles should be fought only when success was reasonably certain, and "war has a higher object than that of mere bloodshed."' This was true enough, and Buell could cite eminent authority for his belief. Yet this war might possibly turn out to be unlike the ones in the textbooks. It might have rules of its own, or no rules at all, as Nathaniel Lyon had discovered in the free-for-all at St. Louis; in which case a man who went by the book could have much trouble.

Buell was beginning to have a little trouble this fall, in point of fact. As much as he wanted anything short of final victory, Abraham Lincoln wanted east Tennessee occupied by Union troops, for reasons both military and political; the occupation would break the all-important railroad line that connected Virginia with the Mississippi Valley, and east Tennessee was full of sturdy Union sympathizers and ought to be liberated. McClellan accepted this and passed the orders along to Buell, and Pap Thomas was eager to make the move just as soon as he got his wagon train in order. But Buell thought the move was all wrong. In a letter to Lincoln he confessed that he was led to prepare for the thrust "more by my sympathy for the people of east Tennessee and the anxiety with which you and the general-in-chief have desired it than by my opinion of its wisdom." East Tennessee, he felt, would have to wait; the important thing was to break the main Rebel line in the West.[8]

The western end of this line was anchored by the powerful riverbank fortress at Columbus on the Mississippi, to possess which Bishop Polk had been willing to fracture Kentucky's neutrality at the beginning of September. The center was based on Bowling Green, where Albert Sidney Johnston seemed to have his principal troop concentration. Eastward, the line tapered off in the mountainous area north and west of Cumberland Gap.

Thus the western end of the line was in Halleck's territory and the rest in Buell's, and before any of it could be attacked properly Buell and Halleck would have to work out a joint plan and make complete arrangements for co-operation. It was taking them a long time to do this. Some of the delay possibly arose because each general knew perfectly well that the man who drove the Rebels out of Kentucky was going to win fame and promotion, so that each one greatly preferred to see the main push take place on his own bailiwick. While they planned, argued, and cajoled one another by mail and by telegraph—for some reason they were never quite able to spend a couple of days face to face and iron out all difficulties—McClellan at long distance called for action and meditated at leisure on the best way to make use of the Army of the Potomac. . . . And the autumn months passed, and Republican leaders muttered that the generals were reluctant to fight, and General Stone was made an object lesson for the hesitant.

In spite of the delays, there was beginning to be action. If Halleck and Buell preferred to wait until everything was ready, each had a subordinate who was ready to fight.

General Grant in Cairo touched it off first. Across the Mississippi from Columbus, some fifteen miles downstream from Cairo, there was an insignificant Missouri hamlet named Belmont, and to this place on November 7 Grant came by steamer, with three thousand soldiers and the gunboats *Tyler* and *Lexington* for escort, on a vaguely defined mission whose final object seems to have been nothing much more complicated than to stir up a good fight.

He got his fight, since there were several Confederate regiments in residence at Belmont. Grant took his men ashore just far enough upstream to be out of range of the heavy guns at Columbus, marched down the Missouri shore, smashed a hastily formed Confederate battle line, and seized the Confederate camp. His troops felt that they had won a great victory and they celebrated by breaking ranks and looting the camp for souvenirs, thus giving the Confederates time to rally and to get reinforcements across the river. In the end Grant's force was driven back upstream, and at the close of day the men hurriedly re-embarked and steamed back to Cairo, abandoning most of their loot and a number of their wounded men. The fight had been brisk enough—each side lost four hundred men or more—and nothing very definite had been accomplished either way. But Grant's men considered that they had behaved very well under fire (as in fact they had) and their morale went up, and the Confederates had been put on notice that they were facing an aggressive enemy.[9]

Belmont had settled nothing, in other words, but it did bring to an end the period of inaction along the Kentucky-Tennessee front. A few weeks later Buell's General Thomas got into a fight that had more important consequences.

Thomas had been edging forward toward the Tennessee border from the left end of Buell's line, getting ready for the anticipated march into east Tennessee. Buell thought he was too far forward, and anyway Buell was thinking in terms of a drive through the Confederate center toward Nashville, so by the end of November Thomas was ordered to pull his men back and await developments near the town of Lebanon in central Kentucky. This apparently encouraged the Confederates, and they thrust a force up through Cumberland Gap and posted it on the north side of the Cumberland River, not far from the Kentucky town of Somerset; and around the first of the year, hampered by bad weather and atrocious roads (it took eight days to advance forty miles), Thomas went lunging forward to drive this force away.

Federals and Confederates finally collided on January 17, 1862, at Mill Springs, otherwise known as Logan's Crossroads. The battle was fought in woodlots and meadows along the edge of a little stream, and untried soldiers on each side formed a line and blazed away manfully. Hardly anyone on either side had ever fought before; when a Confederate firing line sensibly took cover behind the lip of a ravine, a furious Union colonel climbed on a rail fence, denounced the Rebels loudly as dastards, and dared them to stand on their feet and fight like men. The Confederate General Felix Zollicoffer, in the confusion of the action, rode into the Union line and was shot; Thomas got his reserves forward at just the right moment, and the Confederates were finally driven off in rout, abandoning camp and commissary stores, eleven pieces of artillery, and more than a thousand horses and mules. Happy Federal soldiers laid in vast stocks of Confederate rations and amused themselves by cooking flapjacks, made mostly of flour and sugar, living on these so extensively that whole regiments came down with bowel trouble.[10]

This battle had been on a small scale—neither side had more than four thousand men on the field—but it had important results. In effect, the right end of the Confederate line had come loose. The way into east Tennessee was wide open now, if anybody wanted to use it, and Mr. Lincoln hopefully urged Congress to provide for building a railroad from Kentucky down to Knoxville. But Buell continued to think that it would be much better to move on Nashville; and as the winter deepened, General Grant and Commodore Foote unexpectedly helped his argument along by focusing attention on the Confederate center in the most dramatic way imaginable. They moved boldly up the Tennessee River and captured Fort Henry.

3. Come On, You Volunteers!

The high command had been doing a good deal of sputtering during January. McClellan still hoped that Buell could move into east Tennessee, but Buell was insisting that he had to crack the Confederate defenses at Bowling Green first and then move on Nashville; so McClellan told Halleck that he ought to move up the Tennessee River to create a diversion and keep the Rebels from reinforcing at Bowling Green, and Halleck was replying that the Confederate force at Columbus far outnumbered the ten thousand men he had available for such a move. He argued that "it would be madness to attempt anything serious with such a force," and he gave McClellan a little lecture on strategy; to move against two points on the Confederate line would be "to operate on exterior lines against an enemy occupying a central position," a military solecism which "is condemned by every authority I have ever read." Lincoln saw the correspondence, and across the bottom of Halleck's letter he scribbled: "It is exceedingly discouraging. As everywhere else, nothing can be done."[1]

The sputtering continued. Halleck reminded McClellan that the troops he had inherited from Frémont were in a disorganized, near-mutinous condition, and complained: "I am in the condition of a carpenter who is required to build a bridge with a dull axe, a broken saw and rotten timber."[2]

Some of his tools did have a good edge, however, and Thomas's victory at Logan's Crossroads lent inspiration. Grant, Foote, and old C. F. Smith were all convinced that they were facing a bright opportunity rather than a vexing problem, and word of their optimism got abroad. Oddly enough, a false alarm from the East was a spur to action. McClellan learned that General Beauregard was being sent west, to be second-in-command to Albert Sidney Johnston: in addition, he was erroneously informed that Beauregard was taking fifteen regiments with him, and it seemed advisable to do something before these reinforcements should arrive. Halleck finally consented to let Grant make a stab at Fort Henry on the Tennessee River, just over the line from Kentucky, and he found that he could spare fifteen thousand men for the task instead of the ten thousand he had mentioned earlier. He and Buell then began exchanging messages, exploring the possibilities of co-operation, deploring the atrocious state of the roads, and doubting that anything very effective could be done. Halleck told McClellan that unless he got heavy reinforcements he did not believe he could accomplish much, Buell complained that Halleck's move was being commenced "without appreciation—preparative or concert," and he added that the Rebels would probably muster sixty thousand men to oppose the move.[3]

While the high command sputtered, Grant, Foote and Smith moved.

The Tennessee River comes up from the Deep South to meet the Ohio River at Paducah. To the east, the Cumberland River, after rising in the Kentucky mountains, dips to the north, and as it leaves Tennessee to re-enter Kentucky it flows parallel to the Tennessee for a long distance. Just below the Kentucky-Tennessee border, at a place where the two northward-flowing rivers are no more than ten miles apart, the Confederates had prepared two strong points: Fort Henry on the Tennessee, and Fort Donelson at Dover on the Cumberland. Between them, these two forts were supposed to hold the line between Columbus on the west and Bowling

Green on the east, where the main Confederate body was concentrated.

On paper these forts were powerful. What Grant had learned was that Fort Henry, at least, was a hollow shell. It had been poorly situated in lowlands which were subject to flood. The Tennessee was high, as February began, and half of Fort Henry was under water; furthermore, the place was weakly garrisoned, and while the Confederates were trying to remedy matters by building another fort on the western bank of the Tennessee they had not got very far with it.

Early in February, Grant took off. He had approximately fifteen thousand men—a strong division from Paducah under C. F. Smith, another division under an ambitious politician-general from Illinois named John A. McClernand, and a smaller group of reserves under the General Lew Wallace who had hesitantly asked Smith if he should actually accept the responsibility the government was giving him. Also, he had Foote and his gunboats; and since the roads were all but impassable, the entire force was moving up the Tennessee by water.

They anchored a few miles downstream from Fort Henry on the afternoon of February 5, and Foote invited the generals aboard the gunboat *Cincinnati* and steamed up a little way to inspect the Confederate defenses. The river was full of floating mines—torpedoes, they were, in the nomenclature of that day—and the flood waters had torn most of these loose from their moorings and many of them were floating by. Sailors got one of them and brought it aboard the flagship, and Foote and the generals gathered around it on the low fantail deck at the stern while the ship's armorer was called to dismantle the thing and see how it worked.

The mine was an iron cylinder, five feet long by some eighteen inches thick, with three long iron rods protruding from one end to actuate the firing mechanism. While the officers bent over to watch, the armorer removed these rods, took off the detachable end of the tube, and went to work with a wrench on a heavy nut that held the interior works together.

Apparently the torpedo had leaked. Water had entered, and the cylinder was full of air under pressure. As the armorer loosened the nut, this air suddenly began to emerge with an ominous hissing sound, and all hands immediately got the idea that the machine was about to explode. The armorer vanished, Smith and McClernand dropped flat on the deck, and Grant and Foote made for a ladder and went floating swiftly to the upper deck—getting there, breathless, just as the hissing stopped and it became obvious that the torpedo was not going to explode after all. General and flag officer looked at each other sheepishly. Then Foote blandly inquired:

"General, why this haste?"

Said Grant:

"That the navy may not get ahead of us."[4]

Then they returned to the lower deck and the examination of the torpedo was completed.

They would attack the fort next day, and that evening old Foote made the rounds of the vessels in his squadron addressing the crews, exhorting them to be brave men—most of them had never been under fire before—and urging them to put their trust in divine Providence. As a good Yankee, he had a final word of caution for them. When they fired the big guns they must make every shot count: "Every charge you fire from one of these guns costs the government about eight dollars."

While Foote was addressing his crews, Grant got his troops ashore: Smith's men on the western side of the river, to march up and seize the new works the Confederates were building there, and McClernand's on the eastern bank, to march directly on Fort Henry itself. Morning came, the troops began to move, and Foote wheeled his gunboats upstream to convenient range and opened fire. An officer on the *Essex* noticed that the first three shots from the flagship fell short, and remarked that Foote's own gun crews had just wasted twenty-four dollars.[5]

The fight was surprisingly short. The Rebel commander in Fort Henry, rightly judging that the place could not be defended very long, had sent most of his men cross-country to Fort Donelson, retaining only enough to work the guns that bore on the river. The gunboats' fire was accurate (after the initial twenty-four-dollar lapse) and the fort surrendered before Grant had got his soldiers into position.

Somewhat to the army's embarrassment, the Confederate commander came out in a rowboat under a flag of truce, boarded the flagship, and made his surrender to ·Foote, who sent a detail ashore to hold the place until the soldiers could get there. The fort was so badly flooded that the cutter carrying this detail rowed straight in through the sally port. A Confederate officer said that if the fight had been delayed forty-eight hours the rising Tennessee would have drowned the fort's magazine and the Yankees could have had the place for nothing.

Short as it was, the fight had not been bloodless. Foote's flagship had been struck thirty-two times and two of her guns had been disabled, and the *Essex* had been put completely out of action with a shell through her steam chest and thirty-two casualties. The Confederate gunners had stood up to their work until fire from the fleet had dismounted their effective pieces; but Foote had brought his boats in to close range where his raw gun crews could hardly miss, and he had heavier guns than anything the fort possessed. The whole experience apparently gave sailors and soldiers alike an exaggerated idea of the effectiveness of gunboats against fortifications, which was to have important consequences a bit later.[6]

Grant's men came floundering up presently—the bottom land was all under water and there was a veritable millrace a quarter of a mile wide just outside the parapets—and since he and Foote got on well the navy refrained from crowing too much over its triumph. Smith and his men were brought over from the western side of the river, and Grant sent a wire to Halleck announcing the victory. He added that he would move over and capture Fort Donelson in a couple of days.[7]

Grant's telegram immediately stepped up the exchange of messages in the McClellan-Buell-Halleck triangle. Halleck told McClellan that he could hold Fort Henry "at all hazards," predicted that the Rebels would feel obliged to abandon Bowling Green, and urged that every available man be sent up the Tennessee or the Cumberland. McClellan suggested that perhaps Buell should go to Fort Henry in person—in which case, since he outranked Grant, he would be in command there; Halleck thought that Buell should simply send reinforcements instead. McClellan proposed that Buell take his men up the Cumberland to Nashville while Halleck continued to ascend the Tennessee, with a combined smash at Memphis as the objective. This was a sound idea but impracticable for the moment, since the navy did not yet have enough gunboats to escort transports on two rivers at once. Buell complained that he could not get a clear idea of Halleck's plans.[8]

Meanwhile Grant was taking his men overland to Fort Donelson.

Fort Henry had been comparatively easy, but Donelson would be very tough. Grant was no great distance from Paducah, where Sherman—brought out of his temporary retirement by Halleck and given the post Smith had held—was working hard to funnel more troops to him; but Buell's men in Kentucky were a long way off, and Confederate Johnston had fifty thousand men strung out on the line from Columbus to Bowling Green. Beauregard had joined him—without those reinforcements which rumor had said he was bringing—and he was urging that Johnston concentrate everything he had and smash Grant's force before it was too late. Johnston refused to go along with this and ordered the forces at Bowling Green to fall back on Nashville instead; but he did send twelve thousand men to Fort Donelson, bringing the total force there to seventeen thousand or more. Built on the west bank of the Cumberland, Donelson occupied high ground, with powerful guns to command the river and with extensive entrenchments strung along wooded ridges and hilltops to command the approaches by land. As the head of Grant's column approached the place, the Confederates had more men on the scene than he had.

It had taken much longer than Grant anticipated to get everything ready, and it was not until February 13 that his army was in position. His plan was simple. Foote had gone back to Cairo, leaving his disabled boat there and picking up three others, two of which were the unarmored *Tyler* and *Conestoga*. He was steaming up the Cumberland now with six gunboats, four of them armored, and he was convoying transports bringing Grant reinforcements. Grant proposed to hem the Confederates in by land and have the gunboats close the river front; a sharp bombardment by Foote, then, might make a successful infantry assault possible, and the Confederate garrison could be captured entire.

February 14 came in cold after a sharp night. It had been unseasonably warm during the cross-country march from Fort Henry, and many of the green troops had blithely thrown away their overcoats; some units had even left blankets behind in camp on the Tennessee. The men put in a miserable night. They were so close to the Confederate lines that fires were not allowed. But as the sun came up the air moderated a bit, and in midafternoon the soldiers' spirits rose; out of their sight, beyond the hills and the trees, there came a heavy, measured thud-thud of the big naval guns. Foote was bringing his four armored gunboats up to give Fort Donelson what he had given Fort Henry.

It might have worked if he had kept his distance His guns outranged anything the Confederates could fire at him, and when he opened the shooting at a distance of two miles his gunners were hitting regularly and doing substantial damage. But at Fort Henry he had finished things off fast by closing to point-blank range, and he tried the same thing here. The result was sheer disaster. At close range his gunners consistently overshot, and the Confederate gunners found their targets and pounded them hard. In a short time the squadron had to withdraw, two boats disabled, the others damaged, many men killed, Foote himself badly wounded. If Fort Donelson was going to be taken, the army would have to do it. Glumly Grant admitted that he might have to settle down for a siege.

Fortunately the Confederate command was very nervous. Top Confederate in the place was Brigadier General Gideon Pillow, a gray-whiskered veteran of the Mexican War who was to bear one distinction, and only one, out of the Civil War—he was the only Confederate general to whom Grant consistently referred in terms of contempt. Even though the naval attack had been beaten off, Pillow figured the place could not be held, and next morning he marshaled a striking column to break the right of Grant's line and open a way for the garrison to escape.

To an extent, the plan worked. McClernand's division held the right: the Confederate assault doubled it back on the Union center, driving Federal brigades in flight and swinging the door of escape wide open. But Grant sent Lew Wallace and his men in to help close the gap, and on his left he ordered Smith to assault the Rebel breastworks in order to ease the pressure on his right. Old Smith, who had said the officer must live for the great day of battle, put his regiments into line, stuck his cap on the point of his sword, and rode ahead of them into a tangle of brush and felled trees, with Confederates on a ridge beyond driving in a hot fire.

Smith's men had never been in action before, and when they entered the underbrush with bullets whining and crackling all around them, they wavered. Smith stormed at them: "Damn you, gentlemen, I see skulkers. I'll have none here. Come on, you volunteers, come on! This is your chance. You volunteered to be killed for love of country, and now you can be. You damned volunteers—I'm only a soldier and I don't want to be killed, but you came to be killed and now you can be!"

Then, without looking back, sitting his horse as if he were on parade, sword held high, he rode on ahead of them. One of his rookies wrote afterward that "I was nearly scared to death, but I saw the old man's mustache over his right shoulder, and went on." Through the underbrush and fallen timber and up the slope they went, the Rebels blistering the hillside with musket fire. Once more the line wavered briefly. Smith beckoned to his division surgeon, who was riding with the staff, and told him: "Hewitt, my God, my friend, if you love me, go back and bring up another regiment of these damned volunteers. You'll find them behind the bushes."

The other regiment came up, the wavering ceased, and a staff officer recorded: "And so the old cock led them with a mixture of oaths and entreaties over the breastwork." On Smith's whole front the Confederates had to withdraw to an inner line. Wallace's men, meanwhile, had regained most of the ground McClernand had lost, and by evening the open door was slammed shut again. Clearly enough, Grant's army—heavily reinforced by this time and strongly outnumbering the Confederates—could drive home a smashing assault in the morning.[10]

It was another cold night, and the Federals huddled in their lines with nothing but the anticipation of victory to warm them. Sometime past midnight Grant was in the little cabin that served as headquarters, his surgeon dozing in a chair, a good fire burning in the fireplace; and General Smith came in, ice on his boots, his great mustachios looking frostier than ever. He handed Grant a letter, remarking, "There's something for you to read, General." Then he asked the surgeon for a drink, took a good old-army pull from the flask that was offered, wiped his lips, and stood before the fire, warming his long legs. Grant read the letter.

It had just come through the picket lines under a flag of truce, and it bore the signature of Brigadier General Simon Bolivar Buckner, an old-time army friend of Grant, now commanding the Confederates in Fort Donelson. Because his two seniors were frightened, Buckner was the residuary legatee of defeat. At a council of war earlier that evening the Confederate commanders had agreed that the fort would have to be surrendered. However, no Confederate general had yet been captured by the Federals, and no one was quite certain that a vengeful Lincoln government might not try captured generals for treason; and so General Pillow, the top man in the fort, announced that he personally was going to make his escape, and he passed the command to the next man in line, Brigadier General John B. Floyd.

Floyd had personal reasons for wishing to avoid capture. He had been Secretary of War in Buchanan's Cabinet, and Northerners believed he had used his official position to stock southern arsenals and forts with extra supplies of weapons against the day of secession. It seemed likely that if they caught Floyd they would make things tough for him. So Floyd said he thought he had better go away with Pillow, and he passed the command on to Buckner. Being made of stouter material, Buckner did not try to duck his responsibilities. If the fort had to be given up and if he was now its commander, he would do what had to be done and would stay with his men, to take what came. So he had written a letter to Grant asking what terms the Federals would give if the garrison should surrender.

Grant read the thing and looked up at Smith, who was twisting his mustache before the fire. Perhaps Grant still felt like the young cadet in the presence of the commandant, for he asked, "What answer shall I send to this, General Smith?"

Smith cleared his throat heavily and barked: "No terms to the damned Rebels."

Grant chuckled, got a pad of paper, and began to write. A moment later he showed Smith what he had written. It was a short message, which would become famous. Curt and to the point, it announced that Grant would offer no terms except "immediate and unconditional surrender," and closed with the blunt statement: "I propose to move immediately upon your works."

"Hmm!" said Smith. "It's the same thing in smoother words!" Grant chuckled again, and Smith stalked out of the room to send the letter through the lines to Buckner.[11]

Buckner thought the letter harsh and unchivalrous, but there was no help for it. Pillow and Floyd had slipped away to the far side of the Cumberland and were on their way to safety. One other soldier had also escaped, a man who was to be worth more to the Confederacy than a dozen Pillows and Floyds: a hard, rough-hewn former planter and slave trader named Nathan Bedford Forrest, now commanding a detachment of Confederate cavalry, one of the authentic military geniuses of the whole war. If they could have caught him and kept him under lock and key to the end of the war, the Federals would have saved themselves much anguish. Forrest had found that the encircling lines were not quite airtight, and he led his troopers out to safety, floundering waist-deep through an icy backwater in the silent night; and Buckner and his troops—something like fifteen thousand of them, with all their guns and equipment—laid down their arms and surrendered when morning came. The North had won the first great victory of the war.[12]

Grant's message was sent all across the North, and people made him a hero overnight; there was something about the hard ring of "unconditional surrender" that aroused vast enthusiasm, and it tickled people that the words fitted Grant's initials.

But it was old Smith who had really stated the terms. As he said, all Grant had done was put them in smoother words.

4. To the Deep South

Fort Donelson was a crusher, and the Confederate high command instantly recognized it as such. The loss of Fort Henry had already cracked Johnston's line, causing him to retreat from Bowling Green to Nashville, and to send Beauregard west to see what could be done with the great river fortress at Columbus. Now with Donelson gone, there was no good place to make a stand north of the southern Tennessee border.

On news of Buckner's surrender, Johnston evacuated Nashville and started south, while Beauregard prepared for the evacuation of Columbus. As far as any plans had been made, Johnston aimed to concentrate his forces at Corinth, Mississippi. Beauregard believed that the Mississippi River could still be held, with strong points at Island No. Ten, New Madrid, and Fort Pillow, but except for this fringe all of western Tennessee was gone.[1]

What gave the defeat the potentiality of outright disaster —aside from the fact that the Confederacy was losing a modest industrial nexus of fair importance—was that it exposed to the Federal invaders the most important railroad line in the southern nation, the Memphis and Charleston, which (after dipping down into northern Mississippi and Alabama) ran east through Chattanooga and Knoxville and gave the Mississippi Valley region a direct connection with Virginia and the Atlantic seaboard. Abraham Lincoln, whose strategic ideas were not nearly as defective as a good many of his generals assumed, had had this line on his mind from the start; it was one of the reasons he was so desperately anxious to get an army down into eastern Tennessee. The value which the Richmond government placed on the line was shown by its reaction to the news of the defeat; it instantly began to strip the southern seaboard of troops in order to give Johnston reinforcements.

Confederate Secretary of War Judah Benjamin wrote to Robert E. Lee, who was then busy perfecting coastal defenses in South Carolina and Georgia, to send troops to Tennessee at once, because the railroad line "must be defended at all hazards." Braxton Bragg, commanding at Mobile, Alabama, was ordered to leave a garrison in the harbor forts and to take the rest of his troops up to Johnston. Benjamin's predecessor in the War Department, L. P. Walker, now a brigadier in Alabama, wrote that it would be better to lose all the seacoast than this railroad, calling it "the vertebrae of the Confederacy." The Confederate government was aware by now that the Federals would soon be mounting an assault on New Orleans via the Mississippi passes, but when Donelson fell the best troops in the Louisiana sector were rushed north, along with much military equipment.[2]

Naturally the northern authorities were jubilant. The chief engineer of the Army of the Potomac wrote to McClellan saying that the victory "knocks all present calculations in the head" and remarking that if McClellan's army did not move pretty soon it might find that the western troops had won the war without its aid. 'We can march anywhere, I take it," he exulted.[3]

This touched McClellan where he was sore. President Lincoln, the Cabinet, and the Republican leadership generally had been getting more and more impatient with him because he was refusing to move, and Lincoln not long since had irritably remarked that if McClellan did not propose to use the army he himself would like to borrow it for a time. Now McClellan was beginning to take fire. To Buell he telegraphed that "if the force in the west can take Nashville, or even hold its own for the present, I hope to have Richmond and Norfolk in from three to four weeks." In a wire to Halleck he was equally optimistic: "In less than two weeks I shall move the Army of the Potomac, and hope to be in Richmond soon after you are in Nashville."[4]

Halleck himself seemed to be slightly unhinged. He reported that the Rebels were reinforcing Columbus (which they were in fact preparing to evacuate) and he warned that they were apt to attack him any day in great strength. To Buell he appealed: "I am terribly hard pushed. Help me and I will help you." He told McClellan that Beauregard was about to come upstream and attack Cairo, called for more troops, and complained: "It is the crisis of the war in the west." He wanted reinforcements, he wanted Grant and Buell made major generals (along with Smith, who he said was the real author of victory at Fort Donelson, and John Pope, who was mounting an assault on the Confederate river defenses), and most of all he wanted advancement for himself. He appealed to McClellan to make him top commander in the West: "I ask this in return for Forts Henry and Donelson." Only by promoting him, he asserted, could the Federals cash in on the situation: "I must have command of the armies in the west. Hesitation and delay are losing us the golden opportunity." Assistant Secretary of War Thomas A. Scott was in Louisville at the time, and Halleck begged him to make Buell co-operate with him, adding plaintively: "I am tired of waiting for action in Washington. They will not understand the case. It is as plain as daylight to me." Then he went over everybody's head and sent a wire direct to Secretary of War Edwin M. Stanton, saying that he had "a golden opportunity" to strike a fatal blow but that "I can't do it unless I can control Buell's army. . . . Give me authority and I will be responsible for results."[5]

Washington's reaction was lukewarm. Even at that distance McClellan could see that Beauregard was not in the least likely to launch an assault on Cairo, and he said so, adding that neither Halleck nor Buell was giving him a clear picture of what was going on. (Buell was telling him that Johnston was concentrating at Nashville, which he was actually abandoning, and was warning that a great battle would be fought there, for which he would need reinforcements.) Halleck was told that neither the President nor the Secretary of War saw any need for changing the western command arrangements at present and was warned that he and Buell were expected "to co-operate fully and zealously with each other." For the time being the only promotion that came through was a major general's commission for U. S. Grant.

Now Grant would outrank Buell if their forces ever came to-
gether.⁶

Grant, meanwhile, wanted to keep moving. He was no
man for fuss and feathers; when a romantic staff officer, his
mind full of the pageantry of formal warfare, asked him on
the morning of Donelson's surrender what arrangements
were being made to parade the captured Rebels for regular
surrender ceremonies, Grant said that there would be no
ceremonies: "We have the fort, the men and the guns," and
that was enough. To make a show of it would only mortify
the beaten Confederates, "who after all are our own countrymen."

Grant wanted to push on up the Cumberland toward Nashville. The first objective was the town of Clarksville, twenty-
five miles upriver from Donelson, where the railroad line
from western Tennessee crossed the Cumberland on its way
to Bowling Green. Learning that the Rebels were leaving the
place, Grant sent C. F. Smith up to hold it, notified Halleck
that he was doing so, and offered to push on and take Nashville if anybody wanted it.⁷

Taking Clarksville smoothed the path of invasion. The
roads were in bad shape, but Buell could move by rail to
Clarksville and could go from there to Nashville by boat,
and at last he got under way. Unable to get any clear direc-
tive from Halleck, Grant went on ahead, hoping to meet
Buell at Nashville and find out what the plans were; and
soon after Buell's advance brigade entered the place—led
by the Ormsby Mitchel who had seen poetry and romance in
a moonlit reveille in a Kentucky camp—Grant was there, too,
trying to work out some scheme for co-operation.

Nashville was a prize. Johnston had left in a hurry, abandoning huge quantities of supplies—half a million pounds of
bacon, much bread and flour, and bales of new tents, the
latter greatly welcomed by the Federals, who had left their
own tents far behind them. The Federals were having their
first experience in occupying a Confederate capital, and they
found numerous timid citizens who were ready to turn their
coats and cuddle up to the invaders: dignified gentlemen
who called on generals to explain that they personally had
always been Union men, to identify leading Rebels in the

community, to tell where Confederate supplies had been hidden, and in general to make themselves useful. Mitchel felt that the town looked desolate and deserted, said the Rebels were disheartened and confused, and complained bitterly that Buell had no idea what to do next.[8]

By February 25 Nashville was under control, and Buell's advance guard began cautiously to push southward to see where the Confederates might have gone. Smith was at Clarksville, and Grant's army—a solid outfit of four full divisions now, thirty thousand men, twice as big as the one he had led east from Fort Henry—was concentrated in the Clarksville-Donelson area waiting for orders. And Grant was beginning to discover that he was in serious trouble.

The tip-off came first from a staff officer friendly to Grant, Lieutenant Colonel James B. McPherson of the engineers, who came up to Donelson and remarked that all sorts of wild rumors were floating around in St. Louis: Grant was alleged to be drinking hard, and his troops were said to be wholly out of control. Halleck was reacting to these rumors like a regular gossip, passing them on to McClellan in a way designed to make Grant look like an alcoholic incompetent. He was complaining that he could get no word of any kind from Grant, that Grant had left his command without authority to go off on a fruitless trip to Nashville, and that his army "seems to be as much demoralized by the victory of Fort Donelson as was that of the Potomac by the defeat at Bull Run." With overtaxed virtue Halleck concluded: "I am worn out and tired with this neglect and inefficiency." He added that Smith was about the only officer who was equal to the emergency.

Halleck followed that, next day, with an even more damaging thrust. He told McClellan that he was informed that "General Grant had resumed his former bad habits," which presumably would account for "his neglect of my oft-repeated orders." McClellan of course knew perfectly well what "his former bad habits" meant, and he naturally told Halleck that if he felt it necessary he should not hesitate to put Grant under arrest and give the command to Smith: "Generals must observe discipline as well as private soldiers." Next day Halleck sent Grant a stiff wire: "You will place

Gen. C. F. Smith in command of expedition and remain yourself at Fort Henry. Why do you not obey my orders to report strength and positions of your command?"⁹

So Grant was in heavy trouble, hardly a fortnight after he had taken Fort Donelson. Part of the trouble, apparently, came because Halleck all along had distrusted him; it appears that even before the Henry-Donelson expedition Halleck had planned to find a new commander, and had not acted simply because he had not found the right man. It is also possible to suspect that Grant was getting a little too much fame and glory for Halleck's taste, and Halleck's own attempt to wangle top command in the West had failed. In any case, it was trouble and Halleck was doing about as much as he conveniently could to get Grant clear out of the war.

But the trouble looked worse than it was. Lincoln would always react in favor of a fighting general. The "unconditional surrender" motif was something none of his other generals had yet shown him, and he was not disposed to let Grant be crushed without formal charges and a regular hearing. So on March 10 Halleck got an admonitory note from Lorenzo Thomas, the prim paper-shuffling adjutant general of the army.

By direction of the President, said Thomas, the Secretary of War ordered that Halleck make all of these vague accusations good. There would have to be some specifications: Did Grant leave his command without authority; if so when and why? Had he definitely failed to make proper reports? If he had done anything "not in accordance with military subordination or propriety," exactly what was it, with dates and details?¹⁰

In other words, Halleck was being told from the very top to put up or shut up. If he had something on Grant, now was the time to spell it out; if it could not be spelled out, forget it and get on with the war.

Simultaneously Grant sent Halleck a formal letter asking to be relieved of his command.

Then it all blew over. Halleck could not formulate charges against Grant because there was nothing to formulate. He got out of it, finally, by sending Thomas a letter explaining that if Grant had gone to Nashville he had really done it from the best of intentions and for the good of the service; that any irregularities in his command had taken place in Grant's absence and in violation of his orders and were doubtless, under the circumstances, regrettable but unavoidable; that Grant had explained everything satisfactorily; that the interruption of telegraphic connections between Grant and St. Louis accounted for the failure to make reports, and that all in all the whole thing had best be forgotten. (Nothing more was said about the resumption of bad habits; a rumor which, incidentally, was completely untrue.) To Grant, Halleck sent a message saying that he could not be relieved from his command, that all anybody asked of him was that he "enforce discipline and punish the disorderly" and that everything now was fine: "Instead of relieving you, I wish you as soon as your new army is in the field to assume the immediate command and lead it on to new victories."[11]

If Smith felt any soreness over the role he had been called on to play, he never showed it. He continued to do his job as a soldier, cursing the volunteers in a way they did not mind and teaching them how soldiers should behave, and his junior officers stood in the utmost awe of him. Two of them, one evening, found in somebody's back yard a flourishing bed of mint, which they plucked and took to their quarters, combining the mint with commissary whiskey and what not to make mint juleps; having done which, it occurred to them that Old Smith would probably appreciate a drink. Filling a tall glass, they set out for the general's tent.

It was dark, and the tent flaps were drawn. Through them came a gleam of light; Old Smith was in his cot, propped up on pillows, reading by the light of a bedside candle. The two officers stood in front of the tent, trying to muster nerve to intrude on the august presence. Finally one grew bold enough to rap on the tent pole. From within came a hoarse profane question: Who was it, and why was he bothering?

The officer who was holding the glass quaked, not daring to go inside. He managed at last to part the tent flaps a few inches and thrust his arm inside, the frosted julep glass in his fist. There was a dead silence, while the old soldier stared at this apparition. Finally the beautiful truth dawned on him, and the two officers heard a gruff harrumphing and an amazed "By God, this is kind!" The general's hand came out and the glass was taken, and there was a sniffing and a tasting and a muttered "Kind indeed!" Then the general drained it, the empty glass came back, and the two officers crept away. To the end of his days Smith never knew where the drink came from.[12]

Neither Old Smith nor anybody else stayed put very long at Clarksville. They were going on up the river, into the beginning of the Deep South; and it seemed for a time that spring as if the whole war had come loose from its hinges and perhaps a quick ending to it lay not far ahead.

The victory at Fort Donelson stirred people. So far the people of the North had had Bull Run defeats, and losing battles at Wilson's Creek, and reasonless Ball's Bluff tragedies, and cautious McClellan had gone on with drilling and preparation as if a long war lay ahead. Here, suddenly, was a reversal. Fifteen thousand armed Confederates had been swallowed at a gulp, the war had been pushed from mid-Kentucky all the way back below Tennessee, and in Grant's curt "unconditional surrender" note there had been a sure, confident note that Northerners had not yet heard. Off in Missouri the 15th Illinois, which had detested Grant ever since he ordered its colonel about the summer before, began to admit that perhaps this Grant was not so bad after all. It was ordered down to join his army now, and when it got to Fort Henry and found itself boarding vessels in a fleet of fifty transports and sailing up the Tennessee with colors flying and bands playing, it agreed that the war was fine, exciting, and grand. All through the western theater, regiments that had been doing the drudgery of training-camp or border-patrol duty found themselves hoping to be sent to Grant's army. Victory lay up the river somewhere and everybody wanted to be in on it.[13]

Up the river, or down another river; for the Mississippi moved south not too far west from the valley of the Tennessee, and Union strength was being felt there too. Blustering John Pope, for whom Halleck had vainly sought promotion, who despised volunteer troops and seemed to long for the old-army days of obedient regulars, was taking the Confederate post at New Madrid, Missouri, and with the aid of

Foote's ironclads was putting in motion the offensive that would soon take Island No. Ten and open the river all the way to Memphis. In the southwest a cautious sobersides of a professional soldier named Samuel Curtis was taking an army down to the farthest corner of Missouri, crossing into Arkansas, and routing a Confederate force at Pea Ridge, following Pathfinder Frémont's old trail and giving the Confederates such a setback that Halleck exultantly (and prematurely, as it turned out) was notifying Washington that the rebellion in Missouri had finally been crushed—"no more insurrections and bridge-burnings and hoisting of Rebel flags."[14]

From the Atlantic seaboard the news was equally good. Army and navy together were exploiting the break-through into the North Carolina sounds, hammering Confederate forts into submission, seizing New Bern and Roanoke Island and opening the way for sea-borne invasion. Farther south the navy had broken its way into Port Royal, South Carolina, getting possession of a deep-water base for its whole southern blockading fleet and raising an obvious threat to Charleston. Another amphibious expedition was hitting the Georgia coast and would soon control the sea approaches to Savannah; and in the Gulf, a fleet under a sprightly old salt named David Glasgow Farragut was inside the passes at the mouth of the Mississippi, heading for New Orleans.

There was a feeling of triumph in the air, and no one felt it more than stolid, unemotional Grant himself. Back in command with the blots off his record, Grant was going up the Tennessee, his own headquarters at the town of Savannah, Tennessee, a strong advance-guard posted at Pittsburg Landing, ten miles upstream. He was being reinforced, he would shortly have from forty to forty-five thousand men in his command, and Buell was under orders to march overland to the Tennessee and join him with perhaps thirty thousand more. The objective seemed to be a railroad-junction town, Corinth, Mississippi, twenty miles below Pittsburg Landing, a place where the north-and-south Mobile and Ohio Railroad crossed the all-important Memphis and Charleston. Johnston and Beauregard were pulling their forces together there, and it was clear that the next thing to do was to go down to Corinth and smash them.

Grant believed it would be simple. He was getting, as a matter of fact, a slight case of overconfidence. Donelson had been a hard fight, but it should have been harder, and Grant was beginning to suspect that perhaps the southern heart was not in this war—a gross misconception, as he would find out before he was much older. To Halleck, on March 21, Grant wrote: "The temper of the Rebel troops is such that there is but little doubt but that Corinth will fall much more that the great mass of the rank and file are heartily tired."[15]

Writing to his wife, Grant was even more optimistic. He asserted that " 'Sesesch' is now about on its last legs in Tennessee," and said that he wanted to push on as rapidly as possible to save hard fighting. There would, he felt, be some more fighting, but not too much more: "A big fight may be looked for someplace before a great while which it appears to me will be the last in the west." He added: "This is all the time supposing that we will be successful which I never doubt for a single moment."[16]

He could not move just yet, however. Halleck was being cautious. He saw Corinth as the objective, but he would not attack it until Grant and Buell's forces had joined, at which time he himself would come down and take active command. Grant was ordered not on any account to bring on a general engagement until all of this took place.

Halleck had finally won what he wanted most—top command in the West. Washington was reshuffling its command setup this spring. McClellan's reluctance to move against Richmond (despite his statement to Buell that he expected to be there soon after the Federals were in Nashville) had worn the administration's patience too thin; he was no longer top commander of all the country's armies but was leader of the Army of the Potomac alone; and as it demoted him the administration gave Halleck control over Buell's department as well as Halleck's own. On paper it seemed a logical move, for Halleck's forces were winning victories as winter ended.

Grant was getting one welcome addition to his command this March, although he did not yet know how welcome it would finally be. William Tecumseh Sherman, who had been funneling troops to him from Paducah, brought an untrained new division up the river and took his post at Pittsburg Landing—took post there just in time to exercise command, for Old Smith had skinned his leg jumping from a steamer to a rowboat, the insignificant hurt had become infected, and he was now hospitalized in Savannah in the fine old mansion that Grant had taken over for headquarters.

The Sherman who took over at Pittsburg Landing was a different sort of man from the nervous, jittery Sherman who had lost his poise and his command in Kentucky. Halleck had not known how to handle Grant—had done his best to drive him clear out of the army—but he had found the right touch with Sherman, and that effervescent soldier's self-confidence had returned. In Kentucky he had fretted and worried over reports of Confederate activity, fearing that each thrust by a half-organized cavalry patrol betokened an immediate attack in force. Now, holding the advance and peering south from his tent pitched near gaunt Shiloh meeting house a few miles from the landing, Sherman was less than a score of miles away from the main Confederate army, but he was taking no alarm. Confederate skirmishers were infesting his front, but he was calmly reporting that they were simply trying to find out how many Yankees there were around Pittsburg Landing. He was scorning to entrench his command, and Grant was not telling him to entrench, either; there was no need for it—before long Buell's army would arrive, and then Halleck would come, and they would sweep grandly down and whip the Rebels at Corinth.

Spring was coming on, southern winter was balmy, and a soldier in the newly arrived 11th Iowa doubtless spoke for all of his fellows when he wrote in his diary: "It is warm and dry—it is delightful. There is nothing of importance going on."[17]

5.

A Long War Ahead

1. *Hardtack in an Empty Hand*

SHILOH CHURCH had been built for the Prince of Peace and
it had been named for an Israelite town in Ephraim, where
the Tabernacle and the Ark of the Covenant had stood and
where the boy Samuel had heard voices and seen a mighty
vision. It was a bleak frame building on a hillside in a clearing, with the road from the steamboat landing going past
on its way to Corinth, and like the peach trees whose pink
blossoms caught the April sunlight, the little church had
been put there as a hint that life was not all bleak and
barren. But Shiloh would get a terrible name now, for
armies with banners had gathered around it and in thousands
of families it would become a name for horror and desolation.

They were not really armies, although that is what men
called them. They were just collections of very young men,
most of whom knew nothing at all about the grim profession
they had engaged in, all of them calling themselves soldiers
but ignorant of what the word really meant. Day after tomorrow they would be soldiers, but now they were civilians,
gawky in their new uniforms, each one dreaming that battle
would be splendid and exciting and that he himself would
survive; and they came from North and South, from farm
and canebrake cabin and from small town and busy city,
trudging the dusty roads and tensing themselves for the
great test of manhood which seemed to lie just ahead.

General Johnston and General Beauregard had joined forces
at Corinth, and they had brought forty-five thousand men up
to smite the Yankees in the fields and woodlots above Pitts-

burg Landing and drive them into the river. Grant had about the same number of men, waiting in their camps for the word to move down to Corinth and win the last great battle in the West. With a few exceptions—each army had a sprinkling of men who could call themselves veterans, because they had been in one fight—these soldiers were completely green. A Confederate brigadier confessed later that until he got to Shiloh he had never seen a gun fired, nor had he heard a lecture or read a book on warfare; and there were Confederate batteries whose members had never even heard the sound of their own guns, ammunition having been too scarce to permit target practice. In the Union army conditions were little better. The colonel of an Ohio regiment remarked that before Shiloh his men had not put in as much as ten hours on battalion drill, and there were many regiments whose men had received their muskets while on the way to the field and who had never so much as loaded and fired them until the battle began. Not even at Bull Run had two more pathetically untrained bodies of men been thrown into combat.[1]

The Confederate commanders knew perfectly well that the Federals were going to come down to drive them out of Corinth just as soon as Buell's army joined Grant's, and Johnston made up his mind to beat the Yankees to the punch. On April 3 he put his army on the road for Pittsburg Landing. The march was slow, disorganized, and noisy, as might have been expected of untrained troops; not until the evening of April 5 did Johnston have his men in position before the Union lines, and the men had made such a racket—whooping, yelling, and firing their muskets just to see if the things would really go off—that Beauregard wanted to cancel the whole plan and go back to Corinth, on the sensible ground that even the most inattentive Yankees could not help knowing that they were about to be attacked.

Beauregard should have been right, but he was not. Amateurish as the Confederate advance was, it was no worse than the state of the Federal defenses. Officers and men in Grant's army knew that quite a few armed rebels were in their front, but nobody in the green front-line regiments knew anything about outpost duty; reports that went back to the rear were garbled and incomplete, and the notion that the Confederates would obligingly wait to be attacked at Corinth was overriding. Grant had six divisions in his army, five of them sprawled out between Shiloh Church and Pittsburg Landing. The sixth, under Lew Wallace, was placed at Crump's Landing, four or five miles downstream, on the western side of the Tennessee. It seemed to Grant that the Rebels might be planning to assault this isolated force, and while Johnston's men were floundering up from Corinth, Grant warned Sherman to "keep a sharp lookout for any movement in that direction" and alerted other division commanders to be ready to send help to Wallace's men in case help was needed.' But neither Grant, Sherman, nor anyone else in authority had any idea that a head-on attack on the Shiloh position was remotely likely. The advance elements of Buell's approaching army began to reach Savannah on April 5; in a day or two the Federal armies would be in full contact and there would be nothing to worry about.

It rained on April 5, and when the sky cleared at sunset the air was cool, and in the woods and half-cleared fields near Shiloh Church the opening leaves gleamed wet and green. There was a peach orchard a mile east of the church, and a little way back of it there was a country road, worn down by erosion so that its bed was a couple of feet lower than the featureless landscape it crossed; and in the orchard and in front of the sunken road and around the unpainted church thousands of Union soldiers had pitched their tents, with other thousands not far in their rear. The ground was good and the air was clear, the great victory at Fort Donelson lay comfortingly at the back of everybody's mind, the new leaves and the pink blossoms on the peach trees were good to look at, and an Illinois soldier in Sherman's division wrote: "We were as happy as mortals could be." Early in the afternoon, with the day's drill over, regiments broke rank and hundreds of boys scurried down to Owl Creek for a swim. They were wholly unworried. There had been intermittent sputterings of rifle fire out on the picket lines for two or three days, but the men had got used to it; the high command was not fretting about it, so why should they?'

In the Tennessee River the wooden gunboats *Tyler* and

Lexington lay at anchor not far from the landing. Downstream at Savannah there was Grant, in the house where Old Smith was nursing his infected shin. Grant had just received a dispatch from Sherman saying, "I do not apprehend anything like an attack on our position";[4] he endorsed this, saying that he felt the same way, and passed the reassuring news on to Halleck. And over the wooded plateau and the peach orchard and the river there lay an immense quiet and peace, the last hope of a war that would soon be over because the other side had lost the will to fight.

Within a few miles of Shiloh Church, Albert Sidney Johnston had finally shaken off Beauregard's insistence that he give up the offensive and go back to Corinth, declaring: "I would fight them if they were a million." His battle orders were drawn and issued: the Confederate army would move forward at dawn.

Five in the morning of April 6; patrols from the Union advance elements had gone forward a mile or two to see whether anything solid lay back of the Rebel skirmish parties that had been so much in evidence lately. As they went, Johnston was giving his general officers final instructions, closing with the remark: "Tonight we will water our horses in the Tennessee River." The Union patrols kept on going, and before long they collided with Rebel skirmishers. For a little while there was a spat-spat of casual rifle fire, doing no particular harm, alarming nobody; then, up behind the Confederate advance guard, there came the enormous solid mass of a Confederate battle line, banked up to the full depth of three army corps, extending off to right and left through the woods and the underbrush beyond vision. There came heavy rolling volleys and the sound of thousands of men yelling with the crash of field artillery exploding sullenly underneath.

Back came the Union patrols, and in the camps men fell in line and made ready. The advancing Confederates could see white tents on the hillsides, with ordered ranks drawn up in front of them, guns on higher ground, and all along the front they settled down to a savage fire-fight at the closest range. Great banks of dirty-white smoke hung in the air, caught by the foliage, seeping up above the tree tops as if the wilderness were on fire, and a prodigious fury of noise rocked and thundered, to be heard at army headquarters far downstream.[5]

Grant was at breakfast. He cocked an ear, quit his breakfast, got his staff and horses down to a steamboat, and took off for Pittsburg Landing with all speed. One of Buell's brigadiers had just come up, and at the headquarters house he listened uneasily to the rising noise off beyond the horizon. He had gone up to Old Smith's bedroom, to call on that disabled warrior, and Smith chaffed him, laughing at him for imagining that a real battle was in progress. This, he said, was just an affair of the pickets; green soldiers who had never fought before must not worry so; down here they were used to operations on a large scale. But the racket did not die down; it became an unbroken muffled roar, it sounded louder moment by moment and seemed to be getting nearer. At last Old Smith admitted that it might be a little more than skirmish-line stuff; part of the main army might be engaged.[6]

Part of the army was indeed engaged—all of it that was within range of Confederate weapons. Grant had had two divisions in front, and these offered a furious resistance, slowing down the Rebel assault and here and there driving it back with heavy loss, while the troops in the rear were hurried forward. In many of the Federal front-line regiments the men had heard the outpost firing and had assumed that the pickets were simply discharging their muskets to see if the previous day's rain had dampened the powder charges —that was a common affair in this undrilled army. But they sent men forward to investigate, and the men came scampering back, reporting that "the Johnnies are there thicker than Spanish needles in a fence corner," and in no time the fighting became general.[7]

Some units broke apart at the first shock, losing all cohesion and running for the rear, every man for himself. The colonel of the 71st Ohio took one look at the oncoming battle line, put spurs to his horse, and galloped back for the river landing and safety. The lieutenant colonel tried to rally the crumbling regiment as an Alabama regiment came shouldering its way through the saplings; he was killed, and the 71st ceased to exist as a fighting force. Sherman rode up to

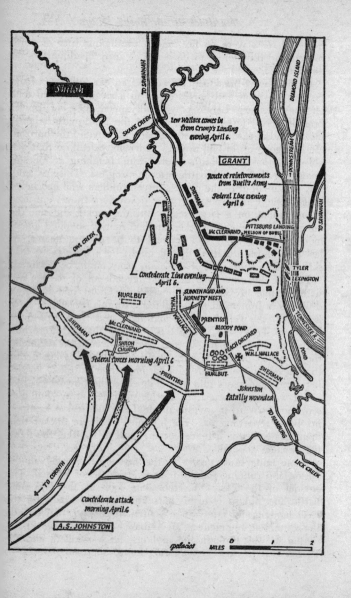

Shiloh

TO SAVANNAH

SNAKE CREEK

DIAMOND ISLAND

Lew Wallace comes in
from Cromp's Landing
evening April 6.

DOWN STREAM

GRANT

Route of reinforcements
from Buell's Army

SHERMAN

Federal Line evening
April 6

TO SAVANNAH

OWL CREEK

PITTSBURG LANDING

McCLERNAND   NELSON OF BUELL

Confederate Line evening
April 6.

TYLER
LEXINGTON

TENNESSEE R.

HURLBUT

SUNKEN ROAD AND
HORNETS NEST

W.H.L. WALLACE

PRENTISS

BLOODY POND

POND

SHERMAN

McCLERNAND

SHILOH
CHURCH

PEACH ORCHARD

W.H.L. WALLACE

Federal forces morning April 6

HURLBUT

SHERMAN

PRENTISS

Johnston
fatally wounded

TO HAMBURG

TO CORINTH

LICK CREEK

Confederate attack
morning April 6.

A.S. JOHNSTON

palacios   MILES   0   1   2

the 53rd Ohio, told its colonel to hold his ground and he would be supported, and rode off to another part of the field. His face gray as ashes, the colonel lay down behind a log; then, springing to his feet, yelled, "Fall back and save yourselves," and headed for the rear. Most of the men followed him. Officers rallied a handful and got help from an enlisted man, Private A. C. Voris of the 17th Illinois, who had fought at Fort Donelson and knew about battle. Voris came over and went along the line, showing nervous recruits how to load, aim, and fire, telling them: "Why, it's just like shooting squirrels, only these squirrels have guns, that's all." The fragment finally fell in with an Illinois regiment and fought the rest of the day.[8]

The Confederate attack was being driven home with fury, and the Union line could not hold long. Regiments that were not entirely routed fell back doggedly, firing from behind trees and logs, rallying briefly around the batteries; they were driven from their camps, and the jubilant Rebels ran on through the tented streets, some of them pausing to pick up loot and souvenirs. The first resistance had been spirited, despite the runaways; one Union brigadier reported that he lost more men in the first five minutes of the fighting than he lost all the rest of the day.[9]

Green troops, one officer said after the war, had this characteristic; they usually would either run away at once or not at all. Both armies were leaking men to the rear at a prodigious rate, but the men who did not run were fighting like veterans. The division that had been posted in front of the sunken road fell back to that eroded lane, found it a made-to-order trench, and got down in it to make a new stand. Wave after wave of Confederate troops charged them, running in through the brambles and the tangled woods, and were driven back by a deadly fire. The 15th Iowa, which had reached Pittsburg Landing that morning, found itself in this road, the men loading their weapons there for the first time in their lives; they had come up through a disorderly crowd of fugitives, who cried out that this was the Bull Run story all over again and that everything up front had been cut to pieces, but the Iowans were game enough and they hugged the ground in the road and opened fire. One private, appar-

ently convinced that he would never get out of this place
alive, was heard to call despairingly to his company commander: "Captain, if I'm killed, don't bury me with a Republican!" In the peach orchard men lay flat to fire, and such a
stream of Rebel bullets came in that the blossoms were all
cut to pieces and floated down on the firing line like a gentle
pink rain.[10]

Most of the soldiers knew nothing of tactics, and when
they had to go from place to place they simply went as the
spirit moved them: a charge was a wild rush forward, a retreat was a similar rush to the rear, and the only rule was to
keep an eye on the regimental flag and go where it went.
Brigade and regimental organization was lost, and men fell
in with the first fighting group they came to and fought without orders. An Ohio soldier, wounded, was told to go to the
rear. He wandered off, found fighting going on wherever
he turned, and came back at last to tell his company commander: "Cap, give me a gun—this blamed fight ain't got
any rear." The 15th Illinois came up from the river, fell in
beside a six-gun battery, and found the rifle fire heavier than
anything it had dreamed of; one man, getting ready to fight,
found his musket stock shattered by a bullet, saw another
bullet puncture his canteen, and was relieved of his knapsack
when a bullet cut its strap. An Iowa boy, lost from his own
outfit and fighting with the Illinois soldiers, got a bullet
through the creased crown of his hat, looked at the hat and
saw four neat holes in it, and hoisted it gaily on his ramrod
for his comrades to see; then a shell burst overhead and he
was killed, the Confederates swept in and captured the guns,
the Illinois regiment broke, and the survivors fell in with
scattered men from other broken regiments a quarter of a
mile to the rear and began to fight all over again.[11]

Behind the lines there was complete chaos. On the roads
leading back to the river landing there was an immense
disorganized huddle of routed men, teamsters and their
wagons, dismounted cavalrymen, reserve artillery, ambulance details bringing back wounded, artillerymen who had
lost their guns. The wildest rumors were afloat: half of the
army had gone, the Rebels had reached the river landing,
there were no officers left, the whole army had been sur-

rendered. One panicky soldier at the landing tried to get others to help him fell trees and build a raft; perhaps they could float down the river to Paducah and safety.¹²

The panic and the scare stories were all at the rear. Many men were gathered there—before the day was over a good fourth of Grant's army was huddling under the riverbank or wandering about in a vain hunt for someone who could turn chaos into order—but up front some of the deadliest fighting in American history was going on, and the terrible clamor of battle kept mounting to a higher pitch while all the woodland smoked and flamed.

In the 16th Wisconsin, made up of backwoodsmen, the men said they were going out on a turkey shoot when they went up to the front. A private found himself in line beside the colonel, who had picked up a musket and was firing with the rest, and the private asked how many Rebels the colonel had shot. Pausing to make a careful reply, the colonel said that he had fired thirty-seven cartridges and so of course should have hit thirty-seven men, "but I don't feel certain of six." In a lull that descended on one part of the field an Illinois captain found himself commanding his regiment, all superior officers having been shot, and since both his division and brigade commanders had also been hit there did not seem to be anybody to tell him what to do. He heard very heavy firing in the woods somewhere off to the right, so he collected what was left of the command and moved over to get in on the fight. An Iowa colonel came to the field drunk, maneuvered his regiment with reckless inconsequence, and was removed by his brigadier from command and placed under arrest; sobering somewhat, he picked up a musket and fell in with another Iowa regiment. Someone recognized him and asked him what he thought he was doing. He replied simply: "I am under arrest and hunting a place to fight." He stayed and fought, too, acting as private soldier for the rest of the day. An army surgeon who had once served in an artillery company found four guns standing idle on a hill, dead and wounded men lying all around, surviving gunners having fled. He rounded up men from a nearby infantry regiment and got the guns back into action; they fought for half an hour, until a caisson was exploded and two of the guns were disabled.[13]

The area in front of the sunken road saw especially bitter fighting. The Confederates assaulted this strong point so many times the defenders lost all count, and Southerners called the place "the hornets' nest." On the right and left, Federal troops gave ground, and victorious Confederates came in and got the road from three sides, but the division that was holding it stayed put. Its commander was an Illinois politician, Brigadier General Benjamin Prentiss, who had been a volunteer captain in the Mexican War, had had a tiff with Grant over rank in the old days at Cairo, and who was turning out today to be considerable of a soldier. He held his line, although the rest of the battle was obviously moving back to the rear, and his men fired so hard and so fast that an opposing Confederate felt that if he could just hold up a bushel basket it would be filled with bullets in no time. Also, these hornets'-nest people killed the Confederate commander, Albert Sidney Johnston.

In spite of this valiant stand Grant's army was being pushed back to the river. Grant himself had got to the scene and was doing all that a commander could to hold the position, but the southern attack was being driven home with a grim determination not to be expected of men who were tired of the war and ready to quit. (The determination converted Grant completely; after Shiloh he expected a war to the finish, not to be ended until the Confederacy had simply been made incapable of fighting any longer.) He sent for Lew Wallace's division to come up, drew up his siege guns and reserve artillery on high ground in front of the river landing, and he did his best to get the disorganized fugitives back into battle and bolster his sagging line.

There was not very much he could do. His army had simply been caught off balance, and the Confederates were pressing their advantage. Grant's front line that dawn had not contained one regiment that had ever been under fire before; many of these regiments had evaporated completely, and short of the line of guns by the river landing there was no good place to make a stand. An energetic Confederate general rounded up sixty pieces of artillery and put them in line to hammer at the hornets' nest at the murderous range of three hundred yards. Prentiss's men held their ground, but the men on their flanks were driven off; the peach orchard, dead bodies and broken trees and bloody ground, pink blossom petals strewn over all, was gone now, and the division was nearly surrounded. Men who tried to get to the rear found that to retreat was worse than to stay in the sunken road; the sixty Confederate guns were firing just a little high, and charges of canister were ripping the saplings and brambles fifty yards back of the line, creating a deadly zone no one could cross. Late in the afternoon Prentiss saw that he could do no more, and he surrendered with some two thousand of his men. They were prisoners, but they had kept the Union army from being destroyed.

Dusk was coming on. Part of Grant's army was cowering by the riverbank, another part had been shot, and part had been captured. Most of the rest had been completely scrambled, regiments and companies all intermingled so that nobody knew where anybody was. Quite characteristic was the experience of an Ohio officer who, trying to lead a lost detachment back into action, met a major on Sherman's staff and asked where his brigade was. The major confessed that he had no idea; he himself was so completely lost that a moment before he had found himself trying to report to a Confederate brigadier well inside the Confederate lines. The Ohioan never heard the rest of the story because just then a charge of Rebel canister came by, the major's horse ran away, and the Ohio officer saw no more of him.[14]

As a general said afterward, both armies by late afternoon had ceased to bear much resemblance to organized armies; they were "mere fighting swarms," with nothing but the flags to give them unity—the flags and the terrible determination that seemed to live in the hearts of these northern and southern boys who had never fought before but who, pitched into one of the war's most dreadful battles, were showing an uncommon capacity for fighting.

By dusk the pressure eased. The Confederates had gained much ground, but by now they were in no better shape than the Federals, and the last attack that might just possibly have broken Grant's final line and killed his army could not be mounted. (Many of the untrained Confederate soldiers had gone off, boy-like, to gawk at the big haul of prisoners taken when Prentiss surrendered.) Also, help was at hand at last.

Lew Wallace could have saved the day, but somehow he had got lost or had been directed wrongly, and he had not been able to get up from Crump's Landing in time to help. But Buell's advance guard was on the scene at last, and when the steamboats brought his men over the river and the men tramped up through the backwash of wounded men, fugitives, and displaced persons the real danger was over. Buell's men looked scornfully at the disorganization they saw all about them and came tramping up the slope to the high ground full of cocky energy, flags flying, all their bands playing. Grant's men raised a wild, half-hysterical cheer at the sight of them; one wrote that men wept for joy and said that the woods fairly quivered with the sound of the yelling, and an Iowa soldier confessed: "Never did strains of music sound so sweet as did the patriotic airs played by the brass bands marching at the head of each regiment."[15]

Some of the beaten men who had been hiding by the river called out to Buell's men not to come ashore—the day was lost, the Rebels were winning everywhere, they would be butchered—and Buell himself became convinced that his arrival had come just in time to prevent a great disaster. But by the time his troops began to form along the line marked out by Grant's artillery the crisis was over. The new line was stabilized, the exhausted Confederates just could not fight any more until they had had a night's sleep, and Lew Wallace's division was coming in at last to provide a solid stiffener. Buell's troops simply provided the clincher.

It rained hard that night; there were more wounded men than the overtaxed surgeons and stretcher-bearers could begin to care for. Officers were busy all night trying to reassemble scattered commands, and gunboats *Tyler* and *Lexington* had found a place where they could fire their big guns— much heavier than anything the army had—down the length of the Confederate battle line; they kept it up at intervals all night long, and only a completely exhausted man could hope to get any sleep. By morning Grant was ready to take the offensive, and shortly after daybreak he sent the men forward, Buell's troops on the left, the men of his own army on the right, in a huge counterattack.

Grant had a strong advantage in numbers by now, with Wallace's and Buell's men on the field, but the Confederates were very stubborn. They had not done any fighting before to speak of, but they did not propose to give up this fight until they had to, and they were hard to convince. Step by step they were driven back until most of the ground they had won the day before had been taken away from them, but they were not to be hurried, and some of this day's fighting was as hard and as costly as anything that had happened on the first day. A regular army artillerist was told to take his six guns and blast some Rebels out of a thicket in his front. He hammered the place with canister and with shell, but it was a long time before this particular knot of resistance was broken. When he got to the place afterward he found one hundred dead Confederates and twenty-seven dead horses, not to mention a wrecked caisson, bushes uprooted by canister, and any number of young trees that had been splintered and knocked down by shell fire. . . . These Confederates had needed a great deal of persuading.[16]

But the tide had turned. By midafternoon Beauregard could see that his army had been fought out and that there was nothing to do but get back to Corinth as quickly as possible. The shattered Confederate army withdrew, and the Union army—equally shattered, except for its reinforcements —moved forward just far enough to make certain that its foes were really retreating, and then went into camp. It had lost thirteen thousand men and it had just been through two of the very worst days of the war. If the Southerners proposed to go back to Corinth, nobody near Pittsburg Landing wanted to keep them from doing it.

The battlefield was a fearful place, with unattended wounded men lying everywhere and hideous numbers of dead bodies turning black and swollen under the April sun. Burial details worked all week, sometimes digging regular graves, sometimes doing little more than tossing dirt over dead bodies. In one place a great trench was dug to hold seven hundred dead Southerners. . . . A few weeks later a western regiment came up to the landing on its way to join the main body and tramped glumly across the littered fighting ground. The men passed one makeshift burial place from which, in ghastly symbolism, a lifeless arm was raised from the earth, an empty hand groping with stiff open fingers for the sky. A soldier looked at it, broke ranks, took a hardtack from his haversack, and put it in the open hand. Then he rejoined his comrades and the men tramped on to the front."

2. Springtime of Promise

It had begun with flags and cheers and the glint of brave words on the spring wind, with drumbeats setting a gay rhythm for the feet of young men who believed that war would beat clerking. That had been a year ago; now the war had come down to uninstructed murderous battle in a smoky woodland, where men who had never been shown how to fight stayed in defiance of all logical expectation and fought for two nightmarish days. And because they had done this the hope for an easy war and a cheap victory was gone forever.

It had been possible, before, for a Northerner or a Southerner to believe that the other side was really not very much in earnest and would presently give up. Grant had had that delusion before Shiloh; so, perhaps, had Johnston, who whistled his men north from Corinth with contemptuous remarks about "agrarian mercenaries" in the northern army.[1] After Shiloh no intelligent man could feel as Grant and Johnston had felt.

For Shiloh underlined one of the basic facts about the war —that it was being fought by men of enormous innate pugnacity: tenacious men who would quit a fight once begun only when someone was *beaten*. North and South had not gone to war in a mere fit of peevish irritability; the men they sent into their armies had something on their minds and were desperately in earnest.

Yet the spring when this fact became obvious was also, for the North, the spring of greatest promise—the spring in which final victory, if it could not be inexpensive, could at least be considered fairly near.

On paper, Shiloh was a draw; actually it was one of the decisive battles of the war. It was a battle the Confederacy simply had to win. For it had been a blow struck to restore a disastrously lost balance, a desperate attempt to re-establish the Confederate frontier in the Kentucky-Ohio country, a crucial effort to save the Mississippi Valley. It had failed, and the fact that it had come close to being a dazzling victory did not offset the failure. Robert E. Lee, serving (with sadly inadequate authority) as Jefferson Davis's general supervisor of military operations, recognized the crisis immediately. While Richmond was still celebrating what it believed to be a great triumph, and while Beauregard was reassembling his exhausted army in Corinth, Lee was wiring Atlantic coast commanders to send reinforcements west at any cost, warning: "If Mississippi Valley is lost, Atlantic States would be ruined."[2]

That was just another way of saying that the outcome of the war would depend on what happened along the Mississippi, and in this spring of 1862 the Mississippi was visibly being won by the North. Federal John Pope, all bluster and heedless energy, had been doing his job. He had taken New Madrid and Island No. Ten, Federal rams and gunboats had smashed a makeshift Confederate fleet that protected Memphis, and before long Memphis itself would be evacuated; the river was open, or as good as open, all the way to Vicksburg.

Worse yet, as far as the Confederacy was concerned, the Mississippi was being lost at both ends. Since early winter the Federals had had troops on Ship Island, that Gulf-coast sandspit within reaching distance of the mouths of the Mississippi. Unaccountably, the Confederate high command had ignored this threat, even though it obviously meant that the Federals were meditating an attack on New Orleans. One reason, perhaps, was the fact that the Federal troops there were under command of Ben Butler, the one-time Democrat who had laid such a heavy hand on the Secessionists in eastern Maryland in the spring of 1861. At the end of February, Confederate General Mansfield Lovell, commanding at New

Orleans, was writing contemptuously that Butler's Ship Island expedition was harmless: "A black Republican dynasty will never give an old Breckinridge Democrat like Butler command of any expedition which they had any idea would result in such a glorious success as the capture of New Orleans."[3]

There was much about Ben Butler that Lovell did not then understand, to be sure; but a more solid reason for optimism lay in the two forts that guarded the entrance to the Mississippi, Forts Jackson and St. Philip, downstream forty miles from New Orleans. These were solid masonry works, plunked down in almost impassable swamps. It was an unshaken military axiom just then that unarmored ships could not fight forts; these forts could be approached only by water; —let the Federals assemble all the warships they chose, therefore, the southern approach to New Orleans was safe. A somewhat makeshift assemblage of river gunboats had been brought down to help the forts. There were fire rafts and river obstructions, and the New Orleans shipyards were building two prodigious ironclads, *Louisiana* and *Mississippi;* once these monsters were afloat and in commission, no imaginable power could come in through this gate.

Nevertheless, as the winter progressed things looked more serious. A brash young Federal naval officer named David D. Porter had sold the idea that these forts would be much less formidable if they were properly shelled; and he had got together twenty schooners, each one bearing a ponderous mortar capable of tossing thirteen-inch shells. Neither mortars nor shells existed when he brought his idea forward, but the North had a great military asset which had been overlooked— the great forges and foundries of Pittsburgh, operating on the iron ore that was coming down in ever-greater quantities through the Soo canal from the Lake Superior ranges. These turned to promptly, and by the time Porter had his schooners stripped for action the mortars were ready to be installed, along with thirty thousand of the heavy shells. By the middle of March these ungainly vessels had been towed across the bar and were creeping upriver, hugging the banks, looking for their spots.

Still another asset the Federals brought to the scene: a

youthfully jovial flag officer in his early sixties named David Glasgow Farragut.

Farragut had been in the navy for more than half a century—had served as a very juvenile powder monkey on the famous frigate *Essex* when she cruised the Pacific in the War of 1812, and was still spry enough for a midshipman. He had a habit of turning a handspring on every birthday and told an amazed junior that he would not think he was growing old until he found himself unable to do it. He had been living in Norfolk, Virginia, when the war started; had warned his secessionist fellow townsmen, "You fellows will catch the Devil before you get through with this business," and then had closed his house and gone north to stick with the old flag. Now he was in command of the fleet that had been appointed to attack New Orleans, and he was getting heavy sloops and gunboats up into the river. It was hard work—the mouths of the river were silting up, and his heaviest warships had to be left out in the Gulf—but at last he got the most of his fleet anchored three miles below the forts. There he made ready, perfectly confident that he could rush the forts and take New Orleans, and eleven days after the battle of Shiloh he signaled Porter to cast his mortars loose and commence firing.[4]

By now the Confederate command was awake to the peril, but by now it was too late. The huge new ironclads were not quite finished; troops had been sent north to fight at Shiloh and defend the upper river—if New Orleans was in danger, men had felt the danger would be coming downstream, not up from the Gulf—and General Lovell was complaining bitterly that his defenses were manned entirely by "the heterogeneous militia of the city, armed mostly with shotguns, against 9 and 11-inch Dahlgrens."[5] His river fleet suffered from divided command and from bitter rivalry among leaders. New Orleans was suddenly looking very naked and undefended—and then Porter began tossing his thousands of heavy shells into the forts, dismounting guns and smashing emplacements and letting floodwaters into the parade grounds, while Farragut stripped his warships for action, weaving anchor chains along the sides for armor, smearing paintwork with Mississippi mud to reduce visibility at night, waiting for the moment when the bombardment would soften the defenses enough to make a bold dash possible.

The moment came soon after midnight on April 24. Red lanterns were hauled to the masthead of Farragut's flagship, the wooden steam sloop-of-war *Hartford*, and with a great creaking of windlasses and clanking of anchor chains the ponderous fleet got under way and started upstream.

It was an eerie business; pitch-dark night all around, broken by a wild red glare as the Confederate fire rafts were pushed out into the current. Fort Jackson lay on the western shore of the river, with Fort St. Philip lying opposite and a little farther north; Farragut's ships had to run straight between the two, fire rafts floating down on them, Confederate gunboats lying off to deliver a raking fire. Porter's mortars had hammered the forts mercilessly, but there were plenty of guns still in position, and men to fire them, and as the smoky light of the burning rafts lit the night the forts opened fire with everything they had. A cigar-shaped Confederate ram, almost invisible on the black water, had come down to help discomfit the Yankees; great clouds of smoke went billowing out from forts and ships, to lie on the water and create blinding pockets in the firelight; a tugboat was out in the night, trying to shove one or another of the burning rafts up against some Union warship. Farragut's navigators had to feel their way along, the ships jarring and shaking with the shock of heavy broadsides, guns going off everywhere, great noise and red-smoky darkness all about, outright disaster lurking not far away. Disaster almost came, at last, when *Hartford* ran aground by Fort St. Philip and the tug jammed a blazing raft under the ship's side; quick spirals of flame began to snake up the rigging, Rebel gunners were hitting their mark, and the men on *Hartford's* littered gun deck flinched and began to draw away. But old Farragut was shouting down from the poop: There was a hotter fire than any Rebel raft could show for men who failed to do their duty, and how about giving that tugboat a shell where it would do the most good? The gun crews ran back to their posts, a fire-control party got to work on the flames, the tug staggered off with a shell through her vitals, the raft drifted away, *Hartford's* hull plowed out of the mud, and the fleet went on upstream.*

And then suddenly it was all over. Most of Farragut's ships were above the forts, the Confederate gunboats had been sunk or driven ashore, and by daybreak the old admiral was anchoring his fleet halfway between the forts and the city, giving decent burial to his dead and making repairs to damaged hulls and rigging. The forts still held out, but they were dead ducks now, wholly cut off, their garrisons on the edge of mutiny with fatigue, battle-weariness, and a general sense of defeat; they would surrender presently and be occupied by Union troops, and New Orleans would surrender, too, as soon as the fleet got there, because with the forts and gunboats gone it had no means of defense.

Rain was coming down as Farragut's ships came steaming up to the New Orleans levee. Onshore there were thousands of people, jeering and cursing and shouting impotent defiance at the Yankee ships; and on *Hartford's* deck an old tar lounged negligently against a ponderous nine-inch gun, the lanyard in his hand, patting the side of the gun and smiling serenely at the yelling crowd.' Officers came ashore, United States flags blossomed out over public buildings, and in a short time Breckinridge Democrat Butler would be on the scene with occupation forces. The victory was complete, city gone, forts gone, the two unfinished ironclads destroyed; and by the end of April the Confederacy owned no more of the Mississippi River than the stretch between Baton Rouge and Vicksburg.

So the war was looking up, in the spring of 1862. On the seacoast the navy was tightening its blockade. It owned deep-water harbors in South Carolina now as bases for its blockaders, the army had knocked Fort Pulaski to pieces at the mouth of the Savannah River, the North Carolina sounds were under almost complete Union control, and hopeful people in Washington were beginning to ask if Farragut could not simply go steaming on up the Mississippi and open the river singlehanded. (Not yet did they realize that running past a fort was not the same thing as destroying it.) The general idea set forth in Scott's Anaconda Plan seemed to be working; perhaps if the armies got busy now victory might be very near.

This meant opportunity for generals; especially for Henry Wager Halleck, commander in the West.

Halleck had assembled a huge army near Pittsburg Landing: Grant's army, Buell's army, and the army with which Pope had been opening the upper Mississippi. He had come to the spot himself to take active field command—for the first and only time in the war—and he had given Grant a dubious sort of promotion, making him second-in-command of the united army and giving the troops Grant had been leading to George Thomas. Grant was finding that his job carried a fine title and prestige but no responsibility and little authority; for the time being he was on the shelf and he was bitterly dissatisfied.

Halleck may have been led to shelve him by the criticism that came down on Grant after Shiloh. Grant had won the battle, to be sure—or at any rate the battle had been won and he had been in command when it happened—but the fame he had won at Fort Donelson had been rubbed down a good deal.

The Confederates had hit him at Shiloh when he was not expecting it, and northern newspapers made a big thing of it. The first account of the battle to reach northern newspapers had been written by a correspondent who got to Shiloh on the second day of the fight and picked up his news from members of the rear echelon—the panicky crowd that hugged the bank by the steamboat landing, circulating doleful rumors of catastrophe. From these he got a fine collection of scare stories—a whole division had been captured, sound asleep, at daybreak; men had been bayoneted in their tents; some regiments were surprised at breakfast and ran away, leaving the Rebels to eat the meal—and all of this got printed and talked about all across the North.[8] In addition, some of the officers who ran away and were cashiered for it had political influence and defended themselves by asserting that the whole army had been shamefully caught unawares. Grant, of course, was held responsible—Grant and Sherman—and the old story about Grant's fondness for whiskey was told and retold. Sherman was fuming at a great rate, denouncing all of these stories as tales "gotten up by cowards to cover their shame," but for a time Grant was under a cloud.[9]

By the end of April, Halleck had assembled 120,000 men. Not twenty miles away, at Corinth, was Beauregard, getting reinforcements for his shattered army but still able to muster less than half of Halleck's numbers. He could be swamped any time Halleck chose to make a solid lunge at him, and after that nothing on earth could keep Halleck's soldiers from going anywhere in the Deep South they wished.

Halleck recognized his opportunity; unfortunately he also recognized a vast number of dangers, including some that did not exist. Grant had been bitterly criticized because he had not entrenched at Shiloh. Halleck would not lay himself open to the same criticism; accordingly, whenever his vast army halted it entrenched, turning each camp into a minor fort. It spent so much time digging trenches, indeed, that it had little time left for marching. An Illinois soldier recalled that they spent two hours every evening digging trenches and then got up at three in the morning to stand in line in the trenches until daybreak; they marched, he said, from a quarter of a mile to two miles each day. There were times when it appeared that Halleck was going to burrow his way to Corinth.[10]

Roads were very bad and there were numerous swamps, and when an unpaved road crossed a swamp it had to be corduroyed. Ten-foot logs would be cut and laid side by side across the roadway, from solid ground to solid ground. Sometimes the watery mud was so oozy that many layers of logs had to be piled up. Often enough the nearest wood was half a mile away, and the troops would have to carry the logs in, six or eight men to a log. When finished, these roads were both atrocious and dangerous, the sole advantage being that they could at least be used by a moving army, as roads of bottomless mud could not. If an unskilled driver let his horses get too near the edge, one wheel of wagon or gun might slip off the logs into the mud, in which case the whole business would capsize—whereupon all the soldiers in the vicinity had to get into the swamp and hoist everything back on the road again. Sometimes, when mud and water were very bad, a horse that slipped off the corduroy was simply left to sink down out of sight and die. Years after the war an Indiana veteran remembered with distaste "the black slimy water and the old moss-covered logs" of those Mississippi swamp roads."

When the roads were not too wet they were apt to be too dry. Mississippi heat was something new, even to boys who knew what heat could be like in Illinois and Indiana. Roads were narrow, and they frequently ran between tall pines that met overhead, cutting off all air and sunlight. The soil was a fine sandy-white loam, and in dry weather a road would be ankle-deep in dust; and a moving column would kick up unending clouds of it, so that a road through a forest would be a choking tunnel in which some men would collapse from exhaustion while others would stagger along, retching and vomiting. One veteran wrote feelingly: "You load a man down with a sixty-pound knapsack, his gun and forty rounds of ammunition, a haversack full of hardtack and sow belly, and a three-pint canteen full of water, then start him along this narrow roadway with the mercury up to 100 and the dust so thick you could taste it, and you have done the next thing to killing this man outright."¹²

The army did move, and with infinite caution it approached Corinth, averaging less than one mile a day. In some way Halleck was getting fantastic reports about Confederate strength. It was believed at headquarters that Beauregard would presently get sixty thousand fresh troops; then credit was given to a report that one hundred thousand Rebels were waiting at Corinth, with more coming in daily. Assistant Secretary of War Scott, who was traveling with Halleck as a War Department observer, wired Stanton in the middle of May that "the enemy are concentrating a powerful army" and suggested that Halleck ought to be reinforced. An attack by Beauregard was expected daily, at practically any point along the front, and the army was kept ready to go on the defensive at any moment. A captured army surgeon, recently released, assured Grant that while behind the enemy lines he had learned there were one hundred and forty-six thousand Rebels in Corinth, with enough reinforcements on the way to raise the number to two hundred thousand; he added, not wishing to draw too dark a picture, that a number of these reinforcements would of course consist of old men and boys.[13]

A month after it left Shiloh field the army found itself squarely in front of the Rebel lines at Corinth. Beauregard had received all the reinforcements he was going to get, and he had, all in all, just over fifty-two thousand men.[14] He had not a chance in the world to fight off Halleck's army and he knew it; seeing that the Federal was at last nerving himself for an assault, Beauregard abruptly left the place—left it at night, arranging one final deception for the Yankees by having steam engines come puffing and whistling into town at intervals to the accompaniment of loud cheers. Pope, commanding the Federal advance, heard it all, told Halleck that lots of fresh troops were coming in to Beauregard's aid, and predicted that he would be attacked in heavy force by daylight. Then at last, when the Confederate rear guard blew up such supplies as it could not remove, Pope caught on, and on May 30 his regiments went cautiously forward into an empty town. Beauregard kept on going until he reached Tupelo, fifty miles south. He was not pursued with any great vigor.

For Halleck clung to the thought that the war might be won without very much fighting. To him, the occupation of Rebel territory was the big thing. Here he was, sitting in an important junction town, occupying a healthy stretch of the Memphis and Charleston Railroad; as far as he could see, this was victory. He wrote to Pope that all he wanted was for Beauregard to go far enough south so that he could not menace the railroad line: "There is no object in bringing on a battle if this object can be obtained without one. I think by showing a bold front for a day or two the enemy will continue his retreat, which is all I desire."[15]

Memphis was in Union hands now, and Grant was sent over to take charge of it. This assignment marked the beginning of the upswing for Grant. He had been on the verge of quitting the army during the march down to Corinth, feeling humiliated because Halleck was giving him nothing to do, and Sherman had talked him out of it—Sherman, who had lost his command and been written off as insane early in the war, but who had come back and was now solidly established,

the last of his nervous anxiety having been burned away in
the fires of Shiloh. Now Grant had a job again. Before long
it would grow bigger.

Bit by bit Halleck was scattering the huge army that
Beauregard had not dared to fight. He had to occupy Memphis, Corinth, many miles of railroad, a network of towns
behind the railroad. Also, he was sending Buell east to take
Chattanooga—an eminently sound idea, one which the Confederates just then did not know how they were going to
stop, except that it was all being done very slowly. Buell was
a cautious, methodical man and Halleck was the last man
on earth to make him less so; Buell went inching along
toward Chattanooga, rebuilding as he went the railroad line
which the Rebels had been tearing up, and it was almost an
open question whether he would reach Chattanooga before
the war was over.[16]

Meanwhile the army had lost a good man—old C. F. Smith,
who had damned the volunteers and led them to victory at
Fort Donelson, who had given Grant the framework for his
"unconditional surrender" message, and who should have
been spared for more battles; there was plenty of fighting
ahead, and a man of his kind would be useful. But the old
man had been ill for weeks with his infected leg, and a few
weeks after the battle of Shiloh had died at Savannah, Tennessee. They would miss him.

3.   *Invitation to General Lee*

This was the spring when they could have done it. The irresponsible overconfidence of the old "On to Richmond" days
was gone forever, and there was a sullen new respect for the
fighting capacity of the southern soldier, but the chance was
there just the same. Now was the time to move fast and hit
hard, because the other side was badly off balance. The Confederate war potential, limited in any case by comparison
with that of the North, had not yet been fully developed.
Final victory could be won before summer if the strong
northern advantage was pressed to the limit.

Yet the great Federal offensive moved with leaden feet.

In the West, Halleck was profoundly cautious, inching along with pick and shovel, leaving nothing to the chances that might go against him, blind to the chances that might work in his favor, asking only that Beauregard leave him alone. And in the East, where the Confederate capital and nerve center lay a scant hundred miles from Washington, the Federal command was demonstrating that speed was a word it did not understand.

Richmond had become very important. Not only was it the capital, the living symbol of the Confederacy's ability to exist as an independent nation. In the largely rural South it was now the metropolis, the great industrial center, the heart and core of the war-production machine. Memphis was gone, and Nashville, and New Orleans; now Richmond was the keystone, and if it fell the Confederacy's ability to resist would be fatally limited. To take and hold Richmond this spring was to win it all.

But there were problems. While the Westerners were moving up the Tennessee toward what would soon be the Shiloh battlefield, Confederate Joe Johnston was stoutly entrenched around the old Bull Run battlefield, and McClellan at last moved forward to drive him out. But McClellan's army was more than twice as big as Johnston's, and Johnston had no intention of waiting to be destroyed; he got out of there before McClellan arrived, falling back behind the Rappahannock River and leaving nothing for the Yankees except miles of trenches, a string of log huts and barracks, a number of wooden guns that had been mounted for purposes of deception, and smoldering piles of burned foodstuffs and equipment that could not be carried away. McClellan looked things over, decided that an overland pull down to Richmond would be too risky, and returned to Washington; he would put his army on boats and steam down to Old Point Comfort, where the James River came into the lower end of Chesapeake Bay. From there he would march up the long peninsula between the James and York rivers, striking Richmond from the east, trusting to Federal sea power to protect his flanks and give him his supplies.

The plan was good enough, and the army sailed with high confidence. By the first week in April thousands of troops were going ashore near Fortress Monroe; like their general, the men assumed that they would be in Richmond in a few weeks, and the mere sight of the great fleet of transports and warships, the waving flags and the visible display of northern power, convinced them that they were irresistible. Richmond was perhaps fifty miles away, and in the state of Virginia there were at least twice as many Union soldiers as Confederates. A quick march up the peninsula, one big battle at the gates of Richmond, and that would be that.

Yet the march was not quick. McClellan got his army to the peninsula before Johnston did, and for a few crucial days there was nothing much there to stop him. Yorktown was fortified, and a sketchy line of works ran across the peninsula from York River to the James, but there were no more than fifteen thousand armed Confederates present. McClellan had fifty-three thousand men with him, more were coming down on every boat, and one hard smash would probably have settled things. But McClellan was an engineer and he wanted to study the situation with an engineer's careful eye, and while he was at his studies the local Confederate commander played a game on him.

This officer was General John Bankhead Magruder, an imposing-looking gentleman whose military talents were limited but who for years had been an enthusiast for amateur theatricals, and the show he put on now had a sure professional touch that completely baffled McClellan. Magruder marched his skimpy forces back and forth and up and down, making a great show, behaving as if his force was unlimited, and McClellan was greatly impressed; he concluded presently that the Confederate line was too strong to be stormed, and so he halted his army, began to wheel up a ponderous array of siege guns and heavy mortars, built works for their protection —and, in the end, lost an entire month, during which time Johnston and his army showed up and the invasion came to a stalemate.[1]

Other things went wrong, military errors being cumulative.

The Union navy ruled the waters, and it had been supposed originally that any Rebel line on the peninsula could easily be outflanked: warships could steam up either of the rivers, hammering down any fieldworks that might exist and landing troops in the Rebel rear. But just at this time the navy had utterly lost control of the waters around Hampton Roads, and the flanking device McClellan had counted on was not available. This had happened because when the Federals evacuated Norfolk navy yard in the spring of 1861 they had done an imperfect job of destruction on one warship which they had been obliged to leave behind—U.S.S. *Merrimac,* a powerful steam frigate, temporarily immobilized because of defective engines.

Merrimac had been burned and scuttled, but when the Confederates took over the yard they raised the hulk, found it largely intact, and with vast ingenuity created a new marine monster that almost won the war for them. *Merrimac* was cut down to her berth deck and was given a slanting superstructure with twenty-four-inch oaken walls covered by four inches of iron plating, with ports for ten guns. For *Merrimac's* bow the unorthodox naval architects devised a four-foot iron beak. The defective engines, not at all improved by having spent some weeks at the bottom of the harbor, were more or less repaired, the vessel was rechristened *Virginia,* and early in March this unique creation came steaming out into Hampton Roads to upset Yankee strategy.

She looked like nothing anybody had ever seen before. Before and abaft her superstructure, her decks were just awash, so that from a distance the craft looked like a derelict barn adrift on the tide, submerged to the eaves. She drew twenty-two feet of water, her decrepit engines wheezed and creaked and frequently broke down, she was so unhandy it could take half an hour just to turn her around—and at that moment there were not more than three warships in the navies of the world that would have been a match for her. She cruised about, sinking two wooden warships with ease and driving another ashore, and the frustrated Yankee gunners who fired whole broadsides at her at point-blank range discovered that they might as well have been throwing handfuls of pebbles: the missiles bounced high in the air when they struck, making a prodigious clanging and whanging but doing no particular harm to anyone.[2]

For twenty-four hours the Federal authorities were in a state of panic, the most panicky of the lot being that eccentric war minister, Secretary Edwin M. Stanton. *Merrimac* could destroy the whole Federal fleet, she could steam up the Potomac and destroy Washington, she could go up the coast and clean out New York Harbor, she could go down the coast and obliterate the blockading squadrons; perhaps, in this promising month of March, the whole war would be lost because of this ungainly waddling warship. (In actual fact, *Merrimac* drew too much water to ascend the Potomac and was far too unseaworthy to go out into the open ocean, but Washington did not realize this.) At the very least she could upset all plans for the lower Chesapeake Bay.

Then, just when all seemed lost, another wholly fantastic warship came into the lower bay to restore the balance.

This was U.S.S. *Monitor*, which had been designed, built, and commissioned in the very nick of time. In all the story of Civil War coincidences, none is more remarkable than the one that brought these two ships into Hampton Roads within twenty-four hours of each other.

Monitor was a flat raft, pointed at the ends, her deck hardly more than a foot above water. Near the bow there was a little wart of a pilothouse, near the stern a smokestack; between them there was a ponderous revolving turret containing two eleven-inch guns. She had no masts, she was heavily plated with iron, and she was as complete a departure as *Merrimac* herself from all conventional standards of what a vessel had a right to look like. Orthodox naval men had shaken their heads dolefully when Swedish designer John Ericsson presented the plans for her; the decision to build her seems to have been made largely by Abraham Lincoln himself, who possessed less than his normal allotment of orthodoxy. She was not much more seaworthy than *Merrimac*, had almost foundered steaming down from New York in a storm; and now, the morning after *Merrimac's* spectacular debut, she came chuffing in through the Virginia capes, ready for battle.

The day was March 9, memorable for the most momentous drawn battle in history—a battle that nobody won but that made the navies of the world obsolete. *Merrimac* and *Monitor* circled one another, got in close, and then fired away furiously, but neither seemed able to do the other very much harm.

Merrimac tried to ram once, but the blow was ineffective—her iron beak had been twisted off the day before in the process of sinking a Federal frigate—and at day's end each warship hauled off, battered and dented but fully operational.[3]

Washington was jubilant: *Merrimac* had met her match. But so, for that matter, had *Monitor*—which meant trouble for McClellan. The navy people were too well aware that until more ironclads were built the one they had must be preserved at all costs, and so *Monitor* was kept strictly on the defensive; if she went out and provoked a finish fight she might conceivably get sunk—a disaster too horrible to think about. So for two months the rival ironclads glowered at one another from opposite sides of Hampton Roads . . . and when McClellan asked the navy to go up the James and outflank Joe Johnston's defensive line on the peninsula the navy could not do it. Just by staying afloat *Merrimac* was paralyzing Union activity on the James River.

So McClellan spent all of April preparing to attack the Confederate defenses. He finally got all of his heavy guns into position, ready for a scientific bombardment that would flatten the opposing works, and on May 4—just as he was about to touch it off—he found that the works were empty. Johnston, outnumbered two to one and greatly mistrusting the strength of his fortifications, had waited until the last moment and then ordered a retreat.

That was the end of *Merrimac*. When Johnston retreated the Confederates had to evacuate Norfolk, which the Federals immediately occupied, and *Merrimac* no longer had a home. Her deep draught kept her from escaping up the James, and at last, on May 10, she was abandoned and blown up. She had had just over two months under the Confederate flag, and she had accomplished a good deal more than she usually gets credit for. She was, in fact, one of the reasons why the North did not capture Richmond in the spring of 1862.[4]

When Johnston retreated McClellan followed. His advance ran into Johnston's rear guard in a chain of fieldworks near old Williamsburg and fought a hard, wearing battle that did nothing but produce twenty-two hundred Union casualties and prove that both armies had long since got past the clumsy amateurish stage of the Bull Run era. Johnston kept on retreating until he had backed all the way into the suburbs of Richmond, and McClellan followed at a pace not much faster than the one Halleck had been displaying in Mississippi. May was nearly over by the time the Army of the Potomac was in line near the Confederate capital—badly behind the "three or four weeks" schedule McClellan had so optimistically laid down on February 20.

By now other things were going wrong, most of them growing out of a bitter difference of opinion between General McClellan and the Lincoln administration.

At bottom the difference of opinion reflected divergent ideas on the kind of war the country was fighting. The administration had accepted it from the first as a revolutionary struggle, calling for hard blows hit fast; McClellan always saw it as a traditional war-between-gentlemen affair, of the sort which a professional soldier could play straight. The administration wanted relentless combat but lacked military knowledge; McClellan had military knowledge but could not see that at bottom this was a political war. It was becoming very hard for McClellan and Lincoln to agree about anything whatever.

A disagreement between general and government could have odd potentialities this spring. There was a great division of opinion in the North about war aims. The administration was coming to suspect that to put down the rebellion it would have to destroy slavery—and, with it, the social and economic system for which slavery was the base. It was nearly ready, in other words, to say that it would stamp out everything the South was fighting for. Northern Democrats, on the other hand, wanted nothing but simple restoration of the Union. On almost everything but secession itself they accepted the southern point of view. Northern Democrats were complaining that the Republican administration was growing intolerably oppressive, ruthless, and dictatorial; the Republicans were suspecting that Democrats believed in a soft and ineffective war and stood on the edge of outright disloyalty.

And McClellan embodied the Democratic position. Any military program he might adopt could be considered a Democratic program, and it was all too easy now to consider a

Democratic program treasonous. So when general and administration differed about anything at all—the placement of a division of troops, a proper route for invasion and supply, the appointment of a soldier to command an army corps—neither one could quite trust the other's motives.

The first disagreement had come because McClellan refused to invade the Richmond area until he was satisfied that his army was entirely ready. Because of this disagreement, in mid-March he had been deposed as commanding general of all the armies and reduced to command of the Army of the Potomac. Then, when he did move, there had been an argument over the way in which Washington should be protected.

McClellan felt that if he kept the Confederates busy in front of Richmond the defense of Washington would pretty well take care of itself. Lincoln and Stanton felt that a strong body of troops should be left behind, and when McClellan went down to the peninsula they held back some thirty-five thousand of his troops—under the luckless McDowell, who had commanded at Bull Run—to watch the line of the Rappahannock and upper Virginia. McClellan complained bitterly that he was being sent to do a job with inadequate strength, and he darkly suspected McDowell of wanting to carve out an independent role for himself. In the Cabinet, meanwhile, there were men who whispered that McClellan had tried to leave Washington defenseless because in the depths of his heart he sympathized with the South.

This suspicion led to increasing fragmentation of the Federal forces in Virginia. In the Shenandoah Valley there was a Union army of ten thousand men under Nathaniel Banks, an important Republican leader from Massachusetts who rated a general's commission for his services to the party (he had been Speaker of the House of Representatives) but for no other discernible reason; and farther west, in the western Virginia mountains, there were fifteen thousand more under none other than John Charles Frémont, the Pathfinder himself, uneasily resurrected this spring and given another chance to lead troops in action.

All of these bodies—McDowell's, Banks's and Frémont's—had dual roles to play, and if they were ever to act in harmony the direction would have to come from the War Department, because they were not particularly answerable to anyone else. All of them were supposed, first of all, to protect Washington. In addition, McDowell was expected to march down and help McClellan capture Richmond. Banks was to maintain Union control in the valley, and Frémont was expected to do nothing less than move down the long diagonal into eastern Tennessee, occupying a portion of the vital east-west railway line, bringing aid and comfort to the pro-Union folk in that area, and ultimately capturing Knoxville.

All of this might just possibly have worked if the Confederate defenses had remained properly supine. Everybody was supposed to assume that it would work, anyway, and when McClellan got his men in line before Johnston's entrenchments on the outskirts of Richmond he formed his army on that assumption.

Six miles from Richmond the Chickahominy River flowed sluggishly along, roughly parallel to the James; an unimpressive little stream with marshy banks and an amazing capacity for overflowing them whenever it rained, coming down through an eroded, farmed-out, pine-thicket country where all the roads were bad and no decent maps existed. Because he expected McDowell to come down at any moment, McClellan extended a wing of his army to meet him; formed his troops, that is, astride the Chickahominy, part of them on the south side confronting Johnston and part of them north of it confronting nobody much but prepared to make contact with McDowell. Militarily it was a bad position, for a sudden rain could make the Chickahominy impassable at any moment, but if McDowell showed up on schedule the risk could be taken.

Johnston quickly detected the flaw in McClellan's position, and at the end of May, when a quick downpour turned the Chickahominy into a foaming, menacing torrent, he attacked the smaller part of McClellan's army that lay south of the river, hoping to destroy it before it could be reinforced.

For two days the armies fought, in swamps and clearings around a farm known as Seven Pines and a railroad station called Fair Oaks, and the result was a bloody stalemate. Luckily for the Union, Confederate staff work was wildly inefficient and Johnston's attack was not made as he had planned it; many assault units did not get into action at all, others got in one another's way, and weaknesses in the Union position were not exploited. Also, McClellan's engineers had bridged the Chickahominy, and the bridges held in spite of the flood, so that ample reinforcements could be rushed to the scene. In the end, neither army had lost anything of consequence—except for five or six thousand soldiers on each side, whose loss was just the small change of warfare—and life in each camp went on about as it had gone before. The one significant result of this battle was that Joe Johnston was wounded; to replace him, Jefferson Davis sent in Robert E. Lee.

The defect in McClellan's position remained, for McDowell was still expected. But McDowell never did get there (although a good portion of his troops reached McClellan by water), and the things that began to go wrong now were things happening far from McClellan's lines and altogether outside his control. What hurt most was the intervention of a humorless, gawky, fire-and-brimstone Presbyterian, with a killer's blue eyes looking unemotionally out from under the broken visor of a mangy old forage cap: Thomas J. Jackson, known to fame as Stonewall.

Jackson was the sort of general Lincoln would have wanted, if that makes any difference: a dedicated hard-war man in whose eyes the enemy were a people to be exterminated with Old Testament fury. (What he would have done, as a Unionist leading a punitive column across Georgia in Sherman's place, is something to think about with awe.) Jackson began to take a hand in the game toward the end of March, and before he got through he had fatally disrupted McClellan's plan of campaign.

Late in March, Jackson attacked a Union outpost in the lower Shenandoah Valley, at Kernstown. He was outnumbered, and after a sharp little fight he had to retreat, fairly beaten, but the battle had strategic consequences: Union authorities were impressed by his aggressiveness, figured that he must be much stronger than he actually was, and were confirmed in their feeling that to protect Washington some of the troops McClellan wanted must be held in upper Virginia.

Then, early in May—about the time Johnston was beginning his retreat from Yorktown—Jackson really went into action.

First he moved west and jumped Frémont's advance guard near one of the passes in the Alleghenies. In itself the fight was not especially important, but it completely upset Frémont. The Pathfinder had not changed much since his experiences in Missouri. His hastily assembled army was looking goggle-eyed at "his retinue of aides-de-camp dazzling in gold lace," and the soldiers felt that the pomp and circumstance that surrounded him—very foreign looking and sounding, most of it—was completely out of place in the rugged West Virginia mountains. Frémont seems never to have worked out a clear plan for his projected move into eastern Tennessee, and Jackson's attack thoroughly disrupted any plans he did have. While he was pulling himself together and trying to get ready for what Jackson might do next he was effectively immobilized for more than a fortnight; Jackson contemptuously turned his back on him and hurried back to the Shenandoah for other adventures.

Reinforced by now to a total strength of fifteen thousand men, Jackson moved rapidly toward the lower valley, baffled the expectant Banks by slipping over to the east side of the Massanutten mountain ridge, captured a detachment which Banks had guarding his communications at Front Royal, and compelled the former Speaker of the House to retreat toward Harpers Ferry. Jackson followed, struck him en route, tore his rear guard apart in a savage morning fight at Winchester, and in the end drove him on in a desperate rout that did not end until Banks and his disorganized men were north of the Potomac. Jackson followed closely, and wild rumors went on ahead of him; Washington got the idea that he was about to invade the North, frantic telegrams went out to alert the Northern governors, and McClellan's chance of getting any help from McDowell went down to the vanishing point.

There were plenty of Federals in upper Virginia to overwhelm Jackson's little army, and the War Department barked and sputtered over the telegraph wires to get them into action. Frémont was ordered to march east from the mountains to cut off Jackson's retreat at Strasburg. McDowell was moved west, with an advance detachment marching on Front Royal.

His army reorganized, Banks was ordered to move down from Harpers Ferry. Altogether, something like forty-five thousand Federal troops were converging on Jackson, who was reluctantly pulling back from the Potomac, and it looked as if he might be destroyed.

But there was no co-ordination among the pursuing columns, and Jackson slipped between them unscathed. He moved back up the valley, knocked Frémont back on his heels when that officer chased him, marched east and routed the advance of McDowell's forces, and then calmly withdrew to a pass in the Blue Ridge and awaited further orders.[5]

The result of all of this was that McDowell never did make his move down to help McClellan, and by the middle of June the Army of the Potomac was still waiting, part of it on one side of the Chickahominy and part of it on the other, in a position that fairly invited attack. And the Confederates in front of Richmond were now under General Lee, to whom nobody ever had to extend such an invitation more than once.

4. Delusion and Defeat

The real trouble was away down inside somewhere. McClellan had his problems, to be sure. His government had interfered with his plans, it had promised troops that were not sent, and it had all but openly accused him of wanting to lose the war —or at least of not wholeheartedly wanting to win it. But the tragedy that was about to unfold in the steaming swamps and pine flats around Richmond came mostly from within the man. At bottom, it was the tragedy of a man who could not quite measure up.

McClellan had nearly all of the gifts: youth, energy, charm, intelligence, sound professional training. But the fates who gave him these gifts left out the one that a general must have before all others—the hard, instinctive fondness for fighting. Robert E. Lee was one of the most pugnacious soldiers in American history, and McClellan himself did not like to fight. He could not impose his will on the man who stood opposite him. He was leading an offensive thrust that had taken him to the suburbs of the southern capital, yet it was just a question of time before the initiative would be taken away from him.

By the end of the third week in June, McClellan had an effective strength, present for duty in front of Richmond, of approximately one hundred and five thousand men. They were arrayed in secure fieldworks, safe from any direct counterthrust, and although the humid lowland heat was so oppressive that many men had fallen ill and the air was hideous with the odor of bodies still unburied from the Fair Oaks-Seven Pines battles, morale was high. The men understood McClellan's plan and believed in it: to advance by slow stages, fortifying each gain, wheeling the heavy siege guns forward until finally they could blast the Confederate works out of the way and go on into Richmond.

Lee understood this plan, too, and on the surface it did not appear that there was much he could do to stop it. When he had scraped together the last possible reinforcements (including Jackson's men, who finally slipped down from the valley to join him) he had perhaps eighty thousand men. During most of June his total was far short of that, and it could never go any higher. His defensive works were not nearly as powerful as they were to become two years later. If he was to drive McClellan away he would have to work something like a military miracle.

McClellan's own hopes were high. During the first three weeks of June his dispatches to the War Department and his letters to his wife (as revealing a set of documents as any general ever wrote) were full of promises. He was always going to make his big move in just two or three more days— as soon as the rains stopped, as soon as so-and-so's division joined him, as soon as this or that or the other thing was all ready. The two or three days would pass, the rains would stop, the other things would work out right, but nothing would happen. Never could he bring himself to the point of action.[1]

He believed that he was horribly outnumbered. He had always believed it—even in the fall of 1861, when Johnston waited in his works at Manassas with no more than half of McClellan's strength. He had believed it on the peninsula in

April, when Johnston was writing scornfully that "no one but McClellan would have hesitated to attack." He believed it now. Lee, he was convinced, had between one hundred and fifty thousand and two hundred thousand men, possibly more.

These figures came mostly from Allan Pinkerton, whose intelligence reports were detailed, explicit, incredibly wrong —and believed down to the last digit. What McClellan believed, the whole officer corps believed. The attitude spread like an infection, and finally it was an article of faith all through the army that the Confederates had a huge advantage in numbers and that this invasion was a risky business that must be carried on with extreme caution.

It will not do to blame it all on Pinkerton. He ran perhaps the most unaccountably inefficient intelligence service an American army ever had, but his fantastic reports did not have to be accepted. Away back in Washington, Quartermaster General Montgomery Meigs that spring combed the Richmond newspapers, made a note of all infantry regiments and brigades mentioned, added this to other intelligence that was coming out of the Confederate capital, and made a very fair appraisal of Lee's manpower.[2] What Meigs did could easily have been done at McClellan's headquarters, but nobody made the effort. Back of the blithe acceptance of the Pinkerton reports, obviously, there was a will to believe. McClellan believed that he was outnumbered because it was his nature to overestimate his disadvantages. As a result, it was impossible for him to take advantage of his opportunities.

His opportunities were not going to remain open very much longer. Lee had no intention of waiting to be hit. He proposed to do exactly what Albert Sidney Johnston had done at Shiloh—smite the invader while he was still off balance— and he was aware of the potential weakness of McClellan's right wing, dug in north of the Chickahominy waiting for the absent McDowell.

In the middle of June, Lee sent his cavalry out on a wide sweep to find out if the Yankees had any real protection north and west of that exposed flank. Lee's cavalry was under a picturesque young soldier named Jeb Stuart, who managed to be a headline-hunting showoff and a very solid, energetic cavalry leader at the same time, and Stuart rode completely around McClellan's army: a prestige item that humiliated the Federals and that also gave Lee the information he wanted. (It must be remarked that Stuart did not have much to fight just then. McClellan had plenty of cavalry, but it was all in fragments—one regiment here, another there, stray detachments all over the lot, with no solid fighting corps anywhere; as his army was organized, McClellan simply could not send out a body of cavalry that could meet Stuart on even terms.) As a result of this raid, Lee understood that the way was open for him to jump McClellan's right wing, provided he moved fast.

He would move fast; also, when he moved, he would move with great strength. Lee was a gambler, ready to take long chances because he knew that if he did not take them the law of averages would inexorably catch up with him. Outnumbered though he was, Lee arranged to give himself an overpowering numerical advantage when he made his fight.

North of the Chickahominy, McClellan had the V Army Corps, between twenty and twenty-five thousand men under a handsome, careful major general named Fitz-John Porter. Lee prepared to strike this force with more than fifty-five thousand men.

To do this he would have to press his luck to the uttermost. McClellan's main body was south of the river, facing Richmond—eighty thousand men or thereabouts. Lee calmly arranged to leave twenty thousand men in the trenches facing this host and trust to the great god of battles that they could keep McClellan from marching into Richmond while Porter was being crushed. Most of these twenty thousand, as it happened, were under command of the same John Magruder who had deceived McClellan so outrageously down on the peninsula early in April. Now Magruder would have to play the same sort of game, looking numerous and pretending to be aggressive. If it worked, the rest of the Confederate army could go north of the river, Stonewall Jackson could bring his army down from the valley, and the exposed Federal corps could be hacked to pieces.

So the man who was outnumbered was going to take a long chance, risking his country's independence on his ability to perform a strategic deception; and the man who had all the advantages waited in his trenches, cautiously refraining from doing anything because the chances might possibly go against him; and the war was going to go on, as a result, for nearly three more terrible years.

Even so, McClellan very nearly beat Lee to the punch. On June 25 he carefully moved his skirmish lines forward, south of the Chickahominy. There was some sharp fighting in weedy fields and swampy woods, the Confederates gave ground, and a full-dress attack by three army corps was planned for the next day along a road leading past a place called Old Tavern.³ Meanwhile some of McClellan's cavalry squadrons, ranging off far above the river, picked up a Confederate deserter, a ragged, footsore chap who was willing to answer his captors' questions. He belonged to Stonewall Jackson's corps, he said, and the whole outfit was just a day's march away, hot-footing it down to fall on Porter's unprotected right and rear. McClellan put Porter on the alert, and the plans for a big push at Old Tavern were temporarily laid aside.

They were never picked up again. Next day, June 26, Lee took the initiative, and from that moment on McClellan had to move in step with his opponent. The greater part of Lee's army crossed the Chickahominy, brushed Union pickets out of the suburban hamlet of Mechanicsville, and went charging east across a wide plain that slanted down to shallow Beaver Dam Creek, behind which Porter's men were in line, waiting. Confederate arrangements had got all messed up; nobody made contact with Jackson and his men did not get into action, but the assault was made anyway—a frightful, botched affair that could have been written off as an outright Confederate disaster if either of the rival commanders had chosen to interpret it that way. The Confederates went in, head on, against a trench line that was as strong as a regular fort, and the Federal cannon had a clear sweep across the plain and up and down the creek valley. The Southerners gave up, finally, after dark, fearfully cut up. They had done Porter's men very little harm and had gained nothing worth talking about; furthermore, the Union commanders south of the river were reporting that a number of the Rebel camps opposite them seemed to be deserted, and now was perhaps a very good time for a solid whack at Magruder's lines.

But McClellan had pulled in his horns. From the moment when he learned of Jackson's approach he had gone entirely over to the defensive. He abandoned his supply line, which led from the Chickahominy to the York River, and set about establishing a new one leading down to the James. Porter was told, even before the June 26 attack hit him, to send his wagon trains and siege guns south of the Chickahominy so that he could get away fast if he had to; and both Lee and McClellan, on the night of June 26, were thinking about exactly the same thing—whether the entire Federal army might not presently be destroyed.

Porter's men had won their fight, but they could not stay where they were. Although Jackson had not got into action he was known to have reached a spot where he could come slicing down behind Porter's lines first thing next morning, and so during the night Porter's corps retreated five miles to the east, posting themselves at last in a wide, irregular crescent on rising ground that covered some of the most important bridges over the Chickahominy.

The Confederates took out after them soon after daylight on June 27, broke through a rear guard at Gaines's Mill, and early in the afternoon the biggest assault of the entire war, down to that moment, got under way—fifty-five thousand Confederates, Jackson and his corps in action at last, swarming in through swamps and dense underbrush to attack about half their number of Yankees.

All afternoon Porter's men held their ground. They had a good position, they were supported by some first-rate artillery, and McClellan had brought them to a sharp fighting edge. Long afterward some of the survivors on both sides said that they never had a hotter fight than this one of Gaines's Mill. Along most of the line the Confederates made so many separate assaults that the defenders lost all count of them. Rifle fire reached terrible intensity, splintering muskets in men's hands, cutting down brush and saplings, strewing the fields with dead and wounded. A tremendous clamor of artillery fire shook the air, and heavy siege guns planted south of the Chickahominy joined in the fight, reaching far across the river to send huge shells into the Confederate ranks. Porter wrote afterward that some Confederate assault waves seemed to dissolve as they approached the Union lines, but as fast as one line disappeared another would come up from the rear, the men fairly clambering over their comrades' bodies as they charged up to get within good musket range.'

Then, along toward sunset, there came a lull: hurricane center, with its deceptive peace, one unhealthy patch of clear sky in the murk overhead, the worst of the storm yet to come. Porter began to hope that perhaps the thing was over—and then, from end to end of the line, there was a great new crash of firing, and every man Lee had north of the river came on the run in a final, desperate, all-or-nothing charge. The Union line broke, guns were captured, whole regiments were surrounded and taken, and as darkness came and the triumphant Confederates held the edge of the plateau it was clear that all of the Federals would have to be south of the Chickahominy by morning.

McClellan himself does not seem to have known exactly what was going on this day. His headquarters were south of the river, and he stayed in them, quite as much concerned by the reports he was getting from his commanders there as by the things that were happening to Porter on the north side. For that devotee of amateur theatricals, John B. Magruder, was putting on the best performance of his life today. Hopelessly outnumbered, holding a line that would be pulverized if the Federals ever attacked it, Magruder all day long played the part of a general who was just about to launch a shattering offensive. His skirmish and patrol parties were constantly active, his batteries were forever emitting sudden bursts of fire, he kept bodies of men in movement on open ground in the rear where the Yankees could see them, and with drums and bugles and human voices he caused noises to be made in the woods like the noise of vast assembling armies—and all of it worked.

It worked, partly because Magruder was **very good** at that sort of thing, and partly because the Federal **command** was fatally infected by the belief that Lee had overwhelming force at his command. This was the grand delusion that brought other delusions after it, the infection that made victory impossible. And so the Federal generals told McClellan that a powerful Rebel offensive was on (or, if not actually on, due to start at any moment) and they said that while they hoped that they could hold their ground they could not possibly do anything more than that. McClellan notified Washington that evening that he could not yet be sure where the principal Rebel attack was going to be made. He added that he had that day been assaulted "by greatly superior numbers on this side"—by which, of course, he was referring to nothing on earth but Magruder's shadowboxing.⁵

There could be just one outcome to this sort of thing, and it was ordered that night at a corps commanders' conference in army headquarters: retreat to some safe spot down the James River before these overpowering Rebels destroyed the army entirely.

The retreat was very ably handled. Huge quantities of supplies had to be destroyed, of course, a number of field hospitals and their occupants were abandoned outright, and any detachments that strayed away from camp or march were left behind for the Rebels to capture at their leisure, but the army itself, with its artillery and its immense trains, was neatly extricated from the pocket into which Lee had maneuvered it. Indeed, McClellan conducted the retreat so smartly that Lee lost touch with him for a day or so, and the bright Confederate hope that the Army of the Potomac could be kept from getting to the James never came close to realization. There were furious isolated actions, at places like Savage Station, White Oak Swamp, and above all at the seedy little hamlet of Glendale, but these did nothing but increase the casualty lists on both sides. Lee was never quite able to get around in front and head the retreating Yankees off.

Last act came on July 1. The army was getting away clean by now, the van coming to the James at Harrison's Landing, where there were wide fields for camps, fine mansions for headquarters, deep water for supply vessels and protecting gunboats. Lee was following hard, furious because his enemy was getting away alive, and it was going to be necessary to fight one more rear-guard battle. The road to Harrison's Landing led up over a broad, undulating height called Malvern Hill, and McClellan told Porter to take his own corps, as much of the rest of the army as he thought he would need, and all of the reserve artillery, and make a stand there.

Porter did as he was told. His position was immensely powerful—so much so that he needed few troops besides the men of his own hard-fighting corps. He had long ranks of artillery ranged hub to hub where they could sweep every field of approach, he had siege guns farther back, and in the river there was a naval squadron that could toss horrendous large-caliber shells into the Confederate ranks. If Lee had one more attack in his system, the army was going to be ready for him.

The attack came late in the afternoon. Lee had had much trouble getting his army into position—the roads were bad, the maps were poor, and officers and men alike had been worn to a frazzle by a week of fighting and marching—and when the Confederates tried to move up their artillery to soften the Yankee line with gunfire, Porter's gunners all but murdered them; fifty Federal guns, at times, would turn on one Confederate battery trying to get into position, killing horses and men, smashing caissons, knocking guns off their carriages, and leaving a horrible pile-up of wrecked wood and metal and torn bodies. On no other field in the war did artillery have such dominance as the Federal guns had here at Malvern Hill.

Yet Lee's assault was made; made, finally, by fourteen brigades, which struggled to cross open ground covered by one hundred guns, with solid Federal infantry waiting with musket fire for close range. Some of the men did reach the Union lines, briefly. Others managed to hold advance positions long enough to inflict a painful fire on Porter's men. But most of the attacking columns were simply destroyed. The Confederate General D. H. Hill, who led one of the divisions in this attack, wrote afterward of his amazement at discovering that more than half of the six thousand casualties the Confederate army suffered that day were caused by cannon fire. This fight, he said, was not war, it was just plain murder; and on reflection he added that with Yankee artillery and Confederate infantry he believed he could whip anybody on earth.[6]

Murderous the fight had been, and when night came and the hot cannon were quiet at last, the Union position on Malvern Hill was wholly unshaken. Lee's army, in fact, had had something like a disaster. The important factor, however, here as in the fight at Mechanicsville, was that neither McClellan nor Lee was prepared to act as if there had been anything but a Confederate victory.

McClellan conceivably might have resumed the offensive next day. He had a firebrand of a division commander, one-armed Phil Kearny, who stormed and swore in great fury because McClellan would not make a drive for Richmond the next morning, and even Porter—very careful and intensely loyal to McClellan—wondered if the army might not have won a great victory on the heels of Malvern Hill. But McClellan would not hear of it. He had Porter bring his men and guns down off the hill after dark, and by the morning of July 2 the Confederates had the place to themselves. McClellan's army was safe within its lines at Harrison's Landing, and the great campaign was over.

The soldier who had fought with all the odds against him had taken hair-raising risks and had won; the soldier who had had all of the advantages had refused to risk anything and had lost; and now the last chance that this ruinous war could be a relatively short one was gone forever.

6.

Turning Point

1. *Kill, Confiscate or Destroy*

AFTER THE SPRING of 1862 the Civil War began to dominate the men who were fighting it. They still had the option to win or to lose, but they could no longer quite be said to be in charge of it. Coming of age, the war began to impose its own conditions; finally it came to control men instead of being controlled by them.

Until that spring ended, the situation was still more or less fluid; the war might yet be disposed of in such a way that it would not become one of the great turning points in history. But after the western army had been scattered and ordered to occupy territory instead of destroying Confederate fighting power, and after the eastern army had been driven into its muggy camp of refuge at Harrison's Landing, the situation began to harden. From now on many things would happen, not so much because anyone wanted them to happen as because the pressure of war made them inevitable.

This began to be visible that summer in the West.

Grant was holding Memphis, western Tennessee, and northern Mississippi—one division here, two divisions there, detachments spraddled out for hundreds of miles to guard bridges, railroad lines, junction towns, and river ports. Buell was marching east to take Chattanooga. He was moving along the line of the Memphis and Charleston Railroad, repairing it as he went, condemned to a snail's progress. Ahead of him he had Ormsby Mitchel's division holding a stretch of northern Alabama.

Mitchel was a voice crying in the wilderness. He had been

in Alabama since early April, when the rest of Buell's people
went down to fight at Shiloh and take part in the Corinth
campaign. Mitchel had gone to Huntsville, where he seized
the Memphis and Charleston machine shops, and he fanned
troops out to east and west, taking special pains to take the
railroad bridges over the Tennessee at Decatur and at Bridgeport. He kept pestering headquarters with urgent messages,
asserting that from where he was he could see the end of the
war. If Buell came over fast, he said, he could get into
Chattanooga without trouble; after that he could capture
Atlanta, and from Atlanta he could march all the way north
to Richmond, because all of that part of the Confederacy
was "comparatively unprotected and very much alarmed."[1]

Mitchel may very well have been right, but he could not
get anyone to listen to him—except for Halleck and Buell,
both of whom were irritated. He was told to break the railroad bridge at Decatur so that Rebels could not use the
Memphis and Charleston if they regained possession of it,
and after that he was to sit tight and await developments. He
obeyed, fuming with impatience. As a diversion he sent out
a handful of men on a long-shot raid to break the railroad
that led from Chattanooga down to Atlanta; the raid failed,
after a spectacular locomotive chase that has provided material for novelists, dramatists, and feature writers ever since,
and most of the raiders were caught and hanged as spies.
But finally, after Corinth was taken, Buell was sent over
toward Chattanooga, and Mitchel was sternly rebuked for
having destroyed the bridge at Decatur and was told to rebuild it.[2] He was also told to tighten up on discipline because
his troops had been misbehaving badly.

Specifically, there was the case of the 19th Illinois and
Colonel John Basil Turchin.

The 19th Illinois was a more or less typical midwestern
regiment, but Turchin was neither typical nor middlewest-
ern. He had been born in Russia forty years earlier, had been
educated at the Imperial Military School in St. Petersburg,
had served on the Russian general staff, and had fought in
the Crimea. In 1856 he came to America and went to work
in the engineering department of the Illinois Central Railroad,
and when the Civil War started he got into uniform and

became colonel of this 19th Illinois. He was a stiff drillmaster —he seems to have been a friend of the departed Elmer Ellsworth, whose amateur Zouaves cut such a swath on militia parade grounds just before the war—and when the 19th left Springfield late in the summer of 1861 it was considered something of a crack outfit.

The first thing that happened to the 19th was a train wreck, which occurred in Indiana while the regiment was on its way east to join the Army of the Potomac. The wreck was a horror, killing twenty-four men and injuring one hundred and five, as heavy a toll as a regular battle would have taken, and while the regiment was recuperating its orders were changed and it was sent down to Kentucky to join Buell's army. Buell was impressed by the 19th's smart appearance at drill, and Colonel Turchin soon had command of a brigade in Mitchel's division.

Whatever its achievements on the parade ground, the 19th had a heavy hand with occupied territory. One of the northern Alabama towns was held by the 33rd Ohio, which did so much looting that on complaint of the citizens its colonel was rebuked and the regiment was withdrawn. The townsfolk exulted only briefly, for the 33rd was replaced by the 19th Illinois; and according to army legend, before the day was over the luckless citizens were begging the authorities to let them have the 33rd again—compared with the Illinois regiment, it was a model of decorum.

The real trouble, however, came in the town of Athens, Alabama, where one of Turchin's regiments was shot up by lurking guerrillas. Turchin considered this a gross violation of the laws of war, and anyway he seems to have had a czarist officer's notions about the way people ought to behave in occupied territory. He called up his 19th Illinois and drove the guerrillas away, and after things were under control he told the boys to go ahead and take the town apart—"I shut mine eyes for one hour." One hour was all the 19th needed. When it got through, Athens looked as though it had been hit by Cossacks. Citizens later contributed forty-five affidavits alleging that personal property to the value of more than fifty thousand dollars had been carried off. Turchin was court-martialed and dismissed from the service (although somebody eventually pulled wires in Washington and got him reinstated); but what had happened really did not have very much to do with him, anyway. It was the Illinois boys and not the Imperial Russian officer who had carried off watches, jewelry, heirlooms, and oil paintings, and all that had been needed to set them off had been one signal.[3]

It was recalled afterward that a detachment of men from the 19th, given horses and assigned to work as scouts and couriers, promptly became famous as "the forty thieves," and the regimental historian confessed that "perhaps there was some slight reason" for this title.[4]

Colonel Turchin may have been unique, but the 19th Illinois was not; it was just about average, and the average soldier in the western armies was learning to regard himself as a cross between licensed freebooter and avenging angel. In northern Mississippi a soldier was writing to his sister: "Our men are using this country awful rough. Such animals as chickens, fences, swine, etc., are entirely unseeable and unfindable within fifteen miles of where our camp has been this last week." Oddly enough, this reflected high morale: "I never saw men in as good spirits and as confident as this army now appears . . . I can't see why people will stay at home when they can get to soldiering. I think a year of it is worth getting shot for to any man."[5]

The generals tried to stop this sort of thing, but they never came close. These volunteer soldiers were bound to get out of hand once they got into what they considered enemy country. Lieutenants and captains lived on terms of approximate equality with their men. They could not be severe with them; would not, in any case, the idea not entering their heads; and although generals might issue stern orders against looting and robbery, these orders were almost completely ignored at the operating level. Subalterns who were Pete and Joe to their men could not keep the army from trailing a cloud of stragglers wherever it went, and the stragglers were under no man's control. Any farmhouse within ten miles of camp, one soldier estimated, would get at least fifty uniformed visitors a day, begging and cadging what they could and stealing anything that was not offered to them.[6]

The official records for this period are full of stiff orders from—of all people—William Tecumseh Sherman, who asserted passionately: "This demoralizing and disgraceful practice of pillage must cease, else the country will rise on us and justly shoot us down like dogs and wild beasts." Even John Pope, whom the people of Virginia would soon consider the very author of lawless war, made himself highly unpopular with his volunteer troops by his efforts to restrain them. He met a party from the 27th Ohio bringing in a wagonload of fence rails for firewood, made them return the rails, and then ordered their colonel to "put these —— —— —— in the guard house until they could be court-martialed and shot as an example to the rest of the —— —— volunteer ——"[1]

None of this did any good (and the volunteers went unhanged) for the fact was that the army saw nothing in the least wrong in taking what it needed from the people of the South. Higher officials were infected as well as enlisted men. Stout German-born General Osterhaus furiously denounced a soldier who was brought before him for killing a cow until he learned that his own cook had the animal's liver and was preparing it for the general's supper. Then he changed his tune: "Ah, dot is it, den? Vell den, you always bring me de livers and den I never know nuttin' about de killin' of de animals." A Wisconsin colonel, lecturing two culprits who had been caught looting, said sternly: "Now boys, I have to punish you. I am so ordered by the general. I want you two to understand that I am not punishing you for stealing, but for getting caught at it, by God!"

An Indiana soldier said that "the generals were slow to adopt the confiscation idea" and issued all sorts of orders against foraging, but "in time the veteran learned to circumvent all such orders, and to modify the cruel penalty by a system of division with the officers in command, who allowed the boys to construe orders to suit their needs." Highhanded foraging, he confessed, had "marvellous beauties." Almost universally, in eastern and western armies alike, company and regimental officers did not even pretend to try to enforce orders against foraging.[8]

In part, this was just what was bound to happen in a civil war in nineteenth-century America. The rowdy strain was coming to the surface again; it had been called up to help create the war, and there was no way to repress it. Army life at any time lifts from men the feeling of personal responsibility for their acts; it was doing this now in a land where the strain of irresponsibility ran high at the best of times. An army of invasion composed of volunteers who considered themselves free citizens despite their uniforms and their oaths of enlistment was going to "use this country awful rough," and that was that.

But that was not all of it. Super-patriots back home were demanding a hard war. Newspapers in Chicago and other northern cities sharply condemned the court-martial of Colonel Turchin, complaining that Buell was altogether too kind to the people of Alabama and Tennessee, who, being in a state of rebellion, needed to be punished. The soldiers sympathized with this criticism—the more so, perhaps, since at the moment the war was not being prosecuted very energetically. To protect Rebel property was beginning to look like being soft with rebellion itself; an officer too alert to prevent foraging and looting might very well be an officer secretly in sympathy with the Confederacy. (General Buell was growing immensely unpopular with his men for this reason.) Anything that hurt anyone in the South, probably, would ultimately hurt the rebellion; secession was treason, men who supported it were traitors, and the worst that happened to them was no more than they deserved.[9]

It was expressed very clearly by the men of the 12th Wisconsin, who occupied Humboldt, Tennessee, that summer. They took over a print shop and for a time got out a weekly newspaper, with enlisted men as editors. The paper spoke the private soldier's mind, and one of its editorials hit the keynote: "The time for negotiating peace has passed; henceforth let us *conquer* a peace. Let the blows fall thick and heavy, and keep on falling. Let us lay aside the 'pomp and circumstance' of war, pull off our coats, and 'wade in.' . . . Let our divisions move on, kill, confiscate or destroy, throw every sympathy to the wind that might stand in the way, and bring the traitors to a traitor's fate by the shortest and quickest way."[10]

The shortest and quickest way, as far as the private soldier was concerned, was to hit hard at anything that stood in his path—to devastate country as well as to fight enemy armies; in general terms, to wreak vengeance on all inhabitants of the Confederacy. The judge advocate in a court-martial in Buell's army summed it up a little later when he defined "a vigorous war policy" as one in which the man who actively or passively aided the secession movement "is considered to have no rights that the government is bound to respect."[11]

Quite simply, this meant that the institution of slavery was doomed. The great majority of Union soldiers had entered the war with no particular feeling against slavery and with even less feeling in favor of the Negro. They had no quarrel with the idea that the Negro was property; indeed, it was precisely that fact that was moving them and writing the institution's doom. Because looting and foraging held "marvellous beauties" for the army of occupation, because ruining a farm seemed one way to strike at the enemy, and because general hell-raising was fun anyway, they were commissioning themselves to strike at Rebel property—and here was the most obvious, plentiful, and important property of all. With the Negro's ultimate fate they rarely bothered their heads. It was enough to know that the South would have a hard time functioning without him.

U. S. Grant got this idea ahead of his troops. Grant had never been an anti-slavery man. He had once owned a slave himself, his wife had owned several, his wife's family had owned many. But as early as the fall of 1861 he was writing to his father, saying that while he wanted to whip the rebellion but preserve all southern rights, "if it cannot be whipped in any other way than through a war on slavery, let it come to that." In the summer of 1862 he saw the myriad contrabands that were following northern armies, and commented: "I don't know what is to become of these poor people in the end, but it weakens the enemy to take them from them." Somewhat later he told his friend Congressman Elihu B. Washburne: "It became patent to my mind early in the rebellion that the North and South could never live at peace with one another except as one nation, and that without slavery."[12]

Not only was the Negro a visible and easily removable piece of Rebel property; he was also a very helpful fellow,

and Union soldiers who found him so began to feel a vague
sort of sympathy for him. Ormsby Mitchel's men were learning
that contrabands would give full information about movements of Confederate troops, and if they were utterly unable
to estimate numbers correctly—when asked how many Rebels
were in a given detachment they would usually say, "Three
hundred thousand!"—their services nevertheless were invaluable. When Buell sternly ordered Mitchel to keep fugitive
slaves out of his lines, several of Mitchel's officers came to his
tent, laid down their swords, and said they could not obey
the order. This was plain mutiny, but Mitchel ignored it and
wrote his own angry protest at Buell's order direct to Secretary Stanton. An Ohio soldier, musing on the rights and
wrongs of the situation, wrote down his thoughts:

"The white Rebel, who had done his utmost to bring
about the rebellion, is lionized, called a plucky fellow, a
great man, while the Negro, who welcomed us, who is ready
to peril his life to aid us, is kicked, cuffed and driven back
to his master, there to be scourged for his kindness to us
. . . There must be a change in this regard before we shall be
worthy of success."

This soldier saw at a Tennessee crossroads one day a road
sign that read: "Fifteen miles to Liberty." He reflected: "If
liberty were indeed but fifteen miles away, the stars tonight
would see a thousand Negroes dancing on the way thither;
old men with their wives and bundles, young men with their
sweethearts, little barefoot children all singing in their
hearts."[13]

. . . The war itself, in plain words, was going to destroy
slavery; not the fevered arguments of the abolitionists, nor
the stirring of vague humanitarian sentiments among the
northern people, but simply the war, and the fact that men
were going to do whatever they had to do to win it. Lincoln
himself was governed by this as much as was the most heedless soldier in the ranks.

For Lincoln this was an uneasy summer. The military
machine had slowed almost to a stop and there did not seem
to be any easy way to get it started again. He had brought
John Pope east from Mississippi and had created a new army
for him in upper Virginia, an army made up of the baffled

fragments that had tried so clumsily to round up Stonewall Jackson a few weeks earlier. This had led to the immediate resignation of John Charles Frémont, but so far it had had no other good result. A week after Malvern Hill, Lincoln went down to Harrison's Landing to talk to McClellan, who was jaunty and confident and who thought that he could yet take Richmond if he were properly reinforced. (That phantom, nonexistent Rebel army of the Pinkerton reports was still being taken seriously at headquarters.)

McClellan had another thought, which he put on paper for the President's benefit. He believed that the Union armies would refuse to fight if this war became a war against slavery.

In a long memorandum McClellan spelled out his ideas of what war policy ought to be: "Neither confiscation of property, political executions of persons, territorial organization of states or forcible abolition of slavery should be contemplated for a moment." Military power should never be used to interfere with "the relations of servitude"; where contrabands were pressed into army service, their lawful owners should be properly compensated."

It was a bad time for a general to hand that sort of document to Lincoln, who was not contemplating property confiscation, political executions, or territorial organization of rebellious states, but who had reached the conviction that he could not win the war without coming out against slavery.

Lincoln was a mild-mannered prairie politician who, in his own brief time as a soldier, had been told to go to hell by red-necked volunteers and had been ordered by a court-martial to carry a wooden sword for gawky unofficerlike ineffectiveness; but of all the leaders of the North, he more than any other had the hard, flaming spirit of war—the urge to get on with it at any cost and to drive on through to victory by the shortest road. So far he was little more than a name to the men in the ranks, and McClellan was the man they adored above all others; but of the two, it was the President and not the general who understood what was on the enlisted man's mind.

Lincoln had said that if he did anything at all about slavery he would do it solely because he believed that it would help to win the war. Now the machine was stalling, and he had to get it moving again; and he had concluded that to do this he would have to call on the emotional power of the anti-slavery cause. The thoughts that would finally become the Emancipation Proclamation were taking shape in his mind when he visited McClellan; less than a week later, back in Washington, he would voice them to two members of his Cabinet. In the previous autumn he had rebuked Frémont for proclaiming abolition prematurely in Missouri; early this spring he had similarly rebuked General David Hunter for doing the same thing along the Carolina coast; now he was making up his mind to proclaim it himself . . . and the general of his principal army was telling him that the soldiers would not fight if he did.

Lincoln went back to Washington. Not long after, he called Halleck east and made him general-in-chief, in command of all the armies.

On form, the appointment looked good. The biggest gains had been made in the West—Missouri cleared, Kentucky saved, half of Tennessee in hand, armies of invasion poised in northern Mississippi and Alabama, with another army and a strong fleet in New Orleans—and all of this except the New Orleans business had been done by men under Halleck's orders. The fact that a great chance had been missed on the slow crawl from Pittsburg Landing to Corinth was not yet apparent—not in Washington, anyway, although Grant and Ormsby Mitchel had been smoldering over it—and neither was the folly that had dispersed Grant's and Buell's armies and substituted the occupation of territory for a drive to destroy Rebel armies. In July 1862 the performance sheet made Halleck look like a winner, and so Halleck was summoned to Washington to take the top command.

It would take time for him to get oriented. This time would be a free gift to the Confederacy, which was led by men to whom it was dangerous to make gifts. And as a result this would be the summer of the great Confederate counterattack, with final Confederate independence looking more likely for a few brief haunted weeks than at any other time in all the war.

2. *Cheers in the Starlight*

Major General John Pope was an odd figure. Montgomery Blair once remarked venomously that he was a cheat and a liar like all the rest of his tribe, and while a disgruntled Blair was apt to be harsh in his judgments, Pope did have a pronounced ability to irritate people. He came on from the West exuding headstrong energy and loud bluster, and for a few weeks he held the center of the stage; then he evaporated, exiled to the western frontier to police the Indian tribes, leaving hard words and recriminations behind him. He had been given a comparatively minor part to play, and he almost succeeded in losing the war with it.

The War Department brought him east in a well-meant effort to get a little drive into the Virginia campaign, and it turned over to him some fifty thousand troops that were scattered all across northern Virginia and told him to weld them into an army and go down and fight Lee. Pope did his best, but the odds were all against him. It would have taken a good deal of time and some really inspired leadership to make a cohesive army out of the fragments that had been given him, and Pope did not have either.

To begin with, there was McDowell's corps. These men, who had marched vainly back and forth across upper Virginia while the Army of the Potomac was fighting in front of Richmond, still considered themselves McClellan's men. They did not like McDowell—for some incomprehensible reason they considered him disloyal to the Union cause—and they resented the orders that had held them away from McClellan's command.

Next came the mountain army with which Frémont had vainly contemplated making a dash down into eastern Tennessee. About half of this corps was made up of German troops, and there was a noticeable lack of harmony between these and the native American regiments; the latter had not cared at all for Frémont, and when he was replaced by Franz Sigel, who had campaigned with varying success in Missouri, they liked Sigel no better. Their spirits were not improved when they learned that the rest of the army was lumping themselves and the Germans together, indiscriminately, as a Dutch outfit.

Lastly, there was the corps which Nathaniel P. Banks had led up and down the Shenandoah Valley. These men had never had any luck. Stonewall Jackson's men had run rings around them and had seized their supply dumps and trains so consistently that jeering Rebels referred to Banks as their favorite commissary officer. The human material in this corps was good enough—which, for the matter of that, was true of the other two corps as well—but the men had never won anything so far and they seem to have been dismally aware that under Banks they were not likely to win anything in the future.

Pope tried to fit these three groups together into an army. To raise the men's spirits he issued a spread-eagle proclamation, announcing that out West the Union armies were used to looking upon the backs of their enemies; he hoped that eastern armies would get the same habit, and from now on they would forget about defensive positions and lines of retreat and would devote themselves entirely to the attack. He was quoted as saying that his headquarters would be in the saddle, which led the irreverent to remark that he was putting his headquarters where his hindquarters ought to be, and instead of inspiring the men his impassioned words just made them laugh. In addition, Pope published harsh rules to govern the conduct of Rebel civilians within the Union lines, threatening wholesale imprisonments, executions, and confiscations. Nothing much ever actually came of these rules, but they did win for Pope a singular distinction: he became one of the few Federal generals for whom General Lee ever expressed an acute personal distaste. Lee remarked that Pope would have to be "suppressed"—as if he were a lawless disturber of the peace rather than an army commander—and he undertook to see to it personally, a fact that was to have extensive consequences.

Pope was moving down the line of the Orange and Alexandria Railroad, preparing to descend on Richmond from the northwest while McClellan's presence on the James forced the city's defenders to look toward the southeast. But Pope and McClellan were too far apart to co-operate effectively, and they were such completely dissimilar types that it is hard to imagine them working together anyway. McClellan remained in his camp, making no offensive gestures, and Lee presently concluded that it would be safe to send Stonewall Jackson up to look after Pope.

Jackson had not lived up to his reputation in the Seven Days' fighting, but he seemed to be himself again now and he moved with vigor. Some word of his move got to Washington, which began to suspect that the Pope-McClellan operation was not going to work very well, and Halleck, the new generalissimo, went down to Harrison's Landing to talk to McClellan. And now, once more, McClellan tripped over his wild overestimate of Confederate manpower.

It was essential to the present operation that McClellan move to attack Richmond. He could do this, he told Halleck, if he had thirty thousand more men. Halleck told him twenty thousand would be tops and asked if he could make the move with those reinforcements; McClellan said that he would try, although he was obviously dubious about it—for Lee, he assured Halleck, commanded two hundred thousand men.[1]

Halleck quickly reached what would seem to be a logical conclusion. If Lee's army was bigger than Pope's and McClellan's combined—which was what McClellan's estimate said—then it was obvious folly to let him occupy a position between them. There was only one thing to do: fuse these two Union armies into one and have them operate as a unit. To do this without uncovering Washington, it would be necessary to withdraw McClellan from the banks of the James. Early in August the orders went out. McClellan was to get his men north as quickly as possible so that he and Pope could join forces.

Bringing McClellan north was what really untied things. To get all of his men, guns, and equipment from the James to the upper Rappahannock and the Potomac would be a slow process. While it was being done the Army of the Potomac would be entirely out of action and the initiative would be with the Confederates. For some weeks to come they would be the ones who would be calling the signals.

They would be calling them in the West as well as in the

East; indeed, during this summer the entire direction of the war would be in their hands, and the Confederate forces that had been doomed to an almost hopeless defensive in May were being given the chance to stage an all-out offensive in August. For Grant's army was divided and immobilized, and Buell was painfully creeping along a shattered railway line, stitching it together as he went, and the Richmond government got reinforcements over into Mississippi from the region beyond the river, posted these where they could watch Grant's men, and sent Beauregard's old army swinging up through mid-Tennessee toward Kentucky in a hard counterblow that canceled all Federal strategic plans.

It was Beauregard's army no longer. After his retreat from Corinth, Beauregard became ill and took leave of absence. He had never been able to get along with Jefferson Davis anyway, and Davis now replaced him, giving the army to scowling, black-bearded Braxton Bragg, who was always able to get along with Davis but who could hardly ever get along with anybody else.

Bragg was a fantastic character, as singular a mixture of solid competence and bewildering ineptitude as the war produced. He distrusted democracy, the volunteer system, and practically everything except the routine of the old regular army, and just before Shiloh he had complained that most of the Confederate soldiers had never fired a gun or done a day's work in their lives. He was disputatious to a degree, and in the old army it was said that when he could not find anyone else to quarrel with he would quarrel with himself. A ferocious disciplinarian, he shot his own soldiers ruthlessly for violations of military law, and his army may have been the most rigidly controlled of any on either side.

This summer he was at the top of his form. He took his army off toward the east and then went up into Tennessee, smoothly by-passing Buell and heading straight for the Ohio River. In Kentucky, it was believed, the people would rise enthusiastically to welcome him, and he carried wagonloads of muskets to arm the recruits that were expected there. From eastern Tennessee a smaller Confederate army under Kirby Smith drove the Federals out of Cumberland Gap and moved north simultaneously. It would join up with Bragg's men somewhere in Kentucky.

While this was going on—causing Buell to forget about Chattanooga and the railroad and to start backtracking feverishly in an effort to overtake Bragg—Lee in Virginia was devoting himself with deft persistence to the task of suppressing Pope.

Jackson had the first part to play. He struck Pope's advance at Cedar Mountain a few days after McClellan had received his orders to evacuate Harrison's Landing and head for the transports at Hampton Roads, and opened a furious attack. Pope's advance was composed of Banks's corps, and these men put up an unexpectedly stout fight, knocking Jackson's men back on their heels and for an hour or so giving them a good deal more than they could handle. But Jackson had a huge advantage in numbers, and by dusk he had driven Banks's corps off in rout with heavy loss. Pope's main body came up next day, and Jackson drew off to wait for Lee and the rest of the Army of Northern Virginia.

He did not have long to wait, for McClellan's departure freed Lee of concern for the James River area. Pope presently found himself up against the first team, and he was woefully outclassed. Lee quickly maneuvered him out of the triangle between the Rapidan and Rappahannock rivers and made him draw back; then, anxious to finish him off before McClellan's men could come up and give Pope the advantage of numbers, Lee divided his army and sent Jackson off in a long sweep around Pope's right flank, to strike at his supply base at Manassas Junction.

Jackson reached this base and destroyed it after a spectacular two-day march around and through the Bull Run Mountains. Utterly confused, Pope turned to strike him, fumbled in the attempt, and at last came upon him in a secure position overlooking the old Bull Run battlefield. And there, for two days at the end of August, Pope's men fought a second battle of Bull Run—a bigger, harder, bloodier battle than the first, in which steady slugging replaced the stumbling retreats and panics of the first engagement, and in which General John Pope, from first to last, never quite knew what was going on.

Lee reunited his divided army on the field of battle, while Pope supposed that only Jackson's corps was present. Mistaking a rearrangement of the Confederate lines for the beginning of a withdrawal, Pope exultantly telegraphed Washington that the Rebels were in retreat and that he would pursue them with horse, foot, and guns. Then, just as what Pope imagined to be his pursuit was getting under way, Lee struck him hard in the flank with James Longstreet's thirty thousand veterans, and Pope's army was broken and driven north across Bull Run in a state of confusion little better than the one that had been seen at the end of the first battle a year earlier. A good part of McClellan's army had joined Pope just before the battle, but these men fared no better than Pope's own soldiers; and as September began, the whole disorganized lot was withdrawing sullenly into the fortifications around Washington, and almost all of Virginia was back in Confederate hands.[2]

And here was a cruel end for all of the high hopes which the spring had created—Virginia lost, most of Tennessee lost, Bragg's victorious army heading for the Ohio River and reclaiming Kentucky as it went, brushing aside the green Federal troops which midwestern governors were hastily sending down into that state, while Buell came plodding north in ineffective pursuit. Lee's hard-fought soldiers went splashing across the Potomac fords, their bands playing "Maryland, My Maryland," while Bragg openly made plans to inaugurate a Confederate governor in Kentucky's capital city of Frankfort. And in Washington it seemed a question whether the demoralized men who had been whipped at Bull Run could possibly be pulled together into an effective army in time to accomplish anything whatever.

All of this came just as Abraham Lincoln was preparing to issue a proclamation of emancipation for Negro slaves.

He had made up his mind this summer. The base of the war would have to be broadened and an immeasurable new force would have to be injected into it. It would become now a social revolution, and there was no way to foretell the final consequences. At the very beginning Lincoln had accepted secession as a variety of revolution and had unhesitatingly used revolutionary measures to meet it, but he had clung tenaciously to the idea that the one ruling war aim was to restore the Union, and he had steered carefully away from steps that would destroy the whole social fabric of the South.

But it could not be done that way. The necessities of war were acting on him just as they acted upon the private soldier. To a correspondent, this summer, he was writing that he had never had a wish to touch the foundations of southern society or the rights of any southern man; yet there was a necessity on him to send armies into the South, and "it may as well be understood, once for all, that I shall not surrender this game leaving any available card unplayed." To another correspondent he was writing that there was no sense to try "rounding the rough angles of the war"; the only remedy was to remove the cause for the war. To do this he would do everything that lay ready for his hand to do: "Would you drop the war where it is, or would you prosecute it in the future with elder-stalk squirts charged with rose water?"³

He would not use elder-stalk squirts. There was no way now to avoid the fundamental and astounding result. Come what might, Lincoln would free the slaves, as far as the stroke of a pen on a sheet of paper could accomplish that.

Yet he could not do it now. Secretary Seward, who had talked of a higher law and an irrepressible conflict long before the war began, was warning him: Issue your proclamation at this moment, when our armies have been beaten and we are in retreat all along the line, and it will look like nothing more than a cry for help—an appeal to the Negro slaves to rise and come to our rescue. You cannot issue it until you have somehow, somewhere, won a military victory. . . . Lincoln reflected on that matter and put his draft of the Emancipation Proclamation away in a cubbyhole in his desk. This war could not be turned into a revolutionary war for freedom while it was in the process of being lost. Everything had to wait for victory.

A victory was needed for more reasons than one. Overseas, the British Government seemed to be on the verge of recognizing the Confederacy as an independent nation—an act that would almost certainly bring effects as far-reaching and decisive as French recognition of the American colonies had brought in 1778. Prime Minister, Foreign Minister, and Cabi-

net seemed at last ready to take the step. They would wait
just a little while to see what came of Lee's invasion of the
North. Then, if all went well . . .

Then the wild impossible dream would come true, America
would become two nations, and the outworn past with its
beauty and its charm, its waste and its cruelty and its crippling limitations, would reach down into the future. Here
was the crisis of the war, the great Confederate high-water
mark. Never afterward was a final southern victory quite as
close as it was in September 1862. The two halves of the war
met here—the early formative half, when both the war and
the change that would come from the war might still be
limited and controlled, and the terrible latter half, which
would grind on to its end without limits and without controls.

By one of the singular ironies in American history, the man
who was standing precisely at this point of fusion—the man
through whom, almost in spite of himself, the crisis would be
resolved—was that cautious weigher of risks and gains,
General McClellan.

McClellan had been quietly but effectively shelved. When
his army came north it was fed down to Pope by bits and
pieces, until by the final day of the Bull Run fight all of it
was gone and McClellan was left isolated in Alexandria,
across the river from Washington, a general without an army.
He had not formally been removed from command, but his
command had been most deftly slipped out from under him.
The thing had been done deliberately. Secretary Stanton
disliked and distrusted him, such men as Treasury Secretary
Salmon P. Chase considered him no better than an outright
traitor, and the Republican party leadership was almost
mutinous against Lincoln for having supported him so long;
and, anyway, it appeared that victory just was not in the
man. He had been set aside, and the war would go on without him.

But the trouble was that at this particular moment Mc-
Clellan was indispensable.

He had warned Lincoln that Union soldiers would not fight
in an avowed war against slavery, and there would be time
enough later on to find out whether that was so; but what
mattered most right now was that this could never be turned

into a war against slavery or anything else unless the Army
of the Potomac very speedily won a victory over Robert E.
Lee, and there was not a remote chance that it could do that
now without General McClellan. Its elements had been
thrown in with Pope's and had been beaten. Pope was wholly
discredited, and the dispirited troops who were retreating
into the Washington lines were not, at the moment, an
army at all in any real sense of the word. They never had
been an army, as the word is properly understood; they were
young men who had heard bugles and drums and had seen
flags waving and had felt something outside of themselves
come in and move them; and now they were tired, dirty, unhappy, conscious that they had been beaten because they
had been poorly led, the flame gone out of them. They were
ready to quit and they could not conceivably be turned into
a useful army again, in time to do any good, by anyone but
the one man who had trained them, the man in whom they
had unwavering confidence, to whom they had given a
mystic and inexplicable devotion. And that man, of course,
was McClellan.

Neither the War Department nor the Cabinet could see
this, but Lincoln could, and he acted on what he saw—risking that which he dared not lose in order to win that which
he had to have. He put McClellan back in command and in
effect told him to pull the army together and go out and
whip the Army of Northern Virginia.

. . . It became a legend, and a true thing to be remembered
in the long years of peace, how McClellan this one time rose
to a great challenge and met it fully. He was a small man,
and he missed many chances, and he probably was afraid
of something; not of death—there is much testimony about
his courage under fire, and he had picked up the hard West
Point training—but of life and the things that can go wrong
in it; but for **one** evening of his life he was great, and the
Confederate **tide beg**an to ebb as the sun went down over
the Virginia **hills to** the sound of men who cheered as if they
had touched the shores of dream-come-true. McClellan rode
out from Alexandria on his great black war horse, a jaunty
little man with a yellow sash around his waist, every pose

and gesture perfect. He cantered down the dusty roads and he met the heads of the retreating columns, and he cried words of encouragement and swung his little cap, and he gave the beaten men what no other man alive could have given them—enthusiasm, hope, confidence, an exultant and unreasoning feeling that the time of troubles was over and that everything would be all right now. And it went into the legend—truthfully, for many men have testified to it—that down mile after mile of Virginia roads the stumbling columns came alive, and threw caps and knapsacks into the air, and yelled until they could yell no more, and went on doing it until the sun went down; and after dark, exhausted men who lay in the dust sprang to their feet and cried aloud because they saw this dapper little rider outlined against the purple starlight.[4]

And this, in a way, was the turning point of the war. It was odd that it should happen this way, because this war was one of the great hinges of history, a closing and an opening of mighty doors, and McClellan believed that it was something very different—a bit of a disagreement among gentlemen, which would be settled presently in the way of gentlemen so that everyone could go back to what they had had before the disagreement began; and no one would go back to anything after this. McClellan rode down the roads to the sound of a mighty cheering and a great crying, and because he did the war would go on and on to its destined end, with McClellan himself fading out of it in an extended anticlimax and with most of the men who called out to him dying or drifting off into the limbo of old soldiers who have had it.

No one could ever quite explain it. The men who threw their caps and yelled themselves hoarse and of their own will became a solid army again could never quite find the words for it, and the best McClellan himself could say finally was: "We are wedded and should not be separated"—which, after all, perhaps was the obscure essence of it. But whatever it was that really happened, it would finally give Abraham Lincoln what he was looking for. And American history would be different forever after.

3. *High-Water Mark*

The tension became almost unendurable, yet it lasted just a little more than a fortnight. Then it snapped, in a great explosion of fire and sound and violence, and the war came to a climax in its worst single day of death.

The Army of Northern Virginia had crossed the Potomac, and no one knew just where it was. No one could be sure, either, where Bragg's western army had gone. The rumor suddenly reached Washington that Bragg's men, having given Buell the slip, were coming east to join Lee, over whatever impossible mountain route across eastern Tennessee and Kentucky, and Lincoln was anxiously wiring the western commanders, asking them: "What degree of certainty have you that Bragg with his command is not now in the valley of the Shenandoah, Virginia?"[1]

Buell scoffed at the notion, which in point of fact was rather fantastic. Yet Buell was not the man to give reassurance. He had been outmaneuvered; Bragg had got away from him, and Buell was now in the act of chasing him up to the Ohio. The administration was impatient with him and planned to remove him; did actually send orders to George Thomas to take Buell's place and was dumfounded when Thomas calmly replied that it would not be fair to remove Buell right now and that he would greatly prefer not to take the offered promotion. Buell stayed on, in uncertain tenure, while Halleck told a friend that the administration was going to guillotine all losing generals; the hard policy of the French revolutionists—win or be dropped—was going to prevail from now on. It might be unjust, Halleck admitted, but it was inevitable; the cause had to have victories.[2]

It would have to have three victories, for the Confederacy was striking in three places at once. The rough timing that co-ordinated Bragg's offensive with Lee's had been extended to Mississippi. There a tough little Confederate army had been put together, led by Earl Van Dorn, a handsome, curly-haired soldier who had been a friend of Sherman at West Point; a dashing, romantic chap who had a reputation as a ladies' man and who would one day die of it, dodging any number of Yankee bullets on the battlefield to take one from an angry husband in his own office. . . . Van Dorn had Pap Price with him and some stout fighters from beyond the Mississippi, and he was sliding forward now to attack Grant, or possibly to slip through Grant's lines and join Bragg in Kentucky—a possibility which, Halleck was warning Grant, "would be most disastrous."[3]

But the victory that was needed most and first would have to be won in the East; the West was where the North finally would have to win the war, but the East was always the place where the North could lose it, and the danger was never greater than in September of 1862.

McClellan hastily reorganized the Army of the Potomac, got most of it north of the river, and took it cautiously north and west through Maryland, with cavalry patrols sending blind groping tentacles out in front reaching for Lee's army.

If McClellan's men had been in the lowest of spirits after the second battle of Bull Run, they had high morale now. Getting up into western Maryland was like getting back home. Civilian sentiment here ran strongly for the Union. As the army marched through towns and villages, people lined the streets to wave flags and to cheer, offering food and drink to any men who could break ranks and help themselves. The soldiers were no longer moving in a vacuum; they were touching the solid core of national sentiment once more, and they did not have to draw all of their inspiration from the little general who led them. They exulted in the welcome they were getting, told one another that they were in God's country once more, and whenever they set eyes on McClellan they cheered until their voices broke, crowding close around him, trying to touch at least the horse he rode, assuring the man that they would do whatever he asked them to do.[4]

McClellan was as cautious as ever. Lee's army lay on the western side of South Mountain, a high ridge that takes off from the Potomac as a continuation of the Blue Ridge and runs in a long slant for sixty-five miles to the north and east. The passes were held by Lee's cavalry, and from the loyal people beyond the mountain came all sorts of unreliable rumors about Lee's strength and movements. Halleck kept sending messages of warning: If McClellan slid too far to the right Lee was apt to come past his left and seize Washington, if he held to the left Lee might go around his right, too rapid an advance would be dangerous, to advance too slowly would permit Lee to invade Pennsylvania . . . and so on and so on, every warning underscoring the hesitancy that McClellan carried with him in any case, the unspoken threat of the guillotine always felt.

What McClellan would finally have done if he had been left to himself is beyond imagination; what actually happened was a dazzling stroke of pure, uncovenanted good luck that cleared up the fog of doubt and put the game squarely in his hands. To this day no one has known quite how it happened, and it is probable that no one will ever know, but some Confederate officer lost a copy of Lee's orders outlining all of his plans and movements, and this copy was speedily brought to Union headquarters, authenticated, and laid before McClellan.

Now McClellan knew where Lee was, what he was trying to do, and exactly where he proposed to go.

There was a Federal garrison of ten thousand men in Harpers Ferry, and Lee did not wish to leave this garrison lying across his line of communications. He knew that McClellan's army had been badly disorganized at Bull Run and that it would take a little time to pull it back into shape, and McClellan was not in the least likely to move fast anyway. It seemed to Lee that it would be safe to delay the invasion while he gobbled up the Harpers Ferry people, and this he undertook to do, dividing his army into four parts in order to do it.

With Longstreet and Longstreet's command, Lee himself moved up to Hagerstown, Maryland, not far from the Pennsylvania border—there was some chance that Pennsylvania militia, stirred by the rising threat to the homeland, might come down to make trouble, and it was well to hold Hagerstown in some strength. One division of troops under D. H. Hill was placed at Boonsboro Gap, the principal pass through South Mountain, where the main road from Washington came west. All the rest of the army was sent down to surround and capture Harpers Ferry, part of the men swinging back into Virginia to come on the place from the south and west, the remainder going down through Maryland in the lee of South Mountain, Stonewall Jackson in command of the lot.

The pieces of the Army of Northern Virginia, accordingly, were very badly separated. McClellan was at Frederick, Maryland, just a short march from Boonsboro Gap. He was closer to the head and the tail of Lee's army than the head and tail were to each other—and with Lee's orders on his desk McClellan knew all of this, and Lee did not know that he knew it. The utter destruction of Lee's army was a definite possibility.

One thing McClellan did not know, and because he did not know it his movements would have a halting, trance-like quality. He did not know that Lee's army was woefully, tragically understrength.

The army had fought hard and it had marched hard, and it was very close to sheer exhaustion. Thousands upon thousands of men had left the ranks, too worn down to go any farther. (The fact that many of these men had no shoes and that Maryland had hard roads on which a barefooted man could not march had a good deal to do with this.) Other thousands had innocently left the army when it crossed the Potomac, on the simple ground that they had enlisted to defend the South from invasion, not to invade the North; the idea that the homeland could be aggressively defended on northern soil was just a little too intricate for them. All in all, it is probable that Lee lost between ten and twenty thousand men from these causes in the first two weeks of September. Of enlisted infantrymen, present for duty equipped, Lee may have had fewer than forty thousand all told. His army was smaller than it was at any other time in the war until the final agonizing retreat to Appomattox.

Yet McClellan lived by the old faith. He still thought that he was outnumbered.

He was not taking as many men into Maryland as he had had on the peninsula. In the middle of September the Army of the Potomac numbered just over eighty-seven thousand, and by no means were all of these combat soldiers; nearly one fifth of the army, at this stage of the war, was occupied on various noncombatant assignments and could not be put on the firing line in battle. McClellan, of course, knew this—he always was acutely aware of his own army's weaknesses—and he could not, for the very life of him, see that the other army was much worse off than his own. The shadowy, unreal host which outnumbered him from the beginning was still opposite him. Luck might have given him the greatest opening any Union general ever had, but when he set about exploiting it he would be very, very careful.[5]

His first moves were simple and direct.

He sent one corps to break through the mountain at Crampton's Gap, five or six miles to the south of the main pass near Boonsboro; if it moved fast, this corps ought to be able to rescue the Harpers Ferry garrison before Jackson swallowed it. With the rest of the army McClellan moved straight for Boonsboro Gap, planning to get to the far side of the mountain and destroy the separate pieces of Lee's army before they could reunite.

The start was made promptly enough, and in each of the passes the Confederates were so greatly outnumbered that they had no chance to fight more than a delaying action. They hung on stoutly, however, aided considerably by the Pinkerton delusion as to numbers; D. H. Hill had five or six thousand soldiers to defend Boonsboro Gap, and the Federal command thought that he had thirty thousand, which meant that the attack could not be driven home until most of the army had come up. In the end, Hill hung on all through September 14, retreating only after night had come. Crampton's Gap was lost sooner, but McClellan's corps commander there, General William B. Franklin, did not think it safe to march boldly for Harpers Ferry until the next morning. When morning came it took time to get his troops moving, and before he could accomplish anything Harpers Ferry had been surrendered and the Confederacy had picked up ten thousand Yankee prisoners, vast quantities of small arms and military stores, and a useful supply of artillery. Jackson rode through the town after the surrender, a remarkably uninspiring-looking man in dusty uniform with an old forage cap pulled down over his eyes—he could no more look like a dashing soldier than could U. S. Grant. One of the surrendered Union soldiers studied him, remarked that he didn't look like much, and then added bitterly: "But if we had him we wouldn't be in the fix we're in."[8]

September 15 saw McClellan through the South Mountain gaps, and Lee was trying desperately to pull his army together before the Yankees could destroy it piecemeal. Lee thought at first that he would have to get everybody back into Virginia as quickly as possible, but when he learned about the capture of Harpers Ferry he changed his mind. He would reassemble at Sharpsburg, a little country town a dozen miles south of Hagerstown, near the Potomac, behind the meandering valley of Antietam Creek; if McClellan wanted to fight they would fight there, and afterward it might be possible to go on with the invasion of the North. In any case, the fight would enable the Confederacy to get the military loot south from Harpers Ferry.

So what there was of Lee's army was ordered to take its place on the rolling hills west of Antietam Creek, and there the advance guard of the Army of the Potomac found it on the evening of September 15.

There, too, the Army of the Potomac faced it all day of September 16—the day on which it was proved afresh that Lee could put up a consummate bluff and that McClellan could never in the world call the bluff. For half of the undersized Confederate army had not yet come up from Harpers Ferry, and if McClellan had simply ordered an advance all along the line the Confederates who were present must, beyond all question, have been driven into the river, Lee in person with them: But McClellan made no advance that day. He needed the time to think things over, to examine Lee's lines at long range, to get his guns into position, to talk with his subordinates, to weigh the risks which he would not take. He presented Lee with twenty-four hours, which was not five minutes more than the absolute minimum Lee had to have for survival, and when at last the Union attack was made—at misty dawn on September 17—the Confederates had just enough men on hand or coming up to make a fight of it.

There never was another day like Antietam. It was sheer concentrated violence, unleavened by generalship. It had all of the insane fury of the Shiloh fight, with this difference: at Shiloh the troops were green and many of them ran away at the first shock, while those who remained fought blindly, by instinct. At Antietam the men were veterans and they knew what they were about. Few men cut and ran until they had been fought out, their formations blown apart by merciless gunfire; and those who did not run at all fought with battle-trained skill, so that the dawn-to-dusk fight above Antietam Creek finally went into the records as the most murderous single day of the entire war.

It began with a Federal attack on the Confederate left, under Stonewall Jackson, posted in a cornfield and two wood-lots in front of a whitewashed Dunker church. Joe Hooker, the handsome, profane, hard-drinking and hard-fighting commander of McClellan's right wing, smashed the cornfield and its occupants with the concentrated fire of three dozen field-pieces and then sent his army corps swinging straight up toward the Dunker church, which marked the high ground that anchored this end of the Confederate line. Some of the Confederate units here were mangled almost beyond repair, but just as Hooker's men neared the little church Jackson brought up reinforcements—John B. Hood's Texas brigade and three tough little brigades from D. H. Hill's division—and the Federals were driven back to their starting point, a good fourth of their number shot down, half of the remainder driven off in disorganized flight.

All of this took about an hour, or perhaps a little longer, and accomplished nothing at all except the creation once more of an appalling list of casualties. Now McClellan sent in another army corps, the men who had followed Banks on his luckless adventurings in the Shenandoah Valley and who had fought so stoutly at Cedar Mountain. (Banks was no longer with them; he had been replaced by an old regular, Joseph K. F. Mansfield, a red-faced soldier who wore a pleasing fringe of white hair and whiskers.) The cornfield and part of the woods were regained and then largely lost again; Mansfield was killed, Hooker was wounded, two army corps had been used up, another hour had passed, and the casualty list was substantially longer.

Now McClellan sent in a third corps, the largest in the

army, eighteen thousand men or thereabouts under old Edwin Sumner, who had been an army officer since 1819, possessed a great roaring voice that could carry the length of an active battle line, and was known by his troops as the Bull of the Woods, or just Old Bull. He was a simple, straightforward sort of war horse; forty years in the regular army had harrowed out all of his complexities, leaving nothing but a devotion to duty and an everlasting respect for the military hierarchy and its system of discipline. He would never get used to the volunteer army; would stare, shake his head, and swear in utter disbelief when he saw some stripling in his early twenties wearing a major's shoulder straps—in the prewar army, field officers were invariably gray-haired.

This morning Sumner was to take his three divisions and crush the Rebel left. He rode with the leading division, led by John Sedgwick, and forgot about the other two, which as a result came into action too late. Sedgwick and Sumner rode across the ground that had been so terribly fought over, got into the farthest fringe of woods, and seemed to have the Dunker church plateau firmly in their possession— and then were hit in the flank and rear by a fresh Confederate division that had just finished the long hike up from Harpers Ferry and whose attack now took them completely by surprise. Sedgwick was wounded, more than a third of his men were shot, the rest were driven off in complete disorder, and the triumphant Confederates swept back across the cornfield and the scarred little woodlots until the long line of Federal guns—fifty or more of them, drawn up in a solid rank to support McClellan's right—blasted them, stopped their advance, and made them beat a sullen retreat.

With one division wrecked, Sumner went back to put the rest of his corps into action. He sent his men up out of the creek valley some distance south of the cornfield and the Dunker church, and they ran into a Confederate battle line posted in a sunken lane that zigzagged along the reverse slope of a long ridge. As the fighting in the Dunker church area burned itself out, this sunken road became a new cockpit. The Confederates here were as secure as the Federals had been in that other sunken lane at Shiloh, and Federals who tried vainly to drive them out wrote afterward that they met here the heaviest fire they saw in all the war.

Sumner's two remaining divisions came in in disjointed fashion, one at a time. (Thousands of men were shot that day because McClellan could not, from first to last, put on one co-ordinated offensive.) The first one to attack the sunken road was led by William French, a stout, choleric man who was a doughty head-down fighter but nothing more. His battle line got to the crest of the ridge, drove off the Confederate skirmishers who held the place, paused briefly for breath, and then went rolling on to attack the sunken road; and the Rebels hunkered down behind their natural breastwork, let them come in close, and then broke them and drove them back with tremendous rolling volleys of musketry. French's men re-formed, tried it again, broke again, tried once more, and then lay on the ground and kept up such fire as they could while they waited for the other division to come up.

This one was commanded by a stout fighter, Israel B. Richardson, a Mexican War veteran who seems to have patterned himself after old Zachary Taylor, cultivating a rough-and-ready air and disdaining to wear anything resembling a proper uniform. He led his men in person, stalking along on foot with a naked sword in his hand, using the point of it to drive skulkers out from behind haystacks and outhouses, blaspheming them in a voice that rose above the din of battle. A house was on fire at one end of the ridge, and the smoke from its burning mingled with the heavy battle smoke, and the men climbed the ridge in a choking fog. Richardson finally got an Irish brigade and some New Englanders up on high ground where they could enfilade part of the sunken road, some of the Confederates broke and ran for it, and at last the whole line caved in. The sunken lane was taken—it was so full of corpses that for the rest of the war veterans referred to it simply as "Bloody Lane"—and the whole center of Lee's line was a frazzled thread, so worn that Longstreet and his staff were helping exhausted gunners work a battery, while D. H. Hill took up a musket and rallied a handful of stragglers for an abortive counterattack.

Lee's army could have been broken then and there, but Richardson went down with a mortal wound—this was a bad day for general officers—and he was the only driver on this part of the field. McClellan had two spare army corps ready and waiting, but he used one to hold the right of his line (he feared that Lee would hit him with a counterattack) and he held the other one in reserve, and the assault died out after Bloody Lane had been won.

By now it was noon, and after a time the left of McClellan's line took up the battle. General Burnside was in command here, with four divisions, and he put them into action hesitantly, one at a time, taking long hours to win the crossings of Antietam Creek and get to the high ground overlooking Sharpsburg. By midafternoon, however, despite all the delays, the high ground was taken, and once more utter defeat for Lee's army was in immediate prospect. But, once more, Confederate reinforcements came up just in time— A. P. Hill's division, brought up from Harpers Ferry in a man-killing forced march that left half of the men gasping by the roadside, too dead-beat to march another step, but that brought the other half in on Burnside's flank just in time to stave off defeat. Burnside reacted nervously to the flank attack, pulled his men back, sent word to McClellan that he thought he might possibly hold on if he were reinforced . . . and at last the sun went down and the battle ended, smoke heavy in the air, the twilight quivering with the anguished cries of thousands of wounded men.

Lee's men had taken a dreadful pounding and they had astounding losses—more than ten thousand men between dawn and dusk, a good fourth of all the men he had on the field—but they had not quite been driven out of Sharpsburg and the high ground. McClellan had lost even more heavily, with more than two thousand men killed in action and near-ly ten thousand wounded, of whom upward of a thousand would die; but he had men to spare. Two corps had hardly been engaged at all, and reinforcements were coming up. By every dictate of military logic, Lee would have to cross the Potomac and get back to Virginia as soon as darkness came; if he stayed where he was one more day, the Army of the Potomac could pulverize him.'

But Lee did not retreat. He pulled his frayed lines together, brought up stragglers, and next morning, with fewer than thirty thousand infantrymen in his command, he calmly waited for McClellan to renew the fighting. (Of all the daring gamblers who ever wore an American military uniform, Lee unquestionably was the coolest.) His bluff worked. McClellan pondered, waited for reinforcements, laid plans for an all-out offensive for tomorrow, or day after tomorrow, or some other time, and let the entire day of September 18 slip by, two exhausted armies facing each other under a blistering sun, the heavy stench of death fouling the air, nervous sputters of picket-line firing rippling from end to end of the lines now and then, nothing of any consequence happening.

That night Lee ordered a retreat. Even McClellan was likely to attack if he was given time enough, and the Army of Northern Virginia just could not afford a finish fight here, with the river at its back. These twenty-four hours of silent defiance had restored Confederate morale, and as the tired Confederates crossed the river and tramped back into Virginia they felt that they had somehow won a victory. McClellan let them go unmolested. His men, like Lee's, felt proud of what they had done, but they were not disposed to claim a sweeping triumph. The most they were prepared to say was voiced by one of McClellan's division commanders, the tough and grizzled George Gordon Meade: "We hurt them a little more than they hurt us."

But the soldiers could not see all of it. Incomplete and imperfect as it had been, Antietam was a decisive Union victory. It had broken the great southern counteroffensive, it had given Lincoln the opening he needed, and it would change the character of the entire war, turning it openly and irrevocably into a war against slavery. As the long gray columns crossed the river and started plodding down the Virginia roads, the South's high tide had begun to ebb.

7.

I See No End

1. *The Best There Was in the Ranch*

PRESIDENT LINCOLN had the Cabinet in, and he made a ceremony of the business. Here was the paper, ready to be signed, dignitaries looking as impressive as might be; fifty miles up the Potomac there was the stricken field of Antietam, the autumn air tainted with death, every house and barn for miles around serving as a hospital, a bruised army in bivouac nearby. What was being done at the White House had been ratified in advance by what had been done around the Dunker church and in the cornfields and woods, along the sunken road and by the crossings of the sluggish little creek. Twenty-five thousand Americans, North and South, had been shot in order that Lincoln might sign the Emancipation Proclamation.

Looked at objectively, this proclamation was nothing much. It was not, technically, a proclamation at all but an official warning that if the rebellion did not cease by the end of 1862 a proclamation would be issued. It declared slavery extinct in precisely the areas where the Federal government at the moment lacked all power to enforce its decrees—in the states that were in rebellion; it let slavery live on in states like Maryland and Kentucky, which had remained in the Union and in which the government's power was unquestioned. It was of dubious legality, and in any case it hardly said more than an act of Congress which had been passed two months earlier—the Confiscation Act, which granted freedom to the slaves of all persons thereafter found guilty of treason and of all persons who aided or supported the rebellion. If the President was going to declare himself on slavery, this preliminary proclamation was just about the least he could say.

Yet it closed a great door in the face of the southern Confederacy. It locked the Confederacy in with the anachronism that was the Confederacy's dreadful, fatal burden. Europe could not intervene now; the Civil War had been turned into something that no British statesman could touch. The South would be limited to its own resources, which were visibly inadequate. It could never get the help it needed from outside. Almost indiscernibly, but with grim finality, it had been isolated.

Beyond this, the stakes of the war had suddenly become incalculable. If the war should be won, the nation would for all time be wedded to the idea that all of its people must (as the proclamation said) be forever free. Free society and racism were defined as incompatibles. The race problem would have to be faced now, because by no imaginable subterfuge could it be dodged, and in time—in one generation, or in two, or in ten—it would have to be solved. People were committed to it now, the compact signed in the blood and fire of a war that went closer to the heart and the bone than any other experience in national history. An ideal that might be humanly unattainable had been riveted in so that it could never, in all the years to come, be abandoned.

The immediate effects of the proclamation were curious. First of them was the fact that it quietly cut the ground out from under the feet of General McClellan.

Not long after the document was signed and issued, McClellan met with a few officers in his headquarters tent. He wanted advice: what should he do about the proclamation? Democratic politicians and high army officers, he said, had been urging him to come out in open opposition to it. Should he do so, or should he keep silent? The proclamation seemed to him to be unwise and unsound, although he suspected that if he denounced it publicly some people might look upon his act as a species of military usurpation; still, he had been assured that the Army of the Potomac was so loyal to him that it would, to a man, enforce any decision he might make regarding war policy. What did these friends think he ought to do?

The friends spoke up promptly and sensibly. McClellan had been listening to dangerous nonsense, he must on no account let himself be made leader of the opposition, the people who were egging him on were his worst enemies; and anyone who supposed that this army would support open defiance of civil authority was imagining a vain thing, and skirting the edge of treason as well. . . . With all of this McClellan at length agreed. He concluded at last to issue a short address to his troops, reminding them that, however they might feel as citizens, they were bound as soldiers to accept and obey the decrees of the government.[1]

His address neither disturbed nor excited anyone very much; and anyway, McClellan's position by now was nearly hopeless. The war was calling for hard men, and he had no hardness. He could not, under any imaginable circumstances, move out to hound an enemy into the last ditch with no thought for anything but the knockout punch. He was not hounding anyone after Antietam. Through the rest of September and all of October he was waiting north of the Potomac, reorganizing and refitting, giving Lee the chance to do the same. (The Confederate army that had hardly numbered thirty thousand men when it retreated across the Potomac would contain seventy-five thousand men when next it went into battle; Lee used the time McClellan gave him to excellent advantage.) And the patience of President Lincoln was being pulled out past the breaking point.

With the Emancipation Proclamation, Lincoln had changed the war, for himself as well as for everyone else. The war now had been pushed past settlement; the unconditional surrender, the penitent submission to national authority, which the government would always insist on, had become something that Confederate leaders would not even consider. Lincoln might continue to try to rally all parties and all factions to his support; increasingly, now, he would have to rely on the bitter-enders, the radicals, the men who tried furiously to make the southern revolution recoil on itself and destroy everything that had bred it. . . . It was not a good time for a Federal general to seem hesitant or lukewarm.

Senator John Sherman of Ohio was writing this fall to his brother, General William Tecumseh Sherman, remarking that old-line regular army officers seemed to fight more from a sense of duty than from "an earnest conviction that the rebellion must be put down with energy." This would never do, and perhaps the only salvation was for "the people to resort to such desperate means as the French and English did in their own revolutions"; ultimately, the nation perhaps could do worse than "entrust its armies to a fanatic like John Brown."[2]

Halleck had cited the parallel of the French Revolution, and now John Sherman was doing it; and when safe, cautious men like these drew that comparison, something was afoot. General Sherman was replying gloomily and cryptically that "the northern people will have to unlearn all their experience of the past thirty years and be born again before they will see the truth." Northern armies, said the general, moved into the South as a ship moves into the sea—the vessel plowed a furrow but the wave immediately closed in behind and no permanent mark had been made; "I see no end, or even the beginning of the end."[3]

No end; but a turning of the tide, in the West as well as in the East. All along the line the Confederate armies had been advancing; now, in weeks, every advance was checked and the great Confederate counterstroke had failed everywhere.

In Kentucky it seemed for a time that everything was being lost. Numbers of untrained Union regiments were hurried down to delay the Confederate advance until Buell could get there, and the oncoming Confederates had rolled over these with disdainful ease, taking prisoners and guns and driving the survivors in headlong retreat; but Bragg unaccountably missed his major opportunities, and by October his advance had changed from a menacing drive into a series of rather aimless maneuverings across north-central Kentucky. The Kentuckians had not risen in universal greeting, as had been expected. They had been cordial enough, but few recruits had come forward, and the wagonloads of muskets and equipment brought north for their benefit remained largely unopened. And while Bragg moved his men this way and that, following no discernible rational purpose, Buell finally got his army around in front and made ready to attack the invader.

Buell's army had had its troubles. It had made a long retreat from the Tennessee-Alabama sector, and the men in the ranks had seen no sense in any of it; they could see only that they were giving up much that they had gained earlier, they were striking no blows at the Confederacy, and the farther they marched the worse their morale became. In addition, Buell had lost one of his most trusted subordinates, the three-hundred-pound ex-naval officer, William Nelson, who had done so much a year earlier to help keep Kentucky in the Union.

Buell lost him in the simplest and most irreversible way imaginable. General Nelson was murdered: shot to death in a Louisville hotel lobby, before a large number of witnesses, by one of his own subordinates, a brigadier with the pleasing but improbable name (for a Union general) of Jefferson Davis. The loss of General Nelson was bad enough. What made it much worse, as far as Buell was concerned, was that he could never get Davis punished for it. The whole business was a startling example of the amount of leverage that a determined hard-war politician could exercise, and the utter helplessness that could affect an army commander whose politics were suspect.

Nelson had been feuding with Governor Oliver P. Morton of Indiana, a diligent Republican and one of the party leaders whose support Lincoln was not on any account going to forfeit. Davis (whose quarrel with Nelson was relatively unimportant—one man was overbearing and the other was insubordinate, and both were hot-tempered) was one of Morton's pets. Buell, who was outraged and was demanding justice, had just had to beat a somewhat inglorious retreat all across Tennessee; furthermore, he had had sharp arguments with Tennessee's Union war governor, a bitter-end anti-Confederate named Andrew Johnson, who considered him unsound and probably disloyal and who had a voice that would be heard in Washington. Because of all of this, nothing ever happened to Davis. He was not even spoken to harshly; instead, he was soon restored to duty and served throughout the war, a slim, dark-bearded man with haunted eyes, looked upon by subordinates with a certain amount of awe.⁴

Buell's luck was not in, this fall, and it was at its worst when he tried to find a replacement for Nelson. He picked Charles C. Gilbert, a regular army captain of the crisp, take-his-name-sergeant variety, who in some vaguely irregular way had recently become a general. Buell and Gilbert believed that he was a major general, the War Department held that he was properly only a brigadier, and the United States Senate finally decided that he was no general at all, refusing to confirm his nomination and letting him slip back to his captaincy. But in his brief career as general Gilbert commanded a third of Buell's army, and he offered a perfect illustration of the complete inability of a certain type of regular army officer to understand or to lead volunteer troops.

The army had been pushing along hard for days and the men were dead on their feet. Near midnight one exhausted column dropped by the roadside for a short breather when Gilbert and his staff went trotting by. Gilbert saw the sleeping men and was offended that nobody bothered to call them to attention and offer a salute so he collared the first officer he saw—a sleepy captain of infantry—and angrily demanded:

"What regiment is this?"

"Tenth Indiana."

"Damn pretty regiment. Why in hell don't you get up and salute me when I pass?"

"Who in the hell are you?"

"Major General Gilbert, by God, sir. Give me your sword, sir, you are under arrest."

This racket roused the regiment's colonel, who came up to defend his captain. Gilbert turned on him furiously, saying that he should have had the regiment lining the road at present-arms when the corps commander rode by. The colonel replied with some heat: his men had been marching day and night for a week, and he "would not hold a dress parade at midnight for any damn fool living." The 10th Indiana, retorted Gilbert, was no better than an armed mob, and he would disgrace it; he would take its colors away that the army might know its shame.

The regiment was awake and on its feet by now, and the color sergeant took a hand in this row between colonel and major general. He would kill General Gilbert, he announced loudly, if he so much as touched the regiment's colors. There was a loud murmur of approval, and one enlisted man shouldered his way up to General Gilbert and cried: "Here, you damned son of a bitch, get out of here or you're a dead man." Someone fired a musket, and some other person thrust a bayonet into Gilbert's horse, causing the poor beast to spring in the air and take off at a headlong gallop. Gilbert's staff followed, more horses were jabbed as they went by, and as the general disappeared in the darkness, still unsaluted, the 10th Indiana called after him, in confused angry chorus, that it would happily shoot him if it ever saw him again. . . . It took a certain knack to handle western volunteers, and not all regulars had it.[5]

On the evening of October 7, Buell had his army up near the town of Perryville, Kentucky, spraddled out on high ground west of the village along a stream known as Doctor's Creek. Bragg's Confederates were in and around Perryville, and apparently neither commander had a clear idea of what either he or his adversary was going to do next. The weather had been hot and water was scarce, advance elements of the two armies began to fight for possession of the pools of water in the little creek, and on October 8 they blundered into a battle that the generals neither desired nor understood. The Confederates attacked the left end of Buell's line with vigor, routed the greater part of one army corps, and brought on an unusually savage and expensive fight. On the Federal side there was an almost complete breakdown of communications, and Buell (who was several miles away) did not even know that a battle was going on until it was all over. He found out finally, at dusk, after he had lost some four thousand men. Concluding that the Confederates would renew the attack the next day, he made ready to receive them, and starchy General Gilbert (whose troops were accusing him of posting guards about the water holes to reserve the water supply for headquarters) pessimistically believed that the Confederates were about to win a great victory. But Bragg had had enough. Kentucky had not risen to support him as he expected, there seemed to be armed Yankees all over the state, and—inexplicably—he abandoned his offensive plans just when he might have made something of them, and started his army back to Tennessee. A Confederate private, remarking that even if Perryville was a meaningless battle it was the hardest fight he was ever in, summed it up: "Both sides claim the victory—both whipped," and Buell moved forward with great caution, not so much to pursue his antagonist as to escort him out of the state. A Union cavalryman wrote in disgust that his fellows believed Buell to be "either incompetent, a coward or a traitor."

In Washington both the White House and the War Department implored Buell to take off the wraps and show a little drive. Specifically they demanded that he march his army over into east Tennessee, as he had been ordered to do a solid year earlier. Buell agreed that there would never be real security for Kentucky (where he felt obliged to leave thirty thousand troops to guard communications and repel raids) until east Tennessee was occupied, but he remarked that there were problems. He could reach east Tennessee only by moving over two hundred miles of very bad mountain roads; he would need a supply train of ten thousand wagons, which he did not have, and the move would stir up a hornets' nest anyway because the Rebels would consider it the most dangerous thrust of the war and would muster all their resources to stop it.

This did not placate Mr. Lincoln at all, and Buell got a very stiff note from Halleck: if east Tennessee was the heart of the enemy's resources it might as well be the heart of Buell's, and his army could support itself there if a Confederate army could. He could get his supplies from the countryside, seizing what he could not buy, which is just what Bragg was doing on his present retreat. The President, said Halleck sharply, "does not understand why we cannot march as the enemy marches, live as he lives and fight as he fights, unless we admit the inferiority of our troops and our generals."

Luckless Buell had all of McClellan's fatal reluctance to move until everything was just so and, like McClellan, he was describing all of his deficiencies and putting an undue strain on presidential patience. Meanwhile, down in Mississippi there had been an important development.

From the Memphis area Grant had sent troops north to help Buell, and as a result he was short-handed; and while Bragg was moving up toward Perryville, Confederate Van Dorn with twenty-two thousand men swept in to recapture Corinth and knock out the keystone of Grant's defensive line. There were perhaps twenty thousand Federals in Corinth, rattling around in the old defensive works Beauregard had laid out for an army two and a half times that large, and they were commanded by a heavy, red-faced, impulsive general named William S. Rosecrans, whom they were about to elevate to fame and a dazzling opportunity.

Rosecrans was a genial, likable sort; a West Pointer who was a little more excitable than a general ought to be but who was never in the least afraid of a fight. An Ohioan in his mid-forties, he had taught at West Point, had left the army to make money in business, and had come back in the spring of 1861 as captain of engineers; it was remembered that he had helped McClellan lay out Ohio's first camp for recruits back when the war was young. He was a devout Roman Catholic, brother to the Bishop of Cincinnati, and although Ohio Democrats offered to back him for office—even for the presidency—he steadfastly refused to mix politics with military matters.

At Corinth his troops put up an enormous fight. Van Dorn massed his assaulting column and drove it in over a partly cleared field littered with stumps and fallen timber. It broke the Union advance line and came to close quarters around a strong point called Battery Robinet, where men fired so fast that their muskets became too hot to handle and too foul with burned powder to be reloaded. Ohioans and Texans fought hand to hand, with bayonets and clubbed muskets and fists, until at last the steam went out of the attack and Van Dorn's men ran back, leaving the field strewn with broken bodies. That evening, October 4, the Confederate army drew off in retreat, and fiery Rosecrans visited Battery Robinet, bared his head, and told his soldiers: "I stand in the presence of brave men, and I take off my hat to you."

Not far away, Union stretcher-bearers picked up a wounded

Rebel officer, shot down near high-tide mark of the assault on the battery. As they did what they could to make him comfortable he told them: "You licked us good today, but we gave you the best we had in the ranch."⁸

In a sense he was speaking for the whole Confederacy.

Terrible battles and dramatic counterstrokes lay ahead, but the South had just made its supreme effort. It had mounted an offensive that went all across the board—a co-ordinated attempt by three armies to win final control of the war, to prevent the inexorable invasion that would desolate southern farms and towns and ruin the proud, static, dream-possessed society that had supposed it could live on in a world of infinite change. It had given the best there was in the ranch, but it had been licked, and now there was a new war to fight; a war that must finally turn into a grim, all but hopeless fight to stave off disaster.

The Federals would pick up now where they had left off last spring, the initiative once more in their hands. They would have some different generals, however. After Antietam, Corinth, and Perryville, the area in which men like McClellan and Buell could be used narrowed to the vanishing point. General Halleck and Senator Sherman had said it: nations in revolution used up their generals pitilessly. This nation was in revolution now; it would do the same.

So Buell was removed, and Rosecrans took his place, the administration being impressed by his avoidance of politics and his uncomplicated willingness to fight. (Grant was not as pleased with him as Halleck and Lincoln were. He felt that Rosecrans should have followed up his Corinth victory by destroying Van Dorn's army; any battle that left the enemy with any appreciable number of survivors was apt to strike Grant as imperfect.) And McClellan was removed, taking his farewell from the Army of the Potomac amid hysterical cheers, the men lamenting his departure so bitterly that timid folk in Washington worried needlessly, lest the army mutiny and depose the government. McClellan went home, out of the war forever. Bumbling, well-intentioned Burnside took his place, and the Army of the Potomac gloomily began to move down the Rappahannock River toward a sleepy little city named Fredericksburg.

The reverses of spring and summer had been canceled out. Thousands of men had been killed, tens of thousands had been wounded, there was bleak acceptance of tragedy in homes all across the land, and now there would be a fresh start, a new war with a different goal. The hard year 1862 was ending, to give way to a harder year, and in Virginia, in Tennessee, and in Mississippi the armies would move from their camps, drums muttering in a steady pulse-beat rhythm as the nation resumed its march into the mysterious future.

2. There Was No Patience

The armies were moving south, and the land they were entering was not wholly strange. The hills and woods were like those in the North, and men from midwestern farms could look appreciatively at the countryside and feel almost at home in it.

An Indiana soldier in Rosecrans's army, looking about him in Tennessee, remarked that "a more beautiful country than middle Tennessee would be hard to find anywhere on the map of the United States," adding that although the land had been tilled for fifty years by slave labor it still produced plenty of corn. He confessed: "Even to men familiar with the rich soil of the Wabash and Ohio River valleys, the long lines of corncribs, full to bursting, on these Tennessee plantations were a marvel." Reflecting on all of this plenty, he confessed that the men of his regiment were foraging quite liberally. The provost guard, he said, never got into action "until many a chicken had squawked his last squawk, and many a pig had squealed his last squeal."[1]

An Iowa boy wrote to his sister with even more enthusiasm. The soil here in Tennessee was not deep, he said, and an Iowa farmer would hardly think of trying to make a crop on it, but it would raise good corn or wheat and would do even better with cotton.

"Farming," he explained, "is carried on entirely differently than at the North. Instead of the beautiful little farms and houses, every quarter or half mile along the roads, you see the large plantation or mansion. . . . In front of these planters' houses are beautiful lawns of five or six acres, covered with the most lovely shrubbery peculiar to the South, and shell or gravel walks winding round and round until they reach the house. They look quite as lovely in the dead of winter as any we see in the North in mid-summer."

Scribbling away at this letter and thinking of the charming society that lived in and about these mansions, the young Iowan fell into a daydream that carried him in an unexpected direction and forced him to cut his reverie short on the edge of disloyalty:

"I imagine, should I have come down here before the war, I should have been enchanted by these bewitching scenes and would have loitered in some of these parks, some warm summer day, and met one of those lovely Southern belles—declared my love—asked her hand—and been accepted; the result would have been disappointment, estrangement and separation, with love unworthy a son of the Northland."[2]

In the Shenandoah Valley, Union soldiers were learning that southern civilians could be exactly like the folks at home and that there could be a touch of friendship now and then between the invaders and the invaded. The 13th Massachusetts was appealed to by a valley farmer for protection against foragers, and the colonel detailed four men to guard the place. The farmer insisted that they stay in the house and make themselves comfortable; he would go about his duties and would call them if any prowlers appeared. His wife would not let them bunk down in the yard when night came, but put them in bedrooms with soft mattresses and clean white sheets, told them to sleep until they were called in the morning, served breakfast at eight-thirty—hominy and bacon, potatoes and fried chicken, hot biscuits and coffee, all they could eat. When the regiment finally had to move on and the detail was called away, the farmer went to the colonel to testify what fine young men these soldiers were, and his wife sent a huge basket of biscuits and cakes for them to take with them. All the rest of the war the 13th Massachusetts nursed this memory.[3]

It was not all sweetness and light. Most of the northern soldiers had farm backgrounds, and as they went south they looked appraisingly at southern fields and farms; they remembered the infinite number of pre-war orations by southern patriots describing the "sacred soil" of Dixie, and they picked the words up and made a sneer out of them. A Pennsylvania private, moving down toward Fredericksburg with the Army of the Potomac, took a top-lofty attitude toward farming practices in the Old Dominion as his regiment came over the Potomac:

"We crossed the Long Bridge and set foot on the 'sacred soil'; the soil may be sacred, but we sacrilegious Yankees can't help observing that it is awfully deficient in manure."

There came to the armies this fall many new recruits, and the fact that they were coming in now, after the ebbing of the tide, reflected the defects in War Department planning.

Edwin M. Stanton was an energetic and competent Secretary of War, but he gave way at times to freakish impulses, and one of these had seized him in the spring of 1862: he had closed down all army recruiting stations and stopped enlistments, which was practically equivalent to announcing that the war was about over and that no more men would be needed. His timing was unfortunate, because a series of Union reverses immediately took place—heavy casualty lists East and West, defeat in the Shenandoah Valley, defeat at Richmond, Rebel armies of invasion slipping the leash and taking the initiative everywhere. More recruits were badly needed, but the high enthusiasm of early spring had cooled, and when the recruiting stations were reopened they did not do a very good business.

To get more men a publicity operation of considerable magnitude was needed, and it was promptly arranged. The governors of the northern states got together and framed a public appeal to the President, asserting—with blithe optimism—that war spirit was running high and that they would be happy to raise new levies if the President thought he needed them. Mr. Lincoln, in turn, publicly appealed to the governors to get him three hundred thousand men and to get them sooner rather than later. A big recruiting campaign was launched in July, someone wrote a patriotic song with the line, "We are coming, Father Abraham," and with much drumbeating and oratory the men were obtained.

They spent the summer in training camps, and in the fall

they began to reach the armies in the field. Their uniforms were unfaded and unwrinkled and, like all green soldiers, they were heavily loaded down with all sorts of surplus equipment. The veterans jeered at them unmercifully, calling out "Fresh fish!" whenever a new regiment showed up, and making caustic remarks about their possessions.

"Knapsacks," wrote one veteran scornfully, "were a foot above their heads; overcoats, two suits of clothes and underwear, all kinds of trimmings, bear's oil for the hair, gifts from loving and well-meaning friends but useless to the soldier. On the back of their knapsacks were strapped fryingpans, coffee pots and stew pans, pairs of boots hanging to the knapsacks, blankets and ponchos, making in weight one hundred pounds to the man, while the vet carried about twenty-five pounds."

In the Army of the Potomac, old-timers hooted at the new 118th Pennsylvania, which came in equipped with oversized knapsacks, extra pants, and other incidentals, and told the recruits to throw all that stuff away (starting with the knapsacks themselves) and roll up their essentials in their blankets. A rolled blanket could be tied in a horse-collar loop and worn over the shoulder; it weighed little and there were no straps to cut a man's collarbones on a long march. The Pennsylvanians refused to take this advice and kept their ponderous knapsacks, and a Massachusetts veteran remarked that the boys would learn: "I don't suppose there was a spare shirt in my company."[5]

Men of the 103rd Illinois, coming down to join Grant's army, were told that they did not amount to much—they had enlisted only to escape the draft, wear a uniform, get free rations, and enjoy the privilege of marching along with the veterans; when a real fight began they would all scatter and the veterans would have to do the work. When the 24th Michigan arrived near Antietam battlefield to become part of the Potomac army's crack Iron Brigade, the men were treated as outcasts for two solid months; the veterans had heard that these Michigan boys had enlisted only because high bounties were being offered, and they refused to treat the recruits as comrades until after they had proved themselves in battle.[6]

Although the veteran refused to carry any more equipment than he absolutely had to have, he considered it his duty to replace his used garments with any new ones that could be lifted from the recruits, and he devised ingenious ways to do this. The commonest was for the old soldier to wander into a green regiment's camp, select an innocent-looking recruit, sit down beside him, and give him friendly advice about the evils that would befall a man who kept too much in his pack. The recruit would be impressed and before long would be opening his knapsack and pulling out spare pants, shirts, and boots whose weight (according to this expert advice) he would find oppressive. At this point the veteran would peel off his own worn clothing, put on the new, give the recruit a fatherly pat on the back, and strut off to his own regiment. If on arrival he was asked how he had got his new clothing he would grin and say: "By giving a recruit good advice."

There was one noteworthy thing about the new soldiers: they believed in foraging with a free and heavy hand. War propaganda had begun to take effect, and recruiting-campaign orators were no longer simply appealing to love of country and the desire for adventure; they were demanding that the South be made to sweat for the crime of secession, and recruits had been receptive. New soldiers in camp around Memphis considered themselves entitled to take anything edible: "They would slaughter a man's hogs right before his eyes, and if he made a fuss cold steel would soon put a quietus on him." Commanding generals tried in vain to restrain them. William T. Sherman was especially strict, breaking offending non-coms to privates and ordering men tied up by their thumbs all night long, but it did very little good. On the march in northern Mississippi, Grant's men developed the playful habit of setting fire to dead leaves caught in the angles of rail fences; if this fired the fences and in turn set houses and barns ablaze, nobody cared. Along the line of march, any house whose occupants had fled was certain to be burned. An Ohio artilleryman remarked that "the cotton gin was then like the coal-breakers in the time of a great strike—many are burned; among soldiers and miners there is a lawless element that delights in destruction." Gaunt, blackened chimneys stood where burned houses had been, and when soldiers saw one they would point to it and call: "Here stands another Tennessee headstone."[8]

These Tennessee and Mississippi civilians were lucky in just one respect: the Federal armies which were advancing on them at least contained few Kansas troops. The Kansans, rejoicing in the nickname of "Jayhawkers," were the most notorious freebooters and pillagers of all, and where they marched in Missouri or Arkansas they left a red scar on the land. They brought a personal venom into the war; they remembered the bitter lawlessness of the border troubles of the 1850s, they felt that they had a grudge to pay off, and anyway they tended to be a rowdy untamed crew operating under an uncommonly sketchy discipline. So notorious was their reputation that even their own army was wary of them. A Wisconsin cavalry regiment, moving east from Arkansas, told how in a camp beyond the river one of the Wisconsin troopers had died and a detail went out to the cemetery and dug a grave for him. While funeral services were being held back in the camp, the 5th Kansas found it necessary to bury one of its own men. Going to the cemetery, the Kansans found the open grave dug by the Wisconsin men; they buried their own man in it, put in earth, and went back to camp. When the Wisconsin funeral procession got to the spot and saw what had happened, the men instantly and unanimously accused the Kansans. In all the army, they declared, only the Jayhawkers would be capable of stealing a grave!"[9]

Armies are strange human societies—rootless, wholly self-contained, creating derisive legends and folk tales as they tramp along toward death and destiny. These soldiers liked to tell tales about themselves; tales like the one about the teamster in the Indiana regiment who was the champion sprinter in his brigade. He was so prodigious a runner, indeed, that he beat every other runner in camp and finally, inspired by his speed, ran all the way out of the army, was listed as a deserter, and was never seen again at all. They cherished the memory of the Irish private's wife, in an Illinois regiment. By some superhuman effort this woman managed to get all the way from Chicago down to Nashville to visit her husband, and by some even more unimaginable effort she had brought with her a five-gallon keg of whiskey for his refreshment. But when she reached camp she found that he had basely deserted both the army and herself—whereupon, undaunted, she erected a tent, peddled the whiskey to her absconding husband's comrades at fifty cents a drink, and so raised a stake for her future support.

There was a tale about an Iowa cavalry regiment that had a very fat trooper who was unhorsed one day in a clash with Rebel cavalry and who, his own regiment riding off in rout, sought to escape capture by crawling under a small culvert. This bridge was treacherous—two limber stringers, with cross-wise planking, spanning a very shallow ditch. It sagged when it bore a load, and the fat cavalryman became stuck, face down, under the middle of it as the Rebel troopers went over it at a pounding gallop . . . and the Iowan got the father and mother of all spankings, so that he was totally unable (after he had been extricated) to sit in a saddle for months to come.[10]

There was also a Kentucky regiment which swore that one of its members owned a lifetime furlough signed by General George H. Thomas himself. This soldier, it was said, quite early in the war had been notified that his wife was dying, and he obtained from the general a pass permitting him to go home and to stay there until after her death. Most considerately the lady had then recovered, and it seemed likely that she would survive for at least fifty years more; and her husband, who cherished her, stayed at home with her, except that now and then he would go back to camp for a friendly chat with his comrades. . . .[11]

Increasingly the men ran into the problem of slavery, and as they did they began to encounter an arrogance in the southern attitude toward slavery that increased their own antagonism. Slavery seemed to be central. It was the one sensitive, untouchable nerve-ending, and to press upon it brought anguished cries of outrage that could be evoked in no other way.

A Union general in Kentucky wrote reflectively that he had recently called off an advertised property sale in a county-seat town on the ground that since half of the residents were excluded from the town as pro-secessionists the sale could not be fair. Nobody complained in the least, he said, at the prohibition that was put on sales of land and livestock, but the fact that slave auctions were also barred drew furious protests. "A single Negro," wrote the general, "is sufficient to demand the attention of the Governor." The peculiar institution's chief peculiarity, it began to appear, was the fact that it was wrapped in a special kind of inviolability. It could not simply be left alone, it had to be given favored treatment; its claims were positive and not negative.

The Union soldiers which this general commanded (he wrote) were new men from the Northwest, recruited that summer. When fugitive slaves came into camp these boys would shelter them; yet there were not really very many cases of this kind, after all, "and had the owners been satisfied to exercise a little patience when the fugitives could not readily be found the soldiers would soon have got tired of their new playthings and turned every black out of camp themselves."[12]

But there was no patience. The slaveholder was driven on by a perverse and malignant fate; he could not be patient, because time was not on his side. Protesting bitterly against change, he was forever being led to do the very things that would bring change the most speedily. He was unable to let these heedless Federals get tired of their new playthings. He had to prod them and storm at them, and because he did, the soldiers' attitude hardened and they grew more and more aggressive.

They were growing aggressive just as President Lincoln himself was doing, and for much the same reason.

Lincoln had promised to decree emancipation by the first of the new year; and as his armies began to move late in the autumn, he sent a message to Congress on December 1 suggesting the adoption of a constitutional amendment providing for gradual, fully compensated emancipation all across the land, in loyal states and in rebellious states alike.

Geography, said Lincoln, was controlling; there could not be two nations here, the land itself would compel a reunion even if the attempt at secession won; and without slavery, the effort to force a separation could not long continue. Why not meet the inevitable halfway? Compensated emancipation would be expensive but would not cost as much as the war itself was costing; also, it would kill no young men. To save their country, men must disenthrall themselves from the dogmas of the past. To give freedom to the slave was to preserve it for all others, and "the fiery trial through which we pass will light us down, in honor or dishonor, to the latest generation."[13]

It was no use. The peculiar institution's inviolability ran across the North as well as across the South; for emancipated slaves might demand jobs in mill and shop and elsewhere, might someday have to be treated like ordinary human beings, would infallibly compel all sections, sooner or later, to face up to the problem of race relations. Neither above nor below the Mason and Dixon line could the thing be treated rationally. The fiery trial Lincoln was talking about was an ordeal no one could avert.

It did not, as a matter of fact, seem a promising time for the Lincoln administration to propose vast new experiments, for the administration just now was in trouble. It had done very badly in the fall elections, losing seven important states to the Democrats and retaining control of Congress by an extremely thin margin. As far as anyone could see, neither emancipation nor the way the war was being run had made a very good impression on the voters. Each would have to justify itself, and during the immediate future it would all be up to the armies.

There were three principal armies, owning a common background and sharing a common heritage, yet somehow standing in the oddest contrast to each other.

There was McClellan's old army, the Army of the Potomac —"General McClellan's bodyguard," Lincoln once called it in a despairing moment; the only American army ever to be suspected (however falsely) of a desire to overthrow the government and set up a military dictatorship. The army was jaunty, setting much store by military formalities, consciously serving what was imagined to be a romantic ideal; and it had acquired thus early a dark foreknowledge of disaster, a remarkable reputation for bad luck, and a fine legend that would survive years of war and win a place at last in the national memory. It could fight hard, it could endure a fantastic amount of killing, serving faithfully under any general who came along; it could, in short, do practically anything except win the war. Without suspecting it, the army was a Cinderella.

Then there was Rosecrans's army, recently taken over from luckless Buell, officially styled the Army of the Cumberland. It was not unlike the Potomac army in some ways—it had been schooled to a certain amount of spit-and-polish discipline (not all of which quite registered) and taught to admire parade-ground formality—but it never acquired any glamor, in its own eyes or in anybody else's, and its reputation was that of an enduring work horse. It would finally go under the command of George Thomas, and far ahead of time it was beginning to resemble him: it was unbreakable, somewhat plodding, with an unexpected volcanic capacity for exploding all over the landscape just when an explosion was most needed. All in all, it may possibly have been the best army of the lot, but its great day was far in the future.

Finally there was Grant's army, eventually to be known as the Army of the Tennessee. Never was there an army quite like this one. It was half instrument of destiny and half frontier mob, an army that refused to accept discipline and that stamped its own imprint on its generals; predominantly and eternally, it was an army of enlisted men. Taking nothing very seriously, it would go across the land like the embodiment of wrath, pillar of fire by night and pillar of cloud by day to mark its passage, both pillars largely of its own making. For the moment it was an army forgotten, lying in obscure camps far to the south, not yet ready to trample out the way that was appointed for it. The other two armies would take the stage first, to fight terrible battles on frozen fields, providing unendurable drama at a price almost too great for payment.

3. *Thin Moon and Cold Mist*

Winter was approaching, a winter of cold blue moons and frozen fields, with deadly rivers winding across landscapes that had a doom on them. There was the Rappahannock, coming down from the Virginia piedmont and broadening out for a lazy curling route to the sea, the lovely town of Fredericksburg drowsing on its right bank just below the fall line; and in Tennessee there was Stone's River, the market town of Murfreesboro lying just to the south of it, rolling Tennessee farm country all about. Two rivers and two towns, drawing the tide of war to them, with two Union armies coming in and two Confederate armies making ready for defense. Rappahannock and Stone's rivers would be crossed, and Fredericksburg and Murfreesboro would be occupied, but many young would die before it was done.

In Virginia, whiskered Burnside considered his problem and made up his mind to do other than as McClellan had planned. The Army of the Potomac lay east of the Blue Ridge, on the Orange and Alexandria Railroad, with Lee's army grouped loosely in its front. It seemed unlikely that Lee could be outmaneuvered here, which is what McClellan had contemplated, and Burnside decided on a long sweep to his left; he would go forty miles to the southeast, cross the Rappahannock quickly at Fredericksburg, and so compel Lee to come down and fight him at a disadvantage.

In Tennessee, Rosecrans had his Army of the Cumberland at Nashville. As far as he could learn, Bragg's army was at Murfreesboro. Rosecrans would march down and fight, and when Bragg had been crushed, the way to Chattanooga and eastern Tennessee might at last be open. Grant, meanwhile, from the Memphis area, could perhaps do something about taking Vicksburg and opening the Mississippi all the way to New Orleans.

It was Burnside who got started first. Through dismal late-November weather his men plodded cross-country amid failures of supply and equipment that told an ominous tale about defects in army management; and they got to the Rappahannock at the town of Falmouth, opposite Fredericksburg and a mile upstream, before Lee realized what was going on. Lincoln had told Burnside that his plan might work if he moved fast, and in the beginning Burnside moved very rapidly. At the end of a fortnight everything had worked as he had hoped. It remained now to cross the Rappahannock, base himself in Fredericksburg, and then go driving on to a region where Lee would have to come and attack him.

Crossing the Rappahannock, however, presented problems. There were places above Fredericksburg where sturdy men could easily wade the river, but it seemed to Burnside that it would be very rash to put troops across until he could build proper pontoon bridges for his supply trains; and when he made ready to do this he found that the pontoons he had been counting on were not there.

They were missing because—to put it at its simplest—this was an army in which some arrangement or other was always going wrong. Men could be recruited, fed, drilled, and disciplined in large numbers; they could even be led into a battle, after a fashion, with their own bravery making up for many failures in leadership; but to take care of the daily routine of housekeeping and maintenance was for some reason beyond the capacity of this army's authorities. Burnside had ordered pontoons sent to Fredericksburg to be ready for him when he needed them, but in some way his orders had gone astray; the pontoons were not where everybody supposed they were, and anyway, when the orders finally reached them, nobody remembered to explain to the men in charge that there was a great hurry about things. So the Army of the Potomac sat in idleness by the Rappahannock while these mistakes were set right; and because it took a long time to set them right, Lee brought his army to Fredericksburg, arrayed it carefully on high ground back from the river, and calmly waited to see what Burnside would do next.[1]

Burnside would do just what he had set out to do, for there was a great stubbornness in him—a great stubbornness, and nothing more. He had said he would cross at Fredericksburg, and at Fredericksburg he would cross, even if destruction awaited him. By December 11 everything was ready, pontoons and all, and on the next morning the engineers came down to the water to build the bridges.

The Confederates were waiting, and from houses and riverside shacks they laid fire on the river, killing many of the engineers. Bridges half built, the engineers had to stop, while more than one hundred Federal guns hammered the town, pulverizing houses, knocking bricks and timbers into the empty streets, and sending a great cloud of smoke billowing up toward the autumn sky. Silence again, and a new rush by the engineers; then Rebel sharpshooters, little harmed by the fire that had wrecked the town, opened fire again, more of the engineers were killed, and once more the bridge-building failed.

In the end Burnside's men took some of the ponderous pontoons, filled them with infantry, paddled them across the river in spite of the musketry, and drove combat patrols through the town, gouging the sharpshooters out of their holes. This ended the resistance. By midafternoon the bridges were finished, and at last the great, sinewy Army of the Potomac began its crossing. It moved glacially, hour after hour, the enormous blue columns coming down the banks to the river and swaying endlessly over the bridges, flooding the town and fanning out into an open plain just downstream; it moved with flags and with bands and with a great rumbling of moving cannon, making a display of might that impressed the waiting Confederates, impressed even Lee himself. Yet this Union army which seemed to move so irresistibly was in fact plodding blindly into a trap.

Fredericksburg was deceptive. The Rappahannock, coming down the distant Blue Ridge on a general easterly course, turns south just above the town, and for a time it flows very nearly on a north-to-south line, with Fredericksburg lying on the west bank. An army crossing the stream and entering Fredericksburg finds a shallow open plain west of the town, extending for several miles downstream; and just beyond the plain, perhaps three quarters of a mile from the river, there is a long chain of wooded hills running roughly parallel to the river. To get out of the town and make any progress whatever, the army must start by passing that chain of hills.

It looks innocent enough because the hills are not very high, and toward the south they trail off into gentle rolling country where the railroad to Richmond curves past them. But the hills are just high enough to make an ideal defensive position, and in December of 1862 all of Lee's army was securely posted along the crest, with guns ranked so that they could comb all of the plain, lines of infantry at the foot of the hills and other lines higher up. Facing the town itself, as it happened, a sunken road ran along the foot of the hills, with a stone wall nearest the town, the road packed full of Confederate infantry, with many guns just above. In all the war no army moved up against a tougher position than Burnside's army encountered at Fredericksburg. Without a miracle, the Confederate position here could not be taken by storm.

The Army of the Potomac having crossed the river—having committed itself to an advance at this spot—there was nothing whatever for it to do but try the impossible, and this Burnside ordered it to do. He put half of his army in the town itself and ranged the other half near the river on the open plain to the south, and on the morning of December 13 he called for a two-pronged attack. One column would issue from the town, swarm over the stone wall and the sunken road, and reach the heights there; the other would go out a mile or so to the south, hitting for the place where the wooded hills sloped down to meet the plain; and the man apparently believed that Lee's army would be broken and driven in flight, with the two assault columns triumphantly joining hands on the far side of the ridge.

There was a fog that morning, and for several hours the plain was invisible while many divisions of Federal troops got into position, steeples and chimney tops of Fredericksburg just visible above the banked mist to the waiting Confederates on the hills. Then the sun burned away the fog, and all of a sudden the whole panorama was in the open—a breath-taking sight, one hundred thousand men, fighting men ready for work, an army with banners uncoiling in the sunlight, gun barrels gleaming. Lee watched from the highest point on the ridge, and the sight took hold of him—this strong warrior who held himself under such iron control— so that he burst out with something like a cry of exultation: It is well (he said) that we know how terrible war really is, else we would grow too fond of it. . . . Then the moment of high drama passed (unforgettable moment, hanging suspended in the memories of that war forever after) and the fighting began.

The fighting was sheer murder. Coming out from the town, Burnside's men crashed into the stone wall and were broken. Division after division moved up to the attack, marching out of the plain in faultless alignment, to be cut and broken and driven back by a storm of fire; for hour after hour they attacked, until all the plain was stained with the blue bodies that had been thrown on it, and not one armed Yankee ever reached even the foot of the hill. The plain was filled with smoke, shot through with unceasing flashes of fire, and the wild rolling crash of battle went on and on through all the afternoon and there seemed to be no end to it. Burnside was east of the river, encased in the ignorance that besets headquarters, sending over orders to carry on with the attack. His men obeyed every order, until whole divisions had been cut to pieces and the town and the sheltered banks by the river were clogged with men who had been knocked loose from their commands, but from first to last it was completely hopeless. Never, at any time, was there the remotest chance that this attack could succeed.

Downstream things were a little better, although not enough better to help very much. A column led by that grizzled, bad-tempered soldier named George Gordon Meade —a hawk-nosed Pennsylvanian, this man, with goggle eyes and a straggly gray beard and a great simple fidelity to his duty—got into a wooded swamp where the Confederate line was low and punched a small hole in the defenses. Stonewall Jackson was there, and just for a moment it seemed that he might be in trouble; but he brought up reinforcements in a vicious countercharge, the Federal support troops that might have helped Meade's boys did not appear, and after a while the Federals came staggering back out of the swamp and the underbrush and the hole in the Rebel line was plugged up for good. By sunset the attack was a hopeless failure at both ends of the line; the Union army had lost twelve thousand men, and the Confederates waited confidently to see if the Yankees cared to have another try at it next day.[2]

The Yankees did not care to. Burnside, to be sure, remained stubborn; he even had some wild idea of going into Fredericksburg, rallying the shattered formations, and personally leading a forlorn-hope attack on the deadly stone wall, but he was talked out of it by his subordinates. For a night and a day his beaten army clung to the ground, looking

dumbly up at the armed heights; then, on a night of wind
and sleeting rain, the army gave up, pulled its ponderous
length back across the bridges, and the attack was given up
for good. The great battle of Fredericksburg was over. In
front of the stone wall lay hundreds and hundreds of dead
bodies gleaming nakedly in the cold December light; during
the hours of darkness needy Confederates had come out from
their lines to take the warm uniforms which these Yankees
would never need.

The Yankees who had not been shot and who went into
dispirited camp on the far side of the river had uniforms
enough but needed other things; chiefly hope, good management, reason to believe that their terrible fighting was taking
place to some good purpose. The high command was quarrel-
ing with itself, Burnside and his subordinates bitterly at
odds over the way the wasted battle had gone. The administration, already depressed enough by an unhappy congres-
sional election and still carrying the commitment to make the
Emancipation Proclamation good by the first of the new year,
was aware that Burnside would not do for this army, and it
was not aware just who could properly be put in his place.
Handsome Joe Hooker, hard-drinking and hard-fighting,
looked like the ablest soldier among Burnside's lieutenants,
but he was talking too much just now. He would say presently that what the country needed was a dictator; in saying it,
he may well have had himself in mind, and word of what he
had said would get back to Lincoln. If the President's anxious
gaze turned away from Virginia that December and fixed
itself on Tennessee it is not to be wondered at.

In Tennessee, Rosecrans at last had his army, on the
move. December was getting on and the roads were not
good, but the army was in tolerable spirits; it was facing
south again, the long frantic race back to the Ohio River was
forgotten, and this new general—"Old Rosy" to all ranks—
seemed to be a promising sort. He showed himself about
the camps, his huge red nose a beacon as he poked his face
into mess shacks or inspected waiting lines of infantry. At
reviews he liked to rein in his horse and give his men
soldierly advice: "Boys, when you drill, drill like thunder. . . .
It's not the number of bullets you shoot but the accuracy of

aim that kills men in battle. . . . Never turn your backs to the foe; cowards are sure to get shot. . . . When you meet the enemy, fire low."

He liked to stroll through regimental camps in the evenings, and if he saw a light burning in a tent after "taps" he was likely to whack the canvas with the flat of his sword. At such times the men in the tent were fond of shouting profane abuse, and when the general's crimson face came through the tent flaps they would offer profuse apologies, swearing that they had thought him a rowdy wagon driver who was in the habit of annoying them, and insisting that they really had not heard the lights-out call.

Old Rosy was able to take this sort of thing in good part. His officers found him convivial and approachable, fond of bantering with his staff members. He seemed to have studied his profession attentively, and in conversation around the mess table he could display a vast theoretical knowledge of war. When he discussed some immediate problem he was apt to cite parallel cases out of the textbooks. It was noted that in battle he became restless, was likely to talk so fast that he could hardly be understood, and all in all generated a high pitch of excitement. But he was a friendly man and he worked hard at his job, and after the aloof, enigmatical Buell he seems to have been a relief.[3]

Washington had been reminding him that what it wanted most of all was a Federal army moving into east Tennessee, but Rosecrans was beginning to see Buell's point of view—that such a move was easier to plan in Washington than to execute on the spot. He concentrated at Nashville, perceived that Bragg and the Confederates were concentrated at Murfreesboro, less than thirty miles away, and on the day after Christmas, 1862—a gloomy day, low clouds everywhere, a chilling mist in the air, with intermittent rain coming down to soak men's clothing and spoil the roads—Rosecrans called his army out of its tents and set off southeast to find Bragg and fight him.

He was starting out with some forty-three thousand men. There were more than that in his command, but he was in enemy country infested by a great many highly active Confederate raiders, and he had to leave extensive details behind to guard bridges, supply lines, and wagon trains. Unfortunately most of the men taken for these details came from the troops of Rosecrans's best corps commander, George Thomas, who would be short one entire division when the army went into action. Thomas, who had turned down the chance to replace Buell before Perryville, seems to have felt hurt when the government finally gave Buell's job to Rosecrans, and Halleck was soothing him with kind words by letter—soothing him, as it finally would prove, not too effectively.'

Corps commanders with Thomas were Thomas L. Crittenden, son of the distinguished Kentuckian who had tried so hard and so unsuccessfully to work out a compromise between North and South in the final months before Sumter, and Alexander McD. McCook, a cheerful, bluff regular whose men had done most of the fighting at Perryville and who possessed a division commander who was just beginning to attract notice as a furious driving fighting man—a brand-new brigadier, recently a colonel of cavalry, by name of Philip Sheridan. Rosecrans spread his three corps out over the wet roads, and after marches made slow by sporadic skirmishing and cavalry fighting his troops pulled up in front of Murfreesboro on the evening of December 29.

On the following day, noticing that Bragg had all of his army drawn up in front of the town ready to fight, Rosecrans spread his own troops out into line—McCook off to the right, Thomas in the center, and Crittenden massed on the left, on the edge of icy Stone's River, which came wandering down to curve west between Bragg's army and Murfreesboro. As night came down, both Bragg and Rosecrans were determined to fight as soon as there was daylight.

By the oddest chance, each general had formed precisely the same battle plan—to hold with his right and attack with his left. Rosecrans would send Crittenden's corps over the river to come in on Bragg's right flank, breaking it and driving it out of action, while the rest of the army held on and waited for the breaks; Bragg, in his turn, proposed to mass troops on his left and crush the Federal right, trusting to elements on high ground behind the river to keep his right safe. Conceivably, the two armies might swing around each other like the halves of a revolving door. Even more conceivably, the army that struck first might very well win the battle.

The night was cold and the ground was wet, and campfires were alight. It occurred to Rosecrans to deceive his opponent and make him think the Federal right was longer and stronger than was actually the case, so campfires were lighted where no men camped, for two miles beyond McCook's right. The strategy apparently backfired; Bragg saw and believed but simply ordered his own assaulting columns to sweep more widely to the west, which meant that when they struck they would extend far beyond McCook's flank.[5]

Dawn came in cold and sullen. Awakening Federals felt that they had picked a gloomy place for a battle. Everything was wet, with soggy clumps of black cedars massed in ominous-looking bits of forest, deserted cotton fields all about with cotton wool still visible in the open bolls. They did not have long to reflect on this, because Bragg's men struck with overpowering might at the moment of dawn, completely canceling all of Rosecrans's plans and compelling him to throw his entire army on the defensive.

The men at the right end of McCook's line got it first, and it came with very little warning. They had been turned to at the moment of daylight, and while they were still blinking the sleep out of their eyes they made out an appalling mass of Confederates coming at them from the south—four solid columns, a brigade to a column, with immense reserves taking shape in the gray half-light beyond. The Confederates came quietly, slipping out of cedar thickets without noise, swinging into battle line and charging on the dead run, raising the Rebel yell only when they actually reached the Union line. In five minutes from the moment the Federals first saw their foes one of the most desperate battles of the war was in full blast.

McCook's line was hopelessly swamped, hit from the flank and in front by seemingly limitless numbers, and it dissolved almost immediately. An Illinois soldier remembered, as characteristic of the scene, watching a Federal battery which had been firing canister and which started to limber up to withdraw to better ground; the Rebels, he said, swept it with one inconceivable volley which killed seventy-five horses and left the men unable to move a single gun—whereat the surviving artillerists abandoned their guns and fled for the rear. Men in reserve a mile behind McCook's line hardly heard the crash of battle when fugitives from the front came scampering through their camps, spreading panic in their flight. An Indiana regiment remembered with grim amusement a captain who had been so afflicted with rheumatism that he could walk only with great difficulty, with the help of a cane. Caught up in the rout, he dropped the cane and went to the rear at a breakneck run, so that his men (whom he rapidly outdistanced) guffawed and pointed and cried: "My God, look at the captain!"[6]

McCook's corps was routed, all of Rosecrans's right wing had vanished, and now everything was up to Pap Thomas, who had his two divisions posted on high ground near a railroad crossing and a four-acre plot of dark cedars known locally as "the round forest." Thomas was imperturbable. He got reinforcements from Crittenden's corps (which had long since abandoned any idea of crossing the river to hit the Confederate right), and his men held their ground, pouring out an enormous volume of fire that some of the men felt was louder and more ear-shattering than any other fire they heard in all the war. Charging Confederates were seen to pause in the cotton fields and stuff cotton in their ears to deaden the sound.[7]

While Thomas held, Rosecrans was riding about the field in a fury of activity. An officer who rode with him that day said that from dawn to dusk the general did not stay in one spot as long as half an hour.[8] His chief of staff, riding beside him, was beheaded by a cannon ball, blood spattering Old Rosy's uniform; and with his riding and shouting Rosecrans got together a long line of guns at the right of Thomas's position and formed a new line of infantry from regiments that had been driven out of McCook's position earlier. By afternoon the Union army was drawn up in an arrowhead formation, right and left wings standing almost back to back; and there, finally, as the cold day waned, they made their stand and held on grimly, beating off the last of the Rebel attacks.

There was a council of war that midnight, Rosecrans and his principal commanders; and Thomas tilted his chair back and went sound asleep while the generals asked one another whether the army could possibly stay where it was. The word "retreat" came to Thomas through his sleep; Rosecrans was asking him if he could protect the rear while the army withdrew. Thomas opened his eyes and said flatly: "This army can't retreat," then went back to sleep. His word held. The idea of retreat was abandoned and Rosecrans decided to hold his army in position and fight.[9]

It was a hideous night. A mist lay on the field, with a thin moon shining through it; a cold wind swayed in the cedars, the mud froze, no one was allowed to light a campfire, and the air was full of a steady crying and groaning from the thousands of wounded who lay all about, untended. In the morning a red sun came up, tinting the mist so that all the landscape looked bloody. One soldier on the skirmish line remembered being so stiff with cold that he had to take his right hand in his left and force his finger around the trigger of his musket before he could fire.[10]

New Year's Day was anticlimax. Bragg had driven his enemy to the edge of destruction; now, unaccountably, he failed to resume his attack, and the day passed with nothing more than skirmish-line firing. Bragg wired Richmond that he had won a great victory, but he refused to try to make anything of it. Not until January 2 did he resume the attack. This time he tried to hit the Federal left; the ground was unfavorable, and a great bank of the Federal artillery caught his charging brigades in flank and broke them apart, crushing the attack almost before it got started. Bragg waited some more—and then at night ordered a full retreat, drawing his army miles to the rear and leaving Rosecrans in full possession of the field. Unable to believe their good fortune, the Federals realized that they had, in a way, won a victory. At least they had the battlefield, along with thirteen thousand casualties. If they could pull themselves together they could continue the invasion. But Stone's River was not a field they ever cared to remember.

4. *Down the River*

The war was expanding at the end of 1862. Its potentialities were becoming immeasurable; so was the cost of fighting it, as the twenty-five thousand Federal casualties of Fredericksburg and Stone's River attested. Burnside had been hopelessly beaten, and Rosecrans had been brought to a full stop. It remained to be seen whether U. S. Grant could do any better.

Grant held western Tennessee and was responsible for the territory north of it all the way back to the Ohio. He had some forty-eight thousand men in his command, although he had to use a good half of these to guard railroads, highways, supply dumps, and what not in his rear, and during the early fall he had been unable to advance. But after Bragg's thrust into Kentucky was turned back, Grant was promised reinforcements, and it seemed to him that if he attacked the Confederates in his front vigorously he could keep them from bothering his rear too greatly. At about the time when Burnside began his unhappy move from the Blue Ridge foothills to Rappahannock tidewater—early in November—Grant started south. He proposed to clear the last Rebel resistance out of western Tennessee and then strike down into Mississippi, where the Confederate General John C. Pemberton was waiting for him with an army that Grant believed to be about the size of his own.

Vicksburg was the objective, and Vicksburg was a hard place to reach, principally because of the existence of the Yazoo Delta.

The Yazoo River is the product of a large number of smaller streams, and it begins to be a river at a point near the Tennessee line, not far inland from the Mississippi itself. It wanders east into the state of Mississippi, picking up more rivers as it goes, drops south, and at last comes back to flow into the Mississippi a few miles above Vicksburg. To the east of the Yazoo there is high ground, but to the west of it—between the Yazoo and the Mississippi—there is a vast lowland, 170 miles long by 50 miles wide, a Venetian complex of sluggish streams, bayous, backwaters, and interconnecting sloughs, with a flat country all around subject to flood when the waters are high. As roads and wheeled transport existed in 1862, no army of invasion could hope to march across this Yazoo Delta. To reach Vicksburg, Federals in western Tennessee would either have to go straight down the Mississippi by steamboat or march down east of the Yazoo and come up to Vicksburg from the rear. The Yazoo country was an impassable barrier.

In the Mississippi the Union had a powerful naval squadron led by Admiral David Dixon Porter—an impish, long-bearded man of the rough-sea-dog type, too outspoken for his own good, and given to embroidering the tale of his own exploits, but for all that an energetic and capable naval officer. It was perfectly possible for Porter to steam down and bombard Vicksburg, but the place could never be captured that way; it lay upon high bluffs, and Confederate engineers had turned it into a fortress. It had to be approached from the east, and the army that tried to get there from western Tennessee would dangle at the end of a very long supply line, exposed to incessant Confederate raids.

Nevertheless, Vicksburg was all-important. As long as it held out the Mississippi was closed, and the administration was being warned that unless the river could be opened fairly soon the farmers of the Middle West, who felt, with reason, that the eastern railroads were gouging them mercilessly, might become highly sympathetic to the Confederacy. Furthermore, Vicksburg connected the two halves of the Confederacy; if it fell the South would automatically lose an irreplaceable part of its strength.

Accordingly, Grant began to move. He had no sooner begun than he discovered that something very mysterious was going on far to his rear.

One of Grant's principal subordinates was Major General John A. McClernand of Illinois, a wiry, aggressive, ambitious man whom Grant eyed with deep distrust. McClernand was a Democratic politician; he had spoken up boldly for the Union cause after Fort Sumter, when the administration was in a mood to prize pro-war Democrats, and he had been made a general as a reward. There was nothing wrong with his fighting heart, but he was an unskillful soldier and he had so much seniority that he outranked everybody in Grant's army except Grant himself. Grant had felt no especial sense of loss when late in August he got orders from Halleck detaching McClernand and sending him back to Springfield, Illinois, to help organize new volunteer troops. But by the end of November, Grant began to realize that McClernand was up to something.

In its great need for more soldiers that summer, the administration had played with the idea of getting some combination military and political hero to do a recruiting job. Mayor George Opdyke of New York, chairman of a big-name National War Committee, had asked Stanton to let either Frémont or Ormsby Mitchel tour the North to raise a special corps of fifty thousand men. Stanton had turned him down; the administration wanted no more of Frémont just then, and Mitchel had been ordered to duty along the Carolina coast (where he would presently die of a fever); but the basic idea was appealing, and shortly thereafter McClernand had come in with a plan of his own.

Let him go through the western states, he pleaded, getting and organizing recruits, then; when a force of perhaps thirty thousand of all arms had been raised, let him take it and move boldly down the Mississippi, answerable to no one but Washington. He would capture Vicksburg; this would open the river to the Gulf, split the Confederacy, assuage midwestern farmers, dampen the rising tide of northern Copperheads, and possibly win the war.[1]

Lincoln and Stanton told him to go ahead, and McClernand went west, conferring with governors and other men of influence and then taking to the stump to raise volunteers. He was popular with western Democrats and he was a good stump speaker, and before long new volunteers began to appear in quantity, especially in Illinois. McClernand busily organized them into regiments and wrote jubilantly to Stanton, who assured him that "everything here is favorable for your expedition," told him to make frequent reports, and added: "I long to see you in the field striking vigorous blows against the rebellion in its most vital point."[2]

That McClernand was raising and organizing troops was, of course, public knowledge, but the rest of the program was top secret. Plenty of rumors were afloat, however, and these reached Grant; and then, on November 10, after he had wired Halleck asking why the reinforcements that had been promised him were not arriving, Grant received a very odd reply. A number of regiments were on the way, said Halleck, and more would quickly follow, and "Memphis will be made the base of a joint military and naval expedition on Vicksburg."

Since Grant's own plans called for an overland hike on the eastern side of the Yazoo Delta country, this sounded very much as if someone else were coming in to supersede him, and that someone could only be McClernand. Grant sent Halleck an anxious inquiry.

Halleck was playing his cards carefully. He had no use for McClernand, an independent Vicksburg expedition struck him as absurd, and if in the preceding winter he had tried to elbow Grant out of the army he was very much on Grant's side now. Studying the McClernand case, Halleck discovered that the administration had put in McClernand's orders a little escape clause, and of this Halleck now was prepared to take full advantage.

The War Department on October 20 had given McClernand confidential orders instructing him to do all of the things he had asked to be allowed to do. Among other things, these orders told McClernand to send the new troops he was raising to Cairo, Memphis, or such other place as Halleck might direct, "to the end that, when a sufficient force not required by the operations of General Grant's command shall be raised," McClernand might lead his men against Vicksburg.

Halleck was a good lawyer, and he saw through all of this without difficulty. The troops would go forward, as fast as McClernand got them ready, into Grant's department. On arrival, it might easily turn out that they would be "required by the operations of General Grant's command," especially if McClernand himself did not at once go with them. Blandly Halleck wired Grant that he was not being superseded; all troops entering his department were under his command.[3]

Grant put Halleck's messages on top of all the rumors he had been hearing and worked out a new program. He would march down into Mississippi as he had planned, following the line of the Mississippi Central Railroad, which goes roughly parallel to the Yazoo, thirty or forty miles farther inland. Simultaneously a joint army-navy expedition would leave Memphis for Vicksburg. It would include some of the troops that had been in the department all along, and all of the McClernand troops that had arrived, but it would be under the command of William Tecumseh Sherman.[4]

Together, these two thrusts might be very effective. Grant's own advance should force Confederate Pemberton to come up to meet him. Meanwhile Porter and his gunboats would convoy Sherman clear down the Mississippi to the mouth of the Yazoo. By ascending the Yazoo a short distance Sherman could put his army ashore at the foot of the Chickasaw Bluffs, just a few miles north of Vicksburg. If the Confederate defenders were kept busy opposing Grant's thrust from the north, Sherman could storm the bluffs and take the city; if the Confederates concentrated against Sherman they could not very well keep Grant from moving on down the railroad. And, in any case, the big Vicksburg expedition would be put in motion without McClernand.

McClernand, meanwhile, back in Illinois, was happily sending new regiments down to Memphis, where Sherman was hastily giving them brigade and division formation and preparing to march them on transports. By the middle of December, McClernand was reporting to Washington that he had sent most of his men and that there was nothing of importance remaining for him to do in Illinois: might he not now be ordered to go to Memphis and assume the promised command?

The orders did not come, but news of what was going on at Memphis did, and on December 17 McClernand sent an outraged wire to Lincoln: "I believe I am superseded. Please advise me."[5] To Stanton, on the same day, he telegraphed a similar complaint.

Stanton sent him the most innocent of replies, brimming with reassurance. McClernand was not being superseded; Grant had been ordered to form the troops in his department into four army corps, McClernand would be named commander of one of these, and as soon as Grant signed the papers McClernand could go south, assume command of his troops, and head for Vicksburg. Simultaneously orders to proceed with the corps formation and the appointment of McClernand went from the War Department to Grant.

There was a letdown in this. Being a corps commander under Grant was not quite the same as being an independent army commander. There was also a catch in it. Grant made out the orders next day, December 18, and wired McClernand that his corps was ready and that it would "form a part of the expedition on Vicksburg"; Grant hoped that when McClernand reached Memphis he would find all preparations complete and the expedition ready to move.[6] The catch lay in the fact that there was somehow a delay of several days in the transmission of this wire. By the time McClernand reached Memphis—he came down by special steamboat as soon as he got Grant's message—he found that the expedition had not waited for him. Gunboats, transports, and two solid army corps, one of them belonging to McClernand and the other subject to his orders because he outranked its commander, had gone on down the river without him. There was nothing for him to do but go chugging down-river after it, fuming and fruitlessly demanding an explanation.

McClernand, in other words, had been given a neat double shuffle. He had dreamed up the expedition and he had brought in most of the troops for it, men who might not have enlisted at all without his efforts; now the expedition had moved out from under him, and although he would eventually overtake it, the moment of glory might easily elude him. He was never able to prove a thing on anybody, although it was clear some very fancy footwork had been performed. Many years afterward Grant confessed: "I had good reason to believe that in forestalling him I was by no means giving offense to those whose authority to command was above both him and me."[7]

Perhaps the Confederates helped a little, although the price of their help came high.

Grant's army was moving down the line of the Mississippi Central Railroad while all of this was going on. It got as far as Oxford, thirty-five miles below the Tennessee line; some twenty miles in its rear, at the inconsiderable town of Holly Springs, Grant had established a huge supply dump. The country was wooded and thinly populated, and the inhabitants seemed to hold unanimous anti-Yankee sentiments of considerable bitterness. One reason, perhaps, was that the western troops were doing an uncommon amount of senseless looting. A Union officer remembered seeing in one occupied town a cavalryman staggering off carrying a huge grandfather's clock. Asked what on earth he proposed to do with it, the man explained that he was going to dismantle it "and get a pair of the little wheels out of it for spur rowels."⁸ The idea took hold, and other cavalrymen were doing the same. Meanwhile the roads were poor, the weather was wet, most of the streams were swollen, and the army had no pontoon train.

Then, just as things seemed to be going well, two Confederate cavalry leaders taught Grant a lesson about the evils of exposing a long supply line to enemy action.

The first was curly-haired Earl Van Dorn, old-time friend of Grant at West Point, who brushed aside an incompetent Yankee cavalry force, scared a timorous infantry colonel into surrender, and seized the supply base at Holly Springs. The gray troopers made holiday in this town, burning more than a million dollars' worth of Federal supplies and leaving Grant's army in danger of starvation.

Worse yet was the incredible feat performed by Nathan Bedford Forrest.

Forrest took a newly recruited cavalry detachment, imperfectly mounted and largely unarmed, and swung far up into Tennessee, gobbling up one Federal base after another, seizing enough horses and arms so that his whole outfit could be fully equipped, cutting the railroad in several places, and destroying courier routes and telegraph lines so effectively that for days Grant was entirely cut off from communication with the rear echelon. It is possible that this was what delayed his message to McClernand: possible, too, that the complete silence (its cause not then known in Memphis) led Sherman to hurry off to Vicksburg in the belief that Grant had plunged deeply into Mississippi. McClernand, at any rate, was never able to prove that this was not the case.

The real importance of the raids, however, was that they brought Grant's army to an abrupt standstill. All hands were put on half rations, and to keep his army from starvation

Grant sent his wagons out into the country to seize supplies. They got so much stuff, incidentally, that Grant's eyes popped out, and in the months to come he reflected long and hard on the likelihood that an army in Mississippi could abandon its supply line entirely and live off the country.° This conclusion came to him later, however; at the time he could only call off his advance and wait while communications were restored. He could not get word to Sherman, and that officer sailed down-river for Vicksburg, confident that everything was going according to schedule.

Late in December, Sherman's flotilla entered the mouth of the Yazoo, and the soldiers went ashore and made ready to assault Chickasaw Bluffs. As far as Sherman knew, Grant was approaching Vicksburg from the northeast, and the Rebels must be too busy fending him off to make a good defense at the bluffs.

Disillusionment came quickly. Pemberton did not have to worry about Grant, and he had plenty of men waiting for Sherman's attack. The position on Chickasaw Bluffs was so strong that when it was properly manned it could not possibly be stormed, and when the Federals made their attack on December 29 they were quickly defeated, with over seventeen hundred casualties. Sherman got his men back on the boats, moved out of range, and glumly wondered what to do next. The expedition was a flat failure, and it seemed advisable to do something to put a good face on matters. He and Admiral Porter talked things over and agreed that something might be salvaged from defeat by making a quick stab at Confederate Fort Hindman, otherwise known as Arkansas Post—a stronghold forty miles up the Arkansas River, which entered the Mississippi seventy miles above Vicksburg. No real attack on Vicksburg, Sherman argued, could be made until this post was reduced; besides, a victory there would help the North forget about what had happened at Chickasaw Bluffs.¹⁰

No sooner had they agreed on this than the steamer *Tigress* came in bearing McClernand—angry and eager. McClernand issued a proclamation assuming command of everything—between the men who had come down with him and the ones Sherman had led, there were now thirty-two thou-

sand Federal soldiers in the vicinity—and he announced that
this would hereafter be known as the Army of the Mississippi.
Sherman would command one corps in this army and the
other would be under General G. W. Morgan.[11] This rubbed
Sherman where he was raw; he felt that Morgan had let him
down badly in the fight at the bluffs by failing to attack as
ordered, but McClernand was boss and there was no help for
it.

McClernand did respect Sherman as a soldier, and when
the Arkansas Post idea was explained to him he immediately
approved it. He had reached the scene on January 3, and by
January 10 his army and Porter's flotilla had gone up the
Arkansas River and were hammering away at the fort.

The fort caved in quickly, the Federals took nearly five
thousand prisoners, and here was a neat little success to
counterbalance Chickasaw Bluffs. McClernand, Sherman, and
Porter dropped down the river again to a point near the
mouth of the Yazoo; and Grant, who had returned to Memphis, got the news.

Grant was not in a mood to give McClernand a thing, and
when he learned that the expedition had gone into Arkansas
—this news reached him before he learned of the victory
itself—he assumed that it was all McClernand's doing, and
he wrote indignantly to Halleck denouncing it as a senseless
wild-goose chase. Then later returns came in: news of the
victory, and the information that the idea had been Sherman's.
Grant promptly reversed himself and sent Halleck a message
praising the move which he had just condemned and calling
it an essential step in the Vicksburg campaign.[12]

At the same time he reversed his earlier strategic plan.
It was obvious that the original route down the line of the
railroad was very long and risky; obvious, too, that there was
going to be a major drive down the river whether Grant liked
it or not. McClernand had so much rank that wherever he
went he would be in command unless Grant himself were
present, and it was impossible for Grant to think calmly
about things that might happen to an army in the steaming
mud flats just north of Vicksburg with impulsive, unskilled
McClernand in charge.

Grant would put all his eggs in one basket. The attack on

Vicksburg would be made from the river. As large an army as Grant could assemble would be concentrated there, and Grant would go down to take personal command. On January 30, Grant joined McClernand, Sherman and Porter at Milliken's Bend on the west bank of the river, ten miles above Vicksburg, and the decisive campaign of the Civil War had its beginning.

It would begin very slowly, and for a long time it would look like nothing so much as failure. Grant's earlier impression that Vicksburg could not be attacked from the north and west —the only directions from which an army at Milliken's Bend could conceivably approach it—was eminently correct. Ideally, it would have been much better to bring everyone back to Memphis and make a fresh start down the eastern side of the Yazoo Delta. But this just was not in the cards. The move down the river had been approved at Washington. Withdrawal now would be an unmistakable confession of defeat; the political situation in the North was excessively delicate, and it seemed likely that Fredericksburg and Stone's River were, between them, about as large a budget of bad news as the citizenry would be likely to accept. There was nothing for it but to go ahead.

8.

Swing of the Pendulum

1. *The Hour of Darkness*

PROFOUND CURRENTS were moving in America that winter,
but they had not yet fused to form one great tide that would
carry everything along with it. They were still separate, often
in conflict, with deep swirling eddies to mark the points of
tension, and with odd backwaters where things seemed to
drift upstream; and no one could say how the business would
finally be resolved.

The three armies lay in their camps—in Virginia, in Tennessee, and along the Mississippi—and nothing seemed to be
going right with them. Afterward men looked back and said
that, taking everything together, this was the Valley Forge
winter of the Civil War: the winter of misery and despair, of
cold and hunger and of a seeming breakdown of all the
arrangements that had been made to feed and clothe and
usefully employ the men who had been called into the army.
Certainly there was reason to draw the Valley Forge parallel,
for in some ways the winter of 1862-63 marked the bottom of
the depression.

Burnside made one more effort to use the Army of the
Potomac after it had crawled back across the river to recuper-
ate from the Fredericksburg defeat. In the middle of January,
after a long spell of mild weather had dried the unpaved
Virginia roads, he tried a march up the Rappahannock River
to the fords that lie upstream from Fredericksburg, thinking
to cross the river and come down on Lee's flank. What luck
he might have had with this move will never be known,
for a howling rainstorm descended just as the army started

to move, roads and fields turned into quagmires, and inside of twenty-four hours the whole army was hopelessly stuck in the mud. Pontoon trains and artillery columns were utterly helpless, bogged down so that they could not move at all unless men got shovels and dug them out. Infantry and cavalry could waddle along after a fashion, pounds of bulbous clay sticking to each helpless foot, but anything resembling an actual military movement was out of the question. After two days of it Burnside admitted that he was licked, and the army stumbled back to camp.

The camp to which it returned was cheerless enough, even without the humiliating knowledge that one more move had ended in defeat.

The Burnside regime had never quite been able to make regimental and brigade commanders keep house properly, and the log-and-canvas shelters which the men had put up over shallow pits in the ground were little better than pigsties. The commissary had broken down; in this safe camp no more than fifty miles from Washington, men were dying of scurvy because they had nothing but salt pork and hardtack to eat. Hospital arrangements were in a complete mess—no heat in the tents, no proper food for sick men, nursing so inefficient that some patients actually froze to death in their cots. Things, in short, were in a very bad state, and army morale reflected it.

Not only were the men grumpy toward their commanders— one corps defiantly refused to raise a cheer for Burnside at a review, even though all of the officers rode up and down the line, swinging their caps and chanting: "Hip—hip—hip—" They were casting dark looks at President Lincoln himself. The Army of the Potomac was in theory the army that contained the largest core of anti-slavery sentiment, yet with everything going wrong the men found the Emancipation Proclamation hard to swallow.

One New Englander wrote savagely in a letter to his family: "I don't feel as much like fighting as I used to for it looks to me as if fighting for the Union and Constitution is played out and that now we are fighting for the Abolition of Slavery. Speaking of Abe, I have gone clean back on him! He may be a very good rail splitter but rather a poor President

I reckon. . . . Let the Nigger go to hell for all of me, and if a man wants to preach abolition, emancipation or any other ism he must find somebody besides me to preach it to." A New Yorker reflected on the abysmal failure of leadership and wrote to his mother: "Perhaps Old Abe has some funny story to tell, appropriate to the occasion. . . . I am sick and tired of disaster and the fools that bring disaster upon us."[1]

Many people back home were feeling the same way, and the letters the soldiers received reflected it. An Illinois officer in the Army of the Cumberland wrote that the home folks were "writing letters which would discourage the most loyal of men." He put in most of his time, he said, "talking patriotism at the boys and doing good, round, solid cursing at the home cowardly vipers who are disgracing the genus man by their conduct." In the big Union base at Nashville there were so many prostitutes that an Ohio soldier declared the army's very existence was threatened; the authorities finally took a provost guard, rounded up fifteen hundred of the women, and moved them under guard all the way to Louisville, with stern orders not to come any farther south. While Rosecrans worked to reorganize his army and get it in shape for the spring campaign, he feared that he was about to be attacked: he wrote Halleck that Bragg was being reinforced and would soon take the offensive. He demanded reinforcements and complained that Rebel cavalry was constantly annoying him. Meanwhile his winter camps were wet, muddy, and uncomfortable, and there was a great deal of pneumonia.[2]

Grant's Army of the Tennessee found itself strung up and down the western bank of the Mississippi for fifty miles. The river was abnormally high, much of the bottom land was under water, and only the levee itself seemed to offer camping space. Unending rains beat upon the levee, every company street was ankle-deep with black gummy mud, and there was sickness everywhere. A man in a newly arrived Indiana regiment reported that "scarcely a man had anything like good health," and said that "the levee for miles is almost one continued mass of graves"; men had to pitch their tents on top of new graves, and the evil scent of death was always in the air. A doctor reported that steamers fitted as hospital ships would come down, load up with sick men, and then reveal a complete lack of nurses, so that helpless invalids had to look out for themselves; on one such steamer, he said, twenty-two men died overnight, "and I believe before God some of them died for want of proper nourishment."[3]

All sorts of wild rumors went through camp. Some men asserted that the northern states were going to call their regiments home, and it was believed that if a man ran away from the army his home-state authorities would give him protection. When the mails failed to reach the army for a time it was reported that peace had been declared and that Grant was purposely stopping letters and newspapers "for fear we could not be held in subjection if we knew the state of affairs." There was an epidemic of desertion, and an Ohio veteran wrote: "Now the hour of darkness began." In some regiments the sick men outnumbered the well. On top of everything else the army failed to get its paymasters around on time and the soldiers were broke.[4]

All of this made it look as if the bottom had fallen out of the tub, and the Union cause seemed to be dipping down toward acceptance of defeat in January and February of 1863. But if there was reason for gloom there was also, in these armies and in the country behind them, reason for quiet confidence. Under the dejection there was a certain toughness; the sulkiest of complaints could come from men who really had no idea of quitting; and soldiers and civilians alike had deep reserves of strength and hope, to be drawn on when most needed. It is not hard to find signs that the will to win was still powerful.

In Iowa an unusual job of recruiting had just been completed. Early in January this state sent to St. Louis, to go marching through the streets to the rendezvous at Benton Barracks, the 37th Iowa Volunteer Infantry, numbering 914 rank and file; a regiment like all others except for one thing— everyone from colonel to drummer boy was safely past the upper military age limit of forty-five years. (Many of the men were over sixty, some were in their seventies, and one sprightly private confessed to the age of eighty.)

This was Iowa's famous "Graybeard Regiment," recruited by special arrangement with the War Department as a means of showing that there were plenty of draft-proof citizens who

were perfectly willing to go to war. There was a tacit understanding that the regiment would be given guard and garrison
duty as much as possible, but there was nothing binding
about this. The 37th was in no sense a home-guard outfit; it
had enlisted for the full three years and eventually it was to
campaign in Missouri, Tennessee, and Mississippi, hiking in
the rain and sleeping in the mud like anybody else. During
its three years only scattered detachments got into actual
fighting—the total casualty list was only seven—but 145 men
died of disease, and 364 had to be mustered out of service
for physical disability, and when the regiment at last was
paid off, in May of 1865, it was revealed that more than
thirteen hundred sons and grandsons of members of the regiment were in Federal military service. So old were these men,
and so young their state, that not a man in the regiment
could claim Iowa as his birthplace. There had been no Iowa
when these Iowans were born.[5]

An army surgeon in a Kentucky regiment who went down
the river with McClernand's flotilla and saw Sherman's men
just after their repulse at Chickasaw Bluffs noticed no signs of
depression among them. Instead, he found these soldiers "the
noisiest crowd of profane-swearing, dram-drinking, card-play-
ing, song-singing, reckless, impudent dare-devils in the world."
An Illinois recruit who came to the army at this time said that
the men thought more of Sherman than of any other man alive
but that they never raised a cheer for him when he rode along
the lines.[6]

For the Westerners did not often cheer their generals. In
the Army of the Potomac it was different. During the Mc-
Clellan regime, staff officers would ride ahead of the commanding general when he was about to make an appearance,
and would see to it that a cheer was raised; a cheer was
accepted as part of the routine, and for the most part the
men offered it willingly enough. Officers sometimes went to
great lengths in this business. When the Irish Brigade was
paraded to get its first look at its new division commander,
General Israel B. Richardson (who was to be killed at Antietam), a member of Richardson's staff galloped over to the
brigade just before the general arrived and made a speech
about Richardson's many virtues.

"And what do you think of the brave old fellow?" he demanded. "He has sent to this camp three barrels of whiskey, a barrel for each regiment, to treat the boys of the brigade, and we ought to give him a thundering cheer when he comes along."

Naturally the Irishmen gave Richardson a tumultuous reception—not knowing that the staff officer had unblushingly lied to them and that no whiskey had been sent.[1]

The Easterners took their cue from McClellan, who liked cheering; the Westerners may have taken theirs from Grant, who didn't care. An officer remembered seeing Grant one night while the army was crossing a bayou on a pontoon bridge during a forced march; he was in the saddle, solid, erect, and brown, keeping the traffic moving with repeated orders: "Push right along, men—close up fast and hurry over." The men all turned to look at him, made note that the commanding general was in their midst, but said never a word. Looking back on it afterward, the officer mused: "Here was no McClellan, begging the boys to allow him to light his cigar by theirs, or inquiring to what regiment that exceedingly fine-marching company belonged. . . . There was no nonsense, no sentiment; only a plain business man of the republic, there for the one single purpose of getting that command over the river in the shortest time possible."[2]

The Westerners would go where the generals told them to go, and within reasonable limits they would do what the generals told them to do, but they insisted on being unmilitary about it. But when the Potomac soldiers flatly refused to cheer Burnside, it was a sign that they had written him off.

At Murfreesboro the time of sickness and depression did not last long. Rosecrans got his supply lines working in spite of the Rebel raiders and saw to it that there was plenty to eat. The men cut cedar boughs to shade and protect their tents, camps were made clean and were kept well policed, and before long an Ohio private was confessing that "we may be said to have enjoyed all the comforts which can fall to a soldier's lot." The army had been badly mangled at Stone's River; Rosecrans was going to let it get plenty of rest before it began a new campaign. He carried this prescription so far, indeed, that by spring both Halleck and Grant were complaining that his army was not pulling its weight.

Rosecrans himself had put in some of his spare time examining statistics, as a result of which he told his troops that they were going to have to brush up on their marksmanship. In the Stone's River fight, he said, a comparison of Federal ammunition expenditures with Confederate casualties showed that it had taken 145 rounds of musketry to hit one Rebel and that a Yankee cannon had to be fired twenty-seven times to inflict a single casualty.[9]

A resident of Tennessee who had seen a good deal of both Union and Confederate armies wrote out a comparison of his own, basing much of it on what he saw in Rosecrans's camps.

The Federal soldiers, he said, managed their camps better than the Confederates. Even if they were to be in a place only a few days, men would scurry around to build little beds —usually by driving forked sticks into the ground and laying saplings or planks across them—and they would build little shelters for their cooking stoves. Confederates seldom bothered with such comforts. Where a Union camp would be bustling with activity, a Confederate camp was apt to be a scene of idle relaxation. Union animals were better fed and groomed than those in a southern camp; guns and equipment were kept better polished, and the camp itself was usually cleaner.

But the Confederates were incomparably the more orderly. A Confederate detachment might camp in a place for weeks, without a single hen roost being the poorer; but "when the Union troops came around we all had to look out for our money, jewels, watches, vegetables, pigs, cows and chickens." Much of the Federal looting was senseless, with men taking things that could be of no earthly use to them. The Tennessean remembered one outfit that stole a shipment of two hundred Bibles and then tore the books up and used them to build fires. The Tennessean believed that these Federal habits developed partly because the men felt themselves to be in enemy country, where anything was fair game, and partly because the Yankee armies contained so many foreign-born and so much "riff-raff from the large cities."[10]

One Confederate very well qualified to pass on soldierly attributes was studying the western armies that winter—

Joseph E. Johnston, recovered now from the wound that had put him out of action at Seven Pines, and sent west by Jefferson Davis to co-ordinate the effort of Bragg's and Pemberton's armies. Johnston did not enjoy this assignment; the armies were quite a distance apart, it was almost impossible for one man to exercise any real control over both, and most of the decisions he had to make were, he felt, policy matters on which Richmond itself ought to pass. Anyway, Johnston had been comparing the Federal armies in Tennessee with the Army of the Potomac back in Virginia, and he was warning the Confederate Secretary of War not to underestimate the Westerners who were serving under Grant—"his troops are worth double the number of northeastern troops."[11]

The Potomac army was being brought out of its black mood as winter drew on toward spring. Burnside was finally removed, and Joe Hooker at last got the command he had wanted so badly—got it, and a canny letter from Abraham Lincoln telling him that those cracks about the need for a dictatorship had been heard and would be remembered and that what was wanted from Hooker was military victory, as soon as possible.

Somewhat to everyone's surprise (for the man was thought to be nothing more than a hard-driving fighter), Hooker turned out to be a first-rate military administrator. His contribution to the ultimate northern victory, indeed, was not really a matter of fighting at all; it consisted in the fact that he got the Army of the Potomac back on its feet, shook the kinks out of it, and left for his successors a first-rate fighting machine that would go on functioning to the end of the war.

Hooker did all of this by a common-sense process of removing the causes of bad morale.

The camps were laid out anew, the old pigsty bunkhouses were abandoned, and Hooker's inspectors saw to it that the soldiers lived in as much comfort and cleanliness as a winter camp might afford. The commissary system was overhauled so that vegetables and potatoes and fresh meat reached camp in quantity; scurvy disappeared, and a clean and well-fed army suddenly discovered that it did not have nearly as much sickness as it had had before. At the same time, Hooker reformed the hospital system so that sick men could get decent care and food, and the appalling death rates abruptly came down.

Hooker's men had been almost unendurably homesick, and so Hooker gave them furloughs. (Most of the desertions that had been taking place were caused not so much by a conscious decision to leave the army as by a simple desire to get home and see the folks.) At the same time, he tightened up on the security system so that real deserters would have a much harder time getting away from camp.

Finally, Hooker put everybody to work. There were drills —company and battalion drills, brigade and division drills— hour after hour, day after day, with big reviews on weekends and all the pomp and grandeur of war to raise men's spirits. Cavalry was reorganized as a unified corps and was told that the commanding general expected it to get out and fight. Cavalry rose to the occasion. Before long even the captious Federal infantry was admitting that "our cavalry is something to talk about now," and was confessing that "Hooker is entitled to the credit of making the cavalry of use instead of ornament."[12]

As all of this happened, the Army of the Potomac began to cheer again. Hooker would stage enormous reviews, with whole army corps marching back and forth on the dusty plains above the river; sometimes President Lincoln would be there, listening with a faint sense of unease to Hooker's boasts that this was "the finest army on the planet" and that the question was not whether the army would capture Richmond but simply *when*. There was a great jubilant shouting when Hooker rode along the lines. The man had an air; he saw to it that his staff and escort were well mounted and neatly garbed, and to men who thought themselves disillusioned about war he brought back an enduring touch of the color and flashing gaiety of war's romance. He made army life exciting, and under the excitement he infused a sense of great power and growing strength.

The careful, cautious soldiers were being weeded out. McClellan was gone, the cries of the soldiers who adored him still echoing in his ears, and the kind of war he was able to fight was gone forever. Buell was gone, as well, his kind of war also done for; and the War Department was bearing down brutally to prove to reluctant officers that the day of hard war had arrived. Fitz-John Porter who had led McClellan's V Corps so ably on the peninsula, had been cashiered, convicted by court-martial of refusing to carry out John Pope's orders at Second Bull Run. The facts that his conviction and sentence were outrageously unjust and that Pope had in his befuddlement issued impossible orders were beside the point; Porter was simply a victim, beheaded to show the career soldiers that the administration was very much in earnest. Ruthlessly trampling a man underfoot, the administration was also trampling down (as one combat veteran put it) "the damnable heresy that a man can be a friend to the government and yet throw every clog in the way of the administration and prosecution of the war."[13]

2. Stalemate in the Swamps

The great river which western men believed to be the sign and symbol of the nation's destined unity came down from the north with silent power and without haste. It brimmed over its banks, creating ponds and bayous and meaningless tangled waterways all over the flat country on either side; it spun great lazy loops and curves far to the right and the left, and it was swollen now from incessant rains, tearing at its neglected levees as if it might yet flood the war itself out of its broad valley. It was brown with silt; a steamboat captain assured gaping Illinois recruits that if a man drank Mississippi River water for as much as a week "he will have a sandbar in him a mile long."[1]

Half of the country seemed to be under water, a primeval swamp that nevertheless was a settled land with farms, villages, and here and there the bottomless trace of a muddy road. Below the horizon, out of sight except to the patrols and scouts, rose the great land mass where Vicksburg had been built. Its massive bluffs faced the river and swung northeast just below the mouth of the Yazoo, and with entrenchments and heavy guns and an endless chain of rifle pits the Confederacy had made here a stronghold which was the proud and arrogant reminder of the division that had come upon the nation.

One great stretch of the river the Confederacy still controlled—the part that lay between Vicksburg and Port Hudson, a Louisiana town just north of Yankee-held Baton Rouge. This piece of the river, measured along its innumerable curves and bends, was perhaps two hundred miles in length, and as long as it was held the Confederacy was still a united nation. For this was the gateway to the rich trans-Mississippi empire. Into the big river, not far above Port Hudson, flowed the Red River, which came southeast from Arkansas across Louisiana; and down the Red River, for shipment east, the trans-Mississippi sent invaluable supplies—quantities of horses, herds of cattle, munitions brought into Texas by blockade-runners, stout reinforcements for the Confederate armies. Until the Federals could seize this stretch of the Mississippi, opening it to their own traffic and sealing it off to the Confederates, they could not win the war for the valley, and if they could not win the war for the valley they could not save the Union.

According to plan, this part of the river was to be attacked from both ends at once. At the northern end there was Grant, operating against a steady background of complaints from General McClernand, who was bitter because his "Army of the Mississippi" had evaporated and because he himself now commanded nothing more than the XIII Army Corps. At New Orleans, preparing to move north and seize Port Hudson, there were twenty-five thousand Union troops under command of Major General Nathaniel P. Banks.

Banks was a devoted Republican who had had troubles and who was about to have more. In Virginia he had had to fight against Stonewall Jackson, which had tested him beyond his strength. He had been picked for this job in Louisiana partly because as a man of influence with the voters back home he was too good to waste, partly because a combination of circumstances had made it necessary to get Ben Butler out of there, and partly because—to an administration which correctly saw this as a political war but which did have its problems in finding the proper political instruments to use in it—he and John McClernand had for a time looked like the two halves of a perfect whole.

Banks and McClernand, it had been thought, could open the valley between them, and Banks's appointment was the obverse face of the mysterious commission that had been given McClernand. When their forces were joined Banks would take top command, and then they would occupy Texas, complete the mopping up of Louisiana, start healthy shipments of southern cotton moving back up the river, and make it possible to bring this part of the South back into the Union.

The reconstruction problem, in fact, was at the core of Banks's assignment. President Lincoln was groping desperately for a way by which seceding states that were firmly held by Federal troops could somehow be brought back into their old relationship with the central government. He had a scheme now for the discovery and careful cultivation of the little islands of Unionist sentiment which were known to exist in the South. If these were brought along properly, it might eventually be possible to restore the old Union without treating the occupied areas as conquered provinces; the new Union, in other words, might be caused to grow painlessly and naturally out of the deep roots of the old, with a final reconciliation that could help to heal the dreadful scars of war. It was worth trying. Banks understood all about it and believed in it, and to make a good start at it was one of his primary functions.[2]

But he must also lead troops in the field; must open the Port Hudson gateway while Grant opened the one at Vicksburg. Banks was now preparing to do this, but there were still a good many armed Confederates on the march in Louisiana, with a good many more just above them in Arkansas. Banks was worried by these; he would have to do some subsidiary campaigning before he could move on Port Hudson. The political problem was taking half of his attention, and he was not a very skillful strategist anyway. All of which added up to the fact that if the Mississippi was to be opened most of the work would have to be done by Grant's army.

For the immediate present Grant's army could not fight because it was quite unable to get to any place where a proper fight could be made. It was on the wrong side of the Mississippi and it was north of Vicksburg; to make its fight it would somehow have to get downstream, cross the river, and come at Vicksburg from the east. It did not occupy a very good place from which to make such a move, and before it could do anything at all it would have to get down in the swamps and do a great deal of old-fashioned hard work with pick and shovel. The source of its labors lay in an abortive move which the Federal high command had tried a number of months earlier.

Shortly after the capture of New Orleans old Admiral Farragut had taken his salt-water ships up the river to bombard Vicksburg, on the off-chance that the city would cave in as quickly as New Orleans had done. It was a vain hope, and before long Farragut went steaming back down the river, better informed about the strength of this fortress on the bluffs. But a modest detachment of troops had gone upstream at the time, to camp across the river from Vicksburg, and it had occurred to the authorities that it might be possible to by-pass Vicksburg entirely by having these troops dig a canal.

Vicksburg lay near the northern end of a sharp loop in the river, and the land just across the river was actually a long, flat, narrow peninsula. If a suitable ditch could be cut across the neck of this peninsula, it was thought, the river's powerful current would scour it out, the river would presently shift its channel and flow through this expanding ditch, and Vicksburg would be left high and dry, an inland city without military importance. The ditch had been begun, and although the project had lapsed the idea still looked good—especially to President Lincoln, who had all of a frontiersman's interest in tinkering, particularly when a river which he himself had once navigated was involved. Grant was under orders to do all he could to finish the job.

Grant and his engineers had little use for the plan. The half-completed canal had been planned wrong. Its upstream end led out of a backwater, where the current was unlikely to make itself felt, and the downstream end would hit the river at a spot the Confederates could easily reach with the guns at Vicksburg. To make matters ever so much worse, the river was very high just now, and the land that would be crossed by canal was half under water—too wet for diggers but not wet enough for steamboats. But orders were orders, and after the engineers had redrawn the plans so that the canal, if completed, might have a better chance to work as it was supposed to work, thousands upon thousands of soldiers were given picks and shovels and told to get busy.

There was another construction project on the agenda, for that matter. Fifty miles above Vicksburg a lost crescent of a slough known as Lake Providence lay in the flat land a few miles west of the Mississippi. A series of connecting streams led out of Lake Providence and flowed ultimately into the Red River. If a channel could be cut from the Mississippi into Lake Providence, and if the tortuous waterway leading from the lake to the Red River could be made passable for steamboats, it might be possible for Grant's army and Porter's navy to go steaming triumphantly down, enter the Mississippi a little way above Port Hudson, and then steam back to approach Vicksburg from the south, with a moderately secure supply line behind them.

Like the plan for a canal at Young's Point, this idea looked a good deal better than it really was. The route would be fantastically roundabout—Grant estimated that it would involve a detour of something like 470 miles before it could get him to Vicksburg—and there was something unreal about the thought that a steady stream of transports, freighters, and other craft could ply such a waterway, deep in enemy territory, without interference. Besides, when the engineers got to work they found that many miles of the projected waterway were full of trees. These could be cut down in time, but to do it so that loaded steamboats could safely float over the stumps would call for specially designed underwater saws, to say nothing of many man-hours of labor.

Lake Providence, in short, was no better than the canal. Both ideas had to be followed up; there was a whole army of strong young men who had nothing else to do, and it seemed to Grant that they might as well be working as idle. Furthermore, all of this activity was likely to confuse the Confederates and keep them from finding out what the real objective was. But while the men toiled in mud and swamp, Grant had very little hope that the result of their labors would ever really amount to very much.[3]

He still had his original problem: how to get his army to a spot where it could attack Vicksburg with some chance of success. For a time it looked as if the answer might lie up the river.

Across the Mississippi from Helena, Arkansas, and just a few miles downstream—two hundred miles above Vicksburg, or thereabouts, as the winding river went—there was a lackadaisical chain of bayous, flooded swamps, and inconsequential streams known as Yazoo Pass which began just under the lee of the Mississippi levee and communicated at last with the Coldwater River, which fed into a stream known as the Tallahatchie, which in turn went into the Yalobusha, which finally, some 250 desolate miles later, went into the Yazoo. If the levee were cut, boats from the Mississippi could go down this intricate waterway. With any luck they could come out on dry ground a little distance above the mouth of the Yazoo— dead north of Vicksburg, where an army would have the option either of hitting the Chickasaw Bluffs which had stopped Sherman or of circling east and coming up to the fortress from the rear.

This was worth a try, and late in February an expedition got under way—twenty thousand infantry in transports, with a force of navy gunboats to clear the way. Army engineers blew up a mine to break the levee, a miniature Niagara went boiling through Yazoo Pass, and presently eight gunboats and two rams, followed by transports bearing the army's advance guard, went hopefully into the waterway.

Naval officer in charge was Lieutenant Commander Watson Smith, and from the start he found himself mixed up in a sailor's nightmare. The stream he was to follow wound and turned on itself interminably and was full of snags that could rip the bottom out of an incautiously piloted gunboat; there was a powerful current that made it impossible to steer properly, and when the flotilla made three miles a day it was doing well. Smith was a salt-water sailor, and here he was with a squadron of valuable warships navigating in waters where one of the hazards was the chance that the branches of overhanging trees would knock down his smokestacks. The stream was narrow, and artful Confederates swarmed all about, felling trees to clog the waterways. Between the navy and the army engineers, these obstructions were removed—young Colonel James H. Wilson of Grant's staff would send an entire regiment ashore, tail them onto cables, and have them haul the felled trees out by sheer strength and awkwardness. It worked so well, he said, that he never afterward wondered how the Egyptians had hauled their great blocks of stone to build the pyramids—obviously they did it by everyday manpower. In one way and another, this amphibious expedition got deeper and deeper into the half-drowned country of the Yazoo Delta.[4]

March wore away, and the sailors and soldiers inched their way down toward the Yazoo River. They got, at last, after a good deal of pulling and hauling and worrying, to the place where the Yalobusha flowed into the Yazoo; and here, on the only bit of dry ground visible for miles around, the Confederates had built a stout little fort of cotton bales and scooped-up earth, which they called Fort Pemberton. It mounted very few guns, but as things worked out, these few were more than enough.

The river was narrow, and the gunboats could approach just one at a time, in line ahead. Of the eight gunboats, only two were proper ironclads, and these had been hastily and poorly built; when they steamed up for a duel, the Confederate gunners racked them, receiving little damage in return. The logical thing to do now was to land infantry and let it storm the fort, but there was no dry ground for infantry to land on; everything all about was water, with a few muddy tussocks here and there, sprouting dejected pine trees and offering no place for infantry maneuvers. Commander Smith fell ill—he had been having a tough time for a month, and a battle like this in a mosquito-infested swamp was something no navy training had prepared him for—and eventually he turned over the command to a junior and went back to the big river to die of a fever. The junior concluded that nothing more could be done here, and although young Colonel Wilson swore in a fine fury and denounced all weakhearted sailors, it was clear that the game was up. With everybody feeling humiliated, the expedition turned about and floundered back to the Mississippi. Fort Pemberton had stopped it cold.[5]

Admiral Porter, meanwhile, had thought up a similar and equally complicated venture.

Not far above the place where the Yazoo flowed into the Mississippi, a lazy stream known as Steele's Bayou came wandering out of the delta to join the big stream. A venturesome steamboat man who went up Steele's Bayou could before long turn to his right on a little ditch called Black Bayou, which in turn would put him into Deer Creek, which was narrow and shallow and generally mean. Upstream a way there was the mouth of Rolling Fork, which—since all rivers in this land of mud and water seemed to interconnect, flowing impartially in both directions as the state of the water directed —led into the Sunflower River, which in its own good time fed into the Yazoo.

Theoretically a flotilla might leave the Mississippi via Steele's Bayou and, with perseverance and good luck, get into the Yazoo far above Vicksburg. It could then put an army ashore on the high ground back from the Mississippi, this army could take the fortifications on the Chickasaw Bluffs from the rear, its supplies could come to it through this marshy labyrinth—and, in fine, Vicksburg itself could be captured.

Admiral Porter was a man of limitless energy. He sold the idea to Grant—who, all else failing, was about ready to buy anything—and Porter himself would go along to make sure that it worked. Porter got together five of his best gunboats, along with some tugs and a pair of mortar boats, and Grant ordered Sherman to take some troops and accompany the flotilla on land, to clear out any obstructive Rebels who might try to bar the way. In the middle of March—while Commander Smith was still plowing doggedly on toward Fort Pemberton— this odd expedition turned up the narrow bayou and went steaming off through the forest.

It met all of the troubles which Commander Smith's troop had met, most of them multiplied by five. The waterway was painfully narrow. Felled trees and bridges blocked the way at frequent intervals; Porter used his powerful ironclads as tanks and sent them driving through such obstructions, knocking logs and timbers out of the way with prodigious crashing and banging, clouds of black smoke pouring from funnels, everybody dancing and swearing with excitement. The river was full of sunken logs, and donkey engines came into play as these were hoisted out with block and tackle. At times the stream was so narrow that the leading gunboat would be pinched in between the trees that grew out of the half-submerged banks and brought to a standstill. Then there would be much huffing and puffing, and the vessel would drive its way through by brute force, knocking over the trees as it went.

Things got worse and worse. The waterway wound and twisted incomprehensibly, so that there were times when all five gunboats, each dutifully following the tail of the next ahead, were steering in five different directions. Up in front there were web-footed Confederates who kept felling huge trees to block the channel, and each tree had to be fished out individually. All sorts of wildlife, from squirrels to raccoons, came aboard the boats as the overhanging trees were jarred; at times sailors stood by with brooms to sweep overboard such lesser vermin as snakes and bugs.

Then a new obstacle developed. Porter found himself leading his boats into a narrow channel which was all overgrown with young willows. Helpful Negroes explained that in seasons of low water all this country was a second-growth forest from which slaves cut numerous young willows to make baskets; with the water high, the limber little saplings came up like swamp grass through the middle of the stream, forming a yielding but impenetrable barrier that would catch the vessels' hulls, slow them to a halt, and make further advance practically impossible. Porter gave saws and knives to all hands, set up rope-and-plank outriggers, and put his people to work hacking and slicing away at the miserable green withes; with a whole ship's company at work, a gunboat might gain three or four feet after an hour's work.

Ominous noises began to come, to disturb the admiral's mind still more. A steady chop-chopping showed that the Confederates were felling trees to block the waterway—but they were felling these trees *behind* the flotilla, not in front of it; they knew it could not possibly advance much farther,

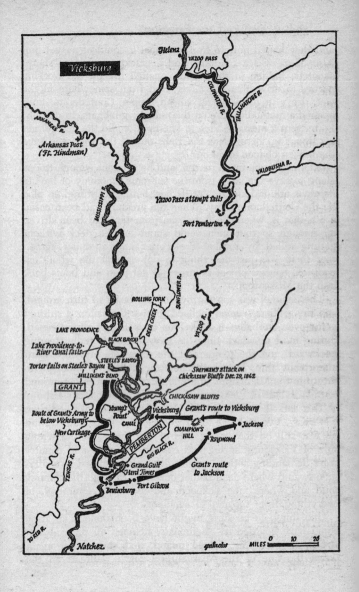

Vicksburg

Helena

YAZOO PASS

COLDWATER R.

TALLAHATCHIE R.

ARKANSAS R.

Arkansas Post
(Ft. Hindman)

YALOBUSHA R.

MISSISSIPPI R.

Yazoo Pass attempt fails

Fort Pemberton

ROLLING FORK

SUNFLOWER R.

DEER CREEK

YAZOO R.

LAKE PROVIDENCE

BLACK BAYOU

Lake Providence-to-
River Canal fails

STEELE'S BAYOU

Porter fails on Steele's Bayou

HILLIKEN'S BEND

Sherman's attack on
Chickasaw Bluffs Dec. 29, 1862

GRANT

CHICKASAW BLUFFS

Young's
Point

Vicksburg

Grant's route to Vicksburg

Route of Grant's Army to
below Vicksburg

CANAL

PEMBERTON

CHAMPION'S
HILL

Jackson

Raymond

New Carthage

BIG BLACK R.

TENSAS R.

Grand Gulf
Hard Times

Grant's route
to Jackson

Bruinsburg

Fort Gibson

TO RED R.

Natchez

spelncizs

MILES

0   10   20

and they hoped now to trap it so that it could never get out. Also, there was a snapping and a cracking as Rebel sharpshooters, hidden in the woods, opened fire on the working parties to drive them to cover; and from somewhere in the wet, leafy invisibility up ahead, some Confederate guns opened a methodical fire on the unlucky gunboats. In despair, Porter sent a message back to Sherman: could the general get his troops up here, clear the Rebs out of the way, and give the navy a chance to go on?

Sherman came up in person, and he brought enough troops along to save the navy from the supreme ignominy of having its crack admiral and one of its best flotillas captured en bloc by the Confederate army. When the pressure had been eased a bit—that is, when the Rebel sharpshooters had been driven off enough so that men could stand on the deck without getting killed by musket fire—Porter and Sherman agreed that there was just one thing to do: call off the whole expedition, confess abject failure, and get men and boats back into the Mississippi.

The channel was too narrow for the boats to turn around, and the soldiers seemed inclined to give the sailors a spirited going-over, verbally; it took four days to get disentangled, during most of which time the navy was dejectedly steering backward, and the tempers of the naval officers were worn abnormally thin; but in the end the flotilla did manage to return to the Mississippi, and one more attempt to get around to the soft side of Vicksburg had to be written off as a failure.°

This left it up to Grant. One canal, one lake-and-river waterway, two stabs at the Yazoo Delta; all had failed, and he was still on the wrong side of the river and the wrong side of Vicksburg, spring was coming on, press and country were demanding action, and his army was camped in a fifty-mile swamp where dead bodies oozed up through the clammy mud and where men sickened and died, day after day, of everything from malaria to smallpox.

One thing, to be sure, might have been done. The army could have boarded its steamboats, steamed all the way upstream to Memphis, moved inland, and started out again down the line of the Mississippi Central Railroad on the route that had been tried in December. It was the obvious course—perhaps the only course left.

But Grant would not follow it. The temper of the country, as far as the most sensitive political weather vanes could determine, was bad; one blatant confession of defeat, such as this return to Memphis, might be one ounce more than the country would stand. For the sake of the war effort itself, the thing could not be contemplated. Besides, there was a stubborn streak in U. S. Grant: a deep psychological reluctance, visible from early childhood, to retrace his steps or turn back from a goal he had set for himself. He could not turn back and he would not turn back; and he sat in his cabin on the headquarters steamer at Milliken's Bend, smoking cigars until the room was blue with drifting smoke, staring into the shifting wreaths of vapor, saying nothing to anyone, and quietly evolving the plan that would take Vicksburg.

3. *The Face of the Enemy*

Part of the time the enemy was the terrible curse of war itself; mud, weariness, the steady erosion of human values, the ugly sickness that came upon young men who ate bad food, wore shoddy clothing, and went to sleep wet to wake up cold. At other times it was the visible human foe in gray and butternut, who bore the same curse himself but who always stood ready to fill the hills and woods with fire and smoke and the echoing crash of gunfire. But underneath everything else the real enemy was a deep blindness of the spirit, an ancient constriction of the mind that fatally narrowed the circle of humanity. This enemy had to be defeated at any cost, even though final triumph might be delayed for generations; the war was just a skirmish in the unending fight, but if it was to repay any part of its cost the skirmish must make final victory a little more likely.

Nobody had consciously made up his mind to fight this enemy. The decision was subconscious; it was being worked out painfully, far below the surface, by men who went about their jobs in the steaming swamps along the Mississippi and in the echoing drill fields above the Rappahannock. Trying to win the visible war, they were being forced to grapple with a foe within themselves—the blind, arrogant assumption that some people are by birth and by nature superior to others, so that anything that democracy might finally do must be funneled out through an opening too narrow for any but the lucky few to pass.

This enemy appeared in many forms. It peered out, mocking and hideous, from an order issued early in the winter by U. S. Grant, which read as follows:

"The Jews, as a class violating every regulation of trade established by the Treasury Department and also department orders, are hereby expelled from the department within twenty-four hours from the receipt of this order.

"Post commanders will see that all of this class of people be furnished passes and required to leave, and anyone returning after such notification will be arrested and held in confinement until an opportunity occurs of sending them out as prisoners, unless furnished with a permit from these headquarters."[1]

Back of this order there were two moving causes, one obvious and immediate, the other coming out of the air men breathed in those days, as old as sin and no better to think about.

The obvious immediate reason was cotton. Northern mills and northern exporters desperately needed cotton, and with the war on they were getting very little of it. Whenever a Union army got down into cotton country the speculators would follow if they had half a chance, and there seemed to be nothing at all that they would not do, no length of bribery or chicanery they would not approach, in order to get cotton and send it north. Ormsby Mitchel had got into trouble in 1862, when his men held northern Alabama, because of cotton. To pay the cost of operating a railroad line he held, he had seized Rebel cotton, had invited New York dealers to come in, had sold the cotton to them to get the funds he needed, and then he had helped the dealers move their cotton north. Only the fact that he was an administration pet, probably, had saved him from dismissal. In New Orleans the cotton speculators were everywhere; in Memphis they were sniffing about, frantically eager for any chance to buy cotton and move it north.

What had touched Grant off, apparently, was an alliance made by his father, Jesse Grant, a shrewd little leather merchant who had business dealings in Ohio and Illinois and who possessed both an unerring eye for the main chance and a total lack of understanding of the standards which ought to guide the father of a major general.

Jesse appears to have formed connections with some cotton dealers, and he took them down to see the general. Grant was highly cordial, until he discovered that what his father's friends really wanted was special consideration in the matter of getting permits to buy and ship cotton. In their corrupt innocence they had supposed that the fix was in when they went to headquarters with the commanding general's father. These dealers happened to be Jewish, and when Grant's wrath exploded—he sent his father and his father's friends back to Ohio on the next train—it left him with a hot resentment that broke out a few days later in the form of this order expelling all Jews from the department.[2]

But the invisible cause of the order—the thing that turned it from a simple tightening up of controls on illicit cotton brokerage into a blind, shotgun blast at the Jewish people— was the fact that Grant at all times reflected the age in which he lived; and this age, which lived by the American dream and which was now paying a stupendous price to broaden it, had nevertheless failed almost totally to understand the dream's power and splendor. It was an age in which race prejudice in all of its forms could stalk unchecked and almost unrebuked.

For Americans of the blood interpreted their birthright narrowly and guarded it with fierce jealousy, treating those whose origins were not as theirs with fear, hatred, or contempt. The country was changing. Year after year the packet ships had been bringing in more and more folk from beyond the ocean, people drawn by many factors, among which was the wild and intoxicating notion that to be an American need not be exclusively a matter of birth. It could also be a matter of conscious choice; one could elect oneself a member of this free society, breaking with the past, sharing in the great pilgrimage toward a dazzling future not because one had been fortunately born but because one wanted to share in it. People came from all over—from Germany and from Ireland and from many other places—bringing languages and creeds and folkways that the nation had not known before and that struck many of the native-born as bewilderingly strange and therefore ominous.

It was not yet a decade since a powerful political party had grown up, built entirely on this fear: the Know-Nothings, who campaigned unashamedly on blatant prejudice, electing governors and senators, coming tolerably close to winning the presidency itself, and demanding that all newcomers be excluded or reduced to second-class citizenship. People who were not infected by this fear nevertheless tended to deny full humanity to the newcomers by seeing them as stereotypes, usually more or less comic. Germans were "Dutchmen," fat and rather stupid folk who talked an amusing brogue and drank too much beer; Irishmen were clumsy bog-trotters who talked an even funnier brogue and who were devoted to whiskey; Jews were bearded, hook-nosed sharpers who peddled goods from wagons and who could be denounced and expelled en masse by an angry general; and Negroes—

Negroes were in some inexplicable manner what the war itself was mostly about. Their status seemed mysteriously to be changing, and as it changed—*if* it changed—there must be corresponding changes in each of the social levels that lay above, and finally in the way Americans looked upon their fellow human beings. For the most fundamental change of all was that it was becoming necessary to look upon the Negro as a man rather than as a thing. Let that once take hold, and racism in all of its forms must receive a mortal wound, even though it might be a very long time dying. What was won for the least of these would finally be won for everybody; and once a common humanity was admitted, an incalculable victory would have been gained, because sooner or later admission would have to be acted on.

Yet victories are won in odd ways, sometimes by men who are thinking about something very different. The General Grant who could express a subconscious but profound racial prejudice in his order expelling the Jews—an order that, by direction of President Lincoln, he very shortly withdrew—could at the same time be working most effectively to destroy racism's foundations, not because he understood what he was about, but simply because he wanted to do everything possible to win the war. One of the instruments he would use would be the Negro as a soldier, the ex-slave put into uniform and empowered to make war against the men lately his masters. The government had come to that step this winter, and colored troops were being raised wherever there were Federal armies.

This decision to use the Negro as a soldier did not necessarily grow out of any broad humanitarian resolve; it seems to have come largely out of the dawning realization that, since the Confederates were going to kill a great many more Union soldiers before the war was over, a good many white men would escape death if a considerable percentage of those soldiers were colored.

Halleck put the thing quite bluntly in a message to Grant in March. It was good policy, he said, to withdraw as many slaves from the South as possible; equally good policy, having withdrawn them, to use them to help win the war. They could certainly be used as teamsters and as laborers, and some people believed they could be used as combat soldiers. Grant must try, and if he found—as he undoubtedly would—that many of the people in his army objected to it, he must ride their objections down and see that this new policy was carried out.

"There can be no peace," wrote Halleck, "but that which is forced by the sword. We must conquer the Rebels or be conquered by them. . . . This is the phase which the rebellion has now assumed. We must take things as they are."

This new phase of the rebellion was a good deal broader than Halleck dreamed. To accept the Negro as a soldier was to state, in a back-handed but decisive way, that the base of membership in the American community had been immeasurably widened. Once widened, it could not again be narrowed. The war henceforth would be fought for this, even though some of the men who were most effectively fighting it had no idea that the base was not already quite wide enough. For the war had become a breaking up of the foundations of the great deep, and to "take things as they are" meant to change things to their fundamentals.

Grant dutifully went to work—this chore came upon him while the various mud-and-water expedients were being tried above Vicksburg—and he instructed corps, division, and post commanders to speed the organization of the Negro regiments. He warned dissenters: "It is expected that all commanders will especially exert themselves in carrying out the policy of the administration, not only in organizing colored regiments and rendering them effective, but also in removing prejudice against them."[4]

Removing the prejudice would not be easy. Soldiers who disliked slavery very often looked upon the slaves themselves as subhuman creatures who belonged neither in the army nor in America itself. An Illinois veteran wrote from Tennessee that he and many others would be emancipationists "if the brutes could be shipped out of the country," but that did not seem to be possible. Slavery, he admitted, was "an awful sin," but if Negroes had to remain in America they ought to remain as slaves; the only suggestion he could make was that they be transferred from Confederate masters to masters thoroughly loyal to the Union.[5]

An Ohio soldier reported that there was intense opposition in his division to the recruiting of Negro troops, which at times "assumed the character of anarchy," with officers and enlisted men vowing that they would throw down their arms and go home if Negroes became soldiers.

This anarchic opposition was quickly tamped down, partly because of Grant's orders and partly because of the unexpected intervention of a rather unlikely hero—lanky, dry-as-dust Lorenzo Thomas, adjutant general of the army, the paper-shuffler from Washington who had been sent to the Mississippi Valley on a mixed mission that seems vaguely to have included the task of telling the War Department just what Grant was up to out there. Part of Thomas's job was to speed the raising of Negro regiments, and he took to this with crusty enthusiasm. He called troops together and warned them that Negroes fleeing from slavery were to be made welcome: "They are to be received with open arms, they are to be fed and clothed; they are to be armed." He was empowered, he added, to dismiss from the army "any man, be his rank what it may, whom I find maltreating the freedmen. This part of my duty I will most assuredly perform if any case comes before me."

The division in which the Ohio soldier had reported so much discontent was drawn up in hollow square and addressed by Thomas. Men who left the army because of the recruiting of Negroes, he warned, would be considered guilty of treason and would be shot, and there would be courts-martial for all who interfered with the program. The boys talked it over around campfires afterward and concluded finally that "a Negro could stop a bullet just as well as a white man," and that "for everyone so sacrificed there would be just that many more white soldiers to return north to their families and friends."[6]

Undeniably the Negro could stop a bullet. He could also help meet a draft quota back home, and northern state officials who were finding it increasingly hard to raise troops began to look his way optimistically. The only trouble seemed to be that most northern states did not, after all, contain so very many colored folk; the source of supply, untapped though it was, did seem to be limited. In Massachusetts the state authorities sent agents far afield, recruiting Negroes wherever they could find them, and forming two whole regiments of them. This led Governor John A. Andrew into trouble. He had promised the Negro recruits that they would be treated precisely as white soldiers were treated, and he presently learned that by a War Department ruling the colored soldiers could be paid no more than ten dollars a month, of which three dollars would stand for a clothing allowance. Since white troops got thirteen dollars a month in addition to their clothing, this represented a substantial difference. Andrew stormed down to Washington to get the ruling changed, failed, and then went back to Boston and got the legislature to agree to make up the difference with state funds.[7]

Negroes could stop bullets and meet draft quotas; they could also open the avenue for promotion to white soldiers. The new colored regiments would need officers. The officers, except in the rarest cases, would not be colored; they would

be white men, combat veterans, selected from the ranks of
the line regiments, given a quick course of sprouts in an
officer-training school, and then commissioned as lieutenants,
captains, or even better. The veterans perked up their ears
at this news. Some of those who had been most bitter about
the new program became reconciled to it when they considered that they themselves, as a result of it, might wear
shoulder straps. There was no lack of candidates for the
training schools. (A veteran in the Army of the Potomac complained that the selection board was biased; soldiers who
might have won commissions in their own regiments if va-
cancies existed, he asserted, were passed over, while the
young sprigs fresh out of college who had never seen gun
smoke got in with ease.) In one way or another, colored
regiments were called into being, officered, and put to work.[8]

There was a great deal of self-interest in the decision to
turn Negroes into soldiers, but there was also the pressure
of sheer necessity. The contraband slave was becoming
uncommonly numerous; simply by his presence—by his insistence on fleeing from bondage and by his mute faith that
the nearest Federal army would be his sure protector—he
was compelling the authorities to do something with him,
and very often the easiest thing to do was to put him into
uniform.

In Virginia in 1863 this problem was not quite so acute.
The Army of the Potomac had not penetrated very deeply
into Confederate territory; it was living in a war-ravaged
area in which there were not very many slaves, and the
contrabands who did come in could easily be shipped back
to Washington—where, for the most part, the government
utterly failed to devise any intelligent system for handling
them. But in the West so many slaves were seeking refuge
with the Federal armies that some sort of action was imperative.

Shortly before the new policy was adopted a Union force
came back to its base at Corinth, Mississippi, after some
foray deeper into the state, and when it marched in it was
followed by hundreds upon hundreds of fugitive slaves.
The army command at Corinth did not want these people—
had, in fact, very little idea what it could do with or about

them—but it could not send them back, and it fenced off a big camp, put the ex-slaves into it, detailed a couple of infantry regiments to guard it, and plucked a chaplain from the 27th Ohio and told him he was in charge. The soldiers objected to guard duty, declaring that they had come down to Dixie to fight Rebels and not to be policemen for a lot of runaway slaves, and the chaplain came up with an idea. Let him (he urged) form a few infantry companies from among the men in the contraband camp; with a little drill and the proper direction they ought to be able to stand guard over their own people.

The commanding officer agreed that this was a good idea. He had no legal authority to do anything of the kind, but he dug up rifles and uniforms, detailed a few line sergeants to act as officers, and before long here was a detachment of illegal but effective Negro troops, pleased as could be with their uniforms and their responsibility, and the Corinth contraband camp was in effect taking care of itself.⁹

These contraband camps were not usually very inspiring places to look at. There was a huge one on a levee not far from Vicksburg, crammed with fugitives who huddled without shelter, subsisted on army rations, got no real care from anyone, and died by the dozen from bad sanitation, exposure, overcrowding, and general homesick bewilderment. Yet the faith that had brought them here—a faith that freedom was good and that the road to it somehow led through the camps of the Union army—did not seem to leave them, even when their camp became a shambles. A Wisconsin soldier who was detailed for duty around this camp looked on in silent wonder at the prayer meetings that were held every night. There were no lights; none was needed, he thought, since the leaders of the meeting had no Bibles or hymnals and could not have read them if they had them; there was just a great crowd of men and women, dimly seen, bowed to the ground, swaying rhythmically as they prayed that God would set His people free and would send His blessing down on Massa Lincoln, Massa Grant, and all of Massa Lincoln's soldiers.

Before and after the prayers the air would be tremulous with music, which was of a kind the Wisconsin boy had never heard before. "I beg you," he wrote, "not to think of it as being like the jargon of the burnt-cork minstrels who sing for money. I cannot describe the pathos of the melody nor the sweet tenderness of the words as they arose on the night air."[10]

Almost to a man the male contrabands were eager to enlist when the chance was offered. Yet disillusionment usually came soon afterward. It was hard for generals to think of them as combat troops; for the most part the Negro was looked upon as a sort of servant to the white soldiers, he got much more than his share of fatigue duty, and in some camps he was excused from drill altogether so that he might dig ditches, raise fortifications, and perform other pick-and-shovel work. When they were kept at this non-military work, it was noted, most colored soldiers became restive, sullen, sometimes insubordinate.[11]

In the main, though, the newly enlisted Negro was intensely proud of his status as soldier. His pride could be surprising at times, because it seemed to go deeper than mere pride in a musket and a uniform and became pride in a new status as a human being. When Governor Andrew of Massachusetts induced the legislature to appropriate money to equalize the pay for the state's two colored regiments, he and the legislators got an abrupt shock. The paymaster went to pay the men and they refused to take the money. They appreciated what the state of Massachusetts was trying to do, they said, but they would serve without any pay until their enlistments ran out rather than take from the Federal government less money than the Federal government was paying its other soldiers. It was a matter between themselves and Uncle Sam—*their* Uncle Sam—and they would not let Massachusetts make up the difference. (The business caused a stir in Congress; ultimately, many months later, Congress revised the law and equalized the pay scales for white and colored troops.)[12]

Yet if the decision to put a uniform on the Negro had been taken partly from selfishness and partly because of necessity, and if the new recruits found that soldiering was not quite the stirring and uplifting thing they had supposed it would be, something momentous had nevertheless been taking place with the formation of the Negro regiments. Tough old Senator

Zachariah Chandler, militant anti-slavery man from Michigan, who had shared the common abolitionist fear that the Emancipation Proclamation might someday be withdrawn, exulted: "Every Negro regiment of a thousand men presents just one thousand unanswerable arguments against the revocation of the President's proclamation." And the eloquent former slave Frederick Douglass, who had worked and hoped long to see his people brought to freedom, saw even more in it than that:

"Once let the black man get upon his person the brass letters, U.S.; let him get an eagle on his button, and musket on his shoulder and bullets in his pocket, and there is no power on earth which can deny that he has earned the right to citizenship in the United States."[13]

4. *End of a Campaign*

It was time to shoot the works. The canals could never be made to work if they were dug until kingdom come, the intricate network of waterways could never be used, and to take everybody back to Memphis and start all over again was out of the question. Grant sat in what had been the "ladies' parlor" of the headquarters steamboat, moored up by Milliken's Bend, and smoked his cigars and looked into the blue clouds, and at last he made up his mind. He would defy the Confederate guns and military precedent, move straight down the river, abandon his communications, and gamble his army's existence that he could outmaneuver and outfight his enemies and finally come up to Vicksburg from the east. There would be no more grubbing in the mud and playing it safe; he would let everything ride on one turn of the card, winning or losing all of it at once.

It was perhaps the crucial Federal military decision of the war; and it was made by a slouchy little man who never managed to look like a great captain, who had a casual unbuttoned air about him and seemed to be nothing much more than a middle-aged person who used to be a clerk in a small-town harness shop—a man who unexpectedly combined dogged determination with a gambler's daring.

During the winter things had been working for him west of the big river. In December the Confederates had assembled a sizable army in Arkansas, and for a time it looked as if they might upset everything by making a bold dash up into Missouri. But the capture of Arkansas Post—that strange, unpremeditated thrust which had been designed to do little more than take the sting out of the Chickasaw Bluffs fiasco—had knocked one prop out from under this plan; then a Federal army came down from Missouri, whipped a Confederate force at Prairie Grove, and knocked out the other prop. By mid-January the Rebels had retreated to Little Rock, the Federals from Missouri were continuing to put pressure on them, and the southern hope that Arkansas troops might relieve the strain at Vicksburg had gone to seed. Whatever he might do when spring came, Grant could at least be confident that nobody in Arkansas could offer much interference.[1]

It did not seem that he could be confident of much else. When the country looked his way it believed that it saw an army hopelessly bogged down, and incompetently commanded to boot. Newspapers complained bitterly, circulated the old tales about drunkenness, enlarged on the sickness and inactivity of Grant's troops, and demanded that he be removed. (Hot-tempered Sherman rose to high fury at this and asserted that "with the press unfettered as now we are defeated to the end of time." It would not do, he added, to say that the people must have news; every soldier wrote home regularly, and that was all the news the people in the North needed.)[2] Lincoln stood by Grant, remarking bluntly, "He fights!" to a caller who asked why he did not fire him; but Secretary Stanton had his doubts. To settle them, Mr. Stanton sent a civilian representative down to Vicksburg to keep an eye on things and make daily reports. This emissary was Charles A. Dana, one-time member of the transcendentalist troupe at Brook Farm, later an editor for Horace Greeley's New York *Tribune,* now a vaguely titled special commissioner for the War Department.

The grapevine told Grant that Dana was coming, and some of his staff officers proposed that Mr. Dana be pitched neck and crop into the Mississippi on arrival. John A. Rawlins,

Grant's dedicated, consumptive little chief of staff, squelched such talk, and when Dana arrived early in April he was given a pleasant welcome and was lodged in a tent pitched next to Grant's. Somewhat to everybody's surprise he took to Grant at once. What Mr. Stanton heard about Grant began to be more favorable.[3]

Meanwhile the army got ready to move. There were between forty and forty-five thousand men in the dreary riverside camps, divided into three army corps: the XIII, under McClernand, the XV, which was Sherman's, and the XVII, commanded by curly-bearded James B. McPherson, former engineer officer on Grant's staff—a pleasant-mannered, capable Scot whom Grant trusted deeply, whom Dana liked, and whom Sherman was beginning to pick as one who might someday rise above Grant himself.

Grant's plan was simple. He would march downstream on the west side of the river, coming out at some point twenty or thirty miles below Vicksburg. Admiral Porter would bring gunboats and transports down and ferry the army over to the eastern bank. There Grant could do one of two things—go on down the river, meet Banks (if by chance Banks had begun to move) and capture Port Hudson, basing his troops thereafter on New Orleans; or he could swing east to the Mississippi state capital and railroad center, Jackson, destroying Confederate installations there and then wheeling west for a decisive blow at Vicksburg itself.[4]

A great many things could go wrong with such a plan. All told, the Confederates had more soldiers in Mississippi than Grant had, and it was perfectly possible for them to swarm in on him and beat him—and to be beaten so far down in enemy territory, without any open road for retreat, would be to meet complete and final disaster. There was also the prospect that once he crossed the river Grant would have no secure line of supply. His army might simply be starved into surrender if the Confederates played their cards right and had a little good luck. It was certain that the whole proposition would scare cautious Halleck right to the tips of his wispy hair. Therefore, Halleck would not be let in on the secret until it was too late for him to countermand it.

The immediate danger was that the expedition might not even be able to get off the ground.

Primary objective of the troops would be a Confederate strong point known as Grand Gulf, on the eastern side of the river and perhaps twenty-five miles south of Vicksburg in an air line—substantially farther by the twisting course of the river. To get at Grand Gulf the Federal troops must first march down the west side of the river to New Carthage; twenty miles or thereabouts as the roads lay. Between Milliken's Bend and New Carthage lay a somber expanse of flat country, swamps, winding streams, sluggish crescent-shaped bayous, and an inadequate grid of atrocious roads. High water had swollen the waterways and left the land partly flooded. Grant had no pontoon train, and the streams that had to be crossed must be bridged by some on-the-spot operation; the only timbers available would be those taken from plantation houses, barns, and other buildings in the immediate vicinity. There was a great shortage of engineer officers and an almost total lack of trained engineer troops.

Still, the army probably could get to New Carthage or some other point on the river if it floundered along relentlessly. But it would be in a very bad fix if it reached New Carthage and then found that Porter and his steamboats could not also get there; and to reach that part of the river, Porter's vessels would have to run the gantlet of the Vicksburg batteries—many heavy guns, sited both at water level and on top of the high bluffs, ready to blast clear out of the water anything that floated. The run would of course be made at night, but the Rebels kept a careful lookout and had details ready to set fire to houses on the western bank. Any ships that passed the Vicksburg waterfront at night would assuredly be silhouetted against a background of rising flame.

A gamble, in other words, with the odds none too favorable. Sherman, who was beginning to believe in Grant as he believed in no other living man, thought the idea little better than lunacy. When the move finally began he wrote home glumly, "I feel in its success less confidence than in any similar undertaking of the war," and he steeled himself only by reflecting that co-operation was his duty. McPherson had no higher opinion of the scheme. Oddly enough, it was jealous

McClernand who endorsed it; he was a troublemaker and a malcontent, but there was nothing wrong with his nerve and he felt that Grant's move was right.[5]

Right or wrong, it was the move Grant would take. Through March he waited, making preparations for the cross-country march, getting such reinforcements as could be sent to him from Missouri, and waiting for the high water to subside a bit. Then finally, in mid-April, the expedition took off.

The soldiers were in good spirits. Some inkling of the risk that was being taken seems to have filtered down to them, but it did not matter; anything was better than staying in the swamp digging hopeless ditches, and movement was always stimulating. Some of the new troops came rolling down from Memphis by steamboat, moonlight on the river, music from regimental bands floating across the water, men lounging by the railing in conversation or stretched out on deck looking at the pale night sky; they were glad to get to the Vicksburg sector, and afterward they recalled the first leg of the trip as a moving romantic experience that remained fixed in the memory. A Wisconsin regiment that had toiled for months on obscure campaigns in Arkansas was brought over to join Grant's army, and when the homesick boys from the north woods got out on the surface of the Mississippi they remembered that the headwaters of this muddy stream flowed somewhere past Wisconsin; they ran to the lower deck of their transport, lowered canteens and buckets over the side, and gulped down long drafts of water: "We drank and drank until it ran out of our noses, just because it came from the glorious north."[6]

When the cross-country march began it was night—black night, mysterious, with a rain coming down; in the bayous and swamps men heard odd roaring noises and were told that these were made by alligators. Roads became almost impassable, so that wagons and guns stalled repeatedly and had to be hoisted out by sheer strength. Feeling themselves overburdened, some of the men dropped their overcoats and blankets by the roadside; later they learned that although spring days were hot, here in the Deep South, it could grow chilly late at night. Men in the advance guard swarmed around every plantation they came to, collecting skiffs and dugouts, for it seemed as if most of the country was under water.[7]

When streams were encountered they were quickly bridged. These western soldiers knew how to use axes and were handy with all of the frontier's makeshifts; they knocked down buildings, built leaky but serviceable pontoon boats, tied them together with timbers and laid planks taken from barns and gin-houses; an amazed engineer officer saw three floating bridges thus constructed and wrote in wonder that they "were built by green volunteers who had never seen a bridge train or had an hour's drill or instruction in bridge building." A soldier in McClernand's corps asserted that his comrades built almost two thousand feet of bridges, and added that they constructed a wagon road almost all of the distance to New Carthage. Here was an army with some rather special capabilities. . . .[8]

As they marched, some of the men heard a dull booming in the distance. Porter's fleet was running the batteries, and the Vicksburg defenders were firing at him with everything they had.

Porter made his dash on the night of April 16, steaming out on the black river with seven ironclads, assorted wooden gunboats and rams, and three transports loaded with stores. Coal barges were lashed to the sides of the boats, both for protection and to give the navy a supply of fuel in a stretch of river where no supplies could be had. On the deck of the headquarters steamer, moored upstream just out of range of the Confederate guns, Grant and his staff watched. Grant's family was visiting him at the time, and Mrs. Grant sat beside the general; a staff officer perched in a chair, one of the Grant children in his arms, and as the crash of gunfire rocked the night the child clung to him desperately, tightening its arms about his neck every time the baleful light flashed on the dark sky.

The business looked and sounded worse than it was; Porter's flotilla got through, with one transport sunk, another banged up substantially, and only minor damage to the other boats. By now the navy was confident that it could make a dash past almost any fort without too much risk; what it could not do here at Vicksburg was stay within range and hammer the enemy into surrender. Porter made contact with the army below Vicksburg, and in a few days he arranged for half a dozen more transports, each one loaded to the guards with army rations, to come on down and join in the game.⁹

These transports were ordinary river steamers with civilian crews, and the crews promptly walked ashore, announcing that nobody had hired them to run the Vicksburg batteries; whereupon it developed that this army which could build its own roads and bridges could also operate its own steamboats. Grant called for volunteers from the army to operate the boats, and he got more than he needed—so many, indeed, that the men who volunteered finally had to draw lots to see which ones would be used. The men who were told they would not be needed felt aggrieved and tried to bribe their way aboard; one man who got a billet on a steamer reported that a comrade offered him $100 for his place. . . . This was a jack-of-all-trades army. One single regiment contributed one hundred and sixteen river sailors, from captains, pilots, and engineers down to deckhands and firemen.¹⁰

The transports made the dash. With the rations they brought the army at least would not starve before it crossed the river; and it was time now to get over to the other shore and get on with the campaign. Grand Gulf, however, turned out to be an obstacle—too strong to be reduced by naval gunfire, it offered no good ground upstream for an attack by the army. Run the batteries again, then, while the army slogged on through the mud to the vicinity of Hard Times Plantation; take the troops over at undefending Bruinsburg, and they could go inland and take Grand Gulf from the rear.

While all of this was going on, of course, it was necessary to deceive the Rebels. The troops that went downstream were McClernand's and McPherson's; Sherman, still darkly pessimistic, took his corps up around the mouth of the Yazoo and made motions as if a new attack on Chickasaw Bluffs was in preparation. With much puffing and chugging of steamboats it was easy to play the same game that Confederate Magruder had played so well at Yorktown and in front of Richmond. Confederate Pemberton was completely taken in, and he conceived that he was about to be attacked from the north.

Meanwhile, from the area near Memphis, Grant launched a cavalry raid to spread more confusion. Three cavalry regiments under Colonel Benjamin H. Grierson were sent down, roughly paralleling the line of the Mississippi Central Railroad, with orders to move straight south, do all the damage and spread all the alarm possible, and come out (if lucky) in Banks's lines at Baton Rouge, which was six hundred miles off.

The expedition was oddly but effectively led. Grierson was an unlikely choice for dashing cavalry commander; he had been a middle-western music teacher before the war, with a habit of organizing amateur bands in small towns, and he had hated horses for many years because a horse had kicked him in the face when he was a child. When the war came he was prompt to volunteer, but he wanted to do his fighting on foot; when an unexpected chain of circumstances brought him a commission in the cavalry he tried hard, but without success, to get transferred to the infantry. A cavalryman in spite of himself, he became a good one, and it was Grant himself who named him to lead this raid.

Grierson started out on April 17, the day after Porter's gunboats had run the Vicksburg batteries. He dodged the Confederate parties that tried to catch him—greatly aided by the fact that most of the Confederate cavalry had been sent to Tennessee to help Bragg—and between cutting Rebel communications and creating the impression that a heavy mass of Yankee infantry was apt to follow in his wake he added substantially to Pemberton's confusion. After an exciting sixteen days, in which it looked repeatedly as if he would lose his entire command, Grierson reached safety at Baton Rouge, his men worn out and in tatters and all the country behind him boiling with alarms and excursions.[11]

And Grant got McClernand's and McPherson's men over the Mississippi, defeated a Confederate force in a sharp little fight a few miles inland, occupied Grand Gulf, and sent word for Sherman to hurry on down and join him.

He also learned that Banks was nowhere near Port Hudson; the plan to join forces and work upstream toward Vicksburg could not be carried out.

The obvious play-it-safe step for Grant now, was to settle

down at Grand Gulf, establish a secure base of supplies, and wait for Banks to get ready. It was a step that Grant had no intention of taking. He had seized the initiative; after long months of apparent inaction he had the jump on his opponent and he proposed to keep it at all costs. In and around Vicksburg there was Pemberton, with an army which then was nearly the size of Grant's own; over in the Jackson area there was (or very shortly would be) Joe Johnston in person, assembling troops which, if they were added to Pemberton's, would give the Confederates a numerical advantage. What Grant wanted to do was slice in between these two generals, knocking them apart, destroying the route by which Rebel supplies and reinforcements could reach Vicksburg, and lock Pemberton up in the riverside fortress before the enemy had time to figure out what was going on. To do this Grant would have to keep moving.

He moved. The rations that had come downstream by boat were unloaded and distributed. When the troops started to move inland, men lugged boxes of hardtack on their shoulders and rolled barrels of salt pork along the ground. Grant's wagon train had not arrived, and he refused to wait for it. Instead he swept the countryside, seizing everything that moved on four feet, from blooded horses to oxen; farm wagons, buckboards, carriages, and surreys were rounded up, and a tatterdemalion wagon train of sorts was created; then, on May 7, the army left Grand Gulf and set off northeast, getting on the high ground and moving away from the river.[12]

Sherman got his men to Grand Gulf, looked things over, and saw that the whole army had to move by one road. Frantically he sent a message on to Grant: stop everything where it was until new roads could be built, because the movement of supplies from Grand Gulf would create a traffic jam that would tie everything in a hard knot. Back came Grant's amazing answer: there would be no supply line, he would not try to maintain contact with Grand Gulf at all. The army would live off the country, and the beggar's-opera wagon train would serve to carry food levied from the plantations—that, and the army's priceless supply of ammunition. Sherman blinked and began to adjust himself to a type of warfare he had not dreamed of before.[13]

Strong in Grant's memory was the lesson he had learned at Holly Springs in December, when Van Dorn had destroyed his base of supplies and he had to seize food from the planters to keep his army from starving; Mississippi was full of food, and an army that moved fast and kept on moving could support itself for weeks. . . . The Van Dorn who had taught him this lesson came to the end of the trail just at this time; he was shot to death, in his own headquarters, by a civilian who believed that his wife and Van. Dorn had been too friendly.

The army swept inland, heading in the general direction of Jackson, sixty miles away. Grant got off a message to Halleck, telling him what was being done. The message would be a long time reaching Halleck; it had to go upriver by steamboat, all the way to Cairo, Illinois, before it could be put on the wires, and the answer would have to come back in the same way. Halleck would infallibly tell Grant not to do what he was doing, but by the time his answer was received the job ought to be just about finished. Grant set out in the early days of May with a great feeling of relief and freedom.[14] For the next fortnight he would be entirely on his own.

The army stepped out confidently, glad to be on the road again after the dreary months around Milliken's Bend. Everything worked. Day after day Grant's impromptu wagons lumbered out around the country, accompanied by details of gleeful infantry; evening after evening they returned to camp, bringing incredible numbers of cattle, sheep, pigs, chickens, geese, and ducks. As these reached camp, other details would butcher and dress the animals, while the commissaries issued corn meal freshly ground on plantation mills. Of its own supplies, the army was issuing nothing much but coffee, sugar, and salt; Mississippi provided all the rest; the soldiers gorged on fresh poultry, roast pork, and beefsteaks. They ate so much of this, in fact, that some men were heard to say that they would be glad to get back to army hardtack and bacon eventually; their fare now was so rich they were getting tired of it.

None of this foraging slowed the army's progress. It went knifing across the state toward its objective, and luckless

Pemberton was approaching complete confusion. The Yankees had been ineffective all winter, and the Vicksburg area had been quiet; now it had blazed up into incomprehensible activity, and the Confederate commander could not cope with it. He drew his forces together to repel an anticipated dash at Vicksburg, and Grant's army slid past him, moving east. Pemberton thought to stop him by cutting his lines of communication, and got nowhere because there were no lines to cut; Confederate regiments marched around helplessly seeking the nonexistent.

A small part of Pemberton's army made solid contact around the town of Raymond, a dozen miles west of Jackson, and was crumpled and driven back. Rain came down, and the Union soldiers went splashing through ankle-deep pools in roads and fields to attack the Confederate defenses at Jackson.

These defenses were not strong. Joe Johnston had arrived at last, but he had no more than six thousand troops with him, and after a brisk fight Sherman's and McPherson's men knocked these aside and went whooping into the capital on May 14. They reported that the streets were full of disorderly elements—Confederate stragglers, skulkers and deserters, displaced civilians from everywhere, fugitive Negroes, and a growing assortment of Federals who had dropped out of ranks to have fun, everyone apparently bent on picking up any valuables that might be found. There was a good deal of looting and destruction, which grew worse as Federal troops began ripping up railroad tracks and wrecking foundries, warehouses, and other installations useful to the southern war effort. Someone had released the convicts in a local prison, and these joined in the looting until Federal patrols at last restored something resembling order. For a time Jackson knew all of the woes of a conquered town.[15]

Grant now was where he wanted to be, interposed between Pemberton and Johnston, and he proposed to make the most of it. He waited in Jackson only long enough to wreck the place, then turned and headed for Vicksburg, determined to keep his rivals apart and to drive Pemberton back into the Vicksburg lines.

Unluckiest of living generals at that point was Pemberton.

He was that rarity, a Northerner born and bred who had cast his lot with the Confederacy—for principle (he was a confirmed states'-rights man) and because his wife lived in Virginia. Southern xenophobes had muttered against his appointment, and he was a rigid, austere man, lacking the personal gifts that could win doubters to his side. Now Johnston was ordering him to leave Vicksburg and bring about a Confederate concentration, while Jefferson Davis was ordering him to hold Vicksburg at all hazards. Pemberton's own idea seemed to be that he could perhaps do a little of both. He did not know exactly where Grant was or what he was up to, he was the victim of conflicting orders, the sands were running out for him—and, all in all, his number was up and there was very little he could do about it.

He fought Grant on May 16 at Champion's Hill, a hilly wooded area halfway between Jackson and Vicksburg. (Johnston was out of touch, off to the northeast, hopelessly out of the play.) There was a hard, wearing battle; McClernand's troops drove Pemberton's lines back, came to a halt, and were themselves driven off by a savage counterattack. Not all of Grant's army was up, and McClernand was handling his corps inexpertly; Grant intervened, pulled John A. Logan's division out of line and ordered it into action.

Logan was a unusual soldier—a swarthy man with a great shock of black hair, profound drooping mustachios, and an ability to lead men in battle which contrasted oddly with his complete lack of any military background. He had been a politician before the war (still was one, for the matter of that, and would go on being one until he died) and he had been such a partisan Democrat that after Fort Sumter people in Illinois had wondered if he might not come out openly for the South. He finally began to make speeches for the Union, was rewarded (after the innocent custom of the day) with a colonel's commission and was now a general; and Grant felt that he was well qualified to handle more than a mere division. There was a homespun informality in the behavior of Logan's soldiers. In this Champion's Hill battle, one lanky private who apparently had been wandering about on his own hook sauntered up to Logan (who was on horseback, surveying the scene), gestured largely off to the right, and remarked, man-to-man fashion: "General, I've been over on the rise yonder, and it's my idee that if you'll put a regiment or two over there you'll get on their flank and lick 'em easy." Logan looked, concluded that the advice was sound, sent over two regiments—and presently drove the Rebels in retreat.[16]

However it was done, the field at last was won, and Pemberton went west in full retreat, making for the only haven that was open to him—Vicksburg. He turned next day for a rear-guard action at a crossing of the Big Black River, was quickly driven off, and rode on to the entrenched lines around his fortress city. He reflected sadly that this date was the anniversary of his entrance into West Point—one date, he said, would mark both the bright beginning and the ignominious end of his military career. He had no illusions about what would happen once Grant drew in his lines around Vicksburg and settled down to a siege.

During the fight at the Big Black a self-important staff officer from Banks's army came riding up to Grant, all in a lather, bearing a dispatch from Halleck—at last!—sharply ordering Grant to stay in Grand Gulf, abstain from adventures, and wait until Banks was ready to move. Grant tore the dispatch up, the staff officer began to sputter angrily, and then Grant heard cheering, saw that his men had broken the Confederate line, and rode off to see about it. Recalling the business twenty years later, Grant said that the officer was still protesting when he rode off; and he added dryly that as far as he could remember he never saw him again in all his life.[17]

9.

The Trees and the River

1. *Final Miscalculation*

Joe Hooker was another man who had a river to cross. The Rappahannock was not a coiled tawny flood running through bottomless swamps; with daring and good management the crossing could be made whenever he chose. As with Grant, the real tests would come afterward—cruel test of battle for the troops, searching test of lonely responsibility for the general.

He could count on the troops. The Army of the Potomac had been tried in fire. It had learned war in the Seven Days', at Second Bull Run, at Antietam, and at Fredericksburg; it had known great discouragement and swift revival, acquiring a sinewy elasticity thereby, and its volunteers had lost just enough of their innocence to reach a sharp fighting edge. They could do just about anything their commander asked them to do; if he could use them to their full potential, they might win the war.

The question mark was Hooker himself. He was slim and handsome, with rosy cheeks and cold eyes, a hard-drinking, hard-living man with some coarseness of fiber. At his headquarters there was a glitter of arrogance, and in his speech in this spring of 1863 there was a contemptuous confidence in victory, a glib preacceptance of triumph that might just possibly hide a deep inner uncertainty.

Hooker led more than one hundred and twenty thousand men—battle-tested and well drilled, equipped with everything a rich government could provide. The Confederate Army of Northern Virginia, which he was about to fight, seemed badly overmatched. Lee had had to detach Longstreet and most of Longstreet's corps to accomplish some food-gathering and Yankee-repelling mission in the watery flat country back of Norfolk, far below Richmond. As April ended, Lee's army contained no more than half as many men as Hooker's—men more poorly clad, more poorly fed, and less well equipped. By any test the Federals seemed to have all of the advantages.

Yet there would be a test that would go beyond a counting of battalions and a weighing of metal. What really lay ahead, as the serpentine body of the Army of the Potomac moved out of its camps and flowed purposefully down to the river crossings—while the bands played, and the endless length of the artillery columns jolted over the uneven roads, and new blossoms and young leaves touched the bleak woods with delicate color—what would matter the most in all of this would be the result of a searching inquiry into the character of two men—two men, in all of these scores of armed thousands—Lee and Hooker. These two men would not see each other. In all the wild battle shock of colliding armies they would not come within miles of each other. Yet they were the real antagonists. More than any other campaign in the Civil War, the campaign that began when Hooker put his army in motion at the end of April would depend on the stamina of the rival commanders.

It would be a moral issue, finally—a test of inner integrity and manhood. In this test Hooker would be so badly overmatched that it would be no contest.

Hooker's plans were excellent, and so was his execution of them . . . up to the moment of testing.

He was far too intelligent to cross at Fredericksburg, as Burnside had done, and so commit his army to the impossible task of driving Lee's army from its impregnable trenches. Instead he would go far up the river, crossing both the Rappahannock and the Rapidan twenty or twenty-five miles northwest of Fredericksburg, and then he would swing down and come in on Lee's flank and rear. Hooker had created an effective cavalry force and he would use it to screen this march, so that Lee would not know about it until it was too late for him to make an effective reply. The Army of the Potomac was in perfect condition, stripped for action, wagon trains cut to a minimum; it would move fast, it would fight where all the chances would be in its favor, and, fighting so, it ought to win.

So went the plan. So went the execution, too, until the time came when everything depended on Joe Hooker. Then the whole business fell apart like a sheet of soggy blotting paper, and the South won a spectacular victory . . . from which, finally, it could gain no lasting advantage.

Hooker's troops began to march on April 27. (Grant was nearly ready to put his men across the Mississippi; Grierson was riding hard for Baton Rouge.) Three army corps crossed the two rivers and drove swiftly in toward Fredericksburg, marching through a confusing and almost roadless jungle of second-growth timber known as the Wilderness, and going into bivouac on the last day of April at a crossroads by a pillared brick mansion: Chancellorsville. Two other army corps, left in Fredericksburg in the competent hands of General John Sedgwick, began to cross the river there, as if the Burnside fight were to be repeated, and two more Federal corps waited at the river fords a few miles upstream from Fredericksburg, where they could quickly join either wing of the army. Hooker himself went to Chancellorsville, and as April ended he could boast that he had done—so far—exactly what he set out to do and that he had done it very well.

He had at Chancellorsville very nearly as many soldiers as there were in Lee's entire army, and they were hardly more than ten miles from Fredericksburg, right behind the great crescent of trenches with which the Confederates had surrounded that town. Abundant reinforcements were close at hand, and Sedgwick with forty thousand men was squarely in Lee's front—a solid rock against which Hooker's force could smash the Army of Northern Virginia. On the morning of May 1, Hooker put his men on the roads and they started east, moving in to make a finish fight of it. Hooker was confident, and the soldiers were confident. Even crusty George Meade, commander of one of the three army corps at Chancellorsville—a man who rarely bubbled with enthusiasm for anything—was showing his elation. "Hurrah for old Joe!" he cried to a brother officer. "We're on Lee's flank and he doesn't know it."[1]

Lee knew it well enough, but he refused to let it bother him. Technically he was in a desperate fix. If he stayed where he was he would be·crushed between Hooker and Sedgwick. If he turned to meet the Chancellorsville thrust he would have to strike at a force that could quickly be made much stronger than his, and John Sedgwick would be right on his heels. If he tried to retreat toward Richmond, Hooker could easily cut across, strike him in flank, and cut off his escape. All of the choices open to him were bad, and it did not seem that there was very much that he could do about it.

Yet he seemed quite unworried. He left some ten thousand men to hold the line against Sedgwick, and with everybody else he set out for Chancellorsville to meet Hooker. Somewhere around noon on May 1, Confederate and Federal skirmish lines collided three miles east of Chancellorsville. When Federal battle lines came up behind the skirmishers they met a line of Confederate infantry, well posted, with field artillery in action. The commanders of the Federal advance confidently prepared to shoulder this roadblock aside and get on with the war, and they sent news of the encounter back to headquarters.

That put it up to Hooker, and he immediately began to wilt. Things were going precisely according to plan. Only the night before he had issued a big-talk statement to his troops, announcing that the enemy "must either ingloriously fly, or come out from behind his defenses and give us battle on our own ground, where certain destruction awaits him." The enemy was following the script; he had come out from behind his defenses and he was giving battle, and it was on Hooker's own ground at that. But instead of going on to apply the bit about certain destruction, Hooker began to wonder if there might not be something ominous about this development. He concluded, apparently, that there was; and he called off the advance and ordered his army to retire into improvised trench lines around Chancellorsville. And in those lines, as May Day came to an end, his army prepared to spend the night.

Hooker was still talking it up. He told his ranking officer, General Darius N. Couch: "It's all right, Couch, I've got Lee just where I want him." To other officers he remarked that Lee's army was now "the legitimate property of the Army of the Potomac"; to still others he boasted that not even God Almighty could deprive him of the victory that he was about to win. But Couch concluded that under all of this fine talk Hooker was already a beaten man, and no one since that time has seen any reason to think that Couch was mistaken.

While Hooker made windy brags and put "the finest army on the planet" on the defensive, Lee sat on a cracker box a few miles away and held a conference with Stonewall Jackson. They had, by the most favorable estimate, fewer than forty-five thousand men with them; except for the force left at Fredericksburg, that was all the army there was, and they were in the immediate presence of eighty thousand Federals. But Lee was in charge of the battle now, and not Hooker, and what Lee wanted to discuss was the best way in which Hooker's army might be wiped out. He and Jackson talked and they made a plan, and promptly the next morning they set about putting it into execution.

The plan was the distilled and concentrated essence of extreme daring.

Jackson would take twenty-five thousand men, march the length of Hooker's front, circle around until he was due west of him, and attack his exposed right flank. The march would take the better part of the day, and to form line of battle in the trackless wilderness where Hooker's flank rested might take hours; it would be early evening before Jackson could make his fight. Until then Lee with fewer than twenty thousand men would have to confront Hooker and his eighty thousand. Indeed, merely to confront him would not be enough; he would have to pretend to be fighting an offensive battle, and the pretense would have to be convincing, because if Hooker ever found out what Jackson was up to or learned how small Lee's force really was he could destroy the Army of Northern Virginia before the sun went down.

Hooker would find out nothing, for Lee had him in his hands and was toying with him. Jackson made his march (it was discovered, but in the paralysis that had come upon his spirit Hooker was quite unable to interpret the meaning of his discovery; he concluded finally that part of Lee's army must be retreating, and he sent out a couple of divisions to prod the fugitives along). Lee gave a masterful imitation of a general who is about to open a crushing attack all along the line, and kept Hooker looking his way without inducing him to look so attentively that he could discover anything. And a little while before sundown Jackson struck Hooker's exposed flank like the crack of doom.

One Federal army corps was driven off in rout, the right half of Hooker's line was disrupted, and Jackson believed that if the attack could be pressed the Federals could be cut off from the Rappahannock crossings and destroyed utterly. But effective woods fighting in the darkness was impossible, the Confederate battle line was all confused . . . and Jackson himself, at last, was shot down and had to be carried to a field hospital with a wound that would kill him within the week. The fighting died out, with a confusing and malignant sputter of picket-line firing and sudden, meaningless cannonades, around midnight. In the streaky moonlight that lay on the narrow lanes and the crowded clearings, one Federal division collided with other Federal troops and fought a savage battle. Massed Federal artillery, hastily dug in on high ground near the Chancellorsville house, sprayed the landscape with gunfire; Yankee cavalry blundered into marching columns of Confederate infantry, and there were blind slashing and firing; and neither Hooker nor any of his generals quite realized that although their army had been jarred off balance it nevertheless lay between the separate pieces of Lee's army, with an excellent chance to turn Lee's victory into defeat when daylight came.

With daylight the Confederate attack was renewed. Jeb Stuart, the jaunty cavalryman with the plumed hat and the floating cloak lined with scarlet, was called away from his mounted men and given control of the fight Jackson had commenced, and while he desperately reorganized the mixed-up southern infantry elements his gunners moved fieldpieces into an open meadow which the stumbling Federals had abandoned, and from this vantage point his artillery hammered at the Federal guns and blanketed Chancellorsville clearing with a storm of shell. One missile knocked down a pillar of the Chancellorsville mansion. Hooker, who was lounging against the pillar, was thrown down and stunned. The will to strike a counterblow flickered and died in the Federal commander, and by noon his troops were fighting a rear-guard action, pulling back to form a great defensive horseshoe covering the Rappahannock bridgeheads. The two wings of Lee's army came together again, and the huge northern army was shoved and huddled into its new lines, all notion of an offensive fight gone forever. Hooker was not thinking of anything larger than the hope that the army might avoid annihilation.

Back at Fredericksburg, John Sedgwick came into action. His men hit the Confederate trenches on the high ground west of town, captured the heights that Burnside had been unable to take in December, and started off to rescue Hooker. But Lee, as calmly as if he had been directing maneuvers back in the Richmond training fields, left a few brigades to keep an eye on Hooker's host and with the rest of his army turned, boxed Sedgwick's tough soldiers up in a bend of the Rappahannock halfway between Fredericksburg and Chancellorsville, and after a wearing day's fighting compelled them to retreat across the river, glad enough to escape alive. Then— as smoothly as if this shuttling back and forth against impossible odds were all part of the normal routine—Lee regrouped his army in front of Hooker's horseshoe bridgehead and prepared for a new blow that would complete the rout of the Army of the Potomac.

This blow he never had to make, for Hooker had had enough. His men occupied a powerful position, with good trenches on high ground and abundant artillery. He greatly outnumbered Lee, and nearly half of his soldiers had not yet been in action at all; by the book, any Confederate attack now could lead to nothing but a Confederate defeat. But Hooker folded up, once and for all, and on a dark and rainy night he pulled his troops back, crossed to the north side of the Rappahannock, and marched back to his camps opposite Fredericksburg, abandoning the campaign that had been planned and begun so ably. He had been hopelessly beaten, he had lost seventeen thousand men, some of his generals were almost in a state of mutiny—tough little Couch was declaring that he would never serve under Hooker again and was asking the War Department for a transfer—and his soldiers were angrily inquiring how they had lost a battle in which so many of them had not even had a chance to fight.

By any standard, this was a personal triumph for Lee. It had been the story of the Seven Days' all over again, with all of the highlights and the shadows intensified; the man with all the odds against him had taken desperate chances and had seen them pay off, while the man with everything in his favor had gone nervous and had seen his chances evaporate like the gun smoke shredding out over the forests of spiky pines and saplings. At no other time in the Civil War did the moral superiority held by one general over another stand out so clearly as a decisive factor in battle.

And yet this dazzling victory was sterile. Not only had it cost the Confederacy more than the Confederacy could afford to pay—it killed Stonewall Jackson, who was literally irreplaceable, and it put twelve thousand of other ranks out of action to boot—but it left the high command facing a problem that proved finally to be beyond solution.

Hooker had been whipped, and the spring invasion of Virginia had been canceled. But the war was not a duel between generals, and the enormous forces it had set loose would not finally dispose of themselves just because one man was stronger than another. Chancellorsville with its great flame and smoke and noise had done little more than give the Confederacy time to take a second look at its desperate predicament.

Destiny lay in the West. Grant had Vicksburg surrounded now. His army held a great semicircle that ran east of town from the Chickasaw Bluffs and curled around to the banks of the Mississippi a few miles downstream. Within this semicircle Pemberton and his thirty-one thousand were locked up, helpless; outside the semicircle Joe Johnston and an inadequate army tried in vain to find some way to crack the shell. Grant had been reinforced, he was receiving all the supplies the North could send to him, and he was able without effort to hold Johnston off at arm's length while he waited for Vicksburg to fall. Three hundred miles to the northeast, Rosecrans was beginning to move with his Army of the Cumberland. Bragg, who opposed him, was outnumbered. In Mississippi and Tennessee the doom of the Confederacy was beginning to take visible form. Against long odds, battles might be won in Virginia, and the Yankee invader might be made to retreat across the Rappahannock, perhaps even across the Potomac; but Vicksburg would fall and Tennessee would be lost, and if these things happened the Confederacy would be a cut flower in a vase, seeming to live for a time, but cut off forever from the possibility of independent existence.

This was the reality that demanded the attention of the Confederate government as the spring of 1863 drew on toward summer.

Perhaps there was no really good answer. General Longstreet, who had missed Chancellorsville and who was consulted by President Davis in Richmond, urged that troops be taken from Lee's army and sent to Tennessee; given such reinforcements, Bragg could perhaps defeat Rosecrans and compel Grant to draw back from in front of Vicksburg. Secretary of War Seddon believed that reinforcements from Lee's army might go direct to Mississippi, so that Johnston could smite Grant's iron ring directly. There was no certainty that either of these expedients would work; they were just cards that might possibly be played.

Lee could read the future no better than anyone else. He did point out that the government must in effect decide whether to hold the line in Mississippi or to hold it in Virginia. To give up Virginia would be to give up Richmond, national capital, symbol of nationhood, source too of essential munitions and manufactures; loss here would probably mean speedy loss of the war itself, whereas the doom that would descend in the West would at least come more slowly. Furthermore, it would not do to wait and defend Virginia passively. Chancellorsville had humiliated Hooker's army but had not crippled it; in a month or two the Federals would inevitably be ready to invade Virginia anew. Better (argued Lee) to defend Virginia by fighting in the North. A battle won above the Potomac might convince war-weary Northerners that the Confederacy could never really be beaten; it might induce the government at Washington to recall Grant and Rosecrans for home defense; it might even bring reality to that will-o'-the-wisp of southern dreams, recognition of the Confederacy by England and France. It might, in short, be the stroke that would change everything, and at the very least it would take the contesting armies out of ravaged Virginia for a time.[2]

Few soldiers called on by government for advice are ever able to speak with the overpowering prestige that was Lee's in the spring of 1863. When he proposed that he take the Army of Northern Virginia and march into Pennsylvania, the issue was settled. Only Postmaster General Reagan, of all the Cabinet, continued to argue for a troop transfer to the West; President Davis and everyone else backed their winning general, as they were humanly bound to do, and by the middle of May the invasion of the North was ordered.

Probably no other decision could have been made, given all of the circumstances. Yet once again there had been profound miscalculation: the latest in a series of miscalculations, all of them fatal.

It had been calculated that in the concept of the Union of the states there was not anything so compelling that men would fight and die for it; that the institution of slavery could be made to live on in a world that was dreaming broader dreams; that this war (which itself had come against calculation) could be waged as a formalized contest that would go by familiar rules and not as an upheaval of terrible infinite forces that would go by no rules ever heard of and would forever change the people who were fighting it. Of these miscalculations the Confederacy was dying a slow death; to them, now, there was added the hopeful belief that if the brilliant stroke that had been so dazzling at Chancellorsville could just be repeated in Pennsylvania, all that had been lost could be happily redeemed.

Fog of war lay on the land, and men had to make the best decisions they could by the murky light that was available. The men in Richmond determined that the Army of Northern Virginia must march to Pennsylvania, and there it did march, pulling the Army of the Potomac after it—a fated, tragic march that led to the nation's most unforgettable single moment of tragic drama, but that led away from the main current of the war itself. Between them, the two armies that had to make this march would pay fifty thousand casualties for it.

2. *Moment of Truth*

Most of the men in the Army of the Potomac had been soldiers for very nearly two years. In those years a man who had been in all of the army's battles—and very few had been in all of them—might have known as many as twenty days of actual combat. All the rest was monotony; endless days in camps, hour upon hour of work on the drill field, long marches on bad roads with hot sun and dust or cold rain and mud for accompaniment. The soldier's greatest enemy always was simple boredom. The high adventure of army life came down at last to the eternal performance of dull tasks and to an unbroken routine of physical discomfort.

Life after Chancellorsville went on much as it had always gone. The troops were sullen and perplexed, yet there was no great drop in morale as there had been after Fredericksburg. The memory of the terrible battle in the blazing thickets seemed to be dulled very quickly. The old routine caught men up again; by its very familiarity it brought a revival of spirits; by the end of May it was almost as if the battle had not been fought. The army was living wholly in the present.

Yet with all of this there was a growing sense of great things to come. Chancellorsville had settled very little; it had been prelude, not finality, and army life was in a condition of unstable equilibrium. The desolate camping ground by the Rappahannock could not be a permanent abode. There was a rising tension, a dim foreknowledge of approaching climax. The big showdown that had seemed so near when the army moved for the Rappahannock fords at the end of April had not come off; it would come, and when it came it would be cataclysmic, bringing a day of violence worse than anything that had gone before.[1]

The army's failures had always been failures at the top. It was a great army, capable of great deeds, but no commander had ever used it with full throttle. McClellan, Pope, and Burnside had been either too cautious or too clumsy. Hooker, in a way, had been worst of all; crusty General Meade expressed the common feeling when he wrote to his wife that Hooker "disappointed all his friends by failing to show his fighting qualities at the pinch."[2] The army sensed that it would not fight another battle under Hooker, and the national administration had a firm conviction on the matter; the general remained in command, but he was operating on borrowed time, and although he was irritating his subordinates now by trying to find a scapegoat for disaster it seemed likely that when the next fight came someone else would be in charge.

The next fight would come soon. Across the river there was a stir in Lee's camps. Behind the cavalry screen the Confederate divisions began shifting toward the northwest, moving for the gaps in the Blue Ridge to reach the Shenandoah Valley, which offered a sheltered route to northern territory. Yankee cavalry crossed the river and provoked a savage fight at Brandy Station early in June, taking Jeb Stuart somewhat by surprise and getting a line on the Confederate movement. A bit later Hooker's soldiers read a grim omen in the fact that all civilians and sutlers were ordered outside the army's lines.

Lee was moving in a wide arc, beginning a fateful invasion of the North. Hooker thought of pitching into him en route; considered, too, the idea of moving straight for Richmond, believing that this would speedily call Lee back. But Washington ordered Hooker to play a strict defensive game, and by the middle of June the Army of the Potomac was on the move, marching for the Potomac crossings above Washington, circling warily to keep itself between the invader and the national capital.

As the two armies quickened their pace everybody watched —governments in Washington and Richmond, plain people North and South—as if the focus of the entire war centered here, with its final result and meaning depending altogether on what came of this desperate movement. Quick spurts of fire sparkled along the slanting fields, the copses and stone-fenced farms and drowsy hamlets on the eastern slopes of the Blue Ridge, where hard-fighting cavalry patrols probed and sparred, fighting simultaneously for concealment and discovery. The Army of Northern Virginia became mysteriously elongated, advance guard splashing across the Potomac shallows above Harpers Ferry, rear guard lingering near Fredericksburg, other elements strung out between. Lincoln reflected that so long an animal must be very slim somewhere, and he suggested that it might be broken in half if the thinnest spot could just be found. But War Department distrust of Hooker was too solid by now, and Hooker could not take the initiative; he was crippled by the Chancellorsville failure, and neither he nor anyone else could prevent what was coming. All of the chances that had been missed in two years of war were piling up, generating a pent-up violence that must be discharged finally in one shattering explosion. What was coming was fated. The war was following its own grim logic, and the men who seemed to control it were being carried by a tide they could neither direct nor understand.

Mid-June brought sweltering heat, with heavy dust in the torn roads, and the divisions of the Army of the Potomac were driven on in a series of forced marches which the men remembered as the worst they made in all the war. Men died of sunstroke or fell out by the roadside and staggered on to overtake their units after dusk, and the moving army trailed a soiled fringe of beaten stragglers; regiments would make camp at night with fewer than half of their men present, and the laggards would come stumbling in at all hours, exhausted.[3]

(In the West, Grant clamped a tighter grip on Vicksburg and waited for the end, and Joe Johnston vainly sought guidance: seeing that it could not possibly hold both, did the Confederate government prefer to give up Tennessee or Mississippi? Rosecrans got his army ready for movement, and in Arkansas a Confederate column began a hopeless attempt to drive the Federals away from Helena and the rivers; yet those who watched the war kept looking to the North, to Pennsylvania, where Lee's forward elements curled east toward York and Harrisburg, and as June came to an end they found themselves looking at a quiet little market town known as Gettysburg.)

Gettysburg was a dot on the map marking a place where all the roads crossed; a pleasant little town lying amid rolling hills and broad shallow valleys, a blue mountain wall rising a score of miles to the west, rival armies moving toward it without design, as if something in the place drew them irresistibly. All of Lee's army was north of the Potomac by now, connected with its southern bases by the thinnest of threads; it was on its own in a strange land, scooping up supplies from the fat Pennsylvania farming country, driven by an inexorable compulsion—lacking a supply line, it must eternally keep moving, because if it did not it would starve, and whenever and wherever it found its enemy it must strike without delay, no matter how the odds might look.

Hooker's army was above the river too, although Lee did not know it; Jeb Stuart, most famous of cavalrymen, had slipped the leash and gone off on a wild, meaningless raid that took him out of the play and left Lee groping in the dark, condemned at last to fight a battle in which he could not maneuver. But the Army of the Potomac was not Hooker's army any longer. As June ended, the War Department at last extorted from Hooker the thing it desired but hardly dared ask for—Hooker's resignation; and now Hooker was off in retirement and George Gordon Meade was in charge, his army loosely spread out across western Maryland, cavalry patrols groping north and west to see where the Confederate strength might be.

Confederate strength was coming together fast, and it was all heading for Gettysburg. Lee had finally learned that the Army of the Potomac was north of the border, looking for him, and when the news reached him his own troops were strung out along sixty miles of Pennsylvania highway, from Chambersburg in the west to the neighborhood of York and Harrisburg in the east. It was necessary for him to concentrate east of the mountains and to do it at once, and couriers had been riding hard to call the scattered divisions together. The Gettysburg area was the handiest place for them to meet, and so to Gettysburg they were coming; and at daylight on July 1 a Union cavalry division that had bivouacked on a low ridge just west of town saw the head of a Confederate infantry column coming toward it.

Stolid General John Buford, who commanded the cavalry, put his dismounted troopers in line, unlimbered his artillery, sent riders pelting south to notify Meade that the Rebels

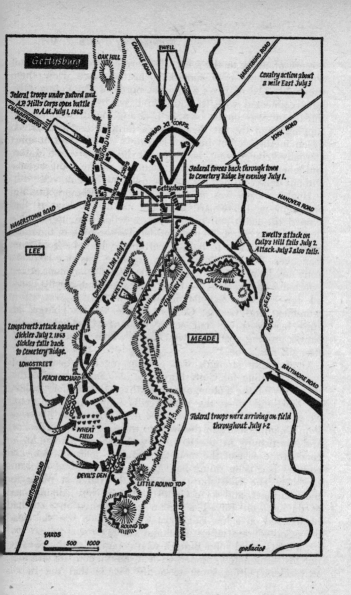

Gettysburg

OAK HILL

CARLISLE ROAD

EWELL

HARRISBURG ROAD

Cavalry action about a mile East July 3

Federal troops under Buford and A.P. Hill's Corps open battle 10 A.M. July 1, 1863

CHAMBERSBURG PIKE

HOWARD XI CORPS.

YORK ROAD

BUFORD

REYNOLDS I CORPS.

Gettysburg

Federal forces back through town to Cemetery Ridge by evening July 1.

SEMINARY RIDGE

HAGERSTOWN ROAD

HANOVER ROAD

Ewell's attack on Culp's Hill fails July 2. Attack July 3 also fails.

LEE

Confederate Line July 3.

PICKETT'S CHARGE

CEMETERY HILL

CULP'S HILL

ROCK CREEK

MEADE

Longstreet's attack against Sickles July 2, 1863. Sickles falls back to Cemetery Ridge.

CEMETERY RIDGE

LONGSTREET

BALTIMORE ROAD

PEACH ORCHARD

Federal troops were arriving on field throughout July 1-2

WHEAT FIELD

Federal Line July 3.

EMMITSBURG ROAD

DEVIL'S DEN

LITTLE ROUND TOP

TANEYTOWN ROAD

BIG ROUND TOP

YARDS
0   500   1000

gpalacios

had been found, and opened fire. And from the moment when cavalry and infantry began to exchange long-range shots—firing tentatively, as if they were probing this embryonic battle to see what it might amount to—the two armies were committed to their most terrible fight.

Gettysburg was an act of fate; a three-day explosion of storm and flame and terror, unplanned and uncontrollable, coming inevitably (as the war itself had come) out of the things that hard-pressed men had done in the light of imperfect knowledge, the end result of actions that moved with an inexorable logic toward a fundamental and astounding goal. It would come to symbolize all the war, as if the blunders and the heroism, the hopes and the delusions, the combativeness and the incomprehensible devotion of all Americans had been summed up once and for all in one monstrous act of violence. It was enormously destructive, its significance was not seen until long after it had ended, and—to make it finally and perfectly characteristic—it opened and closed with moments of heartbreaking drama.

Buford's cavalry had to hold the ridge until some of Meade's infantry could come up. The Confederates got an infantry division in line and began to move forward, and ragged smoke clouds hung over the ridge as the firing grew heavier; then, in the middle of the morning, the leading brigade of General John Reynolds's I Army Corps came swinging up the Emmitsburg road from the south, Reynolds himself galloping on ahead to see Buford and get a line on the fight. As the Federals came nearer they left the road and headed cross-lots, taking a short cut to the scene of action; and some impulse made the commander of this leading brigade shake out the battle flags and put the fife and drum corps at the head of the column to play the men into battle. On they came, five regiments of lean Middle Westerners, roar of battle just ahead, shrill fifes playing "The Campbells Are Coming," eighteen hundred veteran soldiers tramping along in step.* This battle of Gettysburg would begin with a flourish and a snatch of music, with the shock troops giving a last salute to the fraudulent romance of war before plunging into the storm. Then the music ended, the infantry ran out along the ridge, and the fight was on.

This day began well for the Federals, but it ended disastrously. Reynolds's men knocked the first Confederate attack back on its heels, capturing a Rebel brigadier and mangling a couple of Confederate brigades almost beyond repair; but Confederate reinforcements were reaching Gettysburg faster than the Federals, and the battle lines grew and grew until they formed a great semicircle west and north of the town, Federals outnumbered and outflanked, Reynolds killed and his army corps cut to pieces. Another Yankee corps, the XI, came up and went through town on the double, colliding head on with Confederates who were marching south from Carlisle. These Confederates cut around both flanks of the XI Corps' line, crumpled them, punched holes in the line, and late in the afternoon drove the survivors back through the village in rout; then the line west of town caved in, and by evening the Federals who were left (they had had upward of ten thousand casualties) were reassembling on the high ground south and east of Gettysburg, grimly determined to hold on until the rest of the army came up, but not at all certain that they could do it.

Perhaps Lee could have driven them off that evening and clinched things. Most of his army was on the scene by now, and the Federals were badly outnumbered; one final drive in the Stonewall Jackson manner might have done it. But Lee was fighting blind. The cavalry that might have told him where all of Meade's men was still absent, an exhausted column riding hard somewhere off to the east, and Jackson was in his grave, and by the time the southern generals had conferred and considered and weighed risks, night had come and it was too late. The battle would have to be resumed next day.

July 2 came in hot after a windless night in which a full moon lit the dreadful debris on the fields and hills where men had fought on the first day. Meade was on the scene now, most of his army in hand and the rest coming up fast. He held good ground: Cemetery Hill, a massive height on the southern edge of town, wooded Culp's Hill half a mile to the east, and the long crest of a ridge that ran south from the cemetery, taking its name from it—Cemetery Ridge—which ended in two rocky knolls a mile or more away, Little

Round Top and Big Round Top. On these heights the Army of the Potomac waited while Lee prepared for a new assault.

Running parallel to Cemetery Ridge, a mile west across a shallow open valley, was a similar rise in the ground, Seminary Ridge, taking its name from a Lutheran theological institute. On this ridge, looking east, was perhaps half of the Confederate army. The rest of the army was in position in and on both sides of Gettysburg, facing south—an awkward position, since it compelled the smaller of the two armies to occupy the longer line and gave Meade the advantage of a compact central position; wherever they made their fight, the Confederates would have to come uphill.

One Confederate did not like the looks of it at all. James Longstreet was a stubborn, opinionated man, and on July 2 his opinion was that Gettysburg was not a fit place for the Confederates to fight—an opinion that he clung to with massive stubbornness. Better, he argued, to maneuver, sliding far around the Union flank and finding some position in which the Army of Northern Virginia could sit tight and let the Yankees do the attacking. But Lee looked east from Seminary Ridge, saw the ranks of the waiting Federals, and made the inescapable decision: The enemy is there, and there I will attack him. Longstreet argued, grumbled, and sulked, but it made no difference. Here the fight had started and here it would have to end.

It was well on in the afternoon before the Confederates could make their attack; and this second day at Gettysburg was made up of many separate fights, each one a moment or an hour of concentrated fury, with a blinding, choking fog of blue powder smoke over the hillsides and the rocky woods, hammered down by unending deafening noise, sparkling and glowing evilly with constant spurts of fire. In the batteries the slim iron rifles and the squat brass smoothbores bounded backward at each discharge, their trail-pieces tearing the ground; sweating gunners manhandled them back into place, rammed home fresh charges, stood aside for a new salvo, and then ran in to lay hold of wheels and handspikes to make ready for another blast. Above all the racket there was the sound of men cheering and cursing and the fearful screaming of wounded horses, and all the ground was covered with dead and wounded. Ragged lines of infantry swayed in and out of the shifting veils of smoke, battle flags visible here and there, generals riding, gesturing with swords, couriers going in on the gallop with orders that might or might not be heeded. Commanding officers sent troops forward, called up reinforcements, peered anxiously through their glasses at the murk that hid the battle from their sight. They had called this violence into being but they could do no more with it. This was the soldiers' fight now.

East of Gettysburg there was Culp's Hill, high and covered with trees, anchor of the right end of Meade's bent line. Confederate Richard Ewell sent his men in long battle lines forming in the flat ground and running forward into the woods. They found the Federals posted in solid breastworks of earth and felled trees; they struggled up the smoke-drenched hillside, stumbled back down, tried again, won a foothold that threatened the Union army with disaster—and could not quite make it, while the chain lightning of the flashing guns laced in and out among the tree trunks and sparkled in the hot woodland dusk.

South of Gettysburg there was high ground along the Emmitsburg road, and here, against Meade's orders, General Dan Sickles had posted the III Army Corps. Longstreet drove his own army corps in on these men amid an immense bombardment, a cannon ball took off Sickles's leg, and the III Corps was broken up and driven back in confusion, although it made a bitter fight of it before retreating. There was a peach orchard, where men fought hand to hand with bayonets and musket butts amid little trees shattered by shell fire. There was a wheat field, grain trampled flat and strewn with dead bodies, where Northerners and Southerners knelt thirty paces apart and blazed away with unremitting fury; the Federals lost the field, brought up reinforcements and regained it, then lost it for good when a new Confederate attack was driven home. Near the wheat field there was a great tangled area of boulders and stunted trees known as the Devil's Den; it earned its name that afternoon, while men fired from behind rocks and trees, wounded men dragged themselves into rocky dens and crevices for shelter, and

Yankee batteries in the rear blasted the place indiscriminately with shell and solid shot. East of Devil's Den there was Little Round Top, swept by southern rifle fire, defended by last-minute Federal reinforcements who ran panting along the uneven hillside to drive back the Confederates who had swept through Devil's Den.

Sickles's line was pulverized, and fresh troops who came in were broken and driven back, and for a time there was a great gaping hole all along the left of Meade's line. But Little Round Top held, and a line of Federal guns was posted in a farmyard, where it held off Longstreet's charging men until Meade could get fresh infantry on the scene. At one time a Confederate division charged all the way to the crest of Cemetery Ridge, and the Army of the Potomac was in danger of being broken in half; but the invaders could not stay, a series of disorganized but effective countercharges cut them and drove them back, and when darkness came at last the Union left continued to hold the high ground. Over near Culp's Hill there was a final flare-up, and once again disaster came near; charging Southerners broke an infantry line and got in among the Yankee guns on Cemetery Hill, but a Union brigade ran in at the last moment, fighting in pitch-darkness with only the spitting fire from gun muzzles to tell where the battle line was, and the Southerners drew off at last and retired to the plain north of the hill. The second day at Gettysburg came to a close, and as the guns were stilled a constant, agonizing chorus of cries from the helpless wounded men filled the moonlit night; thousands upon thousands of maimed lay in field and woods and on the rocky knolls, all the way from Round Top and the wheat field around to Culp's Hill.

In the rear of the Army of the Potomac there was a great confused huddle of bewildered fugitives, walking wounded, wrecked artillery units, and panicky non-combat details. During the night and early morning the last of Meade's reinforcements came up through this backwash. A gunner in the VI Corps remembered how the stragglers and wounded men told doleful tales of defeat—"there was all kinds of stories flying round in the rear, some telling us that we were whipped to death and that any God's quantity of our artillery was captured"; but when the replacements got to the battle line they found everybody confident. A wounded infantry colonel assured them that "we are just warming them and giving them the damnedest whipping they ever got,"⁵ and when daylight brought a renewal of the Confederate attempt to seize Culp's Hill the Federals steadied and beat the attack off with smooth competence.

After the fight for Culp's Hill ended, there was a lull, and the hot noon hours of the third day passed with nothing to break the stillness but an occasional sputter of skirmish-line fire. The thing had not been settled yet. The armies had not quite fought themselves out; the Army of Northern Virginia had enough strength left for one final assault, and the Army of the Potomac was still strong enough for one more desperate stand. It would happen now. Everybody knew it, and the armies waited, tense, while the sun beat down on the steaming fields.

While they waited, there was a restless stir of movement along the center and left of the Confederate line. Rank upon rank of artillery took position in the open, west of Emmitsburg road; behind, in the woods along Seminary Ridge, troops were on the move, glint of sunlight on rifle barrels visible now and then to the waiting Federals a mile to the east. Meade had predicted the night before that if Lee attacked again he would hit the Union center: he had tried both flanks and had failed; only the middle line was left. Meade was right. Lee was massing strength for one last great blow, aiming it at the strongest part of the Union line, where the chance of success was little better than Burnside's chance had been in front of the stone wall at Fredericksburg. Lee was used to long odds, he had the habit of success, and there was in him a deep confidence that his men could do anything if they were once properly thrown into action. The point they would strike was marked by a little clump of trees—center of the target for Lee's final shot.

He would throw them into action here and now, in spite of the odds, trusting that the valor of an infantry which he believed to be unconquerable would make up for all of the mistakes that had been made. A courier rode out from Longstreet's headquarters with an order for a battery commander; two guns were fired with a breathless, measured interval between—and then, at one o'clock, came the explosion, and the whole line of Confederate guns opened in a thunderous bombardment. Federal gunners on Cemetery Ridge ran to their pieces to reply, Yankee infantry huddled behind low breastworks, dazed by the storm, and the fifteen thousand Southerners who had been appointed to charge across the valley knelt in the woods behind their flaming guns and waited likewise, while the ground trembled and a great smoke-fog filled the open space between the ridges, and the war's supreme hour of tension tightened toward its breaking point.

It was the most prodigious bombardment of the war. The roar was continuous, so intense that artillerists could hardly hear the reports of their own guns; men who thought they had seen and heard the ultimate at Antietam or Gaines's Mill found that this went beyond anything they had known or imagined. It was the utmost the two armies could do.

Yet it was oddly inconclusive. The guns swept Cemetery Ridge with flame and with fragments of flying metal; they killed men and animals, broke gun carriages to fragments, exploded caissons. Over the heads of the waiting Confederate infantry the Federal shells ripped branches and ugly jagged splinters from trees, killed crouching men who never saw the battle, filled the air with the sound and the scent of violent death. But the great assault, when it came, would go about as it would have gone if there had been no bombardment at all. The Federal power to resist was not materially weakened—except that some of Meade's batteries ran out of long-range ammunition and would have to wait for their attackers to get to close quarters; the Confederate power to attack was as strong as it was before the guns went off; and the power and the fury that had beaten upon the rocky hills were no more than the overture for the moment that lay just ahead.

That moment would linger and shine in the American memory forever, the terrible unforgettable moment of truth that would symbolize inexpressible things. It blotted out other scenes then, and it still does. A few miles to the east, all but unnoticed by the armies themselves, Union and Confederate cavalry were fighting a desperate mounted battle, charging lines crashing into each other at full gallop as if these troopers by themselves would win the day and the war; and if Stuart's worn brigades had managed to break through they could have gone all across the defenseless rear of the Army of the Potomac, where they could have made vast trouble. But they did not break through; they drew off at last with heavy losses—and afterward all anyone would say was, "Oh yes, the cavalry fought at Gettysburg too, didn't it?" And far down in Mississippi a white flag was coming out through Pemberton's lines, and for the second time in his life Grant was being asked what terms he would give to a surrendering army; yet then and now, to look at that hour is to see it through the eyes of the sweating Federals who crouched on Cemetery Ridge and squinted west, peering toward the afternoon sun.

What they saw was an army with banners, moving out from the woods into the open field by the ranked guns, moving out of shadow into eternal legend, rank upon endless rank drawn up with parade-ground precision, battle flags tipped forward, sunlight glinting from musket barrels—General George Pickett's Virginians, and ten thousand men from other commands, men doomed to try the impossible and to fail. It takes time to get fifteen thousand men into line, and these Southerners were deliberate about it—perhaps out of defiance, perhaps out of sheer self-consciousness and pride. Then at last they had things the way they wanted them and they went marching up toward the clump of unattainable trees, and all the guns opened again, and a great cloud of smoke and dust filled the hollow plain.

Lee watched from the crest of Seminary Ridge, and because of the smoke he could see very little. Meade saw nothing at all, for he had been busy about headquarters duties far behind the lines, and although he mounted and rode for the front he did not get there until it was all over. The rolling cloud crossed the fields and went up the slope, and the crash of battle rose higher and higher as the men came to grips with each other on Cemetery Ridge, choking fog hiding the battle flags, Federals from right and left swarming over to join in the fight. Then suddenly it was finished. The charging column had been broken all to bits, survivors were going back to the Confederate lines, the smoke cloud was lifting as the firing died down—and the battle of Gettysburg was ended.

Ended; yet singularly incomplete, not to become a rounded whole until months afterward. It was the queer fate of the men who fought over the great question of Union that this most desperate and spectacular of all their battles should not be entirely comprehensible until after all of the dead had been buried, the wounded tended, the field itself made into a park, and the armies gone far below the horizon, fighting other battles in other places. Then the President would come and speak a few sentences, and the deep meaning of the fight would at last begin to clear. Then the perplexing mists and shadows would fade and Gettysburg would reveal itself as a great height from which men could glimpse a vista extending far into the undiscovered future.

Meanwhile they had to get on with the war. Lee would hold his lines until the next day, withdrawing sullenly, a third of his army out of action; Meade would follow with great caution, well aware that he had lost fully a quarter of his force and that Lee's army was still dangerous as a wounded tiger; and in the end both armies would return to Virginia, and the most that could surely be said was that one more attempted Confederate invasion had been driven back. But far to the west the great valley had been opened, and now an Illinois farmer could send his wheat down-river to New Orleans and the outside world, as if 1861 had never happened.

3. *Unvexed to the Sea*

When Grant's army first came up to Vicksburg, on May 18, the men thought that perhaps it was going to be easy. They were cocky. In less than three weeks they had crossed the Mississippi, marched far inland to seize and despoil the capital of the state, beaten the Confederates in battle wherever they met them, taken several thousand prisoners, and forced Pemberton to pull his army back inside of his fortified lines. They had lived, while doing all of this, off the fat of the land; and although they had fought hard, marched hard, and lived hard, there had been about the whole expedition some of the aspects of an especially unrestrained picnic. The soldiers were beginning to believe that they could do just about anything they wished, and it seemed likely now that with one sharp rush they could capture Vicksburg and end the campaign.

Grant himself seems to have felt very much the same way. He suspected, in addition, that the Confederates were badly demoralized. They had just retreated pell-mell into the works after being decisively whipped in the open field, and if they could be hit hard before they had a chance to get set, the blow might be decisive. Grant spent twenty-four hours arranging his three army corps in front of Pemberton's works, and then on the afternoon of May 19 his signal guns boomed and the attack was made.[1]

It did not turn out to be easy, and if the Confederates were demoralized they concealed it admirably. The ground was made for defense, and these Southerners speedily demonstrated anew the truth of an old military axiom—that even badly beaten troops can do very well if they are put into good fieldworks and allowed to fight on the defensive. They proved it now so conclusively that they kept Grant's army out of Vicksburg for a month and a half.

Vicksburg was on an uneven plateau, and the ground all around the town was hilly and rolling, seamed by an infinite number of ravines and gullies that ran in all directions and tended to have very steep walls. It made ideal defensive ground, and Pemberton's engineers had laid out their lines with skill. They put strong redoubts on commanding heights, connected these with a chain of rifle pits, and arranged it all so that every ravine or hollow that led up to their works could be swept by artillery and musketry. In effect, any assaulting party would either have to scale a precipitous bluff or must come up through the narrow end of a funnel, with Rebel marksmen enjoying a clear shot all the way.

The attack on May 19 was bound to fail, and it failed quickly. Grant's troops dashed at the Confederate works, were rebuffed, and then began to dig trenches of their own within easy musket shot of the enemy lines. They still were not convinced that the Vicksburg trenches could not be stormed, and when Grant conferred with his corps commanders he found that his generals were not convinced either—nor, for the matter of that, was he himself. It still seemed as if one determined push ought to take the town and everything in it; Grant was fully aware that Joe Johnston, off to his rear somewhere, was striving to assemble an army large enough to raise the siege—and, all in all, it seemed advisable to try it once more.

The new fight was made on May 22. It cost the Union army rather more than three thousand men and gained nothing worth talking about. The experience of a brigade in McClernand's corps was typical.

Sent in to make its attack, this brigade had to advance by the flank, in column of fours, up a winding gully. The approach was fairly well protected from Confederate fire, but precisely at the point where the gully broadened and gave the troops room to deploy it exposed them to destruction. The leading regiment, reaching this spot, formed column of companies and went forward on the double. The first blast of Confederate fire annihilated the leading company outright —of thirty-two men, all but one were either killed or wounded —and the succeeding companies fared little better. Most of the brigade wound up at last hugging the ground at the bottom of a railroad cut and praying for darkness. At the top of the slope Confederates were lighting the fuses of shells and then rolling the shells downhill on their heads. Now and then the Federals would manage to pick one up and toss it back before it exploded. After night came what was left of the brigade crept back to the rear to reassemble.[7]

Somehow, during this fight, McClernand got the idea that he was winning. In two or three places his men actually reached the first line of Rebel trenches; McClernand saw their flags there and sent word to Grant that he had cracked the Confederate line and that he could go on in and take Vicksburg if McPherson and Sherman supported him properly. Grant was skeptical, but he had the other corps renew their efforts—only to learn later that McClernand's optimism was simply the delusion of an unskilled soldier still obsessed by the belief that he would be the hero who would take Vicksburg, open the Mississippi Valley, and win the war. Sherman and McPherson, whose men lost heavily in the extra attacks because of McClernand's claims, were furious, and Grant made up his mind that as soon as Vicksburg fell he would send McClernand home.[3]

For Vicksburg was bound to fall, eventually. Grant's line of encircling trenches ran thirteen miles, from the Chickasaw Bluffs north of town all the way to the Mississippi on the south, and if the Federals could not force their way in, the Confederates had even less chance to force their way out. On the men, the food, and the ammunition that he had in Vicksburg to begin with, Pemberton would have to make his fight; and there was not a chance that what he had would be enough. Joe Johnston was still in Grant's rear, and because Rosecrans had not yet taken the offensive in Tennessee, Johnston was getting reinforcements; but Grant was being reinforced too, and he was able to form a defensive line of his own, some miles to the east of the lines he had drawn around Vicksburg, to hold Johnston at arm's length. Porter and his ironclads held the river, and at night the naval mortars tossed huge shells into Vicksburg, wrecking homes and killing civilians and driving the citizens to live in caves dug in ravines. All the Federals had to do now was to hold on and eventually the fortress was bound to fall.

The soldiers settled down to it as philosophically as they could. An Iowan wrote home that "we are all as dirty as hogs" and infested with vermin; they had not had their clothes off for four weeks, and in the trenches they could hardly get enough water to drink; to make any attempt to keep clean was completely hopeless. Men in a Wisconsin regiment dug a hundred-foot well but got only a little muddy water for their pains. Most of the troops had to send details all the way to the Mississippi to bring back water in barrels —"and poor stuff it is when they get it." A Rebel prisoner boasted that Pemberton's army had enough corn and bacon to last a year and said it could never be starved out. Fever and ague were common in the Federal trenches, and many men were on the sick list.[4]

Yet Federal morale remained good. The men were proud

of the campaign they had made, and they were strategists enough to know that they had the Confederates in a box. They told one another that they would be in Vicksburg by the Fourth of July; meanwhile they worked night and day to make their own trenches strong. Sandbags were piled along the parapets, leaving loopholes for muskets; heavy logs were then laid on top of the sandbags, and along most of the line a man in the trenches could walk erect in comparative safety. Gunners in an Ohio battery boasted that they had built a regular fort, with walls eight feet high, and at the gun ports they put a casing of saplings around their sandbags so that the blast from the muzzles of their guns would not tear the gunny-sacking. Two miles away they could see the cupola of the Vicksburg courthouse, and when nothing else was going on they would train their guns for extreme elevation and amuse themselves firing at it. They never knew whether they actually hit it.[5]

Grant was the one whose morale suffered. It was strange about Grant: he would go down in history as a stolid, unemotional slugger, yet in reality he was a man who liked to keep moving, and the dull routine of the siege was almost more than he could take. Military routine of any sort bored him; military life itself, with its unimaginative ritual and its way of doing things by rote, he detested. With nothing to do now but watch his men perfect their trenches and start digging the long, slanting ditches that would ultimately get them close to the Confederate lines, Grant became bored. It is alleged that he took to drink, went on an epoch-making bender in the cabin of a supply steamer anchored up the Yazoo, and was saved from exposure and disgrace by a newspaper correspondent who got him out of the place, sent word to Grant's adjutant general, Colonel Rawlins, and finally managed to smuggle Grant back to headquarters, unseen, in an ambulance. Rawlins was waiting, pale with suppressed fury, when the ambulance pulled up. Grant buttoned his uniform coat, got out of the vehicle as steadily as if he had never so much as sniffed at a cork, gave Rawlins a quiet "Good evening," and walked off to his tent, seemingly as sober as any man alive.[6]

So, at any rate, ran the story which the correspondent put

in his memoirs years later. It is an unsupported story and there are flaws in it, and it does not really matter very much whether it is true or not. For it is to be noted that while Grant might drink too much on occasion, he never let it get in the way of serious business. He drank when things were dull—drank, apparently, from loneliness as much as anything; Rawlins always breathed easily when the general was able to have Mrs. Grant in camp with him. Throughout the war the times when liquor was a problem to Grant were the times of inaction. When the chips were down Grant could stay sober.

He emerged from this spree, if he really had it, just in time to get rid of McClernand. McClernand was clearly not up to the command of an army corps, and both Sherman and McPherson were disgusted with him; unfortunately he outranked everyone in the place except Grant, and if anything happened to Grant he would automatically take command of the army. The War Department had long since quietly let Grant know that if he wanted to dismiss Mc-Clernand his action would be upheld in Washington. Now, not long after the failure of the assaults on the Vicksburg lines, matters came to a head.

McClernand had undertaken to congratulate the men of his army corps on their bravery in the recent battle. His congratulations took the form of an official order, which claimed for McClernand's corps credit for just about everything that had been done during the Vicksburg campaign and broadly implied that the corps would have taken Vicksburg if the rest of the army had done its part; and this order McClernand incautiously sent off to a St. Louis newspaper, in which it was immediately printed. This not only sent Sherman and McPherson to Grant's tent with fire in their eyes; it was technically a breach of army regulations, which forbade any officer to publish an official paper without his superior's permission. Naturally McClernand had never cleared this paper with Grant, and now, on June 18, Grant formally relieved McClernand of his command and sent him back to Illinois, turning his corps over to General E. O. C. Ord.

Back in Illinois, McClernand fumed and cursed and cried

for justice, wiring Lincoln that he had been relieved "for an omission of my adjutant." Justice—or at least reinstatement—he could not get. Lincoln sent him a soothing letter, which probably did not really soothe him very much, and declined to intervene. McClernand had played his part: he had put at the service of the administration his political and popular influence in Illinois, and he had brought together and organized a substantial number of highly useful soldiers who might not otherwise have got into the army at all. By these acts he had helped to give the Vicksburg expedition the weight and the impetus it needed . . . and now he was out of the war, milked dry, discarded, shelved where he could give neither Grant nor any other general any further worry. He seems to have felt that he was the victim of a put-up job. . . .⁷

Up and down the long lines the Federal trenches were inched closer to the defensive works. Sharpshooters were constantly busy, and the artillery was always active. There were casualties every day, and a man in the 12th Wisconsin wrote that "it looked hard to see six or eight poor fellows piled into an ambulance about the size of Jones's meat wagon and hustled over the rough roads as fast as the mules could trot and to see the blood running out of the carts in streams almost." Firing died down at night, although the naval batteries and the army siege guns kept booming away; in the darkness the glowing fuses of the mortar shells could be seen, rising high above the town in great parabolas, the explosion lighting the sky like lightning, and every morning the hour of dawn brought a sudden step-up in the firing. Infantrymen learned to sleep soundly even in the rifle pits, despite the racket and the danger. In twenty-four hours the average soldier on the firing line would use from fifty to one hundred cartridges.⁸

Grant was steadily reinforced. He had seventy-five thousand men in his command now, and Joe Johnston could easily be held at a distance while the job of throttling the Vicksburg garrison went forward methodically. The Federals made a number of sap rollers for protection as they extended their trenches. Two empty barrels would be placed end to end, encased in a binding of saplings and filled with dirt;

with the open ends plugged, this provided a heavy, bullet-proof roller, and men could crouch behind it and dig in comparative security.

There was no drama in all of this and very little excitement; just a remorseless, constant tightening of the bonds around the fortress. The men understood that all of this drudgery was much more economical of life than any series of open assaults would have been, and they took to it willingly enough. A general explained their attitude:

"The veteran American soldier fights very much as he has been accustomed to work his farm or run his sawmill; he wants to see a fair prospect that it 'is going to pay.' His loyalty, discipline and pluck will not allow him under any circumstances to retreat without orders, much less to run away, but if he encounters a resistance which he thinks he cannot overcome, or which he thinks it would 'cost too much' to overcome, he will lie down, cover himself with a little parapet, and hold his ground against any force that may attempt to drive him back.'"

There were strange interludes now and then; facing each other at close range, week after week, the men of the opposing armies developed an odd sort of fellow-feeling for each other. One day the men in one Federal trench saw the Confederates opposite them standing on top of their parapet, looking toward them; they climbed into the open themselves and looked at their enemies, and when someone yelled across and asked the Rebels why they were standing up like that, the reply came back: "Because you are." Then a lad in the 11th Wisconsin cried impulsively: "I'm going down into the ravine and shake hands with them Rebs." He ran downhill to a little creek, a Confederate ran down to meet him, and presently hundreds of men from both sides were down there, shaking hands, talking, and picking blackberries. The Confederates asked the Federals how they liked the Mississippi climate, said that they had been getting mule meat for breakfast, and did not seem to feel that they could hold out much longer. Then at last a Confederate officer came out and scolded the men for fraternizing; the Confederates reluctantly went back to their trenches, the Federals did the same, and in another minute the firing had been resumed as if there had never been a break.

Pickets grew friendly. One night a party from the 33rd Illinois was at work digging a trench out toward the Confederate line; unwittingly the men pushed their work until they had gone through the Rebel picket line, and the Confederate pickets protested at this infringement of their territory. Their officer of the guard came out and remonstrated: this was irregular, the Unionists were trespassing on Confederate soil. A Union officer replied that they did not mean to trespass, but they were under orders—they had been told to dig in this direction, picket line or no, and what could they do about it? The Confederate officer at last agreed that there was nothing that could be done about it, and he added despondently: "I suppose it really makes no difference, you'll soon have the place anyway."[10]

Closer and closer came the lines, until in places they were only a few yards apart. Now the Federals began to make tunnels under the Confederate lines, planting mines and exploding them. These were small-scale affairs and caused relatively few casualties; they did result in marvels now and then, as when one mine blew a Negro camp cook in the Confederate army clear over inside the Union lines. He was unhurt, oddly enough, and the Iowa outfit that captured him put him in a tent and exhibited him to the curious for several days, charging five cents a head.[11]

Inside Vicksburg food supplies were running low and hope was gone. The bombardment went on without a letup. Union trenches were so close in some spots that only a wall of earth separated attackers and defenders. Before long, obviously, the Federals could make a concerted rush that would break the defensive line once and for all. Luckless Pemberton held a council of war, confessed that there was no chance that Johnston could break the Federal cordon and relieve the Vicksburg garrison, and remarked that as far as he could see they could do one of two things—surrender now, while it might still be possible to get decent terms, or make one wild, desperate attempt to cut their way out—which would be completely hopeless but which probably would kill a good many Yankees. Most of the generals voted for surrender, and Pemberton agreed. On July 3 a white flag went through the lines, and before long Pemberton and Grant were standing under a tree talking things over.

Grant began by restating the old "unconditional surrender" theme. He did not really mean it, however, and in the end Pemberton was given terms so lenient that Halleck, back in Washington, rapped Grant's knuckles for not being sterner. In effect the Confederates were allowed to come out of the citadel, lay down their arms, and then go to their homes under parole. Grant believed that it would take half of the summer, and be infernally expensive as well, to ship the whole lot all the way north to a prison camp; besides, he felt that Pemberton's men were so discouraged that very few of them would ever return to the army even if they were finally exchanged. (Several hundred of the men refused to sign their paroles, preferring to be sent north as prisoners of war so that they could not under any possibility be forced back into the army; Federals who mingled with the prisoners heard many say that they had "done their last fighting for the South.")[12]

In any case, the Confederate flag came down on July 4, and Grant found himself in possession of thirty-one thousand prisoners, one hundred and seventy-two cannon, and more than sixty thousand small arms, many of which were better weapons than his own men were carrying. A number of Federal regiments rearmed themselves with captured rifles after Vicksburg. It was noted that the victorious Unionists did no cheering when the Confederates laid down their arms—except that one division raised a cheer for "the gallant defenders of Vicksburg." As soon as the ceremonies were over the men of the two armies were mingling on friendly terms, and Confederates who had been eating mule meat got Yankee hardtack and bacon for supper. One Union sharpshooter, seeing a Confederate officer on a distinctive white horse, called out to him: "Mister—you man on the little white horse! Danged if you ain't the hardest feller to hit I ever saw; I've shot at you more'n a hundred times!"[13]

That night, for the first time in a month and a half, no guns fired anywhere along the Vicksburg front. Federal soldiers found it impossible to get to sleep; the unfamiliar quiet was somehow oppressive and disturbing."

Far downstream, at Port Hudson, Banks had at last brought up the army that did not come up in time to meet Grant, and Port Hudson had been under siege since May 23. The business was a small-scale replica of Vicksburg—seven thousand Confederates in the trenches, fourteen thousand Federals outside trying to get in, capture by assault impossible, escape for the beleaguered garrison impossible also. After the fall of Vicksburg a broadside announcing the event was tossed over inside the Port Hudson lines. It brought a defiant shout: "That's another damned Yankee lie!"—but when all the Federals began to cheer and their bands started giving patriotic concerts up and down the lines, the defiance began to fade, and by July 9 Port Hudson was surrendered, lock, stock, and barrel. There were no longer any Confederate troops or fortifications anywhere along the Mississippi River. From St. Paul to the Gulf, the stream was open.

What had been accomplished required no elaboration. The event spoke for itself. It was the logical conclusion of all that had been done in the West since the war began. The strong hand in Missouri, the slow advance up the Tennessee and the Cumberland, the fights at Fort Donelson and Shiloh, at New Madrid and Island No. Ten, at Corinth and Perryville and Stone's River, the long months of sickness and discontent in the muddy swamps and bayous—all of these made a coherent pattern, and no one needed to wait for a presidential speech to explain it. It was all going just about as Winfield Scott had thought it might, in the dim days before Bull Run, although the dropsical old general himself was rusticating at West Point, knowing of the war only by the echoes that came up the Hudson. The Confederacy was broken now, and the break would be permanent; would be followed, inevitably, by others. Mr. Lincoln would use great phrases to tell of Gettysburg, but Vicksburg he could sum up in one terse sentence:

"The father of waters rolls unvexed to the sea."

10.

Last of the Might-Have-Beens

1. *Pursuit in Tennessee*

IT WAS BELIEVED that the Middle West now was back where it had been in 1860. The Mississippi Valley was open again, and it was an article of faith that this river was the all-important highway to the markets of the world. The West was free; the terrible threat of isolation posed by secession was ended, and the farmers and traders of the continental interior no longer had to see a closed door at the mouth of the great river. They could also count themselves relieved from economic bondage to the merchants and bankers of the East.

Yet war is fought in a fog, and men are not always able to understand just what they have done. The Mississippi would never again be what it had been before—not even when the last vengeful guerrillas had been driven from the canebrakes and cured of their new habit of taking shots at passing steamboats. The road to the outer world would run east and west now, river or no river, war or no war. Not again would there be the lazy life of drifting downstream with the tide, high-pressure engines swinging paddle wheels in slow, splashing rhythm, corn and wheat and pork and mules and lumber borne away by the Father of Waters to the great ships waiting at the New Orleans levee. The dike that had obstructed the river was broken, but the old flow would never quite be resumed. The West had won the most significant campaign of the war, but it had not brought back the past. That was gone forever. Now the West must face east, not south. And the entire country must look to the future rather than to the past.

That the capture of Vicksburg would have unexpected results was no more than natural. It had been thought of as something that would soothe the rising war-weariness west of the Alleghenies and make farmers feel that they would gain by the war; it turned out to be the stroke that would decide the war itself, or at least would go far toward doing so, and Sherman was exultantly writing to his brother, the senator, that Federal armies "will be in Mobile in October and Georgia by Christmas if required." He was talking with southern men of repute and position, and he reported: "The fall of Vicksburg has had a powerful effect. They are subjugated."

Sherman could have been right. From a soldier's viewpoint, all the logic was on his side; having lost the valley, the Confederacy could not hope to win the final decision. Yet the war was turning into something that no one battle or campaign could settle. It was no longer a mere matter of armies; it was turning into the first of the great modern wars, releasing unsuspected energies even as it brought infinite destruction, and its proper target now was not so much the opposing armies in the field as the will to resist, the capacity to keep on struggling for survival, in the hearts of the people themselves. Grant had wrecked the transportation and manufacturing nexus at Jackson, Mississippi, as an essential preliminary to the taking of Vicksburg. More and more the war would follow that pattern. The morale of a Mississippi planter or an Ohio farmer would finally come to be fully as significant as the condition of Bragg's or Grant's soldiers.

Odd things were beginning to happen. There was, early this summer, for a sample, the matter of John Hunt Morgan's raid into Ohio and the possibly related business of Clement Vallandigham and his effort to become governor of Ohio.

Vallandigham was a northern Democrat who believed that the sheer weight of the northern war effort was crushing domestic liberties; believed, also, that under almost any circumstances it would be better to have Democrats in power than to have Republicans. He had been campaigning in Ohio with great vigor, uttering words that seemed cal-

culated to discourage northern recruiting efforts and to bring
about a readiness to accept a negotiated peace; and Ambrose
E. Burnside—who, after Fredericksburg, had been gently removed from combat leadership and given the quiet post of
command in the peaceful Ohio country—concluded that Vallandigham was an outright traitor, and he sent a file of
soldiers to arrest the man and throw him into prison. The
Lincoln administration, perceiving that this was making a
martyr out of a sensationally effective Democratic vote-
getter, canceled the imprisonment and sent Vallandigham
into exile; sent him, in the month of May, through Rosecrans's lines below Murfreesboro and straight into the southern Confederacy. Vallandigham went to Richmond and
talked with important people there, and it seems that an
unreal vision began to dawn.

Vallandigham represented many things, all of which could
be summed up under one general heading: trouble for the
Lincoln government. He was appealing to Northerners who
were tired of the war. Many of them were basically sympathetic to the South. They had a shadowy, semi-military, semi-
secret organization, cross between political chowder club
and village lodge, known as the Knights of the Golden Circle,
and some of them at least talked as if they favored a new
secession movement in the Northwest, with further fragmentation of the Federal Union. Somehow, the Davis administration reasoned, it ought to be possible to make use of them.

So while Vallandigham flitted off stage—he went by sea
to Canada, and in Ontario waited the right moment to return
to the United States—John Hunt Morgan took off on a strange,
abortive, extra-military sort of expedition north of the Ohio
River.[2]

Morgan was a Kentuckian: one of the legendary southern
horsemen, all dash and gallantry and unrestrained individ-
ualism, who looked more important at the time than they do
in retrospect. He commanded cavalry under General Joe
Wheeler, who in turn was answerable to Bragg, and while
Grant was tightening his net around Vicksburg and Rosecrans
at last was showing signs of activity Bragg had Wheeler
send Morgan and some twenty-five hundred troopers up
into Kentucky on a raid designed to break up the Louisville

and Nashville Railroad and destroy Yankee supply depots. Morgan set out, calmly ignored his instructions, got his command across the Ohio River west of Louisville, circled up through southern Indiana, and then went zooming off across Ohio, commandeering horses and supplies as he went, while Burnside spattered the Middle West with telegrams to get militia and Federal troops up to head him off.

As a military move, Morgan's raid was totally ineffective. Ohio was presently aswarm with troops, and Morgan and nearly all of his men were at last rounded up and captured after a wild dash that accomplished little more than to dampen the sympathies that a number of Ohio farmers had previously felt for the Confederacy. (Morgan's troopers treated Ohio farms the way Grant's men had been treating the farms in Mississippi, and the Ohioans did not like it.) Morgan and his principal officers were lodged in the Ohio penitentiary (from which place, some months later, they mysteriously contrived to escape) and a Federal general who had helped to capture them wrote that the whole affair had been a great lesson on the weakness of Copperheadism in Indiana and Ohio: "He who witnessed the great exhibition of patriotism and love of country in these mighty states on the passage of the Union army and then could doubt the ability and purpose of the people to maintain the government has certainly been 'given over to hardness of heart, that he may believe a lie and be damned.' "³

Which was probably quite true. Yet the Morgan raid was an odd business altogether. Whether or not it grew out of the vision created by Vallandigham's visit to Richmond, it was at least a significant symptom: the Confederacy would fight behind the lines in the North if it saw a chance, and it would strike at home-front morale and home-front economics as well as at Federal armies in the field. It had, in other words, no faintest intention of quitting; it would go on fighting with any weapon that was handy as long as it had the capacity. Still clinging to legalism, Jefferson Davis was finally beginning to realize that he was fighting a revolution.

General Grant, meanwhile, wanted to get on with the war. Counting prisoners of war and casualties in the preliminary fighting, the Confederates had lost more than forty thousand men in the Mississippi Valley campaign—the equivalent of the army that fought at Shiloh. Although many of the Vicksburg parolees would presently show up in Confederate armies again without benefit of formal exchange, this represented a loss which the Confederacy could not possibly make good. Grant had seventy-five thousand men with nobody much to fight. It seemed to him that he ought to go marching across the South, knocking all of the underpinnings out from under Bragg's army in Tennessee; he could take Mobile, cross Georgia, and in general pull the Confederacy apart without serious opposition. He wanted to move.

Pemberton had no more than signed the surrender papers when Grant was striking at Joe Johnston. Sherman took off on July 5, marching for Jackson again, with elements of three army corps in his command. The weather was blistering hot, and the men had been standing in trenches for weeks and were not used to long hikes; water was scarce, shoes and uniforms were in bad shape, and some of the soldiers were sore because they had never so much as set foot inside the fortress they had just captured. No matter; they marched east, Johnston faded back before them, and Sherman was a driver—regiments would slog the dusty roads all day and make camp after dark, with stragglers hobbling in until midnight. An Ohio battery went lumbering over the field of Champion's Hill, where it had been furiously engaged in mid-May; to their astonishment the men found that the very field they had occupied, all torn and trampled the last time they saw it by the clash of opposing armies, had been plowed and planted with corn, and the corn now stood four feet high, as lush and peaceful-looking as if there had never been a battle within fifty miles of the place.[4] The road was lit with pillars of fire and of smoke by night and by day; cotton gins, farmhouses, anything that would burn went up in fire, and the colonel of one regiment, eying a pillared plantation manor house, burst out angrily: "People who have been as conspicuous as these in bringing this thing about *ought* to have things burned. I would like to see those chimneys standing there without any house." A few days later, when the army marched back from Jackson—which by now was getting to be pretty shopworn—the plantation displayed nothing but blackened chimneys.⁵ Even the fences had been burned.

But although Grant had no trouble in driving Joe Johnston away, he got nowhere with his plan to keep the war moving. General Halleck had other ideas.

In some ways General Halleck was ideally fitted to be general-in-chief in the Civil War. He was a born gossip and politician, and for this if for no other reason he could understand that the administration's chief problems were political rather than military. If a Buell had to be fired and a Ben Butler had to be retained because of political reasons, Halleck could understand it and he could adjust himself to it, and he could soothe other generals with chatty, half-indiscreet letters of explanation. But war itself he looked on as something out of books. The books said that when you invaded an enemy's country the big idea was to occupy territory, and this now was Halleck's obsession.

Grant's army was split up. He must hold the ground he had conquered, with detachments here, there, and elsewhere to symbolize Federal occupancy. Also, he must send help to others; so part of Grant's army went to Arkansas to quell Rebel armies which, having been amputated from Richmond by the victory at Vicksburg, could no longer be of real concern. Another part had to go down to Banks, who was nursing some plan for seizing Texas—another amputated area outside the main stream of the war. Still more had to go to Missouri, and there were forts and outposts in Mississippi and along the river to be manned. As a result, a Confederacy which was off balance and helpless in mid-July was given the rest of the summer to recover. That the rest of the summer was not time enough was more or less incidental; the breathing spell was granted, and instead of invading Alabama and sweeping up the Gulf Coast, Grant found himself visiting New Orleans to help Banks stage an elaborate review of troops—an event that bored Grant so excessively that he may have taken to the bottle again; best horseman who ever attended West Point, he suffered the indignity of falling out of his saddle at the review, injuring his leg so badly that he was crippled for weeks.⁶ Wherever this war might be won, it was not going to be won in the Deep South in the summer of 1863.

It was the post-Shiloh period all over again. The one-two punch was lacking. The administration was not cashing in on its victories. It was trying this summer to break its way into Charleston, South Carolina, in a combined army-navy operation. Charleston was not especially important, but it was a symbol; it was where secession began. To take the place and make it feel the final rigor of war looked like a worthy goal, and so an immense effort was under way. It had been supposed that the new monitors were shotproof, and so a flotilla of these dumpy ironclads led the way in the first bombardment of Fort Sumter; they proved to be a good deal less than shotproof and were so badly hammered that the naval commander, Admiral du Pont, halted operations and announced that the navy alone could never in the world open Charleston Harbor. The ironclads went to drydock and Admiral du Pont went into retirement; but although Admiral Dahlgren, who replaced him, was a sturdier sort, he had no better luck than du Pont had had, and as the summer grew old a dreary amphibious operation was under way, with the navy firing thousands of shells while it risked valuable ships, and with the army landing on sandy beaches and painfully trying to storm Confederate forts that turned out to be all but literally impregnable. Men and energy were consumed freely, but nothing in particular was accomplished.

One bit of legend was created in this attempt to take Charleston. On a sandy spit of land by the harbor entrance there was a Confederate stronghold called Battery Wagner, which the Federals had to take if they were to mount siege guns to reduce Fort Sumter; and the job of taking this place was given to the 54th Massachusetts, a regiment of colored troops—one of the two which had refused to accept pay unless the pay scale recognized them as full-fledged human beings who earned the same pay as white soldiers earned. Colonel of the 54th was young Robert Gould Shaw, a blue-blooded Bostonian who saw the war as a holy cause. He had led the 54th in a grand review on Boston Common before coming south, and his mother had looked on with intense pride to see her only son riding at the head of soldiers who had come up from slavery to manhood, and she had cried: "What have I done, that God has been so good to me!" Now the 54th charged across the sand to attack Battery Wagner, and there had been insufficient preparation. Shaw got his first line on top of the parapet, there was a flurry of bitter hand-to-hand fighting, and then Shaw was killed and a great many of his men were killed. The attack failed, and white colonel and colored privates were buried together in a common grave just outside the fort. Much later Battery Wagner was taken, and siege guns pounded Fort Sumter to rubble, but Charleston was not taken. Yet the memory remained, and the surviving soldiers of the 54th raised money to build a memorial to their colonel on Boston Common, and many Northerners remembered Mrs. Shaw's cry . . . "that God has been so good to me!"[7]

In Virginia nothing much was happening. It was as if the two great armies there were still exhausted by Gettysburg; they moved back and forth, from the Rapidan almost to the Potomac, sparring constantly, occasionally stirring up a minor fight, but accomplishing nothing of importance. It seemed certain that there would be no major offensive in Virginia until the next year.

But in Tennessee, toward the end of June, the armies at last began to move.

Rosecrans's Army of the Cumberland had been enjoying a rather pleasant war these last six months. It had been inactive ever since Stone's River, and the camps around Murfreesboro began to look permanent. The men had made themselves comfortable, company streets had been precisely laid out by military engineers, and with logs and shelter-tent halves the men had made pleasant little homes; arbors of evergreen were arranged at tent entrances to provide shade, there were strict rules about keeping streets and tents clean and properly policed, and every evening the regimental bands played while the soldiers lounged about, smoked, played cards, and told tall tales. Even the men on picket duty felt that they had it easy; in Tennessee, they said, the mockingbirds sang all night long, and their songs made a man feel that he had company.[8]

Both Grant and Halleck had long been urging Rosecrans to move, but he had found reasons for delay. He argued that by staying where he was he was keeping Bragg and Bragg's Confederate army up in central Tennessee, too far from Mississippi to send help to Joe Johnston; if he moved forward, he said, Bragg would retreat, and every mile of retreat would make it easier for him to interfere with Grant's campaign against Vicksburg. Besides, said Rosecrans, it would be bad strategy for him to fight while Grant was fighting: it was a military axiom that no nation should fight two great battles at the same time. With this point Grant took issue. He was not familiar with the axiom, he said, but now that it was stated he did not think much of it. It would be bad, he admitted, to lose two great battles at one time, but it would not be at all bad to win two.[9]

In any event, the final week in June made it clear that Grant would presently have Vicksburg, and on the twenty-third of the month Rosecrans pulled his army out of camp and started south.

When the move came the soldiers welcomed it. They had been in camp too long. If life there was pleasant it was also dull, and as one veteran remarked, "We were simply rusting our lives away to what seemed to us to be no purpose."[10] The order to strike tents and pack up was obeyed with alacrity.

It was a hard pull that lay ahead. The objective would be Chattanooga, gateway to Georgia and eastern Tennessee, and although Chattanooga was no more than fifty miles away in an air line it lay on the far side of rugged mountainous country that had few inhabitants, few resources, and no decent roads. To get to Chattanooga across that barren upland would be almost impossible; the only good route led southeast along the line of the Nashville and Chattanooga Railroad to the junction town of Stevenson, Alabama, forty miles from Murfreesboro, where this line crossed the Memphis and Charleston. Somewhere near Stevenson it would be necessary to cross the Tennessee River; Chattanooga lay thirty miles east and a little north. The difficulty about following the railroad would lie in the fact that General Bragg and forty-five thousand first-rate Confederate soldiers were strongly entrenched across the line of the Nashville and Chattanooga, less than a score of miles from Murfreesboro.

Rosecrans began his campaign with a good deal of skill. He had approximately sixty thousand men with him, and he had no intention of driving them against Bragg's defensive system. Instead, feinting as if he meant to make such an attack, he shifted his main strength to the east, sliding clear around the Confederate right flank and threatening to cut the railroad in Bragg's rear. Taken by surprise, Bragg retreated; by July 4 he had abandoned central Tennessee entirely, and a gloomy Cabinet in Richmond learned that he had retreated all the way to Chattanooga.

All of this Rosecrans had done expertly and—except for a few minor skirmishes—without fighting. But it had not been easy. During nine days of continuous marching, what Rosecrans described as "one of the most extraordinary rains ever known to Tennessee at that period of the year" came down to turn the soil into a spongy quagmire and to make unpaved roads nearly impassable. The rain kept on, hour after hour and day after day, with no letup: "No Presbyterian rain, either, but a genuine Baptist downpour," an Illinois soldier called it. Men in the 6th Indiana remembered making a night march on a mountain road beside which flowed a little stream, swollen now to a torrent that covered the roadway so that the men marched sometimes in water thigh-deep, everything dark as the pit, rain pelting down mercilessly, men tripping over submerged boulders or stepping into invisible potholes. "It rained so much and so hard," wrote one soldier, "that we ceased to regard it as a matter of any consequence and simply stood up and took it, without attempting to seek shelter or screen ourselves in the least. Why should we, when we were already wet to the skin?"[11]

Over one especially bad stretch of mountain road an entire brigade of infantry was ordered to stack arms and then take station along the road all the way to the summit to help the supply wagons get up the grade. As a wagon or a gun came along, a rope would be attached and a whole regiment would help the mules or horses up the grade, turning the vehicle over to another regiment when it reached the end of its assigned beat and going back downhill to get another. It was fun for a while—it was at least different from ordinary marching—and the men treated it as a lark; but it kept on without a break, day and night, and the soldiers at last began to realize that "it requires a great many wagons to carry 20 days rations for men and animals, in addition to ammunition, medical supplies and other things required by an army." The work went on from a Sunday evening to a Tuesday morning, with regiments working in shifts; during the nights flickering torches sputtered in the rain to light the way. Rosecrans recalled afterward that it took Crittenden's army corps four days of extra-hard marching to advance twenty-one miles. When Bragg finally retreated and the Federals settled down in his old camping ground at Tullahoma, the men were able to get their boots off for the first time since they had left Murfreesboro, and one soldier confessed that "it would be hard to find a worse set of used-up boys."[12]

Yet there were compensations. Veterans of the 104th Illinois remembered being in camp in the Elk River valley, rain still coming down, everything muddy and sopping, camping ground itself no more than just above water; and suddenly officers rode through announcing that Grant had captured Vicksburg, and the mountain gorge rang with cheers. As they yelled the men realized that their own hard marching had been a victory too, with the last armed Rebels chased out of central Tennessee and the road to Chattanooga now lying open; and they forgot about discomfort, short rations, and bad weather, and set about getting the mud off their clothing and making ready for the next move.[13]

The army waited in Tullahoma for nearly two weeks while Rosecrans carried on another long-distance argument with Washington. He was well aware that as Bragg retreated he would be reinforced, and he reasoned that since the Federal army which had just captured Vicksburg had nothing in particular to do it might as well move east and cover his own right flank when he resumed the advance. (Grant was arguing in much the same vein; if he should march on Mobile, he believed, Bragg could not conceivably stay around Chattanooga to fight Rosecrans, and all of the Deep South could be overrun before autumn.) But Halleck had other ideas, and Rosecrans was ordered to keep going. Only one concession was made, and it did not prove very valuable: Burnside was getting together an army of fifteen thousand men with which he would move down through eastern Tennessee and attack Knoxville, where the Confederates had troops under the same General Buckner who had surrendered to Grant at Fort Donelson.

On August 16 Rosecrans put his men on the road again. The rains had stopped and the roads were passable, there was an abundance of blackberries and ripe peaches which marching men could get without much trouble, and there seemed to be plenty of good spring water. Some of the men looked back on the hike down to the Tennessee River as actually almost enjoyable.

Early in September the army came out on the north bank of the Tennessee River, considerably west of Chattanooga. The soldiers had to cross the river and then negotiate a high mountain barrier before they could reach their goal, and it is possible that Bragg could have given them a great deal of trouble if he had made a stand there. But Bragg was taken with a spell of bleak pessimism, in the grip of which he seemed unable to do more than sit and think about all of the doleful things that were likely to happen to him. Rosecrans got all of his men across and then started east, looking for gaps in the mountain wall. Illinois soldiers coming out on the crest of Sand Mountain looked back and saw a tremendous pageant:

"Far beyond mortal vision extended one vast panorama of mountains, forests and rivers. The broad Tennessee below us seemed like a ribbon of silver; beyond rose the Cumberlands, which we had crossed. The valley on both sides was alive with the moving armies of the Union, while almost the entire transportation of the army filled the roads and fields along the Tennessee. No one could survey the grand scene on that bright autumn day unmoved, unimpressed with its grandeur and of the meaning conveyed by the presence of that mighty host."[14]

Bragg apparently felt the same way, for he evacuated Chattanooga and withdrew into northern Georgia, waiting for the reinforcements which an aroused government at Richmond was at last ordering to him. On September 9 Rosecrans sent Crittenden's corps into Chattanooga and ordered the other two to fan out far to the south, to get across the mountains as quickly as possible and cut off Bragg's retreat. Men in the marching columns whooped and yelled when they learned that Chattanooga had been taken. Bragg was in full retreat, perhaps in a panic; all that mattered now was to push on after him, destroy his army, and win the war.

2. *Ghoul-Haunted Woodland*

In the four years of its life the southern Confederacy strove heroically to overtake a will-o'-the-wisp, and the story of its life is basically the story of the pursuit of a marsh fire, a flame dancing elusively in a fog of battle smoke. This phantom took many forms. Sometimes it was the dream of European intervention, and at other times it was the dream of a sympathetic revolt in the North; and always it seemed that if the evasive unreality could just be caught it would confer enduring life on an archaic society trying to become valid in a modern world. Of all of these dreams, none was more constantly and deceptively alluring than the belief that one hard blow might finally knock the North out of the war and bring victory.

There could be, in the fall of 1863, one more hard blow. The fabric of the Confederacy was beginning to wear very thin—Mississippi Valley gone forever, everything west of the river cut off, most of Tennessee lost, blockade tighter than ever, drain on manpower and material resources getting progressively greater; it was hardly possible now to keep from seeing what the final verdict was going to be. But it was not yet settled. Strength remained, and hope, and the determination that could command a final supreme effort. That effort would be made now, and it would be entrusted to that fate-haunted soldier, General Braxton Bragg.

Bragg was concentrating his army near Lafayette, Georgia, two or three days' march south of Chattanooga. He was being strongly reinforced. Buckner was coming down from Knoxville with six thousand men; this left eastern Tennessee undefended—Burnside made Lincoln's dream come true by marching into Knoxville with a small army before August was over—but there was no help for it. Other reinforcements were coming up from Mississippi. Most important of all, James Longstreet and a good part of his hard-hitting army corps were coming down from Virginia. (The card that might have been played in June would be played now.) Longstreet's men were coming slowly, roundabout, by the rickety railroad network that led down through the Carolinas and Georgia, and men were quipping that such poor rolling stock had never been called on to carry such good soldiers, but no other way was open to them; the loss of Knoxville and Chattanooga had cut the Confederacy's only direct east-west railway connection.

When all of these troops reached him, Bragg would command close to seventy thousand men. For once in the war, the Confederacy would go into battle with the numerical odds in its favor. Furthermore, Rosecrans was playing directly into Bragg's hands just now. He was coming over the mountains into Georgia with his troops widely scattered, fairly inviting a ruinous counterblow.

Up to the moment when he occupied Chattanooga, Rosecrans had done extremely well. He had maneuvered Bragg clear out of Tennessee with very little fighting, his Army of the Cumberland was exultant, and if he had pulled it all together and caught his breath before trying to go on all would have been well. But old Rosy had suddenly lost his caution. Perhaps his advance had been too successful. He seems to have become convinced that the Confederates were in a panicky retreat that would go on and on for many days, and all he could think of now was a headlong chase that would cut them off.

Part of his trouble was due to geography. The mountains that slant southwest from the Tennessee River near Chattanooga are immense ridges that run down across the northwest corner of Georgia and continue far into Alabama, and there are not many places where an army can cross them. The most substantial of the lot, Lookout Mountain, is one hundred miles long, and in 1863 its feasible crossings were widely separated. The road to Chattanooga from the west followed the valley of the Tennessee, clinging to a narrow shelf between river and mountain just before it reached the city; the next pass was twenty miles south, and the next one was twenty miles south of that. To bring all of his army up around the tip of Lookout Mountain would delay Rosecrans much more than his optimistic ardor would permit. It seemed better to have Thomas and McCook take their corps across the mountain by the more distant passes and fall on such Confederate troops as they might find after they had crossed. Crittenden, meanwhile, could march down from Chattanooga east of the mountains, following the valley of Chickamauga Creek, and the whole army could reassemble at its convenience somewhere in northern Georgia.[1]

It was moving toward a haunted land. Chickamauga Creek had been named by the Indians, and its name reflected a forgotten tragedy far back in the past; the word was said to mean "River of Death." The stream flowed north through a sparsely settled region of heavy woods and lonely fields, walled in by the mountains, shadowed by fate. In a few days it would earn its grim name afresh.

Bragg had concentrated, and he was waiting east of the mountains. Now the game was going his way. The pieces of the Army of the Cumberland were moving straight toward him, so widely separated that no Union corps could come to the rescue of another in case of trouble. But Bragg was always able to see his problems more clearly than he could see his opportunities. If the Federals did not know where he was, he did not quite know where they were either, his scouting and intelligence service having failed him; and he was complaining that campaigning in this country was confusing because one's enemies might pop unexpectedly out of almost any mountain pass without warning. Beyond the dark shield of Lookout Mountain almost anything might be happening.[2]

Bragg tried to pounce on Thomas and McCook as they came over into Chickamauga Valley, but his own generals had caught the spirit of indecision that infected army headquarters, and the first moves missed fire. General D. H. Hill, who had served under Lee during the Seven Days' and the

Antietam campaign and had been sent down from Richmond to take command of one of Bragg's army corps, watched the confused goings-on and reflected sadly that this army was not handled with the unworried competence he had been used to in Virginia. Hill had been depressed even before he joined Bragg. He had felt "the bitterness of death" in July, after learning of the Confederate defeats at Vicksburg and Gettysburg; the Confederacy, he believed, having been cut in half, would now be beaten in detail, and "the end of our glorious dream could not be far off." But what he saw after he got to Georgia depressed him still more. The men in Bragg's army were as good as any Lee had commanded, but something was seriously wrong at headquarters. Bragg had been given as fine an opening as a general could wish, but it was taking him forever to see it. When at last he did see it he seemed unable to do very much about it.³

The Federals, meanwhile, were beginning to realize that they were in trouble. The private soldiers felt it. On September 11, when Thomas's corps made camp east of the mountain, the men were vaguely uneasy. They sensed that innumerable enemies were all about them, with help a long way off—as veteran campaigners they knew enemy country when they saw it—and they were relieved when they saw Pap Thomas ride up, as stolid and unconcerned as if they were all back in camp at Murfreesboro, and settle himself massively on a stool under a tent fly to read dispatches and write orders. But the uneasy mood returned. Rosecrans had come wide awake at last and he was frantically ordering his scattered troops to concentrate a few miles south of Chattanooga, and the soldiers sensed that the high command had the jitters. As Thomas's men went tramping north, following narrow roads through a gloomy country of limestone rocks and dense cedar thickets, they expected trouble. They had to make a forced march of it and they were kept on the road long after dark, and men who made the march wrote afterward about "the gloom and foreboding stillness of the autumn night." For all that Thomas seemed so leisurely, it was recalled that when he bivouacked after midnight he told an aide not to let him sleep more than one hour.⁴

Bragg's plan—when it finally took shape—was simple. He

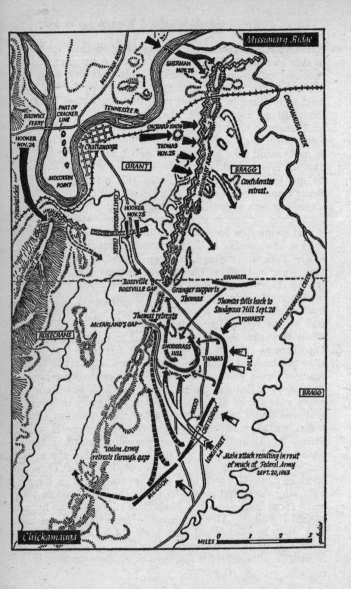

proposed to strike the Union left flank, driving the Army of the Cumberland away from Chattanooga—which was its only possible base of supplies and means of contact with the North —and penning it up in a tangle of dead-end mountain valleys where it could be destroyed. It was a perfectly good plan, and if it had been put into operation twenty-four hours earlier there would have been a Union disaster of the first magnitude. As it was, Bragg's troops did not open their offensive until September 18, and it was the next morning before the battle actually began. Rosecrans had been given just time enough.

He had brought the Army of the Cumberland together in a stretch of comparatively level, heavily wooded country a dozen miles south of Chattanooga. To the east ran Chickamauga Creek, with the Rebels somewhere on its banks and with blue and gray skirmishes contending for possession of the fords and bridges. Off to the west loomed the endless blue mass of Lookout Mountain; and to the north, cutting the army off from the city, was the steep rampart of Missionary Ridge, a somewhat lower height which ran parallel to Lookout Mountain with Chattanooga in the valley between. There was a gap in Missionary Ridge at Rossville, and the road from Chattanooga came down through this gap and ran through the center of the army's area of concentration. This road and the Rossville Gap the army must hold at all costs; to lose them would be to invite outright destruction.

The army occupied a line nearly six miles long, facing the east. Thomas held the left, looking toward the river crossings from which the main Confederate attack was likely to come, and the fighting began a little after dawn on September 19.

It was a bitter, confused fight, waged gallantly by armies whose commanders were not quite sure where their opponents really were. Bragg sent troops in on what he thought was the Federal left, but Thomas had posted his corps farther north than the Confederates supposed, and as the southern advance came groping up through the dark woodland feeling for the exposed flank, he sent a division in and flanked this advance and broke it. More Confederates came up, and the victorious Federal division was flanked and routed in its turn. As the day wore on, this fight for the Union left became the battle, drawing in more and more elements from both armies. The Confederate General Hill (who observed that not even in the brave days of 1861 had he seen southern troops fight with more dash and bravery than they were displaying here) learned something new about the quality of cavalry in the western Confederacy. Hill had always been contemptuous of cavalry, considering it a non-fighting army given to useless riding and sashaying about, and he had once said bitterly that most gray troopers "cannot see, and cannot be made to see, an armed Yankee." But here by Chickamauga Creek he found a line of Rebel foot soldiers fighting desperately and with cruel effectiveness amid fallen trees and brush, and when he asked what infantry this was he was told: Bedford Forrest's cavalry![5]

As the pressure increased, more and more of the Army of the Cumberland was sent to help Thomas—a full division from Crittenden's corps and another from McCook's—and although the Confederates gained ground step by step they took a fearful mauling while they were doing it. When night came, every unit in the Federal army had been in action. They had given ground, but they still held a great crescent covering the Chattanooga road. Most of the fighting had been on Thomas's front, and by dusk he had nearly two thirds of the Army of the Cumberland under his control.

The night was unutterably gloomy—a fever-ridden dream, with lost regiments and brigades moving in and out under the thick of the woodland shadows, hunting new positions as the sluggish mechanism of the high command tried to pull the troops back to a stronger line. By turns the forest was silent with midnight blackness and aflame with the flaring lights of the guns and confused with shattering sound; men felt ill at ease as they tramped along overgrown lanes in the wood, moving from blinding darkness into a dancing play of lights caused by "a display of fireworks that one does not care to see more than once in a lifetime." Nothing had been settled; tomorrow would be worse than today had been; the Rebels were in full strength, and somewhere, somehow, in this vast area of woodland and lost pastures, the showdown would come with the dawn. An Indiana regiment, staggering with exhaustion, found itself by the edge of a stagnant pool, and although dead men and horses lay in the stained water the men broke ranks, ran to the weedy margin, and lay on their bellies to drink. One of the soldiers looked about him at the horrible landscape . . . star-shine faintly reflected in the iridescent water, bloated corpses all about, men gulping a drink from water they would not ordinarily have touched, leafy branches overhead swaying in a ghostly breeze from nowhere, fitful light in the sky as distant guns went off . . . and he thought that this place was exactly like what Poe had been trying to get at when he wrote about the ghoul-haunted woodland of Weir.[6]

Dawn came in foggy, and through the mist and smoke the sun looked red and ominous. Bragg still clung to his original idea: knock loose the Federal left and drive the Union army back into the blind valleys from which it cannot escape. Rosecrans had caught on, and he visited Thomas that night and told him to hang on at all costs; and when morning came and the Rebels' attacks were renewed, all of the reserves of the Army of the Cumberland shifted over to meet the assault. The Confederates drove their charge home, and stolid old Pap Thomas—born and made for moments of defensive crisis like this—notified Rosecrans that he would need help. Rosecrans detached a division from his right, where it did not seem that anything especial was going to happen; the division managed to go astray en route to Thomas and went wandering off in the back area somewhere, and Thomas sent word again for help. Nobody knew that the lost division had not reached him, and nervous Rosecrans concluded that he had all of the Confederacy crowding in on his left and sent more troops. Thomas, meanwhile, irked by the non-arrival of the reinforcements he had asked for, once more called for aid, and to Rosecrans it became obvious that the drive to crack his left flank had taken on gigantic proportions.[7]

This led to disaster. Bragg had received one enormous asset; James Longstreet, in person, had arrived on the scene, had been given full command of the whole left wing of the Confederate army, and had been instructed to strike Rosecrans's right as soon as the fight at the other end of the line was well under way. Longstreet was a man who liked to take his own time getting everything ready before he fought, and he had had precious little time here; but he adapted himself this once, and while Rosecrans was shifting force to the left, Longstreet was lining up half of the Confederate army to hit him on the right. Somewhere around noon, just as the battle on Thomas's front was flaming and crashing all through the woods and ravines, Longstreet massed his brigades and sent them in with the massive, all-out sort of punch that had ruined Pope at Second Bull Run and had almost knocked Meade's army out of the hills south of Gettysburg.

Luck took a hand here; pure, unadulterated chance, which steps in now and then to make a fine hash out of the careful plans of harassed generals.

A little to the right of the center of his line, Rosecrans had a solid division under command of Brigadier General Thomas J. Wood—an old regular from Kentucky, solid and dependable, with a first-rate combat record. Wood had his men in an open field covering one of the lower stretches of the Chattanooga road, half a mile to the south of the sector where Thomas was fighting. The skirmishers along his front were active enough, but nothing very threatening seemed to be impending, and the dense woods a few hundred yards in his front concealed the fact that Longstreet had piled up an avalanche that was just beginning to slide forward. Far back at headquarters Rosecrans got word that a division on Thomas's right needed help. Through some mix-up he got the idea that Wood was the next man in line; and off to Wood, pelting through the underbrush with the dispatch gripped in his teeth, went a blameless staff officer, carrying to Wood instructions to "close up on Reynolds" (the commander of the division that was in trouble) "and support him."

Headquarters had been having its problems. Thomas had been calling for help, help had been sent, the calls were still coming in, and nobody quite knew where everybody was. The order to Wood was pure routine: he should edge over to his left (as headquarters saw it) and lend a hand to the nearest division. What headquarters had failed to notice, however, was the fact that another division of troops held the line between Wood and Reynolds. When Wood got his orders, therefore, it seemed to him that headquarters was telling him to pull his men out of the fighting line, march several hundred yards to the rear, pass behind the division that was immediately on his left, and move up to help General Reynolds half a mile farther north. Figuring that headquarters knew what it was about, Wood gave the order; and his division wheeled about and marched off to the rear at the precise moment when Longstreet's thunderbolt was starting to crash forward through the underbrush and make its strike.[8]

Then everything came unstitched, and all the lower half of the battlefield was a wild swirl of smoke, exploding shells, running men, wild cheers, and desperately galloping generals who were suddenly compelled to realize that the men they were supposed to be commanding had gone completely out from under their control.

The battle had been boiling and steaming for Thomas's men, and they had been holding their own in a vicious toe-to-toe struggle all morning—had been doing a little more than hold their own, in fact, for the Confederates opposite them had gained not a foot of ground and were fought out, gasping for breath, disheartened because every attempt to smash through to the Chattanooga road had run into an unyielding line of stubborn Yankees. Now, without warning, the great blow on the Federal right came in with pile-driver force and struck nothing at all. The result was catastrophe.

The Army of the Cumberland was cut in half. Everything south of the break-through point—including General Rosecrans himself and two of his three corps commanders, McCook and Crittenden—was driven off, generals and enlisted men and guns and wagons all streaming away from the battle, scrambling for a back road that would get them to the Rossville Gap and safety. Coolly taking everything in, Longstreet let them go and swung his victorious column sharply to the right to come in behind Thomas and break the Union army into panicky shreds. Federal control of everything west of the Alleghenies suddenly teetered and rocked, ready to come down in a Humpty-Dumpty crash that could never be repaired.

Pap Thomas, to be sure, was imperturbable. When things were going badly the only visible sign he ever gave was to indulge in a quaint habit of running his fingers through his patrician gray Virginia whiskers. These whiskers now got a furious going-over, but there was nothing else to show that he was disturbed. He methodically set to work to patch up a new line that would hold off the swarming Confederates long enough to avert complete disaster.

What a general could do, Thomas did; no more dependable soldier for a moment of crisis existed on the North American continent, or ever did exist. But what he could do would depend ultimately on the men in the ranks. These were the western farm boys who had gone wet and hungry under Sherman in Kentucky, who had been coldly drilled and disciplined by prim General Buell, who had stood up to the frozen flames at Stone's River and gone slogging over the mountains in the heat of a Tennessee summer: and if enough of these would stop and make a fight of it the day might be saved—not otherwise.

The men who had not been driven completely off the field with Rosecrans and McCook and Crittenden were drifting north, division and brigade organization totally broken up, nobody knowing anything except that all the Rebels in the world had punched a hole in the line and were coming on as if they did not propose to stop short of the Ohio River.

Thomas had the spot picked. His own line was a wide horseshoe, bulging toward the east, a great shallow semicircle of fire and smoke and rocketing noise. Running west from the southern end of this horseshoe was a chain of hills, drawing a name from a log farmhouse owned by one Snodgrass, and this high ground Thomas chose as the place for a rally. One of the segments from Wood's division, scrambling north amid the debris of the break-through, swung around in an open field near the hills and prepared to make a stand. Out of the woods to the south came a battle line in dusty blue, and the men held their fire—these must be some of McCook's troops coming back into action after their rout. The line came nearer, and Thomas himself rode up and peered through the murk at it. Wave all your flags (he told Wood's soldiers) and let them see who you are, but if they open fire let them have it: some of the Rebs are wearing blue here. Thomas galloped away, and the advancing line began to fire. It was one of Longstreet's brigades, wearing

Federal uniforms captured in the sack of Harpers Ferry or some such place, and the Westerners had never seen Southerners in blue. They returned the fire uncertainly, too late to do much good, after a brief stand they had to turn and run for it, and they re-formed at last near the Snodgrass house, dumped fence rails and bits of timber to make a breastwork, and began to fire in earnest.

All along these rolling hills a new Federal line began to take shape. An Indiana regiment came running up, its German colonel carrying his old slouch hat in his hand, rolled up like a club; he was hitting his men on the shoulders with it, shouting, "Go in, boys, and give 'em hell!" and cursing in undefiled high Dutch. An Ohio colonel had his men form in lee of the hill, marched them twenty yards forward to fire, had them return to shelter to reload, and them moved them forward for a fresh volley. In a little hollow just behind the firing line was Thomas himself. A staff officer noted that even in the heat of this furious battle Thomas sent an orderly into a nearby cornfield to collect a few ears of corn for his horse and stood watching the fight while the beast ate. His whiskers were a tangle by now, but otherwise he was cool and controlled. Quietly he told a colonel whose men were in action that this hill must be held at all costs. The colonel turned to him, took courage from his stolid, majestic presence and cried out: "We'll hold it, General, or we'll go to Heaven from it!"

This new Federal line along the hills was not, strictly speaking, a military formation at all. It consisted of fragments of men from a number of commands, a squad here and a platoon there, formal organization completely lost, nobody in particular in general command of anything—except that Thomas was always there, moving back and forth, unhurried, holding this mixed-up line in place by sheer force of his own personality. The Confederates charged in, were driven back, realigned themselves, and moved up again; Federal ammunition ran low, and men went about the field collecting cartridges from the bodies of men who had fallen; and somehow, in spite of everything, the chain of hills was held. Late in the afternoon, help came. Rosecrans had kept a few brigades in what he called his "reserve corps" far off to his left and rear, watching a road from which he feared the Southerners might make a stab behind his flank. This outfit, marooned out of sight, came over finally without orders; its commander, General Gordon Granger—a profane, bearded, rough-hewn regular-army type from the old days—had heard the tremendous crash of the battle action, had figured somebody needed him, and brought his men in just when Thomas needed them the most. They stiffened the patchwork line, and the last Rebel assaults were beaten off.

Far to the rear, that part of the army that had been routed was piling back through Rossville Gap for Chattanooga. It was in complete confusion, a hopelessly disorganized mob. Rosecrans and his officers had ridden about, waving swords and shouting, trying to restore order, but nothing had worked. The formless column was simply streaming north toward safety, and nothing could be done with it. Old Rosy himself gave up at last and rode along with the column, silent, abstracted, seeming to hear and see nothing. As far as he could tell, the entire battle was lost; Thomas was out of sight to the east, probably undergoing destruction, and the only thing that mattered now was to get the survivors into Chattanooga and prepare for a last desperate stand. Once again the Confederates had completely defeated a Union general.

But they had not quite beaten Pap Thomas, or Pap Thomas's men, and—in a measure—these saved the day. They hung on until close to sunset, saving the army; and when Thomas finally ordered a withdrawal and his exhausted brigades began to pull out of line and move back toward the Gap and Chattanooga, the Confederates were too fought out to pursue. Bragg himself was not much more alert than Rosecrans was. Commanders like Longstreet and Forrest urged a smashing pursuit—these Yanks are on the run, pile in after them and never give them a chance for a breather, we can crush the whole army if we keep at it—but Bragg had grown listless. His losses had been appalling, the day had been too much for him—and he went to bed at last, not quite certain whether he had won a great victory or narrowly avoided a humiliating defeat.

In the haunted woodland full night came down on a gloomy timberland where lay more than thirty thousand dead or wounded men. And on the winding road through the Rossville Gap the rear guard of the Army of the Cumberland gloomily plodded on toward Chattanooga. The last stand along Thomas's line had been very fine, and in later years the men would take enormous pride in it, but right now they felt shame and disgrace; they had held on gallantly and they had prevented complete disaster, but still they had been licked and now they were in full retreat. They marched in silence, and one soldier remembered: "While not a word was said, all knew that we were whipped and were retreating from the field. This was new medicine to us . . . it was bitter, and did not go down very well."[10]

3. *The Pride of Soldiers*

There was no way out and there was no way in. Chattanooga lay at the end of the passage. Eastward there was nothing at all, except for General Burnside and the fifteen thousand men with whom he had occupied Knoxville, and these people were one hundred and fifty miles away, utterly unable to do anything except collect cattle and forage from the east Tennessee countryside and wonder how long the Confederates would let them stay there. To the north there was a barren wasteland of mountains which neither man nor beast could cross unless somebody carried food for the journey. To the south there was Bragg's army, its camp-fires glittering at night all along the high rampart of Missionary Ridge, crossing the open plain, and extending across to Lookout Mountain. And to the west . . .

To the west ran the road to the outer world, the road to food and reinforcements and the infinite strength of the Federal government, a road that might have wound across the mountains of the moon for all the use the Army of the Cumberland could make of it.

Lookout Mountain shouldered its way clear to the bank of the Tennessee River, with a highway and a railroad clinging to the slopes of its northern extremity; and armed Confederates lived on top of this mountain, so close that if they chose they might almost have tossed rocks in the river and on the highway and the railroad. Not so much as a case of hardtack, a side of bacon, or a bale of hay could get into Chattanooga for the use of the Army of the Cumberland unless these Confederates consented, and they had drawn their lines on top of Lookout Mountain for the express purpose of withholding their consent. Rosecrans's army was besieged, and although it had escaped destruction at Chickamauga the chances now seemed quite good that it would presently die of simple starvation in Chattanooga. If it stayed where it was it would quickly run out of food—the men were on half rations already, and the horses were dying so fast that it would soon be impossible to move any of the artillery—and if it tried to retreat it would have to go over the mountains north of the river; and the roads there were so bad and so roundabout and the country was so completely empty that an army which tried to retreat by that route would disintegrate in less than a week.

Downstream from Chattanooga, twenty-five or thirty miles away, there was the town of Bridgeport. The Memphis and Charleston Railroad ran through Bridgeport, and from their great supply base at Nashville the Federals could bring vast quantities of supplies to Bridgeport. The trouble was that the Confederates controlled the Chattanooga end of the route. If an army quartermaster at Bridgeport tried to get around this roadblock he would have to make a sixty-mile detour, sending his wagon trains north of the river through the almost impassable mountain country. This had been tried over and over, and the northern road was marked every rod of the way by the bodies of dead horses and the wreckage of broken wagons, but it did not do any good; no wagon train that went this way could carry very much except the forage which its own animals had to eat in order to make the trip. Couriers or small detachments of armed men could make the journey without great difficulty, but no wagon train or large body of troops could do it without coming to grief. The Army of the Cumberland was in a box.

From half rations the army came down to quarter rations. When a commissary wagon jolted by, soldiers would follow, hoping that something edible might fall out so that they could pick it up and eat it. Horses and mules—those that still survived: more than ten thousand of them had died—were allowed three ears of corn each day, and hungry soldiers robbed them so regularly that it was necessary to put armed guards around when the livestock was fed. The horses and mules were so desperate that they gnawed down saplings and hitching posts, and a number of wagons were ruined because the beasts had tried to eat them. After the animals had been fed their inadequate meals, soldiers would search the mud looking for stray grains. Other soldiers risked shots from Rebel pickets to go ranging out through the country between Lookout Mountain and Missionary Ridge to collect acorns.[1]

Yet there was no serious grumbling. The men were depressed because they had lost a battle, but they seem to have accepted the scarcity of food without complaint, confident that sooner or later somebody would do something about it. The Confederates made no hostile moves; felt, apparently, that none was called for, since these Yankees would inevitably be starved into submission before much longer. At night the view was spectacular. An enormous semicircle of twinkling lights, running from the crest of Lookout all the way across the southern horizon to the northern end of Missionary Ridge, marked the Confederate campfires; down below, paralleling this crescent but several hundred feet under it, ran the line of Union fires. The lights lit the sky and almost seemed to dim the stars, and a veteran later remembered the sight as "grand beyond description." Union campfires were rather skimpy most of the time. The only firewood was on the north side of the Tennessee, and the starving horses were too weak to haul it into camp.[2]

The soldiers' confidence that somebody was going to come to the rescue was not misplaced. Washington reacted to the news from Tennessee with almost feverish vigor. Two army corps were detached from the Army of the Potomac, sent west by train and river boat, and hurried down across Kentucky and central Tennessee to Bridgeport; in command was Joe Hooker, recalled from semi-retirement for a job that looked as if it would call for a headlong fighter. Most of the Army of the Tennessee, with Sherman in command, was ordered east from the Mississippi, and it was marching along the line of the Memphis and Charleston, repairing damaged track as it came. And U. S. Grant, still nursing the leg he had injured in his fall from the saddle at New Orleans, was ordered north post-haste. He met Secretary Stanton at Indianapolis and was given command of all Federal operations between the Alleghenies and the Mississippi, except for Banks's enclave in Louisiana; from Indianapolis he went straight to Chattanooga, pausing just long enough to send a telegram on ahead announcing that Rosecrans was relieved from command and that Thomas now would lead the Army of the Cumberland.

Disquieting rumors reached him at Louisville: the Army of the Cumberland was about to retreat. He sent Thomas another wire, ordering him to stay in Chattanooga no matter what happened, and got back the succinct reply: "We will hold the town until we starve." This was taken in the North as a fine bit of bravado; actually, it probably expressed Thomas's objective size-up of the situation—Chattanooga could be held against any assault, but unless a supply line was quickly opened the army was apt to die of hunger.[3]

Just before he reached Chattanooga, Grant met Rosecrans on his way north and the two had a talk. Rosecrans had laid plans for relieving the pressure, and the plans were good; looking back afterward, Grant mused that the only thing he could not understand was why these plans had not been put into operation. When he finally reached the beleaguered town after a miserable ride across the barren mountains north of the river—a very hard ride for a man with a damaged leg, who could hardly stick in the saddle and who could walk only with crutches—he found that things were being done. Chief engineer of the Army of the Cumberland was a General William F. Smith, universally known as Baldy, and Baldy Smith was an operator. He had put together a sawmill at Bridgeport, the motive power a steam engine rifled from some local machine shop, and he was sawing out a large number of planks; with these planks he was building a river steamer, which would be powered by still another steam engine taken from some other local factory, and before long he would be able to move supplies up the river. Meanwhile he had discovered a route by which, with the aid of a few combat troops, a new supply line into Chattanooga could be opened. Grant quickly saw that his own job was not so much to devise new plans as to put additional drive and energy into the execution of plans already made.[4]

Chattanooga lies on the south bank of the Tennessee, and along its waterfront the river flows straight west. Just below the city the river cuts sharply to the south, runs down to the foot of Lookout Mountain, and then makes a 180-degree turn and comes back north for several miles, turning west at last to curve around the northern end of Raccoon Mountain and continue past Bridgeport. As it makes the Lookout Mountain turn it encloses a long finger of hilly land no more than a mile wide, and along the base of this finger, in 1863, there was a little country road that started opposite Chattanooga and came out on the north-and-south stretch of the river at a place called Brown's Ferry. This road was hardly more than two miles long, and it by-passed the Lookout Mountain bottleneck completely. If the river could be crossed at Brown's Ferry, another passable road led across Raccoon Mountain to Bridgeport, no more than twenty miles away. Here, potentially, was a fine supply route, the only trouble being that the Confederates who held Lookout Mountain had troops in the valley between Lookout and Raccoon mountains and so made the Brown's Ferry-Bridgeport road unusable.

These troops could be handled, because Bragg had not put enough of them in the valley to hold the place against a real attack. Hooker was in Bridgeport with twelve thousand tough soldiers from the Army of the Potomac, and Thomas was in Chattanooga with a great many equally tough characters from the Army of the Cumberland; and one night, not long after Grant had arrived, Hooker sent men east over Raccoon Mountain while a brigade of Cumberlands got into flatboats and drifted quietly down the Tennessee, and between them these troops seized Brown's Ferry and drove the Confederates out of the valley between Raccoon and Lookout mountains. The Confederates still held Lookout, but that no longer mattered. A pontoon bridge was laid at Brown's Ferry, and the Federals finally had an adequate, unobstructed road leading in and out of Chattanooga.[5]

It would lead in, mostly, because the only way out that Grant was interested in was the road that led straight south, over the gun-rimmed heights where Bragg's army was entrenched. Hooker had brought plenty of horses and wagons, and now his trains came creaking along the new route with rations and forage for the Army of the Cumberland. The soldiers lined the roads and cheered, dubbed the new route "the cracker line," and spoke admiringly of the ramshackle little steamboat Baldy Smith had built, which helped mightily by carrying bacon and hardtack upstream from Bridgeport to a point within easy reach of Brown's Ferry. The danger of starvation was gone forever. Grant had a breathing space in which to devise a plan for driving the Confederates out of their mountain strongholds.

The breathing space was not comfortable, because Washington was nervous and impatient. Burnside was in Knoxville, and from all the administration could find out, his men there were in as bad a fix as Thomas's men had been in before Grant's arrival. It was believed that if Grant did not smash Bragg very quickly Burnside's little army would be lost en bloc, and Grant was getting almost daily messages—from Halleck, from Stanton, and from Lincoln himself—urging him to move fast.

Burnside's men had had their troubles. The march down from Kentucky had led them over desolate mountains, along roads so bad that hundreds of horses and mules foundered and died. Transport became so inadequate that each soldier had to carry from sixty to eighty pounds on his back, plus eight days' rations. The men tried to lighten this load by eating their rations as fast as they could, supplementing their diet with corn and blackberries gathered along the way. They also threw away most of their inedible freight, and as a result they were poorly equipped when they reached Knoxville. They did not like the rugged mountain country, and one soldier, looking back on the long hike, wrote bitterly: "If this is the kind of country we are fighting for I am in favor of letting the Rebs take their land and their niggers and go to hell for I wouldn't give a bit an acre for all the land I have seen in the last four days."[8]

Still, things were pleasant in Knoxville. Much of Lincoln's old eagerness to get a Federal army into east Tennessee was based on the belief that this area was full of Union sentiment, and the soldiers found that this belief was justified. Crowds lined the streets to cheer when the men marched into Knoxville; one old man stood on the sidewalk, eyes uplifted, crying: "Glory! Glory! I have been enslaved but now I am free." Country people visited the Union camps with gifts of pie and cake and other things to eat, and an Illinois cavalryman noted that "the oft-repeated story of the loyalty of the people of east Tennessee had never been exaggerated." It was not hard to get enough meat and bread from the country around Knoxville to keep the army fed, even if things like coffee, sugar, and salt were almost unobtainable—to say nothing of clothing, medical supplies, and ammunition. The real trouble was that Burnside's supply line, which ran through Cumberland Gap, was so long and difficult that it was in effect worthless. If his army was to be supplied, the supplies would have to come up from Chattanooga, and that could not be done until Bragg had been driven away.[7]

Then, in a misguided moment, Bragg detached Longstreet and sent him off with fifteen thousand veterans to take Knoxville and capture Burnside's army.

Of all the mistakes Bragg made in this fall of 1863—and he made quite a number—this was probably the worst. (Long after the war someone suggested to Grant that Bragg must have supposed that he could afford to send Longstreet away because of the belief that his position on Missionary Ridge was impregnable. Grant looked down his stubby nose, grinned quietly in his sandy beard, and remarked: "Well, it *was* impregnable.")[8] The move did not do Burnside any particular harm, and it fatally weakened the Confederate army for the battle that was about to be fought. But in the early days of November, when news of the move got abroad, it did give Grant some bad moments. The tone of the daily telegrams he was getting from Washington began to be very shrill.

On November 7 Grant ordered Thomas to attack Bragg's right in order to compel Bragg to recall Longstreet and his men. Thomas was as willing a fighter as ever wore a uniform, but he had to reply that he could not comply with this order: he had no horses and no mules, and as a result he could not move one piece of artillery. Grant, in turn, had to tell Washington that he could not attack just yet; he must wait for Sherman and the Army of the Tennessee, and Burnside would have to get along somehow for a few weeks longer.[9]

While Grant waited for Sherman, he began to find that the situation at Chattanooga was in some respects unusual. The Confederates had been holding their dominant position for so long that they seemed to look on all of the Yankees in Chattanooga as their ultimate prisoners; regarding them so, they found little reason to make a tough war out of it. Grant went out one day to inspect the Federal lines, and he reached a point where Federal and Confederate picket posts were not far apart. As he approached the Federal post the sentry turned out the guard; Grant dismissed it and rode on—only to hear, before he had gone fifty yards, another cry: "Turn out the guard for the commanding general!" Immediately a snappy set of Confederates came swarming out, formed a neat military rank, came to attention, and presented arms. Grant returned the salute and rode away. . . . A little later he reached a spring which soldiers of both armies sometimes used. On a log by the spring was a soldier in blue, his musket at his side. Grant asked him what corps he belonged to, and the man, getting up and saluting respectfully, replied that he was one of Longstreet's men. Before they went their separate ways, Union commander and Confederate private had quite a chat.[10]

There were times, indeed, when it seemed that the Union soldiers disliked each other more than they disliked the Confederates. Here at Chattanooga there were elements from three armies—Hooker's two corps from the Army of the Potomac, Sherman's Army of the Tennessee (when it finally arrived; the head of the column reached Brown's Ferry on November 20), and the Army of the Cumberland; and these armies had distinct characteristics. Each was locked in by its own pride and clannish spirit, and each looked on the others as strange and rather outlandish groups. The Easterners gaped at the Westerners, especially at Sherman's men, considered them undisciplined and abominably unmilitary in appearance, and remarked that except for the color of their uniforms they looked exactly like the Rebels. Sherman's men in turn, whooping and yelling as they marched through camp, slouching along with shapeless black hats jammed any which way on their heads, hooted and jeered at the men from the Army of the Potomac and made remarks about "kid gloves and paper collars"—to which the Easterners replied with disdainful comments about "backwoodsmen."

One of Sherman's veterans said he and his fellows had very little use for either Hooker's or Thomas's soldiers, and confessed that "to hear our men talk to them when passing them or their camps marching, you'd think the feeling between us and the Rebels could be no more bitter." The Army of the Cumberland, he said, they could just endure, but the Army of the Potomac—it was too stiff, the men with their jaunty little forage caps looked too neat and tin-soldier-like, and "the 11th and 12th corps Potomac men and ours never meet without some very hard talk." The Westerners noticed, too, that there was a great gulf between officers and enlisted man in the eastern regiments; in Sherman's army a private was quite likely to be on a first-name basis with his company commander."

It was the Army of the Cumberland that was unhappiest in all of this. The men still carried the memory of their defeat at Chickamauga as a stain on their record. They had been whipped in fair fight; they would not be at peace with themselves until they had made up for that whipping—and here were two other armies brought in to rescue them. The plain implication was that they could not get out of their difficulties without help, and the men bitterly resented it; nor did the remarks which Potomac and Tennessee men kept on dropping make the load any easier to bear. The Cumberlands were like a blend of the other two armies. Buell and Thomas were drillmasters as stiff as any the Easterners had seen, and men who served under them learned to button their coats, shine their boots, and say "Yessir" when addressed by higher ranks; but the men themselves were Westerners. They walked with a long stride and they were bigger physically than the men from the East, and they considered that Stone's River and Chickamauga were fights as tough as any the other men had been through. Now here they were, squatting on the plain looking up at the infinite lines of Confederate trenches on top of the Tennessee mountains, and the authorities obviously felt that they could not fight their way out unaided. Far down underneath, their pride in themselves as soldiers had been deeply, grievously damaged.

. . . Under everything, the men had become soldiers. There were men from Ohio (to name a northern state at random) in each of the three armies; and the instinctive loyalty of all of these men went now to the army, not to the state or even to the nation. Far back at the dawn of life these young men had gone to the recruiting station and had taken the oath, and after that there had been a long round of drill, of dull marches across uninteresting country, of hard fighting where the real enemy was death itself, and terror and the danger of crippling wounds, rather than the opposing army in gray. What the war itself was all about had been lost in the shuffle somewhere. All that mattered now was the army itself, the regiment or the corps or the army to which a man gave his loyalty; it was Pap Thomas or Joe Hooker or Uncle Billy Sherman, with the grim stooped figure of Grant somewhere in the background; and in the queer way of soldiers the men could be stirred by an appeal to the badge they wore on their shoulders, or the address that home folk scrawled on an envelope, rather than by the tremendous issues for which, by the books and in theory, they were risking their lives. They could be cynical about everything but their own manhood, and that was somehow wrapped up in the army itself.

The war had had its way with them. They were soldiers: volunteers technically, professionals in all but name, moved now by the mysterious intangibles that go with soldiering. Under everything else, they were fighting not for the Union nor for freedom nor for anything else that carried a great name, but simply for the figure which they would finally make in their own eyes. They were about to go into a great fight, and their pride as soldiers might be the decisive factor in it.

4. *A Half Dozen Roasted Acorns*

Maybe the real trouble was that the battle was too theatrical. People could see too much; most particularly, the Confederates could see too much. They were up in the balconies and all of the Federals were down in the orchestra pit, and when the fighting began, every move down on the plain was clearly visible to the Southerners on the heights. Perhaps just watching it did something to them.

Or it might have been the eclipse of the moon, which took place a night or two before the battle. There had been a great silver light over mountain and plain and rival battle lines, and it died and gave way to a creepy rising shadow as the moon was blotted out, so that the armored ridge was a silent, campfire-spangled mass outlined against a pale sky, with darkness coming up out of the hollows. Both armies looked on in awed silence, and the sight seems to have been taken as an incomprehensible omen of ill fortune. (Ill fortune, but specifically for whom? The Army of the Cumberland decided finally that it must mean bad luck for the Rebs: up on the mountain crest the Johnnies were a lot closer to the dying moon than the Federals on the plain, and the portent of disaster which seemed to be involved in this eclipse must be aimed at those who were nearest to it.)[1]

Or, finally, it may be that everybody had been waiting too long. The armies had been in position for two months, or nearly that, with nothing much to do but look at each other. Day after day and week after week the Confederates had lounged in their trenches, looking down on men who could not conceivably do them any harm, and during all of that time the Federals had lounged in their own trenches, looking up at foes who seemed to be beyond all reach. What would happen when the men finally went into action might be strangely and powerfully affected, in a quite unpredictable way, by those long weeks of waiting and watching.

If justice existed on earth and under the heavens, Braxton Bragg would have been right; his position was impregnable. Missionary Ridge rose five hundred feet above the plain, sparse trees and underbrush littering its steep rocky slope; it ran for more than five miles, from southwest to northeast, and the Confederates had all of it. At its base, fronting the plain, they had a stout line of trenches, and on the crest they had another line, studded with cannon. Halfway up, at the proper places, there were other trenches and rifle pits, manned by soldiers who knew what to do with their rifles when they got a Yankee in the sights. To the west, a detachment held Lookout Mountain—not the crest, which rose in a straight palisade no army could scale, but the steep sides which ran down from the foot of the palisade to the edges of the Tennessee. The detachment was not large, but the mountainside was steep and the Yankees were not up to anything menacing, and it was believed that this detachment ought to be able to hold its ground. Across the flat country between Lookout and the southwestern end of Missionary Ridge, there was a good line of fieldworks held by infantry and artillery. And at the upper end of Missionary Ridge, where the high country came down to the river a few miles upstream from Chattanooga, there was broken hilly ground held by some of the best men in all the Confederacy—the division of Irish-born Pat Cleburne, a tremendous soldier who had trained his men to the precise pattern which had been glimpsed by his pugnacious Irish eyes.

Bragg was right, by any standard anyone could use. His main position could not be taken by assault, not even if nearly a third of the Confederate army had been sent up toward Knoxville to squelch General Burnside.

The Army of the Cumberland held the low ground south of Chattanooga; Lookout Mountain looked down on it from one side and Missionary Ridge looked down on it from the other, and men who had heard about Fredericksburg and Gettysburg, with their doomed charges on high ground, could look up at these heights and have disturbing thoughts. On November 23 Thomas moved his army forward. It drove Confederate skirmishers and advance guards off the plain and seized a little detached hill, named Orchard Knob, which came up out of the flat ground a little outside Chattanooga. If Thomas wanted to order an assault on Bragg's position he had an excellent place to take off from, but there was little reason to think that this would help very much. Missionary Ridge was still five hundred feet high, and it was studded with Rebels from top to bottom.

This was the nut that U. S. Grant was expected to crack, and as he made his plans he did just what Thomas's grumpy men had thought he would do. He gave the big assignments to Sherman and to Hooker, and to the outlanders these officers had brought in with them. The Army of the Cumberland would have the inglorious job of looking menacing and helping to pick up the pieces, while the men from the Army of the Tennessee and the Army of the Potomac had the starring parts.

Grant proposed to hit the two ends of the Confederate line at once. Hooker would strike at Lookout Mountain, and Sherman—moving his army upstream, across the river from Chattanooga, and crossing over by pontoons—would hit the upper end of Missionary Ridge. While they were breaking into the Confederate flanks, Thomas's men could attack the center. The latter attack would not accomplish anything in particular, for it would be suicide to expect troops to take that tremendous height, but if they could apply enough pressure to keep Bragg from reinforcing his flanks their job would be done. Sherman and Hooker would win the battle.[2]

It was ordered so, and the men of the Army of the Cumberland got the full implication of it. They were veterans, and in any ordinary circumstances they would have been happy enough to let somebody else's army do all of the heavy fighting. But these circumstances were not ordinary. Their pride had been bruised badly enough in recent weeks, and now it was being hit harder than ever. In the eyes of the commanding general, obviously, they were second-class troops. They waited in helpless, smoldering anticipation for the battle to begin.

It began on November 24, after a good many delays, when Hooker sent his Easterners forward from Lookout Valley to seize the mountain that looked down on the road and the river and the city of Chattanooga. At the same moment Sherman got his army across the Tennessee, above Chattanooga, and sent it driving in on the northern end of Missionary Ridge.

Hooker's men found their job unexpectedly easy. They outnumbered the Confederates on Lookout Mountain by a fantastic margin—five or six to one, as far as a good estimate is possible—and they clambered up the rocks and steep meadows and drove the defenders out of there with a minimum of effort and a maximum of spectacular effect.

The Cumberlands (and the newspaper correspondents) were all down in the valley, watching. They saw the high ground sparkling with musket fire and wreathed in smoke, and a mist came in and veiled the top of the mountain from sight; and then at last the mist lifted, and the Union flag was flying from the crest of the mountain, the Confederates had all retreated, and Joe Hooker was a fine handsome dashing soldier whose men had scaled a mountain and licked the Rebels in front of everybody. The newspapers blossomed out with great stories about "the battle above the clouds." The left end of Bragg's line had been knocked loose from its moorings, although actually the achievement was not as solid as it seemed. Hooker's men still had to come down the eastern slope and crack the battle line in the plain, and that would take a little more doing.

While Hooker was at it, Sherman's rowdies from the Army of the Tennessee attacked Pat Cleburne's men and found that they had taken on more than they could handle.

Missionary Ridge did not run in a straight line to the edge of the Tennessee River, as Grant and everyone else on the Federal side supposed. It broke up, before it reached the river, into a complex of separated hills with very steep sides, and Sherman's men no sooner took one hill than they found themselves obliged to go down into a valley and climb another one, with cold-eyed Rebel marksmen shooting at them every step of the way—and occasionally rolling huge rocks down on them. By the end of the day the Army of the Tennessee had had some very hard fighting and had not yet gained a foothold on the end of the ridge. Sherman believed (apparently mistakenly) that Bragg was drawing men from his center to reinforce Cleburne, and he called for help.*

When the battle was resumed the next morning, nothing went right. Sherman's men hammered at the northern end of Missionary Ridge and got nowhere. Hooker took his troops down from the slope of Lookout Mountain and headed south, to strike the other end of the Confederate line, but he went astray somewhere in the wooded plain; there was a stream that needed bridging, the pontoons were missing, and this blow at the Confederate left missed fire completely.

On Orchard Knob, Grant and Thomas watched the imperfect progress of this unsatisfactory battle. Sherman continued to believe that the Confederates in his front were being strengthened, and he was calling for more reinforcements. Some of Thomas's troops were sent to him, but he still could not push Pat Cleburne's men off the heights. By mid-afternoon his attack had definitely stalled, with severe losses, and Hooker's push had not materialized. If anything was to be done the Army of the Cumberland would have to do it.

What was planned and what finally happened were two different things. Grant told Thomas to have his men attack the Confederate line at the base of Missionary Ridge, occupy it, and await further orders; the move seems to have been regarded as a diversion that might lead Bragg to strengthen his center by withdrawing some of the men who were confronting Sherman. No one had any notion that the Army of the Cumberland could take the ridge itself. Thomas apparently was dubious about the prospect of taking even the first line of trenches; he was slow about ordering the men forward, and Grant had to prod him before they finally began to move.[4]

The men were impatient, for a powerful excitement had been rising in them all day. They had heard the unending crash of Sherman's battle off to their left, and they sensed that things there were not going right. Straight ahead of them was the great ridge, and they looked at it with an irrational, desperate sort of longing. One of them remarked afterward that they were keyed up to such a pitch that "if General Grant had said the word Missionary Ridge would have been taken in thirty minutes time."[5]

The word came—not to take the ridge, just to take the trenches at its base—and the men surged forward in one of the most dramatic moves of all the war. The battle line was two miles wide, eighteen thousand men in four solid infantry divisions, moving toward an impregnable mountain wall that blotted out half the sky. Flags snapped in the wind, and Thomas's carefully drilled men kept a parade-ground alignment. The Confederate guns high above them opened with salvos that covered the crest with a ragged dirty-white cloud; from some atmospheric quirk, each shot they fired could be seen from the moment it left the gun's muzzle. The Cumberlands kept on going and, from Orchard Knob, Federal artillery opened in support. General Gordon Granger, who had done so much to save the day at Chickamauga, was on Orchard Knob, and he was so excited that he forgot he was commander of an army corps and went down into the gun pits to help the cannoneers. Thomas stood on the hill, majestic as ever, running his fingers through his whiskers. Beside him, Grant chewed a cigar and looked on unemotionally.

The plain was an open stage which everybody watched— the generals back on Orchard Knob and the Confederates on Missionary Ridge. Crest and sides of the ridge were all ablaze with fire now, and the Army of the Cumberland took some losses, but it kept on moving. Up to the first line of trenches at the base of the mountain it went, the men swarmed over the parapet, and in a moment the Confederate defenders were scampering back up the hillside to their second and third lines. The Cumberlands moved into the vacated trenches, paused for breath, and kept looking up at the crest, five hundred feet above them.

The rising slope was an obvious deathtrap, but these men had a score to settle—with the Rebels who had whipped them at Chickamauga, with the other Federal armies who had derided them, with Grant, who had treated them as second-class troops—and now was the time to settle it. From the crest of the ridge the Confederates were sending down a sharp plunging fire against which the captured trenches offered little protection. The Federals had seized the first line, but they could not stay where they were. It seemed out of the question to go forward, but the only other course was to go back, and for these soldiers who had been suffering a slow burn for weeks, to go back was unthinkable.

The officers felt exactly as the men felt. Phil Sheridan was there, conspicuous in dress uniform—he was field officer of the day, togged out in his best—and he sat on his horse, looked up the forbidding slope, and drew a silver flask from his pocket to take a drink. Far above him a Confederate artillery commander standing amid his guns looked down at him, and Sheridan airily waved the flask to offer a toast as he drank. The Confederate signaled to his gun crews, and his battery fired a salvo in reply; it was a near miss, the missiles kicking up dirt and gravel and spattering Sheridan's gay uniform. Sheridan's face darkened; he growled, "I'll take those guns for that!" and he moved his horse forward, calling out to the men near him: "All right, boys—as soon as you catch your breath you can go on again." All up and down the line other men were getting the same idea. Brigadier General Carlin turned to his men and shouted: "Boys, I don't want you to stop until we reach the top of that hill. Forward!" The colonel of the 104th Illinois was heard crying: "I want the 104th to be the first regiment on that hill!" And then, as if it moved in response to one command, the whole army surged forward, scrambled up out of the captured trenches, and began to move up the slope of Missionary Ridge.[6]

Back on Orchard Knob the generals watched in stunned disbelief. Grant turned to Thomas and asked sharply who had told these men to go on to the top of the ridge. Thomas replied that he did not know; he himself had certainly given no such order. Grant then swung on Granger: was he responsible? Granger replied that he was not, but the battle excitement was on him and he added that when the men of the Army of the Cumberland once got started it was very hard to stop them. Grant clenched his teeth on his cigar and muttered something to the effect that somebody was going to sweat for it if this charge ended in disaster; then he faced to the front again to watch the incredible thing that was happening.[7]

Up the side of the ridge went the great line of battle. It was a parade-ground line no longer. The regimental flags led, men trailing out behind each flag in a V-shaped mass, struggling over rocks and logs as they kept on climbing. Confederate pockets of resistance on the slope were wiped out. Now and then the groups of attackers would stop for breath—the slope was steep, and it was easy to get winded— but after a moment or so they would go on again.

Looking down from the crest, the Confederates kept on firing, but the foreknowledge of defeat was beginning to grip them. The crest was uneven, and no defender could see more than a small part of his own line; but each defender could see all of the charging Federal army, and it suddenly looked irresistible. The defensive fire slackened here and there; men began to fade back from the firing line, irresolute; and finally the Federals were covering the final yards in a frantic competitive run, each regiment trying to outdo the others, each man trying to beat his fellows. A company commander, running ahead of his colors, grabbed the coat-tails of one of his men, to hold him back so that he might reach the crest first.[8]

No one could ever determine afterward what unit or what men won the race, and the business was argued at old soldiers' reunions for half a century. Apparently the crest was reached at half a dozen places simultaneously, and when it was reached, Bragg's line—the center of his whole army, the hard core of his entire defensive position—suddenly and inexplicably went to pieces. By ones and twos and then by companies and battalions, gray-clad soldiers who had proved their valor in a great many desperate fights turned and took to their heels. Something about that incredible scaling of the mountainside had been just too much for them. Perfectly typical was the case of a Confederate officer who, scorning to run, stood with drawn sword, waiting to fight it out with the first Yankee who approached him. An Indiana private, bayoneted rifle in his grip, started toward him—and then, amazingly, laid down his weapon and came on in a crouch, bare hands extended. There was a primeval menace in him, more terrifying than bayonet or musket, and the officer blinked at him for a moment and then fled.

As resistance dissolved, the victorious Federals were too breathless to cheer. They tossed their caps in the air, and some of them crossed the narrow ridge to peer down the far side, where they saw what they had not previously seen—whole brigades of Confederates running downhill in wild panicky rout. The Federals turned and beckoned their comrades with swinging arms and, regaining their wind, with jubilant shouts: "My God! Come and see them run!"

General officers began to reach the crest. Sheridan was there, laying proudly possessive hands on the guns that had fired at him. The General Wood whose division had been ordered out of the line in that disastrous mismaneuver at

Chickamauga was riding back and forth laughing, telling his men that because they had attacked without orders they would be court-martialed, each and every one. He found the private who had charged the Confederate officer bare-handed and asked him why he had done such a thing; the man replied simply that he had thought it would be nice to take the officer prisoner.[9]

The battle of Chattanooga was over now, no matter what Sherman or Hooker did. With a two-mile hole punched in the center of his line, Bragg could do nothing but retreat, and as his army began to reassemble on the low ground beyond the mountain, it took off for Georgia, with Cleburne's men putting up a stout rear-guard resistance. Phil Sheridan got his division into shape and took off in pursuit, figuring that it might be possible to cut in behind Cleburne and capture his whole outfit, but his pursuit was little more than a token. The Army of the Cumberland was temporarily immobilized by the sheer surprise of its incredible victory. Nobody wanted to do anything but ramble around, yell, and let his chest expand with unrestrained pride.

Oddly enough, it was a long time before the soldiers realized that they themselves were responsible for the victory. They tended to ascribe it to Grant and to his good management, and they told one another that all they had ever needed was a good leader. One officer who had shared in all of this army's battles wrote that during the uproar of this conflict "I thought I detected in the management what I had never discovered before on the battlefield—a little common sense." When Grant and Thomas came to the top of the ridge the men crowded about them, capering and yelling. Sherman himself was thoroughly convinced that the battle had gone exactly as Grant had planned it; to him the whole victory was simply one more testimonial to the general's genius.[10]

Washington felt much the same way; but Washington also remembered that Burnside was still beleaguered in Knoxville, and when Lincoln sent a wire of congratulations to Grant he added the words: "Remember Burnside." Grant started Granger off to the rescue with an army corps; then, figuring that Sherman would make a faster march—and feeling apparently a little disillusioned about Granger after noticing the man's unrestrained excitement during the battle—he canceled the order and sent the Army of the Tennessee.

Burnside, as it turned out, was in no serious trouble. Longstreet had made a night attack on his lines and had been repulsed, after which he drew his troops off and menaced the Union garrison from a distance. Sherman's men relieved the Knoxville situation without difficulty, except that the pace at which Sherman drove them marched them practically out of their shoes. They found the Federals in Knoxville ragged and hungry—the food allowance had been reduced to a daily issue of salt pork and bran bread, so unappetizing that it took a half-starved man to eat it—but things had not been as bad in Knoxville as they had been in Chattanooga before Grant's arrival, and Sherman and his officers were slightly nonplused when Burnside and his staff welcomed them with an elaborate banquet. One of Burnside's officers explained later that the whole town had been ransacked to get such a meal together; both soldiers and civilians had felt that they ought to make some tangible expression of their gratitude to the men who had raised the siege. Sherman fumed privately over what he considered the military folly of trying to occupy Knoxville at all, and the effort to nudge Longstreet off to a safer distance involved a good deal of highly uncomfortable winter campaigning, but the danger was over. Before too long, full railroad connections with Chattanooga were restored, which meant that plenty of food and clothing could come in. Half of the army came gaily down to the station to greet the first train—a ten-car freight train which, when the doors were opened, turned out by some triumph of military miscalculation to be loaded with nothing but horseshoes.[11]

Back in Chattanooga the soldiers prepared for winter and for the spring campaign that would follow. Grant was turning Nashville into one of the greatest supply bases on the continent, and the railway connection with Chattanooga was being restored and strengthened; in the spring Grant would take Atlanta and Mobile, and he wanted everything ready. Meanwhile he rode out one day with Thomas, Baldy Smith, and other officers to look at the battlefield of Chickamauga. A

young staff officer stuck as close to Grant as he could, hoping
to hear some profound comment by the victor of Chattanooga
on the scene of the most desperate fight the Army of the
Cumberland had ever had. He was disappointed. Grant made
only one remark that the staff man could remember, and
it was nothing much for the history books. Looking about at
one place where all the trees were scarred and splintered by
bullets, the general observed: "These trees would make a
good lead mine."[12]

Pap Thomas also made a remembered remark about this
time. During the battle of Chattanooga it had occurred to
him that the little hill of Orchard Knob would make a
beautiful burying ground for Union soldiers slain in battle,
and not long after the fight he ordered a proper military
cemetery laid out there, detailing whole regiments to help
in the work. The chaplain who was going to be in charge of
burial services when everything was ready came to him and
asked if the dead should be buried by states—Ohioans here,
Hoosiers there, Kentuckians over yonder, and so on. Thomas
thought about it and then shook his head.

"No—no, mix 'em up, mix 'em up," he said. "I'm tired of
states' rights."[13]

States' rights, as a matter of fact, had made its last great
counterattack, and the Confederacy had passed the last of
the great might-have-beens of the war. Its supreme attempt
to restore the lost balance had failed. By making the greatest
effort it could make—pulling together a large army even at
the cost (never risked before or afterward) of taking men
from Lee's army—it had made its final bid for victory at
Chickamauga. It could not again make such an effort, and it
would not again have a chance to make the tide flow in the
other direction. The Army of the Cumberland might have
been destroyed at Chickamauga but was not destroyed; it
might have been starved into surrender at Chattanooga, but
that had not happened; and now Bragg's wrecked army was
recuperating in north Georgia, Bragg himself replaced by
cautious little Joe Johnston, and from this time on the Confederacy could hope to do no more than parry the blows that
would be leveled against it. The dream that had been born

in spring light and fire was flickering out now, and nothing lay ahead but a downhill road.

The shadows were rising that winter, tragically lit by a pale light of southern valor and endurance which were not enough to win and which the victorious Federals glimpsed as they looked back on the immediate past. A man in the 46th Ohio recalled strolling along the fighting line at the northern end of Missionary Ridge, the day after the battle of Chattanooga had ended, and looking down at the unburied body of a dead Confederate, and he wrote:

"He was not over 15 years of age, and very slender in size. He was clothed in a cotton suit, and was barefooted—barefooted, on that cold and wet 24th of November. I examined his haversack. For a day's ration there was a handful of black beans, a few pieces of sorghum and a half dozen roasted acorns. That was an infinitely poor outfit for marching and fighting, but that Tennessee Confederate had made it answer his purpose."[14]

11.

And Keep Moving On

1. *Year of Jubilo*

EIGHTEEN HUNDRED and sixty-four came in, and it would be the worst year of all—the year of victory made certain, the year of smoke and destruction and death, with an old dream going down in flames and an unfathomable new one taking form in the minds of men who hardly knew what they dreamed. Steadily and inescapably a new rhythm was being felt. The revolutionary times which old General Scott had detected away back in the early days, when hotheaded little Captain Lyon had to be equipped with irregular authority to meet a fantastic situation in Missouri, were enforcing their own hard rules. Visibly drawing nearer to its end, the war had paradoxically become a thing that could not be stopped.

Thoughtful Southerners saw the narrowing circle and the rising shadows and cried that the fight must continue to the final limits of endurance. The Confederate Congress, adopting a resolution addressed to constituents back home, touched the edge of hysteria in its fervor. If the Washington government (said this resolution) called for restoration of the old Union it was merely setting a cruel trap for the deluded; there could be no reunion, because the only possible relation between the reunited sections would be that between conqueror and conquered, and "nothing short of your utter subjugation, the destruction of your state governments, the overthrow of your social and political fabric, your personal and public degradation and ruin, will satisfy the demands of the North."[1]

If there was in this the desperate overstatement common to wartime propaganda, there was nevertheless reason for thoughtful Southerners to feel this way. The attempt to make an independent confederacy had been, in a sense, nothing more than a despairing effort to do something about the problem of slavery. The war was a great forced draft applied to a long-smoldering flame, and under its white heat the problem was changing. Not for nothing was slavery called "the peculiar institution," and its chief peculiarity seemed to be that it would not stay put. It changed when it came under examination; the question now was not so much what could be done about slavery as what could be done about the Negro, and this in turn was becoming a problem of what to do about white society itself. There was material here for an almost unlimited overthrow of human institutions, because existing institutions had been built, by and large, on the happy assumption that the basic problem would not have to be faced at all.

Lincoln himself had shared in this belief. Ten years earlier he had confessed that if he had all earthly power he would not know what to do about slavery; it was a wrong that cried for settlement, but millions of Negroes were physically here in America, and if they were not slaves they would be free men, headed for ultimate equality with white men; and "we cannot . . . make them equals." More recently—in the middle of 1862—he had protested to a Maryland correspondent that all thinking Southerners must know that "I never had a wish to touch the foundations of their society." Yet the foundations were being touched with a hand of iron, and no one was more disturbed by this than Lincoln. As recently as July 31, 1863, he had seemed to be less than certain about the Emancipation Proclamation itself. Writing about this proclamation (to a general who had asked for guidance), he seemed to be brooding about a decision not yet final: "I think I shall not retract or repudiate it. Those who have tasted actual freedom I believe can never be slaves or quasi-slaves again. For the rest, I believe some plan, substantially being gradual emancipation, would be better for both black and white."[2]

Yet even as he brooded the decision had been made, if

not by the President, by the war itself. In that same summer Grant had written bluntly: "Slavery is already dead and cannot be resurrected. It would take a standing army to maintain slavery in the South if we were to make peace today, guaranteeing to the South all their former constitutional privileges." And grim Sherman was contemptuously saying: "All the powers of earth cannot restore them their slaves any more than their dead grandfathers."³ Now, early in 1864, Sherman's soldiers were making fairly substantial strides with an operation that the Congress at Richmond would undoubtedly have considered part of the overthrow of the southern social and political fabric; they were doing it in a wild rough holiday mood, with taunting, boisterous laughter, simply as a means of getting on with the war.

Specifically, they were creating a smoky darkness at midday in Meridian, Mississippi, making a wasteland in order that Yankee armies a little farther north might thereafter go about their business with less difficulty.

Meridian lay 150 miles east of Vicksburg, and it was a railroad junction town, a military supply depot, and a modest industrial center. Mississippi produced many Confederate guerrillas, who had a pestiferous habit of riding up into western Tennessee to disrupt Federal supply lines and other arrangements. As far as they could be said to have a base, they were based on Meridian, and Sherman felt that if Meridian became an ash heap the Yankee machine in northern Mississippi and in Tennessee could operate more smoothly. So he brought troops down to Meridian—feinting smartly so that Bishop Polk, Confederate commander in the state, thought that Mobile was being menaced and took his own troops down there to head him off—and on February 14 Sherman's heavy-handed foot soldiers reached Meridian and began to destroy the place. The railroads were torn up for twenty-five miles around; an arsenal, two hotels, various shops and factories, vast quantities of cotton and any amount of food, textiles, army equipment, and unassorted private property were burned. The soldiers said that they had been ordered to lay hands upon every sort of property "which could in any way be applied to aid the Rebel armies"—which, when one stopped to think about it, was a category broad enough to include anything from a railroad bridge to a smokehouse full of bacon—and they were men to whom such orders did not need to be given twice. (A year earlier Sherman had told Admiral Porter that "our new troops came in with ideas of making vigorous war, which means universal destruction," and nothing that had happened in the past year had weakened that notion in them.) The 10th Missouri, it was said, took particular pleasure in the work; it contained men who had been driven from their homes by Confederate guerrillas, and they were out to get even. Their comrades in arms, however, acting without animus, were just about as effective.

In any case, Meridian was thoroughly sacked. Sherman had appointed a solid column of cavalry to come down from the Memphis area and join him, and he had further ventures in mind, but the cavalry ran afoul of Bedford Forrest along the way and went back in ignominious defeat, so Sherman pulled his infantry out, loaded down with all the loot that could be carried (as the Confederates charged) in three hundred wagons which had been appropriated in the nearby countryside. Black smoke lay on the land as the troops marched away, and a scar that would be a long time fading; and as the column swung back toward home territory it was followed, as Sherman recalled, by "about ten miles of Negroes."⁴

No other Yankee raid into southern territory brought back such an array of contrabands—five thousand of them by soldiers' count, at least eight thousand by the estimate of angry Mississippians. These fugitives had swarmed in from long distances, some of them carrying small children, none of them equipped for a long journey. Soldiers said some had come three hundred miles to join the column. Many died along the way. All were hungry and weary, yet they seemed to be cheerful, and while they had no real notion where the Army of the Tennessee was going they knew that its road was the road away from slavery, and they followed it with pathetic eagerness.

A Wisconsin soldier who watched them suspected that the average colored refugee had, deep within him, some very sober thoughts, for all his surface gaiety. "He was not only breaking up old associations, but was rushing out into a wholly new and untried world. . . . He was not certain of a full meal three times a day, or even once a day, and he must have sadly wondered what was to become of him." Reflecting on all of this, the soldier remembered that a number of people in the North and in the South were arguing that the Negro slave was in reality quite satisfied with his lot, and he wrote angrily: "Such talk is mere twaddle.'"

Grant and Sherman were right; slavery was doomed, and the war was passing sentence upon it, no matter what doubts might assail the President. Of all societies, that of the South was least fitted to stand the shock of revolution, and the war was revolutionary. The destruction of Meridian and the ten-mile column of hopeless, hopeful colored folk who trailed out behind the triumphant northern army simply underlined the Confederacy's inescapable problem.

For secession had been an attempt to perpetuate the past: to enable a society based on slavery to live on, as an out-of-date survival in the modern world. Slavery was above all else a primitive mechanism, and the society that relied on it could survive, in the long run, only if the outside world propped it up. But the southern society was not itself primitive at all. It needed all of the things the rest of the world needed—railroad iron, rolling mills, machine tools, textile machinery, chemicals, industrial knowledge, and an industrial labor force—yet it clung to the peculiar institution that prevented it from producing these things itself, and it relied on the rest of the world to make its deficiencies good. Now the rest of the world had ceased to contribute, except for the trickle that came in through the blockade. Instead, that part of the outside world that lay nearest—the North—was doing everything it could to destroy such industrial strength as the South possessed, and what it destroyed could not be replaced. The valor that sent southern youth out to fight barefooted in cotton uniforms with a handful of acorns in the haversack was not enough. Federal soldiers would be destructive because destruction pointed to victory, and as cotton gins and clothing factories went up in smoke the peculiar institution itself would crumble, dim human aspirations seeping down into a submerged layer and undermining all of the foundations.

The southern Congress was quite right; an overturn was coming, and it was precisely the sort of overturn that the men who had created the Confederacy could not at any price accept. No peace based on reunion (the only sort of peace that was really conceivable) could be contemplated, because reunion, by now, inevitably meant the end of slavery. The more hopeless the military outlook became— the more inescapable the cruel parallel between dead grandfathers and slaves escaped from bondage—the more bitterly would southern leaders insist on fighting.

In this fact lay the real horror of 1864. The end of the war could not be hastened, even though it might become visible; it would have to go on until the last ditch had in fact been reached. The peculiar institution was at last taking its own revenge; taking it by the singular dominance it exerted over the minds of men who had gone to arms to perpetuate it.

Six weeks before Sherman made his raid on Meridian there was a singular little meeting one evening in the headquarters tent of General Joe Johnston, commanding what had been Bragg's hard-luck army, at Dalton, Georgia. All corps and division commanders, with one exception, were present; among them, Irish General Pat Cleburne, who had fought so stoutly against Sherman's troops at Chattanooga. General Cleburne had been considering the plight of the South, and he had a paper to present. With Joe Johnston's permission (although not, it would appear, with his outright approval) he read it to the other officers.

The Confederacy, said Cleburne, was fighting a hopeless struggle. It had lost more than a third of its territory; it had lost many men and had "lost, consumed or thrown to the flames an amount of property equal in value to the specie currency of the world." It was badly outnumbered and the disparity was getting worse instead of better, and the Confederate soldier was "sinking into a fatal apathy" and was coming more and more to "a growing belief that some black catastrophe is not far ahead of us." Worst of all, at the beginning of the war slavery was one of the Confederacy's chief sources of strength; now, from a military point of view, it had become "one of our chief sources of weakness."

In any area that had been touched by northern armies, said Cleburne, slavery was fatally weakened, and with this weakness came a corresponding weakness in the civilian economy. The Confederacy thus had an infinite number of vulnerable spots: there was "one of these in every point where there is a slave to set free." The burden could not be carried any longer. Therefore—said Cleburne, reaching the unthinkable conclusion—the South must boldly and immediately recruit Negro troops, guaranteeing in return freedom to every slave who gave his support to the Confederacy. In substance, what Cleburne was asking for was emancipation and black armies. If the peculiar institution was a source of weakness, Cleburne would abolish the institution and turn its human material into a source of strength.

The war, said Cleburne, was killing slavery anyway. From one source or another, the Negro was going to get his freedom; as clearly as Sherman, Cleburne saw that the old relationship belonged in the grave with departed grandfathers. Make a virtue of necessity, then (said this foreign-born general), "and we change the race from a dreaded weakness to a position of strength."

Cleburne's proposal had certain support. It was signed by two brigadiers and a number of field officers from his own division, as well as by a stray cavalry general; and the first signature on the list, of course, was that of Cleburne himself. But the net effect of this modest proposal, dropped thus into a meeting of the commanding generals of the Confederacy's western army, was about the effect that would be produced in a convention of devout churchmen by the unexpected recital of a grossly improper joke. It was received with a shocked, stunned, and utterly incredulous silence. Cleburne had mentioned the unmentionable.

One of the generals who had heard him hastened to write to good Bishop Polk. He began with a simple confession: "I will not attempt to describe my feelings on being confronted by a project so startling in its character—may I say so revolting to Southern sentiment, Southern pride and Southern honor." He went on: "If this thing is once openly proposed to the Army the total disintegration of that Army will follow in a fortnight, and yet to speak and work in opposition to it is an agitation of the question scarcely less to be dreaded." Secretary of War Seddon wrote earnestly to General Johnston, expressing Jefferson Davis's conviction that "the dissemination or even promulgation of such opinions under the present circumstances of the Confederacy . . . can be productive only of discouragement, distraction and dissension." General Johnston passed the word down the line, Cleburne put his paper away and agreed not to press it any farther, and the matter was buried.⁶

It had to be buried, for what Cleburne had quite unintentionally done was to force his fellow officers to gaze upon the race problem which lay beneath the institution of slavery, and that problem seemed to be literally insoluble. It did not, in that generation, seem possible to most men that white and black folk could dwell together in one community in simple amity. There had to be a barrier between them—some tangible thing that would compel everyone to act on the assumption that one race was superior and the other inferior. Slavery was the only barrier imaginable. If it were removed, society would be up against something monstrous and horrifying.

A great many men of good will felt that way. Lincoln himself had hoped that the business might be settled by some scheme of colonization, with freed Negroes transplanted bodily to some other continent in order that a free society might not have to admit them to full membership. Davis, addressing the Confederate Congress at the beginning of 1863, had denounced the Emancipation Proclamation as "the most execrable measure recorded in the history of guilty men"; it was a program, he said, "by which several millions of human beings of an inferior race, peaceful and contented laborers in their sphere, are doomed to extermination." A junior officer in the Confederate War Department, addressing himself to Secretary Seddon about the time Cleburne was putting his own thoughts on paper, had spoken feelingly of "the difficulties and conflicts that must come from exterminating the Negro, which upon this continent is the only mode of exterminating slavery."

None of these folk who talked so lightly of extermination really meant it, of course. It would be left for a much more ruthless society in a far more brutal age to try the actual experiment of genocide. All anyone actually meant was that to make human brotherhood a working reality in everyday life seemed too big a contract for frail human beings. The privilege of belonging to an admittedly superior race—the deep conviction that there actually were superior and inferior races—could not be wrenched out of human society without a revolutionary convulsion. The convulsion was unthinkable, yet it was beginning to take place, even though hardly anyone had consciously willed it; it was coming down the country roads with the swaggering destructive columns in weathered blue, lying across the landscape behind the haze of smoke that came down from the ridges around Gettysburg and Chattanooga, and there was no stopping it. The bugle that would never call retreat had been heard by people who had not previously been allowed to look upon themselves as persons possessing any rights which other people were bound to respect. To end slavery was to commit the nation permanently to an ideal that might prove humanly unattainable. The inner meaning of the war now was that everything which America had done before—its dreams and its hopes, its sacrifices and its hard-bought victories—was no more than prologue to a new struggle that would go on and on for generations, with a remote ideal lying dim but discernible beyond the dust of the coming years.

Here was the real revolution: here was the fundamental and astounding conclusion, which had been implicit in the first crash of the marsh guns around Fort Sumter, which had followed Old Glory and Palmetto Flag down so many streets amid so many gaily cheering crowds. Here was what was being bought by infinite suffering, tragedy, and loss. Here was the showdown, not to be understood at once, not to be accepted for generations, but nevertheless wholly inexorable. Mr. Lincoln was worried and Mr. Davis was desperate, and General Cleburne was quietly snubbed; and down the dusty roads came ten miles of Negroes, bags packed for a journey longer than any man could understand, marching toward a future that could never again be built in the image of the past.

. . . If people could not see it or say it, they could sing it. There was a tinny, jingling little song in the air that year across the North: a Tin Pan Alley ditty, mocking and jeering and pulsing somehow with a *Ça Ira* sort of revolutionary drumbeat. It spoke for the colored folk in a queer inverted way, although it had not yet reached them, and in a ten-cent manner it voiced what the year meant. It was called "The Year of Jubilo":

> *Say Darkies has you seen old Massa*
> *Wid de muffstache on his face*
> *Go long de road sometime dis mornin'*
> *Like he gwine to leave de place?*

It went on, shrill and imperious, the song of the great over-turn, the cheap little tune to which a great gate was beginning to turn painfully on creaking hinges:

> *De massa run, ha-ha!*
> *De darkey stay, ho-ho!*
> *I tink it must be Kingdom Coming*
> *And de year ob Jubilo!*

It would be that sort of year: year of Jubilo, year of over-turn and disaster and ruin, year of infinite bloodshed and suffering, with the foundations of the great deep broken up; hard tramp of marching military feet, endless shuffle of splay-footed refugees running away from something they understood little better than they could understand what they were running toward; the significance of their march being that it led toward the unknown and that all America, like it or not, was going to follow.

2. *Vote of Confidence*

Beyond the war there would be peace. It was still a long way off, and a great many young men would have to die before it could become real, but Abraham Lincoln never took his eyes off it. For the peace would have to justify its cost, which was immense beyond calculation, and if the war was being fought to bring the Union together again, the Union would need to be rebuilt on something better than hatred and suspicion and a sullen longing for revenge. So in the beginning of 1864, Lincoln was reaching out to shape the peace that had not yet been won.

In a moment of candor he once remarked that he could not claim to have controlled events but that events rather had controlled him. All in all, the events of war had not been kind to him. He had become the instrument through which more than he desired was being done. He wanted to restore something—the shape of a lost golden age, perhaps, which early America had thought that it possessed—and the past had gone beyond restoration. Among those who supported him (supported him reluctantly, and only because they could not help themselves) were men who wanted the very destruction and overturn which he himself most dreaded; hard men, made for hatred, to whom reconciliation was a paltry word and who would be happy to play the part of conquerors. As 1864 began, Lincoln was trying to lay his own hands on the peace before victory itself had been won.

In December of 1863 he had set forth his program, which was essentially an effort to get both seceded persons and seceded states back into the Union with the least possible difficulty. Pardon and restoration of full rights would go to any Confederate (with certain stated exceptions) who would swear to support the Constitution and the Union of the states and to abide by all of the Federal government's acts and pronouncements in respect to slavery. And a state itself could return to its old position in the Union whenever as many as ten per cent of the state's voters should re-establish a loyal Union government within that state. In effect, he was trying to get the citizens of southern states to make at least a start in the direction of rebuilding the old Union.

There were difficulties. Radical Republicans were asserting that the southern states, by the act of secession, had in effect committed suicide; they would have to be rebuilt anew, and the agency that must say how and when they could be rebuilt must be the Federal Congress, not the President. Furthermore, the first steps which Lincoln so greatly desired could be taken, obviously, only in such southern states as were already largely occupied by the Union army. The most conspicuous of these was Louisiana, a large part of which had been effectively held since the middle of 1862. Here was the logical place to make a beginning. Yet Louisiana had been ruled for a time by Ben Butler, with whom even the most Union-minded of Southerners would hesitate to co-operate; and after Butler's removal there was divided Federal authority in the state, with purely military problems competing for attention with the problems of reconstruction, and the work went forward very slowly.

Nevertheless, the start was being made, and Major General Nathaniel P. Banks, that devoted politician and maladroit strategist, was in charge of it. As the winter progressed, Banks was calling for elections—election of a civilian governor and election of delegates to a convention that should create a new constitution. (In Washington, bitter-enders like Thaddeus Stevens and Ben Wade were sputtering furiously against all of this, but the work was going forward.) The basic complication lay in the fact that Banks's effort to reconstruct Louisiana politically was going hand in hand with an effort to conquer another section of the Confederacy by force of arms, and under Banks's handling the two projects got in each other's way. Banks was to lead a military expedition up the Red River toward Texas. This would complete the occupation of Louisiana, would enable a Union army to move down toward the Texas border—thereby, presumably, putting the fear into Napoleon III of France, who had been ostentatiously fracturing the Monroe Doctrine by installing luckless Maximilian on the throne in Mexico—and just incidentally it should scoop up considerable quantities of cotton for the hungry textile mills of New England, with whose problems General Banks was closely familiar.

So Banks was a busy man in this winter of 1864, and Louisiana was buzzing with activities which unfortunately were not entirely compatible. In the end, none of these ventures would actually come to anything; Wade and Stevens and their cohorts would scuttle Lincoln's cherished "ten per cent plan," and there were armed Confederates in waiting to defeat the Red River expedition, and the whole program would come to look like an eccentric thrust, a diversion of effort away from the main channels of the war program. Yet it did represent a valiant attempt to shape the war with postwar ideals in mind; an effort to reassert control over those events that thus far had been out of control. Every other ounce of attention had to go simply to the task of making victory certain. Here, at least, was a try at looking beyond victory. It would not work, finally, for a variety of reasons, among them the grim fact that war lays down its own rules, but the motives back of it were good. Not unless it was forced upon him would Lincoln accept the war as a complete uprooting and overturning.[1]

Meanwhile there was the war itself; and in March 1864 the Federal government took the decisive step. Congress created the post of lieutenant general in the regular army and Lincoln gave the job to U. S. Grant; solid insurance, finally, that the war would be fought remorselessly and methodically until the South was capable of no further resistance.

Now Grant was the top northern general, and Halleck was reduced to the position of chief of staff. Broadly speaking, Grant would have a free hand. He could make his headquarters where he chose, and within wide limits he could do as he pleased with the country's armies, with White House and War Department pledged to give him full support. He was the fourth man to hold this position during the war, and he stood in odd contrast to the generals who had gone before.

First there had been Winfield Scott—old, swollen with dropsy, vain and fussy, a stouthearted man and a sound strategist, but so infirm physically he could not mount a horse, could indeed hardly so much as get out from behind his desk without help. Scott had understood the kind of war that was being fought, and he had done his part to get the country off to a good start; his only trouble was that he was fifteen years past his prime, and he had been quietly shelved after a few months, his place taken by the brilliant young McClellan. McClellan, too, had contributed his bit; he had given organization, order, and high morale to the Army of the

Potomac, but he had never understood either the war itself or his own place in it; he had become obsessed by his picture of himself as the virtuous hero forever hampered by scheming and treacherous men of ill will, and the capacity for hard driving fighting was not in him. So he had gone, too, and Halleck had come in: Halleck, the book soldier who quickly reduced himself to the role of paper-shuffler, a man fond of details of office work and given to writing long, gossipy letters to his subordinates, pettish and querulous, wholly unfitted for the direction of a war that went by none of the old rules. Now there was Grant.

He had had his ups and his downs, and nobody in his senses would ever give him any of the nicknames that had been given to his predecessors—Old Fuss and Feathers, the Young Napoleon, Old Brains. He was not a man for nicknames, or for striking attitudes, or for impressing other people. A physician on his staff once asked him about the art of war, expecting a dissertation on Jomini or some other world authority. Grant replied that the art of war was really simple enough; at bottom, it meant to "find out where your enemy is, get at him as soon as you can and strike him as hard as you can, and keep moving on."[7] This uncomplicated creed he had followed ever since Belmont and Fort Henry, and it precisely expressed the quality that Abraham Lincoln had been looking for in his generals for so long a time. Now Lincoln had the man he wanted; from the spring of 1864 the Federal armies would keep moving on, and sooner or later the end would come.

Grant took over the high command in a little ceremony at the White House on March 9, and he got to work at once. As he sat down to survey the situation and figure out the best way to put his little creed into effect, he could see that in a way his task was quite simple. The Confederacy possessed two principal armies—the Army of Northern Virginia, commanded by Robert E. Lee, and the Army of Tennessee, commanded by Joseph E. Johnston. Lee's army was in camp below the Rapidan River, lean and taut and ready for action; Johnston's was encamped in northern Georgia, near the town of Dalton. Behind Lee lay Richmond, and behind Johnston lay Atlanta. These armies and the territories they defended were Grant's destined striking points. To get at them as quickly as possible, hit them hard and keep moving on, was the Federal commander's main responsibility. If they could be put out of action, the war would be won.

There were side shows: most notably, General Banks's expedition, of which Grant heartily disapproved, on the twin grounds that it was not aimed at a vulnerable point and that it drew men and effort away from the real targets. Banks was getting progressively deeper into trouble while Grant was taking over his new job; he captured the Louisiana city of Alexandria and pushed forward hopefully enough, but within weeks he was to be so roundly defeated that he would narrowly escape losing his entire army and Admiral Porter's pet fleet of ironclads along with it. But what he might or might not be able to do would make very little difference. Johnston and Lee were the real antagonists, and the war would be won or lost in Virginia and Georgia. It was these points that got Grant's attention.

In the West things looked favorable. When he moved east Grant gave Sherman top command in the West, and Sherman kept prodigiously busy during the winter getting his supplies and transportation in shape for the big drive. Technically Sherman was what would now be called an army group commander. Under him there were close to one hundred thousand combat soldiers, more than half of whom belonged to George Thomas's Army of the Cumberland. Then there was Sherman's old Army of the Tennessee, led now by James B. McPherson—smaller than the Army of the Cumberland, less well disciplined, cockier and faster on its feet. With these there was a third army, led by General John Schofield: the little Army of the Ohio, really no more than an army corps, its leader the young man who had served as very junior assistant to Lyon out in Missouri in the early days of the war. With these three armies, made as ready as the enormous resources of the North could make them, Sherman was waiting for the signal. His instructions were clear and uncomplicated; as he himself put it later, "I was to go for Joe Johnston."[3]

As Sherman's army went for Joe Johnston, the Army of the Potomac was to go for Robert E. Lee, and it was with this army that Grant himself decided to move. It was believed in Washington that this army needed the all-out drive that only the general-in-chief could provide. George Gordon Meade, its own commander, was a solid and conscientious soldier, but neither he nor any of his predecessors had ever quite been able to make the army fight all out. The Virginia theater of operations was the war's show window, closest to the capital and to the big eastern centers of population, most thoroughly covered by the newspapers, so that it sometimes seemed as if the real war was being fought here and that everything else was a side show; yet the Army of the Potomac, for all the glamor that was attached to its name, was in reality the inglorious hod carrier for the Union cause. It had been blooded at Bull Run, and it had fought on the Virginia peninsula, along the Rappahannock, in Maryland and in Pennsylvania. The evil forces of politics had flickered over it; Robert E. Lee had played cruel games with its generals, deceiving them and leading them on so that they would get many of their men killed to no good purpose. The army had tramped through the choking red dust and the clinging mud of Virginia without seeming to accomplish much, its two victories were purely defensive, and all in all it had never got the habit of triumph. Its men were fatalists, doing the best they could, taking their beatings—Gaines's Mill, Second Bull Run, Fredericksburg, Chancellorsville—and coming back for more, always ready but never really confident, clinging to fond memories of the departed McClellan, and ready enough to admit that the greatest general of all was the man who commanded the opposing Confederate army, General Lee.

The army tended to be suspicious of Grant when he established his headquarters near Meade's. Peppery little General Rawlins, Grant's chief of staff, found the suspicion freely expressed. Officers of the Potomac army would admit that the western troops had done well enough, but would always add: "Well, you have never met Bobby Lee and his boys; it would be quite different if you had." If any of Grant's people expressed optimism about the coming campaign in Virginia, someone was sure to wag his head and say: "Well, that may be, but mind you, Bobby Lee is just over the Rapidan."[4]

Grant did not have a great deal of time in which to pull this army together; just six weeks from the moment he pitched his tents along the Rapidan to the day when the great offensive would start. They were busy weeks. There were reviews, to let the troops have a look at the new general-in-chief and to let him have a look at them; there was an endless bustle of reorganization and re-equipping, a tightening up of details, a ruthless combing out of the snug, comfortable forts around Washington so that more combat men could be added to the army—this latter a move that was highly popular with the veterans, who rejoiced to see the big heavy artillery regiments deprived of their soft assignments, given muskets, and told to soldier it along with everybody else. Grant reorganized his cavalry, bringing hard little Phil Sheridan in from the West to turn the cavalry corps into a fighting organization. As April wore away, the effect of all of this began to be felt, and the army displayed a quiet new confidence. Lee might be just over the Rapidan, but there was a different feeling in the air; maybe this spring it would be different.

Maybe it would; what a general could do would be done. But in the last analysis everything would depend on the men in the ranks, and both in the East and in the West the enlisted man was called on that winter to give his conclusive vote of confidence in the conduct of the war. He gave his vote in the most direct way imaginable—by re-enlisting voluntarily for another hitch.

Union armies in the Civil War did not sign up for the duration. They enlisted by regiments, and the top term was three years. This meant—since the hard core of the United States Army was made up of the volunteers who had enlisted in 1861—that as the climactic year of 1864 began the army was on the verge of falling apart. Of 956 volunteer infantry regiments, as 1863 drew to a close 455 were about to go out of existence because their time would very soon be up. Of 158 volunteer batteries, 81 would presently cease to exist.[5]

There was no way on earth by which these veterans could be made to remain in the army if they did not choose to stay.

If they took their discharges and went home—as they were legally and morally entitled to do—the war effort would simply collapse. New recruits were coming in but because Congress in its wisdom had devised the worst possible system for keeping the army up to strength, the war could not be won without the veterans. Enlistments there were, in plenty; and yet—leaving out of consideration the fact that raw recruits could not hope to stand up to the battle-trained old-timers led by Lee and Johnston—they were not doing the army very much good. Heavy cash bounties were offered to men who would enlist; when cities, states, and Federal government offers were added up, a man might get as much as a thousand dollars just for joining the army. This meant that vast numbers of men were enlisting for the money they would get and then were deserting as quickly as possible—which was usually pretty quickly, since the Civil War authorities never really solved the problem of checking desertion—and going off to some other town to enlist all over again under a different name, collecting another bounty, and then deserting again to try the same game in still a third place. The "bounty man" was notorious as a shirker, and the veterans detested him. Grant once estimated that not 12 per cent of the bounty men ever did any useful service at the front.

There was a draft act, to be sure, but it contained a flagrant loophole. A man who was drafted could avoid service (unless and until his number was drawn again) by paying a three-hundred-dollar commutation fee; better yet, he could permanently escape military service by hiring a substitute to go to war for him. Clever entrepreneurs eager to make a quick dollar set themselves up in business as substitute brokers, and any drafted man who could afford the price—which often ran up to a thousand dollars or more—could get a broker to find a substitute for him. The substitutes who were thus provided were, if possible, even more worthless as a class than the bounty men. Cripples, diseased men, outright half-wits, epileptics, fugitives from workhouse and poor farm—all were brought forward by the substitute brokers and presented to the harassed recruiting agents as potential cannon fodder. The brokers made such immense profits that they could usually afford any bribery that might be necessary to get their infirm candidates past the medical examination, and the great bulk of the men they sent into the army were of no use whatever.

Any regiment that contained any substantial percentage of bounty men or substitutes felt itself weakened rather than strengthened by its reinforcements. The 5th New Hampshire —originally one of the stoutest combat units in the Army of the Potomac—got so many of these people that it leaked a steady stream of deserters over to the Confederacy; so many, indeed, that at one time the Rebels opposite this regiment sent over a message asking when they might expect to get the regimental colors, and put up a sign reading: "Headquarters, 5th New Hampshire Volunteers. Recruits wanted." It is recorded that a Federal company commander, finding some of his bounty men actually under fire, sharply ordered the men to take cover: "You cost twelve hundred dollars apiece and I'm damned if I am going to have you throw your lives away—you're too expensive!"[6]

The war could not be won, in other words, unless a substantial percentage of the veterans would consent to re-enlist, and the most searching test the Union cause ever got came early in 1864, when the government—hat in hand, so to speak—went to the veteran regiments and pleaded with the men to join up for another hitch. It offered certain inducements—a four-hundred-dollar bounty (plus whatever sum a man's own city or county might be offering), a thirty-day furlough, the right to call oneself a "veteran volunteer," and a neat chevron that could be worn on the sleeve.

Astoundingly, 136,000 three-year veterans re-enlisted. They were men who had seen the worst of it—men who had eaten bad food, slept in the mud and the rain, made killing marches, and stood up to Rebel fire in battles like Antietam and Stone's River, Chickamauga and Gettysburg—and they had long since lost the fine flush of innocent enthusiasm that had brought them into the army in the first place. They appear to have signed up for a variety of reasons. The furlough was attractive, and an Illinois soldier confessed that the four-hundred-dollar bounty "seemed to be about the right amount for spending money while on furlough." Pride in the regiment was also important; to be able to denominate one's regiment veteran volunteers, instead of plain volunteers, meant a good deal. In many cases the men had just got used to soldiering. A Massachusetts man wrote home, confessing that he had re-enlisted and remarking, "So you see I am sold again," and then went on to explain why he had done it: "There are many things in a soldier's life that I don't like, and we have to put up with privation and hardship that we should get rid of in civil life. But then again there are things in it that I do like, and if it was not for the distinction that is made between a private and a lunk head of an officer I should like it better than I do." A Wisconsin veteran felt that he and his mates had justified their integrity by re-enlisting: "Out of 614 men present for duty in the Regt., 521 have re-enlisted for three years more. This does not seem to indicate that the soldiers are discouraged, does it?"

In the western armies a company that had re-enlisted to the extent of three fourths of its numbers (this was the percentage required if a regiment was to keep its old number and its organizational status) would parade through the camps, fife and drum corps playing and everybody cheering; the example was contagious and led others to sign up. In many cases men seem to have been moved by nothing more complex than the fact that they were adjusted to army life and liked the comradeship which the regiment offered. An Iowa soldier who re-enlisted and then went home on his thirty-day furlough found himself writing after one week back on the farm: "I almost wish myself back in the army; everything seems to be so lonesome here. There is nothing going on that is new."[7]

Whatever their reason, the men did re-enlist, and in numbers adequate to carry on the war. It was noteworthy that re-enlistments were hardest to get in the Army of the Potomac; when Meade added up the results at the end of March he found that he had twenty-six thousand re-enlistments, which meant that at least half of the men whose time was expiring had refused to stay with the army.[8] Nevertheless, even this figure was encouraging. It was insurance; the army would not dissolve just when Grant was starting to use it.

The big drive would begin on May 4; East and West, the armies would move forward then. Along the Rapidan, the

Army of the Potomac waited, tense but hopeful; and in northern Georgia, Sherman's boys got ready for the long march and told one another that this campaign ought to end things. The night before the Westerners moved, the camps were all ablaze with lights. Candles were government issue in those days, and it occurred to the soldiers that since the candles would be of little use in the weeks just ahead they might as well burn them up all at once. So every soldier in camp lit his candle and put it on his tent pole, or wedged it in a bayonet socket and jabbed the bayonet in the ground, or simply held it aloft and waved it; and for miles across the darkened countryside the glimmer and glitter of these little fires twinkled through the spring night, and the men looked at the strange spectacle they were making and set up a cheer that went from end to end of the army.[9]

3. *The Great Decision*

The story of the Civil War is really the story of a great many young men who got into uniform by a process they never quite understood and who hoped, every individual one of them, that they would somehow live through it and get back home to nurse the great memories of old soldiers. The Army of the Potomac was like every other army. It had its own character and its own involved sets of hopes and dreams and memories, and it crossed the Rapidan River on a sunny day in May 1864 believing that this was the last bright morning and that everything that had gone before would presently be redeemed and justified by the victory that was about to be won.

The trouble was that the Army of the Potomac did not quite understand the kind of war that was being fought now. It had had various commanders in its three years of desperate life. There had been men whom it loved, men who embodied the irrational image which each soldier had once had of his own blue-clad person, men like McClellan and Hooker; and there had been men whom it came to despise, such as well-intentioned Burnside and blustering John Pope; also, there was grizzled, honest, uninspired George Meade, whom it had learned to tolerate. All of these commanders had believed that by bravery, good luck, and perseverance the war could be won right here in Virginia and that the storied Confederate capital at Richmond could at last be brought down in flame and smoke as a final, spectacular climax to a war in which valor would get its proper reward. But now there was stolid little U. S. Grant, who chewed on the stub of a cigar and who never quite seemed to have his coat buttoned, and he saw things differently. The war could conceivably be lost here in Virginia, but it could never really be won here.

Richmond was not actually the goal, despite all of the "On to Richmond" slogans. It was necessary to move toward it, to threaten it, to compel the Confederacy to spend its life-blood in defense of it—and if, at last, the city could in fact be taken, that would be well and good; but for the Army of the Potomac the only objective that now had any real meaning was the opposing Army of Northern Virginia. Lean, swift, and deadly, that army had frustrated every Federal offensive that had ever been launched in Virginia. It had been elusive and unpredictable, and it had moved across the war-torn landscape like a whiplash; now it must be pinned down and compelled to fight when and where the northern commander chose, with never a chance for one of those quick, furious strokes of reprisal which, always before, had restored strategic control to Lee. Quite simply, the function of the Army of the Potomac now was to fight, even if it half destroyed itself in the process. If it never lost contact with its enemy, and fought hard as long as that enemy remained in its front, it would do its part and the war finally would end with the United States one nation.

The real area of decision was in the West. The Confederacy had been fragmented already; it was crowded into the area east of the Mississippi and south of the Tennessee highlands, and now the North had the strength—if it used it right—to drive down into the Deep South, cutting the remnant of the southern nation into bits and stamping the independent life out of each severed piece. Sherman had seen it, and when Grant became lieutenant general Sherman wrote him an impassioned plea: "For God's sake and your country's sake, come out of Washington!" He went on in words that showed his own conception of the strategic task that remained to be done:

"Come west; take to yourself the whole Mississippi valley. Let us make it dead-sure, and I tell you the Atlantic and Pacific shores will follow its destiny as sure as the limbs of a tree live or die with the main trunk. . . . Here lies the seat of the coming empire; and from the west when our task is done we will make short work of Charleston and Richmond and the impoverished coast of the Atlantic."[1]

Grant had to stay in the East, but Sherman had seen it. The fight in Virginia would be essentially a holding operation. Lee must be kept so busy that he could not send help to any other part of the Confederacy, and his army must be made to fight so constantly that it could never again seize the initiative, upset Federal strategy, and threaten a new invasion of the North. If this could be done, victory would be won. The difficulty was that it would mean for the Army of the Potomac an unbroken round of hard, bitter fighting—more fighting than it had had in all of its experiences, without a letup or a breathing spell, an eternity of combat in which no one would be allowed to stop to count the cost.

The men of the Army of the Potomac did not understand any of this as the spring campaign got under way. They marched down to the crossings of the Rapidan on a spring day when the May sunlight was bright, and the wild flowers sparkled along the roadside and the dogwood blossoms lit the gloomy forests, and as the long columns moved down to the river the sunlight glinted on musket barrels and bayonets and trundling brass cannon, and the movement of armed men looked like a vast pageant of immeasurable significance. On the plain above the river the long lines were ranked in brigade and division front, mounted officers gesturing with their swords; and one after another these long polished lines wheeled and broke into marching columns, and the unbroken stream of men in blue swept on down to the pontoon bridges and the fords, flags flying, bands making music, everyone full of hope and the tingling feeling that perhaps the final act had commenced.[2]

Beyond the river there was a vast stretch of dark, almost roadless second-growth timber, known locally as the Wilderness. Somewhere off beyond this forest was the Army of Northern Virginia, and the immediate task of the Army of the Potomac was to get through the forest, reach the open country beyond it, and engage the Confederates in a stand-up fight. The Wilderness itself was no place for a battle. Even the best of its roads were no better than enclosed lanes; its long stretches of forest were full of spiky little saplings and heavy underbrush, there were few clearings, and the whole country was crisscrossed with meaningless little streams that created unexpected ravines or dark fragments of bogland.

Yet it was precisely in the middle of the Wilderness that the great battle began. Lee had no intention of waiting for his enemies to get out in the open country to make their fight. He was outnumbered and outgunned, but here in the almost trackless forest these handicaps would not matter so much; and on the morning of May 5 he drove straight ahead, to find the Federals as quickly as he could and to attack them as soon as he found them. The left wing of his army collided with the right center of the Army of the Potomac a little after daybreak, and after a brief moment of skirmish-line firing the battle got under way.

Grant reacted with vigor. If the Confederates were here in the Wilderness, here he would fight them; orders for the advance were countermanded, and the great ungainly mass of the Federal army turned slowly about and went groping forward through the woodland twilight, men scrambling through almost impenetrable underbrush as they struggled to get out of marching columns into fighting lines. The Confederates were advancing along two parallel roads, the roads three or four miles apart, no place on either road visible from any spot on the other; two separate battles began as the Federals swarmed in to meet them—began, grew moment by moment, and boiled over at last into one enormous fight, with the harsh fog of powder smoke trapped under the trees and seeping out as if all the woodland were an immense boiling cauldron.

Artillery was of little use here; the guns could not be moved through the wood, and if they were moved they had no field of fire. Infantry lines broke into company and platoon units as they moved, sometimes reassembling when the undergrowth thinned, sometimes remaining broken and going forward without cohesion. Men came under heavy fire before they saw their enemies—in most places no one could see one hundred yards in any direction, and as the battle smoke thickened, visibility grew less and less. Often enough there was nothing but the sound of firing to tell men where the battle lines were, and as more and more brigades were thrown into action this sound became appalling in its weight, seeming to come from all directions at once.

It was one fight, and yet it was many separate fights, all carried on almost independently, the co-ordination that existed being little more than the instinctive responses of veteran fighting men. Opportunity and dire peril went hand in hand for each commander, and often enough they went unnoticed because almost nothing about this strange battle could actually be seen by anybody. At one stage the two halves of Lee's army were separated, a wide gap between them, and the Army of Northern Virginia might have been destroyed if a strong Federal force could have gone through the gap. But the gap went undiscovered, and when its existence was sensed a Federal division that was sent up to take advantage of it lost its way in the dense forest, swung half around without intending to, and exposed its flank to waiting Confederates, who broke it and drove it off in retreat. On the Union left, the first Federal elements engaged were driven back, and for a time it was the Union army that was in danger of being cut in half; Hancock's II Corps, which had had the advance, was still off to the south somewhere, hurrying up a narrow lane to get into the fight, and the Confederates had a brief chance to come through the opening before Hancock's men could arrive. But reinforcements came up to hold them off, Hancock got his men on the scene in time, and the Confederates were driven back, outnumbered and all but disorganized.

The woods took fire, helpless wounded men were burned to death, and wood smoke mingled with the smoke from the rifles to create a choking, blinding gloom. Night came at last, and the wild tempo of battle became slower; yet some of the men who fought in the Wilderness felt that the fighting never actually stopped all night long, and there were nervous outbursts of firing at intervals all up and down the lines. Off to the rear, such batteries as had been able to get into position sent shells over at random all through the night, and there was a constant shuffling movement of troops as brigade and division commanders tried desperately to pull their fighting lines together.

The battle flamed up in full strength as soon as daylight came. Hancock, on the Union left, held a strong advantage. Not all of Lee's army was up: Longstreet's corps, back at last from its long tour of duty in Tennessee, was hurrying in from the west, but it had not arrived in time to get into the first day's firing, and A. P. Hill's corps, which held that part of the Confederate line, had been fearfully cut up and was badly outnumbered. Hancock sent his men in at dawn, the Confederates gave ground, and before long the Federal assaulting column had reached the edge of one the Wilderness's rare clearings, a run-down farm owned by a widow named Tapp. Here was Lee himself, with a good part of the Confederate wagon train visible not far to the rear; if this clearing could be seized and held, Lee's right would be broken once and for all and his army would be well on the way to destruction. The Federals paused to straighten their lines and then went pounding in, flags in front, everybody cheering at the top of his voice.

Final victory was not ten minutes away, and the surging blue lines came in toward the guns . . . and then ran into a shattering countercharge. The head of Longstreet's corps had come on the scene at the last crucial moment, and its tough Texas brigade—the Grenadier Guard of the Confederacy, as one historian has called it—struck like a trip hammer. Lee himself was riding in with the men, swinging his hat, his usual calm broken for once by the hot excitement of battle; he would have led the countercharge if the Texans had not compelled him to go to the rear, out of harm's way.[9] The massed Confederate artillery blazed away at point-blank range, the Federal assault came to a standstill and then broke up in a tangle of disorganized fugitives, and the victory that had seemed so near dissolved and vanished while the pitch of battle rose to a new crescendo.

Then, abruptly, the pendulum swung the other way, and

before long it was the Army of the Potomac that was in trouble, with disaster looking as imminent as triumph had looked just before.

Ordered troop movements were almost impossible in the Wilderness, but somehow Longstreet managed one. The left flank of Hancock's corps was "in the air," after the repulse of the attack on the Tapp farm clearing; the Confederates saw it, and Longstreet swung a part of his corps around and came in from the south with a crushing flank attack . . . and suddenly Hancock's line went to pieces, masses of Union troops were going back to the rear, and the Confederates had seized what might be a decisive advantage.

But Hancock was just about as good a man for moments of crisis as Pap Thomas. A north-and-south road crossed the road along which the Confederates were advancing, a mile or so to the Union rear, and along this road Hancock had his men prepare a stout log breastwork. He rallied them here, prepared a solid new battle line, and when the Confederate drive reached the point, it was stopped and then driven back. The woods were on fire all along the front here, Longstreet's men were almost as disorganized by their victory as the Federals had been by their defeat, Longstreet himself was badly wounded—shot by his own men, in the blind confusion, just as Stonewall Jackson had been shot at nearby Chancellorsville a year earlier—and the crisis was met and passed. By the end of the day Union and Confederate armies on this part of the field were about where they had been in the morning, except that many thousands of men on each side had been shot.

One more blow the Confederates swung before the battle ended. The extreme right of the Army of the Potomac, operating in dense woods where no regimental commander could see all of his own men, had an exposed flank. Lee found it, and at dusk the Federal right flank was driven in just as the left flank had been driven during the morning. But John Sedgwick, who was still another imperturbable Union corps commander cut to the Thomas pattern, was in charge here; and as the Rebel drive lost its impetus in the smoky darkness he brought up reserves, stabilized a new line, and got the flank securely anchored. And at last the noise died down, the firing stopped, the smoke drifted off in the night, and the two exhausted armies settled down to get what sleep they could, while the cries of wounded men in the smoldering forest (flames creeping up through the matted dead leaves and dried underbrush) made a steady, despairing murmur in the dark.

. . . The fearful story of war is mostly the story of ordinary men who are called upon to suffer and endure and die to no purpose that they can easily discover; and generally the story of a great battle is no more than the story of how some thousands of these men acquit themselves. But once in a great while the terrible drama of war narrows to a very small focus: to a place in the heart and mind of one man who has been burdened with the great responsibility of making a decision and who at last, alone with himself in a darkened tent, must speak the word that will determine how history is to go.

It was this way in the Wilderness after the two days of battle were over. Here were the two armies, lying crosswise in a burned-out forest, death all around them, the scent and feel of death in the soiled air. They had done all they could, nobody had won or lost anything that amounted to very much, and the men who had to carry the muskets would go on doing whatever they were told even if they were destroyed doing it. But someone at the top must finally say what was going to happen next, and as the night of May 6 settled down this someone was U. S. Grant.

Technically, his army (Meade's army, actually, but from now on to the end people would think of it as Grant's) had been whipped quite as badly as Hooker's army had been whipped at Chancellorsville, almost on the same ground, one year earlier. It had had horrifying losses—seventeen thousand men or thereabouts shot or blown loose from their commands —its flanks had been beaten in, it had completely failed to drive Lee away from his chosen ground, and in 1863, Hooker, no more roughly handled, had gone back north of the Rapidan to recruit and refit and to let Lee decide where the next fight would take place. Now it was up to Grant, and the crucial decision of all the war was his to make.

Grant thought it over, taking counsel of nobody, throughout

the day of May 7. The armies stayed in each other's presence, there was picket-line firing all day long, and although things were easy compared with what happened on the two days before nothing seemed to be settled; as far as the men in the ranks were concerned, the battle was still going on. Finally night came in once more, and after dark the divisions of the Army of the Potomac were pulled out of line and put on the road for another march. And when they moved, they all moved—*south.*

In other words, the battle of the Wilderness was no defeat, simply because Grant refused to admit that it was a defeat. He would keep moving on, which was the great point he had laid down in his offhand sketch of the secret of strategy, and he would move in the direction that made continued fighting inevitable.

The army headed that night for Spotsylvania Court House, ten miles off to the southeast; a country town, like Gettysburg in that its importance derived from the fact that all the roads met there. If Grant could get his men on these road crossings before Lee's men got there, then he would be between the Army of Northern Virginia and Richmond, and Lee would have to do the attacking—which, under the circumstances, could hardly mean anything but defeat for Lee's army. The move failed by a very narrow margin. Lee's advance guards got to Spotsylvania a few rods ahead of the advance guard of the Army of the Potomac, and what began as an affair of skirmishers around a country market town blew up quickly into an enormous fight that seemed to have no beginning, no end, and no visible result.

For the fight that started at Spotsylvania lasted for ten uninterrupted days, and it was even worse than the Wilderness fight had been. It was like the Wilderness in a way, in that so much of the ground was heavily wooded and the troops had to fight blindly, nobody from commanding general down to private ever being quite sure just where everybody was and what was going on. As the fight developed, Grant's army kept on edging around to the left, trying vainly to get around the Confederate flank and interpose between the battlefield and the Confederate capital. It never quite made it, but in the ten days the two armies swung completely around three quarters of a circle, and on May 12 they had what may have been the most vicious fight of the whole war —a headlong contest for a horseshoe-shaped arc of Confederate trench guarding the principal road crossing, with hand-to-hand fighting that lasted from dawn to dusk, in a pelting rain, over a stretch of breastworks known forever after as the Bloody Angle. Here men fought with bayonets and clubbed muskets, dead and wounded men were trodden out of sight in the sticky mud, batteries would come floundering up into close-range action and then fall silent because gun crews had been killed; and after a day of it the Union army gained a square mile of useless ground, thousands upon thousands of men had been killed, and the end of the war seemed no nearer than it had been before.

Yet all of this made no difference. In all the welter of promiscuous killing, one thing had passed unnoticed; the great counterattack in the Wilderness, in which Lee had driven in the Yankee flank and had almost (but not quite) taken control of the battle for himself, was the last great counterblow the Army of Northern Virginia would ever make. The Confederate army was resisting destruction, it could not be driven out of the road, it was killing Yankees at a horrifying rate, but it had lost its old capacity to seize the initiative and turn sullen defensive into brilliant offensive. It was being crowded now, it was being made to fight all day and every day, and this was a war that was bound to go against it. It was not losing, but it was not winning either, and if the Confederacy was to live the Army of Northern Virginia had to win.

Side-slipping constantly, the two armies moved in a wide semicircle: out of the Wilderness and down to Spotsylvania, out of Spotsylvania at last and down to the North Anna, past that to the Pamunkey, over the Pamunkey and finally, as May drew to an end, close to the Chickahominy—down to the ground where McClellan and Lee had fought two years earlier, down to the swampy, pine-studded flatlands where Fitz-John Porter had held his ground through two days of flaming battle, down to the area where the church bells of Richmond could be heard (whenever the guns were quiet, which was not often) and where the Confederates had no room to maneuver. Remorselessly and at immense cost Grant was pinning his enemies down to the place where they could do nothing more than fight a wearing, dogged, and ultimately fatal defense of their capital city.

As June began the two armies faced each other not far north of the Chickahominy, and once more a casual road crossing became a place of vast importance; a sun-baked spot on the featureless plain, Cold Harbor, where a second-rate tavern sat by a dusty crossroads; and here Grant massed his troops and made one final attempt to break the Confederate line and pulverize Lee's army once and for all.

The attempt failed, and the price was high. On June 1, and then on June 3—after a day in which beaten-out armies tried to catch their breath in murderous heat—the Union army came in with old-fashioned frontal assaults on strong Confederate entrenchments. They had no luck. On June 1 they gained insignificant patches of ground; on June 3 they tried again, lost several thousand men in half an hour of unimaginable fighting, and then settled down to trench warfare, with every mile of line spurting flame and death every hour of the twenty-four, the loathsome odor of unburied bodies always in the air, sharpshooters and cunningly posted batteries forever alert to shoot whenever they saw movement. The Union cause apparently was no nearer victory than it had been before the campaign began.

Never had armies fought like this. For a solid month they had not been out of contact. Every day, somewhere along the lines, there had been action. During this month Union losses had averaged two thousand men every single day. Old formations had been wrecked. Generals had been killed—most notable of these John Sedgwick, slain by a sharpshooter in the fighting at Spotsylvania Court House—and no soldier had bathed, changed his clothing, or had an unbroken night's sleep for more than four agonizing weeks. Yet morale, somehow, did not slacken; the men took what they had to take with the matter-of-fact air of old soldiers, and a New Englander in the VI Corps, noting one day that there was continuous firing going on a little way to the right, wrote casually: "I suppose it's skirmishing, as they don't call anything a battle now without the whole army is engaged and a loss of some eight or ten thousands." He added that it was hard to see what would happen to the men if this routine went on much longer—"but this army has been through so much that I don't know as you can kill them off."[4]

Elsewhere in Virginia things had gone badly. When the Army of the Potomac crossed the Rapidan, Ben Butler had started to move up the James River from the Norfolk area with an army of thirty thousand men; his way had been fairly open, and a competent soldier might well have gone on, cut the railroads below Richmond, and made victory certain. But Butler, a man of many parts, was in no part a soldier. He let himself be deceived and then defeated by a scratch Confederate army, and while the Army of the Potomac was slugging its weary way down toward Cold Harbor he and his own army managed to get locked up on a peninsula in the James River, thirty miles below Richmond, known as Bermuda Hundred—theoretically a standing menace to Confederate communications, actually as much out of the war as if they had been transported bodily to South America.

It was the same in the Shenandoah Valley. Franz Sigel had been appointed to lead an army up the Shenandoah Valley, destroying the traditional Confederate granary and avenue of attack and curling in on Richmond, finally, from the west. He had been routed and had been removed from his command, and David Hunter, who took his place, had done very little better—had in fact run into disastrous defeat, at last, near Charlottesville and had in panic had fled off into the West Virginia mountains, leaving the Confederacy in better shape as far as the Shenandoah Valley was concerned than it had been in for two years; and neither Butler nor the Sigel-Hunter move had done the Army of the Potomac the slightest bit of good.

Yet it did not matter. The Army of the Potomac had reached and held its objective—continuous contact with Lee's army, which could no longer make the daring thrusts that in the past had always upset Federal strategy. From now on to the end of the war Lee's role would be defensive. The Army of the Potomac was half destroyed, with its brigades led by colonels, its regiments by captains, and its companies, often enough, by sergeants; but it was carrying out its appointed assignment. Somewhere far ahead there would be victory, even if most of the men who had made it possible would not be around to see it.

4. *A Question of Time*

Shortly after the spring campaign began, Robert E. Lee remarked that Grant's army must on no account be allowed to reach the James River. If that happened, he said, the Army of Northern Virginia would be compelled to withstand a siege, "and then it will be a mere question of time."[1] In six weeks of bitter fighting he had managed to stave off that fate; yet he was now so close to the Richmond fortifications that he could have put his army into them by no more than one short march, and in the middle of June, Grant made a swift, decisive move whose final effect was to force upon Lee the siege warfare that Lee had so greatly dreaded.

The rival armies stayed in the trenches around Cold Harbor for the better part of two weeks, and they were not weeks that any soldier afterward recalled with pleasure. All along the front the two armies were in intimate contact—each one entrenched up to the ears, dug in so that no conceivable frontal attack could ever accomplish anything. There was firing every hour, from dawn to darkness, and at night the pickets were alert to detect any movement, which invariably would call forth a burst of musketry and cannon fire. An unspeakable stench lay over the battlefield, the weather was excessively hot, soldiers were caked with dirt and plagued by vermin and by thirst, and sharpshooters on both sides were ready to drill any luckless soldier who incautiously raised his head above the parapet, even for a moment.

To all appearances, it was deadlock. The Army of the Potomac could no longer sidle to its left, which was what it had been doing all the way down from the Rapidan; its left touched the Chickahominy now, and one more side-slip would do nothing better than put it up against the Richmond trenches, which Grant was no more anxious to encounter than Lee was to occupy. It could not move by its right, for that would take it too far away from its tidewater base and expose its supply line to rupture by Confederate cavalry.

Confederate cavalry, to be sure, was not having things its own way now, as it had had in 1862 when McClellan was on this ground. Phil Sheridan was swinging the Yankee cavalry around like a scythe; had raided far in Lee's rear during the Spotsylvania fight, forcing Jeb Stuart to make a hell-for-leather ride after him, fighting a bitter battle in the very suburbs of Richmond, and—sponging one more of the bright romantic streaks off of the board of this war—killing Stuart himself in the process. Nevertheless, the Army of the Potomac was deep in enemy country, and for its own security it had to keep its line short, which meant that it could not move far from one or another of the rivers where Federal gunboats and supply steamers could anchor.

But there was still a move Grant could make. If he could get his army out of its trenches without tipping his hand, he could leave the Cold Harbor sector entirely, march southeast down to the James River, get over to the southern shore (provided his engineers could throw a pontoon bridge over a deep stream nearly half a mile wide), and drive on for the little city of Petersburg, which lay on the south bank of the Appomattox River, some ten miles from the place where the Appomattox flows into the James. Petersburg was a place the Confederacy had to hold if it meant to hold Richmond; for of the railroads that came up from the Carolinas and brought the supplies which the capital and its defenders had to have, all but one came up through Petersburg. In effect, the North could win Richmond by winning Petersburg. A blow at Petersburg was a blow Lee would have to parry no matter what it might cost him.

The move was handled with skill. Despite the closeness of enemy pickets, Grant got his men out of the trenches without arousing Confederate attention, put them on the roads in the night, moved down and crossed the Chickahominy, and tramped on toward the bank of the James. Lee was a hard man to fool, but it appears that for a day or two this move deceived him; the Army of the Potomac had vanished, and although it had obviously moved off somewhere to the south-east it was well screened behind a cordon of cavalry and infantry and there was no way to tell where it might appear next. It was quite possible that it would wheel and come back up on the north side of the James, and Lee held his army in position to counter such a move. Meanwhile Meade's engineers laid a 2100-foot pontoon bridge over the James—completing the job in eight hours, cutting a long approach road on the northern bank, and performing a prodigy of labor—and the Army of the Potomac began to cross and to march for Petersburg, picking up some of Butler's men from Bermuda Hundred as they went.

Petersburg should have fallen on June 15, for the better part of two army corps reached the place then and found it defended by the merest handful of Confederates under Beauregard—who was aware of his danger and was sending to Lee and to the Rebel War Department desperate appeals for aid. But the attack was muffed. Commander of the Union advance was the same General Baldy Smith who had done so well in the matter of opening a supply line at beleaguered Chattanooga in the preceding autumn. He had won Grant's good opinion then, but today he lost what he had won, and lost as well a dazzling chance to cut the artery that fed the Confederate capital. He seized trenches and guns, won a position from which one determined drive would inevitably have put him into Petersburg—and then grew cautious, concluded that he ought to wait for reinforcements, and let the opportunity slip away.

The next three days repeated the same story. Beauregard began to get reinforcements, but the Army of the Potomac was coming up faster, and on each day Beauregard had ample reason to believe that he was about to be driven away in total defeat. Yet the opportunity was never quite grasped. Union attacks were poorly co-ordinated and driven home without vigor—one reason may have been that the army as a whole was simply exhausted from the work of the past six weeks—and in the end Lee managed to get the Army of Northern Virginia down just in time to make the place secure. By June 20, Grant had called off further attacks and was settling down to make a siege of it.[2]

In the technical sense it was not really a siege, for Petersburg was by no means surrounded. Two railroads to the south were still open, and the roads between Petersburg and Richmond were not cut. The Army of the Potomac was dug in with a rambling arc of trenches and fieldworks that confronted Petersburg only from the east; north of the Appomattox there were other works that ran across the neck of Bermuda Hundred, and above the James, close to Richmond, Federal and Confederate patrols confronted each other, and all along this lengthy line there were intermittent firing and constant sniping while the two armies labored mightily to make their defenses strong.

But although Grant had not done all that he had hoped to do he had finally done one thing Lee was extremely anxious to prevent; he had compelled the Army of Northern Virginia to occupy a fixed position—had put it into a spot from which it could not withdraw and in which the greater resources of the North could be consistently applied with a steadily rising pressure. Freedom of movement was very largely gone now, as far as Lee was concerned, and without it he was condemned to the kind of warfare the Confederacy could hardly hope to win. Lee was pinned; Grant's problem now was to keep him pinned and build up the pressure.

Some freedom, to be sure, was left, and Lee would use it to the very best of his ability, which was great. Union defeats in the Shenandoah Valley had left that area open for Confederate use, and by scraping up detachments from here and there and sending away a part of his own forces Lee made up a small army (twelve or fifteen thousand men, or thereabouts) which began to move down the valley for one more try at upsetting Yankee strategy. The army was led by Jubal Early, who was no Stonewall Jackson but who was a canny soldier and a tough customer to boot, and at the beginning of July, Early started north to see how much trouble he could create.

As it turned out, he could create quite a lot. He got across the Potomac, knocked a pick-up Federal army out of the way on the banks of the Monocacy River, and then went straight for Washington, arriving just north of the city on July 11 and creating in the city a general hullabaloo such as had not been seen since the ironclad *Merrimac* had thrown Secretary Stanton into a panic in the spring of 1862. Government clerks, non-combat soldiers in the quartermaster corps, and convalescents from the hospitals were hastily called out, welded into something resembling a combat outfit along with a handful of state militia, and sent out to hold the fortifications that lay in Early's path. The fortifications were very strong, but this scratch force was very weak, and it is just possible that Early could have plowed on through it and gone into Washington if he had moved fast. He could not have stayed there very long, to be sure, but the amount of harm he could have done to the Union cause just by occupying the town for a few hours is something to brood over.

Grant had seen the move as an attempt by Lee to make him ease the pressure on Petersburg, and he refused to rise to it. At the last minute, however, he realized that his own action in pulling the heavy artillery regiments out of the Washington fortifications had left the city almost defenseless, and he rushed the VI Army Corps up from the Army of the Potomac. It got to Washington just in time to drive Early off.

The VI Corps was probably the best combat unit in the army just then, and it was led by Horatio G. Wright, an unemotional, solid sort of fighting man, who was equal to the emergency. Wright got his men into the trenches north of Washington just as Early was preparing to assault. There was a brisk, somewhat indecisive little battle there—witnessed by Abraham Lincoln in person, who came out to Fort Stevens, in the center of things, and stood on the parapet to watch, almost giving General Wright apoplexy: a stray bullet might easily have killed him—and at last Early drew off, marched west through Maryland, and went back into the Shenandoah Valley. The whole venture had accomplished nothing very much except that it had thrown a prodigious scare into the Federal government and had reminded U. S. Grant that the attempt to take Lee's army out of action would never succeed until the Shenandoah Valley had been made secure. Grant began casting about for ways to do something about this situation.

The valley was important for two reasons. It came up beyond the Blue Ridge, and all through the war it had offered the Confederates a handy approach for invasion of the North; it ran from southwest to northeast, so that a Confederate army that used it moved directly toward the heart of the North, while a Union army that followed it would go off at an angle, away from Richmond and the sensitive areas of the Confederacy. In addition, it was a highly fertile and productive garden spot whose meat, corn, and wheat helped supply Lee's army and the people around Richmond and also served to support any southern army that chose to operate toward the Potomac. Before Lee could be taken out of the war the valley itself would have to be taken out.

Early in August, Grant picked the man for the job—wiry little Sheridan, who had begun his Civil War career as a quartermaster captain in the West, had become a cavalry colonel and then a brigadier and later divisional commander in the infantry, and who was now making the cavalry corps of the Army of the Potomac a fighting unit of considerable prowess. Sheridan was a driver. An echo of his quality comes down from a diary entry made by a private soldier in his command in the fall of 1862, when Sheridan's infantry was moving up the Mississippi to help repel Bragg's invasion of Kentucky. One of the troopships ran aground and seemed unable to get loose. Up came the steamer bearing Sheridan. As the soldier noted: "Rounding to within easy swearing range, he opened a volley of oaths on Captain Dickey [the troop commander aboard] and the captain of the boat which annihilated both of them and caused speedy repairs to be made."[3] Sheridan was the hurry-hurry sort, with a knack for getting up into the front line when a fight was going on, and as the son of an Irish immigrant he seems to have had a good deal of personal feeling against high-born southern aristocrats. If anybody could clean out the Shenandoah Valley, he could.

Meanwhile there was the situation at Petersburg itself. Grant had more men than Lee had—his losses during May and June had been huge, but he was getting reinforcements, and while the quality of the new troops was by no means up to the quality of the men who had been killed he still maintained the advantage—and he was holding his army in its trenches, constantly trying to extend his lines to his left. If he could reach out far enough he could eventually cut the all-important railroad lines, and once that happened Lee would have to come out of his lines and fight. The Army of the Potomac was no longer what it had been earlier in the spring, but for the matter of that neither was the Army of Northern Virginia; an all-out fight on open ground, away from the deadly fortifications, could hardly end in anything but a northern victory.

Grant's problem was far from simple. If he held Lee where he was, the North should finally win—provided Sherman did what was expected of him in the West, provided everything else went right, and provided finally that sheer war-weariness did not induce the people of the North to consent to a separation and peace. (This last was becoming a serious problem, not in the least helped by the terrible list of killed and wounded that had been coming out of the Army of the Potomac since Grant took charge.) But if there was any way to strike one hard blow that would destroy Lee's army and end things quickly, that way had to be tried. Late in July it appeared that such a way might be at hand.

This came about because in the IX Army Corps there was a regiment made up largely of coal miners—48th Pennsylvania, recruited mostly in and around Schuylkill County, a veteran regiment that had served with distinction in Tennessee during the previous year. This regiment had a section of trench opposite a Confederate strong point, and it occurred to the former coal miners that they, if permitted, could easily dig a tunnel under the open space between the lines, hollow out a cavity under the Confederate trench, and explode enough blasting powder there to crack a big hole in the Confederate lines. Their corps commander was Ambrose E. Burnside—this bumbling, bewhiskered man had had many ups and downs, and after occupying Knoxville he had been brought back this spring to the Army of the Potomac—and when the idea was presented to him Burnside liked it. Meade, to whom Burnside went with it, had very little confidence in it, and the army engineers derided it and held that it was wildly impractical; but the army was not actually doing anything in those days except hold its lines and exchange tons of metal every day with the Confederates, and it was agreed at last that these Pennsylvanians might as well be digging a tunnel as sitting on the fire step ducking enemy explosives. So the orders went out, the miners dug their tunnel —it was upward of five hundred feet in length, much longer than anything military sappers had ever thought practical before—and by the end of the month eight tons of powder had been put in the end of it, a long fuse had been laid, and it was time to touch it off.

Grant and Meade had not been enthusiastic about the project, but they concluded that if it was to be done at all some real weight ought to be put behind it, and so elaborate plans for a break-through were made. A feint was ordered on the far side of Bermuda Hundred to draw Confederate reserves out of Petersburg; Burnside was told to attack with his entire corps; another corps was alerted to be ready to go in beside him, heavy masses of artillery were put in line to bombard the Confederate position as soon as the mine was sprung—and just at dawn on July 30, after an agonizing delay during which a daring soldier had to crawl into the tunnel to splice a defective fuse, the thing blew up with a shattering crash that opened a 150-foot crater where the Rebel strong point had been and gave the Federal army a clear shot at Petersburg.

Trench warfare had all but made offensive movement impossible. The weapons of the Civil War era were muzzle-loaders, primitive enough by modern standards, but they were rifles and they were highly effective at tolerably extensive ranges, and men properly protected by fieldworks were almost completely invulnerable. But the explosion of the mine had suddenly restored open warfare. For several hundred yards the Confederate defenses had in effect ceased to exist. All that Burnside's men had to do now was drive on through the opening and they would cut Lee's army in half.

The opportunity was completely lost. The mine itself could not have worked better, but the arrangements for exploiting it could not have worked worse. Federal defensive works had not been leveled so that the assault wave could make a real charge; the first regiments that advanced came through in dribbles and then discovered that they totally lacked leadership. Burnside was far to the rear, looking on from an artillery emplacement; the division commander who should have been directing things was in a dugout getting drunk as fast as a jug of commissary whiskey would enable him to do. Instead of marching on through to the naked Confederate rear, the Federals huddled aimlessly in the crater, helping half-buried Confederates to dig themselves out, picking up souvenirs, and waiting for orders. Reinforcements came up, and they also got into the crater, until this great hole in the ground was packed full of blue-clad soldiers. Minutes passed, half an hour, an hour—and the Confederate high command had the time it needed to piece a new line together in the rear. When the assault finally began to move it ran up against the same old, fatal obstacle—well-manned fieldworks that could not be carried by direct assault.

Of all the missed chances of the war, this one probably was the most tragic and the most inexcusable. Grant commented bitterly after the affair had finally ground its way to complete futility that he had never before seen and never expected again to see such a wide-open opportunity to carry an entrenched position. To underline the pathetic story of mismanagement, when the attack had finally bogged down and it should have been obvious that there was no point in carrying it any farther, Burnside sent in a division of colored troops to leap-frog over the earlier waves and break the Confederate line. The Confederates were waiting now, and the colored division was butchered. (It had originally been slated to lead the entire charge, and the men's morale had been high. Grant had canceled these arrangements, arguing that the offensive was a chancy affair at best and that if it failed people would say the army had put the colored troops in front because it was willing to sacrifice them. But they had been sacrificed anyway, not when they had a chance to win, but after defeat had become certain, and the morale of the survivors dropped to zero.)[4]

By midday the attack had been given up. New lines were formed, the Union army glumly counted several thousand casualties (and, it may be, took comfort from the fact that it had gained an acre or so of wholly worthless ground), and the war went on as before. There remained, as tokens of what had been tried, nothing but a prodigious hole in the ground—

it is still there, an item to be looked at when folk tour the Petersburg battlefields—and the record of a solemn court of inquiry, which looked at the dreary record of mistakes and oversights and expressed certain conclusions, as a result of which Burnside was finally removed from his command.

And it began to look to many folk in the North that the Confederacy perhaps could never really be beaten, that the attempt to win might after all be too heavy a load to carry, and that perhaps it was time to agree to a peace without victory. This sentiment would affect the presidential election, which was only a few months away. Conceivably—even probably, as things looked in midsummer—it could bring about the election of a President who would consent to a division of the country if he could get peace in no other way. It was not long after the battle of the Crater that Abraham Lincoln wrote out a despairing yet defiant little document, which he signed, sealed, and put away for later use:

"This morning, as for some days past, it seems exceedingly probable that this administration will not be re-elected. Then it will be my duty to so cooperate with the President-elect, as to save the Union between the election and the inauguration; as he will have secured his election on such ground that he cannot possibly save it afterward."[5]

It might come to that, and it might not. Victory was only a question of time, but time moved now with unendurable slowness, each moment bought by a new record of men killed and maimed, a new scar of loss and suffering laid on a people who had already endured much. The people themselves would finally decide, and they would decide by showing whether their endurance went all the way to the foundations of the American dream.

12.

We Will Not Cease

1. *That Bright Particular Star*

SHORTLY AFTER the Army of the Potomac crossed the Rapidan and plunged into the Wilderness, ninety thousand young men led by William Tecumseh Sherman abandoned their camps in the neighborhood of Chattanooga and started to walk in the general direction of Atlanta, one hundred miles to the southeast. As they began to move, the last act of the war was opened.

Most of the ninety thousand were veterans, and most of them came from the western states. It was noticed that they averaged a little larger than the Easterners—army quartermasters had found that when they ordered shoes for these men they had to specify larger sizes than were ordered for the Army of the Potomac'—and they were loose-jointed, supple, rangy, tramping off the miles with a long, swinging stride as if they were used to long marches. They had walked across Kentucky and Tennessee and Mississippi, and some of them had gone far out in Missouri and Arkansas as well; they had been burned a deep mahogany color by three years of southern sunlight, and they were men without inhibitions or reverence. If an officer or courier rode by and the men felt that his horse was skinny and underfed, whole regiments would begin to caw lustily, until it appeared that a convention of derisive crows was in session. Frank Blair—the same who had, as a civilian, exercised so much extra-legal power in Missouri back in the war's youth—was a major general commanding the XVII Army Corps now, and he drove his men hard in forced marches to overtake the rest of the army;

415

and when he came in sight his troops began to cry "Bla-a-a-i-r! Bla-a-a-i-r!" like a herd of indignant sheep, the bleating call running from one end of the column to the other. Passing a country cemetery, Illinois soldiers saw one of their number who had collapsed, from heat and weariness, amid the gravestones; they gave him a casual look and agreed that he was in luck to have had his sunstroke so handy to a convenient burying ground.[2]

Quiet little Joe Johnston, with his winsome smile, his courtly air, and his ability to lash out with a deadly counter-attack against any people who looked like enemies, was waiting for these rowdy marchers with both barrels loaded. His army—it contained probably something like sixty thousand tested fighting men—had been in camp around the town of Dalton, Georgia, which was on the upper end of the railroad line that went from Chattanooga down to Atlanta, and between his army and Sherman's there was a range of high hills known as Rocky Face Ridge, crossed by a highway that came through a gap with the unappetizing name of Buzzard's Roost. At Buzzard's Roost, Johnston had his men dug in, and if the Yankees came this way there would be feathers in the air.

Sherman sent Thomas and Schofield and their men—roughly two thirds of his entire force—up to the slopes, and there was a deal of skirmishing and sparring for a day or so while the Westerners tapped the Confederate defenses to see if they were as strong as they looked. Sherman himself had no taste for butting his army's head against field fortifications; he wrote that this Buzzard's Roost place was a "terrible door of death" and he sent curly-bearded McPherson and the Army of the Tennessee off to the right in a swift, wide flanking movement. McPherson got his men, after a day or so, far beyond Johnston's flank and came through Snake Creek Gap toward the town of Resaca, ten miles to the south of Dalton; it was on the railroad, and if McPherson could seize it Johnston's men could be driven off into the mountainous country to the east and annihilated at leisure.

McPherson could not quite make it. A cordon of Confederate troops held Resaca, McPherson felt there were too many of them to push out of the way easily, and although

Sherman, when he learned that his advance guard had reached the edge of the town, hammered the table and exulted, "I've got Joe Johnston dead!" things did not work out as he had planned. McPherson's men were delayed, Johnston got the rest of his army down there on the double, and after a couple of days of fighting, the flanking advance was resumed.[3]

Sherman was not duplicating Grant's program in Virginia. Grant was driving in to fight wherever and whenever a fight could be had; Sherman wanted to maneuver rather than to fight, and when Johnston developed an uncanny ability to block the road with fieldworks Sherman refused to assault them and cast about instead for ways to go around them. In the Army of the Tennessee he had the perfect instrument. It had been his own army; men said that for at least two years it had never had either a brigade or divisional drill, and its soldiers had seen enough of war to place a high value on the art of self-preservation. The men refused to let the wagons carry their spades; they insisted on lugging these tools themselves, and when they came in contact with the enemy their first impulse was to dig trenches in which they could escape enemy bullets. They could size up Confederate defensive works at a glance, and if the works looked too strong they simply did not believe in attacking them—unless they could use their spades and burrow their way forward in security. But they could march, and when a long hike would save their necks they would willingly hike until their legs were ready to fall off.[4] So Sherman used them as his flankers. When he found Johnston's army in his front—as he invariably did: Johnston had a sixth sense for determining where the Yankees were going to show up next—Sherman would put Thomas's tough veterans in line and open a hot skirmish-line fire and send McPherson's boys off on a wide swing around the Confederate flank.

Every day the armies were in contact. Every day there were firing and casualties and the wearing labor of digging trenches and rifle pits under the hot southern sun. But every day, too, Sherman would be trying to get around his enemy and reach some place where the Confederates could be caught off balance and compelled to fight in the open, and the Army of the Tennessee marched many miles and lashed out constantly toward the Confederate rear, avoiding head-on attacks like those of the Wilderness and Spotsylvania Court House.

Johnston side-stepped and retreated to meet these threats, and the two armies went down through northern Georgia in a series of movements that were almost formalized, like some highly intricate and deadly dance. Johnston could never quite make a permanent stand, Sherman could never quite force a decision, and slowly but steadily the tide of war went on south toward Atlanta, while both governments began to worry. It seemed in Washington that Sherman was not really getting anywhere; Johnston was too elusive, every move Sherman made was countered by a skillful southern move, and although Sherman's men were getting farther and farther into Georgia they did not seem to be able to win any real victories. In Richmond, on the other hand, there began to be complaints that Johnston could manage a retreat with the utmost skill but that he could not really fight. In Virginia, Lee was killing Union soldiers by wholesale; in Georgia, Johnston was never making a real stand-up fight, and he was getting backed up closer and closer to Atlanta, which the Confederacy could not afford to lose.

The Union soldiers themselves had mixed feelings. In early June an officer in the Army of the Tennessee wrote that he never saw soldiers in better spirits; they trusted Sherman implicitly, and "if we get to Atlanta in a week, all right; if it takes two months you won't hear this army grumbling." Yet the marches were hard, men were too busy to do much foraging—and as a result had to live on hardtack and bacon, so that some of them began to come down with scurvy and the rear areas were full of "black-mouthed, loose-toothed fellows" hankering for fresh food and a little rest.[5] For three weeks there were heavy rains and the roads turned into quagmires; in open country men and vehicles left the highway and plodded through the wet fields, so that after they had passed it was impossible to tell where the road itself had been—everything was plowed up, trodden down, and turned into a general all-inclusive slough.

The armies moved south through places like Adairsville

and Cassville and Allatoona, where Sherman again swung wide in a flanking maneuver and had a hard three-day fight at a country hamlet known as New Hope Church. Then Johnston pulled back to a prepared position on Kenesaw Mountain, and Sherman seems to have got wind of the fact that his men were complaining that there was too much marching going on. He decided, after an extended stalemate, that this time they would make a frontal assault.

The assault was made on June 27, with picked divisions driving up the mountainside toward an open plateau and a little peach orchard, and it was a flat failure. Secure in deep trenches, with head logs running along the parapet and defending infantry snug behind impenetrable defenses, the Confederates blew the assault column all to bits, inflicting a loss of three thousand and suffering hardly any loss themselves; and Pap Thomas, whose men had paid for most of this venture, looked the situation over and remarked to Sherman that "one or two more such assaults would use up this army."

Sherman himself had something to say about this, as it happened. He seems to have felt that Thomas, with his care to save the lives of his men, was being a little too cautious. To Grant, just at this time, he wrote a complaint: "My chief worry is with the Army of the Cumberland, which is dreadfully slow. A fresh furrow in a plowed field will stop the whole column, and all begin to entrench."* But if this feeling existed, he would bow to it. There was no way to get over Kenesaw Mountain—not with all of these armed Southerners waiting there in snug rifle pits with loaded rifles in their hands—and after a few days Sherman began the old flanking maneuvers all over again, swinging out in a wide arc, driving his troops in on Johnston's flank and rear, and ultimately—without another real battle—forcing his antagonist to leave his impregnable lines and come down in the open country to go on with the dance. Nothing at all had been gained at Kenesaw Mountain, except that the Episcopal bishop who served the Confederacy as an army corps commander, General Leonidas Polk, was killed by a cannon ball during the fighting in that area; but by July 9 Joe Johnston had been forced to pull his men back across the Chattahoochee River and put them in the trenches around Atlanta itself.

This did not sit well in Richmond. Jefferson Davis was a man under unendurable pressure. He had to save a country that was dissolving under his eyes, he could not take the long view because the government he headed was dying of steady constriction, and he felt—as he was bound to feel —that his General Johnston should have been able to keep Sherman's army away from the gates of Atlanta. By telegraph he asked Johnston what he proposed to do next. Johnston not only disliked Davis personally; he distrusted him as well— early in the war, when he was commanding Confederate troops in Virginia, little General Joe had expounded his plans to the President and Cabinet and had seen a faithful résumé of them in the Richmond newspapers next day. Now he answered with icy reserve, saying in substance that he would fight Sherman whenever he saw a chance to do so with advantage.

Mr. Davis had had enough. He had nine more months— no more than that, although the future was hidden from him —in which he could exercise the functions of President of a free nation, and while this time lasted he would live up to his role. He sent Johnston a curt message, telling him that since he had not been able to stop Sherman, and since he expressed no especial confidence that he could ever stop him, he was removed from command of his army, which would now go under the control of General John B. Hood.

Johnston replied with equal acidity. He remarked that after all General Sherman had not come any closer to At- lanta during the spring campaign than Grant had come to Richmond—the distances covered, as he pointed out, were just about equal—and he added a final kicker that did him no good but served to discharge a little venom: "Confident language by a military commander is not usually regarded as evidence of competency."

This was true enough, but it did not help. On July 17 Johnston went into retirement, and the General Hood who had fought so hard on so many fields, getting a crippled arm at Gettysburg and an amputated leg at Chickamauga, took his place; and Sherman's officers learned of the change and believed that it might work to their advantage.

Sherman talked to General Schofield, who commanded the Army of the Ohio. Schofield had been a fellow cadet of Hood at West Point, and he remembered the Confederate commander as a man whose intellectual gifts were limited. Schofield recalled that Hood came near flunking out of the Academy because of his difficulty in mathematics; Schofield had coached him, and once, in despair, Hood had blurted out: "Which would you rather be, an officer of the army or a farmer in Kentucky?"—implying unmistakably that he himself would prefer to be a farmer. Schofield managed to get Hood through his difficult mathematics class, and he thought of it now and remarked ruefully that he "came very near thinking once or twice that perhaps I had made a mistake."

At any rate, Schofield gave Sherman warning. Hood was not too smart, but he was combative as anyone who ever lived: "He'll hit you like hell, now, before you know it." It was reported in the Federal army that a Kentucky colonel, hearing of the change in Confederate command, went to Sherman and told him of an old-army poker game he had once witnessed. "I seed Hood bet twenty-five hundred dollars with nary a pair in his hand." However the news came to him, Sherman had fair warning that if he had had trouble in compelling Joe Johnston to meet him in knock-down combat he would have no such trouble with Hood.[7]

This was demonstrated before he was very much older. He got his troops across the Chattahoochee, sent them straight in at Atlanta, and immediately ran into the furious pugnacity of General Hood.

Thomas had the direct approach, and he got his Army of the Cumberland across Peachtree Creek, no more than five miles from the center of Atlanta, while McPherson was taking his Army of the Tennessee off to the east on another of those wide flanking movements, planning to come in on the Confederate stronghold from the vicinity of Decatur. While Thomas was crossing the creek and McPherson was moving east, on July 20, Hood struck, and struck hard.

He had not picked the best man to strike. Thomas was as

good a defensive fighter as America ever produced, and although the attack caught him at a disadvantage he refused to let the fact bother him. He had sent his leading corps across the creek and had it in position on a hill overlooking Atlanta, when Hood's men came out and opened a smashing assault, coming around both ends of the advanced line and getting in behind it. But Thomas led two batteries over the creek, prodding the horses to a gallop with the point of his sword—he was not being "Old Slow Trot" today—and his guns broke the Confederate assault waves and drove them back, other troops came up, and at the end of the day Hood's first massive counterstroke had definitely been a failure. Thomas remarked once that he believed he could whip the Confederates here in front of Atlanta with his own Army of the Cumberland alone, without help from McPherson or Schofield. This battle of Peachtree Creek seems to have confirmed him in this belief.[8]

But Hood had unlimited energy. If he could not blast Pap Thomas off the ground above Peachtree Creek he would try something else; and as Sherman drew his net in around Atlanta, Hood saw an opening and struck again, with concentrated fury.

While Thomas was crossing Peachtree Creek, McPherson had taken his Army of the Tennessee off to the east. He occupied the town of Decatur, five miles east of Atlanta, and then he moved toward the city; and as he moved—somewhat incautiously, perhaps, in the belief that Thomas was giving the Confederates all they could handle—he exposed his southern flank, and Hood hit him there on July 22, slashing vigorously with his shock troops, striking a blow that might crumple the whole Union left and compel the invaders to draw back north of the Chattahoochee.

McPherson was one of the attractive men in the Union army. He was young and brilliant; had been an honor man at West Point, was loved by Sherman as that grim soldier might have loved a gifted younger brother, and he wore a trim curly beard and had dancing lights of laughter in the corners of his eyes. He was thought to be somewhat Puritanical—he had said once that if to be a soldier a man had to forget the claims of humanity, "then I do not want to be a soldier"—yet he was full of life and bounce, and in captured Vicksburg he and brother officers had strolled through the streets in the evening, serenading southern belles with sentimental vocalizing after the camps were still. . . . What had they sung? "Juanita," perhaps?

> *Far o'er the mountain*
> *Breaks the day too soon. . . .*

It does not matter much. McPherson was engaged to Miss Emily Hoffman of Baltimore, and he had planned to take leave in the winter of 1864 and go north and marry her. But the winter became very busy, and after Grant was summoned east and there were promotions all along the line Sherman had called McPherson in and had told him he could not have leave just now; McPherson was an army commander, the army had to be made ready for hard fighting, and his leave would have to wait until fall, or until next winter, or until some other time. McPherson had acquiesced, and he was still a bachelor; and now, late in July, he was bringing his army in on Atlanta from the east while Thomas's men buried the dead in front of Peachtree Creek, and Hood caught his formations off guard and was threatening to inflict a ruinous defeat.

McPherson was at lunch when the news reached him. He got his horse and galloped off to the scene of action, and along the way advancing Confederate skirmishers had found a gap in the Union lines and were pushing through for the rear. McPherson ran into some of them, wheeled to retreat, and was shot dead from the saddle; and farther on his leading division repulsed a frontal attack just in time to turn around and meet an attack that was coming in from the rear. General John A. Logan succeeded to McPherson's command and rode down the fighting lines, his felt hat clutched in one hand, his black hair and mustachios streaming in the wind, crying out to his men: "Will you hold this line for me? Will you hold this line?" The men liked Logan, and as they plied ramrods in hot musket barrels they began to chant his nickname—"Black Jack! Black Jack!" They held the line, beating off assaults that seemed to come bewilderingly from all directions;

and as the hot day wore away, the Army of the Tennessee at last managed to hold its position, Hood's counterblow was broken, and by evening the Union army was safe again.[9]

Grim General Sherman wept unashamedly when McPherson's body was brought to headquarters. After the battle he wrote to Emily Hoffman in Baltimore, the girl who by now would have been Mrs. McPherson if Sherman had not intervened; a girl from a strongly southern family which had not approved of her engagement to this Union general. When the telegram that announced McPherson's death came the girl heard a member of her family say: "I have the most wonderful news—McPherson is dead." Emily Hoffman went to her bedroom and did not come out of it for a solid year, living there with curtains drawn, trays of food brought to her door three times every day, speaking no word to anyone. To her, Sherman poured out his heart in a long letter:

"I yield to no one on earth but yourself the right to exceed me in lamentations for our dead hero. Rather the bride of McPherson dead than the wife of the richest merchant of Baltimore. . . . I see him now, so handsome, so smiling, on his fine black horse, booted and spurred, with his easy seat, the impersonation of the gallant knight."

Lamenting thus, Sherman thought of the fire-eaters who had helped bring on the war, and he lashed out at them: "The loss of a thousand men such as Davis and Yancey and Toombs and Floyd and Beechers and Greeleys and Lovejoys, would not atone for that of McPherson." Then, looking darkly into the mist of war that still lay ahead of him, this uncontrollable fighter tried to put a personal grief into words:

"Though the cannon booms now, and the angry rattle of musketry tells me that I also will likely pay the same penalty, yet while life lasts I will delight in the memory of that bright particular star which has gone before to prepare the way for us more hardened sinners who must struggle to the end."[10]

The bright particular star was gone forever, and something that could never be regained went out of the war when McPherson died, just as had happened with the deaths of thousands of other young men who might have swung a golden light across the dark infinite sky; and meanwhile there was Hood's army in Atlanta, still defiant and still dangerous, and the war could not stop because something irreplaceable had been lost, even though many women had to retreat to darkened rooms to live in the muted dusk of grief. The war had to be won and a good part of it was up to Sherman, and he had to get on with the job.

He had not managed this battle too well, as a matter of fact. While the Army of the Tennessee had to take the pounding, Sherman had let Thomas's and Schofield's men remain out of action. They might have been sent in with an offensive that would have taken Atlanta then and there, for Hood was holding the lines in their front with one corps while he massed everything else against McPherson. A brilliant strategist, Sherman was not always a complete master of battlefield tactics.

But there was no time to waste in mourning lost opportunities. With this battle out of the way Sherman resumed his attempt to outflank the defenders; and he had the Army of the Tennessee, still bearing the grime of battle, set out on another of its long marches, pulling it behind the rest of the army in a wide arc so that instead of facing Atlanta from the east it was, a few days later, approaching the town from the west. Hood shifted strength to meet it, detected an opening once more, and on July 28 came out with another savage attack at Ezra Church, west of Atlanta. Again the Army of the Tennessee beat off the attack, and when it ended, Hood's army was very nearly fought out. It had struck three times to drive the Yankees away from Atlanta, and each blow had failed. After Ezra Church a Yankee picket called out to a weary Confederate: "How many of you are left, Johnny?" The Confederate's reply was brief and eloquent: "Oh, about enough for another killing."[11]

Sherman shifted his command arrangements just before Ezra Church. He refused to retain Logan as commander of the Army of the Tennessee; there was a coolness between Logan and Thomas, and cordial co-operation between the two seemed unlikely. McPherson's old job went to Oliver Otis Howard, a prim sobersides of a New Englander who seemed excessively pious and strait-laced for this army of free-thinking Westerners but who, for some inexplicable reason, was doing a much better job with them than he had been able to do when he led troops in the more sedate Army of the Potomac. Howard had lost his right arm fighting under McClellan at Fair Oaks in front of Richmond; he never drank and never swore, and on Sundays he liked to visit hospitals and distribute religious tracts and baskets of fruit. He was never brilliant but he was reliable, and Sherman—his exact opposite, in most respects—had come to trust him.

Now Sherman settled down to put Atlanta under siege. He brought guns up and kept the town and its defenses under heavy bombardment, he refused to assault the strong Confederate trenches and he kept shifting his troops farther and farther around toward his right, trying to cut the railroads that linked Atlanta with the rest of the South so that he might capture both the city and the Confederate army that defended it.

And the month of August slowly wore away, while Sherman played what looked like a waiting game and people in the North began to feel that neither his army nor Grant's would ever win a clear-cut, decisive victory that would bring peace nearer.

2. Wind across the Sky

The people of the North were about to decide whether they would carry the load any longer. They would decide by means of a presidential election, which would finally be interpreted either as a decision for war to a finish or as a vote to give up and let things slide. In midsummer it looked very much as if the Lincoln administration would be beaten.

The war had gone on for more than three years. It had touched every family circle in America. Every isolated farm, every peaceful village, and every great city knew perfectly well what names like Stone's River and Chickamauga and Cold Harbor meant; and by now many folk were wondering if the terrible price they were paying was really going to buy what they wanted. The Confederates still held Richmond, Atlanta, and the heart of the South. Lee's army was secure and defiant behind the Petersburg trenches. Hood's army hung on in Atlanta. Early's men continued to hold the

Shenandoah Valley; and although the United States flag waved within eyesight of the two great citadels, the North had spent very close to one hundred thousand casualties to put it there, and nothing to speak of had come of it all. If people were beginning to question whether all of this was worth going on with any longer, it is not especially surprising.

Yet there was still the old dream: one nation, running from ocean to ocean, a land in which ideals that had never amounted to much elsewhere could finally be made real; a country whose inner meaning would finally be freedom and unity for everyone. In all human history no people had ever served a greater dream, and it was not to be given up easily. So there was a balancing of costs and possible gains all across the North this summer; and for their reading matter people had fearful lists of men killed and maimed, and stories about hard battles and endless marches, and subtle hints that perhaps it all could be ended if the government would just stop being so stiff-necked . . . and, here and there, bright patches in a dark fabric, things like Abraham Lincoln's letter to a Mrs. Bixby, who had lost two or three or five sons in battle action: ". . . the solemn pride that must be yours to have laid so costly a sacrifice on the altar of freedom."

The Republicans had renominated Abraham Lincoln, largely because they could not help themselves. More and more, control of the party was passing into the hands of bitter men who hated and wanted to destroy. To them it seemed that the President was not tough enough. He had moved slowly on the matter of emancipation, he was openly trying now to arrange things so that the states lately in a condition of secession could quietly be restored to the Union, and he had grave doubts about the status of the Negro once slavery had died. Like everyone else, these men could see an almost insoluble problem arising after the war, and—like some of the leaders in the South—the only answer they could see was the brutal one of extermination;[1] yet where certain Southerners assumed that it was the colored race that must be exterminated, these men believed that it was the Southerner himself. Let the terrible pounding of the war (they argued) continue until everything that had supported slavery and secession had been ground down to dust; the wreckage might provide a suitable foundation for the building of a new society.

They were busy this summer trying to shelve Lincoln. Such men as Roscoe Conkling, Speaker of the House of Representatives, Horace Greeley, erratic editor of the New York *Tribune*, and David Dudley Field and Henry Winter Davis were meeting quietly and were arranging for an extraordinary convention in Cincinnati late in September to concentrate Union strength "on some candidate who commands the confidence of the country, even by a new nomination if necessary."[2]

Meanwhile there were the northern Democrats. They were looking more and more like a peace party, even if the price of peace might be acceptance of a division in the nation. The Vallandigham who had been exiled from Ohio and sent south had crept back into the country by way of Canada, and when the Democratic convention met in Chicago late in August his voice seemed to be dominant. The delegates met (in an atmosphere rendered slightly murky by the presence of numerous ineffective but busy Confederate agents) and nailed this plank into the party's platform: "This convention does explicitly declare, as the sense of the American people, that after four years of failure to restore the Union by the experiment of war . . . justice, humanity, liberty and the public welfare demand that immediate efforts be made for a cessation of hostilities, with a view to an immedate convention of the states, or other peaceable means, to the end that at the earliest practicable moment peace may be restored on the basis of the federal union of the states."[3]

If an armistice and a general convention could restore the Union, that might be all to the good; as a practical matter, the war, once dropped, could never be picked up again, and everybody knew it. This plank supported Lincoln's contention that the Democratic nominee, if elected, would have won the election on grounds that would make victory impossible. The bitter-end Republicans were not in the least surprised when the Democratic convention which had adopted this declaration went on from there to nominate as its candidate none other than the one-time hero of the Army of the Potomac, General George B. McClellan. Had he not always been a soft-war man?

By the end of August, then, that was the situation. Fighting men on both sides appraised it in the same way. Someone sounded Grant out on the matter of Lincoln's possible replacement, and Grant exploded angrily: "I consider it as important to the cause that he should be elected as that the army should be successful in the field." On the Confederate side, valiant General Stephen D. Ramseur of North Carolina wrote to his wife that men just back from the North were saying that McClellan would be elected and that the election would bring peace, "provided always that we continue to hold our own against the Yankee armies."[4]

If they could hold their own . . . continued stalemate could actually mean victory for the Confederacy. It believed itself to be unconquerable, and men could argue that in this dreadful summer it was proving itself so. Hang on, keep the Yankees from making any visible gains, let war-weariness carry the election—and that will be the end of it. So ran the southern hope; so, also, ran the genuine possibility.

The great struggles of history are not always visible and dramatic. They can take place out of sight, in the hearts and the minds of millions of men who have a choice to make. It went thus in 1864. The final word about the Civil War would be spoken by the people back home, most of whom had never seen a battlefield, carried a musket, or known what it was like to watch pain and death take form in the red-gray mist of smoke and flame. Out of what they felt, the choice would come.

The wheel had swung full circle. In 1861, war had come because emotion took charge when hard decisions were to be made. Emotion would take charge again this year; emotion, springing from no one could say what involved thoughts and deep griefs and hopes, given final form perhaps by the news from the battle fronts. In one way or another the men of the North would decide whether they wanted to go on to the finish or give up and write off all that they had suffered and all that they had once hoped for. Their verdict would be final. Lincoln knew it, and the little slip of paper he had filed away in a pigeonhole shows what he feared the decision might be like: shows, too, that if the decision was unfavorable to everything he had lived for he would get around it if he possibly could. There have been few bitter-end fighters in all history quite as tenacious as Abraham Lincoln.

Then, at the moment when despair was deepest, a great wind swept across the sky and drove the clouds off in shreds, and it was possible to see the sunlight once more. To begin with, there was Admiral Farragut and Mobile Bay.

The venerable admiral, who would not consider himself old until he found himself unable to turn a handspring on his birthday, had assembled a powerful fleet at the mouth of Mobile Bay, and early in August he struck with it. Mobile was important, the Confederacy's last port for blockade-runners on the Gulf coast (except for ports in Texas, which, having been cut off, hardly counted any more). Grant had wanted to take Mobile right after Vicksburg fell, but Halleck had ruled otherwise. Now Farragut would try it. The town itself he might not get, but if he could run past the harbor forts and anchor his fleet inside the bay, the port would be closed, and one more Confederate gateway to the outer world would be sealed off—those gateways to the outer world, whose help must come in if the Confederacy was to live.

August 5, and a hot sunny morning; Farragut's wooden sloops of war came steaming in toward the mouth of the bay, topmasts and upper yards sent down, everything cleared for action. The ships were in double file, with the monitors going on ahead; the sun came down hard on the flat iron decks of these latter, making the heat below almost unendurable. Along the channel the Confederates had planted mines—"torpedoes," as the word was used in those days—and on the east side of the channel was powerful Fort Morgan, a masonry work of great strength which Farragut could not hope to pound into submission; his best chance was to run past it, as he had run past the New Orleans forts. Then the fort would be isolated, and the army could bring in troops and siege guns and reduce it at leisure.

Inside the bay the Confederates had a small fleet. Except for one vessel, the ironclad *Tennessee*, this was made up of light gunboats that could never stand up to Farragut's ships at close range, but the exception might make all the difference.

The *Tennessee* had been built on the Alabama River, near Selma, after the *Merrimac* pattern—low in the water, with a slant-sided citadel armored with five- and six-inch iron plating, heavily armed, with a ram bow. She was clumsy and her steering mechanism was exposed, but at that moment she may have been the most formidable warship afloat. With her consorts she waited in the lee of Fort Morgan while the Federal fleet came in through the windless morning, black plumes of smoke trailing off on the smooth water.

At the start there was trouble. The torpedoes were a menace, and when the fort and the Confederate ships opened fire the Union fleet fell into confusion. Monitor *Tecumseh*, at the head of the line, put her forefoot on one of the torpedoes and blew up, going to the bottom like a stone and carrying her captain and most of her crew down with her. Ships behind her sheered off, slowed down, and stopped. Farragut, in the flagship *Hartford*, was astern of them; he scampered up the rigging to a point just below the main top, peering ahead into the smoke while an anxious junior passed the bight of a line around him to keep him from falling into the water. For the fleet to stay here, huddled under the fire of the fort's big guns, was to invite complete destruction. Angrily Farragut demanded to know the reason for the delay.

Torpedoes ahead, he was told: *Tecumseh* is gone already, and if we go on we will lose more ships.

Farragut exploded: Damn the torpedoes! Full speed ahead! The line began to move again; firing mechanisms in the torpedoes proved defective—*Hartford* brushed against one, but it failed to explode—and the fleet exchanged enormous broadsides with the fort while it plowed on into the bay. The fight was hot and heavy while it lasted, and *Hartford* took a brutal pounding. An army signal officer who was stationed aboard her recalled afterward that he had read, in stories about sea fights, tales about decks running with blood and had thought it all imagination; he really saw it this morning.

The fleet passed the fort at last and got well inside the bay. The Confederate ships drew off briefly, and Farragut had his ships anchor and repair damages. Then *Tennessee* came steaming in to the attack, and the fight was renewed—a whole fleet coming to grips with one grim black ironclad. One of the wooden sloops rammed *Tennessee*, hurting the Confederate not at all but wrecking her own bow; another tried to ram, missed, and crashed into *Hartford*, almost sinking the flagship, and again Farragut sprang into the rigging for a better view of what was going on. The guns of the fleet could not penetrate *Tennessee's* mailed sides, but they kept hammering, surrounding her and penning her in; a monitor held position just astern of the big ironclad and slammed away with fifteen-inch solid shot; *Tennessee* lost her stacks, her steering failed, she was helpless, her gun ports could not be opened—and finally, with the other Confederate ships sunk, the fort by-passed, and no hope remaining, she pulled down her flag.

Farragut's victory was complete. His men had paid for it—one hundred and forty-five killed and one hundred and seventy-four wounded—and some of his ships were badly wracked, but he had Mobile Bay. Mobile was no longer a seaport, Fort Morgan would fall whenever an effort was made, and here, suddenly, was encouraging news for war-weary people in the North.[5]

It was followed a few weeks later by even better news. Sherman captured Atlanta.

Sherman had been extending his lines around to the east and south of the city, trying to cut its railway connections, and at the beginning of September he finally succeeded. He hoped to bag Hood's army as well—after all, this army was really his primary objective—but the Hood who could not quite tell when to go in and slug and when to spar and play for time was canny enough to keep his army from being involved in the loss of the citadel, and when he saw that Atlanta could not be saved he got his army out intact. In a sense he kept Sherman from getting the prize he wanted. But in the end it did not matter.

It did not matter because the news that Atlanta had fallen was a mighty intoxicant for the people back home. Mobile Bay, then Atlanta—the war was being won, after all, the stalemate was being broken, and certain victory lay not far away. Even sedate General Thomas lost his control when news of the triumph came to him; he skipped, combed his whiskers with eager fingers, and, as Sherman reported, did everything but actually caper.

Washington got the news on the night of September 2 in a wire from General Henry W. Slocum. Slocum commanded the troops Hooker had had earlier—Hooker disliked Sherman, and when command of McPherson's army went to Howard he resigned in a huff—and Slocum messaged Stanton: "General Sherman has taken Atlanta." A day or so later Sherman sent his own message, beginning: "So Atlanta is ours, and fairly won." Wild rejoicing went all across the North, and Grant ordered his batteries in front of Petersburg to fire a hundred-gun salute, with all guns shotted and trained on the Rebel works.

This was not the end of it. Before the end of September Phil Sheridan won a smashing victory over Jubal Early in the Shenandoah Valley.

Sheridan had been slow getting into action. He had a strong advantage in numbers, but guerrilla warfare in the valley had been carried to such a pitch of perfection that he had to use a good many of his men to guard trains and supply lines, and he seems to have overestimated Early's strength. In addition, he was not altogether sure of the quality of all his troops. He had the VI Corps from the Army of the Potomac—as good a combat outfit as there was in either army—but the rest of his men did not seem quite so solid, and he had taken his time about launching an offensive. But on September 19 he was ready, and he came down and crushed Early in a hard, sharp battle near Winchester.

The battle began badly. Somehow Sheridan's marching orders got fouled up and his troops came to the field slowly. The first attack was knocked back on its heels, and around midday it looked as if the Confederates might win an unexpected victory. But Sheridan was all over the field in person, riding at a pelting gallop on his big black horse, his hat gripped in one fist and his starred battle flag in the other; he reorganized his lines, brought up his reinforcements, and at last drove home an irresistible charge, a whole division of mounted cavalry shearing in behind the

Confederate flank, every man in action—and Early's army went hurrying south through Winchester, and for the first time in the war the North had won a victory in the Shenandoah.

The victory would have consequences. Sheridan would go on, devastating the rich valley farmland with cold, methodical effectiveness, so that it never again could serve as a base of supplies for Confederate armies. Early would counterattack a month later at Cedar Creek, catching Sheridan's army off guard (with Sheridan himself absent) and coming close to driving it north in rout. But Sheridan made a dramatic twenty-mile ride to the scene from Winchester, rallied his stragglers, pulled the lost battle out of the fire, and closed the day by giving the Confederate army such a furious beating that it no longer had any weight as a dangerous combat force.

The war was being won, and the election would be won, too, because it was obviously absurd now to campaign on a plank stating that the war effort was a failure. And to cap it all, McClellan himself pulled the main prop out from under the Democratic platform by the simple process of refusing to accept it.

McClellan had had his troubles and he undeniably had his faults, but now and then he could measure up. He had done so after Second Bull Run, when he pulled the Army of the Potomac together and prepared it for Antietam. He did it now, when—quietly and with dignity—he gave the lie to the bitter-end Republicans who had considered him little better than a traitor, and showed that although he might not swallow the Republican version of the war program he was as determined as anyone to insist on a restored Union and an end to the Confederacy.

The Democratic committee went to McClellan to give him formal notification that he had been nominated. McClellan responded, as a candidate always does, but he did not quite make the response he had been expected to make. Blandly he remarked that as far as he was concerned the party's platform meant that the North was not to offer peace on any terms short of a reconstructed Union. To take anything less, he added, would be to insult and affront the thousands of northern soldiers who had died in battle. The Democrats might look like a peace party, but their candidate had his own ideas.

As the upswing developed, the move to find a new candidate in place of Lincoln withered. Pathfinder Frémont had been brought out, dusted off, and put in position as a species of third-party candidate, to bid for the votes of rock-ribbed abolitionists. He quietly retired, the Republican radicals dutifully lining up behind President Lincoln. Salmon P. Chase, the dignified Treasury Secretary who had always imagined himself as the statesman destined to come in and supply the firm hand Lincoln lacked—Chase, too, was in retirement, no longer a member of the Cabinet, an aspirant for the presidency whom no one could ever take quite seriously. Lincoln had a clear road at last.

In the West and the South, Thomas and Sherman prepared their armies for the mopping-up process; and in the long lines that ran down the James River and half encircled Petersburg, the Army of the Potomac held its ground, pinning Lee's army there by sheer weight, taking daily casualties and looking less and less like the gallant host that had marched down to the Rapidan in May with bands playing and flags afloat, but still holding on with an unbreakable grip. Autumn was wearing away, and the Confederacy's last winter was drawing near.

3. The Grapes of Wrath

On November 8 the people of the North re-elected Abraham Lincoln and endorsed a war to the finish. One week later General Sherman and sixty thousand veterans left Atlanta on the march that was to make that finish certain—the wild, cruel, rollicking march from Atlanta to the sea.

Two months had passed since the capture of Atlanta. A part of this time had been spent in resting and refitting the army. Several weeks more had been consumed in a fruitless chase of John B. Hood, who still commanded forty thousand good men and who circled off to the northwest, molesting Sherman's supply line and hoping to draw the invaders off in retreat. Sherman had tried to catch and destroy this Confederate army, but he had not had much luck, and he complained bitterly, if illogically, that the real trouble was Hood's eccentricity: "I cannot guess his movements as I could those of Johnston, who was a sensible man and did only sensible things."

In mid-October Sherman gave up the pursuit entirely and made his plans for the next campaign. Back to Tennessee went Thomas and Schofield, with something fewer than half of the men who had occupied Atlanta. They would see to it that Hood's Confederates did nothing to upset the military balance; with the rest of his men Sherman would drive for the seacoast.

He had an extended argument over the telegraph wires with Grant on this point. Grant suspected that it would be wise to dispose of Hood before going off on a new campaign; he doubted that Thomas would have quite enough force to protect everything if Hood should march up into mid-Tennessee, and he felt that the navy ought to seize and prepare some seaport city as a base before Sherman moved east. But Sherman convinced him at last that his own plan was sound. He had written off Hood entirely—"Damn him, if he will go to the Ohio River, I will give him rations," he growled at one point—and he was convinced that nothing would bring the war to a close so speedily as a visible demonstration that a large Union army could go anywhere it chose to go in the Confederacy.[1]

Jefferson Davis had recently visited Georgia, rousing the people with valiant speeches in which he predicted that Sherman would be overwhelmed in the Southland as Napoleon had been overwhelmed in Russia. To Grant, Sherman wrote contemptuously:

"If we can march a well-appointed army right through his territory, it is a demonstration to the world, foreign and domestic, that we have a power which Davis cannot resist. This may not be war but rather statesmanship."[2]

Grant's consent was won at last. Thomas moved his Cumberlands back to Tennessee—the men tended to be a little sullen, feeling that they would have to do any fighting that remained while the men with Sherman would have all of the fun—and the Army of the Tennessee went to work to ruin Atlanta before beginning the march to the coast.

Atlanta was pretty tattered already. The repeated bombardments during the siege had destroyed many houses, and when Sherman occupied the place about half of its normal population of thirteen thousand had fled. Sherman ordered the rest of the civilians out of town and managed to deport some sixteen hundred of them; to Halleck he wrote that "if the people raise a howl against my barbarity and cruelty, I will answer that war is war and not popularity-seeking." During the long Federal occupancy of the town the deserted buildings got rough treatment from the soldiers, who never had any qualms about destroying dwellings that were not currently inhabited. And finally, when it was time to leave, Sherman ordered complete destruction of all factories, railroad installations, and other buildings that might be of any use to the Confederacy.

The soldiers went to their work with zest. By now they understood industrial warfare, they could equate wholesale destruction with a blow at the enemy's war potential, and anyway it was fun to wreck everything. Troops who marched through Atlanta while the destruction was going on wrote of "flames illuminating the whole heavens . . . the pandemonium caused by the flames, the yells of the soldiery, the explosion of shells and ammunition." As the men moved out of town it would happen that groups would break ranks and go back to set fires on their own account; one man in such a group wrote that they were moved by a "desire to destroy everything, and fearful that some old rebel's property would be saved." Other men wrote that going through Atlanta "the smoke almost blinded us," and they concluded that "everything of importance" was on fire.[3]

Sherman had ordered that no fires be lit except when he himself was present; he wanted the destruction confined strictly to warehouses, factories, and the like. But flames from these buildings spread to others, wandering bands of carefree privates lit fires on their own hook, and an Illinois veteran who had a part in these forays said afterward that "several general officers were there, but they stood back and said nothing, allowing the soldiers to pursue their course."[4] The firing went on all night long, with the band of a Massachusetts regiment playing gaily in an open square. Later, soldiers under Sherman's orders worked to check the flames.

Smoke filled the sky like a gigantic ominous signal as Sherman's army pulled clear of the city and started for the sea. The army was moving in four columns, widely spread out—XV and XVII Corps, under Howard, on the right; and XIV and XX, under Slocum, on the left. Orders were that there should be an average pace of fifteen miles a day. Transportation was cut to a minimum, and there was no supply line. The army would feed itself with what it found in Georgia along the way.

And so began the strangest, most fateful campaign of the entire war, like nothing that happened before or afterward. These Federals were not moving out to find and destroy an armed enemy; the only foe that could give them a fight, Hood's army, was hundreds of miles off to the rear, and everybody knew it. They were not being asked to hurry; fifteen miles a day was much less than these long-legged marchers could easily make, and everybody knew that too. Their mission was to wreck an economy and to destroy a faith—the economy that supported the thin fading fabric of the Confederacy, the faith that believed the Confederacy to be an enduring creation and trusted in its power to protect and avenge. As they moved down the red roads of Georgia, cutting a swath sixty miles wide from flank to flank, they were the conscious agents of this destruction; men who trampled out the terrible vintage of the grapes of wrath, led by an implacable general who was more and more coming to see a monstrous but logical destiny in his mission.

To Emily Hoffman in Baltimore, Sherman had written (in the days when strong young General McPherson still lived) words that partly expressed his feelings: "We of the North have rights in the South, in its rivers and vacant land, the right to come and go when we please, and these rights as a brave people we cannot and will not surrender." He had made it much more explicit in a long letter to Halleck: "I would banish all minor questions and assert the broad doctrine that as a nation the United States has the right, and also the physical power to penetrate to every part of the national domain, and that we will do it; that we will do it in our own time and in our own way; that it makes no difference whether it be in one year or two, or ten or twenty; that we will remove and destroy every obstacle—if need be, take every life, every acre of land, every particle of property, everything that to us seems proper; that we will not cease until the end is attained. That all who do not aid are enemies, and we will not account to them for our acts."[5]

Sherman's language was often a great deal rougher than his actions, and neither on this nor any other campaign was he out to "take every life." But he was undoubtedly moving consciously as an avenging agent, and his soldiers saw themselves in the same role; they were supposed to wreck all railroad lines and any factories or depots or other industrial installations, and in addition the army had to do a great deal of foraging if it was going to survive—and altogether here was the recipe for wholesale destruction.

Every morning each brigade would send out a detail of foragers—from twenty to fifty men, led by an officer and followed by a wagon to bring back what was seized—and this detail, whose members knew the route the army was following, was not expected to return to camp until evening. The foragers were ordered to stay out of inhabited dwellings and to seize no more food than was actually needed, but they were under the loosest sort of control and in any case they were joined, followed, and aided by a steadily growing riffraff of armed stragglers, who were known contemptuously as "bummers" and who knew very little restraint of any kind. Between the regular foraging parties and the lawless bummers, plantations that lay in this army's path were bound to have a very rough time.

There were some large and imposing plantations in the territory the army was crossing; Georgia was fat and fertile, the barns and smokehouses were crammed, and the men felt that they were in a land of surpassing richness. Earlier, on the way from Chattanooga down to Atlanta, they had felt that Georgia was a pretty poor state and remarked that they never saw any residences to compare with the regular farm buildings north of the Ohio. But the army had not gone two days on its move east from Atlanta before an Illinois soldier was writing that he "could begin to see where the 'rich planters' come in," and he added: "This is probably the most gigantic pleasure excursion ever planned. It already beats everything I ever saw soldiering and promises to prove much richer yet."

The whole Army of the Tennessee was making the same discovery, and it was responding with joyous whoops; and as it moved, the great march to the sea began to resemble nothing so much as one gigantic midwestern Halloween saturnalia, a whole month deep and two hundred and fifty miles long. A captain looked back on it all as "a kind of half-forgotten dream, now gay and lightsome, now troubled and gruesome." He recalled that there was "no fighting worthy of the name" and said that he and his mates "occupied ourselves chiefly in marching from one fertile valley to another, removing the substance of the land." Typical was one veteran's comment: "Our men are clear discouraged with foraging; they can't carry half the hogs and potatoes they find right along the road." In spite of the strict orders that no man not assigned to one of the regular foraging parties should leave the ranks to take any civilian property, it was admitted that "there is scarcely a one that does not forage from morning to night if he gets a chance," and the army reveled in elaborate menus—"we live on sweet potatoes, turnips, flour, meal, beef, pork, mutton, chickens and anything else found on the plantations."[8]

Eight days after it had left Atlanta the army reached Milledgeville, then the capital of Georgia, and one man recorded that "the army had lived high on the products of Georgia and were growing fatter and stronger every day." Perhaps unnecessarily, he added that "they had come to look on the trip as a grand picnic, and were not getting tired but more anxious to prolong it if anything." An Ohioan who had joined in much of the foraging saw a justification for it and wrote exultantly: "There is no haggling over prices or terms and no time wasted in coming to an understanding between the planter and a line of bayonets. He silently and with great show of dignity watches the fruits of his slaves' labor leaving the plantation to supply his enemy. He has sown the seeds of treason that have ripened into supplies to meet the demands of this enemy, and all he can do is to grin and bear it."[7]

Near Milledgeville the army had a brush with a few thousand Georgia militia, stiffened by a little regular cavalry. A brigade from the XV Corps routed the militia with practiced ease, and when the men crossed the field after their enemies had fled they saw with horror that they had been fighting against old men and young boys. One Federal wrote feelingly that "I was never so affected at the sight of dead and wounded before," and asserted: "I hope we will never have to shoot at such men again. They knew nothing at all about fighting and I think their officers knew as little."[8]

Plantations were looted outright; men who had set out to take no more than hams and chickens began carrying away heirlooms, silver, watches—anything that struck their fancy. Here and there southern patriots felled trees to obstruct roads, or burned bridges; there was never enough of this to delay the army seriously, but there was just enough to provoke reprisals, and barns and houses went up in smoke as a result. A general remarked that "as the habit of measuring right by might goes on, pillage becomes wanton and arson is committed to cover the pillage." An Illinois soldier confessed that "it could not be expected that among so many tens of thousands there would be no rogues," and another man from the same state burst out: "There is no God in war. It is merciless, cruel, vindictive, un-Christian, savage, relentless. It is all that devils could wish for."[9]

Day after day crowds of fugitive slaves fell in on the roads to follow the army. A "mammy" would show up, bundle on her head, baby in her arms, three small children at her heels; the soldiers would ask where she was going and she would say, "To Savannah, sah"—and officers, who were aware that the army's destination was not known even to the Union rank and file, would wonder how she knew that that was where they were heading.[10] Sherman did his utmost to keep these fugitives from following. It was ordered that the army's progress was on no account to be obstructed or delayed by these hopeful contrabands, but there was no way to keep them from trailing after the soldiers if they chose, and many of them did choose. What became of most of them, no one ever knew. Thousands of Negroes, it was thought, followed the army for a few days and then vanished, going off no one knew where, uprooted persons wholly adrift in a strange and disordered world. In the end, thousands of them did reach the seacoast with the army, but they were only a fraction of the blind, desperate throng that followed for a time and then spun off into unremembered darkness.

They had no historian and they left no records, and the soldiers were by turns amused and bored by them; but as they moved—blindly, hopefully, doomed, going from one misery to another—they gave significance to the entire march, to the long dusty columns in blue with rowdy outriders and with the lines of bayonets that took no arguments from planters. For if this army was destroying much that did not need to be destroyed, it was also destroying slavery; dismantling one of the barricades that stood in the way of the advance of the human spirit, lighting dreadful fires that would finally stand as beacon lights no matter what they consumed.

It was believed that some of the fugitives met death by starvation, yet those who were able to stay with the troops usually got enough to eat. Some queer grapevine of slave-quarter information told the Negroes which regiments in all this army tended to be most kindly and hospitable; also, the soldiers simply had ever so much more food than they themselves could consume. Foragers brought in vast wagon-loads of material that was abandoned to rot. Usually the surplus was given to the Negroes.

So much food was taken, indeed, that the soldiers themselves were almost appalled when they stopped to think about it. In one regiment the men made a rough rule-of-thumb estimate of the requisitions that had been made and concluded that the army must have accounted for one hundred thousand hogs, twenty thousand head of cattle, fifteen thousand horses and mules, five hundred thousand bushels of corn, and one hundred thousand bushels of sweet potatoes. Sherman himself later estimated that his army had caused one hundred million dollars' worth of damage in Georgia. Of this, he believed, perhaps twenty million dollars represented material that the army actually used; the rest was "simple waste and destruction." One officer wrote about burned houses, burned fences, roads cut to bits by marching men, fields despoiled and crossed by innumerable wagon tracks, and concluded that "Dante's Inferno could not furnish a more horrible and depressing picture than a countryside when war has swept over it."[11] As the march went on, it was noted that the word "bummer" changed its character. Originally it had been a term of contempt, applied only to the notorious stragglers who never stayed in ranks, in battle or out of battle, and who were looked down on by all combat soldiers; before the army got to the coast the men were beginning to call themselves bummers, and even Sherman, looking back in post-war years, did not mind applying the word to all of his troops.

The effect of all of this was prodigious. As Sherman had foreseen, the fact that an army of sixty thousand men could march straight through the southern heartland, moving leisurely and taking all the time it needed to destroy the land's resources, without meeting enough resistance to cause even a day's delay, was an unmistakable portent of the approaching end. No one could remain in much doubt about how the war was going to result when this could be done. Furthermore, the march was both revealing and contributing to the Confederacy's inability to use the resources that remained to it. Around Richmond, Lee's army was underfed, short of animals, perceptibly losing strength from simple lack of food and forage; yet here in Georgia there was a wealth of the things it needed, and it could not get them—primarily because the land's transportation and distribution system was all but in a state of total collapse, but also because this invading army was smashing straight through the source of supply. The morale of Confederate soldiers in Virginia and in Tennessee sank lower and lower as letters from home told how this army was wrecking everything and putting wives and children in danger of starvation.

President Lincoln may have had a few uneasy moments while the march was going on. Shortly after it left Atlanta the army was completely lost to sight, as far as the North was concerned. It had no communications whatever, no message of any kind came from it, and the only news was what could be learned from southern papers. This news was worthless, and much of it consisted of hopeful reports that Sherman was being cut off and surrounded by Confederate troops and that his entire army would presently be wiped out. As November came to an end no one in Washington knew where the army was or what had happened to it. Lincoln confessed that "we know where he went in at, but I can't tell where he will come out."

Sherman would come out where he had intended to, at Savannah. The soldiers, nearing the seacoast early in December, found that they had marched out of the rich land of plenty. This was rice country, and although the foragers could load the wagons with plenty of rice they could not seem to find much else. Soldiers learned to hull the rice by putting it in haversacks and pounding it with musket butts, and to winnow it by pouring the pounded grain from hand to hand, and they speedily got sick both of preparing it and of eating it. The country was flat and a good deal of it was under water, and the campaign's picnic aspects abruptly disappeared.

The army came up to Savannah on December 10. Sherman led it around to the right, striking for the Ogeechee River and Ossabaw Sound, where he could get in touch with the navy, receive supplies, and regain contact with Grant and with Washington. The XV Corps found itself making a night march along the bank of a canal; there was a moon, the evening was warm, and the swamp beside the canal looked strange, haunting, and mysterious, all silver and green and black, with dim vistas trailing off into shadowland. The men had been ordered to march quietly, but suddenly they began to sing—"Swanee River," "Old Kentucky Home," "John Brown's Body," and the like, moving on toward journey's end in an unreal night. An Iowa soldier remembered how "the great spreading live-oaks and the tall spectre-like pines, fringing the banks of the narrow and straight canal, formed an arch over it through which the shimmering rays of the full moon cast streaks of mellow light," and the picture stayed with him to old age."

The army went along the Ogeechee River, overwhelmed Confederate Fort McAllister, and met the navy's gunboats and supply ships, and the days of the rice diet were over. Now the men could have army bacon and hardtack again, for the first time in weeks, and after the rich fare they had been getting in Georgia, army rations seemed good. Sherman missed a bet at Savannah, just as he had done at Atlanta. The Confederates had between ten and fifteen thousand soldiers there, and all of these might have been captured, but while he was investing the place Sherman incautiously left open a line of escape, and the defenders got out and moved up into the Carolinas.

Yet this did not really matter in the least. Prim General Hardee, the Confederate commander, might get his garrison away unscathed, but the war would not be prolonged ten minutes by this fact. For Sherman was not fighting an opposing army now; he was fighting an idea, knocking down the last shredded notion that the southern Confederacy could exist as an independent nation, moving steadily and relentlessly not toward a climactic engagement but simply toward the end of the war.

His soldiers found Savannah unlike any town they had ever been in before. They entered the place on December 21, marching formally for a change, with bands playing and flags flying, Sherman himself taking a salute as they marched past. Savannah had a tropical air; the yards were filled with blooming flowers, palm trees and orange trees were to be seen, the houses looked old and inviting, and war seemed not to have touched the city. The men looked about them, reflecting that they had finished one of the great marches of history, and they suddenly went on their good behavior; Savannah was spared the devastation and pillage so many other places in Georgia had endured.

Sherman sent off a whimsical wire to Abraham Lincoln, offering him the city of Savannah, with much war equipment and twenty-five thousand bales of priceless cotton, as a Christmas gift. To Grant and Halleck he wrote urging that as soon as his army had caught its breath it should be allowed to march straight north across the Carolina country. To Halleck he wrote: "I think our campaign of the last month, as well as every step I take from this point northward, is as much a direct attack upon Lee's army as though we were operating within the sound of his artillery."[13]

Everything was working. Lee's lines at Petersburg still held, but now his rear was unsafe. Sherman's army was nearer to Richmond now than it was to Vicksburg, and there was no conceivable way to keep it from coming up. As the year came to an end, the Confederacy had just under four months to live.

4. The Enemy Will Be Attacked

It is possible that the Confederate General Hood made a very serious error in judgment.

When Sherman stopped chasing him in the middle of October and took his men back to Atlanta to prepare to march to the sea, Hood concluded that his own cue was to invade Tennessee from northern Alabama. This invasion might cause the Federal authorities to call Sherman back from his gigantic raid and order him north to meet Hood's threat. If that failed, Hood could perhaps overwhelm Thomas and regain Tennessee for the Confederacy; he might even be able to drive on north into Kentucky and all the way to the Ohio River in a dazzling counterstroke that would upset the balance and put the Confederacy back into the running again. For reasons that seemed good, then, Hood let Sherman go, pulled his army together below the southernmost loop of the Tennessee River, and at last—late in November, heavy rains and a scarcity of supplies having imposed delay —he took off, crossing the river and moving up toward Nashville.

With hindsight it can be argued that this was a strategic error of the first magnitude. Hood's offensive was doomed. Thomas had enough strength to stop him, and although the expedition caused uneasy moments in Washington (and proved especially disturbing to no less a person than U. S. Grant) it ended in sheer Confederate disaster. But the simple fact is that Hood had no good choice to make. The Confederate armies were coming to the end of the tether. There was a good deal of killing still to be done—deaths on battlefield and in hospital, men slain in meaningless little cross-roads skirmishes, typhoid and dysentery and scurvy doing their stealthy work behind the lines—but the verdict was just about in. Confederate armies now could do little more than play out the string.

In any case, Hood made his march, and for the last time the starred red battle flags of the Confederacy moved north, as if the world were still young and hot gallantry could still go up the road with undaunted hope. Hood himself was morose; he was saying that Johnston's defensive tactics on the campaign down toward Atlanta had got the men so full of the notion that trenches were invulnerable that they had lost their élan and would no longer attack in the old-time Confederate style. (The furious attacks they had made against odds in his own battles around Atlanta might have shaken him out of this idea but had not done so; it is conceivable that he was excusing his own failure.) Still, his prospects could have been worse. The Federal forces in Tennessee were scattered and needed reorganizing, and there was a chance that he could move in between them and cause much trouble.

Thomas was in Nashville, trying to reassemble his army. Some of his stout Cumberland soldiers had gone off to Savannah with Sherman, and he did not have all of his old command. Reinforcements were on their way, and he would presently have a first-rate cavalry corps—young James H. Wilson, the former staff officer who had fumed so mightily when the sailors failed to get their gunboats down through the Yazoo Delta swamps a year and a half earlier, was putting together a mighty force of mounted men, all of them to be armed with repeating carbines—but Thomas was not quite ready yet and he wanted time. He had sent John Schofield with approximately twenty-two thousand men down near the Tennessee-Alabama border to delay Hood and gain a little of this time for him, and for twenty-four hours it looked as if Hood might eat Schofield's force at one bite.

Schofield let Hood steal a march on him, and by a fast flank movement Hood brought his troops around to a place called Spring Hill on the Nashville turnpike, squarely in Schofield's rear. Alerted just in time, Schofield turned back in retreat. Hood's men were where they could have broken up this retreat and compelled the Federals to fight an uphill battle for their lives, but Hood's command arrangements got fouled up most atrociously, and in some unaccountable way he let Schofield's army march straight across his front, wagon trains and all, unmolested.[1]

It was an eerie march, as the Federals remembered it. The men were gloomy, knowing themselves outnumbered, the weather had been bad, and Schofield was pushing them along so fast that they did not fall out for meals but simply munched raw salt pork and hardtack as they walked. When darkness came they could see long ranks of Rebel campfires twinkling in the fields beside the road; officers warned them to keep quiet—although a moving army was bound to make a good deal of noise, and the Confederate pickets obviously had discovered them—and at intervals the whole column would break into a lumbering run, coming down to a walk only when everybody was winded.[2]

All night long the march went on, and by daybreak, November 30, the army was out of the trap. Forrest was commanding Hood's cavalry, and in the morning he came slashing in to attack the moving columns. A few infantry regiments wheeled out with fixed bayonets, and some artillery was unlimbered, and when Forrest's men came riding in they were butchered. Watching with horrified fascination, one infantryman saw what artillery could do to mounted men at close range. He remembered: "You could see a Rebel's head falling off his horse on one side and his body on the other, and the horse running and nickering and looking for its rider. Others you could see fall off with their feet caught in the stirrup, and the horse dragging and trampling them, dead or alive. Others, the horse would get shot and the rider tumble head over heels, or maybe get caught by his horse falling on him."[3]

Forrest was driven off and the Federals tramped wearily up to the town of Franklin, on the south bank of the Harpeth River. The bridge had been burned, and Schofield could not get his guns or his wagons across the river until his engineers had built a new one; so he put his infantry in line in a wide semicircle on a rising ground just south of the town and got them solidly entrenched while the engineers went to work.

Hood's army was moving fast in pursuit—Hood was furious because of the chance that had been missed at Spring Hill, and he was blaming everyone but himself for it, repeating his complaint that his soldiers were unwilling to fight unless they could have the protection of trenches. His army came up into contact with Schofield's outposts a little after noon, and Hood immediately decided to attack.

The Union position was powerful, and Forrest argued that it would be better to cross the river, off to the right, and try one more flank movement. But Hood would not listen. He would attack, and he would do so at once, without even waiting for his artillery to come up. He shook his army out into a broad line of battle and sent his men straight in on the strongest part of the Federal line.

It was November 30, a pleasant Indian-summer day with a broad open field rolling gently up to the Union trenches. General Schofield, who was on the far side of the river seeing to the bridge-building job, looked across and saw one of the great, tragic sights of the war. Here were eighteen thousand Confederate infantrymen, more men than had charged with Pickett at Gettysburg, coming forward in perfect order, battle flags flying, sunlight glinting on polished rifle barrels. On came the moving ranks, looking irresistible, battalions perfectly aligned; then the Federal infantry and artillery opened, a dense cloud of smoke tumbled down the slope, and the moment of pageantry was over.

No fight in all the war was more desperate than this one at Franklin. Hood's men charged with a stubborn fury that should have proved to the angry general once and for all that they were not in the least afraid to fight out in the open. They came to close quarters and—incredibly, for the charge was just about as hopeless as Burnside's assaults on the stone wall at Fredericksburg had been—cracked the center of the Union line and went pouring through, raising the Rebel yell. But the break was quickly mended. Ohio and Wisconsin and Kentucky troops came in with a prompt counterattack. There was terrible hand-to-hand fighting in a farmyard and around a cotton gin; a gunner in one Union battery brained an assailant with an ax, and young Colonel MacArthur of the 24th Wisconsin was crying to his men: "Give 'em hell, boys, give 'em hell, 24th!" The Confederates who had broken the line were killed or driven out, and all along the front the firing reached a fearful intensity; some of the Confederates, utterly beaten out, facing this fire at the closest range, were heard calling: "Don't shoot, Yanks— for God Almighty's sake, don't shoot!"[4]

The autumn day ended at last, and the battle ended with it, the shattered Confederate brigades drawing back in defeat. Their losses had been six thousand men killed or wounded, five general officers killed—among them the Pat Cleburne who had mentioned the unmentionable in that officers' meeting the previous winter—and six more generals wounded, one mortally. Nothing whatever had been gained. Late that night Schofield's bridge was finished and his army marched off to Nashville, eighteen miles away, saving all of its guns and wagons.

Federal losses had been much smaller, but they had not exactly been trifling; there had been more than two thousand casualties, and the survivors—making their second consecutive all-night march, with a wearing battle sandwiched in between—were at the point of complete exhaustion. Whenever the column came to a momentary halt, men would drop in their tracks and sleep; some men even slept while they marched, stumbling along blindly, helpless automatons. Some of these said afterward that in this marching sleep nightmares came to them, with the sights and sounds of the day's battle moving through their drugged minds.[5]

They revived when they got to Nashville. The Federal army had held this town for the better part of three years and had surrounded it with powerful fortifications. General Thomas was here with the rest of the army, there were hot coffee and food and good camping ground where tired men could sleep, and there would obviously be no more forced marches in retreat. When Hood's army came up and ranged itself on the hills facing the Union works, the Federals looked out at them and reflected that it was a fine thing to "occupy the favorable side of the fortifications."[6]

Hood came to a standstill here before Nashville. He had

already shot his bolt, although he did not seem to realize it. He had started his invasion with approximately forty thousand men, of whom something better than thirty thousand were infantry, he had seen his army badly mauled at Franklin, Thomas outnumbered him by a substantial margin, and there was no longer anything of much consequence that he could do. Lacking a better course, he dug trenches facing the strong Yankee line and put up a hollow pretense of besieging the place.

It worried Pap Thomas very little, but it very seriously worried General Grant. Sherman once said admiringly that Grant never cared in the least what the opposing army might be doing off out of his sight, but Grant was worrying now; for once in his life he had the jitters. From his headquarters hut at Petersburg it looked as if Hood might be making a wild, desperate thrust that could wholly upset all of the Federal war plans. Grant had Lee penned, and Sherman was disemboweling the Confederacy with torch and sword—and now, at the eleventh hour, this Confederate army was on the loose; it might get away from Thomas and go rampaging all the way up through Kentucky, and it was important to destroy it at the earliest moment. And Grant, the imperturbable, grew highly nervous and bombarded Thomas with daily messages demanding that he attack at once.

Thomas replied that it would take a few days to get everything ready and that he would attack as soon as possible; Grant retorted that there must be no more delay, and went so far once as to write out an order relieving Thomas of his command and turning the whole army over to Schofield. The order was not sent, finally, but the fact that it was drafted was significant. Between Grant and Thomas there was some strange misunderstanding—a feeling, perhaps, on Grant's part that dependable old Thomas could never quite make himself move fast. Thomas sensed what was in the wind, and when Halleck wired that Grant was highly unhappy about his delay he calmly replied that he had done his best and that "if General Grant should order me to be relieved, I will submit without a murmur." Then, just as he was ready to attack, a great sleet storm came down, fields and roads were coated with an inch of slick ice, troop movements became utterly impossible, and a cavalry regiment required to travel to an outpost found that its troopers had to dismount and walk, leading their horses.

The ice lasted for four days, during which time both armies were immobilized. Grant fretted and worried and at last he got hold of Black Jack Logan, who was north at the time, gave him orders relieving Thomas from command, and sent him west to take over.

Logan never quite made it. On December 14—at last—the weather turned warm. There was a steady rain, mud took the place of ice, and Thomas sent off a wire to Halleck: "The ice having melted away today, the enemy will be attacked tomorrow morning." Then he called in his corps commanders, gave them written orders for the next day's attack, went over the orders with them in detail—and finally went to bed in the Nashville hotel room he was occupying, leaving word at the desk for a five o'clock call next morning.'

Morning came, and Thomas packed his bag, checked out, and rode off to field headquarters. There was a fog on the ground, but it drifted away not long after sunrise and the troops were ready to go. Thomas ordered them forward, sending in two brigades of colored troops to hold Hood's right and attacking at the other end of the line with a solid corps of infantry and all of Wilson's cavalry, which trotted forward to attack a prepared infantry position quite as if it had never yet been demonstrated that mounted men could not profitably assault men in trenches.

Everything worked. Hood's line was stretched thin, and although the works his men occupied at the point of attack looked formidable he did not have enough men to hold them. The infantry smashed through, the cavalry curled around behind his left flank, and Hood was driven back for two miles, to take a new, last-hope position on a little chain of hills. He had been badly beaten, and there was nothing he could do now but retreat as fast as the muddy roads might permit, but he was still full of fight, and he hung on for another day of it. His men were full of fight too. A Federal cavalryman who helped escort a bag of prisoners to the rear the next morning noticed that the captured Rebels were still confident: "They say Hood will pay us today for yesterday's reverses. They all assert he is going to capture Nashville before night."[8]

It was not in the cards. Thomas renewed the attack the next morning, and although the Confederates put up a stout fight their case was hopeless. Thomas's IV Corps swarmed up a hill, crumpling the skirmish line and driving on for the trenches. The officer commanding an Indiana regiment spurred forward to be first man through the line, and as he passed his color-bearer he reached out for the flagstaff, to take the flag in with him. The color-bearer refused to let go of it and ran alongside the horse, colonel and private both gripping the same staff; and presently the colonel was pulled bodily out of the saddle and took an undignified tumble in the mud. The color-bearer kept the flag, ran up to the Rebel trench, and drove the base of the staff into the soft earth of the parapet, while the rest of the corps charged through and destroyed the Confederate line. Wilson's cavalry came up on the right, dismounted and acted like infantry—the men had thrown their sabers by the roadside and were working their repeaters like foot soldiers—and finally the whole defensive position caved in and Hood's army fled, leaving most of its artillery behind, while the Yankee cavalry scurried back to reclaim its horses and set off in pursuit.[9]

The victory had been complete. Hood's army was shattered beyond repair, and there was no refuge for it north of Alabama. Young General Wilson drove his cavalry after the retreating army in the pitch-darkness of a windy, rainy night. Forrest was guarding the Confederate rear, and his men fought savage delaying actions in the bewildering dark, crouched behind fence-rail barricades while the Union cavalry charged in across inky-black fields, nothing visible except the sputtering flames from the carbines—and, at intervals, black tree trunks gleaming in the wet, and dark figures moving in and out, when sporadic flashes of lightning lit the night.

It was mean, confused fighting, much of it hand-to-hand. A Union and a Confederate officer came together in the gloom and fought a saber duel on horseback, so close together that they grappled and in some fantastic manner managed to exchange sabers, after which they continued to belabor each other; the duel ended when a stray bullet broke the Confederate's sword arm and he was compelled to surrender. Forrest's men were driven off at last, but they had delayed the pursuit just long enough to enable Hood to keep from losing what remained of his army, and after midnight Wilson called a halt and put his troopers into bivouac.

At this point Thomas himself rode up. "Old Slow Trot" was coming in at a gallop tonight, and his customary dignity and self-control were gone. He greeted Wilson with a whoop.

"Dang it to hell, Wilson, didn't I tell you we could lick 'em?" he demanded. "Didn't I tell you we could lick 'em?"[10]

In Louisville, Kentucky, General Logan got news of the victory, put his orders away, and turned around to go back to Washington. And in Washington, General Grant himself got the tidings. He had left Petersburg and was on his way to Nashville to come out and see to things personally, and he was stopping overnight in Willard's Hotel when the telegram reached him. It told the news of the sweeping victory that removed the last possible doubt that the war would be won on schedule. Grant read the telegram, handed it to an aide with the remark, "Well, I guess we will not go to Nashville," and then dictated a wire to Thomas, offering his hearty congratulations.[11]

Wilson's cavalry kept up the pursuit for ten days, but with the men who remained to him Hood at last got away to the south side of the Tennessee River, at Muscle Shoals. Of the forty thousand with whom he had set out on his invasion, he had twenty-one thousand left, most of them in a high degree of disorganization. His army had been practically destroyed. Fragments of it would be used in other fields later on, but as an army it had ceased to exist. Pap Thomas had shattered it.

Thomas comes down in history as the Rock of Chickamauga, the great defensive fighter, the man who could never be driven away but who was not much on the offensive. That may be a correct appraisal. Yet it may also be worth making note that just twice in all the war was a major Confederate army driven away from a prepared position in complete rout—at Chattanooga and at Nashville. Each time the blow that routed it was launched by Thomas.

With Hood back in the Deep South, out of Tennessee and out of the war, 1864 came to an end. It had been a long year and a hard year, and it had witnessed two things never seen before in all the history of man's warring: the soldiers who had the fighting to do had voted for more of it, with themselves to carry the load, and the people back home, who had had three mortal years of it, had held a free election and had given their government a mandate to carry the war on to a finish. Now the year was ending on a note of triumph. A Confederate army still existed west of the Mississippi but it was completely out of the main channel, and what it did could not affect the outcome; there was another, smaller Confederate army scattered about in lower Mississippi and Alabama, but it too was isolated and helpless. Grant remained in front of Richmond, Thomas held Tennessee, and Sherman was in Savannah. The Confederacy now consisted of the Carolinas and southern Virginia—no more than that. Spring was not far away, and spring would inevitably bring the end.

13.

Twilight and Victory

1. *Reap the Whirlwind*

IT HAD BEEN going on for nearly four years, and there would be about four more months of it. It had started at Fort Sumter, with officers on a parapet looking into darkness for the first red flash of the guns; now Fort Sumter was a mass of rubble and broken masonry, pounded to fragments by the hammering of repeated bombardments, but it still flew the Confederate flag, a bright spot of color to take the morning light that came slanting in from the sea—symbolic, a flag flying over wreckage and the collapse of a dream. Elsewhere, in many states, winter lay on the hills and fields that had been unheard of four years earlier but that would live on forever now in tradition and national memory—Shiloh, Antietam, the Wilderness, Chickamauga, and all the rest. Here and there all over the country were the mounded graves of half a million young men who had been alive and unsuspecting when all of this began. There would be more graves to dig, and when there was time there would be thin bugle calls to lie in the still air while a handful of dust drifted down on a blanketed form, but most of this was over. A little more killing, a little more marching and burning and breaking and smashing, and then it would be ended.

Ended; yet, in a haunting way, forever unended. It had laid an infinity of loss and grief on the land; it had created a shadowed purple twilight streaked with undying fire which would live on, deep in the mind and heart of the nation, as long as any memory of the past retained meaning. Whatever the American people might hereafter do would in one way

456

or another take form and color from this experience. Under every dream and under every doubt there would be the tragic knowledge bought by this war, the awareness that triumph and disaster are the two aspects of something lying beyond victory, the remembrance of heartbreak and suffering, and the moment of vision bought by people who had bargained for no vision but simply wanted to live at peace. A new dimension had been added to the national existence, and the exploration of it would take many generations. The Civil War, with its lights and its shadows, its unendurable pathos and its charred and stained splendor, would be the American people's permanent possession.

At the time it was possible to see only the approaching end and the hard times that had to be lived through before the end could finally be reached. In the North men nerved themselves for the ruthless blows that must be struck against a dying foe; in the South men nerved themselves to endure the blows; and as the year opened, the blows began to fall.

The first one struck Fort Fisher, a sprawling sand-dune fortification at the mouth of the Cape Fear River in North Carolina. Upstream a few miles was Wilmington, the Confederacy's last seaport. Here, and here only, the blockade-runners could slip in from the mist with the cargoes without which the Confederacy could not live. The sullen guns that looked out of the mounded embrasures would keep pursuing cruisers at a distance, and while Fort Fisher stood the South still touched the outside world—still existed, that is, as a potential member of the community of nations rather than an isolated area in which there was a smoldering revolt to be suppressed. Just before Christmas in 1864 the Federal government had moved in to smash Fort Fisher.

Unfortunately the job was entrusted to Ben Butler, who was not up to smashing anything. He had the assistance of a first-class fleet under Admiral David Porter—brought east from the Mississippi and Red River valleys for a job that seemed to need the attention of a top-flight fighting man—but even the help of the United States Navy could not make a successful soldier out of Butler. Butler filled a ship with powder, sent it in under the walls of Fort Fisher, and exploded it, fancying that the blast would level the fort and make the work of his troops easy. The explosion took place on schedule, but it had so little effect on the fort that the Confederates merely assumed that a Yankee boiler had blown up. Butler got troops ashore, considered taking the place by storm, then changed his mind, re-embarked his soldiers, and sailed back to Hampton Roads, reporting that the fort was too strong to be taken.

Butler had tried his luck one notch too far. He was a strange and devious character, a one-time Democrat who possessed much political influence and whom it had always been necessary to treat with extreme consideration. But the Lincoln administration had just won a presidential election and it was clearly winning the war as well, and suddenly both Grant and Lincoln realized that Butler was no longer an untouchable. Admiral Porter, good friend of Grant since the Vicksburg campaign, wrote the lieutenant general that Fort Fisher would fall whenever the army cared to send a competent general down to attend to the job. Butler went back to Massachusetts, a general without an army; a new amphibious expedition was mounted, the army gave Butler's old command to tough Major General Alfred H. Terry—and on January 15, after a prodigious bombardment by the fleet and a smart charge by the sailors and the infantry, Fort Fisher was captured. The South had lost its last seaport. The dwindling armies which were the Confederacy's only hold on life would get no more equipment than that which the South itself could provide, and the South's own resources were coming down close to the vanishing point. In Tennessee youthful General Wilson was putting together a vast mounted army—twelve thousand, five hundred men, all armed with repeating carbines, trained to fight on foot, using their horses only as means of getting from place to place swiftly . . . true mechanized infantry, in the modern sense, except that their means of locomotion consumed hay and grain rather than gasoline. It would be two months before this mounted army was ready to move, but by spring it would go plunging down into Alabama to break up anything it found that had not already collapsed, and there was no conceivable way in which it could be headed off.

And in Savannah, General Sherman was starting north

with his sixty thousand veterans, heading for nothing less than Richmond itself.

The men would make a tough campaign. They had long since come to look on themselves as the appointed agents through which the country would take vengeance on those who had tried to destroy it. To a man, they felt that South Carolina, above all other places, was the spot where vengeance was most called for. (This idea was not unknown, even in the South; many of Sherman's men, despoiling a Georgia town or plantation, had heard their victims express the hope that when they got to South Carolina they would give the people there a full measure of what they were giving Georgia.) Until now these soldiers had performed the act of devastation casually, without animus; in South Carolina they would act with genuine venom. They could march anywhere, over any ground and in any weather; they believed that they could whip any enemies they would ever meet—a belief that had especial justification in the fact that they were certain to meet no enemy whom they did not greatly outnumber—and the rowdy spirit that lies near the surface all across America never found a more complete fulfillment than it found in them. They would go through South Carolina, if General Sherman led them there, like the wrath of an outraged God.

General Sherman would lead them there. This lean, red-bearded, passionate general had come to see himself as an instrument of justice. He could justify brutality in terms of morality; he had a clouded but authentic vision of what America someday would be, and he saw himself and his army as the instruments by which punishment would descend on the unfaithful. An army surgeon who had seen much of him in Savannah wrote that Sherman "differs from most men by being more plain. He dresses plainly, talks plainly, fights plainly, and reaches results so plainly that after they are reached they look as simple as setting an egg on end, which all could do after seeing Columbus do it." What Sherman saw now—saw with terrible clarity, saw it as the private soldiers in his army saw it—was that to break everything loose in South Carolina was to crush the Confederacy's last hope to fragments. He led his army north from Savannah shortly after the first of the new year with "the settled determination of each individual to let the people know there was war in the land."[1]

This was not the picnic hike that had prevailed in Georgia. To go north across the lowlands, Sherman had to cross a flat swampy country crossed by many rivers, most of which were in flood. Joe Johnston, that canny little soldier who was at last being restored to command (now that there was nothing much for a Confederate to command, now that the last hope was evaporating like the mist from damp fields under the morning sun), believed that no army could cross this land in winter with any success. From afar Johnston watched Sherman's progress, unbelieving; and when he saw Sherman's army bridging rivers, building roads across swamps, and wading through flooded backwaters, making just as much time as it had made on the dry roads of Georgia, he wrote that "I made up my mind that there had been no such army in existence since the days of Julius Caesar."[2]

Johnston was right, in a way. This was not actually an army: it was just a collection of western pioneers on the march—men with axes who could cut down a forest and corduroy a road without breaking step, men who would flounder for miles through floodwaters armpit-deep, making nothing of it except for casual high-private remarks to the effect that "Uncle Billy seems to have struck this river endways." They plowed across the bottom lands as if they were on parade; they built bridges, cut roads, marched in ice-cold water as if they were on dry ground, casually burned towns and looted plantations and set fire to pine forests just for the fun of seeing the big trees burn—and came up north, mile after endless mile, carrying the future on their shoulders without realizing it, laughing and frolicking and making a devastation to mark their passage. An Indiana soldier remarked that the men set fire to so much that "some days the sun was almost entirely obscured by the smoke of the consuming buildings, cotton gins, etc." When deep mud bogged down everything that went on wheels, whole regiments were detailed to take hold of drag ropes and haul wagons and guns out of the mire. It was said that when a staff officer complimented one such detail for its effective work a corporal spoke up in reply: "Yes, we got the mules and wagons out, but we lost a driver and a damn good whip down in that hole."[3]

Mile by mile the army moved north. Every evening the mounted foragers would come in to camp, trailed by hundreds of wagons, buggies, and carriages which they had seized at different plantations and had loaded with foodstuffs; in the morning, when the army moved on, these would be set on fire and abandoned, symbols of the offhand hatred which the rank and file nourished for the state where secession had been born. Going through the town of McPhersonville, Ohio soldiers realized that every house in the place was burning, reflected that "this state was largely responsible for the rebellion," and thoughtfully noted: "Our line of march throughout this state was marked by smoke in the day and the glare of fire by night." All along this line of march few buildings escaped the flames; one soldier commented dryly that "where a family remains at home they save their house but lose their stock and eatables." Another Ohioan remarked that "our men had the idea that South Carolina was the cause of all our troubles" and felt that the state itself was hardly worth the effort it took to conquer it: "The soil was sandy and poor. The houses used for habitation were small and built of logs, rough split staves were used for shingles, wooden pegs for nails, there were no doors, neither sash nor glass in the windows, and there were no plastered inside walls." An Illinois soldier estimated that perhaps one house in ten escaped destruction, and noted exultantly: "The rich were put in the cabins of the Negroes; their cattle and corn were used for rations, their fences for corduroy and camp fires, and their barns and cotton gins for bonfires. It seemed to be decreed that South Carolina, having sown the wind, should reap the whirlwind."[4]

There were Negroes in South Carolina, as elsewhere in the South, and here as always the northern soldiers felt that the man with a dark skin was their friend. A Wisconsin soldier drew a moral from the slaves' attitude and wrote: "Their mute countenances in South Carolina were the best arguments in favor of abolition. If this war is a great drama, the slave in the scene has been the star actor and has acted his part well. The volunteer army, so far as I know, are all abolitionists. Men whom the arguments of Phillips, Sumner and Beecher hardened into pro-slavery advocates, by the simple protestations and silent evidences of the cruelty of slavery of the poor demented negroes have been made practical abolitionists. . . . The slaves have furnished us with information of the movements of the enemy, of the roads, of the treatment accorded our men as prisoners. They furnished our men food, shelter, clothing, and piloted escaped prisoners to our lines, all at the risk of their lives."[5]

Men in camp at night would watch foragers come in with vast loads of food and forage, which, they agreed, was evidence that "something besides hell could be raised in South Carolina"; and they added that "from the numerous conflagrations along the way, that much-talked-of place might be supposed to have its location here." Passing through the town of Barnwell, which the cavalry had set on fire—the troopers jested that the name of the place should be changed to Burnwell—the infantry tramped past one blazing house whose despairing owner was trying frantically and ineffectively to check the blaze. A private innocently called out to ask him how on earth his house had ever caught fire.[6]

All across the state the army collected much more in the way of food and forage than it could possibly use. When it broke camp in the morning, officers would order the surplus to be piled up so that it could be brought along later by wagon; doubting that any of it would ever be seen again, the skeptical privates would stuff all they could carry in their haversacks. It was generally understood that the piles of surplus were simply abandoned purposely so that the Negroes and poor whites could have something to eat. Clouds of smoke hung over the line of march every day, and one soldier recalled: "In our march through South Carolina every man seemed to think that he had a free hand to burn any kind of property he could put the torch to. South Carolina paid the dearest penalty of any state in the Confederacy, considering the short time the Union army was in the state; and it was well that she should, for if South Carolina had not been so persistent in going to war, there would have been no war for years to come."[7]

Almost unnoticed, Charleston fell. Sherman's men did not go near it. They simply marched across all of its lines of communications, knifing them so that the storied city dropped into Yankee hands like a ripe peach falling from a tree; the Confederate defenders left the place and the army and navy people who had tried so long to break a way in entered unopposed. (In Washington the War Department made plans for a great ceremony, to hoist the flag over what remained of Fort Sumter on the fourth anniversary of the day the fort had been surrendered to Beauregard. Invalided Robert Anderson, a major general now, would be on hand for the occasion.) Meanwhile Sherman's army came tramping up to Columbia, capital of the state.

Columbia got the full fury of the storm. Confederate cavalry held the place, made just enough resistance to force the Federals to prepare for a regular assault, and then left. Union troops marched in. Here and there little fires started. A great wind came up, the fires spread—and presently most of Columbia was on fire in a senseless, meaningless conflagration that brought the final measure of ruin and despair to the Palmetto State, which had led the South out of the Union.

Concerning the origin of this fire there is still great argument. Sherman held that retreating Confederate cavalry had set fire to baled cotton and that this had caused the great fire; Confederates retorted furiously that Union troops had started the flames and that Columbia was burned wantonly, for sport, by soldiers who had thrown off all restraint. An Illinois soldier denied that Unionists had caused the fire, but he wrote that the soldiers "smiled and felt glad in their hearts" to see the city burning, and another man from the same state confessed that his whole division was drunk and added: "I think the city should be burned out, but would like to see it done decently." Wisconsin soldiers went whooping and yelling past blazing buildings, shouting: "This is the nest where the first secession egg was hatched—let her burn!" An Iowan felt that most of the trouble came because the soldiers looted stores and saloons and got drunk, and wrote sorrowfully that "the splendid discipline so rigidly maintained throughout the rank and file of the army, which had preserved the city and protected the people of Savannah

. . . was viciously and recklessly destroyed at Columbia." He insisted that the fires were not started by the troops who first marched into the city but were the work of individuals and groups from other contingents who had simply wandered in to have fun, and he left a picture of it: "Straggling soldiers, singly and in squads, from the adjacent camps continued to congregate in town, where all joined indiscriminately in the general confusion, wanton plunder and pillage of the stricken city and helpless people. The scene as witnessed at sundown beggared description, for men, women and children, white and black, soldiers and citizens, many of whom were crazed with drink, were all rushing frantically and aimlessly through the streets, shouting and yelling like mad people. The efforts of Colonel Stone and his Iowa brigade as provost guards in the city to preserve order and protect persons and property seemed to be entirely futile."[8]

However it happened, it happened, and Columbia was burned, and there is very little point in arguing over the responsibility for it. Years afterward General Sherman was on the witness stand, being questioned about the business; he insisted that retreating Confederate troopers had ignited baled cotton, and at last he burst out that "God Almighty sent wind" and that flecks of fire had gone streaming across the city, licking down to bring homes and churches and business blocks to ashes.[9] It may have been that way, and it may have been some other way. The one certainty is that if Sherman's soldiers had not found fire in Columbia they would have started fire of their own. God Almighty sent wind . . . or heedless men sowed the wind, in the days when the time of payment seemed remote and unreal, and in the end there was a whirlwind to reap. This, finally, along with much death and heartache, was what came out of pride and anger and general stiffness of the neck, and the smoke of the torment of the people who stood in the whirlwind's path went up without ceasing.

Sherman himself had not willed the fire. In the end he and his generals began to regain control over their men and made a real effort to stop the blaze. This did not help very much. Most of Columbia was destroyed. Almost universally the soldiers shrugged it off—they approved of the fire, and they said that if they had not found the city ablaze they would have left it that way. General Slocum, a proper man who never wanted to be cast in the part of destroying angel, wrote later that he believed simple drunkenness was the real trouble, and he added: "A drunken soldier with a musket in one hand and a match in the other is not a pleasant visitor to have about the house on a dark, windy night, particularly when for a series of years you have urged him to come so that you might have an opportunity of performing a surgical operation on him."[10]

The army stayed in Columbia's ruins for two days and then marched on. The country was swampy and the winter rains had been falling steadily—though not steadily enough to save Columbia—and more than half of the time the soldiers had to corduroy the roads so that the wagons and artillery could move. They met little opposition. General Johnston commanded such troops as the Confederacy had been able to get together—a remnant from the broken army Hood had brought back from Tennessee, the men Hardee had pulled out of Savannah, and a scattering of other levies—but he was too weak by far to meet Sherman in open combat, and to Lee he wrote despairingly: "I can do no more than annoy him." To make things even more one-sided, Sherman was marching now toward strong reinforcements. General Schofield had brought troops east from Tennessee, had taken Wilmington, and was marching toward Goldsboro, North Carolina, to join hands with Sherman.

On March 7 Sherman's army crossed over into North Carolina. An immediate change in behavior took place. Sherman ordered his officers to "deal as moderately and fairly by North Carolinians as possible," and the soldiers were informed that there would be no more burning of property; anyone caught starting a fire would be shot forthwith. But when they marched through the turpentine forests, the stragglers who continued to fringe the moving army set fire to the congealed resin in notches on the trees, and for mile after mile the army moved under a pall of odorous pine smoke. An officer wrote that the flames in the forest aisles "looked like a fire in a cathedral," and one soldier remembered "the endless blue columns swaying with the long swinging step," and said that above the crackle of the flames could be heard the massed singing of "John Brown's Body." When Fayetteville was reached, a Confederate arsenal and machine shop were burned, but nothing else was destroyed. The men apparently had exhausted their fury in South Carolina. They felt that this state was different, and even the bummers were more or less restrained.[11]

Nearing Goldsboro, the army began to run into resistance. There was a sharp little fight at Averysboro, and on March 19 Johnston moved in and struck the exposed left wing of the army, under Slocum, at Bentonville. But Johnston just was not strong enough to win a victory, even when he hit only half of Sherman's army. Sherman sent in reinforcements, Johnston was driven off, and on March 23 Sherman marched into Goldsboro and joined Schofield. Thus reinforced, Sherman now commanded eighty thousand veterans, men as cocky and as sure of themselves as any Americans who ever marched. Johnston could be an annoyance but nothing more. This army could go wherever it wanted to go, and the Confederacy was powerless to stop it.

At Goldsboro the soldiers learned that the old days were over. Foraging parties were ordered to give up their horses, and the bummers and stragglers were quietly warned that they had better rejoin their own regiments and be good. With its own supply line established, the army would no longer support itself by living on the country. It was in North Carolina now, and in a matter of weeks it would rub elbows with the better-behaved Army of the Potomac, and everyone now would mind his manners. The protracted Halloween spree had come to an end. There would be no more fires.

Trailing back behind the army, from Savannah to the North Carolina line, there was a smoking path marked by charred timbers and cold ashes. Houses and towns and cities had been consumed, and South Carolina had been visited by the limitless wrath that had been turned loose by secession. Long ago, in December of 1860, the South Carolina convention had taken a vote, and great placards had put the word on the streets: The Union is Dissolved! Now the placards were gone, along with the gay spirit that had greeted them. Except for the details, the Union had been put back together again.

2. *The Fire and the Night*

On March 22 the youthful General Wilson, commanding twelve thousand and five hundred cavalrymen armed with repeating carbines, crossed the Tennessee River and moved down toward the heart of Alabama. To oppose him the Confederacy had nothing except Bedford Forrest—who, as a matter of fact, was quite a lot—and perhaps half as many troopers as Wilson was leading; troopers much less well equipped, driving east from Mississippi well aware that they were riding off on a forlorn hope. General Wilson was heading for Selma, a munitions center of considerable importance— just about the last one, aside from Richmond, which the Confederacy still possessed—and he moved with full confidence that he had the strength to go wherever he might be told to go.

His men were similarly confident. A young Iowa trooper in the command, who had been feeling poorly all winter, wrote that this expedition was good for him: "Nothing could be better for restoring my health than a campaign like this— the smoky dark pine woods and the color it adds with the splendid exercise of riding thirty miles or more a day will give health when all else fails. I am perfectly contented for the first time, and enjoy it fine."[1]

This feeling of power, of having an irresistible energy that would quickly overcome all obstacles, was felt in all the Union armies. A New Englander in Meade's army noted that increasing numbers of deserters from Lee's troops were coming through the lines every night, and remarked that his comrades discussed this matter just as fishermen back home, in the spring, would discuss the way the fish were running in the rivers; sitting around the campfire in the evening, the men would talk things over and predict that "there will be a good run of Johnnies."[2] In the upper Shenandoah, Sheridan

was crunching in on Waynesboro, where the pathetic remnant of Jubal Early's army held a cheerless winter camp;
Sheridan's tough troopers would attack it, scatter it for keeps,
and then move east to join Grant's army in front of Richmond, leaving behind them a valley that had been gutted as
thoroughly as any place Sherman's army had visited. Down
by the Gulf coast, General Edward R. S. Canby was leading
a Union army in to besiege and capture Mobile. Mobile was
no longer a real seaport, what with Union warships anchored
in the bay, but it was fortified and it held Confederate troops;
Canby would take it, and there would be one less Confederate
flag on the map.

Behind the lines, men looked ahead to the end of the
war and reflected on what the war had meant, reaching
various conclusions. At City Point, the vast Union base supporting the siege of Petersburg, a Massachusetts agent for
the Christian Commission looked on the military cemetery
that had sprung into being there, and he could think only
of the deaths that had come to so many thousands of young
men, Union and Confederate alike. . . . "I thought of the many
homes made desolate by this war. All the way from the left,
beyond Petersburg, to the right of Richmond, all through
the Shenandoah Valley, on the banks of the Rappahannock,
at Fredericksburg, in the Wilderness, our brave boys are
sleeping, making it in truth one vast burial place. Here one
grave, there another, ten, one hundred, one thousand, and
more. . . . Truly all through coming time must the soil of
Virginia be sacred, because moistened by the blood of so
many heroes." In Washington, General Jacob Cox stopped
off to meet with friends on his way to join Schofield in North
Carolina, and he found the die-hard Republicans bitter at
Lincoln for his approaching victory. "Baboon," he said, was
the mildest epithet these men had for the President, and
the politicians were openly vexed at the Union soldiers' habit
of yelling "Hurrah for Lincoln!" to taunt their Confederate
foes. When Lincoln went down to Hampton Roads to talk
with peace commissioners sent across Grant's lines by Jefferson Davis, these Republican leaders denounced him as being
a weak compromiser.[3]

This meeting with the peace commissioners resulted in

nothing, as it was bound to do. Led by wizened little Alexander Stephens of Georgia, Vice-President of the Confederacy, the Southerners came to see Lincoln about some means of bringing peace to "the two countries"; the very phrase (written into their instructions by Davis) was testimony to the Confederate authorities' final flight from reality. There were not two countries now, and there never could be; the Confederacy was a pinched-off triangle of land in southern Virginia and upper North Carolina, beset by overwhelming power; nothing could be more certain than that it would be ground to fragments as soon as spring made the roads dry enough for army movements. Peace for one united country was the only thing Lincoln would consider, and the commissioners were not even allowed to talk about it. . . . Lincoln was prepared to offer terms. He even suggested that if the South should lay down its arms now he would go to Congress and ask it to appropriate money to pay southern slave owners for the slaves who would very shortly be set free; at four hundred dollars a head this would be expensive, but he remarked that it would cost no more than going on with the war a few months longer would cost, and besides, it would not kill any young men. But the subject was inadmissible, and the commissioners returned to Richmond, where Davis valiantly addressed a mass meeting and called for war to the bitter end.

In Richmond men seemed to be in a queer, trance-like state, where the real and the unreal danced slowly in and out before minds that could no longer make sober meaning out of the things their eyes saw. On March 13 (Sherman was nearing Goldsboro, Sheridan was joining Grant, Wilson was beginning to invade Alabama with his mounted army) Jefferson Davis informed the Confederate Congress that "our country is now environed with perils which it is our duty calmly to contemplate";[4] and the Congress was laboring mightily with the very proposal that had got General Cleburne so cold a snubbing a year earlier—the proposal that certain Negro slaves be enrolled as soldiers for the Confederacy.

This idea, born of final desperation, was examined and whittled down and solemnly weighed and assessed precisely as if there was still some question about what finally would happen to slavery. A Virginia correspondent wrote to Davis in mid-February, saying that slavery was an institution "sanctioned, if not established, by the Almighty" as the most humane and salutary relationship that could exist between the white and colored races; nevertheless, he added, the military situation was getting desperate and it seemed undeniable that "the teachings of Providence as exhibited in this war dictate conclusively and imperatively that to secure and perpetuate our independence we must emancipate the Negro."⁵ And on March 23 the Confederate War Department published for the information of all concerned the text of a law just passed by Congress bearing on this subject.

Under this law the President was authorized to ask for, and to accept from their owners, the services of such numbers of Negroes as soldiers as he might consider necessary in order to win the war. These Negroes, once put into service, would be paid, fed, and clad on an equality with white troops, and if the President did not get enough of them just by asking for them he could call on the separate states to supply their proper quotas, provided that no more than 25 per cent of the male slaves of military age in any state could be called into service. As a final rider Congress stipulated that nothing in this law should call for any change "in the relation which the said slaves shall bear to their owners" except by the consent of the owners and of the states in which they lived.⁶

And thus, with Cleburne in his grave, a fragment of his idea was resurrected, as well as might be, and galvanized into a show of life. Nothing in particular would come of it (the sands had just about run out; when the War Department published this interesting law the Confederate government had just ten more days in which it might occupy Richmond, functioning as a government with its own capitol, its own executive officers, the trimmings and trappings of an established bureaucracy), and the enactment comes down the years as an oddity, significant in a way that nobody involved in it ever quite intended.

They never did understand, really, about slavery. Implicit in this deathbed conversion (halting, partial, and hedged with provisos, like many deathbed conversions—for the dying man suspects that he may yet recover) was the real explanation of the reason why the Confederacy had in fact come to its deathbed. Beyond the superior resources of the North—the overwhelming armies, the favor of the outside world, the wealth of supplies, the industrial machine that could produce limitless quantities of anything a nation at war might need—there was the supreme moral issue of slavery itself. Slowly, painfully, and with many doubts, Lincoln had made this issue central in the war. He had been moved, perhaps, less by conscious determination than by fate itself; for slavery, from first to last, had exerted its own force, working through men who would have preferred to ignore it. Its mere existence had lifted the war to a dimension which the Confederacy could not grasp. Beyond all of the orators and the armies, beyond the gun smoke in the valleys and the flashing of cannon on the hills, there always remained the peculiar institution itself—the one institution on all the earth that could not be defended by force of arms. A nation dedicated to human freedom but cursed with this unconscionable barrier to freedom could not engage in a civil war without letting loose a force that would destroy the barrier forever. The war had begun in the flame and darkness of the Carolina marshes, and fire and night as a result had begun to rise around the notion that one kind of man may own another kind. Even at the final minute of the eleventh hour the men who dominated the Confederate government did not understand this, and it was their lack of understanding that had brought them to the end of the tether.

While the southern leaders strove mightily with phantoms, Lincoln stayed close to Grant's army; and early in the spring Sherman left his own army safely moored in North Carolina and came up to City Point to see the lieutenant general and the President.

All three of these men knew that before very long the two generals would be called on to state the terms on which they would accept the surrender of the Confederate armies facing them; and Lincoln's counsel to them could be summed up in his own expression: "Let 'em up easy." Congress would not be in session this spring. If peace could soon be restored, Lincoln might perhaps be able to get the reconstruction of the Union so far advanced that by December, when the legislators did assemble, measures of vengeance and repression would be impossible. This he greatly wanted. He would destroy the Confederate nation forever, and he would also destroy slavery, but the South itself he would not destroy, nor would he inflict any punishment beyond the fearful punishment which the war itself had already inflicted. Under his direction much killing had been done, yet now Lincoln was repeatedly asking the generals: Cannot this thing somehow be ended without any more fighting? Must we go on with the killing? Grant and Sherman were of his mood, yet both of them told him the business was not yet over. There would be another battle, perhaps two, perhaps more; victory would come, but men still would have to fight for it, and the enormous graveyard that stretched from Minnesota to Florida must grow still more crowded before the last bugle call died on the wind.

Sherman went back to North Carolina, and Grant made ready for the final drive.

The Petersburg lines were more than fifty miles long, running from the south of Petersburg clear around to the northeast of Richmond. All through the previous fall Grant had been extending his lines to his left, reaching out to cut the railroads which the South must hold if it would hold the Confederate capital. It had not been easy going. Lee had foreseen each move and had countered it, and Union troops more than once had been defeated with heavy loss; yet the Union line had been drawn out a little farther each time, and to meet it Lee had been compelled—with constantly dwindling resources—to stretch his own line out in response. His army now was not half the size of the army Grant commanded. The realities of trench warfare, to be sure, were such that men vastly outnumbered could hold their ground against almost any direct assault, but the stretching process could not go on forever. Sooner or later Lee could be made to pull his line so taut that it would break.

No one knew this any better than Lee himself. His only hope (if it could really be called a hope) was to evacuate Petersburg and Richmond, get his army down to North Carolina, join forces with Johnston, and beat Sherman. After that (assuming that the combined armies could in fact defeat Sherman's mighty host) Lee and Johnston might just conceivably turn north again and defeat Grant . . . or move off somewhere, form a continuing knot of resistance, and keep the war going a few months longer. This was the only move left on the board. The odds against it were long, but if Lee stayed where he was it was completely certain that in a very few weeks he would be overwhelmed.

Yet he could not move at once. The unpaved roads, wet with winter's rains, were atrocious, and it was an open question whether Lee's horses, worn down by scanty forage, disease, and the lack of replacements, could pull his wagon trains and his guns. If he went south he would have to get some sort of advantage. He could get it only by making a sharp, punishing offensive thrust that would knock the Army of the Potomac back on its heels. Such a thrust, late in March, the Confederate commander undertook to make.

He struck on March 25, in the dark hour just before dawn, driving a column of infantry in on a strong point in the Union line known as Fort Stedman, due east of Petersburg. His men attacked without warning, seized Fort Stedman, went running out along the trenches on either side, and sent a spearhead on through to take secondary Union positions in the rear. If they succeeded they would break the Union army in half, Grant would have to pull his left wing back to repair the break, and the Army of Northern Virginia would have a clear road to North Carolina.

They could not succeed. The forts to the right and left of Stedman held, with a sharp flurry of hand-to-hand fighting. The Confederate force that had gone on to the second line went astray and was overwhelmed by Union reserves. A Federal counterattack was launched, the men who had taken Fort Stedman found themselves under heavy fire, Union artillery plastered the Confederate front—and by eight o'clock it was clear that the attack had been a failure. Remnants of the Confederate force got back to their own lines, the Union repossessed Fort Stedman, and Lee had lost nearly five thousand men. Now it would be Grant's turn.

Heavy rains slowed all movement, and for a few days the armies marked time. Then Grant struck, crowding a full corps of infantry in on the farthest extremity of the Confederate line; and at the same time Phil Sheridan moved out with his cavalry, leaving the trenches behind and moving up through Dinwiddie Court House to a rain-swept crossroads known as Five Forks—a place from which, if they held it firmly, his troops could quickly go storming north and cut the vital railway lines. Lee sent his own cavalry, plus an infantry division under George Pickett, to halt this thrust, and on April 1 Sheridan got infantry reinforcements of his own, overwhelmed Pickett by sheer drive and force of numbers, capturing most of his force and shattering the rest beyond repair—and Lee's flank had been turned at last, once and for all. The next day Grant ordered an assault all along the main lines. General Horatio Wright and his VI Corps found a place where Lee's force had been stretched too thin and broke it—losing two thousand men in the assault, for even when they were woefully undermanned these Petersburg lines were all but invulnerable—punching a wide hole that could not be repaired. On the evening and night of April 2 Lee evacuated Petersburg and Richmond and began his final retreat.

A great fire burned in Richmond when Union troops marched in. Retreating Confederates had fired various warehouses full of goods they could not take with them, and in the wild confusion of defeat these flames got out of hand; the victorious Unionists, coming at last into the capital city of the Confederacy, spent their first hours there as a fire brigade, putting out flames, checking looting, and bringing order back to the desolate town. Lincoln himself came up the James River in a gunboat—he had been at City Point, unable to tear himself away from the military nerve center while the climactic battle was being fought—and he walked up the streets of Richmond with a handful of sailors for an escort, dazed crowds looking on in silence; went to the Confederate White House, sat for a time at Jefferson Davis's desk, and saw for himself the final collapse of the nation he had sworn to destroy.

Most of Grant's army never got into Richmond, and neither did Grant himself. They were on the road, pushing along furiously to head Lee off and drive him into a pocket where he could be forced to surrender. Lee was making a good march of it—his Army of Northern Virginia always could cover the ground fast—but Confederate supply arrangements, never good, broke down completely, and the rations that were supposed to be delivered to him along the way never reached him. He lost a day while his details combed the countryside to impress provisions, and the loss of this day killed off whatever chance he may have had. Sheridan and his cavalry, followed by infantry, outraced him, curled around in front, and compelled him to drift west instead of following the roads that led to Joe Johnston.

It was a forced march for both armies, lit with jubilant hope for one, darkened by gloom for the other, a matter of hard trial for the foot soldiers of each one; a pressing on in the darkness, over bad roads, through a somber country where the fires of spring had not yet burned away winter's brown, barren bleakness. One army had wagon trains filled with food, the other had few wagons and no rations; yet the soldiers of both armies drove on, marching away from mealtimes, knowing only that after four years of it they were at last coming to the end, with tomorrow and all that tomorrow might mean lying somewhere over the next horizon. Meade overtook a part of Lee's army at Sayler's Creek—a soggy little crossing in a bottomland ninety miles from nowhere—and destroyed nearly half of it, taking many prisoners, capturing among others the fabulous General Richard Ewell, who had been Stonewall Jackson's trusted lieutenant back in the day when the future still was fluid. What was left of the Army of Northern Virginia slogged on over bad roads, taking the last lap on the march to extinction and a deathless legend: and the Army of the Potomac followed, pressing close behind, sending swift tentacles out on parallel roads to get in front and stop the march.

It came to an end at last on Palm Sunday—April 9, 1865—when Sheridan and his cavalry and a whole corps of infantry got squarely across the road in Lee's front. The nearest town was the village of Appomattox Court House, and the last long mile had been paced off. Lee had armed Yankees in his front, in his rear, and on his flank. There was a spatter of fighting

as his advance guard tried the Yankee line to see if it could
be broken. It could not. The firing died down, and Lee sent
a courier with a white flag through the lines carrying a
letter to U. S. Grant.

3. *Telegram in Cipher*

Until this Palm Sunday of 1865 the word Appomattox had
no meaning. It was a harsh name left over from Indian days,
it belonged to a river and to a country town, and it had
no overtones. But after this day it would be one of the haunted
possessions of the American people, a great and unique word
that would echo in the national memory with infinite tragedy
and infinite promise, recalling a moment in which sunset and
sunrise came together in a streaked glow that was half
twilight and half dawn.

The business might almost have been stage-managed for
effect. No detail had been overlooked. There was even the
case of Wilmer McLean, the Virginian who once owned
a place by a stream named Bull Run and who found his farm
overrun by soldiers in the first battle of the war. He sold
out and moved to southern Virginia to get away from the
war, and he bought a modest house in Appomattox Court
House; and the war caught up with him finally, so that Lee
and Grant chose his front parlor—of all the rooms in America
—as the place where they would sit down together and bring
the fighting to an end.

Lee had one staff officer with him, and in Mr. McLean's
front yard a Confederate orderly stood by while the war
horse Traveler nibbled at the spring grass. Grant came with
half a dozen officers of his own, including the famous
Sheridan, and after he and Lee had shaken hands and taken
their seats these trooped into the room to look and to listen.
Grant and Lee sat at two separate tables, the central figures
in one of the greatest tableaus of American history.

It was a great tableau not merely because of what these
two men did but also because of what they were. No two
Americans could have been in greater contrast. (Again, the
staging was perfect.) Lee was legend incarnate—tall, gray,

one of the handsomest and most imposing men who ever lived, dressed today in his best uniform, with a sword belted at his waist. Grant was—well, he was U. S. Grant, rather scrubby and undersized, wearing his working clothes, with mud-spattered boots and trousers and a private's rumpled blue coat with his lieutenant general's stars tacked to the shoulders. He wore no sword. The men who were with them noticed the contrast and remembered it. Grant himself seems to have felt it; years afterward, when he wrote his memoirs, he mentioned it and went to some lengths to explain why he did not go to this meeting togged out in dress uniform. (In effect, his explanation was that he was just too busy.)[1]

Yet the contrast went far beyond the matter of personal appearance. Two separate versions of America met in this room, each perfectly embodied by its chosen representative.

There was an American aristocracy, and it had had a great day. It came from the past and it looked to the past; it seemed almost deliberately archaic, with an air of knee breeches and buckled shoes and powdered wigs, with a leisured dignity and a rigid code in which privilege and duty were closely joined. It had brought the country to its birth and it had provided many of its beliefs; it had given courage and leadership, a sense of order and learning, and if there had been any way by which the eighteenth century could possibly have been carried forward into the future, this class would have provided the perfect vehicle. But from the day of its beginning America had been fated to be a land of unending change. The country in which this leisured class had its place was in powerful ferment, and the class itself had changed. It had been diluted. In the struggle for survival it had laid hands on the curious combination of modern machinery and slave labor, the old standards had been altered, dignity had begun to look like arrogance, and pride of purse had begun to elbow out pride of breeding. The single lifetime of Robert E. Lee had seen the change, although Lee himself had not been touched by it.

Yet the old values were real, and the effort to preserve them had nobility. Of all the things that went to make up the war, none had more poignance than the desperate fight to preserve these disappearing values, eroded by change from within as much as by change from without. The fight had been made and it had been lost, and everything that had been dreamed and tried and fought for was personified in the gray man who sat at the little table in the parlor at Appomattox and waited for the other man to start writing out the terms of surrender.

The other man was wholly representative too. Behind him there was a new society, not dreamed of by the founding fathers: a society with the lid taken off, western man standing up to assert that what lay back of a person mattered nothing in comparison to what lay ahead of him. It was the land of the mudsills, the temporarily dispossessed, the people who had nothing to lose but the future; behind it were hard times, humiliation and failure, and ahead of it was all the world and a chance to lift oneself by one's bootstraps. It had few standards beyond a basic unformulated belief in the irrepressibility and ultimate value of the human spirit, and it could tramp with heavy boots down a ravaged Shenandoah Valley or through the embers of a burned Columbia without giving more than a casual thought to the things that were being destroyed. Yet it had its own nobility and its own standards; it had, in fact, the future of the race in its keeping, with all the immeasurable potential that might reside in a people who had decided that they would no longer be bound by the limitations of the past. It was rough and uncultivated and it came to important meetings wearing muddy boots and no sword, and it had to be listened to.

It could speak with a soft voice, and it could even be abashed by its own moment of triumph, as if that moment were not a thing to be savored and enjoyed. Grant seems to have been almost embarrassed when he and Lee came together in this parlor, yet it was definitely not the embarrassment of an underling ill at ease in a superior's presence. Rather it was simply the diffidence of a sensitive man who had another man in his power and wished to hurt him as little as possible. So Grant made small talk and recalled the old days in the Mexican War, when Lee had been the polished staff officer in the commanding general's tents and Grant had been an acting regimental quartermaster, slouching about like the hired man who looked after the teams. Perhaps the oddest thing about this meeting at Appomattox was that it was Grant, the nobody from nowhere, who played the part of gracious host, trying to put the aristocrat at his ease and, as far as might be, to soften the weight of the blow that was about to come down. In the end it was Lee who, so to speak, had to call the meeting to order, remarking (and the remark must have wrenched him almost beyond endurance) that they both knew what they were there for and that perhaps they had better get down to business. So Grant opened his orderly book and got out his pencil. He confessed afterward that when he did so he had no idea what words he was going to write.

He knew perfectly well what he was going to say, however, and with a few pauses he said it in straightforward words. Lee's army was to be surrendered, from commanding general down to humblest private. All public property would be turned over to the United States Army—battle flags, guns, muskets, wagons, everything. Officers might keep their side arms (Grant wrote this after a speculative glance at the excellent sword Lee was wearing) and their horses, but the army and everything it owned was to go out of existence.

It was not, however, to go off to a prison camp. Throughout the war Lincoln had stressed one point: the people of the South might have peace whenever they chose just by laying down their arms and going home. Grant made this official. Officers and men, having disarmed themselves, would simply give their paroles. Then they could go to their homes . . . and here Grant wrote one of the greatest sentences in American history, the sentence that, more than any other thing, would finally make it impossible for any vengeful government in Washington to proceed against Confederate veterans as traitors. Having gone home, he wrote, officers and men could stay there, "not to be disturbed by the United States authorities so long as they observe their paroles and the laws in force where they may reside." When the powerful signature, "U. S. Grant," was signed under that sentence, the chance that Confederate soldiers might be hanged or imprisoned for treason went out the window.

Having written all of this, Grant handed it over for Lee to read.

Lee's part was not easy. He made a business of getting out his glasses, polishing them carefully, crossing his legs, and adjusting himself. Once he borrowed a lead pencil to insert a word that Grant had omitted. When he had finished he raised a point. In the Confederate army, he said, horses for cavalry and artillery were not government issue; the soldiers themselves owned them. Did the terms as written permit these men to take their horses home with them? Grant shook his head. He had not realized that Confederate soldiers owned their steeds, and the terms he had written were explicit: all such animals must be turned in as captured property. Still—Grant went on to muse aloud; the last battle of the war was over, the war itself was over except for picking up the pieces, and what really mattered was for the men of the South to get back home and become civilians again. He would not change the written terms, but he supposed that most of Lee's men were small farmers anxious to return to their acres and get a crop in, and he would instruct the officers in charge of the surrender ceremonies to give a horse or a mule to any Confederate soldier who claimed to own one, so that the men would have a chance "to work their little farms." And in those homely words the great drama of Appomattox came to a close.

The draft of the terms having been agreed on, one of Grant's staff officers took the document to make a fair copy. The United States Army, it appeared, lacked ink, and to write the copy the officer had to borrow a bottle of ink from Lee's staff officer; a moment later, when the Confederate officer sat down to write Lee's formal acceptance, it developed that the Confederate army lacked paper, and he had to borrow from one of Grant's men. The business was finally signed and settled. Lee went out on the porch, looked off over the hills and smote his hands together absently while Traveler was being bridled, and then mounted and started to ride away. Grant and his officers saluted, Lee returned the salute, and there was a little silence while the man in gray rode off to join the pathetic remnant of an army that had just gone out of existence—rode off into mist and legend, to take his place at last in the folklore and the cherished memories of the nation that had been too big for him.

Grant stayed in character. He heard a banging of guns; Union artillerists were firing salutes to celebrate the victory, and Grant sent word to have all that racket stopped—those men in gray were enemies no longer but simply fellow countrymen (which, as Grant saw it, was what the war had all been about), and nothing would be done to humiliate them. Instead, wagonloads of Federal hardtack and bacon would start moving at once for the Confederate camp, so that Lee's hungry men might have a square meal. Grant himself would return to Washington by the next train, without waiting to observe the actual laying down of arms. He was commanding general of the nation's armies, the war was costing four million dollars a day, and it was high time to start cutting expenses. Back in the Federal camp, Grant sat down in front of his tent to wait for the moment of departure. He seemed relaxed and in a mood to talk, and his officers gathered around him to hear what he would say about the supreme moment he had just been through. Grant addressed one of them, who had served with him in the Mexican War . . . "Do you remember that white mule old so-and-so used to ride, down in Mexico?" The officer nodded, being just then, as he confessed later, in a mood to remember the exact number of hairs in the mule's tail if that was what Grant wanted. So Grant chatted about the Mexican War, and if he had great thoughts about the piece of history he had just made he kept them to himself.[2] Meanwhile the Army of the Potomac was alerted to be ready to move on if necessary. It was just possible it might have to march down into North Carolina and help Sherman take care of Joe Johnston.

But this would not be needed. Lee was the keystone of the arch, and when he was removed the long process of collapse moved swiftly to its end. Johnston himself had no illusions. Much earlier he had confessed himself unable to do more against Sherman than annoy him. Now he was ready to do as Lee had done. What remained of the Confederate government—Jefferson Davis and his iron determination, Cabinet ministers, odds and ends of government papers and funds— was flitting south, looking in vain for some refuge where it could start all over again, but there was no place where it could go. Far down in Alabama, General Wilson's cavalry had taken Selma, the last remaining munitions center, had dismantled its productive apparatus with smooth, disciplined effectiveness, and had gone on to occupy Montgomery, where Davis once stood before a great crowd and heard an orator proclaim: "The man and the hour have met!" Mobile had been surrendered, and the Confederate troops in Mississippi and Alabama would lay down their arms as soon as the Federals could catch up with them. Beyond the Mississippi there still existed a Confederate army, but it might as well have been in Siberia. As an obvious matter of inescapable fact, the war was over.

It was over; and yet in this fearful convulsion of the 1860s each ending was always a new beginning, as if the journey that had been begun so heedlessly and with such high spirits must go on and on, consuming decades and generations, making the break with the past absolute. From first to last, nothing had gone as rational men had planned. The nation had put itself at the mercy of emotional explosions, whether these were shared by everyone or afflicted only individuals. Now, with an end in sight, there came a new explosion, a terrible incalculable, as monstrous and as reasonless as the one that had set swords flashing in the starlight above Pottawatomie Creek nearly ten years before. The knowledge of this explosion—though not a full realization of its grim consequences —was with General Sherman when he journeyed out from Raleigh, North Carolina, on April 17 to meet with General Johnston.

It was a strange meeting, in a way, even without the overtone that went with Sherman's secret knowledge. Here was Sherman, whose very name had come to mean unrelenting wrath and destruction. In his own person he seemed to embody everything that a defeated South had to dread from a triumphant, all-powerful North. Yet as he went to see Johnston—they met in a little farmhouse between the lines— he was oddly gentle. He had talked with Lincoln at City Point and he believed he knew the sort of peace Lincoln wanted: a peace of harmony and reconciliation, with no indemnities and no proscription lists. It was the sort of peace Sherman himself wanted. Away back in Atlanta he had told Southerners that "when peace does come you may call on me for anything. Then will I share with you the last cracker, and watch with you to shield your homes and families against danger from every quarter." Now he was prepared to make these words good by an act of peace, just as he had made worse words good by acts of war: and he and Johnston, who had fought against each other so long, sat down now, not quite as friends, but certainly as men who had come to understand and to respect each other.

And over the table where the two soldiers conferred there was the knowledge of the new and fearful thing that had happened.

Just before Sherman left Raleigh, an army telegrapher notified him that a cipher dispatch from Washington was just coming over the wire: would the general care to wait for it? Sherman had waited. Deciphered at last, the message was given to him. It came from Secretary Stanton, and it began: "President Lincoln was murdered about 10 o'clock last night in his private box in Ford's Theater in this city . . ."

Sherman collared the telegrapher: had he told anyone what was in this message? The man said that he had not. Sherman warned him to say nothing about it to anybody—Sherman's warnings could be pretty effective when the black mood was on him—and then he went off to see Johnston, fearful that if the Federal soldiers learned what had happened they might break all restraints and visit the helpless city of Raleigh with a vengeance that would make what had happened in Columbia look gentle and mild. There was among the men in his army, Sherman confessed, a very high regard for Mr. Lincoln.

At the conference table Sherman showed the dispatch to Johnston and saw the beads of sweat come out on the Southerner's forehead. Neither man knew what this insane news would finally mean, although each was perfectly aware that it would bring much evil. But they would proceed with their business as if it had not happened, and their business was to arrange for the surrender of Johnston's army.[3]

As they got down to it, the scope of the meeting unexpectedly broadened. Sherman said that he would give Johnston the same terms Grant had given Lee. Johnston was willing enough; but he was a gray little man who had seen enough of warring, and he unexpectedly proposed that they finish everything at one stroke—draft broad terms that would embrace all existing Confederate armies, from North Carolina to the Rio Grande, so that what they finally signed would put the last southern soldier back into civilian life and restore the Union.

It was just the sort of suggestion that would appeal to Sherman, who thought in continental terms anyway. But he could see two problems. To begin with, he himself had no authority to do anything but accept the surrender of Johnston's army. Even if he signed the sort of document Johnston was talking about it would not be binding until it had been ratified in Washington. In addition, Johnston's authority was no broader than his own; how could he offer the surrender of distant armies that were not under his control? Johnston was unworried. The Confederate Secretary of War, John C. Breckinridge, was not far away; he could sign the document, and his signature would be valid for all Confederates everywhere.

The two generals parted at last, agreeing to meet again the next day and finish what they had begun. Sherman hurried back to Raleigh and ordered all the soldiers to their camps. Then, with everyone under control and no stragglers or off-duty men roaming the streets, he published a carefully worded bulletin announcing the assassination of the President and expressly stating that the Confederate army had had no part in the crime.

There was no outbreak, although what might easily have happened if the men had been at large in the city and had overheard some Southerner expressing satisfaction over Lincoln's death is something to shudder at. The men took the news quietly, but they smoldered. One private wrote that "the army is crazy for vengeance," and promised that "if we make another campaign it will be an awful one." Most of the soldiers, he said, eager to vent their wrath in action, actually hoped now that Johnston would not surrender, and he added: "God pity this country if he retreats or fights us."[4]

Johnston would neither retreat nor fight. He and Sherman met again the next day, Secretary Breckinridge joined the meeting, and what came out of it was more like an outright treaty of peace than a simple surrender document. Going far beyond any imaginable authority that had ever been given him, Sherman stipulated that all Confederate troops should march to their state capitals and deposit their arms there; that the Federal government would recognize southern state governments as soon as the state officials took the oath to uphold the Constitution of the United States; that political rights and franchises of the southern people be guaranteed, and that the Federal government would not "disturb any of the people by reason of the late war." Pending ratification of these terms in Washington, a general armistice was to prevail.[5]

Apparently Sherman believed that he was doing what Lincoln would have wanted done. Certainly he was moved by a warm feeling of sympathy for the South and by a determination to prevent, if he possibly could, any post-war reprisals. For a man who made very hard war he was surprisingly ready to make a soft peace.

But he had gone far beyond anything permissible to an army commander. In effect, he had disposed of the whole reconstruction issue—that dangerous block of political dynamite that had been getting Mr. Lincoln's most delicate, patient handling for two years—and he had readmitted the Confederate states to the Union on (so to speak) their own recognizance. A man who disliked all politicians and who had an ingrained distrust of the democracy generally, he simply was not able to foresee the reaction that would inevitably follow on what he had done, nor could he understand that his government would unquestionably frown on the idea that Confederate armies should carry all of their weapons back home and put them in state arsenals where they could easily get at them again if they decided to fight some more.

When Sherman's terms reached Washington the government almost blew up. It seems very likely that Lincoln would have disapproved of Sherman's treaty if he had still been alive, but his disapproval would have been quiet and orderly. Now Lincoln was gone and the government for the moment was, to all intents and purposes, Secretary Stanton, and Stanton went into a public tantrum. He issued a statement denouncing Sherman and all but openly accusing him of disloyalty and completely repudiating the proposed treaty. The newspapers suddenly were filled with articles bitterly criticizing Sherman and accusing him of everything from insanity to the desire to make himself a pro-slavery dictator. Grant was sent down to Raleigh to make certain that Sherman should give Johnston terms precisely like those that had been given Lee—no more and no less—and from being one of the idols of the North, Sherman almost overnight became the object of a large amount of the bitterest sort of criticism.

. . . In the course of time it would all wash off. The South would forget that Sherman had nearly ruined himself by his effort to befriend it, and the North would forget it also, and after a few years he would be complete villain to one section and unstained hero to the other. Meanwhile, however, the wild uproar over the way in which Sherman had tried to end the war was lengthening the odds against the kind of peace Lincoln would have wanted. By discrediting Sherman for trying to let the South off too easily, the radical Republicans (with whom Stanton was firmly allied) were beginning to build up their case for a peace that would need to be nailed down with bayonets.

On a road a few miles north of Raleigh, General Slocum one day came upon a group of Sherman's soldiers standing around a loaded wagon to which they had just set fire despite the desperate protests of its civilian driver. The wagon was loaded with New York newspapers, just arrived, full of criticism of General Sherman. Slocum remarked that this was the last property he ever saw Sherman's men destroy, and he said that he watched the burning "with keener satisfaction than I had felt over the destruction of any property since the day we left Atlanta."⁶

4. Candlelight

Through four desperate years Abraham Lincoln had been groping his way toward a full understanding of the values that lay beneath the war. He had seen a profound moral issue at stake, and more than any other man he had worked to make that issue dominant. Amid the confusing uproar of battle, the struggle of the place-hunters, and the clamor of the men who were simply on the make, he had listened for the still small voice; beyond hatred and fear and the greed for profit and advantage, he had sought to appeal to the basic aspirations of the human race. Taking final victory for granted, he had worked to give the victory an undying meaning.

Yet a fog of dust and smoke lay on the land, the horizon was forever ringed in murky flame, and wherever he turned —from the beginning of the war to its end—he kept touching a great mystery. Something bigger than men intended seemed to be at work; when he remarked half despairingly that he had not controlled events but had been controlled by them he was referring to the incomprehensible current which was moving down the century, compelling men to accomplish a thing greater than they had willed, moving toward a goal that was visible only at rare intervals. In the end it was not a party or a section that had triumphed but the entire nation, and the dreams and desires that would move the nation's ultimate generations; and the terrible price that was paid was paid by all and not just by the losers.

Over and over throughout the war Lincoln had tried to put this into words. In the spring of 1864 he had written to a correspondent in Kentucky that after three years of warfare "the nation's condition is not what either party or any man devised or expected. God alone can claim it . . . If God now wills the removal of a great wrong and wills also that we of the North as well as you of the South shall pay fairly for our complicity in that wrong, impartial history will find therein new cause to attest and revere the justice and goodness of God." And in the spring of 1865, when he came to take the presidential oath for the second time, and delivered his inaugural address to a crowd that huddled before the capitol under a lowering sky, he carried the thought farther.

". . . Neither party expected for the war the magnitude or the duration which it has already attained. Neither anticipated that the cause of the conflict might cease with, or even before, the conflict itself should cease. Both read the same Bible and pray to the same God, and each invokes His aid against the other . . . The prayers of both could not be answered; that of neither has been answered fully. The Almighty has His own purposes.''[1]

There were a right and a wrong in the war; of that much he was certain. Yet it was beyond human wisdom to make a just appraisal of the extent to which individual men or groups of men ought to receive the praise or shoulder the blame. The loss and the victory were common property now. The blame also was perhaps a common property. The whole war was a national possession, the end result a thing fated by the clouded stars, a great moment of opportunity, of sorrow, and of eternal hope, brought to a people who had touched elbows with destiny. Here was the supreme mystery; apparently an entire nation, wishing much less, had been compelled to help work out the will of Providence. So the President went on, to pose a majestic and unanswerable question:

"If we shall suppose that American slavery is one of those offenses which, in the providence of God, must needs come, but which, having continued through His appointed time, He now wills to remove, and that He gives to both North and South this terrible war, as the woe due to those by whom the offense came, shall we discern therein any departure from those divine attributes which the believers in a living God always ascribe to Him?"

Like Jacob wrestling with the angel, Lincoln had grappled with this question through the years of bloodshed and loss and grief. There had come to him, in his lonely office in the White House, the endless casualty lists, the hard decisions that would mean innumerable deaths, the streaming thousands of people who wanted understanding, or mercy, or power and money in the pocket; and out of all of this he had grasped a vision. A whole nation could atone for a wrong; atonement made, it could then go on, with charity and without malice, to create a new right. It would be hard to do, of course. An intricate network of hot passions and whipped-up emotions would have to be broken, and many ties of self-interest would have to be severed. But it could be done, and the most adroit and skillful political leader in American history would be responsible for it. The spring of 1865 might be the time for it.

But different men had different thoughts about the war and, like Lincoln, they put them in writing. There was old John Brown, who had looked ahead to the war from the shadow of the hangman's noose . . . "the crimes of this land will never be purged away but with blood. I had, as I now think vainly, flattered myself that without very much bloodshed it might be done." If he had hoped to prevent much bloodshed, old Brown had in fact brought much bloodshed on; and he had swung in the air and then vanished, leaving his own blighted heritage to the land. Now there was John Wilkes Booth, who also had thoughts. He jotted them down: "This country was formed for the *white*, not for the black man. And, looking upon African slavery from the same viewpoint held by the noble framers of our Constitution, I for one have ever considered it one of the greatest blessings (both for themselves and us) that God ever bestowed upon a favored nation." The great blessing was gone now, and Booth would strike a blow of vengeance. He struck, and left his own heritage. Lincoln's words spiraled off in the starless darkness, and it would be a long time before anyone could invoke the spirit of charity and call for a peace made without hate.

Lincoln's casket lay beneath the echoing dome of the capitol, and then it was taken all across the country, to be seen by hundreds of thousands of Americans; a great procession of sorrow, skillfully arranged by men who wanted to do precisely what Lincoln himself would not have done.

These were the radicals—the Stantons, the Ben Wades, the Thaddeus Stevenses, the Charles Sumners, and the rest; the party leaders who had fought Lincoln as often as they had helped him, who distrusted his belief in reconciliation, who had opposed his plan for restoring the southern states to the Union, and who saw the beaten Confederacy as a conquered province which they could rebuild any way they chose. Their way would be a harsh one, and its most pathetic victim would be the recently freed Negro. Swearing now that they meant to protect him and help him walk erect as a man, they would make the race problem harder to solve. By the reaction they provoked they would finally help Jim Crow to come in and (for a time) take the place of Uncle Tom.

They are usually pictured as bad men, but the term is too strong. Some of them were bad and some were good, and the most were a mixture of good and bad; the real trouble was that they were men fatally limited—limited and wholly determined, sure of their own rightness, not unlike the men who in 1860 had dreamed of creating a glittering slave empire that would have the future in its keeping. The blame for the chance that was missed after the war ended is like the blame for the war itself; a common national possession.

President Andrew Johnson, who felt as they felt until experience taught him to feel otherwise, had not yet begun to assert himself. When at last he did he would do it ineptly, a man cursed with a genius for making enemies and estranging friends. Right now these men were running the government. The controls were in their hands, and their first effort was to create an atmosphere in which their kind of peace would look just and natural.

So they gave Lincoln a great funeral, inviting the people to look on the clay of the great leader slain in his hour of triumph. With this, and with the public denunciation of Sherman for his overgenerous offer of peace, they could whip up a state of mind in which charity and forbearance could be made to look like a betrayal. The light that had lit the room when Grant and Lee sat down together and that had gleamed brightly between Sherman and Johnston began to grow dimmer and dimmer. Dusk began to steal across the land, with long shadows to cloud men's vision.

Far to the south things went on to their appointed end. In Alabama, Wilson's tough troopers sat by their campfires in awed silence when they were told that Lee and Johnston had surrendered and that the war was over. "They resisted belief," one man recalled long afterward; "they dared not trust the story." Later they learned that Lincoln had been killed, and they saw that the Negroes everywhere were overcome by fear. The slaves had come to believe that it was Lincoln and Lincoln alone who had made them free; if he could be killed, would they not be returned to bondage? "For days the trembling creatures could not be induced to leave the camps, and it was only slowly and with difficulty that they could be made to realize that their former masters were finally deprived of power over them."³

Making a last effort to break a way through to the land beyond the Mississippi, where it might just be possible to keep the war going, Jefferson Davis was captured and brought north to be imprisoned. It was said that when taken he was wearing his wife's cloak and shawl, and the cruel story went abroad that he had tried to escape by disguising himself in woman's clothing—just as, in the early spring of 1861, men had jibed that Lincoln came to Washington crudely disguised in a long robe and a grotesque Scotch tam o'shanter. The last Confederate troops in Alabama and Mississippi surrendered, and then finally the orphaned Confederate army beyond the Mississippi laid down its arms. The last embers of the southern republic had been stamped out. There would be no more shooting. Nothing was left now but the tragic and moving memories which would lie close to the bones of the American people forever.

In Washington there would be two grand reviews to wind everything up; one for the Army of the Potomac, and another next day for the Army of the Tennessee, with President and Cabinet in a reviewing stand by the White House and with jubilant thousands lining the streets to cheer. The armies had marched up from Virginia and Carolina for this final ceremony, crossing many old battlefields as they came. Wisconsin men in the Army of the Potomac remembered tramping past the desolate acres around Spotsylvania Court House and the Wilderness and seeing hundreds of bleached skeletons, still unburied; in one place army surgeons were collecting skulls in gunny sacks. An old man hoeing weeds in a corn patch as the soldiers passed saw what the men were looking at and shook his head sadly. "Ah, sir," he said to one soldier, "there are thousands of both sides lying unburied in the Wilderness."⁴

Sherman's men crossed the Petersburg area, where the rival armies had faced each other in trenches for nine deadly months, and they looked at the fortifications with professional interest. The log huts which the Potomac soldiers had built for winter quarters struck the Westerners as excellent, but the Confederate works were not as imposing as they had expected them to be; out West (they insisted) the Rebs had built much tougher forts than these![5] Sherman's XX Corps came up through Richmond and realized suddenly that it had made the most prodigious swing of any corps in the whole Union army. This corps was composed of the troops Joe Hooker had taken west from the Army of the Potomac in the fall of 1863, when Rosecrans needed rescuing after Chickamauga. Some of the men had come down across the Chickahominy with McClellan in the spring of 1862, getting so near the Confederate capital that they had seen its spires and on quiet mornings had heard the far-off tinkle of its church bells. Then they had retreated down the James, and after that they had fought in such battles as Antietam, Fredericksburg, Chancellorsville, and Gettysburg. Finally they had gone to Tennessee, and they had hiked from Chattanooga to Atlanta and from there to Savannah, and from Savannah they had come north across the Carolinas—and now, at last, they were entering Richmond, three years after first seeing it, from the south instead of from the north.

In due time the armies reached Washington and went into camp. They gave the authorities a certain amount of trouble. To the very end the Potomac soldiers were trimmer, neater, better dressed, and better drilled; Sherman's men had never been very distinguished for any of these virtues, and after their long winter campaign they tended now to be even more ragged and informal than ever. When men from one army met men from the other it usually took little more than a sidelong glance to touch off a fight. In addition, the Army of the Tennessee was bitter about the treatment the government had given Sherman, and in Washington saloons Sherman's officers had a way of jumping on top of bars, and calling for three groans for Secretary Stanton. With the ice thus broken, it would be only a question of time before some Westerner would remark that the Easterners were paper-collar soldiers who had never been anywhere or licked anybody. The riot would begin immediately afterward. Eventually Grant had to put the two armies in camps on opposite sides of the Potomac River. It was noted that farmers whose lands were near Sherman's camping grounds began to complain that their chickens were not safe.

These Federal volunteer armies had existed for four years. For many thousands of young men, army life embraced all that they had ever seen of manhood. Now—suddenly, although there had been much forewarning—there came to all of these the realization that this tremendous experience was over. Never again would they rise to bugle call or drumbeat, make slogging marches in dust or mud, sleep tentless in the rain, or nerve themselves for the racking shock of battle; nor would they ever again go rioting across whole states with a torch for every empty house and a loaded wagon to carry away hams and turkeys and hives full of stolen honey for a campfire feast in the cool evening. They would be cut off, now and forever, from everything they had become used to; the most profound experience life could bring had come to them almost before boyhood had ended, and now it was all over and they would go back to farm or village or city, back to the quiet, uneventful round of prosaic tasks and small pleasures that are the lot of stay-at-home civilians.

They had hated the war and the army and they had wanted passionately to be rid of both forever; yet now they began to see that the war and the army had brought them one thing that might be hard to find back home—comradeship, the sharing of great things by men set apart from society's ordinary routine. They had grown used to it. They wanted to go home, they were delighted that they would presently take off their uniforms forever, and yet . . .

In Nashville, Pap Thomas held a farewell review for the stout old Army of the Cumberland, and as the men prepared to disband they found themselves feeling lost, almost sad.

"None of us," wrote a survivor, "were fond of war; but there had grown up between the boys an attachment for each other they never had nor ever will have for any other body of men." An Iowa cavalryman, awaiting the muster-out ceremony he had so long wanted, wrote moodily in his diary: "I do feel so idle and lost to all business that I wonder what will become of me. Can I ever be contented again? *Can I work?* Ah! How doubtful—it's raining tonight."

In Washington the great reviews were held as scheduled,

toward the end of May. Thousands of men tramped down Pennsylvania Avenue, battle flags fluttering in the spring wind for the last time, field artillery trundling heavily along with unshotted guns, and great multitudes lined the streets and cheered until they could cheer no more as the banners went by inscribed with the terrible names—Bull Run, Antietam, Vicksburg, Atlanta—and President Johnson took the salute in his box by the White House. It was noticed that Sherman's army unaccountably managed to spruce up and march as if parade-ground maneuvers were its favorite diversion. Sherman had apologized to Meade in advance for the poor showing he expected his boys to make; when he looked back, leading the parade, and saw his regiments faultlessly aligned, keeping step and going along like so many Grenadier Guards, he confessed that he knew the happiest moment of his life.

And finally the parades were over and the men waited in their camps for the papers that would send them home and transform them into civilians again.

. . . There was a quiet, cloudless May evening in Washington, with no touch of breeze stirring. In the camp of the V Corps of the Army of the Potomac men lounged in front of their tents, feeling the familiar monotony of camp life for the last time. Here and there impromptu male quartets were singing. On some impulse a few soldiers got out candles, stuck them in the muzzles of their muskets, lighted them, and began to march down a company street; in the windless twilight the moving flames hardly so much as flickered.

Other soldiers saw, liked the looks of it, got out their own candles, and joined in the parade, until presently the whole camp was astir. Privates were appointed temporary lieutenants, captains, and colonels; whole regiments began to form, spur-of-the-moment brigadiers were commissioned, bands turned out to make music—and by the time full darkness had come the whole army corps was on the parade ground, swinging in and out, nothing visible but thousands upon thousands of candle flames.

Watching from a distance, a reporter for the New York *Herald* thought the sight beautiful beyond description. No torchlight procession Broadway ever saw, he said, could compare with it. Here there seemed to be infinite room; this army corps had the night itself for its drill field, and as the little lights moved in and out it was "as though the gaslights of a great city had suddenly become animated and had taken to dancing." The parade went on and on; the dancing flames narrowed into endless moving columns, broke out into broad wheeling lines, swung back into columns again, fanned out across the darkness with music floating down the still air."

As they paraded the men began to cheer. They had marched many weary miles in the last four years, into battle and out of battle, through forests and across rivers, uphill and downhill and over the fields, moving always because they had to go where they were told to go. Now they were marching just for the fun of it. It was the last march of all and, when the candles burned out, the night would swallow soldiers and music and the great army itself; but while the candles still burned, the men cheered.

The night would swallow everything—the war and its echoes, the graves that had been dug and the tears that had been shed because of them, the hatreds that had been raised, the wrongs that had been endured and the inexpressible hopes that had been kindled—and in the end the last little flame would flicker out, leaving no more than a wisp of gray smoke to curl away unseen. The night would take all of this, as it had already taken so many men and so many ideals—Lincoln and McPherson, old Stonewall and Pat Cleburne, the chance for a peace made in friendship and understanding, the hour of vision that saw fair dealing for men just released from bondage. But for the moment the lights still twinkled, infinitely fragile, flames that bent to the weight of their own advance, as insubstantial as the dream of a better world in the hearts of men; and they moved to the far-off sound of music and laughter. The final end would not be darkness. Somewhere, far beyond the night, there would be a brighter and a stronger light.

NOTES

Chapter One: THE HURRICANE COMES LATER

Sowing the Wind

[1] *The Crime against Kansas: Speech of Hon. Charles Sumner in the Senate of the United States, 19th and 20th May, 1856;* Boston, Cleveland and New York, 1856; *History of the United States from the Compromise of 1850,* by James Ford Rhodes, Vol. II, pp. 132-33; *Abraham Lincoln: The War Years,* by Carl Sandburg, Vol. I, p. 103.

[2] *Life of Charles Sumner,* by Walter G. Shotwell, pp. 217, 241; Rhodes, op. cit., pp. 135-36.

[3] *The Crime against Kansas.*

[4] *John Brown, 1800-1859: A Biography Fifty Years After,* by Oswald Garrison Villard (cited hereafter as Villard), p. 93.

[5] Rhodes, op. cit., pp. 155-57; Villard, op. cit. pp. 142-45.

[6] Rhodes, op. cit., pp. 158-60; *A Standard History of Kansas and Kansans,* by William E. Connelley, Vol. I, pp. 551-52; *Bleeding Kansas,* by Alice Nichols, pp. 105-9.

[7] *Alleged Assault upon Senator Sumner; report of the Select Committee appointed under the resolution of the House, passed on the 23rd day of May, 1856;* Shotwell, op. cit., pp. 331-32.

[8] For the conflicting testimony about the seriousness of Sumner's injuries, see the report of the House Committee, cited above. A

grave view of the after effect of the blows is taken in the Shotwell biography of Sumner, p. 342. Brooks's cane appears to have been a hollow affair made of gutta-percha, easily broken. That Sumner was considered, by himself and his doctors, to have been seriously injured is clearly evident in the letters he wrote and received throughout the summer of 1856. (Manuscript collection owned by Mrs. Mary Reeve of Clearfield, Pennsylvania.)

[9] Villard, op. cit., pp. 85, 93, 153.

[10] Rhodes, op. cit., p. 162; Villard, op. cit., pp. 153-54.

[11] This account of the Pottawatomie murders follows Villard, op. cit., p. 155 et seq.

Where They Were Bound to Go

[1] A fascinating description of the Lake Superior-St. Mary's River country before the building of the Soo Canal is to be found in *The Long Ships Passing: The Story of the Great Lakes*, by Walter Havighurst, pp. 43-44, 72, 200. See also *Michigan: A Guide to the Wolverine State*, p. 124.

[2] *History of the Sault Ste. Marie Canal*, by Dwight H. Kelton, pp. 6-15; *Michigan: A Guide to the Wolverine State*, p. 345; *Cleveland, the Making of a City*, by William Ganson Rose, pp. 222-24, 236, 274; Havighurst, op. cit., pp. 230-31.

[3] *Main-Line of Mid-America: The Story of the Illinois Central*, by Carlton J. Corliss, pp. 63-65, 76, 82, 84; Havighurst, op. cit., p. 83, pp. 128-29.

[4] *Life in the Middle West*, by James S. Clark, pp. 10-15, 25. This artless book contains a singularly ingratiating account of life on the Ohio frontier.

[5] Ibid., p. 35.

[6] *Democracy in the Middle West, 1840-1940*, by Jeannette P. Nichols and James G. Randall, p. 31. For a good summary of the change that came over the Middle West in the pre-war decade, see *The Growth of the American Republic*, by Samuel Eliot Morison and Henry Steele Commager, Vol. I, p. 618.

Light over the Marshes

[1] In a speech made at Peoria, Ill., on Oct. 16, 1854. See *The Living Lincoln*, edited by Paul Angle and Earl Schenck Miers, pp. 161-73.

² Capt. James Chester, "Inside Sumter in '61," from *Battles and Leaders of the Civil War*, Vol. I, pp. 20-31. (This work is cited hereafter as *B. & L.*) In the same Volume, see also Gen. Abner Doubleday, "From Moultrie to Sumter," pp. 40-47; in addition, Maj. Anderson's message to Adj. Gen. Samuel Cooper, *Official Records*, Vol. I, pp. 2, 3.

³ Scott's letters are in the *Official Records*, Vol. I, pp. 112, 114.

⁴ *Official Records*, Vol. I, p. 195.

⁵ Ibid., pp. 196-98.

⁶ Ibid., pp. 211, 245, 248, 285; *B. & L.*, Vol. I, pp. 65-66.

⁷ Ibid., pp. 74-76.

Chapter Two: NOT TO BE ENDED QUICKLY

Men Who Could Be Led

¹ *B. & L.*, Vol. I, p. 85.

² Sandburg, op. cit., Vol. I, pp. 211-214. For an appraisal of Douglas's influence in Illinois, See *The Borderland in the Civil War*, by Edward Conrad Smith, p. 179.

³ *The Sherman Letters: Correspondence between General and Senator Sherman from 1837 to 1891*, edited by Rachel Sherman Thorndike, p. 110; *The Blue and the Gray*, edited by Henry Steele Commager, pp. 40, 43; *The Rebellion Record*, edited by Frank Moore, Vol. I, Part 1, p. 45; *B. & L.*, Vol. I, p. 84.

⁴ *Civil War Papers Read before the Commandery of the State of Michigan, Military Order of the Loyal Legion of the United States*, Vol. I, pp. 8-11.

⁵ *The Rebellion Record*, Vol. I, Part 2, pp. 86-87.

⁶ *A History of the Sixth Iowa Infantry*, by Henry H. Wright, p. 11; *The Story of a Cavalry Regiment: The Career of the Fourth Iowa Veteran Volunteers*, by William Forse Scott, pp. 1-3.

⁷ *Army Life of an Illinois Soldier: Letters and Diary of the Late Charles W. Wills*, compiled and published by his sister, p. 8; *History of the Sixth Regiment Indiana Volunteer Infantry*, by C. C. Briant, pp. 4-5; *The History of the 9th Regiment Massachusetts Volunteer Infantry*, by Daniel George MacNamara, p. 11;

The Rebellion Record, Vol. I, Part 1, p. 45; *A Narrative of the Formation and Services of the Eleventh Massachusetts Volunteers*, by Gustavus B. Hutchinson, p. 11.

[8] *Drum Taps in Dixie: Memories of a Drummer Boy, 1861-1865*, by Delavan S. Miller, p. 30; *Civil War Papers Read before the Commandery of the State of Massachusetts, Military Order of the Loyal Legion of the United States*, Vol. II, p. 448; *Story of the Service of Company E and of the 12th Wisconsin Regiment*, written by One of the Boys, pp. 44-46.

[9] *Journal History of the 29th Ohio Veteran Volunteers*, by J. Hamp SeCheverell, p. 21; *The History of the 9th Regiment Massachusetts Volunteer Infantry*, p. 11; *Army Life of an Illinois Soldier: Letters and Diary of the Late Charles W. Wills*, pp. 14, 21.

[10] *Story of the Service of Company E and of the 12th Wisconsin Regiment*, pp. 48-50.

[11] *History of the 124th Regiment, N.Y.S.V.*, by Charles H. Weygant, p. 32; *History of the 33rd Regiment Illinois Veteran Volunteer Infantry*, by Isaac H. Elliott and Virgil G. Way, pp. 7-8; *The Eagle Regiment: 8th Wisconsin Infantry Volunteers*, by a "Non-Vet" of Company H, pp. 40-49, 75 et seq.

[12] *Military Essays and Recollections: Papers Read before the Commandery of the State of Illinois, Military Order of the Loyal Legion of the United States*, Vol. III, p. 402; *A Soldier Boy's Letters to His Father and Mother, 1861-1865*, by Chauncey H. Cooke, p. 3; *Diary of an Ohio Volunteer*, by a Musician, Co. H, 19th Regiment, p. 15; *Story of the Service of Company E and of the 12th Wisconsin Regiment*, pp. 84-85.

[13] *Army Memoirs of Lucius W. Barber, Company D., 15th Illinois Infantry*, p. 12; *A History of the Sixth Iowa Infantry*, p. 20; *B. & L.*, Vol. I, pp. 94-95.

[14] *History of the 51st Indiana Veteran Volunteer Infantry*, by William R. Hartpence, p. 36; J. S. Clark, op. cit., p. 56; *Military History and Reminiscences of the 13th Regiment of Illinois Volunteer Infantry*, prepared by a committee of the regiment, p. 18. An eastern soldier remarked caustically: "The ignorance by our officers has become proverbial and patent to the men and hence the present low standard of discipline in the army." (Manuscript letters of James Gillette, 4th Maryland Volunteers.)

[15] An amusing account of Lincoln's war experience is to be found in Carl Sandburg's *Abraham Lincoln: The Prairie Years*, Vol. I, pp. 154-57, 386.

In Time of Revolution

[1] An excellent study of the problem in respect to the border states is E. C. Smith, op. cit. There is a good brief discussion in Clement Eaton's *A History of the Southern Confederacy*, pp. 34-40.

[2] *Life of General Nathaniel Lyon*, by Ashbel Woodward, pp. 25-30, 204-31, 235, 242.

[3] E. C. Smith, op. cit., pp. 122-30, 228-30; *Official Records*, Vol. I, pp. 654, 656-57, 669-70; *B. & L.*, Vol. I, pp. 119-20.

[4] *Official Records*, Vol. I, p. 675; *B. & L.*, Vol. I, p. 171; *The Mississippi/Valley in the Civil War*, by John Fiske, pp. 10-12.

[5] Fiske, op. cit., pp. 14-18; *Official Records*, Vol. III, p. 4; E. C. Smith, op. cit., pp. 234-36; *The Union Cause in St. Louis in 1861*, by Robert J. Rombauer, pp. 218, 224. Mr. Rombauer doubts very much that Lyon visited the militia camp in woman's dress. Aside from the inherent difficulty of dressing Nathaniel Lyon so that he would look at all feminine, Mr. Rombauer remarks that as a competent officer Lyon undoubtedly had other sources of information about doings in the southern camp.

[6] *Official Records*, Vol. III, p. 5; Rombauer, op. cit., pp. 233-39; E. C. Smith, op. cit., pp. 236-38.

[7] Ibid., pp. 240, 244-50; Woodward, op. cit., p. 261; *Forty-Six Years in the Army*, by Lt. Gen. John M. Schofield, pp. 33-34.

[8] *B. & L.*, Vol. I, pp. 266-67; E. C. Smith, op. cit., p. 252.

The Important First Trick

[1] *Wooden Nutmegs at Bull Run*, by Frinkle Fry, p. 31; *Three Years with the Adirondack Regiment*, by John L. Cunningham, p. 21; *The Rebellion Record*, Vol. I, Part 1, p. 50; *The Soldier Boy's Diary Book; or, Memorandums of the Alphabetical First Lessons of Military Tactics*, by Adam S. Johnston, p. 8; *Military Essays and Recollections: Papers Read before the Commandery of the State of Illinois, Military Order of the Loyal Legion*, Vol. III, p. 426.

[2] *Edward Rowland Sill: His Life and Work*, by William Belmont Parker, pp. 34-36; Cooke, op. cit., p. 10.

[3] *History of the 38th Regiment Indiana Volunteer Infantry*, by Henry Fales Perry, p. 129; *Story of the Service of Company E and of the 12th Wisconsin Regiment*, pp. 88-89.

[4] *B. & L.*, Vol. I, p. 179.

[5] Ibid., pp. 138-39; *Diary of an Ohio Volunteer*, pp. 35, 46, 52.

[6] *History of the Army of the Cumberland*, by Thomas B. Van Horne (cited hereafter as Van Horne), Vol. I, pp. 8-12; *The Wild Riders of the First Kentucky Cavalry: A History of the Regiment*, by Sgt. E. Tarrant, pp. 9-11.

[7] *B. & L.*, Vol. I, pp. 373-77.

[8] See E. C. Smith, op. cit., p. 311: "South of the Ohio River there was no good line of defense for the Southern armies. From the time that Kentucky finally made her decision for the Union, they fought a losing battle."

The Rising Shadows

[1] *The Living Lincoln*, edited by Paul M. Angle and Earl Schenck Miers, p. 639.

[2] There are extensive discussions of Bull Run and of McDowell's problems, in *B. & L.*, Vol. I, pp. 167-259. An uncommonly useful handbook is Joseph Mills Hanson's *Bull Run Remembers*. These two have been heavily relied on in the preparation of this section.

[3] There is a good description of all of this in *Sherman, Fighting Prophet*, by Lloyd Lewis, pp. 177-79.

[4] There are enough accounts of the Bull Run panic to satisfy all tastes. The classic, probably, is that of William Howard Russell, correspondent for the London *Times*. For his and other accounts, see *The Blue and the Gray*, pp. 106-15.

[5] *Official Records*, Vol. III, pp. 48, 58.

[6] J. S. Clark, op. cit., pp. 54-57, 64.

[7] Ibid., p. 66; *Official Records*, Vol. III, pp. 61, 95; *B. & L.*, Vol. I, pp. 289-97.

[8] J. S. Clark, op. cit., pp. 57, 69-70; Schofield, op. cit., p. 45.

[9] *Official Records*, Vol. III, pp. 62, 74; Schofield, op. cit., pp. 44-46.

[10] J. S. Clark, op. cit., p. 72.

Chapter Three: MEN WHO SHAPED THE WAR

The Romantics to the Rescue

[1] For a full presentation of Scott's plan, see *Abraham Lincoln: A History*, by John G. Nicolay and John Hay, Vol. IV, pp. 298-303.

[2] *Mr. Lincoln's Army*, pp. 63-68.

[3] Manuscript letters of John W. Chase of the 1st Massachusetts Artillery.

[4] *Down in Dixie: Life in a Cavalry Regiment in the War Days*, by Stanton P. Allen, p. 145; *The Story of a Cavalry Regiment: The Career of the Fourth Iowa Veteran Volunteers*, p. 27; *A History of the First Regiment of Massachusetts Cavalry Volunteers*, by Maj. Benjamin W. Crowninshield, p. 11.

[5] Miller, op. cit., pp. 19, 27.

[6] *McClellan's Own Story*, pp. 82-83.

[7] Ibid., p. 85.

[8] Frémont's account in *B. & L.*, Vol. I, pp. 278-79.

[9] *Frémont: Pathmaker of the West*, by Allan Nevins, pp. 481-84; *B. & L.*, Vol. I, pp. 279-80.

Trail of the Pathfinder

[1] *B. & L.*, Vol. I, pp. 281, 307-13.

[2] *Personal Memoirs of John H. Brinton, Major and Surgeon, U.S.V.*, p. 32; *The Story of the Guard: A Chronicle of the War*, by Jessie Benton Frémont, pp. 34, 44; *Official Records*, Vol. III, p. 541.

[3] *The History of Fuller's Ohio Brigade*, by Charles H. Smith, p. 67.

[4] *The Eagle Regiment: 8th Wisconsin Infantry Volunteers*, p. 10.

[5] *Army Memoirs of Lucius W. Barber*, p. 21.

[6] *History of the 51st Indiana Veteran Volunteer Infantry*, p. 68.

[7] Schofield, op. cit., pp. 1-30, 49.

[8] Nevins, op. cit., pp. 496-97; *Official Records*, Vol. III, pp. 542-43.

[9] Jessie Benton Frémont, op. cit., pp. 43, 85, 88.

[10] *Official Records*, Vol. III, pp. 466-67.

[11] Jessie Benton Frémont, op. cit., Preface, p. x; *The Eagle Regiment: 8th Wisconsin Infantry Volunteers,* p. 3.

[12] *Official Records,* Vol. III, pp. 469-70.

[13] *Abraham Lincoln,* by Benjamin P. Thomas, p. 276; *Official Records,* Vol. III, pp. 477-78, 485.

[14] Ibid., Vol. VI, p. 788.

[15] Nevins, op. cit., pp. 507, 520; *History of the 16th Battery of Ohio Volunteer Light Artillery,* compiled by a committee, p. 6.

[16] Jessie Benton Frémont, op. cit., p. 85.

[17] *A History of the Sixth Iowa Infantry,* p. 35; *Military History and Reminiscences of the 13th Regiment of Illinois Volunteer Infantry,* p. 27; J. S. Clark, op. cit., p. 64.

[18] *Official Records,* Vol. III, p. 553.

[19] Thomas, op. cit., pp. 278-79.

He Must Be Willing to Fight

[1] *Ulysses S. Grant and the Period of National Preservation and Reconstruction,* by William Conant Church, p. 84.

[2] Ibid., p. 83.

[3] *Personal Memoirs of John H. Brinton, Major and Surgeon, U.S.V.,* pp. 36-37.

[4] *Muskets and Medicine; or, Army Life in the Sixties,* by Charles Beneulyn Johnson, M.D., p. 181.

[5] *Personal Memoirs of John H. Brinton, Major and Surgeon, U.S.V.,* pp. 40, 43, 61; *Letters from the Army,* by B. F. Stevenson, p. 14.

[6] *Guns on the Western Waters: The Story of River Gunboats in the Civil War,* by H. Allen Gosnell, pp. 15, 18.

[7] Van Horne, Vol. I, p. 23; *Personal Memoirs of U. S. Grant,* Vol. I, pp. 265-67.

[8] *Military Essays and Recollections: Papers Read before the Commandery of the State of Illinois, Military Order of the Loyal Legion,* Vol. I, pp. 22-23, 25.

[9] *"Ben-Hur" Wallace,* by Irving McKee, Chap. 1, passim; *Lew Wallace: An Autobiography,* Vol. I, pp. 338-45.

[10] *B. & L.,* Vol. I, pp. 380-81; *History of the 38th Regiment Indiana Volunteer Infantry,* p. 11.

[11] Lewis, op. cit., pp. 189-91; *The Wild Riders of the First Kentucky Cavalry: A History of the Regiment*, p. 30.

[12] *History of the 53rd Regiment Ohio Volunteer Infantry*, by John K. Duke, p. 6.

[13] *Memoirs of a Volunteer, 1861-1863*, by John Beatty, edited by Harvey S. Ford, pp. 70-71, 75-76, 79-81.

[14] *History of the 38th Regiment Indiana Volunteer Infantry*, p. 261.

[15] *The Life of Major General George H. Thomas*, by Thomas B. Van Horne, pp. 1-31; *Military Reminiscences of the Civil War*, by Jacob D. Cox, Vol. II, p. 237.

Chapter Four: TO MARCH TO TERRIBLE MUSIC

Sambo Was Not Sambo

[1] *Ormsby MacKnight Mitchel, Astronomer and General*, by F. A. Mitchel, p. 237.

[2] *Personal Memoirs of John H. Brinton*, pp. 46-47.

[3] *Military Essays and Recollections: Papers Read before the Commandery of the State of Illinois, Military Order of the Loyal Legion*, Vol. III, p. 404.

[4] *History of the 51st Indiana Veteran Volunteer Infantry*, pp. 9-10; *Memoirs of a Volunteer*, p. 95; *The Story of a Cavalry Regiment*, by William Forse Scott, p. 380.

[5] *History of the 33rd Regiment Illinois Veteran Volunteer Infantry*, p. 23.

[6] Cox, op. cit., Vol. I, p. 158; *History of the 77th Illinois Volunteer Infantry*, by Lt. W. H. Bentley, p. 101; *A Soldier Boy's Letters to His Father and Mother*, pp. 30, 36.

[7] Manuscript letters of John W. Chase, 1st Massachusetts Artillery.

[8] For anyone who is interested, the Stone affair is discussed in greater length in *Mr. Lincoln's Army*, pp. 76-83. For a much more pointed analysis, see T. Harry Williams, "Investigation 1862," in *American Heritage*, Vol. VI, No. 1.

War along the Border

[1] *B. & L.*, Vol. I, pp. 632-33.

[2] Ibid., p. 661 et seq.; *Official Records*, Vol. VI, p. 179.

[3] Thomas, op. cit., p. 289.

[4] For a pointed discussion of the ruinous effect of the habit of overestimating Confederate strength (written by a soldier by no means hostile to McClellan) see *Military Reminiscences of the Civil War*, Vol. I, pp. 250-53.

[5] *The Wild Riders of the First Kentucky Cavalry*, p. 109.

[6] *Personal Recollections of Distinguished Generals*, by William F. G. Shanks, p. 258.

[7] *Official Records*, Vol. XVI, Part 1, p. 51.

[8] Ibid., Vol. VII, pp. 530-31.

[9] *The Rise of U. S. Grant*, by A. L. Conger, p. 83 et seq.; *Personal Memoirs of U. S. Grant*, Vol. I, pp. 271-80.

[10] Van Horne, Vol. I, pp. 50-58; *The Life of Major General George H. Thomas*, p. 50 ff; *History of the Tenth Regiment Indiana Volunteer Infantry*, by James Birney Shaw, p. 162; *B. & L.*, Vol. I, pp. 387-91.

Come On, You Volunteers!

[1] *Official Records*, Vol. VII, pp. 527, 532-33.

[2] Ibid., p. 532.

[3] Anyone interested in following this dreary exchange of messages can find them in *Official Records*, Vol. VII, pp. 573-74, 576, 578-80, 583-87.

[4] Gosnell, op. cit., pp. 47-48.

[5] Ibid., pp. 49-50.

[6] *B. & L.*, Vol. I, p. 358 ff.

[7] *Personal Memoirs of U. S. Grant*, Vol. I, p. 294.

[8] *Official Records*, Vol. VII, pp. 590-91.

[9] *B. & L.*, Vol. I, pp. 398-410, 430-36; *History of the Seventh Regiment Illinois Volunteer Infantry*, by D. Leib Ambrose, p. 32; *Personal Memoirs of U. S. Grant*, Vol. I, pp. 298-304.

[20] *Personal Memoirs of John H. Brinton*, p. 121.

[21] Ibid., pp. 129-30; *Personal Memoirs of U. S. Grant*, pp. 308-12.

[22] *B. & L.*, Vol. I, p. 426; *The Army of Tennessee*, by Stanley Horn, p. 98.

To the Deep South

[1] *The Army of Tennessee*, pp. 99-102; *P. G. T. Beauregard: Napoleon in Gray*, by T. Harry Williams, p. 119.

[2] *Official Records*, Vol. VI, pp. 398, 828; Vol. VII, p. 889.

[3] Ibid., Vol. VI, p. 692.

[4] Ibid., Vol. VII, pp. 640-41.

[5] Ibid., pp. 627, 628, 632, 641, 648, 655.

[6] Ibid., pp. 630, 640, 646, 652; *The Rise of U. S. Grant*, p. 192.

[7] *Personal Memoirs of John H. Brinton*, p. 133; *Official Records*, Vol. VII, pp. 637-38, 649.

[8] *Ormsby MacKnight Mitchel, Astronomer and General*, p. 255; *Official Records*, Vol. VII, p. 660.

[9] *Personal Memoirs of John H. Brinton*, p. 131; *Official Records*, Vol. VII, pp. 679-80, 682; Vol. X, Part 2, p. 3.

[10] Ibid., Vol. VII, p. 683.

[11] Ibid., p. 283; Vol. X, p. 32.

[12] *Personal Memoirs of John H. Brinton*, pp. 160-61.

[13] *Army Memoirs of Lucius W. Barber*, pp. 43, 47; *A History of the Sixth Iowa Infantry*, p. 57.

[14] *Official Records*, Vol. VII, p. 647.

[15] Ibid., Vol. X, Part 2, p. 55.

[16] Grant's letters to Mrs. Grant; photostats of manuscript copies furnished by Ralph G. Newman of Chicago.

[17] *Downing's Civil War Diary*, by Sgt. Alexander G. Downing, edited by Olynthus B. Clark, p. 39.

Chapter Five: A LONG WAR AHEAD

Hardtack in an Empty Hand

[1] Lewis, op. cit., p. 217; *Official Records*, Vol. X, Part 1, pp. 252, 262, 288, 290, 411.

[2] Ibid., Vol. X, Part 2, p. 91. This may be as good a place as any to point out that Shiloh is exhaustively covered in *B. & L.*, Vol. I, in articles that extend from p. 465 to 610, that there is an excellent account of the battle in Stanley Horn's *The Army of Tennessee*, pp. 122-43, and that T. Harry Williams discusses it in his *P. G. T. Beauregard, Napoleon in Gray*, pp. 133-49. One of the most moving descriptions is in Lloyd Lewis's *Sherman, Fighting Prophet*, pp. 219-31.

[3] *Army Memoirs of Lucius W. Barber*, p. 48; *Downing's Civil War Diary*, p. 40.

[4] *Official Records*, Vol. X, Part 2, p. 94.

[5] It might be noted that Confederate reports in the *Official Records* do not bear out the rumors that Federal troops were surprised in their tents. Uniformly, the Confederate accounts describe very stiff resistance from the beginning; General Hardee tells of Federal attacks on his skirmishers at dawn, before the main attack got rolling. See *Official Records*, Vol. X, Part 1, pp. 513, 514, 532, 536, 541, 548, 568, 573, 581.

[6] Ibid., p. 331; report of Col. Jacob Ammen.

[7] *Lew Wallace: An Autobiography*, Vol. II, p. 505.

[8] *Ohio at Shiloh: Report of the Commission*, by T. J. Lindley, pp. 37-38, *Official Records*, Vol. X, Part 1, pp. 264-65; *History of the 53rd Regiment Ohio Volunteer Infantry*, pp. 27-48.

[9] *Official Records*, Vol. X, Part 1, p. 133.

[10] *Ulysses S. Grant and the Period of National Preservation and Reconstruction*, p. 135; *Official Records*, Vol. X, Part 1, p. 288; *History of the 15th Regiment Iowa Veteran Volunteer Infantry*, by William Worth Belknap, pp. 84-85.

[11] *Lew Wallace: An Autobiography*, Vol. II, p. 524; *History of the 53rd Regiment Ohio Volunteer Infantry*, p. 49; *Army Memoirs of Lucius W. Barber*, p. 53; *Official Records*, Vol. X, Part 1, p. 226; *Downing's Civil War Diary*, p. 41.

[12] *History of the 53rd Regiment Ohio Volunteer Infantry*, p. 55.

[13] *Ulysses S. Grant and the Period of National Preservation and Reconstruction*, p. 135; *Official Records*, Vol. X, Part 1, p. 158; *A History of the Sixth Iowa Infantry*, p. 80; *History of the 15th Regiment Iowa Veteran Volunteer Infantry*, pp. 83, 110-11.

[14] *History of the 53rd Regiment Ohio Volunteer Infantry*, p. 51.

[15] *A History of the Sixth Iowa Infantry*, p. 89.

[16] *Official Records*, Vol. X, Part 1, p. 375.

[17] *Memoirs of the War*, by Capt. Ephraim A. Wilson, p. 112; *Downing's Civil War Diary*, p. 43.

Springtime of Promise

[1] *Official Records*, Vol. X, Part 1, p. 396.

[2] Ibid., Vol. VI, p. 432.

[3] Ibid., p. 832.

[4] *B. & L.*, Vol. II, pp. 25-29.

[5] *Official Records*, Vol. VI, p. 889.

[6] There are excellent accounts of the running of the forts in *B. & L.*, Vol. II, pp. 33-91.

[7] *B. & L.*, Vol. II, p. 20.

[8] *Ohio at Shiloh: Report of the Commission*, pp. 79-80.

[9] *The Sherman Letters: Correspondence between General and Senator Sherman from 1837 to 1891*, pp. 143-45.

[10] *Army Memoirs of Lucius W. Barber*, pp. 62-63.

[11] *History of the Sixth Regiment Indiana Volunteer Infantry*, by C. C. Briant, pp. 130-31.

[12] Ibid., p. 138.

[13] *Official Records*, Vol. X, Part 2, pp. 166, 172, 214.

[14] Ibid., p. 548.

[15] Ibid., p. 252.

[16] For a discussion of this point, see Van Horne, Vol. I, p. 129.

Invitation to General Lee

[1] *Mr. Lincoln's Army*, pp. 109-12.

[2] *B. & L.*, Vol. I, pp. 693-700. Americans often speak of *Merrimac*

as the world's first ironclad warship; actually when *Merrimac* was rebuilt the British navy had two ironclads in commission and the French had one.

³ Ibid., pp. 701-3, 719-50.

⁴ The point is stressed by Col. John Taylor Wood, CSA, in *B. & L.*, Vol. I, p. 711.

⁵ By all odds the best account of the whole valley operation is the one contained in Col. G. F. R. Henderson's classic biography, *Stonewall Jackson and the American Civil War.*

Delusion and Defeat

¹ The point is discussed in detail in *Mr. Lincoln's Army*, pp. 131-33.

² Cox, op. cit., Vol. I, p. 253; *Official Records*, Vol. XI, Part 3, p. 340.

³ Ibid., pp. 250-51.

⁴ *B. & L.*, Vol. II, p. 337.

⁵ *Official Records*, Vol. XI, Part 3, p. 266.

⁶ *B. & L.*, Vol. II, pp. 394-95.

Chapter Six: TURNING POINT

Kill, Confiscate or Destroy

¹ *Ormsby MacKnight Mitchel, Astronomer and General*, pp. 284-88, 315; Van Horne, Vol. I, pp. 130-32.

² *Ormsby MacKnight Mitchel*, pp. 306-14, 330.

³ *The Nineteenth Illinois*, by J. Henry Haynie, pp. 131-39, 144-46, 159, 165, 167; *Three Years with the Armies of the Ohio and the Cumberland*, by Angus L. Waddle, p. 17; Cox, op. cit., Vol. I, p. 436; *Official Records*, Vol. X, Part 2, pp. 212-13. Details about Turchin's court-martial can be found in *Official Records*, Vol. XVI, Part 2, pp. 273-78.

⁴ *The Nineteenth Illinois*, p. 171.

⁵ *Army Life of an Illinois Soldier: Letters and Diary of the Late Charles W. Wills*, pp. 132, 134.

⁶ Ibid., p. 74.

⁷ *Official Records,* Vol. XVII, Part 2, p. 81; *The History of Fuller's Ohio Brigade,* p. 50.

⁸ *History of the 51st Indiana Veteran Volunteer Infantry,* pp. 26-27, 31; *Letters from the Army,* by B. F. Stevenson, p. 247; *With the Rank and File,* by Thomas J. Ford, p. 120. Some mention should be made of the Union brigadier in Louisiana who solemnly warned his troops not to catch any chickens or geese in such a clumsy way as to get bitten (*History of the 77th Illinois Volunteer Infantry*).

⁹ *Official Records,* Vol. XVI, Part 1, p. 640. Perfectly typical of the Union soldier's attitude is the blunt remark, "We thought anything belonging to a secessionist was for plunder," in the manuscript letters of Elmer J. Barker, 5th New York Cavalry.

¹⁰ *Story of the Service of Company E and of the 12th Wisconsin Regiment,* pp. 125-26.

¹¹ *Official Records,* Vol. XVI, Part 1, p. 644.

¹² *Letters of Ulysses S. Grant to His Father and Youngest Sister,* edited by Jesse Grant Cramer, pp. 69, 88; *General Grant's Letters to a Friend,* with Introduction and Notes by James Grant Wilson, p. 27.

¹³ *Ormsby MacKnight Mitchel,* pp. 317-19; *Memoirs of a Volunteer,* pp. 96, 103.

¹⁴ *Mr. Lincoln's Army,* pp. 155-56.

Cheers in the Starlight

¹ *Official Records,* Vol. XI, Part 3, pp. 337-38.

² Pope's weird account of this campaign and battle is in *B. & L.,* Vol. II, pp. 449-94.

³ *The Living Lincoln,* pp. 492, 493-94.

⁴ *Mr. Lincoln's Army,* pp. 51-54.

High-Water Mark

¹ *Official Records,* Vol. XVI, Part 2, p. 497. For a similar query sent by Lincoln to Gen. Horatio G. Wright at Cincinnati, see p. 496; Buell's reply is p. 500.

² Ibid., p. 421.

³ Ibid., Vol. XVII, Part 2, p. 222.

[4] *Mr. Lincoln's Army*, pp. 167-69.

[5] A first-rate study of the Antietam campaign is to be found in *The Antietam and Fredericksburg*, by Francis Winthrop Palfrey.

[6] *B. & L.*, Vol. II, p. 627.

[7] For a good brief account of Antietam, see Jacob Cox in *B. & L.*, Vol. II, pp. 630-60.

Chapter Seven: I SEE NO END

The Best There Was in the Ranch

[1] *Military Reminiscences of the Civil War*, by Jacob Cox, Vol. I, pp. 358-61.

[2] *The Sherman Letters: Correspondence between General and Senator Sherman from 1837 to 1891*, pp. 164-65.

[3] Ibid., pp. 166, 185.

[4] *B. & L.*, p. 43. This volume contains an extensive discussion of the Kentucky campaign, written by General Buell. Buell was in many ways an unfortunate man; in no way more unfortunate than in the fact that his lengthy, well-reasoned explanations of the things he did during the war have a stodgy, pedestrian quality which makes them all but literally unreadable. See also *The Story of a Thousand*, by Albion W. Tourgee, p. 70 ff.

[5] *History of the Tenth Regiment Indiana Volunteer Infantry*, pp. 171-72; *Official Records*, Vol. XVI, Part 1, pp. 662, 693.

[6] Van Horne, Vol. I, pp. 185-95; *Co. Aytch: Maury Gray's First Tennessee Regiment*, by Sam R. Watkins, p. 81; manuscript diary of Henry Mortimer Hempstead, 2nd Michigan Cavalry.

[7] Van Horne, Vol. I, pp. 197-99, 205; *Official Records*, Vol. XVI, Part 2, pp. 622, 626-27.

[8] *B. & L.*, Vol. II, pp. 737-57; *The History of Fuller's Ohio Brigade*, pp. 86, 89.

[9] *Personal Memoirs of U. S. Grant*, Vol. I, p. 420.

There Was No Patience

[1] *History of the 38th Regiment Indiana Volunteer Infantry*, p. 66.

[2] *A History of the Sixth Iowa Infantry*, pp. 174-75.

[3] *Three Years in the Army: The Story of the 13th Massachusetts Volunteers*, by Charles E. Davis, Jr., pp. 24-26.

[4] *Army Letters, 1861-1865*, by Oliver Willcox Norton, p. 27.

[5] *History of the Tenth Regiment Indiana Volunteer Infantry*, p. 170; *Mr. Lincoln's Army*, p. 199.

[6] *Reminiscences of the Civil War, from Diaries of Members of the 103rd Illinois Volunteer Infantry*, compiled by a committee, p. 26; *History of the 24th Michigan of the Iron Brigade*, by O. B. Curtis, p. 65.

[7] *The History of Fuller's Ohio Brigade*, p. 67.

[8] *Army Memoirs of Lucius W. Barber*, p. 91; *A History of the Sixth Iowa Infantry*, p. 147; *Downing's Civil War Diary*, pp. 80, 92; *History of the 16th Battery of Ohio Volunteer Light Artillery*, p. 35.

[9] *The Story of a Cavalry Regiment*, p. 404.

[10] *History of the 38th Regiment Indiana Volunteer Infantry*, p. 18; *History of the 15th Regiment Iowa Veteran Volunteer Infantry*, p. 85; *The Story of a Cavalry Regiment*, pp. 54-55.

[11] *The Wild Riders of the First Kentucky Cavalry*, pp. 162, 164.

[12] *Official Records*, Vol. XX, Part 2, p. 69.

[13] *The Living Lincoln*, pp. 519-20, 522; *Official Records*, Series 3, Vol. II, pp. 892-97.

Thin Moon and Cold Mist

[1] For an extended discussion of the difficulty in regard to the pontoons, see *Glory Road*, pp. 34-39.

[2] Any reader who wants source references for Fredericksburg will find a tabulation in the "Notes" section of the aforementioned *Glory Road*.

[3] For various glimpses of Rosecrans, see *The History of the 104th Regiment of Illinois Volunteer Infantry*, by William Wirt Calkins, p. 44; *Greene County Soldiers in the Late War*, by Ira S. Owens, p. 27; Cox, op. cit., Vol. I, pp. 111-12, 127, 133.

[4] *The Life of Major General George H. Thomas*, pp. 75-76, 84-89.

[5] Van Horne, Vol. I, pp. 228-29; *History of the Sixth Regiment Indiana Volunteer Infantry*, p. 176.

[6] Ibid., pp. 194-95; *History of the 34th Regiment of Illinois Volunteer Infantry,* by Edwin W. Payne, pp. 43-44.

[7] Van Horne, Vol. I, pp. 234-38; *B. & L.,* Vol. III, pp. 620-29.

[8] *Official Records,* Vol. XX, Part 1, p. 234.

[9] *The Life of Major General George H. Thomas,* p. 97.

[10] *With the Rank and File,* p. 9; *History of the 38th Regiment Indiana Volunteer Infantry,* pp. 61-63; *Echoes of the Civil War as I Hear Them,* by Michael H. Fitch, pp. 105-8; *Greene County Soldiers in the Late War,* pp. 33-35.

Down the River

[1] *Official Records,* Vol. XVII, Part 2, pp. 274, 275, 278, for McClernand's letters to Stanton. His confidential orders, signed by Stanton and dated October 20, 1862, are in the same volume, p. 282.

[2] Ibid., pp. 300, 302.

[3] *Personal Memoirs of U. S. Grant,* Vol. I, p. 426.

[4] Ibid., pp. 427-28.

[5] *Official Records,* Vol. XVII, Part 2, pp. 400, 401-2, 420.

[6] Ibid., p. 425.

[7] *Personal Memoirs of U. S. Grant,* Vol. I, pp. 430-31. There is an appreciative discussion of the little game in Earl Schenck Miers' *The Web of Victory,* pp. 34-35. Lloyd Lewis also examines it in his *Sherman, Fighting Prophet.*

[8] *Under the Old Flag,* by Maj. Gen. James Harrison Wilson, Vol. I, p. 141.

[9] *Personal Memoirs of U. S. Grant,* Vol. I, pp. 434-35.

[10] Lewis, op. cit., pp. 259-60.

[11] *Official Records,* Vol. XVII, Part 2, p. 534.

[12] Lewis, op. cit., p. 262.

Chapter Eight: SWING OF THE PENDULUM

The Hour of Darkness

[1] Manuscript letters of John W. Chase; *War Letters of William Thompson Lusk*, pp. 245, 256.

[2] *Army Life of an Illinois Soldier*, pp. 153-54; *Memoirs of the War*, by Capt. Ephraim A. Wilson, pp. 151-52; *Echoes of the Civil War as I Hear Them*, p. 118; *Official Records*, Vol. XX, Part 2, pp. 318, 323.

[3] Gosnell, op. cit., p. 146; *History of the 83rd Regiment Indiana Volunteer Infantry*, by Joseph Grecian, p. 22; *Letters from the Army*, p. 184.

[4] Manuscript letters of Isaac Jackson, 83rd Ohio; manuscript letters of George L. Lang, 12th Wisconsin; *History of the 77th Illinois Volunteer Infantry*, p. 120, passim.

[5] *Roster and Record of Iowa Soldiers in the War of the Rebellion*, Vol. V, pp. 741-88; *Iowa and the Rebellion*, by Lurton Dunham Ingersoll, pp. 661-63.

[6] *Letters from the Army*, p. 174; *Reminiscences of the Civil War, from Diaries of Members of the 103rd Illinois Volunteer Infantry*, p. 54.

[7] *Mr. Lincoln's Army*, p. 299.

[8] "Some Recollections of Grant," by S. H. M. Byers, from *The Annals of the War Written by Leading Participants*, pp. 342-43.

[9] *Three Years with the Armies of the Ohio and the Cumberland*, pp. 46, 48; *Official Records*, Vol. XX, Part 1, p. 197.

[10] "Characteristics of the Armies," by H. V. Redfield, from *The Annals of the War*, pp. 361-65. Note an eastern soldier's comment: "In manners, in the conduct of soldiers and the discipline, these bundles of rags, these cough-racked, diseased and starved men [i.e., the Confederates] excel our well-fed, well-clothed, our best soldiers." (Manuscript letters of James Gillette.)

[11] *Official Records*, Vol. XXIV, Part 1, p. 222.

[12] *Glory Road*, pp. 156-63; manuscript letters of John W. Chase.

[13] *Service with the Sixth Wisconsin Volunteers*, by Rufus R. Dawes, p. 125.

Stalemate in the Swamps

[1] *Reminiscences of the Civil War, from Diaries of Members of the 103rd Illinois Volunteer Infantry*, p. 15.

[2] See T. Harry Williams, *Lincoln and the Radicals*, p. 275 ff.

[3] *Personal Memoirs of U. S. Grant*, Vol. I, pp. 442-49; *Under the Old Flag*, Vol. I, pp. 154-55.

[4] Ibid., p. 152.

[5] *B. & L.*, Vol. III, pp. 561-63.

[6] Ibid., pp. 563-64; *The Web of Victory*, by Earl Schenck Miers pp. 119-30.

The Face of the Enemy

[1] *Official Records*, Vol. XVII, Part 2, p. 424.

[2] *The Web of Victory*, pp. 54-55.

[3] *A History of the Negro Troops in the War of the Rebellion*, by George W. Williams, pp. 106-7.

[4] Ibid., p. 108.

[5] *Army Life of an Illinois Soldier*, pp. 126, 166-67.

[6] *History of the 53rd Regiment Ohio Volunteer Infantry*, pp. 102-3; George Williams, op. cit., p. 110.

[7] *The Negro in the Civil War*, by Benjamin Quarles, pp. 8-9, 200-1.

[8] *Musket and Sword*, by Edwin C. Bennett, p. 315.

[9] *Personal Recollections*, by Maj. Gen. Grenville M. Dodge, p. 14.

[10] *Story of the Service of Company E and the 12th Wisconsin Regiment*, pp. 188-90.

[11] George Williams, op. cit., pp. 161-62, 166.

[12] Quarles, op. cit., p. 201.

[13] T. Harry Williams, op. cit., p. 291; Quarles, op. cit., p. 184.

End of a Campaign

[1] *B. & L.*, Vol. III, pp. 441-59.

[2] *The Sherman Letters: Correspondence between General and Senator Sherman*, p. 192.

[3] *Three Years with Grant*, by Sylvanus Cadwallader, edited by Benjamin P. Thomas, pp. 61-62.

[4] *The Rise of U. S. Grant*, pp. 288-89; *Under the Old Flag*, Vol. I, pp. 158-60; *The Web of Victory*, pp. 138-39.

[5] Lewis, op. cit., pp. 270-71.

[6] *Story of the Service of Company E and of the 12th Wisconsin Regiment*, p. 179; *A Soldier Boy's Letters to His Father and Mother*, pp. 46, 54.

[7] *Muskets and Medicine*, pp. 73-74, 84; *Downing's Civil War Diary*, p. 113.

[8] *Under the Old Flag*, Vol. I, pp. 168-69; *History of the 77th Illinois Volunteer Infantry*, pp. 132-33.

[9] *Under the Old Flag*, Vol. I, p. 164; *Personal Memoirs of U. S. Grant*, Vol. I, pp. 463-64.

[10] *Ulysses S. Grant and the Period of National Preservation and Reconstruction*, p. 160.

[11] *Personal Memoirs of U. S. Grant*, Vol. I, p. 488. For a first-rate account of the Grierson raid and an appealing sketch of Grierson himself, the reader is referred to D. Alexander Brown's excellent book, *Grierson's Raid*.

[12] *Reunion of the 33rd Illinois Regiment: Report of Proceedings*, p. 13; *B. & L.*, Vol. III, pp. 499, 501.

[13] Lewis, op. cit., p. 273.

[14] *Personal Memoirs of U. S. Grant*, Vol. I, p. 480: "I felt a degree of relief scarcely ever equalled since. . . . I was on dry ground on the same side of the river with the enemy."

[15] *The Story of a Cavalry Regiment*, p. 84; *Three Years with Grant*, pp. 74-75.

[16] *History of the 33rd Regiment Illinois Veteran Volunteer Infantry*, p. 39.

[17] *Personal Memoirs of U. S. Grant*, Vol. I, p. 526.

Chapter Nine: THE TREES AND THE RIVER

Final Miscalculation

[1] *The Campaign of Chancellorsville*, by John Bigelow, Jr., p. 221.

A list of sources for the Chancellorsville portion of this chapter will be found in *Glory Road*, pp. 386-90.

[2] See *R. E. Lee*, by Douglas Southall Freeman, Vol. III, pp. 18-19.

Moment of Truth

[1] *The Road to Richmond*, by Maj. Abner R. Small, p. 94; *The History of the 9th Regiment Massachusetts Volunteer Infantry*, by Daniel George MacNamara, p. 299.

[2] *The Life and Letters of George Gordon Meade*, by Col. George Meade, Vol. I, p. 372.

[3] *History of the 12th Regiment New Hampshire Volunteers*, by Capt. A. W. Bartlett, p. 114; *Three Years Campaign of the Ninth N.Y.S.M. During the Southern Rebellion*, by John W. Jaques, p. 149; *The Story of the 15th Regiment Massachusetts Volunteer Infantry*, by Andrew E. Ford, p. 256; *The Twentieth Connecticut: A Regimental History*, by John W. Storrs, p. 70; *History of the First Regiment Minnesota Volunteer Infantry*, by R. I. Holcombe, p. 330.

[4] In *Glory Road*, this author somehow identified the tune that took the first brigade into battle as "The Girl I Left Behind Me." A courteous letter from the grandson of the Gen. Rufus Dawes who commanded the 6th Wisconsin of that brigade at Gettysburg has provided the necessary correction. Mr. Dawes recalls that as a small boy he often saw his father or one of his uncles come into the parlor where the old soldier was sitting and pick "The Campbells Are Coming" out on the piano, one-finger fashion, "just to see the old man's beard bristle."

[5] Manuscript letters of John W. Chase.

Unvexed to the Sea

[1] *B. & L.*, Vol. III, p. 517; *Three Years with Grant*, p. 89.

[2] *B. & L.*, Vol. III, p. 518; *History of the 33rd Regiment Illinois Veteran Volunteer Infantry*, p. 44.

[3] *Under the Old Flag*, Vol. I, pp. 180-83; *Personal Memoirs of U. S. Grant*, Vol. I, p. 531.

[4] Manuscript letters of Abram S. Funk, 35th Iowa; manuscript letters of George L. Lang, 12th Wisconsin.

[5] *History of the 16th Battery of Ohio Volunteer Light Artillery*, pp. 73, 75.

[6] *Three Years with Grant*, pp. 103-9. For a highly critical analysis of the Cadwallader memoirs, see Kenneth Williams in *American Heritage*, Vol. VII, No. 5.

[7] Lewis, op. cit., pp. 282-84; *Personal Memoirs of U. S. Grant*, Vol. I, pp. 546-47.

[8] Manuscript letters of George L. Lang; *Story of the Service of Company E and of the 12th Wisconsin Regiment*, p. 196.

[9] *Forty-Six Years in the Army*, by Lt. Gen. John M. Schofield, p. 145.

[10] *Story of the Service of Company E and of the 12th Wisconsin Regiment*, pp. 202-4; *History of the 33rd Regiment Illinois Veteran Volunteer Infantry*, pp. 84-85.

[11] *Downing's Civil War Diary*, p. 124.

[12] *B. & L.*, Vol. III, pp. 530-34, 536; manuscript letters of George L. Lang.

[13] *B. & L.*, Vol. III, p. 492.

[14] *Story of the Service of Company E and of the 12th Wisconsin Regiment*, p. 194.

Chapter Ten: LAST OF THE MIGHT-HAVE-BEENS

Pursuit in Tennessee

[1] *The Sherman Letters: Correspondence between General and Senator Sherman*, p. 213.

[2] For a suggestive discussion of the connection between Vallandigham's visit and the Morgan raid, see Howard Swiggett, *The Rebel Raider: A Life of John Hunt Morgan*, pp. 120-26.

[3] *Official Records*, Vol. XXIII, Part 1, p. 640. General Wheeler's report, emphasizing that Morgan disobeyed orders by crossing the Ohio, is in the same volume, pp. 817-18.

[4] *History of the 77th Illinois Volunteer Infantry*, p. 185; *History of the 16th Battery of Ohio Volunteer Light Artillery*, pp. 86-88.

[5] *History of the 53rd Regiment Ohio Volunteer Infantry*, p. 108.

[6] Lewis, op. cit., p. 309; *Personal Memoirs of U. S. Grant*, Vol. I, p. 578 ff.

[7] *The Negro in the Civil War*, pp. 1-11, 13-18.

[8] *Echoes of the Civil War as I Hear Them*, p. 121; *History of the Sixth Regiment Indiana Volunteer Infantry*, p. 203; *History of the 38th Regiment Indiana Volunteer Infantry*, pp. 68-71.

[9] *Personal Memoirs of U. S. Grant*, Vol. II, p. 20; Van Horne, Vol. I, pp. 298-99.

[10] *History of the Sixth Regiment Indiana Volunteer Infantry*, p. 202.

[11] *Official Records*, Vol. XXIII, Part 1, p. 408; *The History of the 104th Regiment of Illinois Volunteer Infantry*, p. 97; *History of the Sixth Regiment Indiana Volunteer Infantry*, pp. 210-11.

[12] *Opdycke Tigers: 125th Ohio Volunteer Infantry*, by Charles T. Clark, p. 81; *Official Records*, Vol. XXIII, Part 1, p. 407; *History of the Sixth Regiment Indiana Volunteer Infantry*, p. 215.

[13] *The History of the 104th Regiment of Illinois Volunteer Infantry*, p. 98.

[14] Ibid., pp. 101, 111.

Ghoul-Haunted Woodland

[1] Van Horne, Vol. I, pp. 317, 320, 322-23, 327.

[2] *B. & L.*, Vol. III, pp. 641-45.

[3] Ibid., pp. 638-39.

[4] *The History of the 104th Regiment of Illinois Volunteer Infantry*, p. 118; *Echoes of the Civil War as I Hear Them*, pp. 134-36. Note the remark of the author of the *History of the Sixth Regiment Indiana Volunteer Infantry*, p. 225: "There was not even a private in the ranks who did not realize the fact that we had a big contract on our hands."

[5] *The Army of Tennessee*, p. 263. This book, incidentally, contains one of the best of all the accounts of the battle of Chickamauga.

[6] *History of the 38th Regiment Indiana Volunteer Infantry*, pp. 89-91.

[7] *The History of the 104th Regiment of Illinois Volunteer Infantry*, pp. 134-35; Van Horne, Vol. I, pp. 342-43, 345-47.

[8] Ibid., p. 347; *B. & L.*, Vol. III, p. 663; Cox, op. cit., Vol. II, pp. 160-61.

[9] *History of the Sixth Regiment Indiana Volunteer Infantry*, p. 239; *Opdycke Tigers*, pp. 106-8, 117, 123-24; *Three Years with the Armies of the Ohio and the Cumberland*, p. 54.

[10] *History of the Sixth Regiment Indiana Volunteer Infantry*, p. 242.

The Pride of Soldiers

[1] *Memoirs of the War*, pp. 208-9; *Three Years with the Armies of the Ohio and the Cumberland*, pp. 57-58; *The History of the 104th Regiment of Illinois Volunteer Infantry*, p. 159.

[2] *History of the 34th Regiment of Illinois Volunteer Infantry*, p. 78.

[3] *Personal Memoirs of U. S. Grant*, Vol. II, p. 26; Cox, op. cit., Vol. II, p. 16.

[4] *B. & L.*, Vol. III, pp. 684-85. This volume contains an amusing account of the building of the river steamer, pp. 676 ff.

[5] Cox, op. cit., Vol. II, pp. 17-19.

[6] *Footprints through Dixie: Everyday Life of the Man under a Musket*, by J. W. Gaskill, pp. 60-62, 64.

[7] *History of the 14th Illinois Cavalry*, by W. L. Sanford, p. 63; Cox, op. cit., Vol. II, p. 84.

[8] *B. & L.*, Vol. III, p. 693 n.

[9] Ibid., p. 694.

[10] *Personal Memoirs of U. S. Grant*, Vol. II, pp. 42-43.

[11] *Civil War Papers Read before the Commandery of the State of Massachusetts, Military Order of the Loyal Legion of the United States*, Vol. I, p. 250; *History of the 3rd Regiment of Wisconsin Veteran Volunteer Infantry*, p. 233 n.; *Army Life of an Illinois Soldier*, p. 218; *History of the 33rd Regiment Illinois Veteran Volunteer Infantry*, pp. 47-48.

A Half Dozen Roasted Acorns

[1] Lewis, op. cit., p. 319.

[2] *The Life of Major General George H. Thomas*, pp. 180-91.

[3] Lewis, op. cit., pp. 320-21.

[4] *B. & L.*, Vol. III, p. 706.

[5] *History of the Sixth Regiment Indiana Volunteer Infantry*, p. 274.

[6] *The Life of Major General George H. Thomas*, pp. 191-92; *Opdycke Tigers*, pp. 164, 169, 172; *The History of the 104th Regiment of Illinois Volunteer Infantry*, pp. 180, 183; Lewis, op. cit., p. 323.

[7] *B. & L.*, Vol. III, p. 725.

[8] *Opdycke Tigers*, p. 166; *The Life of Major General George H. Thomas*, p. 197; *B. & L.*, Vol. III, pp. 725-26; *History of the Sixth Regiment Indiana Volunteer Infantry*, p. 275.

[9] *Ibid.*, pp. 276-78.

[10] *Memoirs of a Volunteer*, p. 263; Lewis, op. cit., pp. 325-26.

[11] *A History of the Sixth Iowa Infantry*, pp. 247-48; Cox, op. cit., Vol. II, pp. 84-85; *Footprints through Dixie*, p. 70; Schofield, op. cit., p. 114.

[12] *Echoes of the Civil War as I Hear Them*, p. 187.

[13] *The Life of Major General George H. Thomas*, p. 213.

[14] *Ohio at Shiloh: Report of the Commission*, p. 204.

Chapter Eleven: AND KEEP MOVING ON

Year of Jubilo

[1] *Official Records*, Series 4, Vol. III, p. 130.

[2] *The Living Lincoln*, p. 162; *Official Records*, Vol. XXIV, Part 3, p. 567.

[3] *General Grant's Letters to a Friend, 1861-1880*; Lewis, op. cit., p. 335.

[4] *Official Records*, Vol. XVII, Part 2, p. 868; *The Story of a Cavalry Regiment*, pp. 186, 207, 216; Lewis, op. cit., pp. 332-33.

[5] *Story of the Service of Company E and of the 12th Wisconsin Regiment*, pp. 249-50.

[6] *Official Records*, Vol. LII, Part 2, pp. 586-92, 598-99, 606-9.

[7] *Ibid.*, Series 4, Vol. II, p. 345; Series 4, Vol. III, p. 86.

Vote of Confidence

[1] See Benjamin P. Thomas's *Abraham Lincoln*, pp. 405-8.

[2] *Personal Memoirs of John H. Brinton*, p. 239.

[3] Lewis, op. cit., p. 345.

[4] *The Life of John A. Rawlins*, by Maj. Gen. James Harrison Wilson, pp. 426-27; *The Life and Letters of George Gordon Meade*, Vol. II, p. 201.

[5] *Official Records*, Series 3, Vol. V, p. 650.

[6] *Drum Taps in Dixie*, pp. 144-45.

[7] *Official Records*, Series 3, Vol. V, pp. 649, 651; *History of the 34th Regiment of Illinois Volunteer Infantry*, p. 96; manuscript letters of John W. Chase; manuscript letters of George L. Lang; Cox, op. cit., Vol. II, p. 92; *Downing's Civil War Diary*, p. 177.

[8] *Official Records*, Vol. XXXIII, p. 776.

[9] *Greene County Soldiers in the Late War*, p. 68; *Echoes of the Civil War as I Hear Them*, p. 197; *Three Years with the Armies of the Ohio and the Cumberland*, p. 66.

The Great Decision

[1] Lewis, op. cit., p. 343.

[2] *The Road to Richmond*, by Maj. Abner R. Small, pp. 130-31; *Recollections of a Private Soldier in the Army of the Potomac*, by Frank Wilkeson, pp. 42-43.

[3] *R. E. Lee*, by Douglas Southall Freeman, Vol. III, p. 287.

[4] Manuscript letters of John W. Chase.

A Question of Time

[1] Freeman, op. cit., Vol. III, p. 398.

[2] See John C. Ropes, "The Failure to Take Petersburg on June 16-18, 1864," in the *Papers of the Military Historical Society of Massachusetts*, Vol. V; *A Stillness at Appomattox*, pp. 183-99.

[3] Manuscript diary of Henry Mortimer Hempstead, 2nd Michigan Cavalry.

[4] *A Stillness at Appomattox*, pp. 219-51.

[5] *The Living Lincoln*, p. 616.

Chapter Twelve: WE WILL NOT CEASE

That Bright Particular Star

[1] *Official Records*, Vol. XIX, Part 2, p. 505.

[2] *Reminiscences of the Civil War, from Diaries of Members of the 103rd Illinois Volunteer Infantry*, pp. 99, 133; *Story of the Service of Company E and of the 12th Wisconsin Regiment*, pp. 281-82.

[3] Lewis, op. cit., pp. 357-58.

[4] "Letters of C. C. Carpenter," edited by Mildred Throne; from the *Iowa Journal of History*, January 1955, p. 84.

[5] *Reminiscences of the Civil War, from Diaries of Members of the 103rd Illinois Volunteer Infantry*, pp. 78, 95.

[6] Lewis, op. cit., pp. 375-78.

[7] Schofield, op. cit., pp. 131, 231-32.

[8] *The Life of Major General George H. Thomas*, pp. 243-45.

[9] Lewis, op. cit., p. 386.

[10] Manuscript letter of General Sherman to Emily Hoffman of Baltimore. Family tradition regarding Miss Hoffman's receipt of the news of McPherson's death, and her reaction to it, related by her grand-nephew, Mr. Walter Lord of New York.

[11] Lewis, op. cit., p. 400.

Wind across the Sky

[1] For slavery as a race problem, see Allan Nevins and Henry Steele Commager, *America: The Story of a Free People*, pp. 214-15.

[2] *Abraham Lincoln*, by Benjamin P. Thomas, pp. 441-42.

[3] *Abraham Lincoln: The War Years*, Vol. III, p. 227.

[4] Ibid., p. 218; Thomas, op. cit., p. 445.

[5] *B. & L.*, Vol. IV, pp. 379-400.

The Grapes of Wrath

[1] Lewis, op. cit., pp. 426, 430.

[2] Ibid., p. 431.

[3] B. & L., Vol. IV, p. 672; *The History of the 104th Regiment of Illinois Volunteer Infantry*, pp. 252-53; *Reminiscences of the Civil War, from Diaries of Members of the 103rd Illinois Volunteer Infantry*, p. 147.

[4] *The History of the 104th Regiment of Illinois Volunteer Infantry*, p. 252.

[5] Manuscript letter, Sherman to Emily Hoffman; *Official Records*, Vol. XXX, Part 3, p. 698.

[6] *Reminiscences of the Civil War, from Diaries of Members of the 103rd Illinois Volunteer Infantry*, pp. 148, 149; *The History of the 104th Regiment of Illinois Volunteer Infantry*, p. 278; *History of the 34th Regiment of Illinois Volunteer Infantry*, p. 106.

[7] *The History of the 104th Regiment of Illinois Volunteer Infantry*, p. 263; *Footprints through Dixie*, p. 124.

[8] *Reminiscences of the Civil War, from Diaries of Members of the 103rd Illinois Volunteer Infantry*, p. 153.

[9] Cox, op. cit., Vol. II, p. 234; *The History of the 104th Regiment of Illinois Volunteer Infantry*, p. 279; *History of the 34th Regiment of Illinois Volunteer Infantry* p. 173.

[10] *The History of the 104th Regiment of Illinois Volunteer Infantry*, p. 258.

[11] *Reminiscences of the Civil War, from Diaries of Members of the 103rd Illinois Volunteer Infantry*, p. 164; Lewis, op. cit., p. 465; Cox, op. cit., Vol. II, p. 234.

[12] *Downing's Civil War Diary*, p. 237; *A History of the Sixth Iowa Infantry*, pp. 379-80, 384; *The History of the 104th Regiment of Illinois Volunteer Infantry*, p. 279.

[13] Lewis, op. cit., p. 471.

The Enemy Will Be Attacked

[1] The most exhaustive discussion of Hood's odd failure at Spring Hill, probably, is that of Stanley Horn in his excellent *Army of Tennessee*, pp. 384-95.

[2] *Footprints through Dixie*, pp. 136-37.

[3] *With the Rank and File*, pp. 18-19.

[4] *The Army of Tennessee*, pp. 399-404; Schofield, op. cit., pp. 177-79; *Opdycke Tigers*, pp. 339-53; *With the Rank and File*, pp. 16-17. Note that the youthful Colonel MacArthur of the 24th

Wisconsin, who was wounded in this fight, later became the father of General Douglas MacArthur.

[5] *Footprints through Dixie,* pp. 142-43.

[6] Manuscript diary of Henry Mortimer Hempstead.

[7] The whole sequence of events is set forth in complete detail in Maj. Gen. James Harrison Wilson's *Under the Old Flag,* Vol. II, pp. 64-93; see also *B. & L.,* Vol. IV, pp. 455-56.

[8] Manuscript diary of Henry Mortimer Hempstead.

[9] *History of the 51st Indiana Veteran Volunteer Infantry,* p. 259; *History of the 14th Illinois Cavalry,* p. 284.

[10] *Under the Old Flag,* Vol. II, pp. 122-23, 126.

[11] Ibid., p. 95.

Chapter Thirteen: TWILIGHT AND VICTORY

Reap the Whirlwind

[1] *History of the 34th Regiment of Illinois Volunteer Infantry,* pp. 179, 191.

[2] Lewis, op. cit., p. 490.

[3] *History of the 83rd Regiment Indiana Volunteer Infantry,* p. 71; *History of the 34th Regiment of Illinois Volunteer Infantry,* p. 354.

[4] *History of the 83rd Regiment Indiana Volunteer Infantry,* p. 77; *History of the 53rd Regiment Ohio Volunteer Infantry,* p. 176; *Reminiscences of the Civil War, from Diaries of Members of the 103rd Illinois Volunteer Infantry,* p. 176; *History of Fuller's Ohio Brigade,* p. 265; *The History of the 104th Regiment of Illinois Volunteer Infantry,* pp. 309-10.

[5] *Echoes of the Civil War as I Hear Them,* pp. 268-69.

[6] *The History of the 104th Regiment of Illinois Volunteer Infantry,* p. 287.

[7] *Downing's Civil War Diary,* pp. 251, 259.

[8] *History of the Seventh Regiment Illinois Volunteer Infantry,* p. 297; *Reminiscences of the Civil War, from Diaries of Members of the 103rd Illinois Volunteer Infantry,* p. 183; *Story of the Service*

of Company E and of the 12th Wisconsin Regiment, p. 407; A History of the Sixth Iowa Infantry, pp. 411-14.

[9] Lewis, op. cit., pp. 506-7.

[10] B. & L., Vol. IV, p. 686.

[11] Downing's Civil War Diary, p. 260; The History of the 104th Regiment of Illinois Volunteer Infantry, p. 309; Lewis, op. cit., p. 509.

The Fire and the Night

[1] Manuscript diary of Capt. Lot Abraham, 4th Iowa Cavalry.

[2] Manuscript letters of Lewis Bissell, 2nd Connecticut Heavy Artillery.

[3] Manuscript letters of David Carpenter, Massachusetts agent for the Christian Commission; Cox, op. cit., Vol. II, p. 397.

[4] Official Records, Series 4, Vol. III, p. 1131.

[5] Ibid., pp. 1067-70.

[6] Ibid., pp. 1161-62.

Telegram in Cipher

[1] Personal Memoirs of U. S. Grant, Vol. II, p. 489. Grant's own account of the surrender proceedings and the version given by Col. Horace Porter in B. & L., Vol. IV, pp. 729-46, have been followed here.

[2] B. & L., Vol. IV, p. 744.

[3] Lewis, op. cit., pp. 534-35.

[4] Reminiscences of the Civil War, from Diaries of Members of the 103rd Illinois Volunteer Infantry, p. 208. A similar note was sounded by an Ohio soldier, who said that "the country will just be riddled and burnt over," adding wistfully: "I only wish that it was in some other state as there are a great many Union folks in N. C., but they will not escape." (Manuscript letters of Frank O. Weary, 29th Ohio Infantry.)

[5] The terms are summarized from Lewis, op. cit., pp. 540-41.

[6] B. & L., Vol. IV, p. 757.

Candlelight

[1] *The Living Lincoln,* pp. 600, 638-40.

[2] *Abraham Lincoln: The War Years,* Vol. IV, pp. 319-21.

[3] *The Story of a Cavalry Regiment,* pp. 509, 522.

[4] *History of the 3rd Regiment of Wisconsin Veteran Volunteer Infantry,* pp. 331-32.

[5] *A History of the Sixth Iowa Infantry,* p. 463.

[6] *History of the 51st Indiana Veteran Volunteer Infantry,* p. 303; manuscript diary of Capt. Lot Abraham.

[7] *Under the Maltese Cross, Antietam to Appomattox, narrated by the Rank and File,* pp. 382-83; New York Herald, May 24, 1865.

ACKNOWLEDGMENTS,
BIBLIOGRAPHY AND INDEX

Acknowledgments

This book could hardly have been written without the help which was provided by a large number of very generous people. Manuscript sources dealing with the lives and thoughts of Civil War soldiers are widely scattered; to get at them a writer is bound to rely on the kindness of those who own them. He thereby incurs a debt which can hardly be repaid but which can at least be gratefully acknowledged.

In preparing this book, the following manuscript sources were used:

Letters of George L. Lang, of the 12th Wisconsin; loaned by Stanley Barnett, of Cleveland.

Letters of Abram S. Funk, of the 35th Iowa; loaned by Mrs. Erie M. Funk, of Long Beach, Calif.

Letters of Isaac Jackson, of the 83rd Ohio; loaned by J. O. Jackson, of Detroit.

Letters of Frank O. Weary, drummer boy in the 29th Ohio Veteran Volunteers; loaned by G. H. Lohr, of Cuyahoga Falls, O.

Memoirs of Elmer J. Barker, of the 5th New York Cavalry; loaned by Dr. E. Eugene Barker, of Albany, N. Y.

Diary of Sgt. John P. Beech, of the 4th New Jersey; loaned by Albert C. Lambert, of Trenton, N. J.

Letters of James Gillette, of the 71st New York State Militia, later of the 4th Maryland Volunteers; loaned by Mrs. Amy G. Bassett, of Huletts Landing, N. Y.

Diary of Henry Mortimer Hempstead of the 2nd Michigan Cavalry; loaned by Miss Helen Hempstead, of Saginaw, Mich.

Diary of Bowman Garrison, of the 7th Pennsylvania Reserves; loaned by Mrs. Charles Haskell Danforth, of Stanford University, Calif.

Diary of Corp. Loring N. Hayden, of the 24th Massachusetts; loaned by Mrs. Genevieve Hayden Berry, of Wollaston, Mass.

Letters of General William T. Sherman to Emily Hoffman of Baltimore; loaned by Walter Lord, of New York.

Diary of Capt. Lot Abraham, of the 4th Iowa Cavalry; loaned by John D. Adams, of Newark, N. J.

Letters of David Carpenter, Massachusetts agent for the Christian Commission; loaned by Mrs. Olive L. Sawyer, of New York.

Letters of John W. Chase, of the 1st Massachusetts Artillery; loaned by Mrs. Margaret J. Collier, of Arlington, Va.

Letters of Lewis Bissell, of the 2nd Connecticut Heavy Artillery; loaned by Carl H. Bissell, of Syracuse, N. Y.

Correspondence of Senator Charles Sumner during the summer of 1864; loaned by Mrs. Mary Reeve, of Clearfield, Pa.

Letter of General Francis Barlow; loaned by his daughter, Mrs. Pierre Jay, of New York.

Letters of General U. S. Grant to Mrs. Grant; photostatic copies provided by Ralph Newman, of Chicago.

Other people to whom thanks for assistance are due include the following:

E. B. Long and Earl Schenck Miers read the book in manuscript and made many helpful suggestions. (It should go without saying, of course, that neither of these gentlemen is responsible for any opinions expressed in this book or for any factual errors which may be found in the text.)

Clifford Dowdey generously sacrificed a weekend to guide me about the fascinating but confusing battlefields of the Seven Days' fighting and shared with me his encyclopedic knowledge of that campaign.

L. Van Loan Naisawald of New York made available the findings of his extensive study of Civil War artillery.

Frank Warner, of Mineola, N.Y., kindly checked the facts in connection with the writing and first singing of the song "Year of Jubilo."

Donald H. Richards, of Durham, N.H., gave me a copy of his excellent manuscript study of the 5th New Hampshire Volunteers.

Lewis Gannett, editor of the Mainstream of America Series, and Walter I. Bradbury, managing editor of Doubleday & Company, performed their editorial functions in a way that made my task much more pleasant and easy.

To the historians and other staff members of the National Park Service at many Civil War battlefield parks I am very deeply indebted. Without exception, these men have had both the will and the knowledge to be of most substantial assistance.

I am particularly grateful to Mrs. Donna Whiteman, of New York, for speedy and competent typing of this manuscript.

Bibliography

General Works

A principal reliance in the preparation of this book has of course been the indispensable *War of the Rebellion: a Compilation of the Official Records of the Union and Confederate Armies,* published by the War Department in 1902. It is cited here as *Official Records;* unless otherwise noted, volumes cited are from Series I. Use also has been made of the *Dictionary of American Biography,* edited by Dumas Malone. In addition, the following works were consulted:

America: The Story of a Free People, by Allan Nevins and Henry Steele Commager. Boston, 1942.

The American Political Tradition and the Men Who Made It, by Richard Hofstadter. New York, 1951.

The Annals of the War Written by Leading Participants. Philadelphia, 1879.

Antietam and Fredericksburg, by Francis Winthrop Palfrey. New York, 1882.

The Army of Tennessee, by Stanley Horn. Indianapolis, 1941.

Battles and Leaders of the Civil War, edited by Robert Underwood Johnson and Clarence Clough Buel. 4 vols. New York, 1884-87.

P. G. T. Beauregard: Napoleon in Gray, by T. Harry Williams. Baton Rouge, 1954.

Bleeding Kansas, by Alice Nichols. New York, 1954.

The Blue and the Gray: The Story of the Civil War as Told by Participants, edited by Henry Steele Commager. Indianapolis, 1950.

The Borderland in the Civil War, by Edward Conrad Smith. New York, 1927.

John Brown, 1800-1859: A Biography Fifty Years After, by Oswald Garrison Villard. New York, 1943.

Bull Run Remembers, by Joseph Mills Hanson. Washington, 1952.

The Campaign of Chancellorsville, by John Bigelow, Jr. New Haven, 1910.

Campaigning with Grant, by Gen. Horace Porter. New York, 1907.

Civil War Papers Read before the Commandery of the State of Massachusetts, Military Order of the Loyal Legion of the United States. Boston, 1900.

Cleveland, the Making of a City, by William Ganson Rose. Cleveland and New York, 1950.

Confederate Operations in Canada and New York, by John W. Headley. New York and Washington, 1906.

Jefferson Davis: The Unreal and the Real, by Robert McElroy. 2 vols. New York, 1937.

Democracy in the Middle West, 1840-1940, edited by Jeannette P. Nichols and James G. Randall. New York, 1941.

The Diary of Gideon Welles, with an Introduction by John T. Morse, Jr. 3 vols. Boston and New York, 1911.

The Emergence of Modern America, 1865-1878, by Allan Nevins. New York, 1935.

Experiment in Rebellion, by Clifford Dowdey. New York, 1950.

Forty-Six Years in the Army, by Lt. Gen. John M. Schofield. New York, 1897.

Frémont: Pathmarker of the West, by Allan Nevins. New York and London, 1939.

Glory Road, by Bruce Catton. New York, 1952.

General Grant, by James Grant Wilson. New York, 1897.

Ulysses S. Grant and the Period of National Preservation and Reconstruction, by William Conant Church. New York, 1897.

General Grant's Letters to a Friend, 1861-1880, with Introduction and Notes by James Grant Wilson. New York, 1897.

Greyhounds of the Sea: The Story of the American Clipper Ship, by Carl C. Cutler. New York, 1930.

Grierson's Raid, by D. Alexander Brown. Urbana, Ill., 1954.

The Growth of the American Republic, by Samuel Eliot Morison and Henry Steele Commager. 2 vols. New York, 1942.

Guns on the Western Waters: The Story of River Gunboats in the Civil War, by H. Allen Gosnell. Baton Rouge, 1949.

History of the Army of the Cumberland, by Thomas B. Van Horne. 2 vols. Cincinnati, 1875.

History of the Army of the Potomac, by J. H. Stine. Philadelphia, 1892.

History of the Civil War, by James Ford Rhodes. New York, 1917.

A History of the Negro Troops in the War of the Rebellion, by George W. Williams. New York, 1888.

History of the Sault Ste. Marie Canal, by Dwight H. Kelton, Captain, U.S. Army. Detroit, 1888.

A History of the Southern Confederacy, by Clement Eaton. New York, 1954.

History of the United States from the Compromise of 1850, by James Ford Rhodes. 9 vols. New York, 1906.

Andrew Atkinson Humphreys: A Biography, by Henry H. Humphreys. Philadelphia, 1924.

Stonewall Jackson and the American Civil War, by Col. G. F. R. Henderson. London and New York, 1936.

R. E. Lee, by Douglas Southall Freeman. 4 vols. New York, 1934.

Lee's Lieutenants, by Douglas Southall Freeman. 3 vols. New York, 1942-44.

The Life of Lieutenant General Chaffee, by William Harding Carter. Chicago, 1917.

Life of General Nathaniel Lyon, by Ashbel Woodward, M.D. Hartford, 1862.

The Life and Letters of George Gordon Meade, by George Meade, Captain and Aide-de-Camp. 2 vols. New York, 1913.

Life in the Middle West, by James S. Clark. Chicago, 1916.

The Life of John A. Rawlins, by Maj. Gen. James Harrison Wilson. New York, 1916.

Life of Charles Sumner, by Walter G. Shotwell. New York, 1910.

The Life of Major General George H. Thomas, by Thomas B. Van Horne. New York, 1882.

Abraham Lincoln, by Benjamin P. Thomas. New York, 1952.

Abraham Lincoln: A History, by John G. Nicolay and John Hay. 10 vols. New York, 1900.

Abraham Lincoln: The Prairie Years, by Carl Sandburg. 2 vols. New York, 1926.

Abraham Lincoln: The War Years, by Carl Sandburg. 4 vols. New York, 1939.

Lincoln and the Radicals, by T. Harry Williams. Madison, Wis., 1941.

Lincoln Finds a General, by Kenneth P. Williams. 3 vols. New York, 1950-52.

Mr. Lincoln's Army, by Bruce Catton. New York, 1951.

The Living Lincoln, edited by Paul Angle and Earl Schenck Miers. New Brunswick, N.J., 1955.

The Long Ships Passing: The Story of the Great Lakes, by Walter Havighurst. New York, 1942.

McClellan's Own Story, by George B. McClellan. New York, 1887.

Main-Line of Mid-America: The Story of the Illinois Central, by Carlton J. Corliss. New York, 1950.

Meade's Headquarters, 1863-1865; letters of Col. Theodore Lyman from the Wilderness to Appomattox. Selected and edited by George R. Agassiz. Boston, 1922.

Michigan: A Guide to the Wolverine State, compiled by workers of the Writers Program of the WPA in the State of Michigan. New York, 1946.

Military Essays and Recollections: Papers Read before the Commandery of the State of Illinois, Military Order of the Loyal Legion of the United States. Chicago, 1891.

Military Reminiscences of the Civil War, by Jacob D. Cox. 2 vols. New York, 1900.

Minnesota: A State Guide, compiled and written by the Federal Writers' Project of the WPA. New York, 1947.

The Mississippi Valley in the Civil War, by John Fiske. Boston and New York, 1901.

Ormsby MacKnight Mitchel, Astronomer and General, by F. A. Mitchel. Boston and New York, 1887.

The Negro in the Civil War, by Benjamin Quarles. Boston, 1953.

The Ohio Gateway, by D. E. Crouse. New York, 1938.

Ohio at Shiloh: Report of the Commission, by T. J. Lindsay. Cincinnati, 1903.

Papers of the Military Historical Society of Massachuetts, edited by Theodore Dwight. 10 vols. Boston, 1906.

Pemberton, Defender of Vicksburg, by John C. Pemberton. Chapel Hill, 1944.

Personal Memoirs of U. S. Grant. 2 vols. New York, 1885.

Personal Recollections, by Maj. Gen. Grenville M. Dodge. Council Bluffs, 1914.

Personal Recollections of Distinguished Generals, by William F. G. Shanks. New York, 1866.

The Rebellion Record: A Diary of American Events, edited by Frank Moore. 12 vols. New York, 1864.

The Rebel Raider: A Life of John Hunt Morgan, by Howard Swiggett. New York, 1937.

Recollections of the Civil War, by Charles A. Dana. New York, 1898.

Recollections of Half a Century, by Alexander K. McClure. Salem, Mass., 1902.

Recollections of War Times, by Albert Gallatin Riddle. New York, 1895.

Reporters for the Union, by Bernard Weisberger. Boston, 1953.

The Rise of U. S. Grant, by A. L. Conger. New York, 1931.

Sherman, Fighting Prophet, by Lloyd Lewis. New York, 1932.

The Sherman Letters: Correspondence between General and Senator Sherman from 1837 to 1891, edited by Rachael Sherman Thorndike. New York, 1894.

Edward Rowland Sill: His Life and Work, by William Belmont Parker. Boston and New York, 1915.

A Standard History of Kansas and Kansans, by William E. Connelley. 5 vols. Chicago and New York, 1918.

A Stillness at Appomattox, by Bruce Catton. New York, 1953.

The Story of Detroit, by George B. Catlin. Detroit, 1923.

The Story of the Guard: A Chronicle of the War, by Jessie Benton Frémont. Boston, 1863.

Tambo and Bones: A History of the American Minstrel Stage, by Carl Wittke. Durham, N.C., 1930.

Three Years with Grant, as Recalled by War Correspondent Sylvanus Cadwallader, edited and with an Introduction and Notes by Benjamin P. Thomas. New York, 1955.

Under the Old Flag, by Maj. Gen. James Harrison Wilson. 2 vols. New York, 1912.

The Union Cause in St. Louis in 1861, by Robert J. Rombauer. St. Louis, 1909.

"Ben-Hur" Wallace: The Life of General Lew Wallace, by Irving McKee. Berkeley and Los Angeles, 1947.

Lew Wallace: An Autobiography, 2 vols. New York and London, 1906.

War Papers, Commandery of Wisconsin, Military Order of the Loyal Legion of the United States. Milwaukee, 1891.

War Papers Read before the Commandery of the State of Michigan, Military Order of the Loyal Legion of the United States. Detroit, 1893.

The Web of Victory: Grant at Vicksburg, by Earl Schenck Miers. New York, 1955.

Wisconsin: A Guide to the Badger State, compiled by writers of the Writers Program of the WPA in the State of Wisconsin. New York, 1941.

Regimental Histories, Soldiers' Diaries and Reminiscences, etc.

Army Letters, 1861-1865, by Oliver Willcox Norton. Chicago, 1903.

Army Life of an Illinois Soldier: Letters and Diary of the Late Charles W. Wills, compiled and published by his sister. Washington, 1906.

Army Memoirs of Lucius W. Barber, Company D, 15th Illinois Infantry. Chicago, 1894.

Battle of Wilson's Creek; reprinted from Articles by Lucile Morris

Upton in the Springfield News and Leader. Springfield, Mo., 1950.

Berdan's United States Sharpshooters in the Army of the Potomac, by Captain C. A. Stevens. St. Paul, 1892.

Co. Aytch: Maury Gray's First Tennessee Regiment, by Sam R. Watkins, with an Introduction by Bell I. Wiley. Jackson, Tenn., 1952.

Days and Events, by Col. Thomas L. Livermore. Boston, 1920.

Diary of an Ohio Volunteer, by a Musician, Co. H, 19th Regiment. Cleveland, 1861.

Down in Dixie: Life in a Cavalry Regiment in the War Days, by Stanton P. Allen. Boston, 1888.

Downing's Civil War Diary, by Sgt. Alexander Downing, edited by Olynthus B. Clark. Des Moines, 1916.

Drum Taps in Dixie: Memories of a Drummer Boy, 1861-1865, by Delavan S. Miller. Watertown, N.Y., 1905.

The Eagle Regiment: 8th Wisconsin Infantry Volunteers, by a "Non-Vet" of Company H. Belleville, Wis., 1890.

Echoes of the Civil War as I Hear Them, by Michael H. Fitch. New York, 1905.

The Fifth Army Corps, by Lt. Col. William H. Powell. New York, 1896.

First Ohio Heavy Artillery History, by H. C. Miller, Gallipolis, O., 1899.

Footprints through Dixie: Everyday Life of the Man under a Musket, by J. W. Gaskill. Alliance, O., 1919.

Greene County Soldiers in the Late War, by Ira S. Owens. Dayton, O., 1884.

History of the 8th Cavalry Regiment, Illinois Volunteers, by Abner Hard, M.D. Aurora, Ill., 1868.

History of the 83rd Regiment Indiana Volunteer Infantry, by Joseph Grecian. Cincinnati, 1865.

History of the 15th Regiment Iowa Veteran Volunteer Infantry, by William Worth Belknap. Keokuk, Ia., 1887.

History of the 5th Regiment Maine Volunteers, by the Rev. George W. Bicknell. Portland, Me., 1871.

History of the 51st Indiana Veteran Volunteer Infantry, by William R. Hartpence. Cincinnati, 1894.

History of the 53rd Regiment Ohio Volunteer Infantry, by John K. Duke. Portsmouth, O., 1900.

A History of the First Regiment of Massachusetts Cavalry Volunteers, by Maj. Benjamin W. Crowninshield. Boston and New York, 1891.

History of the First Regiment Minnesota Volunteer Infantry, by R. I. Holcombe. Stillwater, Minn., 1916.

History of the 14th Illinois Cavalry, by W. L. Sanford. Chicago, 1898.

The History of Fuller's Ohio Brigade, by Charles H. Smith. Cleveland, 1909.

History of the Ninth Massachusetts Battery, by Levi W. Baker. South Framingham, Mass., 1888.

The History of the 9th Regiment Massachusetts Volunteer Infantry, by Daniel George MacNamara. Boston, 1899.

The History of the 104th Regiment of Illinois Volunteer Infantry, by William Wirt Calkins. Chicago, 1895.

History of the 124th Regiment, N.Y.S.V., by Charles H. Weygant. Newburgh, N.Y., 1877.

History of the Second Army Corps, by Francis A. Walker. New York, 1886.

History of the Seventh Regiment Illinois Volunteer Infantry, by D. Leib Ambrose. Springfield, Ill., 1868.

History of the 77th Illinois Volunteer Infantry, by Lt. W. H. Bentley. Peoria, Ill., 1883.

History of the 16th Battery of Ohio Volunteer Light Artillery, compiled by a committee. n.p., 1906.

A History of the Sixth Iowa Infantry, by Henry H. Wright. Iowa City, 1923.

History of the Sixth Regiment Indiana Volunteer Infantry, by C. C. Briant. Indianapolis, 1891.

The History of the 10th Massachusetts Battery of Light Artillery in the War of the Rebellion, by John W. Billings. Boston, 1881.

History of the Tenth Regiment Indiana Volunteer Infantry, by James Birney Shaw. Lafayette, Ind., 1912.

History of the 3rd Regiment of Wisconsin Veteran Volunteer Infantry, by Edwin E. Bryant. Madison, Wis., 1891.

History of the 38th Regiment Indiana Volunteer Infantry, by Henry Fales Perry. Palo Alto, Calif., 1906.

History of the 34th Regiment of Illinois Volunteer Infantry, by Edwin W. Payne. Clinton, Ia., 1904.

The History of the 39th Regiment Illinois Volunteer Veteran Infantry, by Charles M. Clark, M.D. Chicago, 1880.

History of the 33rd Regiment Illinois Veteran Volunteer Infantry, by Isaac H. Elliott and Virgil G. Way. Gibson City, Ill., 1902.

History of the 12th Massachusetts Volunteers, by Lt. Col. Benjamin F. Cook. Boston, 1882.

History of the 12th Regiment New Hampshire Volunteers, by Capt. A. W. Bartlett. Concord, N.H., 1897.

History of the 24th Michigan of the Iron Brigade, by O. B. Curtis. Detroit, 1891.

A Hundred Battles in the West: The Second Michigan Cavalry, by Capt. Marshall P. Thatcher. Detroit, 1884.

Iowa and the Rebellion, by Lurton Dunham Ingersoll. Philadelphia, 1867.

Journal History of the 29th Ohio Veteran Volunteers, by J. Hamp SeCheverell. Cleveland, 1883.

Letters from the Army, by B. F. Stevenson. Cincinnati, 1884.

"Letters of C. C. Carpenter," edited by Mildred Throne; from the *Iowa Journal of History,* Iowa City, January 1955.

A Little Fifer's War Diary, by C. W. Bardeen. Syracuse, 1910.

Memoirs of a Volunteer, by John Beatty, edited by Harvey S. Ford. New York, 1946.

Memoirs of the War, by Capt. Ephraim A. Wilson. Cleveland, 1893.

Military History and Reminiscences of the 13th Regiment of Illinois Volunteer Infantry, prepared by a committee of the regiment. Chicago, 1892.

Musket and Sword, by Edwin C. Bennett. Boston, 1900.

Muskets and Medicine; or, Army Life in the Sixties, by Charles Beneulyn Johnson, M.D. Philadelphia, 1917.

A Narrative of the Formation and Services of the Eleventh Massachusetts Volunteers, by Gustavus B. Hutchinson. Boston, 1893.

The Nineteenth Illinois, by J. Henry Haynie. Chicago, 1912.

Opdycke Tigers: 125th Ohio Volunteer Infantry, by Charles T. Clark. Columbus, O., 1895.

The Passing of the Armies, by Joshua Lawrence Chamberlain, Brevet Major General. New York, 1915.

Personal Memoirs of John H. Brinton, Major and Surgeon, U.S.V., 1861-1865. New York, 1914.

Recollections of the Civil War, by Mason Whiting Tyler. New York, 1912.

Recollections of a Private Soldier in the Army of the Potomac, by Frank Wilkeson. New York, 1887.

Reminiscences of the Civil War, from Diaries of Members of the 103rd Illinois Volunteer Infantry, compiled by a committee. Chicago, 1904.

Reminiscences of the War of the Rebellion, 1861-1865, by Maj. Jacob Roemer. Flushing, N.Y., 1897.

Reunion of the 33rd Illinois Regiment: Report of Proceedings. Bloomington, Ill., 1875.

The Road to Richmond, by Maj. Abner R. Small. Berkeley, Calif., 1939.

Roster and Record of Iowa Soldiers in the War of the Rebellion, published under direction of Brig. Gen. Guy E. Logan, adjutant general. 7 vols. Des Moines, Ia., 1911.

Service with the Sixth Wisconsin Volunteers, by Rufus R. Dawes. Marietta, O., 1890.

The Soldier Boy's Diary Book; or, Memorandums of the Alphabetical First Lessons of Military Tactics, by Adam S. Johnston. Pittsburgh, 1866.

A Soldier Boy's Letters to His Father and Mother, 1861-1865, by Chauncey H. Cooke. n.p., 1915.

The Story of a Cavalry Regiment: The Career of the Fourth Iowa Veteran Volunteers, by William Forse Scott. New York, 1893.

The Story of the 15th Regiment Massachusetts Volunteer Infantry, by Andrew E. Ford. Clinton, Mass., 1898.

Story of the Service of Company E and of the 12th Wisconsin Regiment, written by One of the Boys. Milton, Wis., 1893.

The Story of a Thousand: being a History of the Service of the 105th Ohio Volunteer Infantry, by Albion W. Tourgee. Buffalo, 1896.

Three Years Campaign of the Ninth N.Y.S.M. During the Southern Rebellion, by John W. Jaques. New York, 1865.

Three Years with the Adirondack Regiment, by John L. Cunningham. Norwood, Mass., 1920.

Three Years with the Armies of the Ohio and the Cumberland, by Angus L. Waddle. Chillicothe, O., 1889.

Three Years in the Army: The Story of the 13th Massachusetts Volunteers, by Charles E. Davis, Jr. Boston, 1894.

Three Years in the Sixth Corps, by George T. Stevens. New York, 1870.

Trials and Triumphs: The Record of the 55th Ohio Volunteer Infantry, by Capt. Hartwell Osborn and Others. Chicago, 1904.

The Twentieth Connecticut: A Regimental History, by John W. Storrs. Ansonia, Conn., 1886.

Under the Maltese Cross, Antietam to Appomattox: Campaigns of the 155th Pennsylvania Regiment, narrated by the Rank and File. Pittsburgh, 1910.

A War Diary of Events in the War of the Great Rebellion, by Brig. Gen. George H. Gordon. Boston, 1882.

War Letters of William Thompson Lusk, edited by William Chittenden Lusk. New York, 1911.

The Wild Riders of the First Kentucky Cavalry: A History of the Regiment, by Sgt. E. Tarrant. Louisville, 1894.

Henry Wilson's Regiment: History of the 22nd Massachusetts Infantry, by John L. Parker. Boston, 1887.

With the Rank and File, by Thomas J. Ford. Milwaukee, 1894.

Wooden Nutmegs at Bull Run, by Frinkle Fry. Hartford, Conn., 1872.

Index